An American Abbot

Boniface Wimmer, O.S.B.

Archabbot Boniface Wimmer, O.S.B. (1809–1887), founder of the
Benedictine Order in the United States and first archabbot of
Saint Vincent. (Oil painting by unknown German artist,
Saint Vincent Archabbey Art Collection.)

Jerome Oetgen

❦

An American Abbot

Boniface Wimmer, O.S.B.

1809–1887

Francisco J. Gamboa Félix

The Catholic University of America Press

Washington, D.C.

The paper used in this publication meets the minimum requirements of
American National Standards for Information Science—Permanence of
Paper for Printed Library materials, ANSI Z39.48–1984.
∞

Library of Congress Cataloging-in-Publication Data
Oetgen, Jerome, 1946–
    An American abbot : Boniface Wimmer, O.S.B., 1809–1887 / By
Jerome Oetgen. —rev. ed.
        p.   cm.
    Includes bibliographical references and index.
    ISBN 0-8132-0893-9 (alk. paper)
    1. Wimmer, Boniface, 1809–1887.   2. Abbots—United States—
Biography.   3. Benedictines-United States—Biography.   I. Title.
BX4705.W58034   1997
271′.102—dc21   97-7552

Contents

To be worthy of the task of governing a monastery, the abbot must always remember what his title signifies and act as a superior should. He is believed to hold the place of Christ in the monastery, since he is addressed by a title of Christ, as the Apostle indicates: *You have received the spirit of adoption of sons by which we exclaim, abba, father* (Rom 8:15).

—*Rule* of Saint Benedict

I can glory in one thing alone. At every moment since becoming a Benedictine, all my desires and aims, more or less, directly or indirectly, were to promote the progress of the order. I was always misunderstood in the Old World and I am frequently misjudged in America. Some look upon me as a farmer or adventurer, others censure me for my expenses in the education of scholastics, and a third class calls me a reckless administrator of church property. However, whatever I did, and whatever I do, is intended for the welfare of the order. I may have been at fault at times, but this is certain: the blessing of God was upon the work.

—Boniface Wimmer

Foreword

by Demetrius Dumm, O.S.B.

The task of recalling, evaluating, and reporting the past is never finished. New information appears, new judgments must be made, and fresh insights emerge. Such is certainly the case with the present volume, and we are fortunate that Jerome Oetgen has prepared a second, thoroughly revised edition of his fine work of twenty years ago. He has been able to draw upon important new research in this vibrant period of the Catholic Church in America, and he has matured in his own appreciation of the complexities of this period.

Sometimes it is difficult to recover a sense of past events simply because sources are so meager. Such is definitely not the case with Boniface Wimmer. I recall that Father Felix Fellner, who was well acquainted with Wimmer's story, told my novitiate class that, though Wimmer was a great man, he would never be a candidate for canonization "because he wrote too much." As a matter of fact, his correspondence was not only abundant but it was also frank and personal. One who reads his letters comes away with a sense of having met a real and credible human being.

Drawing largely from this copious correspondence, Oetgen has given us a vivid and convincing portrait of this extraordinary man. One sees Wimmer's tenacity in his early exchange with Bishop Michael O'Connor as he held out for the kind of exemption from episcopal control that the ancient monasteries of Europe had long enjoyed. Modern American Benedictines can hardly imagine how different their lot would be if he had not been successful.

From the earliest days of monasticism, bishops had "raided" monastic communities, seeking the best and the brightest to be ordained (sometimes reluctantly) and assigned to pastoral or adminis-

trative work in the church. One can certainly understand the ratio-
nale of such bishops, but it soon became clear that, as far as the spiritual health of the whole church was concerned, such activities were
indeed shortsighted. It is for that reason that monasteries were later
granted the privilege of exemption from episcopal control. As is clear
from the correspondence, Bishop O'Connor was very reluctant to see
this privilege granted to Saint Vincent. But Wimmer persisted and
prevailed.

This struggle for independence from outside control has some
bearing also on the controversy surrounding Wimmer's relations with
the Benedictine sisters whom he had invited to America and for
whose welfare he felt responsible. Several recent works have told the
story of the early days of the Benedictine sisters in America, including their difficulties with Wimmer, and that is, of course, a welcome
contribution. But Wimmer's story needs to be told also. Oetgen has
now done this in a far more detailed and perceptive manner than was
possible in the first edition.

There were no doubt mistakes and misunderstandings in Wimmer's dealings with the sisters, but it seems clear that it was always his
earnest desire that they should prosper and even, if possible, participate in the privilege of exemption that he had won for his monks.
This is not to say that the Benedictine sisters fared badly under episcopal supervision as their extraordinary contributions to the church
make clear. However, exemption would have afforded them more security in fostering their distinctive spirituality as well as in the disposition of their apostolic activity. After all, the bishops were much
more likely to see them as helpers in education and other apostolic
works than as monastics trying to maintain an atmosphere conducive
to prayer and community support.

People of my generation will easily recall how religious superiors
were pressured to send young sisters into the classroom immediately
after their novitiate with little more than a high school education and,
in some cases, with no aptitude or desire for teaching. We can only
imagine the pain and frustration experienced by these idealistic and
sincere young women. In many cases, they had to acquire their college degree over twenty or more years of summer school. Today, one
can merely speculate about the possibility or consequences of exemption for American Benedictine sisters, but Wimmer was certainly the
only one who could have made it possible.

What emerges most clearly from the Wimmer correspondence is the portrait of a man who knew how to dream without becoming a mere dreamer. It was probably with good reason that his Metten confreres labeled him a *Projektenmacher*, but they did not foresee the rest of the story. For there are dreams that are little more than idle flights of fancy, just as there are dreams that are daring and inspiring without losing contact with reality. The difference becomes apparent when the dreamer comes up against the hard facts of real people and events. The fanciful dreamer will cling to the original untested vision and will inevitably experience disappointment and failure.

Wimmer was no such fanciful dreamer. He was constantly making adjustments as he tested his original plans against the reality of his experience in frontier America. He was forever taking what real life offered him rather than trying to impose his plans on reality. Thus, he quickly left Carrolltown when that site proved unsuitable; he reached beyond German immigrants when he found others in need; he did not spurn city parishes though he preferred a rural setting.

However, Wimmer's blend of dream and reality was most evident in the manner in which he dealt with his confreres. His letters are full of references to moments of both joyful satisfaction and bitter complaint as he struggled to realize his aspirations in a community where he found both obedient and recalcitrant members. Nonetheless, he was never paralyzed by opposition. Rather, he would find a way through the difficulty and sometimes surprise even himself as things turned out much better than expected.

Wimmer's capacity to adjust to reality was also manifest in his determination to resist the strong temptation to become resentful or to hold a grudge. Some of his most talented and trusted confreres turned against him, and he had to change plans because of their disloyalty. But it is with amazement that we note how he called upon these same men to fill other and even more sensitive positions. He may have complained, but he found life too short for recrimination or self-pity.

Oetgen has succeeded admirably in documenting and describing these features of Wimmer's extraordinary career. His work reads so much like an adventure novel that one is reminded occasionally that in this case also facts are stranger than fiction. No one who is interested in the history of religion in America or in the fortunes of the venerable Benedictine Order will want to overlook this fine work.

Preface to the Revised Edition

This volume is a newly revised and expanded version of *An American Abbot*, the biography of Boniface Wimmer published twenty years ago by the Archabbey Press. In the course of revision I have reexamined the original sources, added material from additional sources that have subsequently come to light, and incorporated suggestions made by reviewers and readers of the first edition.

Attempting to improve both the accuracy of the story and the flow of the narrative, I have rewritten substantial portions of the book to make the motives, actions, and consequences of the events described clearer to the reader, but I have left out nothing of importance in the second edition that can be found in the first, although in certain instances, after reexamining the primary sources, following the helpful suggestions of generous and astute readers, and benefitting from new research by Benedictine scholars, I have reassessed and even altered some of my earlier conclusions. The length of the revised edition is consequently about a third greater than the original version. Those who have read the original edition will agree with me, I think, that this is a new book. I would also like to hope that it is a better one.

Three reasons justify a new edition of the life of Boniface Wimmer. The first is that 1996 marks the 150th anniversary of the Benedictine arrival in the United States and the founding of the first American Benedictine monastery at St. Vincent. One fitting way to celebrate that anniversary is to examine once again the character and life of the man who was principally responsible for transplanting the ancient Benedictine monastic tradition from Europe to North America.

A second reason for a new edition of *An American Abbot* is that since the first edition two decades ago, significant developments have taken place in American Benedictine historical studies that shed new light on the life and work of Boniface Wimmer. These developments include the publication of several important scholarly works, chief among which are Sister Incarnata Girgen's *Behind the Beginnings: Benedictine Women in America* (1981), Sister Judith Sutera's *True Daughters: Monastic Identity and American Benedictine Women's History* (1987), Sister Ephrem Hollermann's *The Reshaping of a Tradition: American Benedictine Women 1852–881* (1994), Father Paschal Baumstein's *My Lord of Belmont: A Biography of Leo Haid* (1985), and Father Joel Rippinger's *The Benedictine Order in the United States: An Interpretive History* (1990). The first three of these provide much help to students of American Benedictine history in gaining a clearer understanding of the controversial relationship between Wimmer and the Benedictine nuns who came from Eichstätt in 1852. The fourth is an exhaustive study of one of Wimmer's most distinguished spiritual sons and an examination of the events that led up to and flowed from what was probably Wimmer's most daring missionary venture, the establishment of a Benedictine monastery in Protestant North Carolina. The last is an ambitious and generally successful attempt to examine the extent and significance of Wimmer's and the American Benedictines' contributions to the American Catholic Church.

Developments in the historiography of the Catholic Church in ninteenth-century America constitute a third major justification for a revised edition of this biography. The appearance in the 1980s of such works as James Hennesey's *American Catholics: A History of the Roman Catholic Community in the United States* (1981), Jay P. Dolan's *The American Catholic Experience: A History from Colonial Times to the Present* (1985), Gerald P. Fogarty's *The Vatican and the American Hierarchy from 1870 to 1965* (1985), and Philip Gleason's *Keeping the Faith: American Catholicism Past and Present* (1987) casts into sharper relief the experience of immigrant Catholics in the United States during the nineteenth century and provides new contexts within which to examine and assess Boniface Wimmer and his achievement.

Wimmer's achievement has been generally underestimated in the history of American Catholicism. The reason for this erroneous assessment would seem to be that the principal focus of his missionary labors and apostolic work was on immigrant Catholic communities in rural America at a time when the most dramatic and formative events in nineteenth-century American Catholicism were taking place in the densely populated cities of the land. Modern historians of the Catholic Church in the United States, understandably concentrating on the phenomenon of urban Catholicism, have tended to neglect the story of Catholicism on the American rural frontier where between 1830 and 1860 the majority of the 1.5 million German immigrants to the United States settled. It was chiefly to serve these farm-bound German immigrants that Wimmer came to America in 1846, and for the next forty years, as his evangelization efforts expanded to include Irish, African-Americans, Native Americans, and immigrants from eastern Europe, he consistently exhibited the traditional Benedictine preference for establishing monasteries in farming regions and for working among people of the countryside rather than those of the cities.

Wimmer also contributed to the growth of American Catholicism in the cities, of course, as his work in Newark, Erie, Pittsburgh, Covington, and Chicago shows. However, it was in the rural districts of Pennsylvania, Minnesota, Kansas, Kentucky, Texas, Iowa, Nebraska, North Carolina, Georgia, and Alabama that the most characteristic and distinctive work of Wimmer and the American Benedictines occurred, and insofar as nineteenth-century rural Catholicism has not generated the degree of interest among historians of the American Catholic Church as has the phenomenon of urban Catholicism, Wimmer's incontrovertible contribution to the growth of the Catholic Church in the United States during the formative immigrant era has not attracted the attention it deserves.

Still, John Tracy Ellis called him "the greatest Catholic missionary of nineteenth-century America," and in his own lifetime Wimmer was widely esteemed both by the American hierarchy for his distinguished pastoral work among European immigrants and the freed American slaves and by European ecclesiastical and monastic leaders for the critical role he played in the nineteenth-century revival and development of Benedictine monasticism. Wimmer did not work in the wings but rather on the broad full stage of the great multicultural drama that was the nineteenth-century American Catholic Church. If his role did not often bring him to center stage, he was nonetheless, clearly, one of the key supporting actors. His story forms an important subplot, and this biography is an attempt to assess his part and importance in the play as a whole.

A hundred and fifty years after his arrival in America, twenty-one American Benedictine abbeys and independent priories, with more than 1,200 monks, continue the work Wimmer initiated. The major-

ity of the monastic communities he established during his lifetime—
St. Vincent in Pennsylvania, St. John's in Minnesota, St. Benedict's in
Kansas, St. Mary's in New Jersey, Belmont in North Carolina, St.
Bernard's in Alabama, St. Procopius in Illinois, and Holy Cross in
Colorado—still serve the American Catholic Church in schools,
parishes, and the missions, and other abbeys and priories that derived
from these continue to carry on the work in Canada, Mexico, Puerto
Rico, Brazil, Taiwan, and the United States.

I would like to express my appreciation to the many Benedictine
and non-Benedictine friends who commented on the strengths and
weaknesses of the first edition, who made suggestions on how to improve the story, and who encouraged me to proceed with the revision.
I especially want to thank Father Omer Kline of St. Vincent Archabbey, Father Paschal Baumstein of Belmont Abbey, and Dr. James
O'Callaghan, director of the Latin American Fulbright program at
the United States Information Agency, for their careful reading of the
text of the second edition and their astute and compelling suggestions
for improvements. Of course, what errors and infelicities that remain
are entirely my own.

Finally, I want to express my heartfelt gratitude to Archabbot
Douglas Nowicki and the entire community of St. Vincent Archabbey, my friends and abettors, who made this revised and expanded
edition of *An American Abbot* possible.

Jerome Oetgen
Washington, D.C.

Preface to the 1976 Edition

In a very real sense this biography is the product of many hands. Since 1891, when Father Oswald Moosmüller, O.S.B., published his *Bonifaz Wimmer, Erzabt von St. Vincent in Pennsylvanien* as a premium for the readers of the *Wahrheitsfreund*, Benedictines from the community of St. Vincent and the daughterhouses emanating from it have been conspiring, sometimes in ones and twos, at other times in whole flocks, to gather together all the pertinent material about their founder with the hope that his full story would some day be told. Many of the conspirators are long dead, but their efforts certainly produced results that inspire nothing less than awe in a modern researcher. Among those who helped collect and preserve papers and records dealing with the early history of the monastery of St. Vincent and its first abbot was Boniface Wimmer himself, who commissioned several of his students in Rome to make copies of important documents sent to the Holy See from St. Vincent between 1846 and 1880. Father (later Abbot) Vincent Huber, O.S.B., did considerable spade work in the archives of the Propaganda Fide during the nineteenth century, and his work, together with the work of the early archivists of St. Vincent, Fathers Edward Hipelius, O.S.B., Augustine Schneider, O.S.B., and Oswald Moosmüller, laid the foundation for all future research into the life of Wimmer and the communities he founded.

Like a zealous breed of monastic packrats, monks from St. Vincent and many of her daughter communities collected, filed, and catalogued letters, documents, and assorted memorabilia from Wimmer's period so that today a researcher into the life and work of the first Benedictine abbot in America has hundreds of thousands of pages, both primary and secondary sources, at his disposal. Among the most energetic of these collectors was Father Felix Fellner, O.S.B., who traveled two continents in search of Wimmer letters and documents. Certain historians, outstanding among whom were Fathers Gerard Bridge, O.S.B., and Louis Haas, O.S.B., wrote monographs on Wimmer and the history of the American Benedictines. But Fellner's five-volume *Abbot Boniface and His Monks,* which never quite made it past the editors more because of linguistic deficiencies than any lack of hagiographic zeal on the part of the author, remains the most complete, though somewhat cumbersome, synthesis of all the Wimmer material gathered up to the year 1956. It was Fellner's work that first attracted me to Wimmer, and it was the rewriting of his biography that I first set out to do.

In the nineteen fifties the histories of St. Vincent's first two daughterhouses were published, and the authors—Father Colman J. Barry, O.S.B., of St. John's Abbey, and Father Peter Beckman, O.S.B., of St. Benedict's Abbey—added even more to the Wimmer corpus. Their research uncovered important new documents that were, like the others, collected, filed, and catalogued. In light of research subsequent to Fellner's, therefore, a rewriting of *Abbot Boniface and His Monks* became less desirable than a thorough restudy of all the sources and the compilation of an entirely new biography.

In the nineteen sixties, when Father Matthew Benko, O.S.B., was archivist at St. Vincent, an effort was begun to transliterate many of the letters of Boniface Wimmer from the unfamiliar German script into the much more readable Roman script, and the work was carried on by Father Rhabanus Goetz, O.S.B., and Brother Lambert Berens, O.S.B., when Father Omer Kline, O.S.B., succeeded Father Matthew as archivist.

In 1968 Brother Philip Hurley, O.S.B., began the arduous task of reassembling and recataloguing all the Wimmer papers in the archives of St. Vincent in order to facilitate their study by researchers. By 1970 most of the work was completed, and the papers, now even more neatly collected, filed, and catalogued, were opened for investigation.

My own curiosity about the life and work of Boniface Wimmer, whetted by the availability of the documents, has resulted in the present study. But neither the availability of the documents nor the completion of this work would have been possible had it not been for the untiring efforts of all those whom I have named—and a good many others as well. For that reason this biography is the product of their hands as much as of my own, and in my more sober moments I realize that theirs was the greater task and doubtless the more successful.

I acknowledge this and thank them.

In addition, I would like to thank Father Timothy Fry, O.S.B., editor of the *American Benedictine Review,* who graciously consented to permit expanded versions of four articles that had first appeared in that journal to be included in this biography, and Father Quentin Schaut, O.S.B., who took time from a busy schedule to read the first version of the manuscript and who offered some extremely helpful suggestions which I have tried to incorporate.

Many hands have participated in the Englishing of the letters of Boniface Wimmer, and though the task is not yet complete, those who have worked on the letters in recent years cannot be overlooked. They have included Father Ildephonse Wortman, O.S.B., Father Hugh Wilt, O.S.B., Father Roland Ripoli, O.S.B., Father Warren Murrman, O.S.B., Father Jonathan Murrman, O.S.B., Brother Kurt Belsole, O.S.B., and Brother Aaron Buzzelli, O.S.B, all of St. Vincent. Also Father Anselm Biggs, O.S.B., of Belmont Abbey, Fathers Alcuin Hemmen, O.S.B., and Bernard Sause, O.S.B. of St. Benedict's Abbey, Father Bede Babo, O.S.B., of St. Mary's Abbey, Mrs. Vera Slezak of St. Vincent College, Father Philip Ghys, O.S.B., of St. André Abbey, Sister Imelda Bauer, O.S.B., of St. Joseph's Convent, Sister Gonzaga Englehart, O.S.B., of Mount St. Scholastica, Sister Margretta Nathe, O.S.B., of St. Benedict's Priory, and Sister Gregoria, O.S.B., of Eichstätt all contributed their time and energy by translating hundreds of Wimmer letters. To them grateful thanks are due.

Finally, I want to express my deepest thanks and appreciation to the archabbot and community of St. Vincent for whom this labor was begun and to whom its product is dedicated.

Jerome Oetgen
Latrobe, Pennsylvania

Introduction

Colman J. Barry, O.S.B. (1921–1994)

The publication of the first biography of Archabbot Boniface Wimmer, O.S.B., is a welcome advance in the mosaic of American Catholic literature. This study has been awaited and needed for many years. A lacuna is now filled to the enrichment of us all.

Sebastian Wimmer, priest of the diocese of Ratisbon, who joined the restored Abbey of Metten in Bavaria, was consumed with a drive to go to America to establish the ancient Benedictine way of worshiping and working together, and to build religious community life. Wimmer began this undertaking at St. Vincent, Westmoreland, Pennsylvania, in 1846. This American Benedictine founder represents the intriguing line of diocesan priests—Gueranger, Marmion, Beauduin, to mention three others—who rose up to restore and renew the Benedictines in the nineteenth and twentieth centuries. At a time when organized religious life in great part had become the victim of wars and politics, as well as interior decay, the Holy Spirit moved again in strange and wondrous ways on the American frontier through the service of Boniface Wimmer.

All the ingredients of greatness were in Wimmer: courage, vision, determination, and love of the interior life. There was much personal and communal suffering. There was dedication of heroic proportions given freely by the brethren of St. Vincent. The foundations—priories and abbeys as well as their descendants—stand today on the American continents as witness to the unique founder and his little band.

Saint Boniface of Germany had a worthy successor in Abbot Boniface of America. He established a chain of abbeys against insurmountable odds. At the same time the missionary needs of the immigrant, Indian, and Negro consumed his drive and zeal, day and night.

Missionary advances by religious families continue to offer growth potential for the Christian community. The story of Boniface Wimmer is an important model in that development of God's people on the Way to the Kingdom.

St. John's Abbey
Collegeville, Minnesota

An American Abbot

Boniface Wimmer, O.S.B.

1 ❧ *Thalmassing to Metten*

As USUAL the monks had risen before dawn and assembled in the abbey church to chant the office of matins. *Come! Let us raise a joyful song to the Lord. Let us enter his presence with thanksgiving and sing him songs of triumph!* It was the Feast of the Immaculate Conception, and as they chanted the ancient hymn and bowed their heads to glorify the Trinity, the old abbot lay dying in his cell, with the prior and a handful of monks keeping the deathwatch.

It was a strange sight for his brother monks gathered around the deathbed: this bold and dynamic man, who during the course of seventy-eight years had explored the outer reaches of human energy, who had helped revitalize the ancient spirit of monastic missionary zeal, who had brought the fourteen-hundred-year-old tradition of Benedictine monachism to a new and alien land, dying quietly, unobtrusively, one might almost say comfortably. For more than forty years he had seemed to spurn comfort, but now, his work ended at last, he lay peacefully awaiting the final call.

In the abbey church the acolyte intoned the Twenty-second Psalm: *The Lord is my shepherd, there is nothing that I lack.* The abbot had come to this place forty-one years earlier, bringing a vision not always shared by those with whom he lived. Like the others he had been a monk of Metten and like them could have led a tranquil life in his Bavarian monastery, doing the ordinary things that monks do. When he spoke with his superiors about America, they told him to stop dreaming. Such things were only for the extraordinary. His work had been set down for him: he would be a teacher in Munich.

But though he loved his abbey and his homeland, he would not abandon his vision. There was work to be done across the ocean, and he was called to do it. He protested that it was neither his pride nor any sense of his own extraordinary abilities that motivated his vision. There was a need in America that he felt almost anyone could fill, but if no one else was willing to fill it, he felt compelled to accept the mantle. Once again he petitioned his abbot, and almost as if to unburden himself of a constant and persistent cross, his abbot said that he might become a missionary.

With eighteen young companions he had come to Pennsylvania during the cold October of 1846. From the monastery and school he established at St. Vincent his work had spread to Minnesota in the 1850s and to Kansas when that territory was being bathed in the blood of an undeclared war, the grim prelude to a near-apocalyptic civil conflict that took the lives of a million Americans. It had spread to New Jersey and to Kentucky; to Virginia, Texas, Tennessee, Nebraska, and Delaware; to Illinois, Iowa, Maryland, Georgia, North Carolina, Alabama, Florida, and Colorado. His monks had brought the Word of God to German and Irish, Pole and Bohemian, black and white, as well as to the Native American. In 1887 they labored in nearly twenty dioceses and vicariates of the American Catholic Church, and the following year *Sadlier's Catholic Directory* would say of Abbot Boniface Wimmer's Benedictines that "[n]othing in the growth of the Church in this country exceeds the wonderful development of this community." His life's work had been an extraordinary success; yet in the end he was plagued with misgiving.

He wrote to Abbot Innocent Wolf of Kansas:

I have had the good fortune to do a great deal for the Order of St. Benedict, and I can say, without praising myself, that I have worked for its prosperity as well as can be expected from one with so little talent and learning as I have. All honor for this belongs to God alone, and only trouble arises for me when I try to answer the question: Did I work in the right direction? Did I do my work as it ought to have been done? Would it not have been much better had I settled down somewhere with a few of my followers to lead a religious life in accordance with the Rule of St. Benedict, to live in retirement with them, devoted to prayer, to the praise of God, to mortification and self-denial, to occasional preaching of the Gospel? Would not this have been much better than assuming, or rather presuming, to establish monasteries, schools, and missions—thereby running the risk that I and my companions should appear too worldly-minded, should give too little edification, and should in the long run turn out like bogus monks, neither hot nor cold but lukewarm? The older I become, as I advance in years, the more frequently this question arises in my mind, and my attempts to answer it create more doubts and cause me untold anxiety.

Not long before the final relapse that confined him to his death-bed, Abbot Boniface wrote to Father Celestine Englbrecht:

Today you and I are the only surviving clerics [of those who came to St. Vincent in 1846]. And, if I am not mistaken, of the brothers only three are still alive. Near to death and slowly dying, I naturally think quite often about the days gone by and wonder how things turned out the way they did. No one imagined us capable of accomplishing anything significant, and yet we did accomplish something. God's grace was obviously with us. Our chief object—the establishment of the order in America—has been achieved, and our second major purpose—training and providing a sufficient clergy for our Catholic Germans—is well underway. May unbounded thanks be given to God a thousand times, for He chose and made use of us as instruments for the execution of His designs. For many, our foundations have had serious defects, but it could not have been otherwise without a miracle. . . . Hence we do not want to become faint-hearted or discouraged. Rather we want to work on confidently and courageously as well as we can. Inasmuch as things have come this far only with the evident protection and grace of God, so may we not expect from ourselves success in the future, but again only from the grace and protection of God, who cannot fail us so long as we work not for ourselves, but for Him, for His holy Church, for the order, and for souls.

Prior Michael Hofmayer, who had assumed the duties of administrator of the monastery several weeks earlier, stood by the bed reading the prayers for the dying. He and the others looked at the wasted frame of the once strong and portly man who was never above tucking the pectoral cross into his scapular and joining his monks for a day's work in the fields. In Rome he had been called, somewhat disparagingly, "the farmer-abbot." He gloried in the name. Along with prayer, work was the second pillar upon which a monk built his life, and farmers, he said, were "the backbone of any nation." So while some scoffed, this farmer-abbot built monasteries and schools all over America, educated the children of German immigrants, trained priests to serve in the American missions, and established the first non-Italian Benedictine house of studies in the Eternal City. His appreciation for learning, art, and the humanities never waned. Not long after coming to the United States he said that "a monastic school that does not give just as much attention to art as to knowledge and religion is a very imperfect one. A deficiency in scholarship at the beginning can be more readily excused than a neglect of art." He was a farmer with soul, deeply religious, deeply humane.

The prior watched the emaciated face with its long white beard and perhaps recalled the sensation the flowing whiskers had caused among the clean-shaven cardinals of Rome when the abbot visited the Vatican in 1865. He had been reluctant to arrive in Rome with a full beard and even wrote the abbot of Metten asking what he thought of the idea. Not much, it seems. The Bavarian prelate recommended prudence. Things were done differently in Rome, and officials there didn't always understand, or appreciate, innovation. The abbot of Metten told him to keep in mind that when in Rome he should do as the Romans, but Abbot Boniface decided to take the chance. He arrived unshaven. People gawked at him in the streets. The nuns of a convent he visited were frightened by his "shaggy appearance." The Italian cardinals raised their bushy eyebrows. But in the end the abbot's audacity was vindicated. He was received in audience by the Holy Father, and after hearing of his success in spreading the Benedictine Order throughout North America and bringing the Gospel to the immigrants who were daily arriving on the shores of the new land, Pope Pius IX gave his blessing to the work and dismissed him with the words "Long live Abbot Wimmer and his magnificent beard." From that day on he never shaved, and he urged his monks to follow his example.

Now his long life was coming to its end. It had been a prolonged and difficult race to this unremarkable finish. Along the way he had known many troubles. He wrote Abbot Alexius Edelbrock of Minnesota that while in Rome for the First Vatican Council he had visited the tomb of St. Benedict at Montecassino and prayed for "trials and humiliations, that I might be purified by suffering." They had come, Abbot Boniface said, in ample measure, "[m]uch more abundantly, in fact, than I had anticipated." He had experienced deception, disloyalty, and rebellion among his own brothers. On four separate occasions those in whom he had placed his greatest confidence had turned against him, challenged his leadership and ideals, rejected his vision, and demanded new approaches to monastic life radically different from those he held to so tenaciously.

"The past," he wrote, "often appears to me like a dream. Sometimes I feel like Adam before Eve was made. I see nobody like me. I am surrounded by young monks. I am like an old tree in the middle of young underwood." He listened and he accommodated. He punished and he forgave. But in the end he remained faithful to the vision he had received at Metten nearly half a century earlier.

Abbot Boniface Wimmer died at ten o'clock in the morning on the Feast of the Immaculate Conception, December 8, 1887. A tradition first recorded by his earliest biographer, Father Oswald Moosmüller, says that he breathed his last as the celebrant intoned the Gloria of the solemn high mass in honor of the Virgin, whom the bishops of the United States had named patroness of the abbot's adopted country in the same year that he had come to St. Vincent.

On that day the *Pittsburgh Leader* reported, "In his death the church loses one of its foremost leaders and the Benedictine order mourns a pilot that has guided it safely for many years on stormy seas." On the following day the *New York Herald* noted that, "[h]is acts of kindness and of charity extended to all classes and conditions of society, and there is scarcely a poor family in all the region about the monastery that, at some time or another, has not been the recipient of his bounty." James Cardinal Gibbons, archbishop of Baltimore, wrote Prior Michael Hofmayer, "I know of few men in the country who are more esteemed and venerated by the hierarchy than was good Abbot Wimmer," and Bishop James O'Connor of Omaha, brother of Bishop Michael O'Connor who had welcomed Abbot Boniface and his Benedictines to the diocese of Pittsburgh in 1846, wrote, "No nobler character than he has yet appeared in the Church of the United States. A man without guile, learned, pious, charitable almost to a fault, he was the ideal monk of old."[1]

The life that ended so quietly began amid the rumor of war. Bavaria in the opening days of 1809 was entering its sixth year of alliance with the Emperor Napoleon, and across her eastern frontier the Austrian troops of Emperor Francis I were massing and preparing for battle with the imperial French army. King Maximilian I Joseph, whom Napoleon had personally selected to rule Bavaria four years earlier, ordered the Bavarian forces to march in support of the French and placed his twenty-four-year-old son and heir, Crown Prince Ludwig—the future patron and friend of Boniface Wimmer and the American Benedictines—in command.

The ancient town of Regensburg, located at the point where the waters of the Regen join the Danube and the great eastern river becomes navigable, was a strategic military point. Napoleon hoped to thrust into the heart of Austria and strike at Vienna by way of the Danube. Regensburg would be a major point of embarkation for the offensive against the Austrians, and Marshal Davout, the Bavarian prince of Eckmühl and duke of Auerstedt, was placed in command of the town. The surrounding countryside was alive with marching troops and rumbling caissons, and it was here, in Thalmassing, a small farming village of two hundred people, about eight miles west of Regensburg, that Wimmer was born. The date was January 14, 1809.

Wimmer was the first child of Peter Wimmer and his second wife, Elizabeth, née Lang, of Langenerling. Like most inhabitants of Thalmassing, his forebears had been farmers, but his father had left the soil to operate a tavern on the western edge of the village.[2] At one point a story prevailed in Thalmassing that Wimmer was not born at home but rather in the neighboring forest to which the populace had fled as the armies of Napoleon and Francis I met for battle. History records, however, that in fact the two great armies did not enter the region until the middle of April when the infant was three months old.[3]

Nevertheless, the legend suggests the turmoil and chaos that formed the background of the child's early days. On April 19, 1809, Marshal Davout withdrew his Bavarian troops from Regensburg, and the following day Austrians of the 2nd Army Corps under General Kollowrath occupied the town. A few days later the French and Bavarian allies, marching from the west, began a counterattack, and after a furious bombardment, which turned the lovely town into a blazing inferno, they recaptured Regensburg on April 23. French troops of the 65th Regiment under Colonel Coutard were given the honor of being the first detachment to enter after the Austrian withdrawal, but despite the Bavarian alliance with Napoleon, and no doubt because of the terrible bombardment to which the French had subjected them, Regensburg's citizens greeted the victors with invectives, projectiles, and showers of boiling water. The following day Napoleon set up his headquarters at Regensburg and ordered reprisals against the recalcitrant population.[4]

Although the major part of the battle was fought south of Regensburg, between Eckmühl and Landshut, the marching and counter-marching armies could not have failed to disturb the quiet community of Thalmassing forty miles away. The artillery bombardment and the burning of Regensburg, moreover, certainly rattled the houses and lit up the bedrooms of the small farming village. The story of the population's flight to the forest, therefore, is probably true, and the chaotic conditions that drove Peter and Elizabeth Wimmer with their infant son to the same woods through which St. Boniface had trudged eleven hundred years earlier to bring Christianity to the Germanic tribes were a fitting prelude to the future missionary's formidable life.

In 1809 the Church too was still suffering the chaos, upheaval, and uncertainties of the times. Six years earlier, on February 25, 1803, a congress of liberal German princes, acting under the mandate of Napoleon's imperial French government, had gathered for the notorious Diet of Regensburg and passed an "Enactment of the Imperial Delegates" which amounted to a virtual spoliation of the ancient German Church. Influenced by the enlightened, anticlerical thought of the day, the princes had ordered all the properties belonging to the cathedral chapters and their clergy confiscated. In addition to the confiscation of the episcopal domains, the delegates decreed that

all goods and properties of institutions, abbeys, and monasteries . . . are hereby placed at the free and complete disposition of the respective princes of these territories, to be used to meet the expenses of divine services, education, and other purposes of the common good, as well as to ease their own financial burdens; with the condition that they provide for the proper care of the cathedral churches . . . and for the pensions of the dispossessed clergy.

Two months later Napoleon formally confirmed and approved the decrees of the Diet of Regensburg.[5]

In the general secularization that followed, the German Catholic Church lost more than 1,700 square miles of property, and suffered the confiscation of eighty German abbeys and more than two hundred convents and monasteries. In Bavaria the spoliation of the ancient monastic centers was especially effective under Maximilian Joseph, count of Montgelas, a French emigré who was King Maximilian I Joseph's chief minister. Montgelas was a liberal statesman of the Tallyrand school and one of the most virulent anticlericals of the empire. Under his direction the monks of Bavaria's monasteries were evicted and given miserable pensions; priceless vestments, sacred altar vessels, manuscripts, and books were confiscated, destroyed, or scattered; churches were profaned, torn down, or left to fall into decay; and monastic buildings were converted into military barracks, prisons, or insane asylums. Not since Henry VIII's suppression of the English monasteries in the sixteenth century had Benedictine monasticism in Europe suffered such a devastating blow.

Five months after Wimmer's birth, in June 1809, as the secularization of the European Catholic Church continued under Napoleon and his ministers, the Benedictine pope, Pius VII, issued a bull of excommunication against "the robbers of the Patrimony of Peter, their advisors, abettors, and agents." In retaliation, French soldiers entered the Vatican that same month and took the Holy Father captive, eventually bringing him to Fontainebleau in France, where he remained a prisoner for five years.[6]

It was into an ambience of warfare, political upheavals, and religious turmoil, then, that Wimmer was born. Within a few days of his birth he was taken to the parish church of Thalmassing and there given in baptism the name Sebastian. For the next eleven years he lived with his family in their native village where he received both his primary education and his formal religious training in the parish school. In time a brother, George, and a sister, Anna, were born. A single story survives from this period. It seems that one day, when he was ten, Wimmer and some of his friends were playing in a field with his father's horses. Troubled by a severe toothache, he selected one of the tamer animals, wrapped several hairs from its tail around the bothersome tooth, and whacked the horse's flank with a stick. His novel method of extracting teeth was reputedly successful.[7]

In the parish school at Thalmassing Wimmer displayed a gift for quick learning and a religious bent that led his parents and teachers to encourage his youthful aspirations for the priesthood, and in 1820, at the age of eleven, he was sent to the Latin school at Regensburg to begin preliminary studies for holy orders. A year later he was awarded a prize for scholastic excellence. In his evaluation report that year, one of Wimmer's professors, a man named Mayerhofer, observed that the twelve-year-old student had "a sanguine temperament, possessed good intellectual faculties, and showed a quick and correct judgment in high degree." Mayerhofer went on to say that with so many excellent qualities he would have succeeded in obtaining a higher rank in the class if his previous preparation for this course had not been so meager. He was steady in diligence, indefatigable in work, and attentive in every area of learning. He never entered the classroom unprepared, especially during the second term when his mind was opening more and more. He studied the rules of Latin grammar well, but showed himself less skillful in applying them. In his oral answers he showed a thoughtful disposition and a mature deliberation. His conduct deserves every praise. His morals are pure. His exterior behavior showed that he was open, natural in his ways, and more sedate than is usual in boys his age.[8]

Wimmer's performance in the Latin school remained consistently good for the next five years, and in the autumn of 1826 he graduated with second honors. His final evaluation, signed by Dr. Johann Denk, rector of the school, and Professor G. M. Salfrank, vice-rector and director of the graduating class, noted that he was "a very gifted young man who made good use of his faculties in the best possible manner. The result of this endeavor was very good progress." Only his difficulties with mathematics prevented him from graduating with top honors.[9]

In September 1826, with letters of recommendation from Denk and Salfrank, Wimmer, at age seventeen, went to the diocesan seminary at Regensburg to study philosophy. The following year his superiors urged him to apply for admission to the University of Munich, which he did successfully in the summer of 1827, and the next autumn he entered the university with the intention of taking a degree in theology.

At the time the University of Munich was one of the oldest seats of learning in Bavaria, but in the preceding five decades it had undergone a series of destabilizing blows that had brought it to a low ebb. When Wimmer became a student in 1827, therefore, the university was not a significant center of European intellectual activity, although because of the accomplished faculty its new patron, King Ludwig I, had assembled there, it showed promise of becoming an important academic institution once again.

The university traced its origins to a fifteenth-century establishment in the Bavarian town of Ingolstädt on the Danube, fifty miles southwest of Regensburg. It had subsequently come under the control of the Jesuits in the sixteenth century and thereafter gained renown for its enthusiastic espousal of humanism, its scientific research, and the excellence of its faculties of philosophy and theology. After papal suppression of the Jesuits in 1773, the university was renamed the Ludwig Maximilian University and transferred to Landshut, a town on the River Iser, fifty miles northeast of Munich, where it underwent secularization, became a center of liberal thought and enlightened anticlericalism, and experienced a precipitous decline in academic quality. In 1826 the new Bavarian king, Ludwig I, called for the university's reform, summoned leading German Catholic intellectuals to join its faculties, and transferred it to Munich where he expected it to become a cornerstone of his plan for a Bavarian Catholic revival.

Wimmer was among the first students to enter the newly constituted Ludwig Maximilian University, his entrance papers being approved and signed by its first rector, Dr. F. E. Döllinger. Many of Wimmer's professors during his three years in Munich were scholars who enjoyed international reputation; others were churchmen and writers who would become famous as time went on. King Ludwig I had succeeded in drawing a solid corps of respected intellectuals to his capital city, many of whom were members of the university faculty. Friedrich Wilhelm Schelling, who together with Fichte and Hegel was one of the chief representatives of idealist philosophy in Europe after Kant, was on the faculty and among Wimmer's instructors. The renowned theologian Francis Xavier Baader, one of the most brilliant controversialists and lecturers in nineteenth-century Germany, whose work to bridge the theological gulf between Protestantism, Orthodoxy, and Catholicism laid the groundwork for twentieth-century ecumenism, taught him dogmatic theology. Wimmer's other professors included Joseph Allioli, the famous biblical scholar whose translation of the Old and New Testaments became the standard German Catholic Bible of the nineteenth century, and Joseph von Görres, who was regarded as the single most influential and formative force in nineteenth-century German Catholic thought and who was attracting men of the stamp of Lamennais, Lacordaire, and Montalembert to his famous "Round Table" in Munich and lending his support to movements that would restore Bavaria to what he considered to be its pure Catholic and German traditions. In the same year that Wimmer went to the university, a promising young priest joined the faculty as professor of history. He was the son of the rector and for a while lived with Wimmer in the theological college. His fame would one day spread throughout Christendom, but in 1827 Johannes Ignaz Döllinger was still a junior member of the faculty. The following year he would become one of Wimmer's professors, and forty years later he would gain notoriety as a leader among those European Catholic intellectuals who opposed ultramontanism and who would break with the Catholic Church on the issue of papal infallibility.[10]

Two years of preliminary philosophical studies were a requisite for the study of theology in German universities, and Wimmer spent his first year in Munich completing the studies in philosophy he had begun at the diocesan seminary in Regensburg in 1826. He had hardly embarked on his university career, however, when two crises intervened that threatened to frustrate his aspirations for the priesthood.

The first of these was the death of his father and the consequent financial burdens placed on the family. Peter Wimmer died early in 1827, leaving the tavern in Thalmassing with its modest income to his wife Elizabeth. Feeling herself unable to manage the family's financial affairs alone, Elizabeth Wimmer signed the tavern over to her second son, George, with the stipulation that he pay her an annual rent and share the benefits of his inheritance with his brother Sebastian and his sister Anna. Obviously the intention of Elizabeth Wimmer was to arrange matters in such a way that her eldest son might continue studies at the university while his younger brother and sister remained at home to assist in the family business. It soon became apparent, however, that the financial difficulties resulting from Peter Wimmer's death were much greater than the family had anticipated and that the income from the tavern was not sufficient to support both the family in Thalmassing and Sebastian in Munich. For a while it seemed as if Wimmer might be forced to withdraw from the university because of his inability to pay the costs of living and studying in the Bavarian capital. But he applied to the university for financial relief, and acting on evidence provided by the district court at Thalmassing, which issued a statement declaring that the Wimmer family's financial condition prevented them from paying Sebastian's university expenses, the university authorities agreed to exempt him from the payment of tuition.[11]

Even as Wimmer's financial problems were being resolved, a second crisis developed which in many ways was more threatening than the first to his plans for becoming a student of theology. The attrac-

tions of Munich, with its cosmopolitan airs and sophisticated am-
biance, clearly beguiled the eighteen-year-old tavernkeeper's son from
Thalmassing. He found himself for the first time in his life in a world
unbounded by narrow provincial prejudices and with a whole range
of new possibilities open to him. His enthusiasm for the priesthood
waned, and he began to contemplate abandoning theology for the
study of law. At the same time, his interest in the nonacademic aspects
of student life, as well as news coming out of Greece, had begun to
distract him from his philosophical studies.

Soon after arriving in Munich, Wimmer had joined a student organization called the "Corps Bavaria" which had originally been
formed to assist poor students but which in time had become a kind
of paramilitary society in which such martial arts as drilling and fenc-
ing were learned and practiced. The camaraderie and pseudomilitary
discipline of the Corps Bavaria proved highly attractive to the callow
young student, and eventually he began to spend more hours in the
clubroom than in the lecture halls.[12]

Meanwhile the war for independence that Greek patriots were
waging against their Turkish masters had captured the imagination of
both the Bavarian people and their king. King Ludwig I, whose
brother Otto would later be named king of the Greeks, was first
among Bavarian Grecophiles. He had a deep and abiding love for
classical letters and art and was an enthusiastic student of Greek history and culture. Reflecting his romantic passion for Greek culture
and the classical tradition, his ambitious building programs in Munich and throughout Bavaria were based on classical Greek models.
He was an ardent supporter of the Greek fight for independence, and
following his lead the Bavarian government came to the support of
the Greek patriots. A recruiting office was opened in Munich to draw
volunteers for the Greek cause.

In the student circles of Munich admiration for Greek culture and
fervent support of the Greek independence movement were widespread, and members of the Corps Bavaria—whose distinctive features were beards, military uniforms, and "a white cap that they wore
not only in Munich but also at home"—were caught up in the political passions of the day, spending hours in their clubroom and in the
cafés of Munich discussing the latest newspaper reports from Greece
and the glorious fight for freedom taking place in the nation where
democracy was born. Many of them, like the English romantic poet

Byron, aspired to join the Greek cause and come to the defense of the land of Homer and Socrates.

Apparently Wimmer's only gesture in support of Greek independence in his first year at the university was to name his pet poodle "Phylax." Still, the martial spirit and romantic aspirations of his fellow students were beginning to take their toll on him. His thoughts turned to Greece and the dramatic struggle for independence going on there. At the same time, his financial situation continued to look bleak.

In addition to petitioning the university for exemption from fees and tuition, Wimmer had applied in 1827 for a scholarship to the Gregorium, a residential college for theology students at the university. A scholarship would provide his living expenses and thus ease his financial problems, but when he learned that one hundred and twenty applications had been made for only thirty scholarships, he grew discouraged and decided to take his summer vacation in Thalmassing to think out his future. As one of his early biographers put it, "Hungry and tired, he set out on foot for his home with his faithful dog Phylax. He found that his good mother was as little pleased with his white cap as she was with his determination to study law. She offered no objections, but doubled her prayers."[13]

During the vacation Wimmer heard that the son of a neighbor in Thalmassing was attending the Gregorium, and he visited the young man's family to learn what he could about the life of a student of theology in Munich. The picture the student had painted in his letters home was not encouraging, and Wimmer seemed more than ever determined to abandon his plans to study theology. To turn to law, however, would incur an expense that, after the death of his father, neither he nor his family could afford. There seemed, then, only one alternative attractive enough for him to consider.

When he returned to Munich in the autumn of 1827, he informed his friends that he was bent on joining the Greek fight for independence. They greeted his announcement with general exultation and suggested that they all celebrate the good news in one of the local beer halls. By the time their celebration ended, the recruiting office had closed, but not to disappoint his friends Wimmer patriotically announced that "postponed does not mean abandoned." He would come back tomorrow. The next day, fully determined to join the Greek army, he set out a second time for the recruiting office but once again was delayed on the way and found when he arrived that the recruiters had gone home. Discouraged, he returned to his rooming house where his landlord, Herr Grundner, greeted him with news that he had won the scholarship to the Gregorium. When Wimmer asked how the landlord knew this, Herr Grundner said that the announcement had appeared that day in the Munich *Intelligenzblatt*. "Well, we'll see about it," Wimmer is reported to have said, apparently reconsidering the possible ramifications of a military career. "At least it won't cost me my head."[14]

The next day he directed that his bed and his poodle Phylax be delivered to his mother in Thalmassing, and after shaving his beard, doffing the cap and uniform of the Corps Bavaria, and borrowing a silk hat and a suit of conservative clothes from a friend, he presented himself to the rector of the Gregorium who informed him that with the scholarship came an allowance of money that would permit him to live comfortably in Munich for the next two years. The study of theology seemed attractive to him after all.[15]

Settling down to theological studies with Baader, Allioli, Görres, Döllinger, and his other professors, Wimmer proved an apt student, receiving the grade "excellent" in most of his courses.[16] With his romantic plans to join the Greek army laid aside, his wild oats sown, his ambitions to become a lawyer behind him, Wimmer was ordained to the minor orders on March 18, 1829, by Archbishop Lothar von Gelbstättel of Munich, and at the end of his third year at the university he returned to the diocesan seminary at Regensburg to finish his studies of theology under the direction of Bishop George Michael Wittmann, coadjutor to Bishop Johann Michael Sailer. Two years later, after receiving a dispensation from the Holy See because he had not yet reached the canonical age of twenty-four, Wimmer was ordained to the priesthood with seven other young men in the cathedral of Regensburg by Bishop Wittmann. The date was August 1, 1831, and Sebastian Wimmer was twenty-two years old.[17]

In 1831 the diocese of Regensburg had more priests than positions. The neighboring diocese of Passau, however, had more positions than priests to fill them. In order to assist the neighboring diocese, therefore, Bishop Sailer sent the eight priests ordained in Regensburg to Passau for assignment until the poorer diocese should receive more vocations of its own. Four of the eight were assigned to small country parishes, and four, including Wimmer, were sent to the Marian shrine at Altötting to act as curates. "It was my fate that I should become a priest for pilgrims," Wimmer wrote. He began his service in Altötting on September 1, 1831.[18]

Altötting had been the site of a shrine to the Blessed Virgin since the sixth century, and both Franciscans and Jesuits had ministered to the hundreds of thousands of pilgrims who visited the site before the secularization decrees of the Diet of Regensburg in 1803. In that year the shrine had been suppressed, but in 1826, after King Ludwig I ascended the throne of Bavaria, Capuchin priests were assigned the task of reopening it. Several years later the Capuchins turned the shrine over to the bishop of Passau who established a community of diocesan priests in the place. Father Joseph Albrecht was named superior of the community, and it was under his guidance that Wimmer first took up his duties as a priest.

As many as 200,000 pilgrims visited the shrine at Altötting annually, and Father Wimmer's initial assignment was a taxing one. In addition to ministering to the pilgrims at Altötting, he regularly assisted the pastor of the parish at Neukirchen and other nearby villages. Meanwhile, as he quietly went about his priestly functions in the diocese of Passau, significant developments were taking place elsewhere in Bavaria that forecast a bright new future for the German Church.

After the fall of Napoleon in 1815 the Holy See immediately began efforts to reverse the effects of the secularization decrees of the Napoleonic period. In the early months of 1817 King Maximilian I Joseph of Bavaria dismissed his liberal prime minister Montgelas, and the way was opened for important changes in the Bavarian Church. On June 5, 1817, a concordat was successfully negotiated between the king and Pope Pius VII in which the Church in Bavaria was reorganized. The concordat contained three important provisions. First, though the king and his Catholic successors would retain the right to nominate bishops to the eight Bavarian sees, the pope would once again make the final decision as to who would be elevated to the episcopate. Second, the Bavarian bishops were given unrestricted authority in the administration of their dioceses, especially in the exercise of spiritual jurisdiction and in free intercourse with Rome. Third, while no attempt was made to force the return of confiscated property to the Church, the Bavarian government pledged to provide adequate financial support to dioceses, cathedral chapters, and seminaries, and also to restore some of the monasteries that had been suppressed in 1803.[19]

In spite of the concordat several of King Maximilian I Joseph's anticlerical ministers succeeded in delaying the execution of many of its articles until the king's death in 1825. The new spirit of ultramontanism, however, was gaining strength in Bavaria, and when the crown prince ascended the throne as King Ludwig I, the joy of the Catholic conservative party in Bavaria was unbounded. Born in Strasbourg in 1786, the new king had been the godchild of Marie Antoinette and Louis XVI of France, after whom he was named. Educated in Paris, Ludwig had become an enthusiastic romantic, rebelling against the politically correct Enlightenment principles of his day. He never got along well with Napoleon, who considered him an arrogant upstart, and he was not a favorite among his father's liberal ministers either. When he assumed the crown in 1825, he was regarded by many as the most cultivated monarch in Europe and the darling of the Catholic conservative party in Bavaria.

A disciple of Johann Michael Sailer, the ultramontanist bishop of Regensburg, the new king was not long in fulfilling the hopes of the Bavarian Church. Brooking opposition from remnant members of his father's liberal cabinet, Ludwig began almost immediately to put into effect the articles of the concordat of 1817. He summoned Catholic scholars from all over Europe to the newly constituted Ludwig Maximilian University in Munich, and following the lead of such eminent Catholic apologists as Joseph von Görres, he initiated what would become a virtual Catholic Renaissance in his kingdom.

Central to his plan was the revival of Benedictine monasticism in Bavaria. Under the influence of Sailer he had acquired a deep personal attachment to the ancient Benedictine religious, educational, and cultural traditions, and in 1827 he issued a decree restoring the Monastery of St. Michael at Metten in the diocese of Regensburg.[20]

St. Michael's Abbey at Metten had been founded by Charlemagne in the eighth century and for a thousand years had had a continuous history of Benedictine observance. The secularization decrees of 1803, however, had brought about its suppression along with those of eighteen other Bavarian abbeys. The monks of these abbeys had been dispossessed, given miserable pensions, and scattered throughout the parishes of Bavaria. By 1827 all but six of them had died, and these six were infirm old men. King Ludwig turned to Baron von Pronath,

King Ludwig I of Bavaria (1786–1868). Patron and protector of the
American Benedictines. (Oil painting attributed to Heinrich
Wilhelm Vogel. Saint Vincent Archabbey Art Collection.)

whose family had acquired much of the abbey's property during the
secularization, and asked that he surrender some of his land and
buildings to the Crown so that the abbey might be restored. Von
Pronath agreed, and Ludwig directed the bishop of Regensburg to
look for monks to take up the challenge of a Bavarian Benedictine
revival.

Sailer appealed to the six remaining members of the suppressed
Bavarian Benedictine Congregation, and two of them agreed to help
reestablish monastic life at Metten. Father Roman Raith, O.S.B., had

been a monk of Metten at the time of the suppression in 1803. Since then he had served as pastor in the small village of Oberwinkling in the diocese of Regensburg. He, together with Father Ildephonse Nebauer, O.S.B., a former member of the Benedictine Priory of Andechs who had been serving as administrator of St. Peter's Church in Straubing, twenty-five miles from Metten, returned to the ancient monastery, and on June 3, 1830, in the presence of Bishop Sailer and Johann Mulzer, president of Lower Bavaria and King Ludwig's representative, the two monks officially reintroduced Benedictine monastic life at Metten after a quarter century's hiatus. Bishop Sailer named Father Ildephonse prior of the community.[21]

But the monastery at Metten had been restored in name only. The two old monks who had returned hardly constituted a flourishing community, and though their only duty was to recite the divine office, their age and their poverty seemed to militate against the possibility that Metten would ever again become an important center of Benedictine monastic life in Bavaria.

Bishop Sailer did what he could to help them. He sought vocations for Metten throughout his diocese and urged pastors of several neighboring parishes to come to the monastery's financial aid. Despite the support of both church and state, however, Fathers Ildephonse and Roman discovered their situation at the end of the first year to be extremely discouraging. The financial condition of the monastery became so tenuous that King Ludwig offered an endowment of 50,000 florins (about one million dollars in U.S. currency today) to put it on a firmer footing, but the problem of vocations still remained.[22]

In clerical circles throughout the country the restoration of the Benedictine Order generated considerable interest and became a frequent topic of conversation. Bishop Sailer, whose diocese had an overabundance of priests, began making discreet inquiries among his clergy to see if any might be willing to leave the diocese to join the monastery. Meanwhile, Wimmer and the other Regensburg priests continued their work at Altötting. One evening as members of the community discussed the plight of the two old monks at Metten and the recent inquiries of the bishop of Regensburg, the twenty-three-year-old priest from Thalmassing remarked that he would consider becoming a monk. As a student in Munich, he said, he had studied the history of the Bavarian Church under the brilliant young scholar Ignaz Döllinger and had acquired from his professor a deep appreci-

Metten, Bavaria. Wimmer was a priest of the Abbey of Metten, motherhouse of the first Benedictine monastery in the United States.

ation for the Benedictine missionaries who had brought Christianity to the Germans. While in Munich he had even done research into the history of the Benedictine Order in Bavaria but had thought little of the monastic life since his ordination. A story that circulated many years later indicates that Wimmer's confrere priests in Altötting greeted his casual remark with surprise. Apparently few of them had ever considered Wimmer a likely candidate for the monastic life. Nevertheless, as soon as he made the remark, his superior, Father Joseph Albrecht, said that if Wimmer was serious, he would be very pleased to give him permission to leave Altötting to join the incipient community at Metten.[23] Reportedly Wimmer was shocked by the speed with which his superior agreed to release him from his duties. At first he took it as tacit criticism of his work at Altötting, but when he considered the matter at length he came to the conclusion that perhaps he did have a vocation to the monastic life after all and that since Metten was in desperate need of monks, Father Albrecht was not criticizing his work but in fact encouraging an unconscious aspiration that very well may have come from the Holy Spirit. He consulted Bishop Wittmann, who had been his spiritual guide before ordination and who, upon the death of Bishop Sailer in 1832, had succeeded as ordinary of Regensburg, and when Bishop Wittmann too encouraged him in his monastic vocation, Wimmer wrote Prior Ildephonse Nebauer of Metten to say that he was considering becoming a Benedictine.[24]

Despite the tradition that Wimmer's entrance into Metten was the fruit of a casual remark spoken at a recreation table in Altötting, the first of a series of more than twelve hundred surviving letters he wrote between 1832 and 1887 suggests that he had devoted considerable thought to the question of the monastic life. "I have had a secret desire for a long time," he said,

to enter a monastery, partly to amend my life for the future, and partly to work for the greater honor of God, no matter how weak my strength. In the monastery under your supervision and in union with virtuous and well-educated men, I could work out my own salvation as well as that of others. Divine Providence itself has seemed to work for the realization of my desire. . . . Immediately after my ordination I was transferred to Altötting without having asked for the assignment. Here I learned to value the common life which I had lived in the seminary at the Gregorium in Munich for two years and in Regensburg for one year. I have learned the necessity of the common life.

Wimmer went on to say that in spite of the fact that he had gained much practical pastoral experience at Altötting, the life of the parish priest was not as attractive to him as was the life of a monk. Since coming to Altötting, he had been shuffled from parish to parish in the area. He had worked in the churches of Neukirchen, Ötting, Unterneukirchen, and Altötting, and he said that through all this pastoral labor he had become more convinced than ever of his vocation to the monastic life. He had taken the liberty of having his academic credentials forwarded to the prior of Metten. In the meantime, he awaited final approval from the bishop of Regensburg for his petition to enter the monastery, and when he received that, he would send his formal petition to the prior asking that he be accepted as a member of the Metten community.[25]

Wimmer spent the next six weeks settling his affairs and preparing to enter the monastery. He obtained Bishop Wittmann's permission to apply for the novitiate at Metten; he visited his family in Thalmassing to tell them of his decision; and he sought and received testimonials from his superior, Father Joseph Albrecht, who said of him that during his ten months at Altötting he had shown "indefatigable diligence in the pursuit of studies and in the performance of his official duties; he excelled in true priestly conduct and gained the respect of his superiors, and in all this he deserves the grade 'Excellent.'" The district court at Altötting provided a report that characterized him as a priest who had "demonstrated during his stay here such exemplary conduct that he could be regarded as a model for his confreres. As administrator for the parish of Neukirchen he was praiseworthy."[26]

On July 16, 1832 Wimmer wrote Prior Ildephonse of Metten that nothing now stood in the way of his becoming a Benedictine.

Since my purpose and vocation in life seem to be from God, I come with a most humble and submissive request. I wish hereby to apply formally for admission into the monastery over which God has placed you as prior. Please do not consider my total unworthiness and worthlessness, but rather my sincere and holy resolution to serve God in the most agreeable and profitable manner for my eternal salvation. Please allow me to enter, live, and die in the Order of St. Benedict under your guidance and supervision.

Wimmer told the prior that after much reflection he had discovered that the founders of religious orders, and especially St. Benedict, seemed to have no other purpose than to establish institutions wherein they and their followers would "(1) do penance for sins committed, (2) preserve themselves as much as possible from sin, and (3) find motivation and means to do good." Wimmer said that his own motives for entering the monastery had sprung from these three purposes. His reasons, therefore, for making application were

(1) To do penance for my many sins of the past by which I have offended God. Thus by judging and punishing myself may God not judge and punish me. I have often misused my freedom. Now I offer it to God as a sacrifice so that I no longer possess freedom as men generally do whereby they can do what they want. I do not want any other will than the Rule of St. Benedict and the will of my future spiritual superior.

(2) Flight from the world and its dangers. I know very well that if I wanted to avoid all temptations, I would have to leave the world entirely. I know that wherever I go, the tempter accompanies me. I am also quite aware of the fact that by assuming a more severe way of life, I take upon myself ob-

ligations which as a secular priest I would not have. I also know that by disobeying or by obeying only partially I would sin. I have often found the truth of the psalmist's words, "With the good I have been good, and with the bad I have been bad." The good I expect to find in the monastery, more good at least than bad. I believe that with the grace of God I can become good with them, for I am not good now.

(3) Conversion of morals by the common work and action of all the members of the monastery. In the world I am entirely left to myself. However, I should be a city on the top of a high mountain, visible from afar, a great attraction and protection to all the strangers. But I feel so weak, so unsure of myself, so desolate, so downcast, for I cannot be what I know I should be. I should be a light placed in the lamp stand, so that all in the house may see. But if the light itself is darkness, how can it shine? I should be the salt of the earth that prevents decay wherever applied. I should not weaken. But I am so lukewarm, so poor, so needy. I need the salt myself first before I can be salt to others. My weaknesses will be made bright from their spiritual lamp. My lukewarmness will be made warm by their zeal and fervor. The Rule of the monastery will prevent me from misusing my freedom and give me the means to do only good. Everything in the monastery is arranged around the daily praise and service of God. I am convinced that all I do, if it is according to the Rule, is profitable as soon as done out of obedience, something I cannot say of many deeds I did while in the world.[27]

Two weeks later he received news that his petition had been granted by Prior Ildephonse, and on August 6 he wrote Nebauer to express his gratitude. He said he would not be able to go to Metten until after the Feast of the Assumption because he had promised his diocesan superiors that he would remain in Altötting until the pilgrims visiting the shrine for the great Marian feast had left, but he added that

should you order me to depart sooner, I would be ready at any moment. I do not feel at home here anyway, because I know that I do not belong here any more. From the bottom of my heart I am very happy to be able to enter a monastery. I enter it with the firm conviction that God has led me to it. As regards temporal affairs, I am satisfied, unconcerned, and fear nothing but myself. Mistrust of self was always one of my reasons for entering the monastery. God have mercy on my poor soul that it may rest peacefully.[28]

Wimmer arrived at Metten on September 1, 1832, and in December, sixteen months after his ordination, he entered the novitiate, receiving the name "Boniface" in religion. On the verge of his twenty-fourth birthday, he was the youngest of five priests from the diocese of Regensburg to take the monastic habit. With him as co-novices were Father Leonard Scherr, age twenty-eight, who received the name "Gregory" and who eight years later would be elected abbot of Metten and twenty-four years later be named archbishop of Munich; Father Anthony Leiss, age thirty-seven, who received the name "Rupert" and who would later be named first abbot of the restored abbey of Scheyern; Father Wolfgang Sulzbeck, age twenty-five, who received the name "Francis Xavier" and who would reintroduce Benedictine life in the ancient abbey of Weltenburg; and Father Joseph Bacherl, age twenty-seven, who received the name "Pius" and who would die two years before Father Boniface could introduce the Benedictine Order to the United States.

Many years later, after Wimmer had established the American Cassinese Congregation of Benedictines, parallels would be drawn between him and his patron, St. Boniface of Germany. It would be said that he must have had the intention of becoming a missionary even before entering the novitiate at Metten; otherwise he would not have chosen such a propitious name as he did. But years afterward he wrote to Abbot Utto Lang, who succeeded Gregory Scherr as superior of Metten, that the name had merely been a happy accident: "Of the so-called three great men who entered Metten in 1832, Gregory was named after Gregory XVI (who at that time was pope), Xavier after Bishop Xavier Schwäbl of Regensburg, and I after Dean Boniface Urban of that diocese. I was the least in stature, in fact the 'troublemaker and visionary.'"[29]

On December 29, 1833, a year after entering the novitiate, the five priest-novices professed solemn vows of stability, conversion of morals, and obedience before Prior Ildephonse Nebauer and Father Roman Raith. Because he had petitioned for entrance to the community after him, Father Boniface followed Father Gregory in reciting and signing the vow formula. He was the second monk, then, to make profession at Metten after the restoration, and two weeks later he celebrated his twenty-fifth birthday.[30]

Soon after his solemn profession Wimmer was assigned as assistant pastor in Edenstätten, a village near Metten whose parish the monastery had been given to supplement its income. The newly professed Benedictine, who had entered the monastery because he felt called to

a monastic rather than a parochial vocation, served the people of
Edenstätten for the next twenty-two months. In the meantime,
events were unfolding in Munich whose ramifications would before
long be felt at Metten.

King Ludwig I intended that the revival of Metten be merely the
first step in the restoration of the Benedictine Order in Bavaria, but
in 1834 anticlerical sentiments still percolated among his ministers.
Several of the king's liberal ministers objected to the monastic life in
principle, claiming that it was a moribund holdover from the Middle
Ages completely out of touch with the realities of the nineteenth century. The restoration of Metten particularly galled them because the
monks there, whose only duties were to recite the divine office and
occasionally do pastoral work in nearby parishes, performed no "useful" function in society. The king came under increased pressure to
reverse his decision to restore monasticism in Bavaria. One of his
ministers, Count Ludwig von Wallerstein, visited Metten in 1833 and
reported to the court that the life of prayer and asceticism of the small
band of monks was in "the spirit of the Dark Ages." He recommended that if the king insisted on the monastery's existence, the least
he should require was that the monks adopt "more humane and modern forms of life."[31]

Back in Munich Wallerstein began lobbying for significant changes
in the king's policies with regard to the Benedictines. There seemed
little hope of discouraging the monarch altogether in his plan to restore the abbeys of Bavaria, but perhaps certain accommodations
could be made to the liberal point of view. The monks of Metten, in
Wallerstein's opinion, contributed nothing to the common good. If,
on the other hand, they could be induced to establish a school, they
would become useful to the state and to society, and thereby justify
their existence. This was the suggestion, then, that Wallerstein made
to King Ludwig I after his visit to Metten, and the king was amenable
to the idea. Benedictine monks, after all, had a long and distinguished
history as educators. They had brought not only the faith but also
learning to Germany in the Middle Ages, and there seemed no more
proper work for them than the work of education.

King Ludwig I approved Wallerstein's proposal and directed his
ministers to draw up the necessary plans and instructions for their execution. Wallerstein and his liberal colleagues in the cabinet selected

Augsburg for the experiment. They conceived a plan to revive the Abbey of St. Stephen there and to reestablish the college that the monks had operated before the suppression of 1803. Monk-professors would be drawn from all over Europe, and St. Stephen's Abbey would become the principal Benedictine monastery of Bavaria. To facilitate the project, the king's advisors suggested that he withdraw the endowment of 50,000 florins that he had granted to Metten in 1831 and turn it over to the new community of Augsburg. Finally, they proposed that Metten and all subsequently restored monasteries in Bavaria be established not as independent Benedictine communities but rather as mere dependencies of St. Stephen's, with all their monks transferring their vows of stability to the Augsburg abbey.

The king saw nothing wrong with the plan and was in fact pleased that some of his ministers had finally taken an interest in his monastic projects. On December 16, 1834, he issued a royal patent putting all the recommendations of his advisors into effect. St. Stephen's was restored as the principal abbey of Bavaria, and Father Barnabas Huber, O.S.B., a member of the former Benedictine abbey of Ottobeuron, was named its first abbot; a school for boys was established at the abbey and Benedictine professors from Bavaria, Switzerland, and Austria were invited to join the faculty. St. Michael's Priory at Metten lost its canonical status as an independent monastery and was placed under the authority of the abbot of St. Stephen's. With the king's approval, the government transferred the royal endowment from Metten to the Augsburg abbey, and in the middle of October 1835 several monks from Metten, including Rupert Leiss and Boniface Wimmer, were ordered to Augsburg to become professors in the college there. To many, Metten seemed doomed.[32]

The monks of Metten were profoundly distressed. They quickly recognized the implications of the government's action and knew that Wimmer and his companions would be lost to the community once they reached Augsburg because there they would be required to sign a statement transferring their vows to the new abbey; therefore, with the approval of Bishop Xavier Schwäbl, who had succeeded George Michael Wittmann as ordinary of Regensburg, the Metten monks destined for Augsburg drew up and signed a document in which they renewed their vows of stability to Metten and declared that any efforts to force them to renege on their allegiance to St. Michael's Priory would go contrary to their consciences. With this document in hand, they set out for Augsburg on October 21, 1835, arriving there three days later.

It is clear that from the beginning Wimmer assumed leadership of the group of Metten monks and spearheaded the effort to resist their forced transfer to Augsburg. The boldness, ingenuity, single-minded-ness, and plain stubbornness that characterized his later efforts to achieve whatever objectives he set out to accomplish were fully manifest in his actions following the monks' arrival in Augsburg.

From St. Stephen's Abbey Wimmer wrote Prior Ildephonse Nebauer of Metten that since "things are in order here, something definite can be said about the situation. I will inform you of the situation, for I am sure that even though we are no longer under your paternal care, you will take a warm and intimate interest in our fate. Furthermore, I do not consider myself so separated from you that I do not consider myself as belonging to Metten any more." Father Boniface said that before leaving Regensburg he had visited Bishop Schwäbl and had received from him renewed pledges of support for Metten. Upon reaching Augsburg, he had presented Abbot Barnabas with the declaration that he, Father Rupert, and the others had signed before leaving Metten. The monks from St. Michael's saw immediately "that he was not too well satisfied." Wimmer complained to Prior Ildephonse that there was no monastic spirit at Augsburg, that the enclosure was often violated, and that women frequented the corridors and even the cells of the monks. This was not the kind of environment in which he and the others thought they could faithfully follow the Benedictine Rule. Not long after their arrival in Augsburg, he said, the monks from Metten were presented with a document that demanded that they perpetually submit themselves to the bishop of Augsburg and the abbot of St. Stephen's. The document had been drawn up by royal command and would in effect nullify the Metten monks' previous vows of stability to St. Michael's. The prior of St. Stephen's had given them the document,

but though we irritated him very much, we did not sign it. Rather we sent our Father Rupert to the abbot to remonstrate against this demand. But the angry prior followed him immediately and provoked him further so that Father Rupert could not accomplish anything. The abbot would not hear of a conditional submission. We considered it again and determined not to sign, but rather to return to Metten if we could not stay here as guests. The next day, Tuesday, His Grace the bishop arrived at ten o'clock to induce us to sign. We were ordered to appear before the abbot and there confronted Prior Waible of Einsiedeln, the future prior of Ottobeuron, the reverend prior and master of novices, Father Robert from the Scots monastery in Vienna, together with the bishop. The bishop tried to show us that our insubordination was unfounded. We had to prove that we were justified in being suspicious.

It was difficult, Wimmer said, to defend himself. He and the others did not want to reveal before the distinguished group of church and monastic leaders that they had no confidence in the quality of observance or in the monastic future of the Augsburg abbey. "We could not hide this entirely," he wrote. "They noticed it, and we were reproached for it. The bishop was especially against me, as I seemed to be the leader and was doing the talking for the group." Wimmer and the recalcitrants were accused of rudeness, ingratitude, and narrow-mindedness, but they did not give in. "We profited nothing after disputing for two hours."

One of Wimmer's key objections to transferring his vows to the abbey of St. Stephen's was that in his opinion the Augsburg abbey was too dependent upon the Bavarian government to assure it sufficient freedom to follow the monastic Rule as he and his Metten confreres believed it should be followed. He did not think that the abbot was strong enough to oppose the will of the government when that will ran contrary to the ideals of the monastic life. After the session with the bishop, Wimmer returned to Abbot Barnabas's room and in a two-hour private discussion explained to him all the objections that he and his confreres had to signing the document. "I hid nothing from him, not even my lack of confidence in him regarding his difficult position towards the government, the bishop, and the numerous foreign guests." He said that the Metten monks would all agree to sign if the words "in perpetuum" were deleted from the formula but that they wanted to make no commitments that would preclude their returning to Metten if the Priory of St. Michael should ever regain its independence from St. Stephen's.[33]

In the meantime the bishop of Regensburg was petitioning the royal government in Munich to restore Metten to its former independence. Villagers in the neighborhood of the priory began public prayers to prevent a second ruin of the monastery, and from his cell in Augsburg Wimmer himself began testing the waters of ecclesiastical politics. He secured from Abbot Barnabas a promise to use his considerable influence in Munich to regain for Metten its previous status, and he promised the abbot in return that he would remain in Augsburg for several years to teach at St. Stephen's College. He wrote Bishop Schwäbl of Regensburg, urging him to continue to press for the reinstatement of Metten's independence and telling him that he had learned one reason the royal government was reluctant to support Metten was that officials in Munich had little confidence in the leadership of the prior, Father Ildephonse Nebauer. Should Nebauer be induced to resign (and Wimmer recalled that the prior's appointment had been for only six years) and should a younger, more energetic man be appointed in his place, Wimmer suggested that the king might then be more inclined to recognize Metten as an independent monastery. In that event all things would be set aright and St. Stephen's could go its way while Metten went its own.

In May 1836 Wimmer made an indirect appeal to King Ludwig I through Professor Amandus Höcker, a former Benedictine of the Abbey of Oberaltaich. "Since Easter," he wrote Höcker, "I have been corresponding with the whole world, knocking at the door of every house where I think I might find someone who is interested in our Metten. During vacation I have been traveling to Regensburg and Metten with the sole intention of seeing whether something can be done to make Metten independent again." Wimmer proposed to the king through Höcker that more of the formerly monastic buildings at Metten be purchased from their lay owners so that a school could be started there. Prior Ildephonse could then be replaced as superior by one of the younger monks, whose numbers had increased since Father Boniface had pronounced vows, and there would then be no reason for Metten not to be recognized as an independent monastery. Not only would the superior, whose credit in Munich had declined, be replaced, but the community itself would be more "socially acceptable" to King Ludwig's liberal ministers because it would then be devoting its labors and energies to education.[34]

In June Wimmer wrote the bishop of Regensburg that a petition for the restoration of Metten's independence had been made to the king and that he and his Metten confreres in Augsburg had reason to hope that their plan to restore Metten to its former status would succeed.[35] Less than two months later Wimmer received the assurance of King Ludwig himself that "in accordance with the Interior Ministry's decision on the 20th of last month I have pronounced my intention that Metten be independent or should become so as soon as it has an efficient superior and the means to become an abbey."[36] Wimmer forwarded a copy of the letter to Bishop Schwäbl with the observation that Metten's opponents in the government seemed, through their machinations, to have unwittingly assured the community of something it could not have hoped for until now, namely, that the monastery would become an abbey much sooner than it would have if trouble had not been stirred up by the anticlerical party of the royal court in the first place.

Nonetheless, Wimmer remained cautious and continued his behind-the-scenes efforts to bring about a successful resolution of the affair. With the king's assurance of Metten's independence, he now turned his attention to the election of a prior to replace Father Ildephonse. The abbot of St. Stephen's had gone to Munich to propose that Father Rupert Leiss be appointed superior, but Wimmer pushed for a free election. He had the support of his confreres in this too, not so much because they opposed Father Rupert as superior but rather because they wanted to establish the precedent of freely electing their own superiors and thus achieving greater independence from outside (specifically government) influences on their monastic life. Father Boniface wrote confidently that "it seems that all obstruction will be removed and that nothing will stand in the way of the formal restoration of Metten, even if they oppose it [in Munich] as much as they can." Wimmer ended his letter to Bishop Schwäbl with the wry comment that "our Reverend Bishop of Augsburg will hardly live through the next week. I believe that he has been prayed to death, for if he had not been sick these past three months and therefore forced to be inactive, we could not have accomplished anything."[37]

At the beginning of September 1836 Wimmer and his Metten confreres in Augsburg returned to St. Michael's Priory, and on November 10 King Ludwig issued a royal decree restoring Metten to its former independence, granting it the right to receive novices, and permitting the monks to elect a new prior. Because he had proved to be a stumbling block in the effort to regain the independence of Metten, Prior Ildephonse humbly agreed to step down, and on January 11, 1837, Father Rupert Leiss was elected second conventual prior of the restored community for a term of three years. Five new novices were received by the community. Even though the financial situation of the priory was not as fortunate as the monks might have wished, Wimmer said that he and the others were delighted with the way things had turned out. The priory was now established on a firm footing, and the monks were observing the Benedictine Rule in the manner Wimmer and his confreres believed it should be observed. "Now everyone has his office," he wrote. "The horarium is firmly established and everything works according to plan. Discipline and order reign in the monastery as everyone strives for it willingly." Father Boniface had only kind words for the former prior, Ildephonse Nebauer, whom he had helped force from office.

Since all of us loved and honored him on account of his laudable personality (even if we were less than satisfied with the way he conducted his office), the change has not caused any quarrel or discord. It went off without any offense given or taken by anyone. The fraternal community has not been disturbed in any way. Externally we don't really need anything but good and numerous novices. Debts are part of poverty. . . . Next fall we will open the Latin school, first with two classes, then with four, and by and by—if God grants us success—perhaps the whole gymnasium.[38]

Despite the active part he had taken in the restoration of Metten's independence and the creation of the school, Wimmer's major activity in the months that followed his return from Augsburg centered not on the development of the Latin school or of monastic observance at Metten but rather on the parishes near the monastery. In the closing months of 1836 he was reassigned to the parish of Edenstätten as assistant pastor, and the next year he was transferred to Stephansposching to become pastor of the parish in that village.

Meanwhile King Ludwig I was proceeding with his plans for the restoration of the Benedictine Order in Bavaria. After Metten and Augsburg, the third monastery to be restored was Scheyern in the diocese of Passau. Prior Rupert Leiss was chosen to reinaugurate monastic life at Scheyern in 1838, and the following year he asked Father Gregory Scherr, his successor as prior at Metten, for a practical-minded monk who could take charge of the temporal affairs of the new community. In the summer of 1839 Prior Gregory summoned Wimmer from Stephansposching and assigned him to Scheyern as Leiss's procurator.

Wimmer remained at Scheyern for a year. In 1840 King Ludwig established the Ludwigs Gymnasium, a state college in Munich, and the Hollandeum, a boarding school connected with the college, and turned to the Benedictines of Metten for men to staff the new foundations. Metten had recently been elevated to the dignity of abbey, and Prior Gregory Scherr had been elected abbot. When the king's request came, Abbot Gregory assigned five of the Metten monks to Munich, among them Father Boniface Wimmer, who left Scheyern in the summer of 1840 to take up residence as prefect in the Hollandeum and as professor of Latin and Greek in the Ludwigs Gymnasium. After ten years of priestly and monastic life in the villages and small towns of Bavaria, the former student of von Görres and Döllinger was back in the heady atmosphere of the Bavarian capital once again.[39]

Wimmer took up his new duties as professor and prefect with enthusiasm, but neither his interest nor his involvement in the work of restoring the Benedictine Order in Bavaria to its former greatness diminished. In 1837, while assistant pastor in Edenstätten, he had persuaded some wealthy friends to purchase the former monastery of Mallersdorf from the family into whose hands the property had fallen after the suppressions of 1803. He had spoken with some of his confreres at Metten, and they agreed that it would be advantageous for their monastery to purchase Mallersdorf from Wimmer's friends and establish a dependent priory there. Father Boniface's project called for the opening of a Latin school and minor seminary at Mallersdorf that would serve as training grounds for candidates for the Benedictine Order. The Mallersdorf school, according to this proposal, would be staffed by monks from Metten until the new community had grown strong enough to gain its own independence. Thereafter it would remain a house of studies for candidates for the Bavarian Benedictine monasteries. The idea seemed sound, and Wimmer received encouragement from his friends at Metten to pursue it. By pressing for the restoration of a monastery whose principal purpose would be education and by establishing a high-quality school that would attract potential candidates for the Benedictine monasteries of Bavaria, he hoped to ensure the future of the order in Bavaria. But his project encountered immediate difficulties.

Even as he set about formulating his plan, Metten had opened its own Latin school, and Bishop Schwäbl transferred his minor seminary there, thus assuring it some measure of stability and permanence. Because both the human and financial resources of Metten were strained by the community's obligations to Scheyern, to the

Ludwigs Gymnasium in Munich, and to its own parishes and school, Abbot Gregory Scherr opposed Wimmer's project to take on Mallersdorf as an additional burden. Still, with his customary determination and his disconcerting manner of often questioning and even opposing the judgments and decisions of his superiors, Father Boniface continued to seek support from those who could further his project.

In November 1841 he wrote King Ludwig I to ask for his help in restoring Mallersdorf. He told the king that "no one is more interested in the success of the Benedictine Order than is your Royal Majesty, and for that reason I take the liberty to present this proposal for the restoration of the monastery of Mallersdorf." Wimmer predicted that "the poor, the young, and the people in general—especially the wretched among them and all those who have gone astray—would gain by it." He pointed to the great spiritual benefits that the people in the region around Metten had received as a result of the monastic presence there and noted that the same could be expected to occur in the vicinity of Mallersdorf should the monastery be restored. A school at Mallersdorf, moreover, like the school at Metten, would contribute to the cultural enrichment of the kingdom whose "citizens' sons will receive fine educations and become leaders in their parishes. What a guarantee their religious education will be for the tranquility of the country, for its security and moral strength!" Wimmer remarked that the citizens of Mallersdorf themselves wanted the Benedictines among them once again, and the Benedictines, he said, needed Mallersdorf. "Our order has needed for some time, and still needs, many novices." Many young men could certainly be expected to join the monastery from the region around Mallersdorf, just as many from the district around Metten had joined. So, having argued for the wisdom of the restoration, Wimmer formally petitioned the king to establish Mallersdorf as a Benedictine monastery that would eventually "grow in such a way that all the other privileges and favors that Your Highness has bestowed on Metten will be granted to it."[40]

The procedure for the restoration of Mallersdorf, however, was of a different character from that of the earlier restorations. Metten, Augsburg, and Scheyern had all been restored by royal decree, but now that the Benedictine Order had been established on a firm footing in Bavaria once again, the monasteries themselves possessed the canonical right to decide the question of founding daughterhouses.

In addition to petitioning the government, then, Wimmer found it necessary to seek the formal approval of his own community, which would ultimately be responsible for providing the monks to restore Mallersdorf. By November 1841 Abbot Gregory had assigned nine monks to the king's gymnasium in Munich, and Wimmer, having from the beginning assumed leadership of the Mallersdorf campaign, urged them to support his project. He asked for and received from his eight Munich confreres their written approval and support of the plan, and he sent these letters, with his own petition, to Abbot Gregory in Metten.

Scherr replied several days later that he continued to oppose the establishment of a daughterhouse at Mallersdorf. The community at Metten had already stretched itself thin, he said, and he observed that Metten's own Latin school could easily take on the added responsibility of educating candidates for the order, which Wimmer proposed be the principal function of Mallersdorf. The abbot informed Wimmer, moreover, that the king was currently interested in restoring the monastery of Weltenburg on the Danube, and he suggested that it would be better for the Benedictines to let His Majesty himself choose the beneficiaries of his generosity rather than to spend effort and energy making such proposals as Wimmer's.

Father Boniface and his confreres in Munich answered the abbot immediately. In a letter composed by Wimmer and signed by the others they said that "the information that Weltenburg is to be restored has been received with mixed emotion among us." They were pleased, of course, that King Ludwig continued to concern himself with the order, but they felt that Weltenburg was a less desirable spot to restore another monastery than was Mallersdorf. Unlike Mallersdorf, they said, Weltenburg was in an unhealthy locale, and rather than attract candidates it would discourage them. Moreover, they predicted few monks at Metten would be willing to go to Weltenburg.

Who would want to be prefects over students—if indeed there are any students? Who would want to suffer the death-agony every day, the fear that while taking a walk they might drown in the Danube or fall from the rocks? On weekdays in Weltenburg there are no more than six persons in the church; on Sundays and holy days not more than a hundred and fifty. The Danube, poor roads, snow in winter, floods in spring all cut Weltenburg off from the rest of the world, and snow and water accumulate in the rooms of the cloister for weeks at a time.

As far as the Metten monks in Munich were concerned, these all seemed cogent reasons for discouraging the restoration of Weltenburg and pushing for the restoration of Mallersdorf, but in a personal note to Abbot Gregory Wimmer admitted that "it will be difficult to dissuade the king from Weltenburg. If you want to approve my plan, you will have to insist very strongly that Mallersdorf be raised first and Weltenburg a little later."[41]

In spite of Gregory Scherr's continued opposition to Wimmer's Mallersdorf project, he presented it for consideration to the monastic chapter at Metten, and after a heated debate the monks there approved it, voting to submit the plan, along with the chapter's recommendations for acceptance, to the Bavarian Interior Ministry. Following the chapter's directive, Scherr submitted the plan to the government, but in addition he passed along his own report expressing grave reservations about Metten's capacity to undertake and execute the project. With both the Metten monks' recommendations and Abbot Gregory's report in hand, and together with the knowledge of King Ludwig's preference for the restoration of Weltenburg, the Interior Ministry vetoed Wimmer's Mallersdorf plan. Scherr informed Wimmer of the decision, and in a manner that would characterize his future dealings with those who opposed his projects, Wimmer responded with a scathing letter to his former co-novice and current superior, the abbot of Metten.

I do not want to say that you *alone* are to be blamed that His Majesty did not feel inclined to restore Mallersdorf, but no one can deny the fact that you certainly contributed to the decision. He who is not with me is against me, and he who does not gather, scatters. You have tied my hands and my feet by obedience. You have publicly deprived me of my entire undertaking and by doing so have given well-meaning people the idea that I wanted to restore this monastery for myself and not because its existence would be a good thing *per se*. You did not write the chapter's decision to the Ministry, but rather raised difficulties against it, and you therefore made me seem like a babbler and a liar. . . . To be very frank, you did not want to write about the restoration because you did not approve of it, and though you have done nothing directly, you have indirectly spoiled the plan. . . . You know, of course, that subordinates always talk about their superiors, but what they are saying on this point you do not know. I'll tell you what they are saying. All of them know that you are against Mallersdorf because you are afraid to reduce the income from your own benefice, and also because you will have

fewer students. All of them are displeased with this, and there must be something to it, even if you yourself are not entirely conscious of it. . . . Since you
do not want to send a colony to Mallersdorf, where everybody would gladly
go, you will have to send them to Weltenburg, where no one wants to go. . . .
I feel certain that Metten will have to do penance for this. . . . But I shall
write more about it at another time.[42]

If Wimmer pursued the Mallersdorf question further, none of his
surviving correspondence indicates what additional efforts he might
have made in the wake of his failure to have Mallersdorf restored. He
was branded a *Projektenmacher,* a plan-maker or visionary, by many
of his confreres, and for the rest of his life he bore the stigma of that
epithet, though within a decade he would alter its connotations significantly. By the 1860s he was reminding his confreres in Metten that
he was their *Projektenmacher,* and he was doing it with not just a little
smile of irony. In 1842, however, the epithet stung. His failure in the
Mallersdorf affair humiliated him, and he endured the disparaging
remarks of his fellow monks with a certain pained resignation.

In the bustling and stimulating milieu of Munich, the professor at
the king's gymnasium would find other interests and challenges to divert his mind from the trials of the past. In the Bavarian capital he had
the opportunity to allow his projects for the expansion of the Benedictine Order to mature in a crucible of cosmopolitan ideas and intellectual ferment that the rural life at Metten could have hardly afforded. His Mallersdorf project reached its maturity in the capital,
and it was there that Father Boniface received the unhappy news of its
failure. What relationship this failure had with his next project can
only be surmised, but it is clear that not long after his plan to restore
Mallersdorf had been rejected, Wimmer was on the trail of a new and
radically more adventuresome idea. It was one that would reach its
own maturity only after a hard and bitter struggle.

In Munich Father Boniface had occasion to witness the development of one of the most extensive and epoch-making migrations in
history. The first of several great exoduses of European peoples to the
United States was well underway by the time Wimmer received news
of the Mallersdorf failure. In 1842 100,000 immigrants left Europe
bound for the New World, and ten years later the annual rate would
increase to more than 400,000.[43] According to the most accurate

records available, nearly half of these immigrants professed the Catholic faith. Between 1830 and 1850 Germany provided the second largest contingent of Catholic immigrants to the United States (surpassed only by Ireland), and in the same twenty-year period the number of German Catholic immigrants would increase from a little more than 2,000 in 1830 to 110,800 in 1850.[44]

From Europe, where poverty, famine, war, and revolution drove thousands from their ancestral homelands, the immigrants came to America, settling in nearly every part of the United States and bringing with them both an optimism and a vitality that would dramatically contribute to the creative drive of the American people during the next century. They also brought with them a certain longing for spiritual sustenance and links with the traditions and values of the homelands they had left behind.

In the preceding twenty years mission societies had sprung up in Europe to help address both the spiritual and the cultural needs of the immigrant Catholics in America. The Society for the Propagation of the Faith of Paris-Lyons had been founded in France in 1822 to assist Catholic immigrants in the United States, and in 1829 the Leopoldine Foundation of Vienna had been established in Austria for the same purpose.[45] Both gave financial aid to American bishops whose dioceses were filling daily with emigrants from the Continent. In 1838 King Ludwig I, at the urging of Bishop Frederick Résé of Detroit among others, founded the Bavarian counterpart of the French and Austrian societies. The *Ludwig Missionsverein* was established by royal decree on December 12, 1838. Its statutes stated that its purposes were

the propagation of the Catholic Faith among the heathens and unbelievers, principally in Asia and North America; the support of the necessary churches and educational institutions as well as of the missionaries who undertake this laborious and perilous occupation; the support of the Franciscan Fathers in Jerusalem, the custodians of the Holy Sepulcher and the hosts of the Western Christians who come as pilgrims or visitors, and the preservation of the Holy Sepulcher; and the promotion of the sympathy and cooperation of the faithful for these pious purposes in general.[46]

Shortly after the creation of the Ludwig Missionsverein the directors of the society, with the approval of King Ludwig, decided that management of Bavarian alms would be facilitated if the Society for the Propagation of the Faith at Lyons took charge of the distribution of funds. The French society had almost twenty years' experience administering funds for the North American missions and in that time had developed an efficient infrastructure for delivering the money to the American bishops to assist European immigrants. The arrangement with the society at Lyons worked well for a time, but soon reports began circulating in Bavaria that the plight of German Catholics in America was not being improved by the money contributed by Bavarian almsgivers.

In 1840 awareness of the problem became widespread, and the crisis was brought to a head by the publication in Philadelphia of a pamphlet entitled *The Irish Catholic Episcopal Administration in North America*. Written in German by one Severus Brandus ("Stern Critic") and widely distributed in Bavaria, the pamphlet drew a sad picture of the trials of German Catholics in the United States. Immigrants from Germany were losing their faith in large numbers, it said, and their spiritual and temporal needs were being neglected despite the support they were allegedly receiving from their Catholic brothers and sisters in Bavaria. The accusing finger of the author pointed directly at the Irish bishops and priests of the American Church who were, in his opinion, recklessly misusing the mission alms sent from Europe. These alms, he said, were not going to the German immigrants for whom they were intended but rather were being used by the Irish bishops for Irish immigrants and Irish causes.[47] Although this attack on the American bishops was exaggerated and to a great extent unjustified, the sentiments expressed in the pamphlet gained wide currency and were accepted as fact in Bavaria. In addition, relatives and friends of German- Americans were receiving letters from their compatriots in the United States with similar complaints about the American bishops' failure to provide for the spiritual needs of the German-speaking people in their dioceses, and many of these complaints had been forwarded to the Bavarian hierarchy and the Ludwig Missionsverein.

The directors of the Ludwig Missionsverein began to take note of the complaints and argued that the problem lay with the process by which the mission society in Lyons distributed the funds it received from Bavaria. The French society, it was argued, simply turned over the alms to the American bishops, without stipulating how they were to be spent. The American bishops therefore did not feel obliged to use the money collected in Bavaria specifically for their German-speaking flocks, and thus the intentions of the Bavarian donors were not fulfilled.[48] In July 1844, after considerable discussion and debate, King Ludwig I and the directors of the Missionsverein decided that the collections of the Bavarian society would no longer be sent to Lyons but rather to the Sacred Congregation for the Propagation of the Faith in Rome, which would distribute the funds as needed and in such a way as to benefit German-speaking Catholics in America.[49]

As the difficulties of Bavarian immigrants in the United States occupied the attention of the directors of the Ludwig Missionsverein and the Bavarian Church in general, Wimmer's Mallersdorf project came to a head. Shortly after he learned that it had failed, he too began to take a serious look at the immigration problem that occupied the minds of churchmen in Munich, and not long after writing his bitter letter to Abbot Gregory Scherr of Metten, accusing the prelate of foiling his plans for the continued growth of the Benedictine Order in Bavaria, Wimmer asked his superior for permission to go to America as a missionary. His hope at the time was to go as a single missionary to work among German-speaking Catholics in the United States, as other Benedictines had done before him.[50]

Abbot Gregory denied Wimmer's request but encouraged him in his interest in the American missions and urged him to do what he could to raise funds for Bavarian Catholic projects in the United States. Scherr even sent him money for mass intentions to be forwarded to German priests in America. But for the moment, he said, Father Boniface had to be satisfied with helping his countrymen from afar; his vocation was to remain a monk of Metten.

In the fall of 1842 Wimmer returned to his duties as teacher and prefect at the Ludwigs Gymnasium in Munich, but thoughts of becoming a missionary in America continued to occupy his mind. When the 1842–1843 school year ended, he devoted renewed energy and attention to his hobbyhorse, and in July he wrote Abbot Gregory once again. Thanking him for the recent mass stipends sent from Metten, which he promised to forward to America, he told the abbot that his desire to become a missionary would not be placated by the abbot's financial generosity. He had not abandoned his hopes but had

only consented to remain at my post for another year because bodily infirmities counseled me to postpone my plan for the present. . . . I cannot discard the thought that everyone who feels drawn toward the vocation has the obligation of dedicating himself to a missionary life. I very sincerely believe that religious order priests are bound to carry out such designs more strictly than the secular clergy, and it is a disgrace if we shirk that duty. Our order will certainly gain in membership and become more popular if we achieve something in this regard. The spiritual needs of Bavaria indeed are great, but not so urgent as to stand in the way of such work. Perhaps the fact that we are not making greater progress than we are is a sign from heaven that we are remiss in this work.

Wimmer urged Scherr to consider the value of making Metten a mission house like the medieval monasteries of England and Ireland.

How this would influence the spirit of the abbey! What an encouragement for all it would be if a few—or still better, if many—not only gave up the comforts of home for life in a monastery but also followed the lost sheep to the ends of the world shunning neither poverty nor danger in their attempt to glorify the name of the Lord everywhere. If some, as could be expected, should find in this manner of life not only a slow martyrdom of suffering and hardship, but also a martyrdom that persevered to the end, what a glorious crown would be bestowed on our house!

Father Boniface proposed that Metten could easily take on such a burden, and he set forth the plan that marked the first phase of his emerging concept of the Benedictine role in the American Church. Metten, he suggested, could establish a mission house in Munich where potential missionaries could reside and attend classes at the Ludwigs Gymnasium and the university. A Benedictine would be their superior, and as soon as the students were ordained they would be sent to Metten where they could "be instructed in practical parish work and receive a good foundation for their religious life." These students would ultimately benefit the community of Metten because many of them would decide to enter the Benedictine Order. "They would then be monks and could be transferred to the other side of the ocean to establish firm centers for Catholic life and Benedictine monasticism." Once in America, they could expect candidates to enter the order from the surrounding countryside. The expenses of such an undertaking, Wimmer said, could be borne by the Ludwig Missionsverein.

But gradually enough property could be acquired in America so that we would be able to carry on the work even if the Society should cease to exist. . . . People plant trees, although they know for certain that their fruits will benefit only the next generation. Should we think only of today or to-morrow? The Lord has provided for our needs so wonderfully and so quickly. Should we not put even more confidence in Him? Must we measure everything with a yardstick and constantly keep the rules of arithmetic before our eyes? . . . The harvest is ready, but there are no laborers. Let us not become isolated or transfer this work to others. We belong to the whole world. The heretics are spreading to all parts of the earth, and we are keeping warm behind the stove.

Wimmer ended his lengthy letter to Abbot Gregory with the remark that he would continue to remain a missionary *in votis* and that it depended on Scherr whether or not he ever became one in reality.[51] The abbot replied that he would have to be satisfied with the less spectacular lot.

Frustrated in his missionary ambitions, Wimmer continued to follow events in the American Church and participate in the ongoing discussions in Munich concerning the plight of German Catholics in the United States. In 1843 the superior of the Redemptorist seminary in Altötting, where Wimmer had spent his first year as a priest, informed the directors of the Ludwig Missionsverein that two students from the Archdiocese of Baltimore had been sent to Altötting by Archbishop Samuel Eccleston to complete their studies for the priesthood. So that the German Redemptorist students could take advantage of the Americans' presence and learn English from them, the rector suggested that the Ludwig Missionsverein help finance the education of the American students while they remained at Altötting. The directors agreed. King Ludwig I at once perceived the advantages of training priests in Bavaria for the American missions and asked the directors of the mission society to investigate the feasibility of establishing a mission seminary at Altötting under royal auspices where German students could be prepared to work among German immigrants in the United States.[52]

The Redemptorists and the directors of the mission society studied the proposal for more than a year, and although they eventually abandoned it because they lacked resources for its execution, discussions about the proposal stirred up great interest in Munich. Meanwhile, the Leopoldine Foundation of Vienna, whose interest in German-speaking Catholics in America equaled that of the Ludwig Missionsverein, had sent Canon Joseph Salzbacher of Vienna to the

United States to investigate conditions at first hand. Salzbacher returned in 1843 and two years later published the celebrated account of his visit, *My Journey to North America in the Year 1842*.[53] He reported that while many German Catholics in America were concentrated in cities, others were scattered throughout the land, living on farms or in small communities. Often they saw no priest for several years at a time. The old people among them, he said, remained nominal Catholics, but the younger ones were becoming Protestant in alarming numbers as soon as their parents died. He proposed that the problem could be remedied by sending roving German-speaking missionaries, who would be independent of parish structures, to the United States. They would go from place to place administering to the spiritual needs of the scattered flock and in so doing could save thousands of souls who would otherwise be lost. Salzbacher proposed that the best solution to the problem of training such missionaries was to establish either in the United States or in Europe a seminary whose principal purpose would be to educate young men for mission work among German-American Catholics, and he mentioned that the German Redemptorists of Baltimore were prepared to undertake the work if they could somehow get the means to do it.

About the time that Salzbacher's book was circulating in Austria and Bavaria, a rare German missionary from one of the newest American dioceses was visiting the Continent to raise funds and enlist missionaries for the Germans of his region. Father Peter Henry Lemke was a convert from Lutheranism who since 1834 had worked in the mission fields of western Pennsylvania. For a while he had been assistant to the famous prince-priest of the Alleghenies, Father Demetrius Gallitzin, and after Gallitzin's death in 1840 he had taken on singlehandedly the apostolate to the German Catholics of Cambria County, Pennsylvania. When the diocese of Pittsburgh was created in 1843, the new bishop, Michael O'Connor, agreed to Lemke's proposal that he go to Europe to seek aid for the new diocese.[54]

In May 1845 Lemke arrived in Munich and there met Father Boniface Wimmer. Years later he described the encounter:

One day I dined with the Benedictine Fathers who were members of the Abbey of Metten and had charge of a Latin School. They were very inquisitive about America, and I told them among other matters that I was authorized by the bishop of Pittsburgh to engage German priests and that I would be pleased to become their leader. They only smiled at such an idea, because in those days the good people of Bavaria bothered themselves no more about America than about the moon. After dinner, Father Boniface Wimmer, one of the professors, took me aside and told me that for a long time he had felt inclined to come to America as a missionary. "It is easy," I said, "for a religious to get a dispensation for such work."

Lemke told Wimmer that he would be willing to offer him land to found a monastery and might even consider becoming a Benedictine himself and assisting in the establishment of the order in America. He had written an article for the Mainz *Katholik* in 1835, he said, in which he had asked why the Benedictines had not come to America. "This would be the land for them, if they would commence in the same way as their predecessors did more than a thousand years ago in the impenetrable forest of Germany."[55]

Wimmer's meeting with Lemke, which occurred about the time that Canon Salzbacher's book appeared and news of the failure of the Altötting mission seminary project became known, caused him to reconsider his plans for establishing schools in Munich and Metten to train priests for the American missions and for himself becoming a single missionary in North America. Now he began to envision a new project, and soon after Lemke's visit he wrote Abbot Gregory Scherr from Munich that

[F]or three years in succession I asked your permission to become a missionary. Three times I was appeased. I submitted to this decision and adapted myself to the tasks that were demanded of me, for I knew that . . . "there are ways that seem right to men, but their ends lead to perdition." Still I could never rid myself of this thought, and the desire grew stronger when I heard or read anything about America or its missions.

He went on to report to Abbot Gregory of his recent encounter with Father Lemke:

Your Lordship can easily imagine that although my sympathies for America had somewhat subsided, his descriptions revived them again. When my confreres introduced me to him as a friend of the missions, we soon became acquainted and little persuasion was necessary to make me decide to follow him. He greatly regretted the fact that our order is not yet represented in America and believes that it would well suit American ways if we took up the same work that our forefathers did centuries ago.

Father Peter Henry Lemke (1796–1882). Lemke invited
Boniface Wimmer to establish the first Benedictine
monastery in the United States in the state
of Pennsylvania. He later joined the
Benedictine Order. (ASVA)

Wimmer said that rather than continuing to promote the idea of a
mission seminary in Munich to be operated by the monks of Metten,
he was now thinking in terms of founding a Benedictine monastery
in America that would operate a seminary and train the sons of German immigrants to work among their own people in the American
missions. Lemke had offered land in western Pennsylvania for such
a monastery, he said, and Wimmer himself was ready to lead an expedition of Benedictine missionaries to bring the new project to
fruition. "To accomplish this, however, pioneer monks will be
obliged to work again with the hoe and the plow." The Benedictines,
he insisted, were more suited for the work of evangelizing America

than either the Jesuits or the Redemptorists because the former "generally are not engaged primarily in the care of souls, preferring to establish institutions in which young men of every creed are educated" and the latter "minister to people in the populous districts and therefore are doing little for the farmers, who constitute the best class of people in any country."

Wimmer told Abbot Gregory that he had submitted a request to the Propaganda Fide in Rome through Archbishop Carlo Morichini, papal nuncio to Bavaria, for permission to travel to the American missions. He had also presented to Morichini his "plan of founding a monastery on the property that Father Lemke promised to sell me. Several young men who wish to become brothers and five students have so far expressed their desire to accompany me." Father Boniface reported that Archbishop Morichini had given him every reason to hope that his petition would be granted. "I am sure," he said, "that my departure from Metten will be more a gain than a loss. The blessing of God will be with us; more priests will enter our order, and the unforgettable Mallersdorf affair will prove a success." He ended his letter to the abbot with the hope that Scherr would not "misconstrue my conduct and my intentions."[56]

During the preceding three years Wimmer had become acquainted with many Bavarian churchmen who shared his concerns about the American missions. He had come to know personally several of the directors of the Ludwig Missionsverein, including Father Joseph Ferdinand Müller, chaplain to the court of King Ludwig I, and he actively cultivated the friendships of these acquaintances in order to further his own designs. In May 1845 he sought Müller's help in obtaining for him an audience with the king to discuss his project for establishing a Benedictine monastery in the United States, and in late May Müller informed him that the audience had been arranged. It took place on June 4, 1845, and the following day, the Feast of St. Boniface, Wimmer wrote Abbot Gregory that the king had listened with great interest to his idea for educating priests to work among German-speaking immigrants in the United States. Wimmer said that he had not asked the king for assistance, "although His Majesty seemed to invite me to do so by saying that he has gladly given money to the missions in America in the past." Wimmer reported that King Ludwig, as well as Karl August von Reisach, coadjutor archbishop of Munich, believed that the Benedictines were the order best suited for mission work in the United States. "Therefore," he said, "you see that I am one step nearer my goal, which I hope to reach with God's help."[57] Ten days later Father Peter Henry Lemke gave Wimmer a formal invitation which, in the name of Bishop Michael O'Connor, authorized him to travel to the diocese of Pittsburgh and establish a Benedictine monastery there.[58] Sometime during this period, it appears that Abbot Gregory gave Wimmer the permission he sought, and on June 30 he wrote Scherr that his plans for going to America were proceeding ahead on schedule. He awaited only the Vatican's reply to the petition he had sent in May.[59]

In July the answer came from Rome, but it did not contain the news he had hoped for. Rather than granting him permission to enter the American missions, Cardinal Giacomo Filippe Fransoni, prefect of the Sacred Congregation for the Propagation of the Faith, wrote that because he was apparently needed more by his own community of Metten than by the missions in America, his petition to become a missionary was denied. Fransoni encouraged Wimmer to return with renewed zeal to his work of teaching in Munich, where he could better serve the Church and reap greater rewards for himself and the Benedictine Order than he could hope to do in the United States.[60]

Wimmer was profoundly disappointed by the response from Rome and wrote Abbot Gregory that he could not understand the reasoning of Cardinal Fransoni because he was not really needed at Metten and because Abbot Gregory had already approved his proposal to become a missionary in America "The decision, as you can see, is not satisfactory because the Propaganda directly states that it is not the opportune time for me to leave. I believe that the reasons are not sufficient. I explained this to the new nuncio, who told me that he could give me permission, but advised me to abide by the decision."[61]

Wimmer clearly had no intention of abiding by the decision. In response to the Vatican's refusal he set about drawing up a second petition to Rome. In the meantime, however, Abbot Gregory had had a change of heart. During the summer vacation, soon after the letter from the Propaganda Fide had arrived in Munich and Wimmer had written him of its contents, Scherr informed Wimmer that he was indeed needed at his posts in the Hollandeum and the Ludwigs Gymnasium, and that the permission he had previously given him to work in the American missions was revoked. Abbot Gregory suggested that the German-speaking Catholics of America really had no need for Wimmer's services, and he observed, as Cardinal Fransoni had done, that Father Boniface could do much more for the Church and his monastic community by remaining a professor and prefect in Munich than by going as a missionary to America. Scherr ordered Wimmer, therefore, to remain in the capital and begin preparing for the new academic term.

Wimmer obeyed, but he was furious. Shortly after the school year began, he wrote Abbot Gregory that he intended to submit a second petition to Rome through the papal nuncio and he hoped that Scherr would not humiliate himself by opposing it. Wimmer reminded the abbot that he still had Scherr's letter granting him permission to go to America, and noted that "it would grieve me if in my next petition I should have to call attention to the contradiction between that former declaration and your change of mind during vacation. In any case, such an about-face would appear strange."

Wimmer said that he could easily refute the reasons Abbot Gregory had given for revoking permission. It was nonsense to think that there was no need for priests in the American missions because the bishop of Pittsburgh himself had recently visited Munich in an attempt to recruit German priests for his diocese. "Similarly," he said,

the court chaplain, Father Müller, whom I also visited, has requests from Wisconsin in the United States which are far more pressing than the bishop's. Just in case you are inclined to doubt me, I gladly offer written proof. . . . For three consecutive years I have been put off from one year to the next, and this year I have been completely shoved aside. It is just as if I were a child with some caprice that would easily pass away if one just stalled a bit. A man is as good as his word. That is the way I see it, and you can consider it in no other light either. At any rate I will use every legitimate path leading to my goal.

Wimmer said that he had given much thought to the American missions and did not intend to abandon them: "My poor and forlorn fellow countrymen stand before me and call for help. I should and I do want to help as best I can. I desire to go—as firmly as can be desired—with several others or alone, whichever is possible and more convenient. I will not rest until I have succeeded." He said that he felt ashamed of the Benedictine Order because of its stubborn refusal to respond to a need that was obvious to everyone and was being addressed by all other religious orders in Germany. "Just recently I heard again from the court chaplain, Father Müller, that the Premonstratensians of Wiltau have established a monastery in North America. . . . When I heard this, I began to think that the whole world is getting ahead of us: the Jesuits, the Redemptorists, and now the Premonstratensians. We alone stick to our 'nicely and slowly forward' etc. I have been and still am ashamed of it—ashamed to the very quick." Wimmer ended his letter to Abbot Gregory with a plea that he reconsider his position and let him have a definite and positive reply that he could submit to the papal nuncio in Munich, along with his new petition, as soon as possible. "I have paid my debt to Metten as well as I could. In my thirteen years as a monk I have been kept at home for only two. Thus by letting me help out all over—in Augsburg, Scheyern, and Munich—Metten has already clearly indicated that as much as my weak strength permits, I am to labor more for the good of the whole order than for Metten itself. I am willing to do it; surely you would not want to hold me back."[62]

But it would take Wimmer many more months of pleading, persuading, and cajoling before Scherr would finally see his way clear to let him go, and even then Scherr would have deep reservations. Wimmer's thoughts continued to bend toward America. He was thirty-six years old, and for the second time in his priestly life he was preparing to make a major change of vocation. As strongly as the monastery had called him from the secular priesthood, so now the American missions called him from his monastery. The voices of his countrymen were drifting back, forlorn and homesick, across three thousand miles of ocean, and if no one else was prepared to respond, he at least would not turn a deaf ear. He would go under any circumstance—even alone if necessary.

2 ❧ Answering the Call

In the autumn of 1845 excerpts from the Viennese edition of *Meine Reise nach Nordamerika in Jahre 1842,* Canon Josef Salzbacher's account of conditions among German Catholics in the United States, began to appear in *Sion,* the weekly Catholic supplement of the *Augsburger Postzeitung.* The Bavarian publication of Salzbacher's detailed description of the plight of German-speaking immigrants in North America, and his appeal to the religious orders, especially the Jesuits and the Redemptorists, to step into the breach and supply the American missions with German-speaking priests to preserve the immigrants' faith, rejuvenated the debate that had been going on for several years among ecclesiastics in Munich over how best to serve the spiritual needs of German Catholics in America.

Salzbacher's solution to the problem was for the Jesuits or the Redemptorists to establish in either Germany or the United States a mission seminary to train German-speaking secular clergy for the American missions. These missionaries, working outside traditional parochial structures, would travel about the United States bringing religion and the sacraments to German-speaking immigrants not only in the cities, where many of them had settled, but also in the remoter rural areas, in which many others had established themselves and which were seldom visited by a priest. This was essentially the idea that the directors of the *Ludwig Missionsverein* had attempted to put into motion with the proposed creation of a Redemptorist mission seminary in Altötting. For lack of sufficient financial resources, the mission seminary at Altötting had never materialized, but now that Salzbacher had raised the idea again, churchmen in Bavaria began once more to discuss it in the light of his arguments.

Wimmer too was fascinated by Salzbacher's proposals, but he found himself in disagreement with some key elements of the solution offered by the Austrian priest. In November 1845, only days after sending his letter to Gregory Scherr asking that the abbot reconsider his decision not to permit him to go to the United States as a missionary, Wimmer composed a response to Canon Salzbacher's book in which he outlined his own ideas about how best to address the spiritual needs of German immigrants in North America. Entitled *Über die Missionen* and published anonymously in the *Augsburger Postzeitung* on November 8, 1845, Wimmer's article has been called the "charter of the American Benedictines" because in it he set forth the aims and methods he developed consistently and successfully over the next four decades to establish the Benedictine Order in the United States.[1]

"Every Catholic who cherishes his faith," he said, "must take a deep interest in missionary labors." He continued:

But religion as well as patriotism demands that every German Catholic should take a special interest in the missions of America. To us it cannot be a matter of indifference how our countrymen are situated in America. I, for my part, have not been able to read the various and generally sad reports on the desolate condition of Germans beyond the ocean without deep compassion and a desire to do something to alleviate their pitiable condition. . . . I do not wish to offend anyone, but my opinion is that secular priests are not the best adapted for missionary labors. History shows that the Church has not availed herself of their services to any great extent in missionary undertakings. I do not mean to say that a secular priest cannot labor effectually within a limited territory in America, for there are many who labor successfully even at the present day. But they cannot satisfy themselves. They are in great danger of becoming careless and worldly-minded. I cannot agree with Dr. Salzbacher when he says that the spiritual needs of our countrymen can be provided by perambulating missionaries, who go about like the Wandering Jew from forest to forest, from hut to hut; for unless such a missionary be a *Saint* not much of the spiritual man would remain in him, and even then by such transient visits not much lasting good could be accomplished. The missionary, more than any other priest, stands in need of spiritual renewal from time to time, consolation and advice in trials and difficulties. He must, therefore, have some place where he can find such assistance: this may be given by his bishop but he will find it more securely in a religious community—in the midst of his confreres.

For this reason, Wimmer argued, religious were better adapted to missionary work than secular priests. "All things being equal," he wrote, "a religious priest in community should be able to work more effectively on the missions than the secular priest who stands alone."

The next question, of course, was which religious order was best suited for American missions—"not to convert the native Indians but to provide for the spiritual necessities of German immigrants." Wimmer observed that both the Jesuits and the Redemptorists were doing admirable work in the United States. But, he went on,

the fact that Jesuits generally receive only the children of richer families, many of whom are Protestants, into their institutions, because they depend upon them for their sustenance, and that the Redemptorists are by their statutes required to devote themselves to missionary work, and can, therefore, not be expected to take charge of seminaries, gives us no reason to hope that the spiritual wants of Americans, particularly of German-Americans, will be provided for by native German-speaking priests.

There was, however, another religious order that was perfectly suited, both by its character and by its history, to serve the needs of German Catholics in the New World. "We now come to the Benedictines," Wimmer wrote,

who are not as yet represented in the United States. In my opinion they are the most competent to relieve the great want of priests in America. In support of my opinion I will adduce some facts: but I must again state that I have not the remotest intention of belittling the efforts and successes of other religious orders; on the contrary, I am desirous of seeing them labor in the same field, side by side with the Benedictines.

History abundantly proves:

(1) That we owe the conversion of England, Germany, Denmark, Sweden, Norway, Hungary, and Poland almost exclusively to the Benedictines, and that in the remaining parts of Europe Christendom is deeply indebted to them.

(2) That the conversion of these countries was not transient but lasting and permanent.

(3) That this feature must be ascribed to the fact that the Benedictines are men of stability; they are not wandering monks; they acquire lands and bring them under cultivation and become thoroughly affiliated to the country and people to which they belong, and receive their recruits from the district in which they have established themselves.

(4) That the Benedictine Order by its Rule is so constituted that it can readily adapt itself to all times and circumstances. The contemplative and practical are harmoniously blended; agriculture, manual labor, literature,

missionary work, education were drawn into the circle of activity which St. Benedict placed before his disciples. Hence they soon felt at home in all parts of Europe and the same could be done in America.

Having presented the relevant historical facts and institutional characteristics that made the Benedictines ideally suited for missionary work, Wimmer continued his argument by comparing nineteenth-century North America with medieval Europe and by then concluding that what the Benedictines did in medieval Europe they could do again in modern America.

When we consider North America as it is today, we can see at a glance that there is no other country in the world which offers greater opportunities for the establishment and spread of the Benedictine Order, no country that is so much like our old Europe was. There are found immense forests, large uncultivated tracts of land in the interior, most fertile lands which command but a nominal price; often for miles and miles no village is to be seen, not to speak of cities. In country districts no schools, no churches are to be found. The German colonists are scattered, uncultured, ignorant, hundreds of miles away from the nearest German-speaking priest, for, practically, they can make their homes where they please. There are no good books, no Catholic papers, no holy pictures. The destitute and unfortunate have no one to offer them a hospitable roof, the orphans naturally become the victims of vice and irreligion—in a word, the conditions in America today are like those of Europe 1000 years ago, when the Benedictine Order attained its fullest development and effectiveness by its wonderful adaptability and stability.

Wimmer said that in the United States the Benedictine Order "would be required to adapt itself again to circumstances and begin anew," but that in America it would find fertile ground for the establishment of a monastery whose preliminary work would be pastoral.

Such a monastery would from the very start be of great advantage to German settlers, at least to those who would live near it. They would have a place where they could depend upon hearing mass on Sundays and hear a sermon in their own language; they would also have a place where they could always be sure to find a priest at home to hear their confessions, to bless their marriages, to baptize their children, and to administer the last sacraments to the sick if called in time.

Wimmer envisioned that eventually the work of the monks would expand and the monastery would soon become an important cultural and educational center that would attract German-speaking settlers, students, and candidates for the priesthood. "Such a monastery if judiciously located would not long remain isolated," he said.

All reports from America inform us that the German immigrants are concentrating themselves in places where churches have been erected or where a German-speaking priest has taken up his residence. This would also be found, and to a greater extent, if there were a monastery somewhere with a good school. In a short time a large German population would be found near the monastery, much as in the Middle Ages, villages, towns, and cities sprang up near Benedictine abbeys. Then the monks could expect a large number of children for their school, and in the course of time, as the number of priests increases, a college with a good Latin course could be opened. They would not be dependent upon the tuition fee of the students for their support, which they could draw from the farm and the missions (though these would not be a source of much income in the beginning). Thus they could devote their energies to the education of the poorer classes of boys who could pay little or nothing, and since these boys would daily come in contact with priests and other monks, it could scarcely be otherwise but that many of them would develop a desire of becoming priests or even religious.

Thus, as Wimmer foresaw it, the monastery would become not just a cultural and educational center but a source of missionary priests who would sally forth from the monastic community to bring the comforts of religion and the sacraments to those who would otherwise be deprived of them. "In this way a numerous religious clergy could soon be secured, and then some of the Fathers might be sent out to visit those Catholics who scarcely ever see a priest; occasionally at least they might preach the word of God and bring the consolations of religion even to those who live at a great distance from the monastery; small congregations could be established, and the seminary could soon furnish a goodly number of the secular clergy."

Most of the ideas Wimmer proposed in his anonymous article for the *Augsburger Postzeitung* he had set forth earlier in his correspondence with Abbot Gregory Scherr, but this was the first time he had given them public expression. During the previous year he had had a chance to test these ideas in discussions with noted churchmen, including Father Joseph Müller, chaplain to the court of King Ludwig I, and Father Frederick von Held, C.Ss.R., the Vienna-born provincial of the Redemptorists' Belgian province to which the Redemptorist missions in North America were subject. Now, however, for the first time he laid his plan open to public scrutiny. He was heartened by the response it received.

Three days after the appearance of the article, Wimmer wrote Scherr and enclosed a copy of his article for the abbot's consideration. He noted that many of his Benedictine confreres, as well as non-Benedictine ecclesiastics in Munich, saw great merit in the plan, and he said that though other voices might be raised against it, "I am prepared to explain my statements without contradiction and to prove that the Benedictines, better than priests of any other order, are fit to become missionaries in America not only to the Germans living there but to Catholics generally." He said that he hoped the abbot would now see that the plan was not capricious. He had "considered this earnestly for many years," and the conclusions he had drawn had been reinforced by the support of many who knew the situation in America much better than did the abbot of Metten. He emphasized that his plan did not involve merely furnishing priests for some scattered German colonies in the United States. It had a greater purpose: "to found monasteries of our order and to erect important ecclesiastical institutions." By purchasing land in America, a Benedictine colony would soon admit the possibility of supporting the German-American clergy from its own means and also of procuring assurance of lasting existence in the unforeseen event that the flow of money from Europe should stop.

Wimmer told Scherr that Metten was all but obliged to assist in the project because "God rewards abundantly what one in temporal need mercifully donates." But as the Apostle Paul said, "He who sows sparsely harvests sparsely." Would it not be preferable, he asked, for Abbot Gregory's "name and history to be associated with the memory of a mission similar to that which your great namesake sent from Rome to England" rather than with the recollection that "through your influence such a mission was prevented?" He then offered a half-apology: "Pardon me this language. It seems to be a strong indictment, but it is only an expression of the zeal which I have for your honor." Wimmer denied that he wanted to go to America "to improve my situation or to be a superior myself—though I must admit that I have enough confidence in myself to think that I will be able to found one or more monasteries." Rather, he said, he sincerely wanted to work among the poor Germans in America and to be instrumental in spreading the Order of St. Benedict for which he was willing to make any sacrifice.

Wimmer complained that he could not understand Scherr's refusal to live up to this previous agreement to let him go to the American missions. The response from the Propaganda to his original petition, he claimed, had not been an absolute denial but rather a "postponement" because the officials in Rome thought Wimmer was needed at Metten. Now that it seemed that Metten could do without him, Wimmer wanted Scherr to live up to his original promise: "The word of a prelate must have some value. It must be holy. I will take you at your word, which is holy to me, and I will not let you go so easily. I have it black on white and will not let it out of my hand, except to send it to Rome. Then you will have the choice either of declaring me unfit for this mission . . . or admitting that you simply do not want to live up to your word."[2]

Even without Abbot Gregory's permission, Wimmer was preparing for his departure for America. Through the offices of Court Chaplain Müller he kept in close contact with the directors of the Ludwig Missionsverein, and after publishing his article in the *Augsburger Post-zeitung* he discovered that the king himself had begun to take a serious interest in his plan to establish the Benedictine Order in the United States. Wimmer's earlier audience with the king had failed to produce any tangible assistance, but when Ludwig inquired who the author of the article was and learned that Father Boniface had written it, he summoned the Benedictine to court. This second audience with the king proved highly successful and dramatically advanced Wimmer's project toward its ultimate achievement. King Ludwig listened to Father Boniface's ideas, promised financial support to establish the Benedictine Order in the United States, and urged him to proceed with his preparations. Having received assurances of the king's support, Wimmer turned to other powerful figures in Munich and learned that they too were ready to help him. The directors of the Ludwig Missionsverein pledged financial assistance. The papal nuncio, Archbishop Morichini, expressed renewed interest and promised to use his influence in Rome to obtain the necessary approval from officials at the Propaganda, and Dr. Joseph von Görres of the University of Munich came forward with encouragement and advice.[3]

Despite the encouragement and tangible support offered by secular and ecclesiastical officials in the Bavarian capital, however, Wimmer still had not received permission from Abbot Gregory Scherr to go to America. Nevertheless, confident that Scherr would eventually acquiesce, he proceeded with his plans. In November 1845 he wrote to Father Peter Henry Lemke, who had returned to America a short time earlier, and informed him that his project for establishing a monastery in Cambria County, Pennsylvania, was advancing on schedule. He hoped, he said, to be in America by the following autumn.[4] In the meantime he had begun to recruit candidates for the venture, and by December he had enlisted about twenty young men who were willing to accompany him. About this time he also persuaded Abbot Gregory to submit his proposal for founding a monastery in the United States to the chapter at Metten and to let the monks themselves pass judgment on it. Nearly all the Metten monks in Munich supported the project, and Wimmer felt confident that the rest of the community would support it as well. But he was mistaken.

When the capitulars assembled at Metten, the failure of Wimmer's Mallersdorf project came to mind, and the monks expressed grave doubts as to whether the community's *Projektenmacher* would be able to succeed in an undertaking so ambitious as this latest one. After an extended debate, therefore, they decided not to give him their total support for the establishment of a monastery in the United States. Instead, since Wimmer was so eager to go to America, they recommended to Abbot Gregory that he be given a leave of absence in order to serve in the American missions, with the stipulation that he could be recalled to Metten whenever he was needed there again. Apparently, one of the major reasons for such limited support of Wimmer's plan was that many within the Metten community believed that Wimmer's motives were not as selfless and noble as he claimed them to be. These sentiments were repeatedly voiced during the chapter, with some monks suggesting that Wimmer was a dreamer and a malcontent whose disappointment with the Mallersdorf affair had soured him on his own community and had caused him to want to sever his ties with Metten. The easiest way for him to do this was to go to America and found his own monastery. Others said that he was excessively ambitious and wanted to become an abbot, and since the way to his goal seemed blocked in Bavaria, his plan was to establish his own community in North America over which he could rule as superior.

From several of his confreres at Metten Wimmer learned the gist of the discussions in chapter, and in response he immediately began to compose a series of letters to Abbot Gregory and to Father Utto Lang, O.S.B., a Metten capitular and the future successor of Scherr, in which he defended himself against the aspersions cast upon him by "those who know me so well."

He said, first of all, that though he would go to America as a temporary missionary if ordered to do so by his superior and community, he would not think of applying for such a mission. He wanted not only permission to go to the United States but also the authority to establish a Benedictine monastery there. He had recruited twenty young men who were relying on him, and he could not possibly take them three thousand miles across the ocean if he had to face the possibility of being recalled to Metten at any time. He was obliged to consider the security of his companions because they were sacrificing a great deal to accompany him to a strange and foreign land. If he were recalled, they would be left stranded, leaderless and unable to support themselves. His young followers, Wimmer said, were all ready "to work with hoe and ax and to live as the ancient Benedictines used to live," but he needed assurances from Abbot Gregory and the community of Metten that their hopes would not be dashed soon after their arrival in America. "Give me the liberty to do what I can in America," he pleaded; "I worked for Metten and succeeded as I intended because I could do what I wanted to do. I worked for Mallersdorf and succeeded as long as I could do what I wanted to do. The project failed because others refused to do what I advised. . . . And [in America] I will succeed if I am free to act as I want to. God is my witness that I do everything for Him and for His holy Church and for our holy order."

He expected difficulties at the beginning, he said, but these would not discourage him. He simply wanted assurance from Metten that initial hardships and problems would not provoke the chapter to recall him from the missions. "How long did it take St. Boniface to achieve anything?" he asked. "But he did not give up, and later it turned out to be all right with him."

So Wimmer asked that his release from Metten be unconditional, and if this were not possible, he asked that he be given a guarantee that once he had established a monastery in America, he would be able to transfer his vow of stability from Metten to the new community. Above all, however, he wanted the authority to go to America and establish a monastery, not simply permission to go and act as a solitary missionary subject to recall at any moment. Wimmer had learned that Abbot Gregory had expressed guarded support for such an undertaking during the recent chapter meeting, and he now urged Scherr to make a written declaration to the effect that he was giving his missionary-minded subject the authority not only to go to America but also to found "one or more monasteries in America . . . and that I will be released permanently if I succeed in establishing a community as strong as Weltenburg." He also asked Scherr to inform Archbishop Morichini of his decision.

Wimmer said that he was offended and insulted by the insinuations made about his motives by his confreres during the recent chapter. If Scherr did not trust him to lead the group and wanted to send another priest as superior, he would be happy to follow him, but he said that he resented being "persecuted with suspicion even across the ocean." In a characteristic display of anger and defiance, he wrote:

If I cannot work in America as a Benedictine, I will go in another habit. . . . If you do not trust me to govern a monastery . . . then let another priest go with me. . . . I will gladly serve under him. Something has to be done by us; of this I am firmly convinced. My way can be made more difficult, but it cannot be closed. I can be delayed and retarded, but not stopped. I can be persecuted with suspicion and distrust . . . but I will go my way because I firmly believe that God wills it. I beg again, with all respect, for a definite written decision. I cannot be satisfied with the permission as it was previously given, for it does not suit my plans.

Wimmer closed his letter by saying once again that he ardently wished "that my present superiors would send me rather than dismiss me. In the extreme case that they prove pitiless, I will join another order under other superiors who will fulfill my desire. God knows I do not look for a higher position, but only for the missions."[5]

The persistence that had marked Wimmer's single-minded determination to bring about his plan to establish a Benedictine monastery in the United States finally paid off in February 1846 when he received his abbot's approval of the project and his permission to undertake it.[6] In March he wrote Scherr to thank him for his paternal benediction and to inform him that permission for the mission had also arrived from the Propaganda Fide in Rome. There was still some question as to whether he had been given authority to establish a Benedictine monastery in North America, but both Archbishop Morichini and Bishop O'Connor would support his petition to do so, which he had no doubt would be granted by Rome. In the meantime he had begun making final arrangements for the journey and had already received 6,000 florins from the Ludwig Missionsverein for travel expenses. He was expecting a letter from Father Lemke any day confirming that he was ready to receive the Bavarian missionaries upon their arrival in Pennsylvania.[7]

As Wimmer's travel plans began to take shape, however, he received a letter from several of the young candidates he had recruited, a letter in which they voiced their doubts and expressed reluctance to leave so soon for America. Wimmer had enlisted a number of students of theology for the proposed monastery in the United States and had recruited a far greater number of candidates for the lay brotherhood. Six of the students sent a joint letter to him in February requesting permission to remain in Bavaria to complete their studies and to learn more about the Benedictine life before joining him in the American missions. Three days after receiving the letter, Wimmer penned a reply in which he set forth firmly, unambiguously, and with detail the nature of his vision for the Benedictine Order in America and the implications of that vision for those who wished to join him. His letter to the students articulated both the practical and the theological foundations of his mission to the New World.

"If I rightly understand the tenor of your letter," he wrote,

you wish to inform me that, as matters now stand, you are not satisfied with the hope of becoming Benedictines and missionaries in America, but are anxious to know whether I intend to take you with me at once or leave you in the Institute until you complete your regular course of studies, or send you to one of our monasteries to become acquainted with the Holy Rule. You also intimate that, unless you first live here under the same Rule, you might later regret the step which you are planning to take. I can even see the beginning of wavering in your resolution to follow me. In response I am sending you the following points for your consideration:

(1) You must above all be determined to become priests and good priests.

(2) You must become religious not only to be united to Christ more closely and follow Him more faithfully, but, if necessary, do more for Him, to suffer for Him, and not by any means to go with the intention of becoming priests more easily or, still less, to escape temporal cares.

(3) The vocation to the priesthood in itself is a great grace, and that to the religious state a greater one, because it is a state of perfection, and that to the missionary life still greater, because it is an apostolic vocation.

(4) We should consider it a great privilege that God deigns to use us as instruments in founding an institution which, if the foundation is well laid, will confer untold benefits on the people of the United States. If you consider this well, you will not put yourself forward without vocations. But if you feel the call within you, you will not allow yourselves to be deterred from following this impulse by obstacles, because the greater the sacrifice, the greater the reward. We will be able to say to Our Lord with Peter, "Behold we have left everything and have followed Thee; what therefore will we have?" Undoubtedly he will give us the same answer that he gave to Peter, recorded in the Gospel of St. Matthew, chapter 19, verse 28 ["I tell you this: in the world that is to be, when the Son of Man is seated on his throne in heavenly splendor, you my followers, will have thrones of your own, where you will sit as judges of the twelve tribes of Israel."].

If these are your sentiments, you will never have cause to regret having followed me when you are in America. The main reason is not that you are in quest of beautiful surroundings, a comfortable home, or a life of ease, but that you are seeking the opportunity to carry the cross of self denial after the crucified Jesus, to save or regain souls that otherwise would be lost and for which His blood would have been shed in vain.

What I know of America I have learned only from hearsay and from what I have read about it. I must be prepared to meet all possible emergencies. I am giving up a comfortable and honorable position and cannot reasonably expect another. I am leaving behind relatives who are poor and therefore stand in need of me. I am parting from kind superiors and confreres who honor me and only reluctantly consent that I go. I am renouncing a position in which everything is well ordered to enter upon an entirely new state of life in which everything has to be started anew and be put in order.

I do this because I am interiorly urged, although I take upon myself difficulties, cares, and hardships. My heaviest burden, however, will be that I must carry out my plans with men whose willingness, confidence, and vocation have first to be tested.

You see, therefore, that I have no advantage over you. I am willing to take you along because I am confident that you will gladly share my joys and sorrows in the service of God and of our neighbor. If you join me, you must be animated by the same confidence in me. If you cannot have this confidence in my integrity, my honesty, my zeal, my experience, and my determination, do not go with me. Under such conditions you would not obey, and I could not keep you. Perhaps next to confidence in God, these qualities will often be the only means to console and support us in our difficulties and hardships. Through harmony small things grow; through dissension great things are destroyed.

To that end you should consider it a privilege to be allowed to take part in a work like this. I will be glad to have good and zealous helpers. But you must not imagine that you are doing me a favor by going with me. The reception into a religious order is something that must always be asked for, no matter how welcome an applicant may be to a community. For this reason, do not go with me to please me, but on the contrary, consider yourselves fortunate and honored if you are found worthy to take part in such an undertaking. God is able to raise up children to Abraham from stones. He made Paul out of Saul. If my undertaking is from Him, He will send me colaborers, wherever they may come from. I am sure of this. Therefore I will not persuade or entice you to go and thus render you unhappy if you have no vocation. You will never have cause to cast this up to me. I do not know the future. I only show you the cross. If you take it upon your shoulders, very well. But do not complain afterwards when from time to time you feel its weight. Jesus said to his apostles, "Behold, I have told you beforehand," and "Behold, I send you as lambs among the wolves." And he said it to us also, and I say it to you: if you are afraid of the wolves, if you fear their howling and their teeth, then stay at home. If you have not the courage to do and suffer all things for Christ through his grace, to go wherever you are called by obedience, to allow yourselves to be used as willing tools, then do not go to a monastery and by no means go to America. It is true, in America all are free to profess their respective religions, but non-Catholics are more numerous, powerful, and wealthy than Catholics. We cannot tell whether they will always respect the laws. They may possibly persecute us and even put us to death. I can vouch for nothing. I am prepared for everything, and whoever wishes to follow me must likewise be prepared.

As you desire to go with me, it will not be necessary to complete your course of studies. In America no one will ask you whether you have completed your entire course of studies. However, if you wish to finish it, it must be done before July; and I hope to obtain this favor for you. The preparations for it will have to be made here.

I would not advise you to enter a monastery here to make your novitiate. You would soon become accustomed to many things that you will not find in America, and this would result in unpleasant comparisons. I know of a religious community that receives no one who belonged for even an hour to another community.

If you wish to accompany me at once, I will take you along without much ado. But your decision must be made soon because I will have to make arrangements accordingly, as two may have some difficulty in getting released from army service. You will have time to become acquainted with the

Holy Rule before you leave. As soon as the copies I ordered arrive, we can begin without delay. It will not take long to read it and you need not fear it, for it is very moderate.

You must also get the consent of your parents and guardians. Only after a written statement of this is on hand, will I be able to arrange matters with the government. . . .

If to all this everyone adds good will and fraternal charity, our little monastery will be a veritable paradise. Even if suffering, sickness, poverty, or persecution should occasionally be our lot, as they are not wanting in any place, still they will be like pepper and salt to season the monotony of our daily routine. They will remind us that there is nothing perfect here below and that we must carry the cross of affliction because the road to heaven is narrow and thorny. Let there be no Judas among us. Let no temporal considerations motivate us. Let not ambition be our goal. Do not render my life nor yours miserable through such aims. If you feel that you are weak, it is no disgrace to stay at home, but to come along without being animated by pure and holy intentions would be acting the part of Judas.

From this you know my opinion in the matter. Consider well whether you are satisfied with what I have said. May God guide you in your decision. I will not entice you, nor will I tempt you to go; but I will take you along if you desire to follow me.[8]

It is a measure of Wimmer's self-confidence, the boldness of his vision, and his willingness to take enormous risks to achieve his ends that he planned to establish the Benedictine Order in America not with experienced monks but with young and untried recruits whom he could mold according to his own ideals and interpretation of the Benedictine Rule. Clearly he intended to create something new in the United States, a Benedictine monasticism that, though rooted in European and Bavarian tradition, would develop along new lines and address pragmatically and innovatively the needs of the Church in the New World.

Wimmer spent the next several months outfitting himself and his companions and preparing for the journey to Pennsylvania. From lay and ecclesiastical benefactors in Munich and from Metten itself he collected books, missals, clothes, altar vessels, altar linens, mass vestments, breviaries, and works of art that "would be quite an embellishment in America and very desirable." He was unable to obtain deferments from military conscription for two of the six students and for several of the brother candidates. A secular priest, Father John Aman, who had expressed interest in joining the group, withdrew at the last moment. But otherwise things proceeded smoothly.[9]

In May Wimmer wrote the Benedictine bishop of Linz, Austria, Gregory Thomas Ziegler, informing him of his plan to establish a Benedictine monastery in America and asking for advice and support. Ziegler replied that Wimmer's project was "very pleasing to me. I am perfectly convinced that a country, no matter where it is situated on earth, can be christianized and strengthened in the faith" through the presence of Benedictine monasteries. The bishop said that he would welcome the opportunity to contribute to the undertaking, and he sent an initial contribution of several thousand florins to help pay for the missionary band's passage to the United States.[10]

Wimmer's plan called for the enlistment of a large number of non-clerical lay brothers for the Benedictine colony in America, and since there was no precedent in the Bavarian monasteries for so many brothers (at the time Metten had only three), he began attempting to formulate a spiritual regimen for them. He asked Bishop Ziegler and Abbot Gregory for advice, saying that he had not yet decided whether it would be better to have the brothers join the clerical monks in the choral chanting of the Latin office, to establish a separate choir for them in which they would pray the psalms in German with lessons from the New Testament, or to have them pray the Little Office of the Blessed Virgin in German together with the rosary. This was a question Wimmer would not decide until after the monks had settled in America. In the meantime he attempted to secure enough breviaries to permit the lay brothers to chant the Latin office along with the clerical students and himself.[11]

In the beginning of June Wimmer reported to Abbot Gregory that he had decided to make a major change in his plans. He had determined against going to the diocese of Pittsburgh after all. Father Peter Henry Lemke had not responded to any of his letters, and Wimmer had since then spoken with Redemptorist priests from America who recommended him to Bishop William Quarter of the diocese of Chicago. "Many Germans live there," Wimmer wrote, "but there are no German priests. Some Redemptorist missionaries have advised me to go there because the earth is very fertile, the climate mild, and the price of land reasonable. Besides, there is no fear of jealousy among various missionary groups because there is no competition."[12]

In the weeks that followed Wimmer continued to raise funds and gather supplies for the journey to America. On June 23 he wrote Abbot Gregory that a letter from Bishop O'Connor of Pittsburgh had finally arrived formally inviting him and his Benedictine candidates to the diocese, but the bishop wanted testimonial letters for Father Boniface from the abbot of Metten and the bishop of Regensburg, and Wimmer was still awaiting a letter of invitation from Bishop Quarter of Chicago. "After that I will decide where I will go."[13]

Shortly afterward Wimmer received a letter from Father Lemke in which the Pennsylvania missionary said that he had made all the necessary preparations and was expecting Wimmer and his band in the late summer or early fall. Their forthcoming arrival, he said, was "generally known in the neighborhood, and the people are longing to see the sons of St. Benedict swinging axes in the American forests as they did a thousand years ago in the German forests." Lemke also wrote that he was considering joining the community and taking Benedictine vows himself.[14] On June 30 Wimmer wrote Bishop Ziegler of Linz that he had decided against going to the diocese of Chicago after all and had returned to his original plan of accepting Lemke's offer in western Pennsylvania. It was located, he said, "in the beautiful Allegheny Mountains at the origin of the Susquehanna River, seven hours from Loretto where Prince Gallitzin worked so long and profitably that almost the whole country is Catholic. The place is indicated in Dr. Salzbacher's travel accounts and is better recommended for a Benedictine settlement than is the property in distant Illinois."

Lemke's land, Wimmer said, lay midway between Philadelphia and Pittsburgh and would therefore be an ideal spot for a Benedictine motherhouse where "new arrivals can first become acclimatized and then, if more follow later, can join the train of migration westward."[15]

In mid-July Father Boniface wrote Abbot Gregory telling him that many people, both lay and ecclesiastic, had come forward with donations for the Benedictine mission in the United States and that he had set the final plans in motion for the journey to America.

Now I must humbly ask to be recognized, *formally and in writing*, as the superior of the mission, so that I may have the necessary ecclesiastical authority over my people, and will also be able to prove my legitimate jurisdiction to my future ordinary. I dislike having to make such a request, but it is absolutely necessary that some ecclesiastical title be added to the name of 'the

Reverend Boniface.' If this is not done, authority can hardly be upheld in the land of freedom.

All but one of his novices, he said, were full of confidence and enthusiasm for the mission. The indecisive one, however, was giving Wimmer many headaches. "He is just like an old woman who can never make up her mind. If he does not withdraw by himself, I will advise him to do so. He does not have firm confidence in God or me, and for a decision such as this, one needs to have both." Wimmer asked Scherr to forgive him for "all those things I meant to do well but did badly." Similarly he asked pardon of all his confreres at Metten "for any offenses by which I scandalized them," and he begged that his "future foundation be admitted into the family of monasteries for which prayers are said at Metten, that fraternal charity might increase among them."[16]

Less than two weeks later, on July 25, 1846, Wimmer and his band of eighteen missionaries assembled in St. Michael's Church, Munich, at five o'clock in the morning and attended mass offered for them by Karl August von Reisach, coadjutor archbishop of Munich. When mass ended, the missionaries gathered at the Munich train station, and after bidding farewell to their relatives and friends, they departed the Bavarian capital for Mainz. The following day Archbishop Carlo Morichini, papal nuncio to the kingdom of Bavaria, filed a report to the Propaganda Fide in Rome saying that Wimmer and his party were bound for the diocese of Pittsburgh with the hope of transplanting the Benedictine Order from Europe to North America.[17]

The intrepid band traveled through Augsburg, Ulm, and Stuttgart to Mainz. In Mainz an exuberant Wimmer penned a hurried letter to Bishop Ziegler. "With God's help," he said, "I hope not to disappoint the confidence and expectations which my benefactors, sponsors, and friends have placed in me, and if these hopes of mine are fulfilled, Your Excellency will not regret having found the cause that I represent worthy of your attention, participation, and most gracious support. With a profound awareness of my weakness and feeling the need of strong support from the pious prayers of all God-fearing people, I commend myself once again to your prayers." Wimmer signed himself "Superior of the Benedictine Mission to America."[18]

From Mainz the group traveled down the Rhine to Rotterdam where on August 10, 1846, they embarked on the packetboat *Iowa* for the United States. Daniel Lines was the ship's master. According to the regulations governing the *Iowa*'s voyage, each passenger older than five years had to provide for himself forty pounds of hardtack, five pounds of rice, four pounds of butter, twelve pounds of ham, two pounds of salt, two hundred pounds of potatoes, and four pints of vinegar. Moreover, everyone had to furnish his own bedding, his own kitchen utensils, and—under pain of being rejected or losing his transportation—each had to be on board twelve hours before sailing.[19]

At one time Wimmer's candidates had numbered twenty-five, but their ranks had dwindled to eighteen by the time the pioneer members of the first Benedictine community in the United States boarded the *Iowa*. There were four clerical candidates and fourteen candidates for the lay brotherhood. Accompanying Wimmer and the Benedictine candidates on the *Iowa* was a party of Premonstratensian monks on their way to the new Norbertine monastery in Wisconsin. The leader of the group was Father Maximilian Gärtner. He and Wimmer shared a cabin while the Benedictine and Premonstratensian candidates traveled in steerage.[20]

Among the students thirty-one-year-old Benedict Lawrence Haindl had made his classical studies at the Old Gymnasium in Munich; he later completed his philosophical and theological studies at St. Vincent under Father Peter Lechner and was ordained in 1849. Placidus John Döttl, who was twenty-three, had been educated at the Latin school in Burghausen, Bavaria, and in the New Gymnasium in Munich, where he was preparing for his final examinations when he joined Wimmer's missionary group bound for America. He studied philosophy and theology at St. Vincent and was ordained in 1849. Celestine Charles Englbrecht, at twenty-two the youngest of the first clerical monks at St. Vincent, was in the same class as Döttl in Munich and was ordained with him and Haindl at St. Vincent in 1849. Charles Martin Geyerstanger, age twenty-six, had finished both his classical and his philosophical studies in Salzburg, Austria, and was studying theology at the Ludwig-Maximilian University in Munich when he joined Wimmer's expedition to America. He was ordained in 1847, becoming the first Benedictine monk to receive major orders in the United States.[21] Of the fourteen lay brothers, Conrad Joseph Reinbolt (age 27), Felix Michael Hochstätter (28), Leonard Hiller (27), and George Wimmer, Father Boniface's nephew (24), were farmers; Joseph Sailer (26), Michael Böhm (27), and Peter Seemüller (30) were weavers; Stephen James Weber (26) and Bernard Joseph Eggerdinger (28) were masons; James Reitmayer (33) was a carpenter; Andrew Binder (30) was a leather worker; Englebert Nusser (32) was a blacksmith; Placidus James Wittmann (32) was a locksmith; and Francis Pfaller (25) was a baker.

From Rotterdam the *Iowa* sailed to Havre, and on August 11 a steamer towed her into the open seas. The ship headed north, and the passengers sighted the Isle of Wight that day, but an almost total calm prevented them from continuing on. They turned south, and toward evening on August 11 the ship reached Cherbourg, France. For three days they traveled back and forth between the coasts of France and England, hampered first by calms and then by a violent storm. Wimmer wrote Abbot Gregory from aboard the *Iowa* that the captain "remained on deck continuously. I was there with him until late at night and also very early in the morning. I could not sleep anyway since my bed was constantly tossed to and fro." When day broke on August 14, they saw the English coast for the second time. Passing the Eddystone Light that morning, they saw the coast of Ireland on the evening of August 15. Contrary winds drove them north after they had headed into the Atlantic, and once more, on the afternoon of August 17, they passed the Irish coast. "The ship rocked so much that all tumbled head over heels upon each other and no one was able to walk or stand up." Wimmer reported that nearly all the passengers became seasick during the storm. "Whole families just lay there, so sick they felt they were dying. Whenever we stood or walked we saw people vomiting." He added ironically that "it was especially appetizing when, sitting at table, one after another ran to throw up what had just been swallowed. The cabins, where the sick, lamenting, and shrieking vied with one another at vomiting, were just as bad." Father Boniface boasted of not having become seasick himself. ("On the contrary I can eat and drink more than ever.") But, he said, most of his companions spent the greater part of the journey in agony. "From this Your Lordship can see that the ship is sailing very slowly and that there is little of the pleasure trip in this sea voyage. We have had really favorable wind for only two days. During the rest of the time the wind has been more or less contrary, and thus only partially useful."

Wimmer took the opportunity during the six-week voyage to acquaint his eighteen monastic candidates with the Benedictine Rule and to instruct them in the recitation of the divine office. None but Geyerstanger, who for several months had been a postulant at the Bavarian Benedictine community of Weltenburg, had ever been inside a Benedictine monastery. The others were completely unfamiliar with the monastic regimen. Father Boniface reported that he was assiduously training both the four students for the priesthood and the fourteen candidates for the brotherhood in the rigors of the Benedictine life. They had already created a quasi-monastic community, he said, and their unity had given them strength.

Luckily they are numerous; otherwise they would not fare so well. According to my instructions they pray the rosary, aloud and kneeling, every morning, afternoon, and evening. At first there were difficulties. Some of their fellow passengers laughed, others whistled or sang, and still others did something else. But with patience, earnestness, and, when necessary, measures of greater firmness, they grew more peaceful. By now their prayer is proceeding quite well. I must admit that the many Jews on board are quite tolerant. It was several Württemburgers and Frenchmen who needed to be threatened. We really felt like stuffing their mouths when they purposely disturbed us. After a while even some of the better sailors participated. Certainly I am very well satisfied with my companions.

On August 25, the Feast of St. Louis, the Benedictine and Premonstratensian missionaries gathered together to pray and celebrate the namesday of their mutual benefactor, King Ludwig I of Bavaria. Three days later a potentially disastrous event took place that Father Boniface, in the rough humor of the Bavarian countryside, described as "comical." A storm had torn off a crosspiece from the ship's mast, and the crosspiece fell from the rigging striking the deck directly in front of the kitchen. Because the cooks were in the midst of preparing breakfast, a considerable quantity of smoke was coming from the kitchen. The crash of the crosspiece and the billowing smoke led one of the passengers to assume that the ship had caught fire and he sounded the alarm. The panic that followed could have led to serious injuries to both passengers and crew, but Wimmer's narration of what happened next emphasized only the comedy he saw in the stampede that resulted from the false alarm.

All the people were still in bed, but in a flash they came rushing up to extinguish the fire and save themselves. The first to bound up the stairs was a Jewish boy. He had hardly set foot on the deck when he fell backwards and landed solidly on his posterior. There he lay sprawled out on the deck; his first movement was to stick his hand back there to see if everything was intact. Over on the other side one of my men, Geyerstanger, dashed up in his underpants, trousers in hand. He leaned against a handy water barrel so that he could slip into his trousers, but try as he would, he couldn't do it because of the pitching ship. When he saw it was a false alarm, he had to beat a retreat in his white underpants. There are many other such incidents also; I still laugh when I recall them.

The voyage lasted thirty-eight days. A thick fog on September 1 hindered the ship's progress, and Wimmer reported that a catastrophe was barely averted when the *Iowa* collided with a two-masted schooner in the darkness off the coast of Newfoundland. Only the quick and expert action of the captain saved them. The first sign of land came on September 4 when a gull landed on one of the ship's masts, and on September 14 Captain Lines announced that land had been sighted. The following day a tugboat steamed out to meet the *Iowa* on the open sea and to tow her in to New York harbor. With the other passengers the missionaries passed through customs and into the bustle of the city at 3:30 in the afternoon of September 15, 1846.[22] The achievement of Boniface Wimmer's visionary project seemed to be within his grasp, but immediately he met with frustration and discouragement.

Wimmer had left Bavaria with letters of reference to several bishops and German priests in the United States, and once on land he set out to deliver some of them to the clergy he had been told to contact in New York and its vicinity. He visited and sought the advice of Monsignor John Stephan Raffeiner, vicar general for Germans in the Diocese of New York and pastor of St. Nicholas Parish in Williamsburg (Brooklyn); Father Gabriel Rumpler, C.Ss.R., Redemptorist pastor of the German Holy Redeemer Parish in New York City; and Father Nicholas Balleis, O.S.B., an Austrian Benedictine from the Abbey of Salzburg who for ten years had been a missionary in America and who was now pastor of the German St. Mary's Parish in Newark, New Jersey. Each of these priests insisted that Wimmer's plan for establishing a Benedictine monastery and seminary in Pennsylvania was not in harmony with conditions in America and was in fact doomed to failure. They detailed the unsuccessful attempts of others to carry out similar projects. The Trappist venture in Bishop

John Carroll's time, the Redemptorist seminary in Baltimore, the Jesuit scholasticate in New York, Bishop John Dubois's seminary project in New York, and Bishop Benedict Joseph Flaget's community of religious brothers in Kentucky had all failed, and they predicted that Wimmer's project would too. They considered it "nothing more than a wild venture with absolutely no prospect of success," and they advised him to dismiss the brother candidates, to secure admission for the clerical candidates in an American seminary, and himself to follow the example of Father Nicholas Balleis and apply for incardination in one of the American dioceses as a single missionary to German Catholics.[23]

As if discouragement from these more experienced German priests on the American mission were not enough, Wimmer discovered that Father Peter Henry Lemke of Carrolltown, Pennsylvania, who had promised to meet him and his fellow missionaries in New York, had not arrived. He and his companions were alone and without help in a foreign land, but undaunted he determined to forge ahead with his project. Politely declining to follow the suggestions of his well-meaning advisors and determined to proceed with his plan of going to Pennsylvania with or without Lemke, he and his eighteen companions secured their baggage at the New York customs house and on September 19 went to Grand Central Station to make arrangements for their passage to Carrolltown. In the train station, to their thorough relief and joy, the Bavarian missionaries encountered a breathless Lemke who apologized for his late arrival and offered his assistance. Lemke was not particularly impressed with these "Benedictines." He had expected experienced priests and brothers to come from the monasteries of Bavaria to establish the first Benedictine community in the United States. What he found were Wimmer and eighteen inexperienced young men. Later he wrote:

I hurried to New York, and behold my Benedictines had arrived. Benedictines, did I say? There were nineteen persons whom I met: four students of theology and fourteen others who had agreed to enter as lay-brothers. These were tailors, shoemakers, blacksmiths, hostlers, and brewers, as Father Wimmer could gather in Munich. I must confess, I felt sadly disappointed and doubted that anything could be achieved with such help. But I had given my word to settle them, and took the whole company with their abundant luggage four hundred miles to Carrolltown.[24]

The group left New York by train on Saturday, September 19, and arrived in Philadelphia that evening. Remaining over Sunday in the City of Brotherly Love, where they attended mass at the German parish of Holy Trinity on 6th and Spruce Streets, they departed for Harrisburg at midnight, reaching the Pennsylvania capital at ten o'-clock the following morning. The train ride to Harrisburg was very disagreeable for Wimmer. He wrote that the wood rails were topped with iron bands fastened to them by spikes, which rendered their surface so rough that sleep was impossible. Moreover, sparks from the locomotive repeatedly threatened to set the baggage in the open cars on fire. Near Harrisburg they left the train and traveled eighty miles by canal to Hollidaysburg in Blair County. Wimmer said that the heat made the nights "unbearable" and that the missionaries could find fresh water to sooth their thirst only rarely. As the canal boat made its way slowly to Hollidaysburg, Wimmer reported, he frequently left the deck to walk along the bank for exercise. Two of the candidates for the lay brotherhood, Conrad Reinbolt and Felix Hochstätter, contracted typhoid fever during this part of the journey and had to be left behind in Hollidaysburg to recover.

At Hollidaysburg Wimmer and his companions got their first look at the famous Portage Road that connected Pittsburgh and western Pennsylvania with the East. Father Boniface expressed wonder at the extraordinary system devised by Yankee ingenuity which transported their boat over the ridges of the Allegheny Mountains. He described how the boat was taken apart, loaded on an inclined plane, hoisted to the top of the mountain ("higher than those at home—strange as it may seem, but the absolute truth"), and then lowered down the other side. Having reached the top of the mountain, Wimmer and Lemke left the rest of the missionary company to follow with the baggage and traveled ahead on foot toward Ebensburg, the county seat of Cambria County, and Lemke's holdings at Carrolltown.

Wimmer and Lemke walked along the woodland trails for three hours before they reached the place where Lemke had laid out the village of Carrolltown. As he traveled through the lovely forest, where "there was scarcely a house in sight," Wimmer grew increasingly convinced that Providence had brought him at last to a place where he could firmly establish Benedictine monastic life in the New World. With growing excitement he found himself, like his eighth-century patron, St. Boniface of Germany, a true missionary, treading virgin wilderness, bringing the Cross and the Gospel to a people in need of salvation.

Lemke had begun planning the village of Carrolltown in 1840, naming it after Archbishop John Carroll of Baltimore (1735–1815), the first Roman Catholic bishop of the United States, and though the village itself had not yet begun to take shape, he ministered to the Catholics of the area from his base at nearby St. Joseph's Church, which had been established in 1830 by Father Demetrius Gallitzin, the Russian prince who was the first Catholic priest to complete all his theological studies in the United States and who even before his death had gained renown as the "Apostle of the Alleghenies."[25] Catholics had been settling in Cambria County since the late eighteenth century. By 1846 there were more than three hundred of them in the vicinity of Carrolltown, primarily of German, but also of Irish heritage.[26]

It was the settlement of St. Joseph near the proposed village of Carrolltown that Lemke offered the Benedictine missionaries. Wimmer and his companions arrived at St. Joseph's on September 30, 1846, and began immediately to renovate the house that Lemke had provided them. The St. Joseph's settlement consisted of the house, an adjacent barn, and the church about two miles away. Two meadows nearby were "fairly good," but the fields the monks were to plow had been only partially cleared, and Wimmer complained that dead trees stood about "like so many giant ghosts, their stumps everywhere" and that the land was full of stones. Under such conditions, plowing was extremely difficult. George Wimmer, the son of Father Boniface's younger brother George and one of the brother candidates, complained to his uncle "every evening about the various aches the work caused him."

Wimmer described the region as a "high, stony, barren plateau, little suited for agriculture, but excellent for cattle-raising." It was "totally different from what I was told and what I expected."[27] Nevertheless, he made a preliminary contract with Lemke to purchase the property for $4,300. Within several days of his arrival, he received a letter of welcome from Bishop Michael O'Connor who invited him to Pittsburgh for the forthcoming diocesan synod and for the blessing of St. Philomena's German church in the see city. Wimmer accepted the invitation and met the bishop on October 4. He explained the disappointment he and his confreres had experienced with the property in Cambria County and told the bishop that he thought the price Father Lemke was asking was excessive. The bishop listened sympathetically.

Ever since being named first bishop of Pittsburgh in 1843, O'Connor had been hoping to establish a seminary in his diocese and for a time had entertained the idea of forming one on some property the diocese owned in Westmoreland County.[28] Various experiments and halting starts had failed because the bishop lacked the financial resources as well as an adequate theological faculty for a seminary. Aware that Wimmer had come to the United States precisely for the purpose of educating young men for the priesthood, O'Connor had eagerly accepted him into the diocese, and hearing now that he and his companions were dissatisfied with the location in Cambria County, he offered the incipient Benedictine community the estate in Westmoreland County which was more convenient to the diocesan see than was Lemke's property in Cambria County. St. Vincent Church near Youngstown, the oldest parish in the diocese, was sixty miles nearer Pittsburgh than was St. Joseph's, and on October 5 Bishop O'Connor took Wimmer to the property and urged him to consider making his settlement there.

The parish that had come to be called St. Vincent had been established in 1789 by Father Theodore Brouwers, O.F.M., one of the earliest Catholic missionaries in western Pennsylvania. Brouwers had purchased the property known as Sportsman's Hall from Joseph Hunter in that year, and fifteen months later, after a very brief tenure ministering to the Catholics of the area, he died. On his deathbed he drew up a will that bequeathed the property to any Roman Catholic priest who would take up residence there and work among the Catholics of the region. Moreover, he stipulated in his will that the property be passed down in perpetuity to his successor's successors.[29]

Through his will Brouwers intended to attract missionaries to western Pennsylvania and at the same time to avoid the problems of trusteeship which the American church faced in its early years. But the Franciscan missionary's will posed more problems than it solved. Archbishop John Carroll of Baltimore, in whose diocese the property fell, was plagued with a series of renegade priests who assumed possession of the land within the terms of the will. Some of them were removed from the parish only after lengthy civil court trials. Because of the troubles caused by the Brouwers will, the parishioners appealed to

Sportsman's Hall (1789), the original pastoral residence and chapel for the parish that became Saint Vincent in Westmoreland County, Pennsylvania. (ASVA)

the Pennsylvania legislature to turn over the property to Catholic trustees. The legislature granted the petition, and four decades after Brouwers's death, when the trustees refused to permit the new pastor, Father James Ambrose Stillinger, the right to administer the finances and property of the parish, Bishop Francis Patrick Kenrick of Philadelphia was confronted with the very problem that the Franciscan missionary had attempted to circumvent. In 1831 Kenrick, pledging to respect the desires of Father Brouwers that the parishioners of St. Vincent be attended by a priest, ordered the trustees to relinquish all claims to the parish property and in accord with canon law to turn it over to himself as bishop of the diocese in which it fell. After lengthy negotiations, the trustees agreed to the bishop's demands, and Kenrick confirmed Father James Ambrose Stillinger as pastor. When the diocese of Pittsburgh was created in 1843, Bishop Michael O'Connor assigned Father Michael Gallagher to the parish.[30]

When Bishop O'Connor showed Father Boniface the property in October 1846, St. Vincent consisted of two farms, one of 315 acres and a second, seven miles north of the first, of 150 acres. On the larger farm Father Stillinger had constructed a brick church in 1835 which served the surrounding population of Irish and German Catholics. East of the church, which sat on "a pleasant hill that slopes gently down to the valley on the east, south, and west but which climbs higher toward the northwest," stood a one-story parochial residence which at the time of Wimmer's visit housed a group of seven Irish Sisters of Mercy who had been led to America the previous year by Mother Francis Xavier Warde, R.S.M. The sisters were conducting a school for about twenty girls, but Bishop O'Connor assured Wimmer that they would be moving to a nearby tract of land during the coming spring. North of the church was a two-story brick building recently constructed by the parish to serve as a schoolhouse, and it was here that Father Gallagher was living. East of the parochial residence stood a dilapidated barn and a hewn-log structure built by Father Theodore Brouwers and known as Sportsman's Hall. This building had served as the parish church from 1790 until 1835. In 1846 it was inhabited by a tenant farmer and his family.[31]

The more fertile land of the St. Vincent property, as well as its accessibility to the main road between Philadelphia and Pittsburgh and to the projected route of the Pennsylvania Railroad which skirted the parish farm, favorably disposed Wimmer to accept the bishop's offer and move to Westmoreland County. The fact that the majority of Catholics in the area were Irish rather than German, however, caused him to consider the possibility that his financial support from Bavaria might be jeopardized should he move there from Cambria County. He told O'Connor that he would consider the offer and returned to Carrolltown to discuss the matter with his men.

In Cambria County Father Boniface called a meeting of the missionary group and asked for opinions. He explained the situation and the bishop's offer, saying that St. Vincent was in "an uncommonly beautiful and fertile region" which was far more attractive and arable than the rocky land at St. Joseph's. Acting as spokesman for the others, Stephen Weber, one of the brother candidates, urged that because of the more suitable farmland in Westmoreland County the community move there. The others agreed, complaining that the stumps in the fields of the Carrolltown property were hindering efforts to plant the winter wheat crop. Meanwhile the parishioners of St. Vincent, at the suggestion of Bishop O'Connor, wrote Wimmer on October 11 and urged him to come to Westmoreland County, promising to "do everything in our power to aid you in your benevolent undertakings and console you in the discharge of your arduous duties." The letter, signed by fifty-four members of the parish, was accompanied by a note from the bishop, reaffirming his desire to have the Benedictine foundation closer to the diocesan see than Carrolltown.[32]

On October 12 a special messenger left Youngstown on horseback to deliver the letters to the Benedictine community at St. Joseph's, and on October 15 Wimmer directed that the community collect its baggage and make preparations for the move to St. Vincent. His decision did not please Lemke at all, but Wimmer said that besides offering property inferior to that which the bishop had offered, Lemke had set his price too high and had made his terms too difficult. Wimmer therefore canceled the tentative contract he had made with him and ordered the move. Lemke opposed the decision as best he could and organized resistance among the local German Catholics. The resistance involved their refusal to assist in the transfer of baggage to the new property, so Wimmer was forced to hire several Irishmen from Carrolltown to haul the community's belongings the sixty miles to St. Vincent. Despite the delay caused by Lemke's organized resistance, an advance party of Wimmer's group set out on foot from Cambria County on October 16. After stopping for the night in Blairsville, where they stayed with the pastor of Ss. Simon and Jude Church, Father James Ambrose Stillinger, they reached St. Vincent on October 18. A second group, accompanying several sick members of the community, left a day later and arrived on October 19.[33]

When the Benedictine missionaries arrived at St. Vincent, the pastor, Father Michael Gallagher, turned the parish over to Father Boniface, and on November 5, 1846, Bishop O'Connor came to Westmoreland County and officially appointed Wimmer pastor, stating his willingness "to arrange matters in such a way that the superior of the Benedictine monastery, which is to be established here, will always be pastor." Moreover, he gave the Benedictines permission "to found other monasteries in this diocese in which they can lead a monastic life and devote themselves either to the education of youth, both for the secular and clerical states, or to care for souls."[34] Gallagher agreed to stay on at the parish to assist with the English-speaking parishioners, and in December he entered the novitiate, taking the name Joseph in religion.

On October 24 sixteen of the candidates were invested with the

Benedictine habit in a simple ceremony in the parish church. There
were only six habits for all the novices, and as one was invested, he
would retire to the sacristy, change back into his secular dress, and return the habit to the sanctuary where it would be used in the investiture of another candidate. The two sick members of the community
who had been left at Hollidaysburg, Conrad Reinbolt and Felix
Hochstätter, were invested sometime later.

Two days after the investiture Wimmer wrote Father Joseph
Müller informing him of the move to St. Vincent and revealing his
first impressions of America, impressions based not only on direct
observation but also on his recent discussions with Bishop Michael
O'Connor of Pittsburgh with whom at this stage he enjoyed excellent
relations.

When you see the name of the place where this letter is written, and the date,
you will probably say, "Why is he not at St. Joseph's?" We changed our residence, and now are fifty miles southwest of the first colony, in one of the
most beautiful and salubrious spots in America for a Benedictine monastery.
The Most Rev. Bishop offered me two farms of 315 and 150 acres. They are
the foundation of Father Brouwers, a pious missionary who lived here towards the end of the last century and donated them for the support of the
pastor to minister to the Catholics who are scattered over the whole county.
The bishop also wishes that I start a seminary as soon as possible to educate
youths for the priesthood. There is now no such institution in the country,
but such a school is most necessary for the Church in the United States. The
boys of the wealthier classes of society usually study for secular professions.
For this reason almost all the priests of the secular clergy are of foreign birth:
Irish, German, French. The whole diocese of Pittsburgh has only one native
American priest, and this one [Father James Ambrose Stillinger], although
of German descent, understands only little of the language of his ancestors.
Other dioceses are in similar condition. Therefore priests are not only too
few for the number of people, but being foreigners often do not have the
confidence of their parishioners. Moreover, they themselves come to understand the mind of the people only gradually, especially if in a mixed population they speak only one language.

Irish and German Catholics usually live closely together, and when the
pastor, even if he resides among them, speaks only one language, one part of
the congregation seldom hears a sermon or is without spiritual assistance in
the confessional and in sickness. What is still worse, almost all the schools
are controlled by non-Catholics. Therefore missionary seminaries, not in
Europe but here in America, will be the only means of solving the problem.

Saint Vincent in 1846. Unknown artist's sketch of the church, pastoral residence,
school house, and Sportman's Hall (foreground) as they appeared in the year
that the Benedictines arrived. (ASVA)

Our people are so well convinced of this need that no other method is ever
mentioned. Such institutions must be established on American soil. Likewise everybody concedes that only a religious order can maintain such seminaries for poor boys, because such institutions must have either a sufficient
or an assured income. Lay brothers by their work can procure such support.
Unfortunately, so far such endowments are non-existent; therefore at present only an order that has lay brothers can hope to succeed. A mendicant
order cannot carry out such a plan because it possesses no property. Therefore, the situation confronting us calls for an order which besides priests also
has lay brothers. This is the Benedictine Order with its varied membership.
Here our order has all the opportunities to rise to new life. Earlier I defended
this theory in Bavaria, and now I am very glad to find it confirmed here by
experience.[35]

The settlement at St. Vincent and investiture of the novices formally inaugurated Benedictine monastic life on the continent of
North America. But Wimmer and his companions were not the first

Benedictines to reach America. Discounting legends about Benedictine missionaries who accompanied the Vikings and Columbus before the sixteenth century,[36] history records that the first son of St. Benedict to arrive in the United States was Father Pierre Joseph Didier, O.S.B., a member of the Abbey of St. Denis in Paris. Didier led a group of French refugees from revolutionary France in 1790 and settled with them at Gallipolis, Ohio. When the colonization enterprise failed, he became a parish priest in St. Louis, where he died in 1799.[37] In 1794 Bishop John Carroll of Baltimore received inquiries from Father Michael Pembridge, O.S.B., of the English Benedictine Congregation about the possibility of establishing a community of English monks in America, and in his reply of September 19, 1794, Carroll offered Pembridge and the English Benedictines some property in western Pennsylvania which almost certainly was the land of Father Theodore Brouwers, who had died four years earlier.[38] In the end the English Benedictines did not accept Bishop Carroll's offer and the project came to nothing. The next record of a Benedictine in America does not occur until 1836. In that year Father Nicholas Balleis, O.S.B., of St. Peter's Abbey, Salzburg (one of the German priests who greeted Wimmer when he and his missionaries arrived in New York), was received into the diocese of Philadelphia by Bishop Francis Patrick Kenrick. Balleis served parishes in Philadelphia and Pittsburgh for several years and then was incardinated in the diocese of New York, founding St. Mary's Church, Newark, New Jersey, in 1840.[39] Like Balleis, another Benedictine from Europe came to the United States in the 1840s to work among the German immigrants. Father Florian Schweninger, O.S.B., of the Abbey of Fiecht in Tyrol, arrived in America two years before Wimmer, and in 1846 he was serving in a parish in Utica, New York. Wimmer visited him in 1851, and soon afterward Schweninger went to California where he worked in the archdiocese of San Francisco until his death in 1868.[40]

But none of the Benedictines who had come to the United States before Father Boniface had attempted to introduce monastic life to North America. They had all come as single missionaries to work among the growing number of immigrants there. Wimmer alone had the vision and the drive to transplant the ancient Order of St. Benedict from Europe to America, and on October 24, 1846, his long-held dream was fulfilled.

The community occupied its early weeks at St. Vincent settling into the two-story brick schoolhouse, where they shared quarters with Father Gallagher, and adjusting to life in their new home. After the Sisters of Mercy left, Wimmer, Gallagher, and the clerical novices moved into the one-story parochial residence and altered the building, with its two rooms divided by a narrow hallway and its garret accessible only by ladder, to house twenty people. Wimmer and Father Gallagher occupied one room which during the day served as a study hall. The other room was used as a kitchen, refectory, and infirmary. The novices slept in the garret. Linen ticks, filled with straw from the barn and covered with blankets, served as beds, and nails driven into the walls served as wardrobes. The brothers set to work immediately to construct an outdoor latrine and kitchen. Wimmer wrote to King Ludwig I that these were difficult but rewarding days.

We were only too glad to get up in the morning, since it was so cold that we were freezing even under the woolen blankets. The little money that I still had with me was quickly used up in the acquisition of implements needed to run the farm, in the purchase of horses and cattle. Our food and board during the first year were paid entirely out of our own purse; hence I was soon up to my ears in debt and my credit was very low because people still had doubts about the feasibility of my plan.[41]

Wimmer's plan centered upon the tested Benedictine tradition of acquiring land and cultivating it to support the monks. Since he also intended to establish a school, he conceived the idea of imitating the medieval Benedictine practice of receiving numerous lay brothers into the monastery who would accept the responsibility of manual labor, leaving the priests and clerics free to teach and study. Originally Father Boniface had hoped to integrate the lay brothers into every aspect of life at his new monastery. He wanted them to participate in the recitation of the divine office with the clerical monks as well, but soon after his arrival in America, when he found that the brothers had difficulty learning Latin, he altered his plan, and from then on there developed a division in prayer, work, and horaria between the clerical and lay members of the community.

In his letter to Father Joseph Müller he provided details about the schedule the monks followed in the early days of Benedictine observance in the United States.

Although our various departments have not yet been fully organized, we are keeping the following order as well as we can: we rise at 3:45 to meet in the parish church. Here, at 4 o'clock, I say Matins and Lauds with the four students [clerical novices] in the choir loft, while the brothers recite one third of the Rosary and other prayers in the sanctuary. At 5 o'clock, at a sign, meditation begins which lasts one hour, after which I say the conventual Mass. This is followed by a frugal breakfast for the brothers, and we recite Prime, at which the martyrology and a chapter of the Holy Rule are read. The rest of the morning is taken up with work for the brothers and studies or classes for the students, with a short interruption at 9 o'clock when we recite the Minor Hours.

At 10:45 all are called again to the church for the adoration of the Blessed Sacrament and particular examination of conscience. At 11:00 we take dinner, after which the students have a short recreation and the brothers receive instructions in religious life. At 1:00 the brothers recite the second part of the Rosary, and work until 5:00. During that time the students have classes or lectures, which are interrupted by the recitation of Vespers at 3:00. All attend spiritual reading or explanation of the Holy Rule from 5:00 to 6:00, which is followed by supper. Then a second recreation or housework lasts until 7:30, when the brothers recite the third part of the Rosary, and we say Compline. Finally night prayers and general examination of conscience conclude this daily routine. At 9:00 all retire.[42]

In November the tenant farmer, John Schowalter, sold his fall harvest to the monks and moved out of Sportsman's Hall. This log structure then became the brothers' quarters, and congestion in the schoolhouse eased. The debts Wimmer assumed when he took over administration of the parish amounted to more than $5,000, and because of the community's poverty the first winter promised to be difficult. In a letter to a relative of his in Bavaria, Canon Joseph Meyringer, pastor of the parish church in the village of Pfakofen near Regensburg, Father Boniface described some of the conditions in which he and his young confreres found themselves. "We drink neither beer nor wine nor coffee," he said, "and we eat only dry bread; . . . only Father Gallagher gets butter because he has been used to it for so long."[43] Promised financial aid from Bavaria had not arrived, and the community had to depend largely on the charity of parishioners who themselves did not have a great deal to spare. In some cases nearby merchants offered to sell food and supplies to the monks on credit. Throughout the winter the brothers worked to adapt the buildings for the use of the community, and the four clerical novices studied theology under Wimmer and Gallagher.

Father Boniface was also kept busy in the parish, traveling to missions in Greensburg, Ligonier, Saltsburg, and Indiana, Pennsylvania, in order to administer the sacraments to his widely scattered flock. In December he wrote Archbishop von Reisach:

I am the only pastor in the whole county [Westmoreland], with 42,000 inhabitants of whom scarcely 2,000 are Catholics. We cannot expect many more immigrants because it already has many settlements and land is constantly rising in price. However, once we have several priests in the monastery, we hope to be able to make converts, especially among the Germans, or at least prevent apostasies, which so far have been quite frequent.[44]

Bishop O'Connor, with whom Wimmer had established cordial relations, sent a subdeacon to St. Vincent to finish his studies for the priesthood with the Benedictine novices, and on March 15, 1847, O'-Connor himself came from Pittsburgh to ordain novice Charles Geyerstanger to the priesthood. It was the first ordination of a Benedictine monk to take place in the United States.[45]

Wimmer wrote joyfully to Father Joseph Ferdinand Müller at the royal court in Munich that "the foundation is laid, the beginning made, the temporal support given, not only for me and my companions but also for others who are willing to work with us. What we need now are good priests, or those who can become good priests and who have a true vocation to the religious life. I do not doubt that the Lord will send them because He knows best what is most necessary here."[46]

And Müller in turn wrote the Swiss bishop of Milwaukee, John Martin Henni, that everyone in Munich had the highest hopes for the success of the Benedictine colony in the United States. Wimmer had shown that all the doomsayers were wrong, that it was indeed possible to establish a Benedictine monastery in America. "In New York," Müller wrote, "people wondered when he arrived with so many persons, and they called it a nonsensical undertaking, but just this helps Father Boniface most. Without his personnel he could not have taken charge of St. Vincent and begun his work. . . . If all the Benedictines in Europe who were so inclined could leave, half the Benedictines would emigrate. But the abbots are opposing this. . . . I expect much from this community."[47]

Nevertheless, the decision to transfer the community from Cambria County to St. Vincent had upset several influential members of the Ludwig Missionsverein, who considered the parish in Westmoreland County, with its large debt and preponderance of Irish parishioners, hardly the ideal place for a German monastery. They were not inclined to provide financial support to an undertaking that would chiefly benefit non-German Catholics in America. Müller warned Wimmer not to neglect the Germans in his rush to provide pastoral care for the Irish Catholics in his charge. "Be prudent and careful," he said, "in everything that you are undertaking. Europe and America are watching the progress of your foundation, and, as at all times, every good work has its friends and its foes. As long as no negligence is evident, conscience cannot reproach you. May God bless you all."[48] Two and a half months later Müller wrote more pointedly:

I received your two letters from which I can see that God has directed everything in your favor. You are settled now at St. Vincent. Very well. I ask, however, one thing of you: do not neglect the Germans. You went to America to protect, teach, and look after the Germans. This was also our intention. As soon as you give up that plan, you are lost. Therefore, my dear friend, beware. Experience has taught me this. Far be it from me to prevent any good work, but as soon as you have established your foundation, they [the Irish bishops] will try to change it. . . . If you want to count on our permanent support, I must impress upon you not to neglect the Germans.[49]

To answer some of the objections to his move from Cambria to Westmoreland County, Wimmer wrote Archbishop Karl August von Reisach, now ordinary of Munich and president of the Ludwig Missionsverein. Reporting that he had formally initiated monastic life at St. Vincent four months earlier, Father Boniface said that he was working among both German and Irish Catholics, ministering to the pastoral and sacramental needs of both immigrant groups. "To devote this help exclusively to the Germans," he said,

could not be my intention. Had it been, then closer insight into the native circumstances would have had to convince me that this would not be feasible, or at least not out in the country where in my opinion Benedictine monasteries are chiefly intended to be. Besides, there is hardly one large congregation that is completely unmixed. . . . Usually Germans and Irish, or anglicized Germans, live mixed with one another, and usually the Germans are in the minority.

For that reason he did not "hesitate to take over the parish of St. Vincent and Youngstown, although this is neither unmixed German nor sharply separated from the Protestants." From St. Vincent Father Boniface said that he was in charge of nineteen small towns and there were German Catholics living in each one of them. Wimmer defended his decision to educate both German and Irish students in the school he proposed to establish, because in this way he could contribute to the amalgamation of the two principal Catholic ethnic groups in America, the Germans and the Irish. Wimmer gave a lengthy explanation of the relationship between Germans and Irish in the American Church and begged the archbishop to continue his support of the Benedictine venture in the United States despite the compromise he and his companions had to make as a consequence of the conditions they found in the United States.

I had to modify my original plan of limiting my educational program to German youth. This change became necessary on account of local conditions. I can well see why Germans, living among Irish and American Catholics, cannot establish their own parishes, or have their own pastors, especially in the rural districts. Even if they could afford the expenses, they would be unable to get priests of their nationality because there is a great scarcity of such, and on account of the large and steady immigration this condition will continue for a long time. In most places only English-speaking priests are found. How much could be done for the Faith if the English pastor could also speak German and the German priests be able to preach in English. This could be achieved if English and German boys were educated by teachers who are masters of both languages. I could then educate an English boy for the Germans and a German boy for the English. Naturally my first aim will always be to educate German youths, but under such conditions I cannot refuse to accept English boys. In this way I shall also avoid conflicts with the Irish bishops and at the same time contribute to the amalgamation of the two Catholic elements in the Church of America, which, so far, are *opposing* one another to the *detriment* of both. For this reason I gladly received Father Gallagher into the order, although I do not consider it beneficial for the Church that the two nationalities live together in the same monastery. I will, however, be glad to receive instructions about these matters.[50]

Wimmer's dilemma was not an easy one to resolve. On the one hand, he was obliged to provide pastoral care for German-speaking Catholics in the United States both because of his original commitment and because that was the purpose for which funds had been given him by the Ludwig Missionsverein and other donors. On the other hand, he found conditions in America such that it was difficult if not impossible for him to focus his resources and energies exclusively on the German community. Such exclusively German communities were, as he explained to von Reisach, few and far between in the United States, although one existed in northwestern Pennsylvania at the German colony of St. Marys and others could be found in the West. Soon after arriving in America, however, Wimmer realized that the character of the American melting pot required that he deal with the total Catholic community and not just with one part of it. He quickly understood that by focusing his efforts on one ethnic group to the exclusion of others he and his mission would soon be marginalized, that his work would become ineffective and ultimately irrelevant. For that reason he accepted Bishop O'Connor's offer of the mixed Irish and German parish at St. Vincent, a parish that because of its mixed congregation, and the problems which arose as a result of the "mixture," was in many respects a microcosm of the mid-nineteenth-century American Catholic Church.

Still, his benefactors in Bavaria found it difficult to understand the conditions that forced him to make what they considered an unwarranted compromise of his original commitment, and in his correspondence with them Wimmer continually attempted to justify himself by emphasizing his key objective in the American missions of providing a German-speaking clergy for the German Catholic community in the United States, as well as his secondary objective of helping to preserve the German language and culture among that community. Thus he wrote to King Ludwig I:

We have in mind a considerable number of German boys who are poor but very talented and want to become priests and feel they have a vocation. We hope then to be able to educate them and give them priestly training so that on the one hand they may help to preserve and spread the Catholic religion among our fellow countrymen and on the other hand may win respect and recognition for the German elements in the population through the sound and thorough education of German youth, and in particular to preserve the German culture and language among the Germans themselves.[51]

In April the Sisters of Mercy and their students moved from the parochial residence at St. Vincent to the newly constructed convent and school at St. Xavier's about a mile away. Wimmer and his confrères moved into the vacated building, and Bishop O'Connor, having fulfilled his part of the verbal agreement with the Benedictines by providing them a place to settle, informed Father Boniface that he planned to send seven English-speaking students for the priesthood to pursue their studies under the Benedictines in the small monastic school they had established. He indicated, moreover, that he was hoping to assign an English-speaking diocesan priest to St. Vincent to direct the students' education. O'Connor wrote:

A few months ago I spoke to you about some boys whom you might accept as students. You answered that you would receive them as soon as you were able to move into the pastor's residence, which is now occupied by the sisters. I saw very well that such a request meant a hardship for you, wherefore I did not mention it during my last visit to St. Vincent. Now, however, several reasons urge me to seek better accommodations for them than they have here. This condition compels me to propose the matter sooner than I expected. I also thought that I might better broach the subject before you make changes in the house which you now occupy. This dwelling could very well be used for these boys until you have better quarters. These students, seven in number, are all English boys. I will consider it a great favor if you would be able to take them without too much trouble. If you wish (and most probably this will be necessary now), I can send an English priest along who will give them instructions. It might be advisable that you make inquiries from time to time whether good order is kept and the proper lessons are given. This priest will be told to obey you, and I do not doubt that he will follow these orders. I am only suggesting this not to cause you too much trouble. I will be very glad if you and your men educate these boys. I do not want to increase your expenses in the beginning, and until other arrangements are made, I will pay for them.

Although I will pay for the priest and these boys, you will do me a great favor by accepting them, the sooner the better. Send me, please, an answer as soon as possible by the bearer of this message.[52]

But Wimmer balked at the bishop's request and replied that the community's poverty would allow it to accept neither the diocesan priest nor the bishop's students. His principal concern was that by agreeing to O'Connor's proposal he would lose control of the educational program at St. Vincent.

Wimmer's idea from the beginning had been to establish a gymnasium (or secondary school) at St. Vincent where German-speaking students would study under Benedictine teachers and be subject to the discipline of Benedictine superiors. His plan called for the cre-

ation of an educational environment that would be nourished by
Benedictine spiritual and intellectual traditions and at the same time
by Bavarian Catholic cultural values. While O'Connor's proposal
seemed on the face of it reasonable if not innocuous, it posed serious
difficulties for Wimmer. If he agreed, he would be forced to surrender a significant part of the administration of the school to the diocese and admit English-speaking students who would, he foresaw, soon come to set the cultural and linguistic standards for the
school. He could not accept such a development without abandoning the purpose for which he had come to the United States and
further jeopardizing the support of his financial backers in Munich
who were already questioning his acceptance of the pastoral care of
English-speaking Catholics. He therefore rejected out of hand Bishop
O'Connor's proposal to send the students and an English-speaking
priest to St. Vincent.

The disagreement initiated a tense relationship between the Benedictine superior and the bishop of Pittsburgh that would manifest itself more frequently in the years ahead. Not only was this awkward relationship an example of the historical conflict between episcopal and
monastic interests that had been part of the Church's experience at
least since the Middle Ages, but it was also aggravated by conditions
prevalent in the American Church during the nineteenth century
when German and Irish Catholics engaged in a nationalistic struggle
for dominance.

Tensions between German and Irish Catholics in the United States
had reached a peak by the time Wimmer and his Benedictine candidates arrived at St. Vincent. Complaints had continued to filter back
from German colonists in America to Bavaria and the Holy See that
the Irish bishops of the United States were not devoting sufficient attention and resources to their spiritual needs, and events in the diocese of Pittsburgh, whose bishop was regarded as "anti-German" by
many churchmen in Munich, helped bring the confrontation to a
head just as Wimmer was attempting to establish Benedictine monastic life at St. Vincent.

Shortly before Wimmer's arrival in Pennsylvania, a group of
German Catholic colonists, with support from the Ludwig Missionsverein, had settled in northwestern Pennsylvania, at a place they
called St. Marys. The St. Marys colony was the brainchild of several
German Catholic lay leaders, including the convert Baron Heinrich

von Schröter of Mecklenburg. In 1846, not long after Wimmer's arrival in Pennsylvania, von Schröter visited St. Marys (but not St. Vincent) to inspect the colony and report on its progress. When he returned to Munich, he sought an audience with King Ludwig I in which he recommended that the king use his influence in Rome to have a new American diocese established, with its see at St. Marys, to which a German bishop would be named. The king liked the proposal and instructed his ambassador to the Vatican, Graf von Spaur, to present it to the cardinal secretary of state with the recommendation of the Bavarian government that it be implemented. Von Spaur presented the proposal to Cardinal Leonardo Antonelli in January, and Antonelli passed it on to the Sacred Congregation for the Propagation of the Faith which had charge of ecclesiastical affairs in the United States. In March von Spaur had an audience with Pope Pius IX in which he reiterated the Bavarian government's support for naming more German bishops in the United States and for providing greater support for German Catholics there.

The Bavarian proposal was discussed at the next session of the Sacred Congregation for the Propagation of the Faith with the result that the Congregation informed the American bishops that it encouraged their greater attention to the care of German Catholics in the United States and would welcome the nomination of German priests for new or vacant American sees. To the disappointment of King Ludwig and the Bavarian party, however, Propaganda did not create a diocese or name a bishop for the St. Marys colony.[53]

While Wimmer had nothing to do with these efforts, and in fact was not even aware that they were in progress, the Bavarian efforts to influence ecclesiastical policy in the United States had two immediate and potentially damaging effects on his own struggle to establish an independent Bavarian Benedictine monastery at St. Vincent. First, the Bavarian government's *demarches* to the Holy See, which quickly became known among the American bishops, caused Bishop Michael O'Connor to take a second look at Wimmer's motives and intentions. It was, after all, out of his diocese that the Bavarian government had proposed to carve a German-speaking American diocese. Was Wimmer part of this conspiracy, O'Connor wondered, to wrest control of the American Church from the hands of the Irish bishops who now presided over it? Later, when Father Boniface insisted upon the establishment of an independent priory at St. Vincent exempt from the authority of the bishop of Pittsburgh, it seemed clear to O'Connor that his earlier suspicions about Wimmer's part in a Bavarian conspiracy had been confirmed.

Second, the Bavarian government's efforts to provide greater support for neglected German Catholics in the United States led many of Wimmer's supporters in Munich, including the directors of the Ludwig Missionsverein, to question again his decision to settle at St. Vincent where the congregation was not predominately German. In Bavaria the problems of the American Church were seen very clearly as ethnic problems caused by a conflict between Irish and German interests. The American Church was dominated by Irish bishops. These Irish bishops, according to reports, neglected the German Catholic immigrants. Wimmer had gone to help the Germans in the United States. Why, therefore, was he devoting his time to serving a "mixed" congregation that was predominately Irish? If he acceded now to Bishop O'Connor's proposal that English-speaking students be sent to St. Vincent under an English-speaking diocesan priest, his Munich supporters could only conclude that under pressure from the Irish bishops he had abandoned the Germans, and they would consequently refuse him and his community their further support.

Wimmer found himself in the delicate position of being suspected of duplicity by both Irish interests in the American Church, represented by O'Connor, and German interests, represented by the Bavarian patrons who had provided him the means to undertake his mission to the German immigrants of the United States in the first place.

In May 1847 Bishop O'Connor wrote Wimmer and proposed that a contract be drawn up so that the misunderstanding between them might end. The bishop listed three areas in which he said he expected the Benedictines to contribute to the good of the diocese. The first of these was at St. Vincent itself where the monks were to provide pastoral care for the Catholics of the surrounding countryside. If the German Benedictines could not adequately minister to the English-speaking parishioners, then the bishop reserved the right to assign secular priests to St. Vincent whom the monks would be obliged to support. The Benedictine pastor of St. Vincent, moreover, must be under the jurisdiction of the bishop of Pittsburgh in all matters pertaining to the parochial work of the monks. O'Connor's second area of concern was the pastoral care of the Irish Sisters of Mercy at St.

Xavier's, one mile from the Benedictine monastery. He expected the monks to say daily mass and act as confessors for the sisters and their students. The bishop's third concern was the seminary at St. Vincent, which O'Connor insisted should make no distinction between English-speaking and German-speaking students and should begin to receive diocesan candidates as soon as possible at reduced rates, receiving them gratis once the monastery had achieved a stable financial footing.[54]

Wimmer studied the bishop's proposals and two days later responded with a list of his own expectations. The Benedictines, he said, would be willing to minister to the parishioners of St. Vincent, who included all the Catholics of Westmoreland County; moreover, they would also work in territories outside the county where there were no pastors. But missions outside Westmoreland County would have to be specifically assigned to them by the bishop, and Wimmer expected financial compensation for such work. With regard to the Sisters of Mercy, Wimmer said that he and his priests would be willing to offer mass at St. Xavier's on Sundays and holy days without stipends but that they would expect stipends for all Masses said during the week. Finally Wimmer rejected the third of Bishop O'Connor's proposals, saying that the monastic seminary at St. Vincent would not be bound to receive any specified number of English-speaking diocesan students and that when students were received, they would be expected to pay the customary fees. The seminary, finally, would have to be operated under Benedictine and not diocesan auspices.[55]

On May 13 Bishop O'Connor responded in a mild, conciliatory manner, saying that with regard to the pastoral work that Wimmer was willing to accept, the Benedictine superior was offering more than the bishop had asked. O'Connor, however, continued to insist that the monks offer daily mass for the sisters at St. Xavier's and said that he expected some kind of formal statement from the monks about their willingness to accept diocesan students in the monastery school.

I do not intend to ask anything of you which was not clear from the very beginning, or what has not been clearly agreed upon. You could see what kind of parish [St. Vincent] is and who its members are. You also saw that I had in mind to choose a pastor who besides having the care of souls could also provide for the education of youth, and I gladly granted you the place be-cause you had the same aim. I would not have refused you admittance into the diocese if you had come for any other purpose, nor would I do so now, but it is only just that what was proposed should now be firmly agreed upon.

As you believe that it is not right that your affairs should depend on the will of my successor, it is likewise not right that what has been agreed upon should be refused by your successor.

Therefore it would be well that we make a formal agreement by which I bind myself to appoint one of the monks to hold securely the property of the monastery and by which you and your successors are bound to fulfill what was understood from the beginning. Do not be distressed that if within cer-tain limits I am expecting the diocese to derive the first fruits of your labors.[56]

Wimmer could not agree to the contract proposed by Bishop O'Connor because it did not give him and his successors indisputable title to the land of St. Vincent parish in perpetuity. He feared that without such title, he or his successor could be removed at any time by O'Connor or his successor and that the monastery would then have to be abandoned. As he explained in a letter to the Ludwig Mis-sionsverein almost a decade later, after the dispute had been settled in his favor:

I could well understand the mind of the bishop. In spite of the testimonials from the abbot of Metten and the bishops of Munich and Regensburg, I was still a stranger to him. He granted me the two properties by appointing me pastor, but in case of my death he could have given them to another priest, and in such a case the brothers would have had to leave the place. He could even remove me at his pleasure from the parish. All this caused me great anxiety.[57]

Because the bishop seemed unwilling to grant Wimmer title to the land and continued to insist upon sending English-speaking students to the school, Wimmer began to make plans to leave St. Vincent. He had three options available. The first was a standing offer from Bishop John Martin Henni of Milwaukee to establish a monastery among the German Catholic settlers of Wisconsin; the second was an offer from Benedictine Father Nicholas Balleis to establish a monastery in the German parish of St. Mary's in Newark, New Jersey; the third was an offer of property in the German colony of St. Marys, Pennsylvania. In October Wimmer wrote his friend and advisor, Abbot Rupert

Leiss of Scheyern: "Most likely I will not be here long. But I am torn between Newark and Wisconsin, to which the *German* Bishop Henni has earnestly invited me three times. I thought of Saint Teresa and intend to have nothing further to do with this Irish scoundrel. In reality this changes nothing except the place. We are best under Germans, and never again will I have anything to do with acting as a pastor for the Irish."

Wimmer delayed mailing this intemperate letter to Scheyern, and during the interim he had second thoughts about the place to which he would transfer his fledgling community. In a postscript to this letter he apologized to Abbot Rupert for the tone he had set earlier:

31 October. You see that, as usual in passion, I wrote in somewhat too German a manner. Now I am calmer and not resentful. On October 16 I had to visit the Germans in Indiana [Pennsylvania], thirty-five miles from here, as I do every four weeks. Determined to leave here, I looked around there for a place and three were offered me . . . but in order to have a choice I traveled from there farther north (82 miles) to St. Marys to our dear fellow countrymen. The three developers (Benzinger, Eschbach, and Schröter) happened to be there. . . . I was very urgently invited to move there and was offered gratis as much land as I wanted and where I wanted. I explained I wanted a valley, through which flowed a small stream which could operate a mill and irrigate gardens. . . . I prefer to bury myself in the deepest woods and live for my brothers, doing no pastoral work until we have settlers around us. . . . On the one hand the order must have permanent and incontestable property, and on the other hand the first Benedictines here must be thorough Benedictines. . . . But my people have every confidence in me. They fear and love me, readily follow me, love prayer (many are real men of prayer), pray daily for me too, and so I hope that for a second time God will make a teacher out of an ass, as in Balaam's time.[58]

Learning that Wimmer was determined to leave St. Vincent, Bishop O'Connor too had second thoughts, and in November he wrote from Pittsburgh offering to accept the Benedictines on their own terms. To begin with, the bishop offered to make Wimmer and his Benedictine successors permanent pastors of St. Vincent and thus grant them perpetual rights to the land according to the terms of the Brouwers will. Moreover, other than the normal responsibilities that every pastor in the diocese assumed, O'Connor assured the Benedictines that nothing would be demanded of them with respect to the pastoral ministry. Finally, the bishop gave up entirely his demand that a definite number of diocesan students be educated at St. Vincent at a reduced rate, promising that such students, when accepted by the Benedictines, would pay full expenses.[59]

Three months later, after protracted negotiations, Wimmer and the bishop came to an agreement that, although not entirely suitable to either side, was in the opinion of both the best compromise possible under the circumstances. The bishop acknowledged that the Benedictines had come to the diocese of Pittsburgh in order to establish a monastery "in which boys, especially German boys, would be educated for the clerical state" and promised that Wimmer and his successors, as superiors of the monastery to be canonically erected, would always be pastor of St. Vincent "so long as his term of office lasts" and so long as no canonical impediment stood in the way. With the office of pastor, the Benedictine superior would assume "the rights and obligations which belong to it" and would be subject to the jurisdiction of O'Connor and his successors with the obligation to "render an account in the same manner as other pastors."[60] Wimmer for his part agreed to assume the parish debt incurred by the previous pastor, Father Michael Gallagher, who by now had left St. Vincent.[61] By this agreement the community of St. Vincent was granted a measure of independence from episcopal control, and the operation of the seminary was left in the hands of the Benedictines. O'Connor did not insist that a formal agreement about diocesan students at the monastic school be drawn up. In a blunt letter to Wimmer, however, he did point out his expectations in that regard and emphasized the lengths to which he had gone in order to satisfy the demands of the Benedictines.

I do not demand any obligation which your predecessor did not have when he transferred the property to you. But I want you to accept some students whom I wish to educate for the ecclesiastical state, and I will pay the expenses which you will have. Indeed, the work that you are doing deserves praise. It will be very beneficial to religion, and I will in a special manner be grateful for having it here. I gave proof of this when I transferred the place and the property to you. I am glad to appoint the superior of the monastery as pastor, an act which has no precedent in the United States. In this way he is the only irremovable rector among the secular and regular clergy in this country!

I might have had difficulties finding a man to build up a seminary as you intend to do, but it can hardly be said that this would be impossible. I will say nothing about former times, when men founded monasteries and seminaries for the benefit of others who were not necessarily of their nationality. This has also been done in our age, and in our country, not on account of the love of nation or race, but through Christian charity. What God achieved in other places, He will also be able to do here, and He will raise up men who will found seminaries for all who are Catholics. May His will be done in everything.[62]

Two weeks later Wimmer informed Abbot Rupert Leiss that "the bishop has changed his mind or come to his senses. . . . Since the chief point has been set out, that all my successors are also pastors and the two properties belong to them, our situation is assured, and likewise our freedom, for he abandoned all the conditions with regard to the seminary. Bishop Henni is taking a copy of the document to Rome for confirmation."[63] And to Archbishop von Reisach of Munich he wrote that

just as in the story of Laban and Jacob, the bishop ten times changed the conditions under which he wanted to transfer this place to me in perpetuity, whereas in the beginning he attached no conditions at all. When after much bargaining I believed him to be finally at his goal, there came a new condition; I was therefore completely convinced that I should drop the negotiations and move to another place. When he saw that I was serious, the bishop then withdrew all his conditions except a single one: that I assume the $800 debt of my predecessor here, half payable in four years, half in six, while the bishop himself assumed the remaining $300.

The agreement reached between himself and the bishop, Father Boniface said, "leaves much to be desired." But "it gives me what I first and foremost need: security that as long as Benedictines are here, they will be in possession of this parish and benefice."[64] If Wimmer did not consider the arrangement with O'Connor exactly ideal, it was perhaps because the relationship between them continued to be based on an underlying strain of mistrust, and very soon this mistrust would manifest itself in new tensions that would erupt into a full-scale conflict between the bishop and the Benedictines, jeopardizing the growth and development of the monastery.

In the meantime, however, the future seemed bright enough. On August 18, 1847, reinforcements arrived from Bavaria. Under the leadership of Father Peter Lechner, O.S.B., prior of the Abbey of Scheyern, seventeen candidates for the lay brotherhood, recruited in Munich by Court Chaplain Joseph Müller, arrived at St. Vincent after an incredibly difficult two-month voyage. Immediately Wimmer made Lechner the community's master of novices and named him "prior" while he himself retained the title "superior." Father Gallagher had left the community in June, and to his position as assistant pastor for the English-speaking parishioners at St. Vincent Bishop O'Connor had named Father Thomas McCullough of Pittsburgh. The Sisters of Mercy had recently moved from St. Vincent to the newly constructed convent and academy of St. Xavier's, about a mile from the monastery, and McCullough took up residence with them. Wimmer and the newly ordained Geyerstanger worked in the parish missions while Lechner devoted almost all his time to the education of clerics and novices.

Besides St. Xavier's, there were five mission stations—at Greensburg, New Derry, Ligonier, Saltsburg, and Indiana—attached to the mother church at St. Vincent in 1847. In three of these missions (Greensburg, Indiana, and Saltsburg) the congregations organized by Father Boniface built churches before the end of 1847. Wimmer wrote to Abbot Rupert Leiss:

I have not yet converted any heretics, but quite often, at their request, I have preached in various places and have brought some pretty near the Church. Moreover, I have confessed people who have not been to confession since 1800 and have brought back to the Church people who have not belonged to it for years, have baptized children from ten to fourteen years of age, have baptized adult so-called Catholics, and the more I get to know especially the more remote parishioners, the more wretchedness I find: entire families without baptism, without the knowledge and practice of prayer, without any religion, even though born of Catholic parents: people who have *never* been to confession, never gone to *any* church, even a Protestant church, etc. And these families, many of which have long been lost to the Church, usually become clans, as I have often found, because all marry, and thereby increase the number of our enemies! Or half the children are Catholics, the others Methodists, Presbyterians, brothers or not, often from three to four sects together! How can one who has a heart and a love for God and his fellow men regard this with indifference![65]

Between the summers of 1847 and 1848 the Benedictines established nine more stations in the counties of Westmoreland and Indiana. In June 1848 Father Boniface wrote Bishop Gregory Ziegler of

Linz that in a period of two months he had been at the monastery for only two days. He traveled on horseback, he said.

A bad chair is now and then my bed, on which I sleep sitting up. Sun and moon are my road guides in the beautiful oak forests. My shield is my Jesus, whom I always have with me. Most of the time I have everything that is needed for the Holy Sacrifice of the Mass, so that my horse is a wandering chapel. Always, however, I have been healthy, and never yet have I encountered any considerable misfortune. I always ride in my habit. I understand English now to the extent that I can preach just barely, hear confessions, catechize, and argue with the Protestants, for which there is almost always opportunity along the way.[66]

Meanwhile, at St. Vincent, conflicts had begun to develop within the young Benedictine community. It was integral to Wimmer's plan of establishing a monastery in America that all members of the community participate in the manual labor necessary to make the monastery self-sufficient. Soon after arriving in Pennsylvania he wrote Archbishop von Reisach of Munich that "even the students have to help, notably during the hay making and corn planting seasons." Such work, he said, would not only give them better appetites, but "when they have moistened the ground with the sweat of their brows, it will also give them an understanding of the value of labor and teach them, moreover, to love their new home."[67]

As novice master, Lechner was responsible for training both the clerics and the novices for the priesthood. He inaugurated a rigorous course of studies for the students, and because of the grueling regimen he petitioned Wimmer to relieve them of their duties in the fields. When Wimmer refused, Lechner accused the superior of giving too little attention to the spiritual and intellectual development of his monks. Wimmer responded by reminding Lechner that he, Wimmer, was superior and therefore had the right to decide what formation best suited the young monks. Not to be intimidated, Lechner observed that the monastery at St. Vincent followed the Rule of St. Benedict very haphazardly and that in order to ensure a better observance in the future he should institute a strict and rigorous period of education for the monastic students. The superior's attitudes, Lechner said, especially with regard to manual labor, impeded the spiritual and academic progress of the monks. Wimmer reacted to his subordinate's opposition by asking him to resign his office.

In November 1848 Father Boniface assigned Lechner to Carroll-town where the monks had recently purchased property from Father Peter Lemke with the intention of establishing a second monastery. With Lechner he sent Charles Geyerstanger and four brothers. On the way to Carrolltown, Father Boniface "lectured Father Peter continually, for he caused much annoyance [at St. Vincent]." He told Lechner that his demands for greater severity in the monastic regimen, "such as no meat, no breakfast, etc." were extreme, and he observed that Lechner himself "cannot get along without coffee; he uses it at noon and sometimes at night." Wimmer said that the monks could not do without breakfast and that their sacrifices were great enough, having to drink only water and being deprived of "beer, wine, and most vegetables." Wimmer also said that Lechner's "murmuring about manual labor for the students every chance he gets also annoys me."[68]

Shortly before Lechner went to Carrolltown three young priests, Father Thaddeus Brunner, O.S.B., and Adalbert Pums, O.S.B., of Metten, and Father Andrew Zugtriegel, O.S.B., of Ottobeuren (Augsburg), arrived at St. Vincent to join the growing monastery, and by January 1849 the community numbered fifty priests, clerics, brothers, and novices. Wimmer assigned Brunner and Pums to instruct the clerical candidates and Zugtriegel to assist himself and Celestine Englbrecht with the pastoral work at St. Vincent and in the missions of Westmoreland and Indiana Counties. He soon discovered that with regard to monastic observance the sympathies of both Brunner and Zugtriegel lay with the ideals espoused by Lechner. He was thus forced to contend with more divisiveness in the ranks.

Like Lechner, Brunner and Zugtriegel wanted the Pennsylvania monastery to follow a stricter observance of the Rule and pursue a rigid course of study. In March 1849 Father Boniface wrote Abbot Rupert Leiss of Scheyern, his former confrere at Metten, that he was not in an enviable position.

Not only am I very busy, but also burdened with great responsibilities and troubled by unrest in the community. I am chiefly worried about the difference of opinions with regard to our daily routine. Some consider it too strict, others too lax. Among the later is Father Peter who told me that he has complained to you about the manual labor of the students and the monastic enclosure. We never had any open dispute about these questions, and he never opposed me directly, but I will never give up my conviction that our novices and clerics must work in the field when it is necessary. At present my chief aim must not be to have as many priests as soon as possible, but I must first find means that 30–40 students, with brothers and fathers, can live from the farm. As soon as I am sure of that support, there will be no want of priest candidates. Your Father Peter, however, seems to believe that people can live from the air on five or ten acres of land. Therefore I sent him to St. Joseph's where he will find out that only God can create something out of nothing.[69]

But even with Lechner out of the way in Carrolltown, the monastic ideals he inspired continued to ferment at St. Vincent. Three months after Father Boniface wrote Abbot Rupert, Father Thaddeus Brunner wrote Abbot Gregory Scherr of Metten that he was "convinced St. Vincent is a farm and no monastery." According to Brunner, Wimmer had "thrown himself into a great stream whose waves have covered him, and as a result he cannot see what is going on around him." Brunner complained that the Benedictine superior in Pennsylvania had "entirely given himself over to business affairs, acquiring more land, more cows, and more sheep." He had "quenched every sense and desire for monastic solitude and learning." Moreover, Father Boniface was "seldom at home. Consequently the prescribed spiritual observance is not kept." And when the superior *was* home, he was "always in the kitchen where he laughs and jokes about everything." Brunner observed that "there is no novitiate, and some of the novices do not hear two chapters of the Holy Rule explained to them during the entire year." Brunner's critical letter ended with a note of optimism, however. He said that all would be well, that Benedictine monastic observance in the United States would become exemplary, that in fact the community in Pennsylvania would be saved if Peter Lechner were to take over and implement his own monastic policies at St. Vincent.[70]

Zugtriegel and Lechner also wrote letters to Abbot Gregory in which they bitterly complained of the lack of enclosure and the merry atmosphere that prevailed at the monastery. Like Brunner, Lechner said that Wimmer was "always in the kitchen." He refused to put up a trellis for the enclosure, and his building program was shoddy. "The whole monastery looks like a complicated entanglement." Lechner asked the abbot of Metten to accept what he had written "more as an expression of my anxiety than as a complaint. I pity the superior," he said, "more than accuse him."[71] In July Brunner reported to Scherr that when Wimmer reneged on his promise to let several of the brothers make solemn vows, the community's peace was shaken once again. Lechner, who had recently been recalled from Carrolltown and reappointed as prior, sided with the brothers, as did Zugtriegel and Brunner. Some of these brothers, Father Thaddeus said, "would be worthy to be numbered among the ranks of the saints were they to die." He suggested that to avoid scandal, either the discontented brothers and priests should be allowed to establish another monastery in which they could live in peace or else they should be recalled to Metten. Brunner told Scherr that when he confronted Wimmer about the brothers' dilemma, the superior "told me to pack my bags and go to Carrolltown."[72]

Wimmer had his own complaints to register. Shortly after attending the Seventh Provincial Council of Baltimore, where he had been formally recognized as "provincial of Benedictines" in the United States, he wrote Abbot Rupert Leiss:

In the land of freedom every free man is happy to use his position for the enjoyment of freedom, and so does our good Father Peter. With two other confederates (from Metten and Ottobeuren) he submitted to me yesterday the humble request that I hand over to him a mission under *his* exclusive control, because in conscience he can no longer work *with* me. . . . The men are of the opinion that I should cede St. Joseph's to them. But I can not and will not because I consider it necessary for the greater security of me and mine. . . . I advised them since they don't know where else to turn to go to the State of Indiana (Diocese of Vincennes) to which Bishop St. Palais urgently invited me at the Council of Baltimore. Without an official discharge from me they will not be accepted there, because at the Council I was recognized (and I had nothing to do with it) as *provincialis Benedictinorum.* Hence I must grant this and, in addition, presume your assent. . . . Fortunately, I now have four priests of my own and four theologians to be ordained next year, and hence I can keep all my stations and then run my *own* house, if there are no more strangers in it.[73]

Given the opportunity to establish their own community in the wilds of Indiana, Lechner, Brunner, and Zugtriegel hesitated and decided in the end not to go west but rather to remain in Pennsylvania where they continued to be thorns in Wimmer's side. In a fit of exasperation, Wimmer wrote of Lechner that "to help a good-natured, sanguine fanatic to realize his daydreams I hold to be no vocation," but later he regretted his intemperate remarks. When Abbot Rupert

Leiss wrote urging him to have greater patience with the monks who opposed him, he admitted that Leiss was right and agreed to try to be less combative in spirit. He went on to explain calmly and in more detail the reasons that he could not institute the changes, desirable as they were, urged by Lechner and his "confederates":

In keeping with my character, I wrote impetuously and must apologize for many an improper expression. There can be no question of patience: certainly all must have more patience with me, just as I with them. . . . My situation is surely unenviable: I cannot do many things as they should be done: even now Father Peter is bothering me about enclosure, but it is not *possible* to have one. After I have worked one more year I can comply. I cannot introduce *total* silence in the daytime at work—we would have to become Trappists. I cannot always ask the advice of the confreres—because they are too young and inexperienced, not sufficiently discreet, etc., and would often only hinder me. Peter understands absolutely nothing about secular business—that is just his way. Chapters would be very nice, but when there are fifty members, they become too long; we don't have time. I hold them only on special occasions. In other respects, everything is observed just as it is done in a good monastery. . . . My hands are full of temporal matters. I can go only to Matins and Compline and have only the night to myself. The prayer of the brothers must support me. I cannot study at all and read the newspapers only in part. I would like to be again a prefect among my little ones—but there is no one who can see to the other affairs. However, I must also be pastor in order to know where and how my priests have to work and to be able to supervise them. By the way, I have only one station once every month, sixteen miles from here in the town of Saltsburg, because one must preach there in English—my priests take care of all the nearer and farther stations. Father Peter preaches regularly at home and is *again Prior,* novice master, and professor, but he is too attached to his books and leaves the overseeing etc. to me. There are now more than seventy of us.[74]

The dissension in the community deeply disturbed Wimmer, who continued to hold Lechner, Brunner, and Zugtriegel, the "strangers in the house," responsible. In an attempt to diffuse the tension, he called the community together and explained things as he perceived them. He gave all the reasons he mentioned to Leiss for being unable to establish a strict *clausura,* absolute silence, and regular chapter deliberations, and he told the brothers, who were pressing for formal acceptance as solemnly professed members of the community, that no one would be allowed to take solemn vows, not even the clerical monks, until the monastery had been canonically established. Finally, he threatened punishment for anyone who continued the divisive murmuring. Not long afterward the Bavarian court chaplain, Father Joseph Müller, wrote Abbot Gregory Scherr of Metten and informed him that since Father Boniface had "taken courage and restored his authority" the community at St. Vincent had grown quiet once again. "If anyone asks why this happened," he said, "the answer will be that the Reverend Boniface has stressed the economic affairs more than the educational." Müller said that Wimmer first "must get a firm and orderly household, for how else will he feed so many people?" The court chaplain assured the abbot of Metten that he continued to support Wimmer in every way, and he urged Scherr to do the same. Finally, he passed on a request from the superior in Pennsylvania that Abbot Gregory "send him no other fathers, unless it be Reverend Carl and Reverend Martin."[75]

Despite the hard line that Wimmer had taken, Peter Lechner continued to encourage the young clerics and brothers to strive after a presumably higher monastic ideal than Father Boniface taught. He suggested the Trappist reform as an example of that ideal and urged the members of the community to read the works of de Rancé, the seventeenth-century Cistercian reformer. In July one of the clerics, Jerome Wohlfahrt, applied to Wimmer for permission to transfer his vows to the newly established Trappist monastery of Gethsemani in Kentucky. Wimmer granted the permission and soon afterward four novices also asked leave to join the Trappists. Wimmer agreed. The next to apply was Father Andrew Zugtriegel, who took three lay brothers with him to Kentucky. Finally Lechner himself told Wimmer that he was leaving St. Vincent.

Wimmer watched the exodus with apprehension, complaining that the reformers had deprived the monastery of all its musicians and that he was prevented from continuing his building program on account of the money he had to spend in order to hire a new music teacher. Müller wrote from Munich and offered encouragement, telling him that everything would end well,[76] but to Wimmer the loss of so many members of the community seemed an ill omen for the future of Benedictine life in the United States. He informed Abbot Rupert of Scheyern of Father Peter's departure and expressed his anxieties about the desertions.

Events, however, took an unexpected turn. Before reaching Kentucky Lechner stopped in Pittsburgh where he had second thoughts about joining the Trappists. His presence at St. Vincent had become so divisive that Wimmer refused to take him back and excused him from all further obligations to the Pennsylvania monastery. Now that he considered himself free of the authority of Father Boniface and under obedience to the abbot of Scheyern once again, Lechner turned to Bishop Michael O'Connor and offered himself as a professor in O'Connor's new diocesan seminary in Pittsburgh. Wimmer, regarding the developments with relief, was pleased that he and the St. Vincent community were finally unburdened of the "good-natured, sanguine fanaticism" of Father Peter. "He is a man of feeling such as few are," the superior at St. Vincent wrote to Abbot Rupert.

I love and honor him, but he has caused me more grief, chagrin, and harm than my worst enemy could have caused. If I have not acted properly as superior, or if I have acted too tactlessly against him and you, please excuse me on the grounds of necessity and also of good will: I saw and see no other way. . . .

The consciousness of being surrounded by false confreres, the everlasting opposition, the endless series of impractical proposals, the perpetual complaining when I cannot conjure up everything— this is difficult. But I am unremitting, always well, and delight in the Lord, for it is also a comfort to suffer, especially when it comes not from wickedness but from well meaning but misdirected zeal. I know indeed that this is the case with the Prior, but there I had to prescribe limits, because otherwise the devil could only have made the chasm wider and finally caused a break or tear, and perhaps that is what is happening: as God wills it, but I cannot help it. I need my prestige and hence must maintain it. I do not know what he is engaged in. I hope he does not completely forget himself but remains in Pittsburgh as a professor in the diocesan seminary, where one is now needed. Later I want to report further, but I would advise you not to recall him home, because he will not willingly go or will not go at all and because, for all his piety, he is difficult to manage.[77]

A little more than a year after the exodus, Joseph Müller's prediction that all would end well came true when the group of reformers returned to St. Vincent. They had found life in the French Trappist monastery too exacting for Germans who knew no French and who had even to go to confession through an interpreter. Wimmer received the reform-minded and now humbled monks like the father of so many prodigal sons, but he fairly well gloated when he wrote Abbot Rupert Leiss in December 1850: "My Trappists have all come back, also the musicians, and the loss of several hundred florins, which I suffered on account of them, is compensated by the radical cure of Trappist fever which resulted. Health has been restored."[78]

Neither Thaddeus Brunner nor Andrew Zugtriegel, however, remained at St. Vincent. Both returned to Bavaria to follow their respective vocations. Zugtriegel entered the Trappist Order and eventually became abbot of the Trappist Abbey of Oehlenberg in Alsace. Brunner joined the Benedictine Priory of St. Denis at Schaeftlarn near Munich, where he eventually became conventual prior. In 1851, after all his best efforts to reform the monastery at St. Vincent had failed, Peter Lechner left Pittsburgh and returned to Scheyern to pursue the monastic and scholarly life he had wanted to create in Pennsylvania. He wrote a life of St. Benedict, a Benedictine martyrology, and a three-volume commentary on Sacred Scripture and published numerous other books and articles on theological and spiritual topics.[79] In 1853 he published an account of his American adventure which was not unsympathetic to Wimmer and the work of the Benedictines at St. Vincent.[80] Lechner died in 1874. His monastic reform efforts at St. Vincent ended in failure less because of his own weakness than because of the single-minded determination and indomitable will of the superior with whom he had to contend. Wimmer had a clear vision of the Benedictine role in the American Church and was fierce in his commitment to its achievement. Pragmatic, determined, and undeterred by even the strongest criticism, he pressed ahead with his plan to establish the Benedictine Order in the United States as an active missionary and educational institution. Lechner's efforts to inject a more contemplative spirit in American Benedictine monasticism created a division at St. Vincent that was never fully resolved, and the disparate ideals of those "strangers" in the community who wanted a stricter monastic observance, enclosure, and a life of scholarship and those who desired a more outgoing style of missionary activity, teaching, and pastoral work plagued Wimmer and the community of St. Vincent to the end of Wimmer's life.

3 ❧ The First Years

THE PRINCIPAL AIM of the first Benedictines in the United States was to educate a German-speaking clergy for the growing population of German Catholic immigrants who by the 1840s had become an important presence in the American Church. It was this purpose that inspired Wimmer in Munich and won him enthusiastic support from the *Ludwig Missionsverein* and his other Bavarian benefactors, as well as cordial invitations from three American bishops—Michael O'Connor of Pittsburgh, John Martin Henni of Milwaukee, and William Quarter of Chicago—to settle in the United States and establish seminaries in their dioceses. Wimmer had outlined the details of his plan in the *Augsburger Postzeitung* article that set his missionary venture into motion, and upon his arrival in Pennsylvania he immediately began to put the plan into action.

In his Augsburg article Wimmer said that once the Benedictines established a monastery in America,

> the monks could expect a large number of children for their school, and in the course of time, as the number of priests increases, a college with a good Latin course could be opened. They would not be dependent upon the tuition fee of the students for their support, which they could draw from the farm and the missions (though these would not be a source of much income at the beginning). Thus they could devote their energies to the education of the poorer classes of boys who could pay little or nothing, and since these boys would daily come in contact with the priests and monks, it could scarcely be otherwise but that many of them would develop a desire of becoming priests or even religious.[1]

From the start of the Benedictine presence at St. Vincent Wimmer pursued his educational plan aggressively, and events bore out the accuracy of his prediction. The academic development of the monastic school began just after the monks arrived in Westmoreland County. Instruction was underway within days of their settlement. During the first academic year (1846–1847) Wimmer and Father Michael Gallagher taught philosophy and theology to the four clerical student— Charles Geyerstanger, Benedict Haindl, Placidus Döttl, and Celestine Englbrecht—who had accompanied him from Bavaria, as well as to the subdeacon and candidate for the secular priesthood whom Bishop Michael O'Connor had sent from Pittsburgh. In 1847 Geyerstanger and the subdeacon were ordained and three more Benedictine students of philosophy—Jerome Wohlfahrt, Maurus Zacherl, and Luke Wimmer (Father Boniface's nephew)—arrived from Bavaria, entered the novitiate at St. Vincent, and began their studies for the priesthood.

In June 1847 Father Michael Gallagher resigned as professor and left the community, but within two months Father Peter Lechner arrived from Scheyern, and soon afterward Fathers Thaddeus Brunner and Adalbert Pums of Metten, and Andrew Zugtriegel of Ottobeuren, joined him. Lechner, Brunner, and Pums had charge of the philosophical and theological education of the seminarians, while Wimmer, Zugtriegel, and Geyerstanger attended to the pastoral care of the German Catholics at St. Vincent and in the missions of Westmoreland County. (In the beginning first Father Michael Gallagher and then Father Thomas McCullough served the needs of the English-speaking parishioners at St. Vincent, but later, when they had mastered English, the Benedictines themselves took over these responsibilities.) In the fall of 1848 seven additional clerical candidates—Odilo Vandergrün, Utto Huber, John Kreps, Martin Beck, Severin Webber, Leonard Mayer, and Francis Cannon—entered the monastery and began their studies for the priesthood under Lechner. Thus by January 1849 there were thirteen Benedictine novices and clerics studying philosophy and theology in the seminary at St. Vincent. Three of them, Haindl, Döttl, and Englbrecht, were ordained in April.

Within a year of inaugurating the seminary program in philosophy and theology, the monks opened a gymnasium, or Latin school, to provide secondary-level instruction for young boys who came to St. Vincent for their education. The gymnasium, an essential part of Wimmer's strategic plan to educate a German-speaking clergy for the American Church, opened in the fall of 1847 with eight students who had expressed the desire of entering the Benedictine Order and pursuing studies for the priesthood. By October 1848 enrollment in the gymnasium had risen to twelve, and in December Wimmer wrote Father Joseph F. Müller in Munich that "we have among our [minor] seminarians two from Philadelphia, one from Pittsburgh, three from St. Marys [Pennsylvania], one from Butler [Pennsylvania], and five from this parish. I could not accept more for want of room. In the [major] seminary we have three deacons, nine scholastics, and one Irish School Brother who wants to join us. Thus the school has twenty-five students."[2]

The fourth academic year (1849–1850) opened with an influx of seven postsecondary candidates for the secular priesthood from the dioceses of Pittsburgh, Milwaukee, Baltimore, Philadelphia, and New York, and from then on the ranks of diocesan seminarians at St. Vincent grew almost as dramatically as those of the Benedictine students. Except for two Irish theological students from Pittsburgh and the Irish-born Franciscan brother Francis Cannon, who awaited a dispensation from Rome to become a Benedictine, most of the students, both in the major seminary and in the Latin school, and all the faculty members were from Germany. The American-born secondary students were the sons of German-born parents.

Father Thaddeus Brunner took charge of the gymnasium in 1849 and initiated a rigorous course of studies based upon the program at the monastic school at Metten. He was assisted by Father Adalbert Pums and by two laymen, Mr. S. Breitenfeld of Munich, professor of mathematics, and Mr. Aloysius Pichler, professor of music.[3] While leaving the details of academic administration and instruction to Lechner and Brunner because of his pastoral commitments, Wimmer, who for six years had taught Latin and Greek in the Ludwigs Gymnasium in Munich, guided the development of the schools at St. Vincent. He was especially interested in the growth and progress of the Latin school, and wrote the directors of the Ludwig Missionsverein:

My heart is in this work, and I will spare no expense to teach the students first what is necessary, then what is useful, and finally what is beautiful so long as it contributes to their refinement. I cannot expect that all will become priests because we have to accept boys who come to us only to be prepared for the sacraments of confession and communion. Some, however, will enter the sanctuary, and as they study both English and German they will be able to use both languages for the salvation of souls. Already seven of the older boys have asked very earnestly to become Benedictines. Most probably they will soon be invested with the habit. I am only hoping that they will become good priests, or at least good Catholics.[4]

In 1849 a "commercial department" was opened in the gymnasium when thirteen young boys who did not plan to enter the priesthood arrived at St. Vincent from the German colony of St. Marys to begin their secondary education. The establishment of the commercial department is traditionally regarded as the beginning of St. Vincent College. In 1852, after several more such "commercial" students enrolled, Wimmer wrote Archbishop von Reisach of Munich:

In our minor seminary the instructions in Latin are the same as in Germany, but English is the main branch for the Germans and German the most important for English-speaking boys. Some of these beginners who already show signs of a beard are declining *mensa, mensae* or are conjugating *amo, amas*. Greek is taken less thoroughly. The students are graded in different branches according to their progress but receive instructions in common in penmanship, drawing, and music. One priest is director of the school, and he has two clerics as prefects: one for the ecclesiastical, the other for the commercial students. They rise at 4:30 and retire at 8:30. They take care of their own apartment and in this way we follow the motto: help yourself.

Their meals are the same as ours. This arrangement causes difficulties because our diet differs from theirs at home. At times they show this disposition openly. On abstinence days they hate the "Bavarian dumplings," which they call "metaphysics." Our terms are sixty dollars for board and tuition and five dollars for laundry. Generally, however, they pay less and several orphans are kept entirely free.[5]

The secondary school was modeled on the traditional German gymnasium, and its students ranged in age from ten to seventeen. The distinction between the young boys who were studying for the priesthood and those who were not became fixed very early. The priesthood students, or "scholastics," attended classes with the "commercial" students, but they lived in separate quarters and followed a more demanding course of studies and spiritual exercises. The "scholasticate" was a unique institution. Wimmer designed it along the lines of his proposed monastic school for young Benedictine aspirants at Mallersdorf, which never got beyond the planning stage because of opposition at Metten. In America, however, he was free to do as he pleased, and he therefore created a separate division in the gymnasium for young boys with aspirations for the priesthood and the monastic life. Doubtless it was because of this system that so many of them persevered and eventually became monks at St. Vincent.

The basic elements of Wimmer's program of education derived from nineteenth-century Bavarian practice. The impressive cultural and intellectual spirit in Bavaria during the first half of the nineteenth century was transported by the monks to America. Fathers Peter Lechner, who had charge of the program in philosophy and theology for the seminarians, and Thaddeus Brunner, director of the Latin school, were committed advocates of the Bavarian intellectual and spiritual ideals brought to western Pennsylvania in the 1840s, and their unflinching efforts to transplant intact and undiluted the heritage of Catholic southern Germany sometimes brought them into open conflict with the superior, whose approach to education was more pragmatic and flexible than theirs. While Lechner pressed for more time in the academic schedule for the clerics and seminarians to develop their knowledge and intellectual skills and opposed Wimmer's policy of assigning them to work in the fields, Brunner attempted to impose the same academic standards in the gymnasium as existed in the Latin school at Metten. When he discovered that the young boys who came to St. Vincent were not prepared to meet these standards, he urged that Wimmer end his practice of recruiting farm boys from poor families and focus his educational programs on English-speaking boys from the cities, where elementary education was better and incomes higher. Wimmer refused. "[Father Thaddeus] is not the only one who advocates such a change," he wrote, "but this would stamp me as a traitor to my cause. I did not come to America to make money, and not for the rich English students, but to educate my poor countrymen. I would rather suffer want and continue to work under these poor conditions than serve the world, have a better income, and live comfortably."[6]

With admirable determination and single-mindedness Wimmer pursued his vision of educating poor German boys for the Benedictine Order and the priesthood and resisted strongly and successfully attempts to thwart his purpose by those who did not understand the situation among immigrants in the American Church as well as he did. He was committed to serving the needs of poor German

Catholics in rural areas rather than to catering to the better-off middle-class families who lived in the cities. He realized moreover that much of what he and the others had known in Europe would have to be modified if his American experiment were to succeed. Benedictine education in America could not be simply a carbon copy of Benedictine education in Bavaria. Innovations such as the focus on poor students, the creation of the scholasticate, and the requirement that everyone work in the fields were the result of exigencies that confronted the monks in a new land where conditions were much different from those that prevailed in the old country. Students would plant the corn and make the hay because it was good for them and was necessary for the economy of the monastery and the school. If this meant that they would be unable to study as much as their professors thought they should, then so be it. A studious life untempered by manual labor, Wimmer believed, was barren. A boy studied at St. Vincent to become a good priest or a good Catholic layman, not primarily a good scholar. And physical labor was as important in the moral development of youth as studies because "only God can create something out of nothing." For that reason students would be taught "first what is necessary, then what is useful, and finally what is beautiful."

While insisting upon manual labor and emphasizing the religious and moral training of the boys and young men in the schools at St. Vincent, however, Wimmer created an educational program that neglected neither the intellectual nor the cultural aspects of the students' formation. "In a country like America," he wrote,

where Protestant services are so devoid of everything that elevates the mind and the heart, religion and art must cooperate to give our liturgy an outward splendor, great dignity, and even grandeur to render it dear to the people. The common man cannot enter sufficiently into the innermost spirit of our services. Therefore he is not attracted by its highest aims. Yet to create an attachment to religion is more necessary here than anywhere else because we have absolute liberty as regards religion itself, its practice and the persons who take part in such devotions. This means that the monasteries have a solemn duty to foster art in order to spread and strengthen the faith because farmers and shopkeepers will never do this. Therefore I am firmly convinced that a monastic school that does not strive to advance art as much as studies and religious instruction will be deficient in its work.

In scientific matters short-comings may be condoned more readily, especially in the beginning, but a monastic school that neglects the promotion of religious art must be censured. Heretics have seldom been converted by learned treatises, but almost always found their way to the true faith through the beauties of Catholic worship, the holiness of its ministers, the fervor of its people and its prayers. It will hardly be different in America. *Nil novi sub sole.* I may be mistaken, but observation and experience are on my side.

All this urges me to pay special attention to our school of art. In this respect our minor seminary is well equipped. The department of drawing and painting is taking pride in an exceptionally large assortment of pictures and models for their artistic work. We have about 300 oil paintings, not masterpieces. Many of the religious paintings especially of individual saints could be used for altarpieces. We received most of them from Father Pius Reiser in Munich.[7]

For Wimmer artistic activity in the school was important because it was useful. Through it the mind and heart were elevated, and with it the work of spreading the Gospel throughout an essentially Protestant land would be facilitated. From the beginning the academic program at St. Vincent accented the artistic and cultural heritage of Bavarian Catholicism, especially in the areas of music and painting, and after Lechner and Brunner departed for Europe because of disagreements with the superior, it was Wimmer and the young priests and clerics at St. Vincent who sustained the rich cultural milieu that characterized the monastic school at St. Vincent in the 1850s.

With assistance from Father Joseph Müller the monastery school received hundreds of works of art between 1847 and 1851 from benefactors in Bavaria. The majority of these came from the collection of Father Pius Reiser, a diocesan priest of the Munich cathedral chapter who had been a seminary classmate of Wimmer's in Regensburg, but others came from the collection of King Ludwig I. Because of these and other donations from Europe, the school's art department was especially well equipped, as Wimmer noted in his letter to the Ludwig Missionsverein. Its first director was Father Luke Wimmer, Father Boniface's nephew, who had studied art in Munich before coming to America and entering the monastery at St. Vincent in 1847.

Music too was an essential part of the educational curriculum in the gymnasium. In 1852 Wimmer wrote that St. Vincent's music department was reputedly "one of the best in the country." The school's first professor of music was Aloysius Pichler, a layman from Munich who after borrowing money from the Ludwig Missionsverein for passage to the United States repaid the debt by teaching at St. Vincent for two years. Pichler was followed as the school's music director by Professor Maurice Schwab[8] who was assisted by two talented members of the monastic community, Fathers Leonard and Wendelin Mayer. The Mayer brothers had been musicians before entering the monastery and together with Professor Schwab ("who supervises everything with great enthusiasm and rare ability") they helped create "an orchestra which is hardly surpassed anywhere."[9] The Sunday high mass in the parish church at St. Vincent was frequently performed with full orchestra and chorus, and the works of Mozart, Haydn, and Weber were among those featured both in the liturgy and in public concerts.[10]

Besides the many paintings that Joseph Müller arranged to have sent to St. Vincent, King Ludwig's court chaplain helped to collect books for the library as well. Benefactors, who included King Ludwig I, Bishop Gregory Ziegler of Linz, Father Heinrich Brestlmeyer of Ried, Austria, and the directors of the National Library of Bavaria, donated thousands of volumes to the monastery and school. In 1851 Wimmer wrote Archbishop von Reisach that on account of this generosity the library contained the works of "almost all the Latin and Greek authors of prominence." The theology, philosophy, and history sections were especially well supplied and contained books of "both old and new authors and books essential for the study of Scripture."[11] In addition, by 1851 the library owned an incipient collection of valuable incunabula donated by King Ludwig and other wealthy benefactors in Bavaria. Visitors to St. Vincent in the early years often noted the book collection that Wimmer had gathered. The Austrian priest, Father Joseph Salzman, who came to the United States in 1847 and founded the Salesian seminary in Milwaukee, spent several days at the monastery in 1850 and afterward wrote that the library at St. Vincent was "well stocked and considering that the books were acquired by donations, they represent a good selection, particularly in history and patrology."[12]

With the departure of Father Thaddeus Brunner in 1850, Father Utto Huber, a recently ordained Bavarian priest who had completed his theological studies at St. Vincent, assumed the duties of director of the Latin school. Enrollment continued to grow, and financial conditions began to improve when new students arrived whose families were better able to bear the full burden of tuition expenses. In 1852 Wimmer wrote the directors of the Ludwig Missionsverein of the difficulties the Benedictines at St. Vincent had experienced in establishing their school:

You may well believe that under such conditions it is a harder task to establish a school than to found a religious house. To begin with, there are no funds available. Then I have scarcely any teachers. They must first be trained or rather they have to train themselves. In some cases I must trust in God for friends in Europe to send us professors. The founding of a monastery requires much work, but the establishing of a college demands also much worry. We began very slowly, continued courageously and systematically and finally we are noticing some results. As everything was done for God's glory, the blessing of God is visible in many ways. One of the signs that points that way is the fact that not only poor boys ask for admission, but we have already received applications from well-to-do families, although our institution is still very young. At present we cannot take half of those who are applying because we lack the room.[13]

While educating priests to minister to German-speaking immigrants was the principal aim of the first Benedictines in the United States, Wimmer was profoundly aware that by coming to America and establishing a Benedictine monastery at St. Vincent he was breaking new ground in another important sphere as well. The Benedictine Order, the oldest religious order in the Church, after centuries of prominence and far-reaching contributions to the intellectual, cultural, and spiritual heritage of Christian Europe, had recently undergone a period of retrenchment and dormancy. Wimmer blamed the decline not just on Enlightenment secularism and the Napoleonic upheavals that had resulted in the suppression of the order throughout most of Europe at the beginning of the nineteenth century, but also on the internal complacency, inertia, and general lack of spiritual and monastic zeal that in his opinion had debilitated Benedictine monasticism since at least the middle of the eighteenth century. He had been an active participant in the mid-nineteenth-century monastic revival in Bavaria, a movement that was part of a broader revival taking place in Italy, France, and other parts of Europe. In America he saw himself as someone in a unique position to make significant contributions to the modern development of an ancient Benedictine heritage and tradition by transplanting the order to a new land and transforming it once more into a dynamic force within the Church and society.

The fact that some Benedictines in Europe failed to share his vision of what the order could again become frustrated him. "Our order shows such insignificant growth," he wrote Abbot Sigismund Schulte of Vienna,

and seems to have so little blessing from above because it endeavors only to be a learned and honored society, with scarcely any love for missionary activities. However, during the first thousand years of its existence such work was uppermost in the mind of the Benedictines. When our order withdrew from this field of activities, the friars and the Jesuits took over their labors and became prominent. Christ said, "Go and teach all nations." Stability is a beautiful virtue, but it should not develop into immobility. America would be ours if every monastery in Austria would have a colony here. . . . We will be rejuvenated like serpents if only we cast off the old skin.[14]

Wimmer regarded his role, from an historical perspective, as one of inaugurating another stage in the growth and development of the Benedictine Order. He did not view his work in America as something fundamentally new. Rather, he saw his task as restoring within the order an ancient and venerable missionary dynamic which he believed would help revitalize the monastic institution both in Europe and in the New World. He asserted from the outset that by returning to the spiritual ideals and practices of medieval missionary monasticism, by moving away from narrow interpretations of the Rule and abandoning moribund forms of religious observance, by casting off, as it were, its old skin, the Benedictine Order would renew itself as it had many times in history, would attract young and idealistic candidates for the monastic life, and would once more prove a vital force in the Catholic Church.

Within only a few years of his arrival in Pennsylvania, Wimmer began to realize that his plan was succeeding beyond his most sanguine expectations. His vision had inspired numerous young men in Bavaria. He was astonished at how quickly his work at St. Vincent was attracting, year after year, fresh recruits and, despite the challenges and hardships the community faced in the early years, at how deeply the seed he planted had taken root in American soil. By the fall of 1848 the monastic community at St. Vincent had more than doubled in size. Two years later it numbered more than sixty members. Young men arrived regularly to join the monastery either as clerical candidates for the Benedictine priesthood or as postulants for the Benedictine lay brotherhood. The growth of the community was dramatic, and because of the increased numbers he found the buildings inadequate and was forced to construct new ones. In March 1850 he wrote Abbot Rupert Leiss of Scheyern:

We have built a house sixty feet long, forty feet wide, and three stories high, which attached to the old one is now 100 feet long. It is finished except for the attic under the roof, which is still to be laid. This year I will add thirty-six feet and in another year I will add to the front, then it will be as long as the monastery at Scheyern. A brick barn, sixty feet long, forty feet wide, and forty feet high up to the roof, was built in the autumn and is exactly long enough for the harvest.

Twenty boys obtain a good education. There are fifteen philosophers and theologians. Four clerics will soon be ordained. In a radius of thirty to forty miles we conduct the pastoral care of the Germans and often of the English also. Choir prayer and the brothers' rosary take place regularly; the nocturnal silence is strictly observed; meditation and the examination of conscience are diligently performed, as is spiritual reading. Fresh water is our only drink, our food is ordinary fare. *No* priest and *cleric* takes breakfast (nor do I), apart from the Prior. It is gladly allowed him and prescribed because of his infirmity.[15]

Wimmer continued to strive for a balanced and regular monastic observance within the community. Before leaving Bavaria he had taken counsel with religious leaders there and sought advice on how to lay the groundwork for a spiritual regimen appropriate to Benedictine community life in a new land. He consistently emphasized the prayerful and ascetic dimensions of the Benedictine vocation and urged the young men who joined him to pursue the call to work and prayer with discipline and devotion. He wrote Archbishop Karl von Reisach:

Before my departure from Munich I had a long conversation with your Grace about my plans, and I must say that I never lost sight of the principles that we discussed that day, especially about the development of the religious spirit in the community. To a certain extent the goal has already been achieved. I do not hesitate to say that the Holy Rule is observed here as well as in any Benedictine monastery in Bavaria. As far as my contribution to this success is concerned, I merely explained that manner of life and indicated how it should be observed. I found that everyone accepted these rules with great joy. That spirit has not diminished to this day. With the Holy Rule as our guide, we are trying to lead lives pleasing to God. I can only thank the Lord that He gave me so many men who are following it. Certainly all are not equally zealous, but most of them show eagerness to assist by word and example those who need help. I know well that the great tempter "who goes about seeking whom he may devour" will not turn away from the monastery to find possible victims. But with the help of God, I am hoping that the one or other unfortunate member will not bring the destruction of many.[16]

But even as monastic observance in the monastery and academic programs in the Latin school and seminary progressed smoothly and in harmony with Wimmer's original designs, other developments were unfolding that threatened the future of the Benedictine venture in America. In June 1848 Wimmer petitioned the Holy See through the offices of John Martin Henni, Swiss-born bishop of Milwaukee, that St. Vincent be raised to the rank of canonical priory and made both independent of the Abbey of Metten and exempt in all internal administrative and spiritual matters from the jurisdiction of the bishop of Pittsburgh. In Europe this was the standard procedure for officially establishing Benedictine monasteries, which traditionally were communities independent of one another and exempt from episcopal control. Independence and exemption meant that each monastery, whether a priory or an abbey, was free to develop its own religious observance in accordance with the Rule and the regulations of canon law, that its religious superior (whether prior or abbot) was responsible for the community's internal affairs, administration, and spiritual development and could receive the vows of its members, and that except in those matters having to do with the pastoral care of congregations attended by the monks, the community was not subject to the rule of the local bishop. No other independent, exempt religious community existed in the United States at that time, and Wimmer made a serious diplomatic error by petitioning for canonical status without first obtaining the formal, written approval of Bishop O'Connor.

In the late summer of 1848, during his *ad limina* visit to Rome, Bishop Henni presented Wimmer's petition to Alexander Cardinal Barnabo, secretary of the Sacred Congregation for the Propagation of the Faith. Before Propaganda could act on the matter, however, revolution broke out in Italy. In November 1848 the papacy was driven into exile, and Pope Pius IX was unable to return to Rome until April

1850. Once normal diplomatic channels were reopened, the Holy See acted in favor of Wimmer's petition. In September 1850 Propaganda empowered Bishop O'Connor of Pittsburgh to elevate the community at St. Vincent to the rank of canonical priory, but by then a new controversy had broken out between O'Connor and the Benedictines, and O'Connor refused to act.[17]

The reasons for O'Connor's refusal were various. For one thing, he resented Wimmer's having made his petition to Rome without formally advising him of his intention to do so. For another, he was offended that Wimmer had turned to the bishop of Milwaukee for assistance in making his appeal instead of going through the normal channel, which would have been the bishop of Pittsburgh. But the proximate cause of O'Connor's refusal to act in favor of raising the monastery to canonical status had to do with beer.

The story is this: In 1849 one of Wimmer's nephews had immigrated to the United States from Bavaria with several hundred dollars sent by Father Joseph Müller for the monastery of St. Vincent. The nephew appropriated a large portion of the money for his own use, and in order to repay the debt he asked his uncle to purchase for him a tavern and brewery in Indiana, Pennsylvania, thirty-five miles from St. Vincent, from which he hoped to draw enough income to repay the money he had stolen. Wimmer agreed, but he acquired the business in his own name for security. The nephew failed in the enterprise, and the business came into the hands of Father Boniface, who hired the original owner to operate it.[18] When Bishop O'Connor, a member of the growing ranks of temperance advocates among the Irish American Catholic clergy, learned of the Benedictine enterprise in Indiana County, he demanded that the business be closed at once. Wimmer, son of the tavernkeeper of Thalmassing, agreed to close the tavern but informed O'Connor that he would keep the adjacent brewery open until he had paid off its debts. He insisted that the enterprise was perfectly in harmony with Benedictine practice and pointed to the age-old tradition of Bavarian monasteries' brewing and selling beer to the public as evidence. He refused therefore to close the brewery, and when the bishop objected, he "went from the defensive to the offensive" and told the bishop that "we follow no other canonical laws than those in Europe."[19] As a consequence O'Connor, who was piqued not only by the monks' operation of a brewery but also by the fact that Wimmer had petitioned Rome through the bishop of

Milwaukee rather than himself, refused to exercise his faculties to elevate the monastery to the rank of priory and wrote Rome asking for instructions.

The bishop's refusal dismayed Wimmer and caused him deep concerns about the future of the monastery. Without canonical status he could not legitimately receive the permanent vows of the monks who had joined the community—until now he had allowed them to make only canonically dubious promises to live the monastic life at St. Vincent under his authority and according to the Benedictine Rule—nor could he pursue his goal of spreading the Benedictine Order to other parts of America. Thwarted by Bishop O'Connor in Pennsylvania, therefore, he determined to go to Europe to resolve the matter. In December he left for Munich to seek the support of Bavarian church and government officials.

Wimmer embarked from New York on December 6, 1850, and landed in Le Havre two weeks later. From Le Havre he traveled by rail to Munich where he arrived on Christmas Eve, in time to celebrate Christmas mass with his confreres at St. Boniface Abbey. From Munich he wrote Abbot Rupert Leiss at Scheyern announcing his arrival, but he was circumspect about the chief reason for his journey. Its purposes, he claimed, were:

(1) To obtain one or several men who have completed their theology, if possible one who can teach theology and philosophy to the others. You must not fear that I am counting on Scheyern in this regard. I am afraid of priests because I have been taught by experience. I know of only one whom I would want and with regard to him I already know that I can't have him. (2) To consult with the Bavarian abbots about a number of matters concerning the order in America. (3) To reach a closer understanding with the Missionary Society Committee, especially with the Archbishop, who, by the way, is very favorably disposed towards me and my enterprise. (4) To obtain means for further expansion, which I have reason to expect from King Ludwig.

It would be pleasing to me if you would let the word spread among your people that I am here and after a while will come to Scheyern, and would let me take away some good people as brothers.[20]

The real purpose of his journey, of course, was to gather Bavarian support for his position in the conflict with Bishop O'Connor. In the days after Christmas he met with Archbishop von Reisach and Father Müller and asked for their help, and that of the Ludwig Missionsverein, in obtaining canonical status for St. Vincent from Rome. After consulting with them, he drafted a new petition to the Holy See, explaining his conflict with the bishop of Pittsburgh and requesting again that St. Vincent be made an independent, exempt priory. He sent this petition to the Vatican on January 20, 1851. He also wrote a Jesuit friend in Rome, a former classmate whose name is not revealed in the copy he made of the letter, describing his problems with Bishop O'Connor and asking him to speak with Cardinal Fransoni, prefect of the Propaganda Fide, on his behalf.[21]

The cardinals reviewed the petition at a meeting in April, and Fransoni wrote Wimmer shortly afterward that a final decision would not be made until the Sacred Congregation had an opportunity to gather more information about the case. "The cardinals could not make a decision," Fransoni wrote, "because they have no official report from the bishop of Pittsburgh. But according to the opinion of men who are close to the Propaganda and acquainted with conditions in the United States, the brewing of beer could easily give scandal in that country."[22]

Fransoni had sought advice on the matter from Archbishop John Hughes of New York, who happened to be visiting Rome at the time, and Hughes had strongly defended Bishop O'Connor. But Wimmer was not without his own friends. In January Father Joseph Müller informed him that King Ludwig I had decided to donate 10,000 florins to the Benedictines in America, and Müller recommended that Wimmer write the king to express his gratitude, which he did on January 25, 1851.

In his lengthy letter Wimmer thanked the king for his generous donation, described the monastery and its surroundings in western Pennsylvania, gave an account of the community's development since its beginnings five years earlier, and discussed the progress of the school. Describing those conditions among German immigrants in the United States that called for the kind of education and pastoral care that the Benedictines were providing and which the king's donation would advance, Wimmer said that

in America the Benedictine Order appears to be called to fulfill an urgent need, namely, to come to the aid of this country. Up until now this has indeed been the common feeling everywhere, except that no one has yet been able to come up with the ways and means of providing this aid.

Indeed, there are to be found among Catholics [in America]—not for the Germans of course but at least for the English—quite a lot of fine institutions where the children of wealthy Americans, both boys and girls, can obtain an adequate education. To be sure, this is a rather superficial education because the period of instruction is always for three years only. For the ordinary people, however, this is sufficient and qualifies a young man, according to American requirements, which are not too demanding and give no thought to classical education, to take up immediately special studies in law, medicine, or technical subjects.

There is, however, a dearth of educational institutions for Germans generally, and especially of institutions where German Catholics can get a classical and truly religious education. On the part of the state, nothing is done at all in this matter, since it wants the German element to disappear entirely and is seeking to replace it with all that is English. The Germans moreover, being tossed indiscriminately among the poor and the English, and furthermore being splintered into glaring contradictions through the most diverse religious denominations among them, have had neither sufficient courage and self-confidence (which characterizes German dignity) nor the necessary spirit of cooperation to be able to accomplish anything. Because German history is not taught at all, the first generation already does not know from what German region their parents came, much less the many reasons they ought to have for being proud of their German heritage.

For this only a religious institution can help, one which enjoys earthly security in the possession of large landed property and in the productivity of the soil, so that it will remain independent from the outside and consequently will have no need, for its own survival, to beg the patronage of wealthy factory barons and, in return for fat pensions, put themselves in their employ in the education of their children.

There is, however, something still more depressing, namely, the deficiency and shortage of seminaries where German priests can be educated in order to meet the needs of the German people. Here in this country, with regard to German schools, you cannot expect to get anything from the government. In the same way, you cannot expect anything on the part of the bishops. Most of them are English, or in some instances French, and like the government they are not interested in what is German, much less in promoting German interests. In many ways they show themselves fearful of anything that is German. (There is no doubt that in many cases Germans give occasion for this attitude against them.) . . .

In this matter it is again only the Benedictines who can help in the manner mentioned above. This appears to be the most natural way, and at the same time the simplest and surest. If there were just one monastery like ours in every diocese, by this time a great deal would have been accomplished. Then not only could provision be made for the Germans everywhere with regard to the care of souls, not only would the German character be represented, preserved, and respected everywhere—in the school, in the pulpit, in the confessional, and in books—but also, as the individual monasteries become stronger and more resourceful, you would find that the young men undergoing training in the seminaries would enjoy numerical superiority over the English and also would be far ahead of them in learning and culture.[23]

While he hinted at the tensions that existed between German immigrants and "English" bishops in America, Wimmer did not refer to his conflict with Bishop O'Connor in this or in his subsequent letters to King Ludwig. He did, however, seek the king's assistance for the elevation of St. Vincent to canonical rank. On April 18 he wrote Ludwig, who had been residing in Rome since his abdication following the Munich revolution of 1848 and the scandal that resulted from his celebrated affair with the infamous dancer Lola Montez, asking that he use his influence with the Roman cardinals to obtain a favorable decision for St. Vincent. After receiving this letter King Ludwig took an increased interest in the case, asked the Bavarian embassy in Rome to provide assistance, and interceded personally with the Holy See on behalf of the monks of St. Vincent. When he learned from Propaganda that part of the difficulty lay in Bishop O'Connor's opposition to the operation of a brewery by Wimmer, the king, who considered the operation of breweries natural for Benedictine monasteries, decided that this was the key issue that had to be resolved.

With the king's encouragement several Bavarian friends of St. Vincent began collecting money in Munich to help build a brewery at the monastery and to send a brewmaster back to the United States with Father Boniface. In May 1851 Graf von Spaur, Bavarian ambassador to the Vatican, presented a letter to the Sacred Congregation expressing the Bavarian government's firm support of the American Benedictines,[24] and in June, after receiving a report from von Spaur, King Ludwig informed Wimmer that Propaganda would not oppose raising St. Vincent even to the rank of abbey once the monks were able to come to an understanding with the bishop about building a brewery at the monastery.[25]

Misunderstanding the real problem, the king and several of St.

Vincent's other benefactors had made the question of a monastery brewery the central issue in the controversy. Wimmer clearly had no plans for building a brewery at St. Vincent in 1851. He already had one in Indiana which, while it secured an income and thus paid for itself, also supplied the monastery table with beer. Wimmer's friends in Munich, however, considering the advantages of having a brewery closer to the monastery, advanced the cause in Rome. They also urged the Sacred Congregation to make St. Vincent an abbey rather than a priory.

The central issue, of course, was one of jurisdiction. Who would have ultimate authority over the monastery at St. Vincent, the bishop of Pittsburgh or the superior of the community? In August Bishop O'Connor, whose patience with Wimmer was wearing thin, wrote a clerical friend in Rome asking him to look into the matter before the Propaganda Fide. Outlining the problem for the priest, the bishop said that

the Superior of a Benedictine monastery, had the imprudence if you please, to open a common public house or tavern, of which he gave charge to a scapegrace of a nephew, that had robbed him of some money which he got from the Bavarian mission society. The Superior expected to get the money out of the nephew in this way, by what he would make in that public house. All I could do, would not induce him to desist, until he saw that I refused to do anything towards confirming the monastery, a rescript authorizing me to do it having arrived in the meantime. He then dropped the tavern, and said he would go to Rome. As the scandal had come, I was willing to let him make any statement he liked to make to the Pope, and be guided by anything they would write. Instead of this, he went to Germany and has been getting the King of Bavaria and others, I suppose, to intercede, to have this monastery made an abbey, and thus, set me at defiance. I have written on the subject to the Cardinal. Try and get to see my letters: they will give you more information on the subject. I hope that instead of a miter, he will get what he wants more badly, a good lesson on the shameful manner in which he acted, disregarding all I could say to him. It would be a poor encouragement for us, to stand out for defending the liberty of the Church from the interference from foreign secular powers.

If seculars are to dabble in our affairs, it would be better for us to have to deal with those whom we know, and whom we can call to account, than to have German princes dabbling in our affairs. If I were but to apply to the Secretary of State, he would be only too glad to write a letter to Rome, that would rebut this Gentleman's interference, but thank God, I would scorn to do so, no matter how it ends. If the Sacred Congregation has any regard for our welfare, it will give these people a lesson, that will teach them to mind their own business, and let us alone.[26]

Despite his disagreements with Wimmer, however, Bishop O'Connor wrote the cardinals of the Propaganda Fide in August endorsing the elevation of the monastery at St. Vincent not merely to a priory but to an abbey. Surprisingly, he also gave his approval to the suggestion that Wimmer be named abbot. Nonetheless, he registered objections to the brewery once again and complained about Wimmer's recourse to influential members of the Bavarian government and hierarchy. If St. Vincent were to become an abbey, he said finally, he strongly urged that the abbey be nonexempt and that the abbot be nonmitered.[27]

It is curious that Wimmer did not travel to Rome to confront the issues head-on in the place where their outcome would be determined. Instead, he remained in Bavaria for five months and waged his campaign in the Eternal City through letters. From Munich he visited friends and benefactors in Scheyern, Ingolstadt, Eichstätt, Regensburg, Metten, Passau, and Linz. He raised funds, recruited candidates, and collected vestments, altar furnishings, and books from generous benefactors in each of these places. Then, during the third week of May, with the matter concerning St. Vincent's independence still before the Propaganda Fide, Wimmer departed Munich for Le Havre and the return voyage to the United States. Accompanying him were twenty-one candidates for the monastery and forty trunks and boxes. He landed in New York on June 2 and a week later arrived at St. Vincent. With the arrival of the newcomers the monastery now numbered nearly one hundred men.

In September Wimmer wrote the Holy See once again. Having learned not only that his Bavarian friends had petitioned Rome for St. Vincent's elevation to abbatial status but also that Bishop O'Connor himself favored making the monastery an abbey, he asked officials at Propaganda to ignore his earlier petition for elevation to the status of canonical priory in favor of a new petition for the community's elevation to abbatial dignity.[28]

Weeks passed and the St. Vincent files in the offices of the Sacred Congregation for the Propagation of the Faith grew thicker. In October Bishop O'Connor wrote Cardinal Barnabo that he now had reversed his opinion about the suitability of Wimmer to be an abbot, or even to continue as superior of St. Vincent,[29] and in November he wrote confidentially to Benedictine Father Bernard Smith in Rome that he had conclusive proof that Wimmer was unfit not only to be an abbot but to be a spiritual leader of any sort. "Proofs grow upon me," he wrote,

that the present superior is unfit for his position and that the interests of the community and diocese alike require that there should be a change. I forwarded some evidence of this to the cardinal not long ago. I have learned a few days since from a source of which I can have no doubt that a man who had received some counterfeit banknotes applied to him, I believe in confession, for advice and received for his answer that he might pass them off again on the principle that each one was bound to look to himself. Even when I found him wrong-headed and stubborn, I supposed him pious and well-meaning and was under the impression that he adhered to his notions through a mistaken sense of duty to the order. But many things are leading me to fear that the good spirit is evaporating, and I am decidedly of the opinion that the Holy See would do a most useful if not necessary act by procuring a suitable person or superior from one of the good Benedictine monasteries in Germany, say Metten or Scheyern in Bavaria or Einsiedeln in Switzerland.[30]

In December Father Boniface was forced by financial difficulties to bring the matter of the Indiana brewery to resolution. He had leased the business to a parishioner who "deceived me even more than my nephew and caused me greater losses." He was fortunate, however, because the man also owned a farm which, to make up for the losses, he sold to Wimmer at a favorable price. With the money the Benedictines could expect from the farm, the debts brought about by the misadventure in Indiana County would be paid off, and Wimmer reported that the tavern had already been changed into a residence for the priests of the parish that he had established in the town. "The brewery will not be opened again," he said, "unless I find a good manager. In any case, we will only brew for wholesale deliveries and even the bishop is not against that business."[31]

As it turned out, other differences between Wimmer and O'Connor were also resolved at this time, and with the closing of the brewery the bishop withdrew all his objections to allowing Wimmer to remain as superior of St. Vincent. On February 14, 1852, the same day that it named the German Redemptorist John Nepomucene Neumann bishop of Philadelphia, the Sacred Congregation for the Propagation of the Faith issued its decision elevating St. Vincent to the rank of canonical priory and naming Wimmer prior subject to the authority of Bishop O'Connor. The contretemps surrounding the matter had caused the cardinals to hesitate in raising the monastery to abbatial status. Cardinal Fransoni wrote that this decision was the result of the Sacred Congregation's wish "to see that the community is worthy of such a distinction." He explained to Graf von Spaur that "it will be much better to grant this honor after the canonically established monastery has given proofs of its religious discipline and gained the full confidence of the bishop of the diocese."[32]

In a politic acknowledgment of O'Connor's rights, Fransoni observed that "the bishop should be the judge in that question." At the bishop's insistence, Propaganda also decreed that the priory would be nonexempt. But otherwise Wimmer emerged from the fray victorious. The decree of Propaganda created the first independent Benedictine priory in the United States. It also allowed the monks to brew beer "providing that every disorder is avoided." The Benedictines were not to sell it in taverns but were permitted to distribute it wholesale.[33]

Before receiving the welcome news of the rescript making St. Vincent a canonical priory, Father Boniface wrote King Ludwig I explaining that Bishop O'Connor "wants to help us grow and expand and is even generous with his help. He is, however, pushing me a little too hard; I don't like it and I don't think it is good for an order as young as ours is in this country." The Benedictine superior went on to say that the bishop was "promoting his own interest as bishop and is not always sufficiently concerned with our interests as Benedictines and as monks. Canonical conditions in America are still in their infancy. The will of the bishop is law."[34]

Nevertheless, much to Wimmer's satisfaction and relief, tensions between the first bishop of Pittsburgh and the first Benedictines in the United States had eased. As in the aborted rescript of 1848, O'Connor was given the prerogative of executing the decision as well as the right to decide whether Wimmer should be superior. By now the objections he had had to the quality of Wimmer's spiritual leadership had all been resolved, and he did not stand in the way of his being confirmed as prior.

The bishop's doubts about Wimmer's suitability to serve as superior of St. Vincent could well have been in part the result of the influence of Father Peter Lechner, who, during the critical period when the question of canonical status and the operation of a brewery were being debated, had gone to Pittsburgh to teach in O'Connor's seminary. It may well have been that Lechner voiced his criticism of the kind of religious life being led at St. Vincent as strongly to the bishop as he had done to the abbots of Metten and Scheyern, and it is conceivable that he was for a while able to convince O'Connor that Wimmer was not the spiritual leader St. Vincent needed. But by the time the rescript elevating St. Vincent to the rank of priory came from Rome, Lechner had returned to Scheyern and was no longer on the scene to spread stories of Wimmer's alleged inadequacies.

On July 15, 1852, Bishop Michael O'Connor officially promulgated the document establishing Wimmer's monastery as a nonexempt priory in the diocese of Pittsburgh. Father Boniface was named canonical prior of the community and irremovable pastor of the parish. Moreover, the monastery was given the privilege of brewing beer for wholesale distribution, a privilege the monks did not make use of for eight years. Michael O'Connor still remained, by the grace of God, bishop of Pittsburgh, and considering his attitudes as a temperance advocate toward intoxicating spirits of any sort, Wimmer decided to do nothing to antagonize him further. But when O'Connor resigned as ordinary in May 1860, the Benedictines opened their brewery at St. Vincent, and although the business never became a major source of income for the community, it did, for a period of about sixty years, produce the "St. Vincent Beer" which in its own way helped make St. Vincent famous.[35]

As soon as the canonical status of St. Vincent was secure, Wimmer turned his attention to other important matters. The work of ministering to German Catholics in America remained. To carry out his mission, he left few sources of aid untapped. While in Europe he had visited two convents and urged their superiors to send missionaries to America. The Dominican Priory of the Holy Cross in Regensburg, Bavaria, was one of these. In 1851, while calling on a relative who was a nun in the Regensburg priory, Wimmer raised the question of the Dominican sisters making a foundation in the United States. The superior of the convent, Mother Benedicta Bauer, O.P., told Wimmer that she was unable to take immediate action but that the community remained interested in sending missionaries to the United States. Two years later, after Father Boniface assured her that he would be the "advisor and protector" of any sisters she might send to the American missions, Mother Benedicta began preparing her community for the venture. She wrote Bishop Valentine von Riedel of Regensburg that "Reverend Father Wimmer repeatedly and very earnestly promised his cooperation, that he might, to use his own words, 'make St. Dominic indebted to him.'"[36] On May 29, 1853, Bishop von Riedel drafted a dismissorial letter granting four sisters of Holy Cross Priory permission to leave Bavaria for the purpose of erecting a monastery in America. The sisters—Maria Josefa Witzlhofer, Maria Augustina Neuhierl, Maria Francesca Retter, and Maria Jacobina Riederer—left Regensburg in July accompanied as far as Bremen by Father Joseph Müller who had secured financial support for their journey from the Ludwig Missionsverein.[37]

Mother Benedicta had arranged with Wimmer to have the missionary group met in New York, and the sisters expected Wimmer himself to be there. Wimmer, however, delegated the task to Father Nicholas Balleis, the Benedictine pastor of St. Mary's Church, Newark. Balleis, for reasons unknown, failed to meet or make adequate arrangements for the Dominican sisters, and when they arrived in New York on August 26, 1853, they found themselves stranded and alone.[38] Their situation paralleled Wimmer's own when he and his companions reached New York in 1846 and discovered that Father Peter Henry Lemke was not there to meet and assist them. The bewildering experience of disembarking as strangers in the bustling American ports of entry, far from the familiar world and supporting communities that formerly nurtured them, has shocked and disoriented virtually all immigrants who have arrived on the shores of America both in the nineteenth and twentieth centuries. But the experience of the Dominican nuns who landed in New York in August 1853 was especially distressing because they fully expected Wimmer—who had invited them to come—to be there and to give them the material and moral support they needed to adjust to the new and frightening world they had entered. The fact that neither he nor the priest he had delegated to help them was present to assist them through the confusing and difficult first moments of their arrival was the cause for subsequent frosty relations between the Dominicans and the Benedictines. Indeed, as a result of the incident a tradition grew up in the Dominican community that carried down to the twentieth century that Wimmer and his monks were in general unreliable and disappointing compatriots and coreligionists.[39] But this judgment, though understandable, falters in the light of Wimmer's subsequent actions. By the time they arrived, he had already found Benedictine nuns to fill the posts he had initially envisioned for the Dominicans. Nevertheless, he expended considerable energy and expense to provide the nuns from Regensburg with the essential support and means they needed to establish a permanent community in the United States.

In July 1853, a month before the sisters' arrival, Wimmer had written Abbot Gregory Scherr of Metten acknowledging that he expected the Dominicans and had assumed the burden of assisting them. "In the near future," he said, "I shall have to go to New York again to meet six [*sic*] Dominican Sisters that the Convent of the Holy Cross of Regensburg is sending to me as a cross (as if I did not already have enough crosses). I am to look for a suitable place for them. Already letters for that purpose have been sent East and West."[40]

In May 1852, while attending the First Plenary Council of Baltimore, he had spoken with several priests from the Dominican Priory in Ohio about his idea of establishing a Dominican monastery of nuns in the United States. He intended that the sisters from Regensburg should settle near the Dominican priests in the Midwest, but the sisters themselves expected, upon arrival in America, to be brought to Carrolltown, Pennsylvania, to work alongside the Benedictine priests of St. Benedict's Priory.[41] Before their departure, Court Chaplain Müller had given the nuns a letter of introduction to the German Redemptorists of Holy Redeemer Church in New York City. The news of the sisters' mission reached New York before they actually arrived, and on August 25, 1853, the day before their ship docked, the *Katholische Kirchen-Zeitung* of New York published a brief announcement of their imminent arrival, adding that "they will begin their work of teaching under the supervision of Reverend Boniface Wimmer."[42] When they landed in New York, however, and discovered that Wimmer was not in the city to help them, the Dominicans made use of their letter of introduction and contacted the Redemptorists, who received them and offered them temporary shelter.

Not long afterward, Father Nicholas Balleis arrived at Holy Redeemer Church and took two of the sisters with him back to Newark. Apparently he had not received specific instructions from Wimmer as to what to do with the women and consequently had made no arrangements for them either. Believing themselves neglected by the man who had urged them to come to America in the first place, alone in a strange land, shuffled from place to place, without any permanent shelter or work, the sisters remained in their uprooted condition for several days until Father John S. Raffeiner, vicar general for Germans in the Archdiocese of New York and one of the priests who met and advised Wimmer when the Benedictine mission arrived in the United States in 1846, learned of their dilemma and offered them help. Father Raffeiner brought the Dominicans to his parish in Williamsburg, New York, and gave them what was to become their permanent home in America.[43]

In the meantime Father Boniface arrived in New York to see what had become of the Dominicans. After speaking with Balleis and Raffeiner and learning from the nuns themselves that they were content with the arrangements Raffeiner had made for them in Williamsburg, he sat down to write their superior in Regensburg, Mother Benedicta Bauer. Her daughters were comfortably situated in America, he told Mother Benedicta: "I could come to see them and provide for them only on the fifth day of their arrival. Because for the time being I knew of no place for them in the country, I agreed with the reverend vicar general of New York, Father Raffeiner, that he take the sisters to his parish church in Williamsburg."

Wimmer wrote that the parishioners were happy to receive the sisters and described to Mother Benedicta the location where her nuns had settled. He gave advice concerning financial matters and said that "since you yourself confided your daughters to me, and also the bishop in his testimonials, and the archbishop of New York (also his vicar general) considers me the spiritual director of your sisters, I have, therefore, assumed a definite responsibility for them. I believe that I have the necessary authority to direct the sisters; . . . hence I have ordered Mother Josefa to admit promptly any worthy English postulant who might apply for admission." Wimmer had little confidence in the ability of Father Raffeiner to direct the sisters adequately. "The old priest purposely took the sisters so that he would not be obliged to have a cook and also to save money," he wrote. "He is rich but he is very stingy." Wimmer assured Mother Benedicta that everything would go well, provided "the old priest does not change his mind and if he keeps his word." Father Raffeiner, Wimmer said, "depends and relies considerably on me. I impressed sharply upon the sisters this fact: viz., that they should not be too seriously concerned if they suffered somewhat financially—but I urged them to get in touch with me if they were in want so that I might personally fight it out with Father." Wimmer ended his letter by recommending that Mother Benedicta send more nuns. He had nothing but praise for the four who were already in America, saying that "every beginning is hard. Much must be endured. But whoever means well with God and possesses a good will, God will help in the end. . . . Everything was so well ordered [in the convent] that one cannot help feeling that the will of God is being done."[44]

During the months that followed Wimmer remained in close contact with the Dominicans, helping them establish themselves comfortably and independently in the Archdiocese of New York. He visited them several times, assisted them in acquiring suitable property for a convent in Williamsburg, arranged for German Capuchins in New York to serve as their spiritual directors, and advised them on investing the considerable sum of $3,000 they had brought with them from Bavaria. He also convinced Father Raffeiner to offer them charge of the German parish school in Williamsburg. In December 1853 Wimmer wrote Abbot Gregory Scherr of Metten that with the cash they had on hand the sisters would begin building their convent in the spring.

It appears that God's blessing is resting upon this undertaking. Before the sisters came, two teachers had 150–175 children (boys and girls) in the school. Now the sisters already have 225 girls and are getting more and more. The girls would otherwise have had to attend the non-religious public schools. The large Catholic congregation is pleased with the sisters and is helping them in every possible way. I do not regret all the trouble I had in hunting down a suitable place for them. St. Dominic and the guardian angels of these children, who have been saved, will surely be on my side when I need them.[45]

Two months later Wimmer reported that he had recently been in New York to see to the progress of the Dominican sisters and to make the final arrangements for their foundation in Williamsburg. "After many irksome and prolonged negotiations [with the pastor], I arrived at the point where they could settle themselves formally." He noted somewhat whimsically that a recent disaster in Pennsylvania—the destruction by fire of the Benedictines' gristmill in St. Marys—was his reward for helping the Dominicans. "It was the revenge of the devil because the good sisters are such a great hindrance for him. They now have 243 children in their school, more than half of whom went before to the Protestant school or to no school at all."[46] He was quite pleased with the success he had helped the nuns achieve, and the cross he had borne in the course of assisting them he now passed to the sisters themselves. Satisfied that they would manage quite well independently of his further efforts, he now turned his attention to another group of Bavarian religious women whom he had invited to the American missions.

The Priory of St. Walburga in Eichstätt, Bavaria, was one of the few Benedictine communities in German lands to escape total suppression during the secularization of 1803. While the community lost its lands, was not allowed to accept novices, and suffered the dismissal of its younger sisters, the older nuns were permitted to remain in the convent and continue their monastic life after other Benedictine monasteries had been closed. By 1835, when the priory was fully restored, thirteen of the original nuns still survived and now formed the nucleus of a revitalized community. As was the case even before the secularization of 1803, the nuns of Eichstätt maintained close ties with the monks of Metten after the restoration, and during his trip to Europe in 1850–1851 St. Walburga's was the second convent Wimmer visited with the hope of recruiting missionary sisters to teach German girls in the American settlements where he had established communities of men. Wimmer's intentions were firmly set on the goal of transplanting the Benedictine Order from the Old World to the New, and if his interest in the Dominican nuns in New York was limited, that was certainly not the case with the Benedictine nuns whom he invited to Pennsylvania in 1851.

After returning to St. Vincent from Bavaria in June, Wimmer had written Archbishop von Reisach expressing his eagerness to have them come:

I am too much of a Benedictine to let this chance pass without transplanting the female branch of the order into the New World. We have already had several candidates for such a convent who speak English well. Therefore, if I can get two more nuns and one lay sister to start religious life, we will soon have a community. I am firmly convinced that the old orders, especially ours, if they come out of their seclusion and adapt themselves to modern demands, will have many advantages over modern society in so far as tradition, stability, and discipline are concerned. They are modeled after monarchical principles of the Church and thus ought to have the same advantages as limited monarchies over Republics.[47]

During his stay in Bavaria Wimmer had visited Eichstätt and proposed to Mother Edwarda Schnitzer, O.S.B., prioress of the community, that she consider sending nuns to the German settlement of St. Marys in northwestern Pennsylvania. When he returned to St. Vincent shortly afterward, he wrote Schnitzer reminding her of his earlier proposal and asking that she recruit volunteers from the community to work as teachers in Pennsylvania. Mother Edwarda read Wimmer's letter to the Eichstätt sisters, who agreed to send three members from their priory to the United States. Those volunteering for the mission were the novice mistress, Benedicta Riepp; the portress, Walburga Dietrich, and Maura Flieger, a lay sister in simple vows.

After seeking and obtaining permission for the journey from Bishop George von Öttl of Eichstätt, and receiving the formal invitation of Bishop Michael O'Connor, the three Benedictine sisters left Eichstätt for America on June 12, 1852. Like Wimmer himself and the Dominican sisters from Regensburg who would come a year later, they traveled with funds provided by Father Joseph F. Müller and the Ludwig Missionsverein. On June 18 they boarded the steamer *Washington* at Bremen and, sailing by way of Southampton, reached New York on the evening of July 3, 1852. As in the case of the Dominican nuns, the Benedictines from Eichstätt found themselves alone in New York when they landed on Independence Day 1852. Father Boniface failed to meet them or to arrange for anyone to guide them to St. Vincent. With the same spirit of independence and determination that would characterize their future dealings with Wimmer, however, the nuns managed to reach St. Vincent on their own initiative four days later. A story that is part of the oral tradition of Benedictine women in the United States relates that when the wagon carrying the sisters and their luggage neared the monastery on July 8, 1852, a lay brother working in the fields ran to report to Prior Boniface that "a wagonload of trouble" was coming up the hill. If the story is true, it was one of the most prophetic statements yet made by a Benedictine monk in the New World.[48]

Wimmer found accommodations for the sisters with the family of Maurice Schwab, the Bavarian director of music at St. Vincent, and he informed Bishop O'Connor of their arrival. On July 15 O'Connor visited St. Vincent and formally accepted the Benedictine sisters into the diocese. In a document addressed to Wimmer, the bishop reconfirmed his permission for the Benedictine superior of St. Vincent to "establish a community of German sisters in St. Marys, Elk Co." O'Connor complained that he had "expected to have the matter proposed more formally and documents accordingly issued containing everything necessary for such a purpose." He felt confident, however, "that no difficulty will arise in framing these so as to be satisfactory on all sides." Until the nuns were incorporated at St. Marys, the bishop would require that their property be held in trust for them by Wimmer. Moreover, he required "that their position [in St. Marys] must be such as to enable the bishop to make sure of the preservation of discipline and to feel satisfied that what is commenced shall not be easily abandoned nor without proper cause."[49]

On July 16 Wimmer set out from St. Vincent with the three sisters. In a roundabout journey that took them first to Indiana, Pennsylvania, and then to Carrolltown, where monks from St. Vincent had established priories, they reached the German settlement of St. Marys in northwestern Pennsylvania nine days later. Soon afterward Wimmer wrote Abbot Rupert Leiss that

the Benedictine nuns at St. Marys are starting out in greater poverty even than we did—in one wretched frame building with only $100, which they brought with them. The flour, etc., that they need is supplied by my people. I also bought them a cow. They are full of courage and follow our order of the day. I am paying for a Bavarian and an American candidate to learn English better from the Sisters of Mercy so they may obtain English teachers, because even in totally German St. Marys the children want to and should learn English. Next year we intend to acquire a stone house for them, to be added to the new church, which is not yet completed and is 115 feet long and 60 feet wide. It stands in the middle of the city on a slight mound comprising exactly five acres, which will constitute the monastic garden. But the stumps of the trees that were felled for building the church still stand there. Our monastery is outside the city and facing it. This year the brothers cleared a large area; there is food for next year: but this year I must feed them from here, 108 to 115 miles away! . . . St. Marys demands much help, but I am hoping that the heavenly patroness will assist us and bless our efforts on behalf of this colony.[50]

The sisters opened their school in the fall of 1852, and by January enrollment had grown to about seventy girls. In October 1852 King Ludwig I donated $4,000 to the small community for construction of a convent, but instead of sending the money directly to Mother Benedicta, he sent it to Prior Boniface at St. Vincent. Wimmer used the money to pay for buildings he was constructing at St. Vincent and St. Marys, and he wrote the king that his plans to construct a convent for the nuns had to be delayed on account of efforts to complete a church in St. Marys.

The building of the convent could . . . not be undertaken at once, since no preparations for the same had been made, and furthermore could not be made since the entire colony was busy with the building of a church which had already been started and could not be interrupted. The sisters were prepared to lend me the money, since they were not in a position to use it at once, with the condition that I care for the buying and the obtaining of the immediately necessary arrangements, and then, if time allowed, use the remaining money for building a convent. Meanwhile, they live in a frame building, which the company built for the School Sisters of Notre Dame who were here in St. Marys at the time of Baron v. Schröter.[51]

It was a decision that would later return to haunt him.

Soon after the arrival of the three nuns from Bavaria, twelve young women, ranging in age from thirteen to twenty-one, presented themselves to the small community as candidates for the novitiate. Extant records indicate that six of them were American-born and four European-born. (The places of birth of two of them are not indicated.) Wimmer presided at the investiture of the postulants as novices on October 16, 1853. In January 1854 three more sisters (and either one or three candidates) arrived in St. Marys from Eichstätt. During the next two years several more young women joined the convent, and when Wimmer returned to Pennsylvania in December 1855 after his trip to Rome and Bavaria, he brought with him five more sisters from the motherhouse at Eichstätt. By then the sisters in St. Marys numbered thirty-seven.[52]

The story of the disagreements and conflict that subsequently developed between Wimmer and the Benedictine sisters, to be related in the next chapter, forms one of the darkest and most controversial episodes of American Benedictine history.

By the summer of 1852 the monastery, missions, and schools at St.

Vincent had firmly taken root in the fertile soil of Pennsylvania, and the prospect of a bright and productive future for the Benedictine Order in the United States lay ahead. With the establishment of a community of Benedictine sisters in St. Marys Wimmer had, in the course of six short years, proven beyond doubt to any skeptics who remained that the Benedictine Order was well suited to prosper and grow in the Protestant and often hostile climate of America. Through the monks' hard work, his own determination and single-mindedness, and the indisputable success of the Benedictine settlement in Pennsylvania, Wimmer had justified his vision in the eyes of critics in Europe who believed that his scheme to transplant the order to the New World was simply another pipedream of the *Projektenmacher* of Metten. He now turned to the task of securing the work he had toiled so hard to begin.

In October 1852 there were one hundred and fifteen monks at St. Vincent, fourteen of whom were priests, twenty-one clerics, and eighty lay brothers. In addition, four priests and seven brothers were in Carrolltown, two priests and eighteen brothers at St. Marys, and two priests and four brothers in Indiana, Pennsylvania. Altogether there were more than one hundred and fifty professed monks attached to the Priory of St. Vincent, which merely six years earlier had numbered less than twenty. Nearly sixty boys and more than twenty young men were studying in the gymnasium and seminary at St. Vincent, the majority of them as candidates for the Benedictine Order, and two diocesan priests had recently applied for admission to the monastery. The monks had purchased more land and were erecting new buildings at St. Vincent, Carrolltown, and St. Marys. Numbers were also increasing in the sisters' convent and school at St. Marys.[53]

In 1852 eleven monks were assigned as professors in the Latin school and four in the seminary at St. Vincent. In the Latin school Utto Huber, the director, taught Greek; Augustine Wirth, Rupert Seidenbusch, and Ulric Spöttl, Latin; Luke Wimmer, art; Joseph Billon, French; Valentine Felder, German; Emmeran Bliemel, mathematics; and Leonard and Wendelin Mayer, music. Mr. Joseph B. O'Donahue, a diocesan seminarian, taught English. In the seminary Augustine Wirth taught philosophy; Utto Huber, liturgy; Luke Wimmer, dogma; and Ildephonse Böld, moral theology. While most of the Benedictine professors had graduated from Bavarian gymnasiums, none had any extensive experience as a scholar or a teacher. The majority had completed what little advanced studies they possessed at St. Vincent, and five were still students themselves, pursuing their studies for the priesthood in the seminary even as they taught in the gymnasium.[54]

Four of the monks died in 1852, three of them at St. Vincent—Father Placidus Döttl, Brother Salomon Merk, and Brother Gallus Urban—and one at St. Marys, Father Maurus Zacherl, whom Wimmer had recently sent from St. Vincent to Elk County to recover from illness. They all died of pulmonary tuberculosis, a disease that ran rampant in Roman Catholic religious communities in nineteenth-century America.

In a letter to the abbot of Kremsmünster, Austria, Wimmer outlined the community's progress over the previous six years. He described for his Austrian confrere the work and prayer of the monks at St. Vincent, Carrolltown, St. Marys, and Indiana. From St. Vincent, he said, the monks did pastoral work among Catholics, both English- and German-speaking, in Greensburg, Saltsburg, Johnstown, Jefferson, Summit, Hollidaysburg, and Altoona. He reported that many "fallen aways" had returned to the faith as a result of the missionary labors of the Benedictines. The key to their success, Wimmer said, was an active and dynamic educational and missionary apostolate. Nonetheless, difficulties and frustration pressed in from every side.

It is a toilsome existence—this perpetual building which seems to have no end. This clearing, plowing, and reclaiming of the land in the wilderness. This starting always from scratch, and bringing in all of the necessities from the outside! This universal and persistent shortage of everything, and the ever constantly increasing needs! This being besieged from all sides with demands, and on the other hand the necessity of satisfying those demands by begging from others! This jumble of the most heterogeneous activities, which must somehow be harmonized and directed toward the same final goal!

And yet there is always a true and blessed satisfaction in doing this work; no effort goes to waste; every hardship is rewarded; every seed brings forth some fruit; every brick adds to the structure; on every side there is development where before there was nothing, and where there never would have been anything had not someone weighed the possibilities and put forth the effort. I came here six years ago with four students and fifteen[55] brothers, or perhaps I should say with fifteen builders and artisans. Our residence was a small school house where even in the bitter cold we had nothing but a roof over our heads, and where we slept side by side on our straw mattresses and without bedsteads, ridiculed by some, pitied and commiserated by those more kindly disposed, deceived and preyed upon by many, without money and without credit, and abandoned even by our own people. But what a change has taken place! We have acquired some 3,600 acres of land as our own; now we have a residence, which for size and convenience is better than anything that can be found in the neighborhood. We have a stretch of territory as our mission field which is larger in area than the whole of Austria! Our novitiate is the largest training center for priests in the whole of the United States. Our boys' school for German youth and for the poor is the only one of its kind in this country, except for a few experiments in other places, and as a spiritual *seminarium puerorum,* it is the largest and the only one of its kind in this country; it is the only school which provides training for the youth of both nationalities, at least in as far as it is completely Catholic and unmixed (i.e. open only to Catholics). There is no place in America where prayer ascends to heaven so constantly![56]

From the beginning Wimmer maintained a frenetic pace in pursuing the goals he had set for himself and his community. The missionary work he had begun immediately upon his arrival in America continued to expand at a rate that dismayed and worried his subordinates. Hardly was he properly settled in one place before he was off again to establish another center of apostolic work. Whether he was fully aware of it or not, he had rapidly absorbed what he called the American penchant for gambling. "In America everything is done on credit," he wrote.

The whole American people often appears to me like a mass gambler: everyone gambles, everyone takes risks as far as he can go; many thereby lose everything and many succeed. . . . This spirit of reckless chance-taking, along with such lack of concern for others, underlies the egoism that is so noticeable in the American character and which may be called the key to the tremendous and amazing advance in every area of the country. . . . Talent, energy and luck account for success in everything.[57]

Despite the concerns expressed by many in the community, Wimmer's gambles enjoyed impressive returns. In October 1848 Bishop O'Connor transferred all Catholic missions in northern Cambria County to him, and he immediately began missionary operations in this region. Father Peter Lemke sold property in and near Carrolltown to the Benedictines in 1848, and in November of that year Wimmer sent Father Peter Lechner and several lay brothers to St. Joseph's

Church, Hart's Sleeping Place, near Carrolltown, to establish St. Vincent's first dependent priory. St. Joseph's had been the site of the Benedictines' initial, but abortive, settlement in the United States, and now it became a permanent part of the Benedictine mission. Lemke himself became a member of the St. Vincent community in the closing months of 1851.[58]

During the summer of 1849 Wimmer sent Father Benedict Haindl to Carrolltown as prior, and six months later Father Celestine Englbrecht, another of the original band of Benedictines, joined him. Shortly after taking over the Carrolltown mission the Benedictines began constructing a church in the village of Carrolltown to replace St. Joseph's as the center of Catholic worship in the area. They completed it in December 1850, and Father Celestine, who had replaced Father Benedict as prior, dedicated it to St. Benedict. From this center the Benedictines ministered to Catholics in the small settlements of northern Cambria and southern Clearfield Counties.[59]

Despite their new church, the Benedictines in Carrolltown continued to live in unsatisfactory quarters. Wimmer described the priory as a "miserable log cabin where the monks cook, eat . . . and sleep," but he predicted that the Carrolltown property would "someday . . . be an even more desirable location than St. Vincent itself."[60] Wimmer hoped to build a college in Carrolltown, but his plans for this never materialized. In 1852, however, there was a fully functioning dependent priory, St. Benedict's, at Carrolltown with four priests and seven brothers in residence ministering to Catholics of the district.

A second important offshoot of St. Vincent was the Benedictine priory at St. Marys in Elk County, 120 miles north of St. Vincent. Less than a year after his arrival at St. Vincent Wimmer had visited St. Marys, where a small German colony had been founded in 1843. At the time of his visit the Redemptorist Fathers were ministering to the spiritual needs of a Catholic population driven to the settlement from the East Coast by anti-Catholic fanaticism. The Redemptorists had received a large tract of land for the support of a school and church, but with only three priests and no lay brothers they were unable to develop the potential of the land. Moreover, the colonists were too poor to contribute significantly to their support. In a letter to the Ludwig Missionsverein, which had helped finance the settlement, Wimmer expressed hope that he would soon be able to assign several priests to

St. Marys, but in 1848 the Benedictines at St. Vincent had few priests to spare, and the superior was forced to postpone his plans to send missionaries to Elk County.[61]

In October 1849 Father Bernard Hafkenscheid, C.Ss.R., vice-provincial of the Redemptorists in the United States, informed Bishop O'Connor that the congregation could no longer afford to supply priests for the Germans of St. Marys, and not long afterward the Redemptorists turned their property over to the diocese.[62] The bishop then applied to the Benedictines at St. Vincent for assistance, and Wimmer sent two priests, Fathers Benedict Haindl and Andrew Zugtriegel, to Elk County in the closing weeks of 1849.

The initial Benedictine establishment in St. Marys failed. The colonists came from many different parts of Germany, bringing with them disparate local religious customs which the Bavarian Benedictines were hard pressed to reconcile. Fathers Benedict and Andrew found themselves refereeing arguments among different groups of German Catholics and even defending themselves against the attacks of some of them. Moreover, the same financial difficulties that caused the Redemptorists to fail hampered the progress of the monks from St. Vincent. The people were poor and could not support their priests who, in any event, were not so successful in placating the choleric humors and arbitrating the disputes of the diverse interest groups as the colonists had hoped. In May 1850 fire destroyed both the church and school and badly damaged the monastery. In the summer of 1850, with all signs pointing to a failure of the mission, Wimmer withdrew his men and informed both the colony's trustees in Baltimore and Bishop O'Connor that the Benedictines could no longer be responsible for the spiritual welfare of the German Catholics of St. Marys. "I recalled my Fathers from St. Marys," Wimmer wrote, "because I needed them at home and did not wish to be the tool of some parties in that colony."[63]

The trustees were angered by the decision and expressed their displeasure in a letter to their agent in St. Marys.

We had hoped that the Benedictines would not have disregarded their sacred vocation, but since they have proven themselves induced more by money than by any regard for the salvation of souls to accept a pastoral charge, we do not regret their leaving. We already made many sacrifices to retain the Redemptorists, the School Brothers, and School Sisters, but all has been in vain. Our efforts were not appreciated by them. More money, more money was their cry, their subsistence. Their maxims appear to be: riches for them or desertion of the people. Now we have lost confidence in them and depend entirely on the bishop who so far has proven himself worthy of our confidence, and from whom we have every reason to hope that St. Marys will hereafter not be without a pastor. You know that we have given him all the property which the Redemptorists held and have further obligated ourselves to pay him for the maintenance of pastors at St. Marys five hundred dollars payable quarterly for five years.[64]

Bishop O'Connor appointed a diocesan priest, Father Joseph Schafleitner, to serve the parish, but Schafleitner's efforts to raise money for the rebuilding of the church and school met with as little success as those of the Redemptorists and the Benedictines, and less than a year after his assignment to Elk County the diocesan priest asked to be relieved.

In July 1851 O'Connor appealed to the Benedictines once again. After receiving assurances that the diocese would provide economic support, Father Boniface agreed to send his monks back to St. Marys. He reassigned Father Benedict Haindl as pastor and appointed Father Charles Geyerstanger as assistant. The two priests and four lay brothers went to St. Marys in 1851. In accordance with the agreement between the diocese and the Benedictines, the bishop made Wimmer trustee of all diocesan property in Elk County, and in the fall of 1851 Father Boniface enlarged the land now controlled by the Benedictines by purchasing another tract of seventy acres, which brought the total property to nearly eight hundred acres. In a letter to the archbishop of Munich Wimmer expressed his reservations about the St. Marys mission. "I was not anxious," he said "to take over St. Marys, but the bishop offered it, the colonists desired it, and there was no other institute to give them assistance. Therefore, after I received assurance of a permanent residence and the formal transfer of the parish to the order, I agreed to send two priests." He told the archbishop that the monks occupied a frame building that formerly housed the School Sisters of Notre Dame from Munich who had taught for a while in the school before moving on to Milwaukee. There were four hundred Catholic families to be cared for, and the next item on his agenda was the construction of a new church.[65]

The first winter brought extraordinary difficulties for the Benedictines in Elk County. The intense cold, the worst in the memory of the settlers, was especially difficult for the monks because of the poorly constructed frame building in which they lived. Brother William Lechner wrote that he had to take the baptismal font into the pastor's room to prevent it from becoming "a block of ice." Brother Gammelbert Daschner asked for flour and salt which, he wrote, could not be bought in Elk County at any price. He complained that the animals were starving.[66] With help from St. Vincent the small community survived the cold months and undertook missionary work both at St. Marys and in the mission stations of Kersey, Williamsville, Ridgeway, Emporium, and a number of places along the Susquehanna River.

The third important mission center dependent on St. Vincent was in Indiana, Pennsylvania, site of the brewery that had caused such difficulties between the Bavarian Benedictines and the Irish bishop of Pittsburgh. Within months of his arrival in the United States Wimmer had gone to Indiana to attend to the spiritual needs of the Catholics in the town and the surrounding farmlands, and between 1846 and 1851 monks from St. Vincent continued to serve the congregation with pastoral visits several times a month. During the early phase of his disagreements with O'Connor, when it was not clear that the bishop would give the Benedictines unconditional title to the properties at St. Vincent, Wimmer purchased some land near Indiana and for a while considered moving the entire community there. By 1851, however, the problem of title to the property at St. Vincent had long been resolved and the brewery controversy was on its way to being settled. With the closing of the tavern early in the controversy Wimmer had a vacant building in Indiana, and when a farm near the town, belonging to the parishioner whose financial mismanagement had been the proximate cause of the Benedictines' closing down the brewery as well, came into his possession, Wimmer decided to refurbish the tavern as a residence for a small community of monks. He assigned one priest and four brothers to Indiana toward the beginning of 1852. "This community (Indiana) is small and has been very much neglected," Wimmer wrote,

since they had been without a priest before we took charge. The [fathers] stationed there [have] only one small mission station to take care of; it is 20 miles away, and is, if anything, in even worse circumstances than Indiana itself. But things are improving there now, and many of the "fallen aways" are beginning to return to the faith. We own a beautiful house there and it has five acres of land near the edge of town which is used as a pasture. We also have a farm there which is partly under cultivation by our brothers while the remainder is rented out until we can find time to make a better use of it. We have had this farm for only one year, and I am still heavily in debt for it.[67]

As in Carrolltown and St. Marys, the Indiana priory became the hub of Benedictine pastoral work among Catholics of the neighborhood and throughout Indiana County. However, St. Vincent's dependent priory in Indiana never enjoyed the success of those in Carrolltown and St. Marys, and shortly before the Civil War Wimmer downgraded it to the status of parish and recalled most of the monks to St. Vincent, although a resident pastor remained to minister to the Catholics of the area.[68]

A small community of brothers was also stationed at Chestnut Ridge, some nine miles from St. Vincent, where in 1849 and 1851 the Benedictines had purchased several tracts of woodland, totaling seven hundred acres, to provide lumber for the construction of new monastic buildings at St. Vincent. The monks built a sawmill on the property as well as a house large enough to accommodate ten brothers. Chestnut Ridge became the site of a farm that helped supply the monastery table with food and also served as a place of retreat for monks from St. Vincent and its dependent priories. Wimmer reported that whenever he visited the ridge, "I feel as if I am transferred into the time of Clairvaux or the Cistercians. . . . The land itself is wild and rough, but romantic, and in our hands will certainly in time became a very beautiful place."[69]

By 1852 the principal centers of Benedictine missionary activity in western Pennsylvania—St. Vincent, St. Marys, Carrolltown, and Indiana—were flourishing. From these centers the monks engaged in agricultural, educational, and missionary work. Their pastoral care encompassed the six counties of Westmoreland, Elk, Cambria, Clearfield, Indiana, and Armstrong. In July, on the same day that he promulgated the rescript from Rome elevating St. Vincent to the rank of canonical priory, Bishop O'Connor issued a document granting the Benedictines the right to establish other priories in the diocese of Pittsburgh and recognizing the priories at St. Marys, Carrolltown, and Indiana as the first of these.[70]

In 1853 when the diocese of Erie was formed from Pennsylvania's northwest counties, among which was Elk County, Wimmer could boast that he had now founded Benedictine communities in two American dioceses. St. Marys, situated in the new diocese, came under the jurisdiction of Bishop Josue Mary Young who, two years later, invited the Benedictines to establish a parish in the see city. From the five Benedictine centers of St. Vincent, Carrolltown, St. Marys, Indiana, and Erie, and later from a sixth in Butler, the monks were engaged in mission work in virtually every corner of western Pennsylvania. The Benedictines, moreover, did not confine themselves to work in established mission districts but spread out from these centers to preach the Gospel as their services were needed. The Pennsylvania Railroad was constructing its main line from Philadelphia to Pittsburgh, and the right of way skirted the Benedictine property in Westmoreland County. Wimmer sent priests all along the route, as far as Harrisburg, to attend to the spiritual welfare of two thousand Irish Catholic workmen. When he learned of the magnitude of the drinking problem plaguing the railroad camps, he instructed his priests to urge the Irishmen to turn from their strong spirits to beer, which, he said, was much healthier for them.[71]

As the scope of Benedictine work in America expanded, Wimmer began to focus on the status of the community at St. Vincent. In the document authorizing the elevation of the monastery to the rank of nonexempt canonical priory, the Roman Congregation for the Propagation of the Faith had indicated its willingness to consider the question of abbatial status for St. Vincent at a later date, and Wimmer, encouraged by the rapid expansion of the Benedictine community in Pennsylvania and by the support he received from many friends both in Bavaria and the United States to pursue the matter, wasted little time in formulating a petition to that purpose. Less than a year after Bishop O'Connor promulgated the rescript elevating St. Vincent to an independent priory, Wimmer wrote Abbot Gregory Scherr of Metten that he was drafting a document for Rome in which he would ask that the community be elevated to the rank of abbey.[72]

On December 9, 1853, Archbishop Gaetano Bedini, papal nuncio to Brazil and special envoy from the Holy See to the bishops of the United States, unexpectedly visited St. Vincent with Bishop Michael O'Connor. At the time Wimmer was in St. Marys, but the new prior, Father Demetrius di Marogna, organized a hasty reception at St. Vincent that included greetings to the distinguished visitor delivered by the monks and students in Latin, English, German, French, and Italian. Bedini responded with speeches to the priests in Latin, the brothers in German, the students in French, and the prior in Italian. The student orchestra entertained the guests with a concert, and after spending the night at the monastery, the archbishop and O'Connor went on to Pittsburgh. Di Marogna informed Wimmer of the visit by telegram, and on December 11 Wimmer went to Pittsburgh where he met the Vatican's delegate and asked his assistance in petitioning the Holy See to elevate St. Vincent to an abbey. Bedini gave indications of his tentative support and promised to review the petition carefully, and in a gesture of goodwill and approval of what the Benedictines had already accomplished, he agreed to ordain three Benedictine students of theology, Roman Hell, Clement Staub, and Kilian Bernetzeder, to the priesthood.[73]

Even before Bedini's visit Wimmer had sent two letters to Rome requesting abbatial status for the American monastery. One he addressed directly to Pope Pius IX and the other to Archbishop Carlo Morichini, the former papal nuncio in Munich who had helped him obtain permission to go to America as a missionary and who had recently been named cardinal and transferred to the Roman Curia.

In his letter to the Holy Father Wimmer gave a detailed description of the growth, spiritual development, and missionary work of the Benedictines in Pennsylvania and said that "all this will be perfected and extended if the monastery is raised to the rank of abbey." In his letter to Morichini he asked for assistance in shepherding his petition through the Vatican bureaucracy.[74] Immediately after his meeting with Archbishop Bedini, Wimmer wrote a third letter to Cardinal Fransoni, prefect of the Propaganda Fide, in which he said that the monks at St. Vincent were "not unworthy to be called Benedictines although we cannot claim to be equal to those who were sent by Rome to England and from England to Germany." The community at St. Vincent, however, made every effort to imitate the zeal of their medieval counterparts, he said. "If this monastery meets with your approval, I implore Your Eminence to recommend its elevation to the rank of abbey."[75]

Morichini wrote in January that Wimmer's letter had brought him great joy. He was delighted to learn of the progress of the Benedictine mission in the United States, which he had supported at its earliest stages, but he said that in his new post as head of charitable foundations in Rome for the care of the sick he was not in a position to influence directly any decision on abbatial status for St. Vincent. He promised, however, that he would help the cause as best he could.[76]

Fransoni replied to Wimmer on February 7, 1854. He informed him that he had received the earlier petition and that the cardinals of the Sacred Congregation would consider the question as soon as possible. He told Wimmer that because of the importance of the subject, the matter could not be decided immediately, but he promised to inform him as soon as a decision had been reached.[77] Shortly after writing Wimmer, Fransoni wrote the bishop of Pittsburgh asking his opinion, and O'Connor replied in April that in his view the elevation of St. Vincent to abbatial dignity so soon after its establishment as a canonical priory was not opportune. O'Connor explained that the priests of St. Vincent, though very generous in attending to the needs of Catholics in the diocese, were young, inexperienced, and limited in their education and training. Moreover, he said, Wimmer, because of his imprudence and spirit of independence from episcopal authority, was not in the bishop's opinion a man suited for the dignity and role of abbot. If Propaganda should deem fit to name him abbot, the bishop strongly recommended, as he had done three years earlier, that he be nonmitered and that his term of office be limited.[78]

O'Connor had expressed these same views to Archbishop Bedini during the nuncio's visit to Pittsburgh and had managed to convince the archbishop to support his position in the upcoming discussions in Rome. In July Archbishop Bedini wrote Propaganda reviewing the merits of the case. He reported that the monastery of German Benedictines in the diocese of Pittsburgh was "developing well," and he observed that its superior was "a man full of energy and zeal." Bedini said that it was not because of his disagreement with Wimmer over beer brewing that Bishop O'Connor objected to the community's elevation to abbatial rank. The brewery case, he acknowledged, was closed. O'Connor objected, rather, "because he fears that [the Benedictines] will open their monastery to undesirables in order to increase their membership." Bedini believed that "this may have some foundation, but I do not think it should outweigh all other [considerations]." He summed up his recommendations evenhandedly, making the discreet and diplomatic comment that if Wimmer's request were not granted immediately, "I would approve such a decision. But it will always be a pleasure for me to say something in their praise, and I am hoping for the full approval of the petition when better conditions prevail, which certainly will not be far off."[79]

O'Connor's letter and the intervention of Bedini on his behalf caused further delays in Rome as the cardinals considered the advisability of making St. Vincent an abbey, and by the fall, when no word had come from the Propaganda, Wimmer sensed that something was wrong. He assumed that the request had been denied, so in December 1854 he assembled the capitulars and had them draw up another petition addressed directly to the Holy Father. In their letter to Pope Pius IX the monks said that a year had passed since their first petition to the Holy See and that so far the cardinals of the Propaganda Fide had sent them no information concerning the fate of their request. They were turning, therefore, to the Holy Father himself and were appealing to his "fatherly heart which is very solicitous of the welfare of all your children, especially of the religious, and we implore you to confer most graciously the title and rank of abbey on our monastery with the privilege of electing an abbot in accordance with the Sacred Canons." They admitted that things were not perfect at St. Vincent but said that they could "candidly state that no grave defects exist in essential matters." "We adopted the regular discipline which is observed at the Abbey of Metten," they continued, "and in some matters improved on it. The vow of poverty is strictly observed and the enclosure kept." Meditation, examination of conscience, and spiritual reading were all allotted sufficient time in the daily order. "We have regular chapters of faults, and novices are instructed in asceticism and the observance of the Holy Rule." Under these circumstances they humbly asked the pope "to remove this uncertainty of our condition" by raising the monastery to the rank of abbey.[80]

The letter was signed by Prior Demetrius di Marogna and the other priest-monks of the community and forwarded to the pope through Cardinal Fransoni. Wimmer himself wrote Fransoni ten days later that the monks of St. Vincent were firmly convinced that the success or failure of the monastery and the growth or decline of the seminary "depends on the approval or refusal of this request." "Our monastery," he went on, "cannot last much longer without a permanent superior, and if the monastery must be given up, the institution connected with it will come to naught." Wimmer informed Fransoni that one reason he and the other members of the community were stressing the importance of abbatial status for St. Vincent was that "we look upon our order and our monastery as the treasures closest to our hearts and are seeking to advance both in every way." "If other religious orders and societies have canonical superiors in accordance with their monastic principles, why should we not wish to enjoy the rights and privileges of our order?" He asked the cardinal to consider the matter as soon as possible "because many believe that during the coming winter Europe may again be involved in war, and recourse to the Holy See will take a long time, becoming difficult if not impossible."[81]

The forceful, undiplomatic tone of Wimmer's letter did not please the cardinals of Propaganda, and when Bishop O'Connor returned from Rome, where he had been attending the ceremonies surrounding the proclamation of the dogma of the Immaculate Conception, he brought with him no information about the "abbey question." When the chapter at St. Vincent received no response to its petition, Wimmer decided to return to Europe and take up the cause on the ground on which it would be decided.

Shortly after the new year 1855 he informed the St. Vincent chapter of his intention to travel to Rome. The monks elected Father Demetrius di Marogna as temporary superior during Wimmer's absence, and after consulting with the bishop of Pittsburgh, Wimmer departed for the Continent on January 25. Disembarking in Liverpool, he traveled by rail and channel boat to the Continent where he went first to Brussels to seek the advice and assistance of Count di Marogna, brother of Father Demetrius and Bavarian ambassador to the kingdom of Belgium. He arrived in Munich on February 25 and remained with his Bavarian friends for a month, consulting with the archbishop of Munich, the abbots of Metten and Scheyern, and the secretary and directors of the Ludwig Missionsverein. On March 27 he left Munich, and after a brief stop at the Abbey of Einsiedeln in Switzerland, a monastery that had recently established the Benedictine community of St. Meinrad's in the state of Indiana, he traveled by sleigh over the St. Gotthard Pass to the southern slopes of the Alps and from there by carriage and rail to Genoa where he took a boat for Civita Vecchia in the Papal States. He arrived in Rome on the Wednesday of Holy Week, April 4. The city was crowded with pilgrims, and as a stranger on his first visit to Rome Wimmer found lodgings only with difficulty. He slept in a flea-infested hostelry for three nights, but on Holy Saturday he moved to the Abbey of St. Paul's Outside-the-Walls whose abbot invited him to join the monks for Easter. Later he moved to San Callisto, St. Paul's hospice in the city itself, which was much closer to the offices of the Curia where he would have to argue St. Vincent's case, and most of his correspondence during the following months was dated from St. Callisto.[82]

In the slow manner of the Roman bureaucracy, Propaganda continued to weigh the question carefully and deliberately. It was clear that Wimmer had powerful supporters both in Rome and in Munich. But he also faced opposition, and a significant part of that came from Bishop Michael O'Connor of Pittsburgh. O'Connor's opposition was not unconsidered. In December he had written a second letter to Propaganda expressing his opinion that there was no other Catholic institution in America "which gives so much promise for good as the institute of the Benedictines at St. Vincent." Once again, however, he expressed grave reservations about the suitability of Wimmer for the position of superior, resurrecting the old problems related to the brewery and the manner in which the earlier petition had been made—questions Wimmer believed had long been resolved. "After mature deliberation," O'Connor said,

I must say that if the S. Congregation intends to elevate the monastery to the rank of abbey, Father Wimmer should not continue as superior. To render him justice, I repeat what I wrote in my previous letter: I esteem him as a man of great experience in the management of temporal affairs; he has shown good judgment in the government of the monks, and notwithstanding the faults which he committed, I consider him a man of good habits. Even when I had cause for complaint, he acted, I believe, with a sense of duty about the rights of the monastery.

However, more than once he took such false steps in matters of the greatest importance, that I would ascribe these mistakes to his intellect or his will, or partly to the one or the other. It seems therefore dangerous to appoint him to the post of abbot of a monastery. I may give as an example the affair of the tavern which is well known to Your Eminence.

As he had before, O'Connor also complained that Wimmer had made his petition to Rome in 1849 for the elevation of St. Vincent to the rank of canonical priory not through the bishop of Pittsburgh but through the German-speaking bishop of Milwaukee, John Martin Henni. "I must therefore say he acted very ungratefully toward me."

In order to make satisfaction, Wimmer should be bound "to admit among the boys whom he accepts in his institute a fair number of diocesan students (one-half or one-third as the Holy See may deem proper) gratis or at a very low rate for board and tuition. These students should be selected by the bishop."[83]

The seminary question had once more become the critical one. The bishop wanted more assurances that the Benedictines would serve the needs of the diocese than he now had, and he was using the question of abbatial status for St. Vincent as a lever to achieve the concessions he had been denied when the monastery was raised to a priory. O'Connor bristled in the face of the growing independence of the Benedictines in his diocese, an independence encouraged by Wimmer's influential friends in Munich and Rome. In February the bishop wrote yet a third letter to Propaganda saying that Wimmer was perhaps as good a candidate for the office of abbot as any monk at St. Vincent, but he argued against elevating the community to the rank of abbey. The move was unnecessary, he said. The monks were not mature enough to merit this dignity, and such an action would result in a conflict of monastic and episcopal interests. A permanent abbot in an American diocese, O'Connor observed, would be in a position to challenge episcopal authority whenever it suited him.[84] The bishop of Pittsburgh was using every plausible argument to convince the Holy See that it would be in the best interest of the American Church to curb the growing power of the American Benedictines.

On the same day that Bishop O'Connor penned his letter to Cardinal Fransoni, the Propaganda Fide appointed Abbot Angelo Pescetelli, O.S.B., procurator general of the Italian Cassinese Benedictine Congregation, as defender of the St. Vincent case, and on March 12, 1855, Pescetelli delivered a letter to the cardinals of the Sacred Congregation in which he made an unqualified recommendation that St. Vincent be elevated to the rank of abbey with full rights to elect an abbot. Moreover, with regard to the bishop of Pittsburgh's demand that a definite number of diocesan seminarians be educated at the monastic seminary gratis or at lower rates than normally charged, Pescetelli reminded the cardinals that "Father Wimmer was sent by the Ludwig Missionsverein for the Germans in Pennsylvania. . . . This contract should be kept." Wimmer had, of his own volition, accepted and educated Irish students, and his goodwill could therefore not be called into question. After considering all aspects of the matter, Pescetelli said it was his opinion "that St. Vincent should be declared an abbey and that the community should be granted the right to elect its abbot. This election should be for a term of three years and be confirmed by the Holy See. If the same man is chosen three times by a two-thirds majority, he should be abbot for life." Finally, Pescetelli recommended that the abbey be exempt from the jurisdiction of the bishop "in all its internal spiritual and temporal administration," that traditional privileges be granted the abbot with regard to the pontificals he would wear, and that the abbey be affiliated with the Cassinese Congregation of Italian Benedictines.[85]

Wimmer, who arrived in Rome about a month after Pescetelli had sent his letter to Propaganda, paid his first official call on the cardinals on April 18, 1855. Afterward he wrote Father Demetrius di Marogna that the monsignor who first greeted him at Propaganda addressed him as "Abbate" and said that there was great hope for a solution to the case that would satisfy Wimmer and the monks of St. Vincent. Wimmer was informed of Pescetelli's support and told that "later communications with the bishop [of Pittsburgh] were more favorable than earlier ones." The monsignor even stated "that nothing stood in the way of having the monastery declared an abbey and myself appointed first abbot. From his word I learned that the bishop is demanding that we devote ourselves chiefly to the education of poor boys for the clerical state by accepting his own students gratis or at least at a lower rate than the rest. He also requires that the pastor of St. Vincent be presented to him for approval."[86]

As the days passed Wimmer began to realize that the bishop's expectations concerning free education for the diocesan students and episcopal control of some aspects of the seminary administration were blocking a favorable decision from Propaganda. He learned also that O'Connor objected to the title of exemption for the proposed abbey. With the exception of exemption, these were matters that Wimmer thought had been resolved when Rome raised the monastery to the rank of canonical priory in 1852, but O'Connor, ever concerned that the presence of an exempt abbey in his diocese would limit his own authority and prove more a threat to the orderly functioning of the diocese than a blessing, was determined to defend episcopal prerogatives in face of what appeared to him the growing independence of the German Benedictines at St. Vincent. Wimmer, equally determined, intended to prevent any encroachments upon the authority traditionally granted to Benedictine superiors. "Ecclesiastical history shows very well," he said, "that monasteries have sought exemption for this reason: that bishops with their sometimes troublesome requests and recommendations exhausted those who were not able to resist or did not dare to do so. [Bishop O'Connor] does not love the religious if he cannot use them as he chooses. . . . He has no principles of justice and order as his guidelines, except that of utility."[87] So the Benedictine superior settled down for the fight.

On April 21, 1855, Wimmer received an official request from the secretary of the Sacred Congregation for the Propagation of the Faith that he respond to four objections that Bishop O'Connor had to St. Vincent's elevation to the rank of abbey. O'Connor's objections were (1) that the priests at St. Vincent were all very young and had only recently completed their theological studies, (2) that all the St. Vincent monks were from Germany and by retaining the customs of their native land would cut themselves off from the mainstream of American life, (3) that the proposed constitution for the monastery was not clear enough nor were the limits of the abbot's proposed rights clearly expressed, and (4) that no provision was made in the proposed constitution for the removal of an unsatisfactory superior.

In addition to these objections, the cardinals of Propaganda listed certain requirements O'Connor proposed the Benedictines meet before the Congregation consider elevating St. Vincent to abbatial dignity. These were (1) that the monks would maintain a school at the monastery "for students of the secular clergy," (2) that they would accept some of these students "gratis or at a lower rate than other students," (3) that Bishop O'Connor would be "constantly informed about the course of these students' studies," and (4) that "as ecclesiastical laws prescribe, the priests who are engaged in the missions must be approved by the bishop."[88]

Acquiescing completely to these requirements would, in Wimmer's mind, clearly jeopardize the independence and financial security of the monastery. He was therefore not prepared to accept them in their entirety. Writing to Archbishop von Reisach of Munich, he said that insofar as the first requirement was concerned, "we already made that concession eight years ago." He categorically refused to accept the second, claiming that finances at the monastery would not allow him to educate the bishop's students gratis or at a reduced rate. With regard to the third, he was prepared to agree to it conditionally but wanted to make clear that the bishop "can never be rector of the seminary." Finally, he fully accepted the fourth requirement, provided that "this request contains nothing else than what is explicitly stated."[89]

Meanwhile Father Boniface was enlisting the support of influential friends in both Italy and Bavaria for St. Vincent's cause before Propaganda. He had developed a close working relationship and friendship with Abbot Angelo Pescetelli, who offered invaluable help and advice throughout this period. He sought and received the support of the powerful Baron Ferdinand von Verger, Bavarian ambassador to the Vatican, as well as of other Bavarian civil and ecclesiastical authorities. Several Italian Benedictine abbots lent their assistance, and on April 26 King Ludwig I returned to Rome where he quickly brought his considerable influence to bear on behalf of the American Benedictine petition. "We matter a great deal to him," Wimmer wrote di Marogna of the king. "The students of the German College were with him for an audience recently, and at that time he mentioned us with praise. Have the mass for a King celebrated again each Monday. I forgot this for too long."

Despite all the support he received, however, Wimmer was still not sure what success his case would meet before the cardinals of Propaganda. He was prepared to make concessions, but he also began making tentative plans to leave the diocese of Pittsburgh in the event that Bishop O'Connor's efforts to obstruct St. Vincent's bid for exempt abbatial status should succeed. He wrote Father Demetrius: "It is certain that we must rather give up material advantages than sacrifice a principle. Thus it will be better to burden ourselves with the education of a few boys than put the school under the supervision of the bishop. In case we have to leave the diocese, everything must be done quietly. It will not be fair to cause the bishop a difficulty. Let us pray fervently that the will of God be done. I assure you that I will do everything in my power and shall use all honest means to defend our common rights."[90]

As he planned his strategy and recorded his opinions in letters to friends and responses to the Propaganda Fide, Wimmer learned that he faced a new problem. Some of his straightforward and frank communications with Vatican officials did not please the cardinals. Many of his counterarguments to objections raised by Bishop O'Connor sounded to them like ultimatums. "Prince Hohenlohe believes that I will not be made abbot because Monsignor Barnabo told him that I write too harshly and need to be mortified. It is true. I speak plainly even in Latin. But if I must defend right against wrong, I have a still franker language. At the moment, however, it does not seem necessary."[91]

The question of abbatial status for St. Vincent had still not been decided when on June 19, 1855, Wimmer was called to a private audience with Pope Pius IX. Eight days later he wrote di Marogna that the meeting was only partially successful.

I was in the anti-chamber of the papal apartment at 9:30 for the audience at 10:00 but had to wait until the churchmen who preceded me had come from the Pope's audience room. I had well prepared what I wished to say. Count Talbot introduced me to the Holy Father, who in a white cassock was seated at the table and writing. The room proved almost too small for the three prostrations which the court rules prescribe for such audiences. When I came near and tried to kiss the cross on his slipper, he offered me his ring for the ceremony and gave me a sign to take a seat opposite him at the table. However, I dared not sit down. Addressing me as *abbate,* he first inquired whether I preferred to speak Italian or Latin. I chose the latter but when he continued to use Italian, I tried as well as I could to answer in that tongue. The pope was in a very good humor. He even referred to the beer controversy, stating that selling at retail could not well be granted. This gave me a chance to mention the custom in Germany, and I expressed my thanks to him for having made his wishes known. When I explained that I was defending a principle and that we were drinking only water, he laughed heartily and said: "Yes, St. Paul wrote to Timothy to use a little wine for his stomach!" Finally, after inquiring about the number of fathers, brothers, novices, and seminarians, he said that we could do much for the Church. I was not able to mention any of my subjects which I had prepared because he continued writing from time to time and I did not wish to disturb him during those pauses. After a long delay he said "*A dio,*" the customary sign that the audience was over. Finally he gave me his blessing and I left.

I must confess that I was not quite satisfied with the result of that audience because I could not explain my difficulties. Still, it pleases me to have seen the pope in such a happy frame of mind. Two days later Prince Hohenlohe told me that my report was well received and that I should be satisfied with having achieved so much.[92]

The St. Vincent case was formally presented to the fourteen cardinals of the Congregation for the Propagation of the Faith on July 14, and according to custom Wimmer spent the next ten days visiting the cardinals and answering their questions. He discovered during the ordeal that the defense of his cause written in March by Abbot Angelo Pescetelli was his greatest support. Pescetelli accompanied him on his rounds to the various cardinals and spoke strongly in his favor. On July 19 Wimmer wrote di Marogna that he had received confidential information that the cardinals were unanimously prepared to vote in favor of the American Benedictine petition. One of the cardinals "tried to discover animosity towards our bishop in my explanations," he said, but another "couldn't find enough words to praise" the monks of St. Vincent. This cardinal "urgently advised us, for the sake of peace, to make a sacrifice and take two of the bishop's students gratis each year. I agreed to do so if all else would be granted us." Wimmer cautioned di Marogna to make sure that

nothing is said about the bishop, that he is in no way angered, or that he is given reason to complain. We have won a good many powerful patrons among the cardinals of the Propaganda. Even old Fransoni said to me, "Now the case is ripe for the abbey." In the circle directly around the pope all admire the fact that we have so many brothers. The brothers will be no less proud of the fact that the Holy Father and the cardinals read their names and duties individually. I hope all have continued to pray diligently. I do believe that the happy outcome of our cause is the result of pious prayers which all of you together sent to heaven.[93]

The following day Wimmer received a copy of the Propaganda decree raising St. Vincent to the rank of exempt abbey. The decree also granted the Benedictines in America the right to elect their own abbot for life, established the constitution of the Bavarian Congregation as the norm for the new abbey, made St. Vincent the central monastery of a new Benedictine congregation to be affiliated with the Italian Cassinese Congregation, and imposed upon the new abbey "a special obligation to maintain a seminary for the secular clergy" where the bishop of Pittsburgh would have "equal rights with others in the admission of students." In an additional concession to O'Connor the cardinals gave the bishop of Pittsburgh the right "to watch over the progress and the conduct of his own clerical students."[94]

Two weeks later Cardinal Fransoni submitted the decree to Pope Pius IX who confirmed its contents, although he altered the provision for the immediate election of a lifetime abbot. Instead, the pope appointed Wimmer abbot for three years and directed that at the end of that period the monks of St. Vincent choose a permanent abbot. An apostolic brief was published on September 17, 1855, in which the decisions were officially promulgated and in which Father Boniface was formally named abbot by the Holy Father "in consideration of the eminent services" he had performed for the Church.[95]

The decree of the Propaganda Fide was a clear victory for Wimmer and the American Benedictines in their controversy with Bishop O'Connor. Not only had the community been elevated to abbatial rank and given a "mitered" abbot, but it had also been removed from the jurisdiction of the bishop of Pittsburgh and made exempt. Wimmer wrote King Ludwig thanking him for the crucial support he had provided the American Benedictines during the controversy. He said that the cardinals of the Propaganda, who had voted unanimously to raise St. Vincent to abbatial dignity, wanted "to give Your Majesty joy, and they wanted to protect the Benedictine Order against the attacks of the bishop. Thus, through an act of marvelous condescension, Your Majesty has given a great advantage to religion and to the German situation across the ocean."[96]

To the abbot of the Austrian abbey of Kremsmünster Wimmer wrote that "the order [in America] is now formally instituted and provided for in the future so that with the expansion into other dioceses, the common cooperation will not be disturbed through the influences of the bishops on the individual monasteries, either with regard to the discipline or the goals the communities are to pursue."[97]

In a letter to Demetrius di Margona Wimmer said that he had not expected to be named abbot but rather thought that upon his return to America he would preside over an election at which di Margona himself would be chosen by the St. Vincent community. This had not occurred, he said, because the cardinals of the Propaganda had urged the pope to name Wimmer first abbot. "Thus," he continued, "I have the privilege of being the *first* and *last* and *only* American triennial abbot. What is also something unusual: I am abbot, but *sine benedictione.*" He said he was disappointed that the first Benedictine abbot in the United States would not receive a full liturgical abbatial blessing and explained that in his final audience with Pope Pius IX, the Holy Father gave him a pectoral cross and ring as well as a personal benediction which the pope said was abbatial blessing enough.[98]

Wimmer left Rome on August 6 and arrived in Munich eight days later. For the next three months he traveled through Bavaria and Austria visiting Benedictine communities, attempting to recruit students for St. Vincent, and soliciting donations for the Benedictine work in America. He was frustrated in his efforts at recruitment because both the Bavarian and Austrian governments had restricted the emigration of young men of military age on account of the Crimean War, but his fundraising activities bore abundant fruit. He collected money from friends and benefactors—including Abbot Rupert Leiss, Father Joseph F. Müller, Archbishop Karl von Reisach, several Benedictine communities in Bavaria and Austria, and the Austrian imperial family—throughout the regions he visited, and he received gifts of books for the library and liturgical vessels and vestments for use in the liturgies at St. Vincent. A gift he especially prized was the episcopal ring given him by Archbishop von Reisach of Munich. It had once belonged to the saintly bishop of Regensburg, George Michael Wittmann, who had taught Abbot Boniface theology and twenty-four years earlier had ordained him to the priesthood.[99]

On November 2 Wimmer set sail from Bremen on the *S.S. Washington* with two candidates for the Abbey of St. Vincent, five Benedictine nuns from Eichstätt for the Convent of St. Joseph in St. Marys, and three Ursuline nuns from Austria bound for the American missions. The month-long voyage was difficult and unpleasant. From Newfoundland he wrote Abbot Gregory Scherr that during an especially frightening storm "the ship creaked and squeaked as if it would any minute be shattered to bits. Sleeping was out of the question . . . . This sea voyage is the most terrifying I have ever undertaken." He expressed his deepest thanks to Scherr "for all the love and excellent treatment I experienced in abundance at Metten and in every place where the flag of Metten is hoisted."[100]

Wimmer and his companions landed in New York on November 30 but had to remain in the city nearly a week before they could collect all their baggage from customs. Wimmer took advantage of the stay to call on Archbishop Hughes, Bishop Bayley of Newark, Father Balleis, and other priests with whom he was acquainted. On the evening of December 6 he left New York by train bound for Johnstown, Pennsylvania. The following day five priests from St. Vincent boarded the train in Johnstown to greet the new abbot, and an hour later, at the Latrobe station, another delegation met the entourage and escorted it back to St. Vincent.

It had been almost eleven months since he had last seen his con-

freres, and Wimmer's sentimental heart was bursting with gratitude
and happiness. Mounted on horseback and surrounded by his priests,
he made his way up the hill to the abbey. Parishioners lined the road
and greeted him with waves and cheers. Father Demetrius and the
community welcomed him at the gates of the monastery where a triumphal arch had been erected, and the students' brass band played
Bavarian songs that mirrored the joy all those present experienced
that day. At the monastery gates Wimmer dismounted, and the Benedictine community led him to the church where monks and students
joined him in singing the Te Deum. When the solemn celebration in
the church had ended, everyone repaired to the refectory where a
large banquet was spread. Guests from the parish sat at the abbot's
table. Friends from the neighborhood of the monastery, both Protestant and Catholic, joined the Benedictines and their students in a
grand celebration and feast that overflowed with rich food, Bavarian
beer, and *Gemütlichkeit*. During the meal the St. Vincent community
orchestra entertained the guests, and afterward students from the
gymnasium and seminary welcomed and congratulated Abbot Boniface with speeches in Latin, Greek, German, French, Italian, and
English. The abbot himself said little during the festivities. He
claimed afterward that he was too overcome with emotion to speak.
A week later, however, he wrote Archbishop von Reisach, summariz-
ing what his thoughts had been. "Rome has spoken," he said. "The
abbey is firmly established, the work of expansion can begin."[101]

At Christmas the community held another public celebration, one
highlighted by Wimmer's first solemn pontifical mass as an abbot. It
was an event the community planned meticulously and looked forward to with eager anticipation. On Christmas Eve a violent snow-
storm swept over the countryside, and the monks worried that the
ceremony would be marred by sparse attendance. But at midnight,
when the abbot and the monks entered the church to begin the
liturgy, they were delighted to find the pews and aisles packed with
people. Emotions ran high as Abbot Boniface intoned the Gloria and
the orchestra and choir followed with the strains of Haydn. The mass
was a memorable occasion for both the Benedictine community and
the parishioners of St. Vincent and was spoken of for many years afterward.[102]

As news of St. Vincent's elevation to an abbey spread, Wimmer received congratulatory messages from well-wishers throughout the

United States. Among members of the American hierarchy who wrote were Archbishop John Purcell of Cincinnati, Bishop John Nepomucene Neumann of Philadelphia, Bishop Josue Mary Young of Erie, Bishop John Martin Henni of Milwaukee, Bishop Mathias Loras of Dubuque, and Bishop Joseph Cretin of St. Paul. Doubtless the letter he valued most, however, was the one sent by the bishop of Pittsburgh. Michael O'Connor offered warm congratulations to the new abbot and said that even though he had considered the elevation of St. Vincent to abbatial rank premature, "I gave my consent to the measure" since the Holy See "thought it prudent to proceed to that step." With regard to the "seminary matter," the bishop said he was

sorry that your alarm led you to entertain apprehensions which I beg leave to assure you were unfounded, and I must say again that I regret you did not comply with my request of settling this matter before you left for Europe. However, I do not intend reopening this question at present and may possibly settle it by abandoning all claims on it. I again congratulate you on your safe return and your success. Notwithstanding the light in which I am represented, you may rest assured that I feel the most lively interest and entertain the brightest hopes of the success of your community. Though I may sometimes differ in opinion as to the propriety of some measures, I think I may say with sincerity that it will always afford me pleasure to contribute everything in my power that will increase its prosperity and usefulness.[103]

4 ❰❲ *Growth and Expansion*

THOUGH IT WOULD later be called an "era of troubles," the second decade of the Benedictine presence in the United States began auspiciously. After a ten-month absence Boniface Wimmer returned from Rome in December 1855 with a clear mandate for the expansion of the order in America. The principal questions debated before the Sacred Congregation for the Propagation of the Faith had been settled in his favor, and he came back to St. Vincent with documents elevating the monastery to the rank of abbey and appointing him its abbot for a three-year term. The ground had been broken and a strong foundation laid for the newest edifice of the ancient Order of St. Benedict. Now the abbot turned his full attention to the work of expansion.

In his 1845 article for the *Augsburger Postzeitung* Wimmer had proposed that once a Benedictine monastery were securely established in North America "the Fathers might be sent out to visit those Catholics who scarcely ever see a priest; occasionally at least they might preach the word of God and bring the consolations of religion even to those who live at a great distance from the monasteries; small congregations could be established and the seminary could soon furnish a goodly number of the secular clergy."[1]

As has been seen, by 1856 Wimmer had already established small priories in Carrolltown, St. Marys, Indiana, and Butler, Pennsylvania. From these priories and from St. Vincent itself the Benedictines carried on pastoral work in parishes and mission stations throughout western Pennsylvania. The abbey numbered 188 monks in January 1856. The growth had been phenomenal: in its first decade the monastery had increased tenfold in membership. There were 19 priests, 37 clerics, 22 novices, and 110 lay brothers at the abbey and in the priories and parishes attached to it. The community owned almost four thousand acres of land in different parts of the state. Wimmer reported to the directors of the *Ludwig Missionsverein:*

Our Fathers are doing missionary work in two dioceses (Pittsburgh and Erie), and in some of the priories we have erected there will be found the germs of new seminaries and colleges. [At St. Vincent] there are over forty students pursuing their classical studies, and seventeen of these are candidates for the order. We have a complete course of studies and can take little boys who, as they grow in years, are led from the elementary school through the classical course through philosophy and theology into the sanctuary of the holy priesthood.[2]

Twenty-two students for the diocesan priesthood studied philosophy and theology in the major seminary. Seven of them would be ordained before the end of the year, joining more than two dozen German-speaking diocesan priests in the United States who had been educated at St. Vincent.[3]

Through Wimmer's efforts the Benedictine Order was firmly established in the United States by 1856, and both the vision and efforts of the monks during their first ten years of service in the American Church had borne fruits whose extent and potential astonished everyone. The coming decade would witness even further expansion outside the boundaries of Pennsylvania, but before the new foundations were completely successful, Abbot Boniface would have more problems to contend with, and these would prove threatening indeed to the future of the order in America.

As news of the work of the Benedictines in Pennsylvania spread, bishops in other parts of the United States began to petition Wimmer to establish communities in their dioceses. Concurrently the abbot's plan for further development of the new American branch of the order evolved. The "small congregations" he had envisioned in 1845 were growing large. The communities at Carrolltown and St. Marys were flourishing, and at the Abbey of St. Vincent more than two hundred monks and students bustled about in the daily routine of monastic and academic life.

In January 1856, a month after returning from Rome, Wimmer called together the monks of St. Vincent for the first general chapter of the American Cassinese Congregation. The Roman decree of the previous autumn had established the congregation, and at that time Wimmer had been appointed its president. In 1856 the American

Cassinese Congregation was one of only three national congregations of Benedictines recognized by the Holy See. The Austrian and Italian Cassinese Congregations had survived the Napoleonic upheavals intact, but other European congregations had not. The Bavarian Congregation, for example, had been suppressed in 1803, and despite the restoration of Metten, Augsburg, and Scheyern the congregation itself would not be officially restored until 1858.

Affiliated with the Italian Cassinese Congregation, the American Cassinese Congregation was in 1856 merely a paper organization. At its creation the cardinals of the Propaganda Fide had expressed reservations about its establishment since only one independent abbey existed in the United States at the time. In the expectation of continued growth and expansion of the order in North America, however, and in the likelihood of new independent priories being quickly established, they acquiesced to Wimmer's petition for its creation. Wimmer took the opportunity at the first general chapter to make it a functioning and effective entity.

The meeting opened on January 11, and all the priests of St. Vincent were in attendance except Father Roman Hell, who remained in St. Marys so that the people there would not be without a priest, and Father Peter Henry Lemke, who the previous month had left the priory in Carrolltown without permission and gone to Kansas. Wimmer began by reading to the capitulars the Roman decrees elevating the monastery to abbatial status and appointing him its abbot for a three-year term. He then gave his interpretation of the decrees and spoke to the chapter about the instructions he had received in Rome concerning their implementation. Afterward he read the statutes of the suppressed Bavarian Congregation and informed the community that Rome had approved them for adoption by the American Cassinese Congregation. "Everyone was of good will," he wrote, "and very eager to live according to the newly accepted [statutes]." The remainder of the time the monks devoted to drafting formal letters of thanks to Pope Pius IX and King Ludwig I, discussing monastic discipline in the new congregation, reviewing St. Vincent's financial condition, and especially considering the next stage of Benedictine expansion in America. The meetings lasted four days and were followed by a three-day retreat that culminated with a pontifical mass, the second celebrated by Abbot Boniface. A proud Wimmer wrote his friend Abbot Rupert Leiss of Scheyern that "the church was full of Benedictines:

eighty-three brothers, thirty-seven clerics, nineteen priests, seventeen Maurists (young aspirants in the habit). These seventeen and several others were invested and several made simple profession while others made solemn profession. And all who had already made profession renewed it in accord with the statutes. All received Communion from my hands. This too was a lovely day, a moving celebration! We saw how strong we were and hence decided on a new expedition, which the Prior wanted to lead."[4]

Two months later Wimmer wrote Abbot Gregory Scherr of Metten telling him of the chapter and describing conditions at St. Vincent in the opening months of 1856. While he was absent in Rome, he said, the prior of the monastery, Father Demetrius di Marogna, had been forced to borrow three thousand dollars. This debt, as well as others that had accrued in the course of the previous several months, had been unavoidable since the fall crop had failed. The community faced a financial crisis in 1856 because of this, and Wimmer said that "more than one thing went wrong." He complained that Father Demetrius had erected a building "without having told me." The building expenses amounted to only several hundred dollars, "but the house is constructed in the American style, i.e., not solid in any respect." Considering everything, however, the abbot "was glad that all had a good ending. I know too well that no one, not even the most capable, could handle such a complicated business in so short a time."

In addition to the financial problems, Wimmer discovered that during his absence "there was some dissension in the house, but in the long-run everyone followed the dictate of his conscience as well as he could, and this naturally made me very happy." The abbot expressed his hope to Scherr that financial assistance from Bavaria would come soon and ended his letter with the prognosis that "during the coming summer we shall have to think about a new foundation in the Far West. This will demand much thought, much writing, much concern, and much money to spend. . . . It can be done in no other way. In every place the need is urgent."[5]

The opportunity for a foundation in the West came more quickly than Abbot Boniface anticipated. The initial steps toward the establishment of a Benedictine monastery outside Pennsylvania, in fact, had already been made when Wimmer wrote Scherr in March, and though the seed of this new foundation had been planted in stormy weather, quite independently of Abbot Boniface himself, the harvest, before too many more years passed, would be rich.

Father Peter Henry Lemke, who had invited Wimmer to the diocese of Pittsburgh in 1846 and was professed as a monk of the St. Vincent community in 1852, had been assigned to St. Benedict's Priory, Carrolltown, before the end of his novitiate. Lemke, who was fifty-six when he made solemn profession, was the oldest member of the community, though in order of profession he had relatively low seniority. As one of the pioneer German missionaries in western Pennsylvania he had lived a full and productive life, ministering to the spiritual and temporal needs of the German Catholics in his mission fields. He had founded and laid out the village of Carrolltown in northern Cambria County, and in 1848 he sold some of his property in Carrolltown to the Benedictines of St. Vincent.[6] It was on this property that the monks had established St. Benedict's Priory in 1849.

His peculiar situation as subordinate at the Carrolltown Priory caused Lemke to feel like a stranger in his own land, and he came into open conflict with several of the younger members of the community, especially with the twenty-nine-year-old prior, Father Ildephonse Böld. Although he tried to avoid an argument "with that brainless Wimmer as long as I can help it,"[7] he found his position in Carrolltown stifling and intolerable. Claiming that his novitiate had been invalid because Abbot Boniface had sent him to Carrolltown before he completed it, Lemke decided to leave the monastery. In October 1855, while Wimmer was still in Rome, the disillusioned priest went to Pittsburgh. His plan was to find passage down the Ohio River to Kentucky where he hoped to become a Trappist. In Pittsburgh, however, Lemke met a member of the Trappist community of Gethsemani, and what he learned from this monk convinced him that he had not been called to a Trappist vocation after all. In doubt as to what to do, he met several families who were on the way to Kansas to establish homesteads. This encounter at once reawakened Lemke's wanderlust. He offered himself as their spiritual guide, promised them that he would found a Benedictine monastery in the new territory, and in December left Pittsburgh with them bound for Kansas.[8] When the abbot learned of this unauthorized departure, he ordered the fiercely independent priest to return to St. Vincent, but Wimmer had mixed feelings about his order. "I hope he will obey," he wrote Abbot Gregory. "In a way, though, I would rather not see him come, unless it be dangerous for his eternal salvation if he fails to comply."[9]

Lemke remained in Kansas, where he decided his novitiate was valid after all. He convinced Abbot Boniface to allow him to work among the German settlers in the new territory, and his presence there marked the beginnings of the Kansas Benedictine foundation that would eventually become St. Benedict's Abbey.

Meanwhile a more orthodox plan for a foundation outside Pennsylvania was taking shape at St. Vincent. At the chapter in January 1856 the community had discussed the requests of several American bishops for monastic foundations in their dioceses, and the capitulars agreed that in a short time there would be enough priests in the community to permit a small number of them to establish a missionary colony in another part of the country. But the question of where to send the missionaries arose. Requests had come from Archbishop John B. Purcell of Cincinnati, Archbishop Peter Kenrick of St. Louis, Bishop Mathias Loras of Dubuque, Bishop Frederic Baraga, vicar apostolic of northern Michigan, Bishop John Martin Henni of Milwaukee, and Bishop Joseph Cretin of St. Paul in the Minnesota Territory. Each of these bishops had presented cogent and compelling reasons for the Benedictines to establish a monastery in his diocese. None, however, had been specific about the conditions he would impose upon a monastic community once the monks were sent. Wimmer made it known that he wanted to send his men west because he could clearly see that it was in the West that the future of America lay. But beyond desiring to send his men to the newest section of the country, he wanted to ensure that no difficulties arose between the monks who might go and the local ordinary who invited them. He did not want a repetition of the difficulties he had experienced in the 1840s and early 1850s with Bishop Michael O'Connor of Pittsburgh. Accordingly, he determined that before he would send his monks anywhere, the Benedictines and the host bishop would have to agree that the land on which the Benedictines were to settle would be deeded over to them unconditionally, that the monks would be subject in all internal and monastic matters to the jurisdiction of the abbot of St. Vincent, and that the community would in no way be hampered by the bishop from developing into an exempt abbey like the motherhouse in Pennsylvania. Many years later, Father Bruno Riess, one of the pioneer Benedictines in the West, explained how Minnesota was finally settled on as the place for the first successful Benedictine missionary endeavor outside of Pennsylvania.

It happened in January 1856 that six American bishops sent petitions to the late Abbot Wimmer for the introduction of the Benedictine Order and erection of monasteries in their dioceses. This movement caused some perplexity. Widely divergent opinions and proposals were brought to the front in a chapter in which these applications were considered—one favored acceptance of this, another of that post. The Abbot listened, no conclusions were reached. Finally he arose and said: "We will commit the whole affair to the hands of God—may He decide where we should make the beginning. I shall," he said, "write each of the bishops and tell him of our needs, i.e., the conditions upon which we will be able to correspond with his request. All of these letters I will mail at the same time and the first bishop who will reply satisfactorily shall have our priests." And behold, the voice of God came from the West, from St. Paul, the most distant point which the mails only reached via Dubuque and thence per stage; from St. Paul came the first unconditioned call for Benedictine monks.[10]

In the early 1850s a large number of German immigrants had settled in central Minnesota, and as was the case with their countrymen in western Pennsylvania before the coming of the Benedictines, the spiritual welfare of the Catholics among them suffered neglect for want of priests. When Wimmer and the community at St. Vincent decided to answer the appeal of Bishop Cretin of St. Paul, Abbot Boniface appointed his prior, Father Demetrius di Marogna, to lead the mission. Together with two clerics who were preparing for the priesthood, Bruno Riess and Cornelius Wittmann, and two lay brothers, Benno Muckenthaler and Patrick Greil, Prior Demetrius set out for the West on April 5, 1856. After a brief delay in St. Louis, where Archbishop Peter Kenrick tried unsuccessfully to convince them to abandon their Minnesota plans and remain in his diocese, the group arrived in St. Paul at ten o'clock in the evening of May 2. They met Bishop Cretin the next morning and settled down at the episcopal residence awaiting assignment. On May 7 di Marogna wrote Abbot Boniface from St. Paul that "with the Rule and the Statutes in our hand, while holding fast to the course charted therein, we shall succeed if our plan is from God. We are, after all, only tools in the hand of the Craftsman."[11]

At St. Vincent Wimmer summoned Father Benedict Haindl from St. Marys, where he had been serving as prior, and appointed him to

Father Demetrius di Marogna (1803–1869), the
Bavarian nobleman who served as prior of
Saint Vincent and led the first Benedictine
missionaries to Minnesota. (ASVA)

replace Father Demetrius as claustral prior of the abbey. Haindl, described by one who knew him as "placid, silent, only interrupting his
meditations by taking a pinch of snuff,"[12] had been a member of the
original band accompanying Wimmer to America in 1846. His quiet
and contemplative disposition indisposed him to the practical affairs
of administration, and he had encountered innumerable problems at
St. Marys, especially with the Benedictine sisters there. But as prior at
St. Vincent, where administrative problems were handled almost
exclusively by Wimmer, Father Benedict could live a relatively un-
distracted monastic life and at the same time give an example of
piety and detachment to the rest of the monks. The "dissension in

the house" that had occurred while Wimmer was in Rome centered chiefly around the question of monastic observance. The more contemplative members of the community had opposed Abbot Boniface's active monastic missionary policy ever since Father Peter Lechner's time at St. Vincent in the late 1840s. Although Lechner's opposition had ended with a reaffirmation of the active ideals of the superior, the more contemplative aspects of the monastic life continued to find sympathetic adherents at the abbey. As prior, Father Benedict embodied the ideals of the "strict constructionists." He was at the same time, however, devoted to Abbot Boniface and was therefore in a position to function as an intermediary between any latent reformers in the monastery and the superior.

Father Benedict Haindl (1815–1887), Benedictine
pioneer and one of the first four clerical students
at Saint Vincent Monastery. (ASVA)

In November Wimmer wrote Abbot Utto Lang, who had succeeded Abbot Gregory Scherr at Metten upon Scherr's elevation to the archbishopric of Munich, that a decade after its founding the community of St. Vincent numbered 220 monks and students. "We do lots of studying, working, memorizing, and show much improvement," he reported. Some minor problems had arisen, but they were taken care of speedily. A carpenter, newly arrived from Bavaria, had proven fractious and been the cause of no little annoyance: "In spite of all warnings, he continually murmured, acted foolishly, and made all kinds of noise." When conventional medicine failed to settle the man, "We anointed him with Holy Oil, figuratively speaking. He was firmly tied to a bed and his hind part treated with a good hickory switch, which is excellently qualified to administer such an exorcism on a sensitive spot." The treatment worked so well, Wimmer said, that it was again used on one of the brothers. Once more, after the "hickory oil" was applied, there were no further disturbances. Abbot Boniface offered to send some of this valuable "oil" to Abbot Utto if ever he required any. "Plenty grows all around here."

But there were more serious problems facing the community in November 1856. The recent crop, like the one before, had been a total failure. "Absolutely nothing did well, neither wheat nor rye nor even oats, potatoes, and hay." Wimmer had sent Prior Benedict to Chicago and St. Louis to buy grain, but the expenditure had depleted the community's coffers and Wimmer was in need of cash. The crop had failed because of a long drought that made the ground as hard as rock and dried up all the creeks, springs, and wells around the monastery. "All vegetation disappeared," Abbot Boniface said, "and the soil actually looked burnt. Luckily we never had to cut down our fine oak forest. As a result the heat did not dry up the soil which was shaded by the trees, and the cattle found some grass there." But by August, the monks were feeding the cows hay, and consequently the herd had grown quite lean. On the brighter side, Wimmer reported that he was pleased with the profits made by the community's sawmill on nearby Chestnut Ridge as well as by the gristmill at the abbey, and at St. Marys the monks were in the process of building a new gristmill at a cost of two thousand dollars. During the previous month the abbot had been in St. Marys supervising the construction, helping the brothers clear the land for the mill "until I had calluses on my hands. That was foolish of me, but I like the work and it was necessary."

Despite the hardships, life at St. Vincent as depicted by Wimmer in his letter to Abbot Utto Lang was vigorous and full of hope for the future. So many monks had joined the community that the buildings were "always too small." The abbot was especially proud of the seminary where there were "twenty-three philosophers and theologians and fifteen good, diligent seminarians who received the habit." Young America, he said, had eagerly furnished its quota of diocesan priests educated at St. Vincent for the German immigrants. "From New York to St. Louis, from Richmond to Canada, in two years forty priests have been ordained." Nor did the community at St. Vincent neglect its charitable duty to the poor of the immediate vicinity. In what was the beginning of a tradition that lasted up through the early decades of the twentieth century the monks daily fed and cared for "two, three, four, five beggars and hungry persons. They leave a 'May God reward you' or a bed full of lice. Some come here sick and stay until well; one cannot get rid of them."[13]

Abbot Boniface wrote his exuberant letter to Abbot Utto Lang shortly after his return from Minnesota. Father Demetrius and his small band of pioneer missionaries had settled near the village of St. Cloud, Minnesota, some seventy miles northwest of St. Paul, not long after being received into the diocese by Bishop Cretin, and the abbot visited them for the first time less than six months later. He reached the St. Cloud Priory early in the morning of October 23, surprising the monks by joining them during their recitation of matins. Wimmer brought with him six more missionaries for the community. The newly ordained Father Alexius Rötzer was among this second group of Minnesota Benedictines, as were Frater Paul Stenger, a cleric from St. Vincent, and four lay brothers: Wolfgang Beck, Vincent Hörmann, Roman Veitl, and Veremund Erhard. With these recruits the Minnesota Benedictines now numbered eleven, and the future of the St. Cloud foundation seemed secure.[14]

In the meantime, in Kansas, Father Peter Henry Lemke had been purchasing land and dreaming of a Benedictine community there. Wimmer had rescinded the order for him to return to St. Vincent when it became evident that Lemke would be more of a burden in the Pennsylvania monastery than a boon, and he gave the independent-minded priest permission to continue his work among the German settlers at Doniphan, Kansas. But being neither a particularly stable man nor a very wise administrator, Lemke soon found himself in financial straits. Not long after arriving in Kansas, he had purchased land with the hope of establishing a monastery in the territory, but unable to pay the debts he had accumulated, he appealed to Wimmer for help. Although Abbot Boniface sent what material assistance he could, some of the money forwarded to Lemke was apparently stolen in the mail. The old missionary was left in dire circumstances, and to keep alive he was forced to borrow one hundred dollars from the post-master-storekeeper in Doniphan.[15]

In November 1856 Wimmer wrote the Ludwig Missionsverein that the vicar apostolic of Kansas, Bishop John Baptist Miége, S.J., had requested priests from St. Vincent. "This territory is as far from St. Vincent as Minnesota, but Kansas is not as healthy. God will show us the way."[16] Bishop Miége, encouraged by Lemke to make his petition, responded enthusiastically to the idea of establishing a Benedictine monastery in the Kansas Territory. Wimmer answered, however, that though he would be able to send two monks to Kansas, one stipulation he would have to make was that they not form a community with Lemke. The old monk had proven himself fractious and burdensome to live with in Carrolltown, and his quixotic trip to Kansas was evidence, as far as the abbot was concerned, of a certain instability of character. Miége could have the missionaries, therefore, only if he assured Wimmer that they would not be tainted by a forced association with Lemke. The bishop responded that he would be happy to receive the two monks whom Wimmer offered and would see that "the newcomers are not to live with Father Lemke. I will find a suitable place for them, where I hope, they will be able to do a great deal of good."[17]

On April 9, 1857, the two monks, Father Augustine Wirth and Frater Casimir Seitz, a cleric who had recently completed studies for the priesthood, arrived in Leavenworth, Kansas. A week later Bishop Miége ordained Seitz to the priesthood, and from Leavenworth the two Benedictines went to Doniphan where the bishop had provided land for a monastery. There they began to live a quasi-monastic life marked principally by missionary labors among the German settlers. Father Peter Lemke, forbidden by Abbot Boniface to take up residence with his two confreres, settled down as best he could in Bendena, Kansas, where he remained until the following November.[18]

Lemke's unauthorized activities in Kansas were clearly the cause, though an indirect one, of Wimmer's sending missionaries there in 1857 and eventually establishing a Benedictine monastery in Atchison. The old monk's wanderlust had carried him to a place desperately in need of priests, and his presence in Kansas led Bishop Miége to petition Abbot Boniface for missionaries. In 1882 Wimmer wrote that "Father Henry Lemke played a trick in 1856 by running away from Carrolltown to Kansas (Doniphan) as a fugitive—and this became the cause for the foundation of our abbey there!"[19]

Just as Lemke had preceded Wimmer to western Pennsylvania, so he went to Kansas before the officially sanctioned Benedictine mission. And just as his journey to Bavaria in 1845, when he met Wimmer and suggested Pennsylvania as the ideal place for a Benedictine monastery, had been to a certain extent a venture executed independently of his ordinary, Bishop Michael O'Connor of Pittsburgh, so now his adventure in Kansas was quite independent of any formal commission from Abbot Boniface. This charming consistency in Lemke's extraordinary missionary career might be attributed as much to zeal as to eccentricity. In any event, the trails that he blazed were never far from the more enduring paths of the men who came behind him. In 1856 Father Henry returned to Carrolltown, and in 1858 he went to Europe once more. There he collected money for the missions and published a biography of Prince Demetrius Gallitzen, the famous missionary of western Pennsylvania with whom he had served in his youth. In 1861 he returned to America and took up residence as pastor in Elizabeth, New Jersey. Seventeen years later he retired to Carrolltown, where he wrote his memoirs and died on November 29, 1882, at the age of eighty-six.

While the Benedictine missionaries in Minnesota and Kansas struggled to establish more firmly the newest foundations in the West, Abbot Boniface corresponded with several bishops, including John Nepomucene Neumann, C.Ss.R., of Philadelphia and James Roosevelt Bayley of Newark, New Jersey, about the foundation of monasteries in the East. As early as 1847 Wimmer had written of the advantages a monastery in the East would have for the order. It would put the Benedictines in closer contact with New York and Philadelphia, he said, and would make communications with Europe easier. "[Newark] could be a very fine monastery, a hospice for confreres from overseas, and would be very well situated for an academy. By steamer it is a half-hour from New York and five hours from Philadelphia, where more than 30,000 Germans live; Newark itself has more than 25,000."[20]

Father Nicholas Balleis, the Benedictine missionary from Salzburg, Austria, who had greeted Father Boniface and his group when they arrived in New York in 1846, offered to turn St. Mary's German parish in Newark over to Wimmer in 1847, but even after considering the advantages of a parish on the East Coast, Father Boniface was reluctant to accept the offer since Newark was so far removed from his base of operations in western Pennsylvania. Nevertheless in 1849, after repeated requests from Balleis, he sent Father Placidus Döttl from St. Vincent to assist at St. Mary's. Döttl, one of the four priesthood candidates who accompanied Wimmer to America in 1846, had been ordained in April. He arrived in Newark in May and remained there for six months. In November 1849 Wimmer recalled him to St. Vincent to replace Father Peter Lechner as prior. Later Wimmer sent Father Charles Geyerstanger, another of the original band of missionaries, to assist Balleis. Geyerstanger went to Newark in 1852 and worked in St. Mary's Parish until February 1855.[21]

Negotiations between Father Boniface and Father Nicholas about the possibility of Wimmer taking over St. Mary's Parish continued during the next several years, but even though Wimmer kept in close contact with his Austrian confrere, he repeatedly refused to assume the pastorship, though he did allow Balleis to put some of the Newark property in his name. Then on September 4, 1854, an anti-Catholic riot erupted in Newark, in the course of which St. Mary's Church was ransacked. Balleis, who had been encountering problems even among his own parishioners, with whom he was generally unpopular, became extremely discouraged, and the following week Wimmer went to Newark to console him. While there, he received a request from Bishop Bayley to take over the parish, and on September 12, 1854, he replied that he was "not only indifferent as to who may get charge of this place here, but that I can have no reasonable desire whatever to be charged with it, so much the less as it would take many thousands of dollars to make here an establishment of our order, to get a new Church, a new Graveyard, a Sisterhood for the girls."

Wimmer's reluctance to take over the parish in Newark was based on two principal reasons. First, he did not want to incur the jealousy and antipathy of secular priests who he had heard opposed turning the parish over to a religious order. An even more compelling reason for refusing the benefice, however, was the urban location of the parish. Wimmer believed that the Benedictines' proper ambience was in rural districts, far from the bustle, distractions, and "temptation" of cities. "In the country, far from the noise of cities, we lead a happy life," he wrote;

and if we are not doing first rate we are doing at least well, or if this won't express well in English my mind, if we do not very much for the honor and glory of God, we are doing at least a good deal of it through the grace of God, who is often strong in the weak; how we would do in a city, I do not know; for a short while maybe well enough, after a while maybe bad enough, just in proportion to the exactitude with which we observe our holy rule; but there is the fear, the fear that we might lose the simplicity of our manner, the poverty in our diet, the spirit of self denial and the pure intention in our efforts. . . .

[T]he material advantage that might result from the acceptance can come to no consideration with the spiritual disadvantage that might eventually result from it. I have been offered by several Bishops the finest congregations several times; and I was often blamed by my own folks for neglect of care for the temporal prosperity of our order, when I refused to accept them; but I might say, I became rich when I was anxious to avoid it. We now own 3,600 acres of land of a value short of $100,000, and according to circumstances, far more. Not accounting 20 Novices, I am supporting more than 60 young fellows, most of whom will be priests [one day]; and though they may say the contrary, I dare assert, that for classical learning—latin and greek—there is no establishment in this country where more is being done than here. And in Theology, I should hope we are hardly inferior to other institutions.

Now, Dear Bishop, all this would be impossible in a city to be done; the country, the soil, the industry of the lay brothers, the zeal and frugality of the young priests, and above all the blessing of Almighty God never separated from religious poverty is doing it. Will you blame me then, if in sight of such facts, I am not desirous of a congregation in a city. . . ?[22]

Wimmer had also learned that the bishop entertained a low opinion of Benedictine educational standards. The student of Görres and Döllinger was sufficiently annoyed by the report to spend a considerable portion of his letter refuting what he heard was the bishop's view. "You were told," he said to Bayley, "that the Benedictines were poor men in learning. I trust we know as much as priests in general know." He outlined the educational background of several of his priests at St. Vincent, and as if that were not impressive enough, he interrupted the flow of his English to insert particulars of that background in Latin. "The Benedictines never have been intrusive, never have been aggressive," he continued. "In our forest, on our farms we lead a happy life in retirement from the world and the dangers of the world and doing good as much as we can. Why should we hurry into cities to draw upon us the wrath and hatred of others. . . ?"[23]

Bayley replied less than two weeks later, denying that he had ever thought of the Benedictines as men "poor in learning." "I have always supposed that it was just the opposite of this. At any rate, I am satisfied that they have enough learning for my purpose. . . ." The bishop said that he was of the opinion that Wimmer "would find Newark a very eligible place for founding a house. There are a very large number of German Catholics in the city already—many of these very well disposed, and I believe, that if they were properly managed, they would form a very large and zealous congregation." Moreover, "the proximity of Newark to the City of New York would also be advantageous to you in many respects."[24]

Still Wimmer was not inclined to accept the bishop's offer, preferring that the Benedictines focus their pastoral work in rural areas rather than cities. In February 1855 he was off to Rome to argue St. Vincent's case for elevation to abbatial rank. When he returned the following December, the community of St. Vincent was an abbey and he had been appointed its first abbot. Father Nicholas Balleis, after handing over the deed of St. Mary's Church to the bishop of Newark in the early weeks of 1855, had gone to work in Elizabeth, New Jersey. Bishop Bayley gave care of the parish to Father William Hasslinger, C.Ss.R., but Hasslinger, who was vicar general for all German Catholics in the diocese, remained in Newark only until April 1857. When he was obliged to leave suddenly for Europe, Bishop Bayley in desperation petitioned Abbot Boniface for monks once again, and on account of Bayley's great and sudden need, the abbot dispatched Father Valentine Felder to New Jersey.[25]

On April 17, 1857, Father Valentine presented himself to Bishop Bayley, who immediately appointed him pastor of St. Mary's Church with charge of the six thousand German Catholics in the city. Early in May the abbot himself came to Newark, bringing with him two more monks for the foundation, Frater Eberhard Gahr, a cleric ready for ordination, and Brother Luke Zeume, who was to serve as cook for the small community. On May 17 Gahr was ordained by Bishop Bayley, and two days later Father Valentine wrote Abbot Boniface that all was going well. The Benedictines had purchased three houses adjacent to the parish property, and Felder said he was making one of them ready for the Benedictine sisters expected in Newark in about a month.[26] But less than two weeks later tragedy struck the incipient Newark priory.

On May 28 Father Valentine went to New York City to speak with a contractor about the construction of a new parish church at St. Mary's. Later he visited a priest in the city, and shortly after leaving his companion he was struck down in the street by a trolley car. A police officer had the injured priest carried to a nearby police station where he soon died. The officer reported the death to the New York Chancery, but since Father Valentine had been carrying no identification, twenty-four hours elapsed before Bishop Bayley was notified of the accident. On May 29 he telegraphed Abbot Boniface informing him of the tragedy and recorded in his official register, "Valentine Felder killed almost instantly on Thursday evening between eight and nine o'clock by a City Rail Road car. He was a most amiable, intelligent priest and had already endeared himself to all of us. I celebrated Pontiff. Mass and spoke. Funeral largely attended and his death excited much regret."[27]

The shock of the twenty-seven-year-old Felder's death reverberated back at St. Vincent. He was the ninth of Wimmer's monks to die since the establishment of the Benedictine Order in the United States eleven years earlier, and Abbot Boniface wrote Bishop Bayley that "struck with astonishment as I was at the sad and sudden news, I did not know what to do at first." He decided against going to Newark, however, and opted instead to "go to St. Marys, Elk Co., to detach the Prior of the place, F. Rupert Seidenbusch, to New-Ark. . . . This evening I go to St. Marys. I have to travel 115 miles in a buggy; Thursday evening I'll be there; F. Rupert will leave on Friday if possible . . . and will be on Sunday next in New-Ark."[28]

Father Rupert Seidenbusch was a twenty-seven-year-old native of Munich whom Wimmer described as "superior in ability and intelligence." He had entered the monastery at St. Vincent in January 1851 and was ordained to the priesthood less than three years later. His first assignment after ordination was to the priory in St. Marys, where Wimmer appointed him pastor of the congregation under the prior of the community, Father Benedict Haindl. When Father Benedict was recalled to the motherhouse in 1856 to become claustral prior, Wimmer named Father Rupert conventual prior of the monastery at

St. Marys. He was a talented young priest in whom Abbot Boniface placed much confidence, and his assignment as pastor in Newark indicates the high regard and hopes Wimmer had for the small community in New Jersey.

Father Rupert arrived in Newark on January 11, 1858. His first job was to oversee and complete construction of the parish church begun by Father Valentine. He was instrumental in acquiring more property for the order in Newark, and in July 1858 he introduced Benedictine sisters from St. Marys, Pennsylvania, to the parochial school attached to the parish. He remained in New Jersey until 1862 when he became prior of St. Peter's Priory in Butler, Pennsylvania. In 1863 Wimmer chose him to be claustral prior at St. Vincent. In 1866 he was elected first abbot of the Minnesota Benedictine community and in 1875 became bishop of the vicariate of northern Minnesota.[29]

In the spring of 1858 Wimmer again visited Newark, and in August he wrote King Ludwig I that he was pleased with the progress made by the monks in New Jersey. Contrasting the challenges of founding monasteries in America, where the government's consent was not needed nor its financial support available, with the challenges of founding them in Bavaria, he said, "in this country, when the bishops give their consent, we have full liberty to found monasteries, but in most cases we must furnish everything for them. This gives a special delight to undertake something, particularly when the aim is a noble one."[30]

Meanwhile, the missionary work of the monks in Pennsylvania steadily continued to expand elsewhere under the careful husbandry of the abbot of St. Vincent. In April 1857 Wimmer sent two more priests, Prior Benedict Haindl and Father Clement Staub, to the Minnesota foundation. Within the next six months he assigned three more brothers from St. Vincent to the St. Cloud Priory, and in October Wimmer made his second trip to Minnesota. He was delighted with the work his monks were doing there. They had already established several parishes, and when Father Demetrius di Marogna asked to be relieved of his duties as superior in St. Cloud to become pastor of the one in St. Paul, Wimmer agreed, appointing Father Cornelius Wittmann to replace him as prior. After making a visitation at the newly established convent of Benedictine nuns in St. Cloud, he left Minnesota at the end of October and traveled to Kansas.

Bishop Rupert Seidenbusch (1830–1895). After serving
as prior in Newark and at Saint Vincent, Seidenbusch
became the first abbot of St. John's Abbey, Collegeville,
Minnesota (1866–1875), and later bishop and vicar
apostolic of northern Minnesota (1875–1888). (ASVA)

From the beginning the abbot was less enthusiastic about the
foundation in Kansas than about the one in Minnesota. While he
sent several contingents of reinforcements to the priory in St. Cloud,
he consistently refused to supply the community in Doniphan with
monks from St. Vincent. In June 1857 Father Casimir Seitz wrote him
objecting to his "outspoken unfriendly attitude" toward the Kansas
community. Prior Augustine Wirth was even more specific in his objections to Wimmer's laissez faire attitude toward the monastery in
Doniphan. He said he felt the abbot was treating him "like a step
child." Wimmer had refused to send a brother to cook for the monks,
telling them that they must "help themselves." Prior Augustine wrote:

"You have done nothing more than is right for Minnesota, but nothing at all for Kansas. Minnesota got more than $2,000 from St. Vincent, Kansas not a copper. Minnesota has received five brothers, and you don't know whence to take one for Kansas. You are greatly mistaken about Kansas. I wish you could see it soon, and if you don't like it, I am willing to go back with you."[31]

While Wimmer had already made two trips to St. Cloud, he had not yet visited the monks in Doniphan, so when he announced that he would travel from Minnesota to make a visitation at his most neglected mission, both hopes and apprehension were high in the small Kansas community. The journey was not a pleasant one. Wimmer wrote King Ludwig that the trip down the Missouri River was "unattractive" and "depressing." It compared unfavorably with his journeys to Minnesota, he said, which were always pleasant and comfortable. Once he reached Kansas, he found few things to please him despite the warm welcome he received. He arrived in Leavenworth on November 2, 1857, and sought out Bishop Miége, who provided him with food and lodging for the night. Next day he left Leavenworth for Doniphan. He admitted that the scenery around the priory was not unattractive, despite the flatness of the country, which he complained of. He did little to conceal his aversion to Kansas. The soil was certainly fertile, though he considered it "unhealthful," and he complained about the prevalence of poisonous snakes in the area where the monks had settled. He informed King Ludwig that Father Casimir had recently discovered and killed a rattlesnake in the house where the monks slept.[32]

Although his visit to Kansas did not cause him to abandon the venture there, as the monks had feared, Wimmer continued to question the viability of a community in that territory. While his trip to Minnesota had lasted several weeks, he remained only four days with his confreres at the priory in Doniphan. When he left them on November 6, Fathers Augustine and Casimir were no more convinced of Wimmer's interest in them and their community than before his visit, even though before departing he promised them support and encouraged them to keep up the good fight.

Some months later, after discussing the distant foundations with the chapter at St. Vincent, Wimmer wrote to the directors of the Ludwig Missionsverein about the relative merits of Kansas and Minnesota:

We had a question of deciding which of the two territories, Minnesota or Kansas, should have precedence, considering climate, politics, ethnics, and religion, and which was more suitable for a larger Benedictine foundation, and where the stream of immigration, more or less, demanded our attention, our special spiritual care and help. The result was that in many respects Minnesota was preferred. At present, at least, we cannot plan on a monastery in Kansas supported by farming because that state is lacking in wood and water. However, the priests and one brother had already taken claims, amounting to 480 acres of land and had paid for these; but in the town [Doniphan] the monks were given twelve beautiful building sites, which were enclosed by four streets; since then the town council offered Prior Augustine five acres of land in the town, provided he would build a college there. Since Kansas and Minnesota are equally distant from St. Vincent and are also very far apart from each other, and because Benedictines are needed in both places, a beginning has to be made as soon as possible in one or the other, in order to provide a sufficient number of missionaries within a short time. There is no doubt that both of the foundations, if God's blessing rests on them, will be of great importance to the Church. Father Augustine has manifested so much knowledge and prudence in the founding of the priory in Doniphan, that the young plant promises to grow and flourish under his direction.[33]

Wimmer returned to St. Vincent via St. Louis, arriving at the abbey during the third week of November 1857. Father Amandus Kramer, O.S.B., whom the abbot had appointed prior to replace Father Benedict Haindl, reported that all had remained quiet at the motherhouse since he had left in October. After six weeks on the road, the abbot settled down once again to directing affairs at the monastery and its priories in Pennsylvania.

From St. Vincent Wimmer wrote Abbot Utto Lang that Father Augustine was doing "wonderful work in Kansas. . . . He is busy already erecting a seminary and building several churches." The abbot reported to his Bavarian confrere that the Minnesota Benedictines were encountering difficulties with establishing legal rights to the property they had purchased, and that while attending the Eighth Provincial Council of Baltimore in May he had visited the Government Land Office in Washington to see if he could straighten out the problem. In the meantime he intimated that a sizable donation from Munich would greatly ease the difficulties in Minnesota. He sought no assistance from Bavaria for Kansas.[34]

Wimmer reported that five priests and one deacon had been ordained at St. Vincent on May 29, 1858, and that he had just named Father Peter Baunach, a forty-three-year-old native of Bavaria and a former Redemptorist who had recently pronounced vows as a Benedictine, as novice master. The community of St. Vincent, he said, was strictly observing the statutes of the Bavarian Congregation with one exception: "We do not enjoy beer or wine." During the spring and autumn harvests the novices worked in the fields "and this to their enjoyment. The whole *Cursus Marianus* is part of their daily prayers, and many times the *Via Crucis* is added. They make their meditations with great diligence, and the master of novices often meditates aloud, not from a book but *ex corde*. From time to time one of the novices himself must meditate alone before the others. . . . It gives me great pleasure." Wimmer noted that three novices had recently pronounced temporary vows and that six scholastics had followed them into the novitiate. "I would like to have many more, but the secular students divert many of them because they are always ordained earlier and get good positions without delay—a great temptation for hungry scholars." The abbot added that he was well satisfied with those who decided to enter the monastery. Intellectually they were "far superior to those coming from outside."

Wimmer suggested to his confrere at Metten that he begin at once to establish daughterhouses in missionary countries. "America," he said, "is the turning point in the history of the world. . . . Our order has to blossom once more." He urged Lang to continue subjecting the future professors for the monastic school at Metten to rigorous examinations. All of them would not pass, of course, but there would still be plenty of work for those who failed.

In the missions the Jesuits and Redemptorists have caused quite a sensation in the field of science. But there is no need for them any more. The present generation is not suffering so much from ignorance and heresies, but through atheism and the neglect of the means to their own salvation thousands upon thousands are perishing. The preacher of repentance is necessary—he who awakens men from spiritual lethargy. Two or three practical preachers can do more than twenty professors with their pedantic knowledge. And another point: If our order would dedicate itself more to the interior life, to meditation and contemplation in the monasteries, and to the conversion of people in the outside world, there would be less danger of relaxation of discipline. We shall never do anything outstanding without action in the mission field.

The abbot of St. Vincent suggested to his counterpart at Metten that no matter what he decided to do about the rigorous examination of his professors, he should make every attempt

to abolish the present system of education. That is, we must turn from a desire to know everything to a deep and penetrating scholarship. This means that the priest, like the doctor, must know his Latin insofar as his profession demands, but he must also have sufficient knowledge of [other aspects of] his calling. Our greatest men here cannot even read Latin. I do not sanction this, but neither do I sanction those who have enough trouble learning Latin satisfactorily, wasting time on Greek. . . .

It was Wimmer the pragmatist speaking. Traditional doctrines of education were, in his opinion, out of date, and he urged a more practical approach to learning at Metten just as he had instituted at St. Vincent. His monks were being trained for the missions, for the active life that characterized the American society all around them. If one or two happened to turn out to be real scholars, that was certainly commendable and would doubtless be very advantageous for the community as well. But Wimmer's monks were to be first and foremost teachers and missionaries, and anything beyond what was necessary to train them for this calling was superfluous.[35]

Wimmer's tenure of office as abbot of St. Vincent was to expire on September 17, 1858, and on the following day he planned to have an election of a new abbot "unless Rome sets another date." He admitted that he did not know whether or not he would be reelected. There were forty-eight members of the community eligible to vote, forty-three priests and five subdeacons, and Wimmer wrote that if he had his way, they would choose someone other than himself: "I want to rest, to be unburdened by the business and responsibility which now lie on my shoulders, and I think a young abbot would not like to see me in the monastery. For this reason I would change my living quarters to a priory, or would start again somewhere in the West, or put new life into something already begun, such as in Minnesota which appeals to me especially." Nevertheless, if he were reelected, Abbot Boniface said that he would make

every effort to have one or two new abbeys established by elevating one or the other priory. Otherwise, the work and the worry about so many places, notwithstanding my robust health, would kill me. What is worse, I am not able to look after all these places as I should. If the proverb "Pull, horse, pull" still remains valid, it is also true that the horse is getting old. It is not so lively any more; generally its work is slowing down and becoming sluggish; its eyesight is diminishing; its fresh memory is gone; and it has already had a slight attack of the venerable *morositas senilis.*[36]

Wimmer's drive, pragmatism, and zeal for the missions continued to alienate some of the monks at St. Vincent. There were those who thought that he had moved too fast, that the expansion of the order westward had been precipitous, and that the large debts assumed through land purchase, as well as the abbot's tendency to emphasize the active above the contemplative in monastic life, militated against him as a candidate for the lifetime abbacy of St. Vincent. But if Wimmer had serious concerns about what was developing into an opposition movement at St. Vincent to his active missionary policies, he did not specifically mention them in any of his letters, nor did he let them prevent him from forging ahead with his projects.

More disturbing to him was the opposition to his policies that had begun to emerge in Europe. Father Joseph Müller wrote that Archbishop Scherr of Munich was

not pleased with your undertakings. You are starting too many missions and burdening yourself with too many debts. Before founding new missions, consolidate what you have. If you should not be elected abbot (and there are quite a few who oppose you), who shall bring your plans to fruition? You have accomplished in twelve years as much as other men have in fifty. Your policy, moreover, will ultimately prove detrimental since you always send your best men to the dependent priories.[37]

Wimmer responded unhesitatingly and firmly that the fulfillment of his vision to serve the immigrants, educate priests, and spread the Benedictine Order farther and farther afield would brook no delay. If he were to succeed in what he had set out to do, he would have to continue at the same pace he had maintained up until now. If anything, he must do more: "I do not fear to answer the criticism that I undertake too much, or take on new enterprises too quickly. I always think I am doing altogether too little; I am sorry that the erection of new buildings is proceeding so slowly, as is also the cultivation of the land and the formation of the young, of whom some will run away again, after we have fed and clothed them."[38]

In April 1858 Wimmer wrote Alexander Cardinal Barnabo, the new prefect of the Sacred Congregation for the Propagation of the Faith, announcing his intention to hold an abbatial election when his term of office expired in September. After outlining the progress of the abbey during the previous three years, he requested information concerning procedures for the forthcoming election.[39] As his July letter to Lang shows, it is clear that Wimmer anticipated the possibility of losing the election. In June he had written Father Müller that if he were not chosen he would go west. He also wrote King Ludwig: "We will have our next general chapter in September. At that time an abbot will be elected to govern St. Vincent. It is true, I am abbot for life, but am appointed to rule St. Vincent for only three years. . . . Naturally, I do not know if I will be elected, and I am not sure whether I will accept or refuse the position."[40]

In August Wimmer sent out announcements of the September meeting to all the capitulars of the abbey, but he had still heard nothing from Rome concerning the election, nor had he received answers to the procedural questions he had submitted to the Propaganda in April. On August 16 he wrote the Roman procurator of the American Cassinese Congregation, Abbot Angelo Pescetelli, that "our election will soon be held. . . . I would prefer that Fathers Demetrius di Marogna or Benedict Haindl be chosen for the abbatial dignity. Such a change would allow me to go to Minnesota where I have good friends and where we will be able to build another monastery."[41]

Two weeks later Pescetelli responded that the election would have to be postponed because only recently did

the secretary of the Sacred Congregation give me your letter of April 28 containing queries about the chapter to be held on September 17. The answers cannot possibly reach you before that date. I do not know whether or not the Sacred Congregation has already informed you about the prolonging of your faculties, but I am of the opinion that they will continue until you receive new instructions. You made your application in good time, and it is generally understood in such cases that the faculties last as long as the question is under consideration. For your peace of mind, however, I shall procure a provisional letter, if one has not already been sent. Meanwhile I shall present your case in such a way that the vote will be favorable to you. Who could take your place in carrying out your vast enterprise?[42]

Abbot Angelo's letter reached Wimmer only after most of the capitulars had arrived at St. Vincent for the election. On September 10 a retreat began at the abbey conducted by the renowned Jesuit missionary Father Francis Xavier Weninger, and on September 17 the general chapter was convened. Wimmer read Pescetelli's August 30th letter to the monks, who were disappointed that it suggested that the purpose for which they were assembled had not been approved by the Holy See. But the capitulars were eager to continue with the business before them, and they asked Wimmer "almost unanimously" not to delay the election. Many of them had traveled great distances, some from as far away as Minnesota, to be at the meeting, and the time and expense of their journeys would be wasted were they forced to return home without having chosen a permanent abbot.

The community voted, therefore, to hold the election. Nine of the priests had been forced to remain at their posts in the missions, but four of the absent capitulars chose to vote by proxy. The other five had failed to appoint procurators. Forty-three monks, of whom thirty-nine were in attendance, where therefore eligible to cast votes when the election began.

Bishop Michael O'Connor of Pittsburgh came out to the abbey for the event. Wimmer invited him to supervise the election, but he declined, suggesting that Abbot Boniface himself, together with two or three other responsible monks, direct the procedures. Accordingly, at eight o'clock in the morning of September 18, Wimmer announced that balloting would begin. Mass was celebrated and the traditional prayers to the Holy Spirit said. The monks chose Father Peter Henry Lemke, the oldest member of the community, along with Fathers Benedict Haindl of Minnesota and Augustine Wirth of Kansas, the priors of the abbey's two major dependent priories, to assist Wimmer as tellers.

The election proceeded quickly. The first ballot was cast and the tellers counted the votes. Father Edward Hipelius, secretary to the chapter, then announced the results. One of the forty-three votes was disqualified because it had been sent through the mail by a monk in the missions and opened before the balloting had begun. Forty-two votes therefore qualified, and of these, Father Utto Huber, prior of St. Peter's Priory in Butler, received two; Father Benedict Haindl, prior in Minnesota, one, and Wimmer, thirty-nine. The monks greeted the announcement with cheers and applause. Bishop O'Connor warmly congratulated the abbot whom he had once described as a thorn in his side.

The outcome was a decisive victory for Abbot Boniface who had feared that most of his monks had grown tired of his rule. Despite dissatisfaction among many of the younger men with his missionary activity, virtually everyone agreed that Wimmer was the most qualified person to lead the community. The abbot accepted the vote of confidence from his confreres with grace and humility and promised them that he would take up the responsibilities and burdens of office with renewed zeal and enthusiasm. He made a short acceptance speech, and when he had finished, the entire community went to the abbey church for Benediction of the Most Blessed Sacrament and the chanting of the Te Deum.[43]

The following day the monks celebrated the election with a pontifical high mass and a festive dinner, and two days later the chapter reconvened. All but twenty-seven of the monks had returned to their respective missions and priories, and the remaining capitulars elected Fathers Utto Huber and Leo Rau as assistants to the president for the remainder of the general chapter. The chapter's first order of business was the establishment of independent priories. The abbot-president proposed that the community at St. Cloud in Minnesota be elevated to the rank of canonical priory. The monks discussed the matter at length and then voted. With the exception of two, all favored the elevation of St. Cloud to independent status. Next Wimmer proposed the question of independence for the priory in Kansas. The vote on this issue had the same results as the Minnesota ballot: twenty-five in favor, two opposed. Wimmer then opened discussion on the question of whether to raise the priory in St. Marys, Pennsylvania, to independent status. He himself was not in favor of such an action, but he permitted a lengthy discussion during which several monks observed that an independent monastery so close to the mother abbey as St. Marys was to St. Vincent would drain vocations and material resources from St. Vincent. When the vote was finally taken, Father Edward Hipelius informed the capitulars that only two monks favored independence for the priory in St. Marys. Twenty-five were opposed.

With the issue of the independent priories settled, the capitulars then turned to the question of who would be the superiors in Minnesota and Kansas. Names were proposed for a prior in Minnesota, and on the second ballot sixteen out of twenty-seven votes were cast for Father Benedict Haindl, giving him the absolute majority necessary for election. On the next ballot Father Augustine Wirth was re-confirmed as prior in Kansas by a vote of twenty-four to three. At Wimmer's suggestion the capitulars voted to limit the terms of both Haindl and Wirth to three years and to declare that in the event of a vacancy in either place before the expiration of that term the abbot of St. Vincent would appoint a successor.

The general chapter continued through the following day, and following a practice of the old Bavarian Congregation, the monks passed a resolution to establish a common novitiate and house of studies at St. Vincent for the clerics of the American Cassinese Congregation. The capitulars also agreed that, while the Minnesota and Kansas priories would be independent in their administration, the monks assigned to them would continue to have their stability attached to the mother abbey until arrangements could be made to efficiently distribute the monks throughout the independent houses of the congregation. Finally the chapter confirmed guidelines for the spiritual life of the American Cassinese monks, passed legislation on the structure of the divine office to be followed in the various communities, and directed that a unified observance be kept in all houses of the congregation in accord with the Rule of St. Benedict and the statutes of the Bavarian Congregation. The meeting ended on September 21 with a festive celebration.[44]

Even before the chapter ended Wimmer had written Cardinal Barnabo of the Propaganda Fide giving an account of the abbatial election. He asked that the election be confirmed but said that "if these transactions should in any way be considered doubtful or illegal, I will gladly resign the office which I never sought."[45] Wimmer's failure to wait until the questions he posed to the Propaganda in April had been answered, as well as his initiative in calling an abbatial election without the approval of the Sacred Congregation, raised doubts in his own mind if not about the validity of the outcome, at least about the response the cardinals of the Propaganda would have to the procedures. He had acted, however, in good faith. The Roman decree of 1855 instructed him to call an election for a lifetime abbot in three years, and this is what he had done. Still, the letter from his Roman procurator, Abbot Angelo Pescetelli, which he received after the election machinery began to move, had been explicit. He was to wait until the questions submitted to the Propaganda Fide in April had been answered.

If Abbot Boniface doubted the legality of the election, his correspondence in the months that followed indicates nevertheless that he felt more secure than ever in his position as abbot of St. Vincent. In November he wrote his friend Abbot Utto Lang that "if I were as timid as the directors [of the Ludwig Missionsverein] wish me to be, I would now have no new foundations nor the old one so firmly established. Our motto must be 'Forward, always forward. Long live the American Benedictines. May they, and all Benedictines, flourish and increase.'"[46] And in December he wrote the directors of the Ludwig Missionsverein that "the election opens a new era in the history of St. Vincent. The monastery is now a regularly exempt abbey; for the first time the Chapter has exercised its right of choosing a superior. I must confess that after the election I took the crozier in my hands with greater confidence."[47] Wimmer also wrote King Ludwig that the election consoled him very much. It proved that the harmony of the monastery, which had been disturbed during his stay in Rome in 1855, prevailed once again among the younger monks. "It was with a sigh of relief that I learned they are satisfied with my administration and are willing to work with me as they have done so well in the past."[48]

Toward the end of November, however, Wimmer received the first intimations that the election had not pleased the cardinals of the Propaganda Fide. Cardinal Barnabo wrote that because the questions Abbot Boniface had referred to the Sacred Congregation in April had never been answered, "within a few days that business [of your recent election] will be put before the General Congregation."[49] Shortly afterward Abbot Angelo Pescetelli wrote that Cardinal Barnabo was of the opinion that "the election was irregular. I recommended your case as best I could, but the prefect immediately told me that he could not approve the acts of the chapter without first consulting the other cardinals." Pescetelli had learned that "instead of being confirmed for life, you are to be appointed for another term of three years. . . . Accept this humiliation with resignation and remember that you are doing too much good to please the old enemy, who will not allow you to go ahead without obstacles and without suffering."[50]

Several weeks later the official documents arrived from Rome. A decree from Propaganda, issued on December 20, 1858, confirmed all the transactions of the general chapter held at St. Vincent in September, but a letter from the prefect accompanying the decree chided

Wimmer for holding the election without the approval of Rome. Cardinal Barnabo said that the cardinals of the Sacred Congregation, "after mature deliberation, decided to petition the Holy Father to confirm your election for only three years."[51]

The two apparently contradictory documents caused consternation among the monks at St. Vincent. They considered themselves to have validly elected an abbot for life based upon the Roman decision of 1855, and indeed the Roman decree of December 20, 1858, which "validates and approves all that was transacted" at the general chapter of 1858 seemed to confirm that opinion. The letter of Cardinal Barnabo, however, indicated that all acts of the chapter had been approved *except* the election of Abbot Boniface, whom Rome had merely given another three-year mandate to rule the abbey. Wimmer wrote Pescetelli expressing his bewilderment. "Three years ago the cardinals appointed me abbot for life and the pope limited it to three years. Now the capitulars elect me for life and the cardinals limit it to three years." He said that this might be a sign from heaven that he should not be abbot at all.[52]

Pescetelli answered in April confirming that the abbatial election had been overturned and that Wimmer was indeed given only a three-year extension of his original appointment. He encouraged Abbot Boniface to submit to the decision with humility: "You must, like a sturdy oak, spread your roots deeper and deeper, extending your branches farther and farther."[53] But Wimmer was discouraged by the Roman decision, and in June he wrote Abbot Angelo that at the next abbatial election, scheduled for 1861, he was likely to withdraw as a candidate.[54] In the meantime, he would turn his energies and attention once again to the missions.

The missions were flourishing. In Pennsylvania the Benedictines counted one abbey, six dependent priories, and more than a dozen mission churches. In the summer of 1859 the community at the abbey numbered forty priests, over one hundred brothers, fourteen clerics preparing for ordination, fourteen novices newly entered in the order, and over one hundred students in the gymnasium and seminary. In addition to the fourteen Benedictine clerics, priesthood students from the dioceses of Pittsburgh, Erie, Philadelphia, New York, Baltimore, Milwaukee, and St. Louis studied in the seminary. Wimmer was very proud of the progress of his seminarians. He reported that "in the annual examinations *pro cura*, which all the young priests of the Pittsburgh Diocese must undergo, ours distinguished themselves very well. But I deserve no credit for this. I am merely the janitor. I only see to it that good [order is kept] and the weekly conferences are held."

Dependent priories existed in Carrolltown, St. Marys, Indiana, Butler, Bellefonte, and Erie. Wimmer hoped that some of these communities would eventually develop into independent self-sustaining monasteries, but because he realized that granting independence to any of them too soon would inevitably draw monastic candidates from St. Vincent and hamper the development of the motherhouse, he planned in the short term to maintain the Pennsylvania priories as dependencies of St. Vincent and concentrate on the creation of independent houses in other parts of the United States. As it turned out, none of these Pennsylvania communities ever achieved independent status. In the next century all would be downgraded to the rank of parish, but in 1859 Wimmer classified them as priories and in the long term hoped to establish them as independent monasteries.

Two priests, Fathers Charles Geyerstanger and Kilian Bernetzeder, and twelve brothers from St. Vincent staffed the community's oldest dependent priory in Carrolltown, where they served about four hundred families and attended the missions in St. Joseph, Glen Connell, and Summerhill. Wimmer admitted that in Carrolltown "we have done little with regard to building," but he noted that

we have a beautiful property near the city, with a good coal mine, and one and a half hours from there 800 acres of land with a beautiful new sawmill and a good dairy farm. It was a long time before the land produced anything. On the whole, agriculture here is not a profitable business because the work is very costly, the returns are not great, and the value of the product is slight. It will be quite a long time before [all] the uncultivated land is cleared. Our successors will, of course, do better at it, because they will succeed to all the buildings, equipment, livestock, and beautifully cultivated farms. Mere things, which we first had to create.

At the priory in St. Marys four priests (Prior Aegidius Christoph and Fathers Eberhard Gahr, Ignatius Treug, and Emmeran Bliemel) and thirteen brothers were assigned to serve "a fine, totally German, entirely Catholic congregation, a bulwark of our holy religion in the diocese of Erie, in fact in the whole state of Pennsylvania." Describing St. Marys to Abbot Rupert Leiss of Scheyern, and inviting him to visit, Wimmer wrote:

You will certainly like it, especially once you see the large, beautiful stone church with a 137-foot high steeple on which the gilt cross, from a gentle rise, so warmly comforts the much tried settlers. If we go to the church, we will see the ground for sixty feet excavated for a new building. This will be the [sisters'] convent and should be ready this year. The poor congregation built the church. I gave the timber for it. From Austria came $400, and my priests collected $700. There is still a debt of $1,100. I have to build the convent, for which His Majesty, King Ludwig, generously contributed 8,000 florins. (He also gave 3,000 florins for Newark.) It will be sixty feet long by forty-four feet and three stories high. . . . The church is 132 feet long by sixty-six feet and very lovely. . . . Now through a bit of shrubbery and we are in front of our house and not far from the present convent. Both look pleasant, but both are of wood. Everywhere, however, there is good enclosure, proper parlor, domestic chapel. The location is very fine and will be still nicer when we build our monastery on the edge of the hill, which rises like a terrace on the Elk Creek over our two mills, where the railroad passes. But this won't come about at once. We have there 900 acres of land, 600 in one piece, more than half of which is cultivated; it is of medium quality. The mill does the most there. It has cost much effort to bring it so far; but now it is such a joy that we do not regret the trouble, time, and money. . . . The railroad is now assured. Then it will also become a large city. I have endured out of love of the Blessed Virgin and for her honor.

The monks at the St. Marys Priory served a congregation of two thousand souls and attended Catholics in Emporium, Ridgeway, Kersey, Cooper's Settlement, Frenchville, Clearfield, Warren, and Williamsville, and also served the Irish railroad workers building the railway line north of the town.

At the priory in Indiana, site of the controversial and ultimately failed beer brewing business that had caused such disagreement between Wimmer and Bishop Michael O'Connor of Pittsburgh, there were two priests (Prior Alto Hörmann and Father Magnus Mayer) and several brothers who lived "in a large house with a small church and little income." Wimmer reported that "I had to keep paying for it until I bought a farm two hours from the city. It is a fair place. The priests also take care of Kittanning, likewise an important little town. It is only partially a stronghold of Catholics. They have increased significantly, but it is a blemish on our monastery [that there are not more Catholics there]. Perhaps things will improve." The monks at Indiana also served Catholic communities in Brockville, Mechanics-burg, Terrysville, Plum Creek, and Mahoning. "The town is impor-tant," Wimmer wrote, "but our congregation is small and poor, as is also the church, even though it is built of brick."

The least prosperous dependency in Pennsylvania was St. Peter's Priory in Butler, about forty miles northeast of Pittsburgh. Here three priests (Prior Utto Huber, the sickly Ulric Spöttl, and Joseph Billon) and two brothers were assigned to care for Catholics in Butler City, Donegal, and Great Western. "Neither church nor rectory belongs to us," Wimmer said. "I would be glad to give it up, but the bishop will not take it back."

St. John's Priory at Bellefonte in the diocese of Philadelphia was "situated romantically on a mountain at a huge spring which emerges from the limestone and operates many foundries. There too you will find a beautiful rectory and a really pretty stone church." In 1857 Bishop John Nepomucene Neumann, C.Ss.R., had invited the Bene-dictines to Bellefonte, and Wimmer had assigned two priests (Fathers Odilo Vandergrün and Louis Fink) together with several brothers there. From Bellefonte the monks attended missions in Snow Shoe, McVeytown, Lewiston, and Sinnemahoning.

The most recent priory had been established in Erie where Wim-mer sent Father Celestine Englbrecht and two brothers in July 1859 to take over St. Mary's Parish after receiving numerous requests from his friend, Bishop Josue Mary Young of Erie.

In addition to the dependent priories and their mission churches, monks from St. Vincent served Catholic congregations in other parts of western Pennsylvania, including those at St. Severin, Centreville, Saltsburg, Ligonier, Greensburg, Johnstown, and Altoona. By Octo-ber 1859, thirteen years after settling at St. Vincent, the Benedictines were established in all three Pennsylvania dioceses—Pittsburgh, Philadelphia, and Erie—attending to the spiritual needs of Catholic communities in the Pennsylvania counties of Westmoreland, Indi-ana, Armstrong, Butler, Erie, Cambria, Clearfield, Elk, and Centre.

Outside Pennsylvania monks from St. Vincent staffed dependent priories in Newark, New Jersey, and Covington, Kentucky. Prior Rupert Seidenbusch, together with two priests and three brothers, served the German congregation of St. Mary's in Newark. Eight

Benedictine sisters who had come to Newark from St. Marys, Pennsylvania, in 1857 taught in the parish school.[55] The monks lived

in a very beautiful location, with a view over the whole city and the bay. In the large new church, which cost $24,000, you will have almost nothing to find fault with except the poor glass figures in the sanctuary. Our residence is also beautiful and monastic. In the spacious garden there are enough grapevines to yield twenty-eight gallons of mass wine. Our eight sisters also have a pretty house there, but are getting a still better one. You must not be shocked by a debt of $28,000. There is so much paid off that it will be liquidated in seven to eight years.

As with St. Mary's, Newark, Wimmer hoped that St. Vincent's dependent priory in Covington, Kentucky, would one day become an independent abbey. In February 1858 he had responded to a call for assistance from Bishop George A. Carrell, S.J., of Covington by sending two priests, Fathers Roman Hell and Oswald Moosmüller, to establish a monastery and care for the German Catholic congregation. In the following year Wimmer sent two additional priests, Fathers Alphonse Heimler and Aemilian Wendel; a cleric, Frater Lambert Kettner; and three brothers to Covington.

Covington had two German Catholic congregations, an older one cared for by Father Kihr, a secular priest, and a newer one, St. Joseph's, that the bishop entrusted to the Benedictines. Wimmer reported that some years earlier the trustees of St. Joseph's "had purchased an entire square between four streets, on a site where streets for the expansion of the city were already laid out but small houses were still standing. On this location they built a rather handsome structure, eighty feet long, the ground floor of which they used as a church, the upper story as a school and residence for the priest."

The bishop turned this property over to the monks of St. Vincent who, within a year of arriving in Covington, built a new church on the site and opened a Latin day school for boys. In 1859 five Benedictine nuns from Erie arrived in Covington to take up duties as teachers in St. Joseph's parish school. In addition to St. Joseph's German parish, the Benedictines in Covington cared for four rural congregations outside the city, and Father Oswald, who had "discovered by chance in the ironworks at Ashland, between Kentucky and Virginia, a Catholic congregation of more than 100 families whom no priest had ever visited," traveled as far as the Virginia line to care for the

English-speaking Catholics there. "He had to take charge at once and visit them once a month, thus being absent usually for two weeks since the place is 150 miles away. Of course no school, no church, no cemetery were at hand. Hence everything had first to be obtained and taken there. Even the Catholics did not know that there were so many of them and had to be gradually organized into smaller congregations." Wimmer reported that Bishop Carrell was enthusiastic about the Benedictines' Latin school in Covington, which was needed "on the one hand to obtain candidates for the priesthood, and on the other hand, unfortunately, also for the money." The yearly tuition was $40.00.[56]

In July 1858 Wimmer sent two priests, Fathers Edmund Langenfelder and Francis Cannon, to Omaha, where the vicar apostolic of the Nebraska Territory, Bishop James M. O'Gorman, O.C.S.O., had asked the Benedictines to care for German and Irish settlers. These two priests were placed under the jurisdiction of Prior Augustine Wirth of Kansas, and by March 1859 they were also serving the spiritual needs of Catholic soldiers in the forts along the military road to Utah and even as far as Oregon.

Wimmer was proud of his monks and the work they were doing. He wrote: "My young priests so far give me much cause for comfort and contentment. At home and at their stations they work diligently; there are enough of them; they are zealous for monastic observance; they are loved and respected by the clergy and laity, and they love one another." Nevertheless he admitted to Abbot Rupert his concerns about the extent of St. Vincent's commitments and the strain they were putting on himself and on the abbey. "I am dim-witted for sending so many priests to the missions because now I have to do the work of several. But why should I tell all this to you? I don't want to complain much because it does no good, and in fact I have not much reason to complain. I am still always healthy and vigorous and can endure more than most of my confreres. I am always poor and penniless, but I still have credit, and this enables me to manage."[57]

News of the extraordinary range and success of the missionary activities of the St. Vincent Benedictines circulated throughout Europe and the American Church. At Metten word of the success of the community's *Projektenmacher* caused both astonishment and pride. In Munich readers of the annual reports of the Ludwig Missionsverein dug deeper into their pockets for florins to contribute to the community at St. Vincent. In Rome the cardinals of the Propaganda Fide studied developments in the American Cassinese Congregation and "after mature deliberation" declared themselves satisfied. In the United States requests for more priests to serve the immigrant population continued to pour into the abbey from bishops near and far.

The flood of European immigration to the United States in the 1850s created communities of German-speaking Catholics in many dioceses of the American Church, and bishops were hard pressed for German priests to care for them. To minister to these immigrants, of course, was the principal purpose of Wimmer's coming to America. Nevertheless, in 1859 he still did not have enough priests to supply all the bishops who requested them. Moreover, there were certain conditions he required without which he seldom considered sending missionaries to new places. He always demanded, for example, that the property on which the monks were to settle be turned over to the Benedictines unconditionally so that the monasteries he might establish would be under Benedictine rather than diocesan control. He also preferred to accept parishes and to establish monasteries in dioceses and vicariates on the frontier of the nation rather than in the older centers of settlement. It was therefore with a certain reluctance that he accepted such responsibilities as administration of St. Mary's in Newark. In 1859 Wimmer's thoughts turned mainly toward the West, though in some instances he offered temporary help to bishops in the East. Thus when Archbishop John Hughes of New York asked for a priest to take charge of the German parish in Rondout, New York, Wimmer sent Father Oswald Moosmüller on temporary assignment from St. Joseph's Priory in Covington, Kentucky. But less than a year later Abbot Boniface recalled Father Oswald, despite the protests of Archbishop Hughes, when an opportunity arose to take over a college in Sandwich, Ontario. Moosmüller and several monks from St. Vincent went to Canada to assume administration of Assumption College, but the St. Vincent Benedictines remained there for only a year.

Wimmer received requests from other eastern bishops as well. John Timon, C.M., bishop of Buffalo, asked for priests to take over the German parish in his see city; Bishop John Nepomucene Neumann of Philadelphia, after his success in obtaining Benedictines for the German Catholics of Bellefonte, asked for a priest to attend to the Germans of Bridesburg, Pennsylvania; and John McCloskey, bishop of Albany, wrote that he had a parish in Utica, New York, that he wanted Wimmer to staff. In each case the abbot declined the offer because he had decided to focus what resources he had in the West. Other requests, which either because of a lack of priests or the failure of bishops to meet the necessary conditions, the abbot was unable to fill, came from Thaddeus Amat, C.M., of Monterey-Los Angeles, Patrick N. Lynch of Charleston, South Carolina, Henry Damian Juncker of Alton, Illinois, and Clement Smyth, O.C.S.O., of Dubuque.

On the other hand, when Bishop John McGill of Richmond offered to turn over the German parish of St. Mary's to the Benedictines in 1860, Abbot Boniface accepted the place, sending Father Leonard Mayer to Richmond even while expressing reluctance "to have parishes in cities, especially when the parishes are classified as 'prosperous.'"[58] And in 1861 he sent Father Louis Fink to Chicago when Bishop James Duggan offered the German parish of St. Joseph's to the Benedictines of St. Vincent.[59] He regarded each of the parishes and missions he took charge of as a potential abbey and developed their resources with this goal in mind.

Not all the communities Wimmer established in the West were successful. The most notable example of failure was in Texas. Many of the German immigrants who came to America in the 1840s and 1850s settled on the frontier, and in Texas, a state newly admitted to the Union, a number of German settlements had sprung up. There Bishop John Mary Odin, C.M., of Galveston had been comparatively successful in caring for the Germans in his diocese. Franciscan friars from New York had established a community in San José near San Antonio, and from this base they had worked in the mission fields of German immigrants throughout south-central Texas. In 1858, however, the Franciscans were recalled to New York, and Bishop Odin petitioned Abbot Boniface for monks to continue the mission. In March 1859 he wrote Wimmer offering land, buildings, and five German congregations to the monks of St. Vincent.[60]

Receiving no response from Wimmer, Bishop Odin visited the monastery in Pennsylvania two months later and renewed his offer. At first Wimmer opposed the idea of sending men to Texas. As in the case of Kansas he feared that Texas was not a "healthful" land. There was, moreover, the imminent prospect that the South would secede from the Union, in which case he correctly anticipated that Texas would be cut off from communication with the North. These facts seemed to militate against the advisability of taking over the mission of San José, but in spite of his reservations, Abbot Boniface promised Bishop Odin that he would take his proposal under consideration and called a chapter meeting to discuss the matter. Much to his surprise the chapter favored taking over the mission in Texas, and when several priests volunteered to go, Wimmer gave his assent.[61]

Five missionary monks left St. Vincent on July 1, 1859, traveling by rail to Cairo, Illinois, where they boarded a riverboat for the trip down the Mississippi to the Gulf of Mexico. The leader of the mission was Father Alto Hörmann. Accompanying him were two priests, Fathers Peter Baunach and Aemilian Wendel, and two lay brothers, Michael Böhm and Norbert Rossberger. When the monks reached New Orleans Bishop Odin met them and took them by steamer to Galveston. The Benedictines arrived in Texas during the second week of July.

The monastery at San José that Bishop Odin gave them had been founded by Spanish Franciscans in the eighteenth century. The German Franciscans, who had occupied the buildings before the Benedictines came, had upgraded and modernized the facilities, but Prior Alto discovered soon after his arrival that the monks would have to make extensive repairs and undertake new construction before the monastery would in any way be suitable for the community. From San José the Benedictines ministered to German congregations in San Antonio, Castroville, Neubraunfels, Fredericksburg, and D'Hanis. In October 1859 King Ludwig sent a donation of $1,500 to the Texas foundation, and two months later Abbot Boniface wrote enthusiastically to Abbot Angelo Pescetelli that "conditions in Texas are so favorable that we can hope for success. The bishop transferred San José to us. It consists of a magnificent church and a large monastery which are in the midst of 720 acres of fertile land."[62]

The monks from St. Vincent found an abundant field of labor among the Germans of the surrounding area. Their missionary activity, in fact, was so extensive that any sort of conventual monastic life at San José became all but impossible. The churches and missions they served were numerous and widely separated from one another, and even after more priests came from St. Vincent, including Fathers Amandus Kramer, Theodore von Gründer, and Gallus Erhardt, the fragmentation of the community continued. Missionary labors precluded the possibility of the community's gathering for divine office and sharing the common life essential to Benedictine observance. This was not a new problem for the American Benedictines. Missionaries from St. Vincent in Minnesota and Kansas had faced it before, and only the firm monastic leadership of such priors as Demetrius di Marogna and Benedict Haindl in Minnesota and Augustine Wirth in Kansas prevented those communities from fragmenting as well. Wimmer himself was firm in his insistence upon an appropriate balance between missionary labors and monastic observance in all the communities he founded, and he was tireless in his efforts to achieve such a balance. A key motive of his visits to Minnesota and Kansas was to encourage his monks there to neglect neither their commitment to the congregations they served nor their obligation to create communal Benedictine life in the priories. The fact that he was never able to visit Texas accounts in part for the failure of San José.

But even at San José things might have turned out differently had it not been for political and economic developments beyond the control of the community. In April 1861 the American Civil War broke out, and problems began to multiply at the San José Priory. Early in 1862 Prior Alto Hörmann returned to St. Vincent to discuss the future of the Texas community with the abbot, and because of the Union blockade of the South he was unable to return to Texas. In the meantime the war had begun to cause a financial crisis at the Texas priory where the monks had started construction on a number of buildings. Non-German, Protestant Texans in the neighborhood, moreover, began to look with increased suspicion on the monks who had recently arrived from the North and who like most of their German compatriots in Texas sympathized with the Union's cause. Sickness also visited the monks at San José, and several of them contracted tuberculosis, which accounted for the deaths of four of them.

Cut off from communications with the mother abbey because of the war, the monks in Texas were unable to get word to St. Vincent of Brother Michael Böhm's death for two years. News of Father Amandus Kramer's appointment as prior to replace Father Alto did not reach Texas until after the war, and much-needed financial support from St. Vincent, as well as new monks to replace the sick and dying confreres in San José, could not get through the Union lines. In October 1862 Hörmann wrote the editors of the *Cincinnati Wahrheits-*

freund that "the restoration of San José was making progress until the war rendered all enterprises impossible. But peace must come sometime."[63]

Despite the troubles caused by war, poverty, and disease, the monks in Texas continued their work after the Civil War ended. Their susceptibility to tuberculosis as well as deteriorating financial conditions, however, cast grave doubt on the future of what had begun as a hopeful effort to create a third independent Benedictine monastery in the West. Forced to reconsider its commitment to Texas, the monastic chapter at St. Vincent convened in March 1867, and after lengthy discussion about the viability of the priory in Texas the capitulars voted to return San José, its properties, and missions to the diocese of Galveston.

The failure of the Texas venture, which had consumed eight years, four lives, and incalculable resources, provides dramatic and sobering testimony to the challenges facing the Benedictine missionaries from St. Vincent who went west in the 1850s. It serves also to bring into sharp focus the extraordinary achievement of Wimmer and his monks, who managed to create both strong communities and dynamic missionary and educational apostolates in Minnesota and Kansas that continue to flourish a hundred and forty years later.

Even as Abbot Boniface dealt with the problems in the missions and the numerous requests for priests from bishops all over America, a drama was unfolding within the young and energetic American Benedictine family, one that in many ways would prove the most difficult challenge of his life as an abbot. By 1860 the small community of Benedictine nuns from the Priory of St. Walburga at Eichstätt that he had established in St. Marys, Pennsylvania, in 1852 had developed into a sisterhood of fifty-one women living in five convents in Pennsylvania, Minnesota, New Jersey, and Kentucky. From the beginning Wimmer intended that the communities of monks and nuns should work together in the missions to serve the spiritual and educational needs of German immigrants. His long-term goal was to create several independent monasteries for the nuns, with at least one abbey under an abbess, and to formally unite the Benedictine communities of women and men within the American Cassinese Congregation under the authority of the congregation's abbot-president.

Toward that end he strove to establish women's convents as soon as possible in the places where St. Vincent had founded priories of monks. While the priests would attend to the sacramental needs of the Catholic congregations and establish colleges, and while the brothers would provide the manual labor necessary to create self-sustaining monastic and educational centers, the nuns would establish elementary schools to educate the children of the immigrants and prepare the more capable pupils to enter the gymnasiums operated by the monks.

To a certain extent his plan worked. Eventually communities of Benedictine nuns, like the monks who (except in the case of Erie, Pennsylvania) preceded them, were serving German congregations in St. Marys (1852), Erie (1856), St. Cloud (1857), Newark (1857), Covington (1859), Chicago (1861), Atchison (1863), Richmond (1868), and Carrolltown (1870). Before Wimmer could execute and confirm the amalgamation of the communities of monks and nuns within the American Cassinese Congregation, however, a major conflict arose between himself and the mother superior of the St. Marys convent, Benedicta Riepp, the outcome of which was a Roman decision to institute a separate jurisdictional structure for the Benedictine nuns in the United States and to detach them permanently from the authority of the abbot-president of the American Cassinese Congregation. This decision meant that after 1859 the male and female branches of the order in America would develop independently of one another and that Wimmer's hopes of bringing the communities of monks and nuns together in a coordinated effort to address the pastoral and educational needs of German immigrants in the United States would meet with only limited success.[64]

Explaining the plan and his concept of the authority he held over the nuns to Father Joseph Müller in 1857, Wimmer wrote:

My wish and plan was to introduce [the Benedictine nuns] in most of the places where we have established ourselves, and where it would, because of the school, be helpful or necessary. According to the *jus canonicum,* the sisters always enjoy the same rights and privileges as the monks do; they would, therefore, be exempt here and the President of the Congregation at the time would be their highest superior, as I have considered myself to be. . . . Furthermore, the sisters were invited by and were sent to me; I provided a place for a convent for them, gave them the necessary buildings, made many long and expensive trips, spent very much money for them, brought many of the sisters to the convent, supplied confessors for them, and am also, in many

respects, the head of the order, as founder or co-founder, as advocate, as pro-
moter of vocations for the sisters; and because of their proximity to my
brothers, I am *justified* and *obliged* to be solicitous that they be genuine,
good Benedictines and also good teachers.[65]

   Wimmer's effort to establish the female branch of the order in the
United States was integral to his plan for serving the needs of German
immigrants in America and spreading the Benedictine Order beyond
the limits of Europe. To achieve these twin goals he was influenced by
two overriding factors. The first was his developing understanding of
American conditions and their impact upon his mission. The second
was contemporary ecclesiastical law, which in several important respects applied differently to Benedictine monks and Benedictine
nuns. He recognized that the mission he was undertaking had no pre-
cise precedent. His task required new and imaginative approaches to
the inevitable problems that both the monks and nuns would face if
they were to succeed. At the same time the work of introducing the
monastic institute to the United States offered the opportunity for innovations that from his point of view would benefit both the Benedictine Order and the American Church.

   In the mid-nineteenth century Roman Catholic canon law did not
exist as a fixed and coherent body of legislation, but rather as a disparate collection of conciliar documents, papal decrees, and decisions
of Roman congregations that lent themselves to a wide variety of interpretations.[66] At the time of the Bavarian Benedictine mission to
the United States Benedictine nuns continued to be governed by the
decrees of the sixteenth-century Council of Trent. These decrees confirmed the 1298 papal constitution *Periculoso* of Pope Boniface VIII
and stipulated (1) that monasteries of women observe strict enclosure,
(2) that nuns be bound by solemn vows, and (3) that jurisdiction over
convents of solemnly professed nuns rest with the bishops in whose
dioceses they lay.[67]

   Ecclesiastical law and tradition as it applied to Benedictine women
in the nineteenth century differed significantly from the manner in
which it applied to Benedictine men. While the monks were also
bound by solemn vows, they were in practice less strictly confined to
the cloister by the laws of enclosure than were the nuns. (There had
developed in Europe a long tradition of Benedictine men teaching in
schools and working in parishes; this tradition had been renewed and

strenghened at the time of the nineteenth-century restoration of the Benedictine Order in Bavaria.)[68] By implication ecclesiastical law enjoined nuns from involvement in "external apostolates" because to undertake such activities as teaching would require them to go outside the strict enclosure they were bound to. Nonetheless, after the nineteenth-century Bavarian Benedictine restoration the nuns at Eichstätt, at the urging of the Bavarian government and with the permission of the local bishop, opened a school for girls.[69]

The most important distinction between Benedictine women and men insofar as ecclesiastical law was concerned was in the matter of jurisdiction. As "exempt" religious communities, Benedictine monasteries of men, unlike those of women, did not fall under the jurisdiction of the bishops in whose dioceses they lay but were instead subject directly to the jurisdiction of the Holy See.[70] This meant, for example, that both in law and in practice the Abbey of Metten, from which the first monks came to the United States, was subject in all internal spiritual and administrative affairs to the pope, while the Priory of St. Walburga, from which the first nuns came to the United States, was subject to the jurisdiction of the bishop of Eichstätt.

Wimmer fully understood the implications of the distinct jurisdictional rules governing Benedictine monasteries of men and those of women. He also understood the disadvantages for the nuns of being subject in America to the jurisdiction of bishops. He feared that if they fell under episcopal control, (1) each convent would be under pressure to serve the particular apostolic needs of the bishop's diocese and work in fields and under conditions not necessarily conducive to monastic observance; (2) the nuns, now depending on the bishops or secular priests as spiritual guides, would be deprived of essential training in specifically monastic spirituality which only Benedictine priests could provide them; and (3) the various convents, existing within different dioceses, would be cut off from one another and have little or no opportunity to share experiences and develop a unified observance.

It was to avoid these consequences that Wimmer sought to establish independent communities for the Benedictine nuns in the United States, obtain the same exemption for them that he had obtained for the communities of Benedictine men he had established,[71] and unite them under the president of the American Cassinese Congregation. Wimmer realized that the institution he had in mind for the nuns would be unique both in America and in Europe. In 1852, when the first group of Benedictine nuns arrived from Eichstätt, there were only eight Roman Catholic sisterhoods in the United States and all of them fell under the jurisdiction of the bishops in whose dioceses they lived. But if exemption for the Benedictine nuns would be unusual and its achievement difficult, in Wimmer's mind it would not have been impossible. Already he had achieved several "firsts" for the Benedictines in the United States. He had established the first Benedictine monastery in North America despite the doubts of many church leaders both in America and Europe that he would succeed. He had created the first modern Benedictine monastery whose monks were predominantly lay brothers upon whom the prosperity of the community at St. Vincent depended. He had convinced Bishop Michael O'Connor of Pittsburgh to name him the first "irremovable" pastor in the United States by granting him and his successors perpetual rights to the parish at St. Vincent. And he had persuaded the Holy See to establish St. Vincent as the first exempt religious community in the United States. What seemed unattainable goals to others were merely challenges to meet and overcome for the *Projektenmacher* of Metten.

Wimmer's plan for the Benedictine nuns in the United States was innovative and ambitious. The monastery of St. Walburga at Eichstätt was neither exempt from episcopal control nor did it belong to a Benedictine congregation. But Wimmer knew from history that monastic communities of women had often affiliated themselves with congregations of men. In the seventeenth century, for example, Italian Benedictine convents had been part of the Cassinese Congregation, and in the eighteenth century the Cistercian congregational organization included communities of women.[72] Wimmer regarded affiliation of the American Benedictine convents with the American Cassinese Congregation as desirable and necessary if the Benedictine Order were to prosper and grow in the United States.

He believed, moreover, that as the person who brought the nuns to America and as "provincial of Benedictines," which the American bishops had named him at the Seventh Provincial Council of Baltimore in 1849, he had the responsibility and right to oversee the monastic development of Benedictine communities of women in America and to do whatever was necessary to achieve for them the status of independent, exempt monasteries within the American Cassinese Congregation. If confronted with the objection that exemption and congregational affiliation were not part of the tradition of Eichstätt, Wimmer would have responded that American conditions precluded rigid adherence to moribund institutional structures that prevailed in Europe. His goal was to establish independent, exempt communities of Benedictine nuns who, like the communities of men, would follow the statutes of the Bavarian Benedictine Congregation, observe a limited enclosure, embrace education as their principal apostolic activity, and be united with the communities of men within a single congregational structure.

His vision for Benedictine women in America, though based to a certain extent on historical precedent, anticipated the creation of something new and innovative. To his chagrin, some of the nuns did not share that vision.

Soon after the arrival of the Benedictine nuns in St. Marys, friction began to develop between Abbot Boniface and the superior, Mother Benedicta Riepp. As his letter to Müller suggests, Wimmer considered that as "superior" of the Benedictines in America as well as founder and benefactor of the sisters' community in St. Marys he had both the authority and the obligation to supervise and direct their financial and monastic affairs. Within weeks of the Benedictine sisters' arrival he directed Mother Benedicta to open a novitiate, a right normally granted only to independent communities, and to accept twelve young women from St. Marys, who ranged in age from thirteen to twenty-one, as novices. He wrote the abbot of Metten, "It seems that they are not pleased in St. Walburga that the superior here has, at my urging, opened a novitiate, because they are a branch house of St. Walburga, and should be directed from there."[73] Soon he was working toward gaining complete independence for the St. Marys convent from the Priory of St. Walburga and wrote King Ludwig that "[e]ven in spite of the danger that the motherhouse might withdraw help, I insisted on the erection of an independent novitiate and on the affirmation of self-government so that we here could answer the crying need for religious instruction of the young girls as early as possible and in the widest possible sphere of activity."[74] When Prioress Edwarda Schnitzer of Eichstätt protested, Wimmer wrote, "the sisters of Eichstätt are fools if they expect to understand better what is needed in America than I do here in the place and on the spot."[75]

In 1852 when King Ludwig sent a donation of $4,000 through the prior of St. Vincent to the convent in St. Marys, Wimmer felt strong enough in his position as superior to appropriate the funds for use in constructing a gristmill at St. Vincent and another in St. Marys. When as a result of Mother Benedicta's protests he received a letter of inquiry from Munich, Wimmer wrote King Ludwig to explain that the construction of a convent in St. Marys (the purpose for which the money had been donated) was necessarily delayed on account of the efforts by the colony to complete a church.

I could not have undertaken these two buildings if Your Kingly Majesty had not most kindly directed that for the furnishing and building of a convent for the Benedictine Sisters in St. Marys, 8000 fl. should be stipulated. The building of the convent could, however, not be undertaken at once, since no preparations for the same had been made, and furthermore could not be made since the entire colony was busy with the building of a church which had already been started and could not be interrupted. The sisters were prepared to lend me the money, since they were not in a position to use it at once, with the condition that I care for the buying and the obtaining of the immediately necessary arrangements, and then, if time allowed, use the remaining money for building a convent.[76]

Wimmer's appropriation of funds intended for the sisters indicates the extent of authority he considered himself to hold over them. To confirm and consolidate that authority, he attempted during his visit to Rome in 1855 to obtain approval from the Propaganda Fide to establish St. Joseph's Convent as a canonical priory independent of the motherhouse at Eichstätt. Because of objections from Eichstätt's bishop George von Öttl; from Karl August von Reisach, who before being named archbishop of Munich (1846–1855) and curial official in Rome (1855–1869) had served as bishop of Eichstätt (1841–1846); and from Mother Edwarda of St. Walburga's Priory, his efforts to obtain the community's independence from Eichstätt failed, and when he returned to the United States in January 1856 as newly appointed abbot of St. Vincent and president of the American Cassinese Congregation, his position with regard to the Benedictine nuns in America was canonically unclear.[77]

Still, he considered himself their superior and intended, eventually, to subsume their monastery under the aegis of the American Cassinese Congregation. Presuming the same jurisdiction over the nuns that he exercised over the priories of men he had established, Wimmer did his best to direct their affairs from St. Vincent. He changed the daily *horarium* at St. Joseph's Convent so that the nuns in St. Marys adopted the schedule followed by the monks at St. Vincent. He refused to permit the community to accept new members without his approval, and in some cases (according to Mother Benedicta) he accepted young girls into the convent without consulting the sisters.[78] In analyzing the relations between Wimmer and the Benedictine nuns, the Bavarian Benedictine historian Willibald Mathäser, noted that

the right to govern the Benedictine sisters was really not conceded to Wimmer by Rome. He was, in fact, President of the Benedictines of the Cassinese Congregation, but as such he was not superior of the sisters. With the confused situation in relation to ruling power in the quickly developing Catholic Church in North America, and because Wimmer had brought the Benedictine sisters from Europe and was financially responsible for them, the Abbot of St. Vincent took it for granted that he was also the superior of the sisters. In the uncertainty of governing rights lay the cause of the difficulties between Wimmer and Riepp in the first place.[79]

Given these circumstances, it is not surprising that when the opportunity arose for Mother Benedicta to shake off what seemed to her like a rule of tyranny, she quickly took it.

Not long after the Benedictines from Eichstätt arrived in St. Marys, Bishop Josue Mary Young of the newly formed diocese of Erie (1853) invited them to send sisters to teach in St. Mary's German parish in the episcopal city. Establishing a community of nuns in a city where the monks from St. Vincent had not yet settled seemed to Riepp a good opportunity to gain some measure of independence from Wimmer, so in June 1856 she sent five sisters, two of whom were novices, to Erie. She made the move without consulting Wimmer and apparently before she had made formal arrangements with either Bishop Young or Father Francis J. Hartmann, pastor of St. Mary's Church. When the five sisters—Scholastica Burkhardt, Luitgard Butsch, Anselma Schönhofer, Ruperta Albert, and Frances Knapp—arrived in Erie on June 23, 1856, they discovered that no arrangements had been made for their accommodation. With the help of the pastor of St. Mary's Parish, however, they were put up in private homes until Bishop Young and Father Hartmann could provide more permanent quarters for them.[80]

Mother Benedicta explained to the directors of the Ludwig Missionsverein that one reason she had sent the sisters to Erie was so that they could earn salaries as teachers and thus ease the heavy burden of poverty that weighed down the nuns in St. Marys. The German colony in St. Marys, she said, "is and will remain a poor one, unless a special favor from heaven intervenes. . . . Its only treasures are the monastery for men and the convent for women." She admitted that "a few times I was on the verge of losing courage when I considered the want and poverty in which we have often found ourselves; but I always found hope again in the thought that God does not forsake His own." She reported that

[i]n our community we now number 49, of whom five sisters were transferred to Erie last summer to teach the German and English classes in the German parish there and where they receive a salary on which they can live very comfortably. Our novitiate is still quite strong, and we have to make do with little, especially so since the land here is not very fertile and most of the inhabitants all around us are poor; by the time the necessaries of life are brought from the big cities, they cost a great amount of money. I would gladly comply with the wish of the Honorable Directory and give a longer account of the progress of St. Marys, but the fact is, that as long as I have been here, life has been very monotonous.[81]

Mother Benedicta's decision to send nuns to Erie angered Wimmer. He complained that the sisters who had gone, with the single exception of Sister Scholastica, were not well enough prepared to take on the responsibilities of teaching. He claimed, moreover, that Sister Scholastica, who had been serving as novice mistress, could not be spared by the community at St. Marys. Her absence would be a loss the nuns could ill afford. Abbot Boniface also objected to the sisters' lack of preparation before setting out for Erie. As evidence of this, he pointed to the surprise with which both Bishop Young and Father Hartmann greeted their arrival in Erie. The bishop and the pastor did not know what to do with the sisters, and the sisters, Wimmer said, had only their rash behavior to blame. Furthermore, the abbot objected to the fact that Mother Benedicta had acted irresponsibly in sending two novices with the group to Erie. These young girls were prepared neither to teach nor to lead the monastic life. He wrote that he had vehemently opposed the move.

But nothing helped. At once she sent Sister Scholastica [and the others] to Erie, went along herself, had to spend three weeks in private homes, and Sister Josepha, very unwillingly, had to take her place [in St. Marys]. This was done in the hope that all would be successful in Erie, so that the superior could have her residence there and would no longer be under my authority. However, conditions were very bad; they were barely able to exist; the Reverend Pastor Hartmann, of course, did everything he could for the sisters, but he too is not a hen-pecked hero, and so Erie remained (and still is) a burdensome branch of St. Marys.[82]

In March 1857, while in St. Marys to celebrate the profession and receive the vows of several nuns, Wimmer learned that a number of sisters had grown dissatisfied with Mother Benedicta's rule. These sisters told him that they wanted to leave St. Marys and asked his permission, and help, to go to Minnesota where Prior Demetrius di Marogna had invited them to teach in St. Cloud.[83] Abbot Boniface agreed to let the dissatisfied nuns go to Minnesota, but he stipulated that first they must go to St. Vincent's dependent priory in Indiana, Pennsylvania, where the superior, Prior Ulric Spöttl, would prepare them for the missions in Minnesota. The sisters agreed and left for Indiana soon afterward, arriving on March 26, 1857.[84]

In April Father Rupert Seidenbusch, prior at St. Marys, wrote Wimmer about affairs in the St. Joseph's Convent. Mother Benedicta, he said,

appears to have changed a little outwardly, but inwardly she is the same. She hides everything very well, so that you cannot get at her, but she has her own plans. She appears to have great confidence in Fr. Aegidius, but she does not trust me, because I am too much on your side. The rule is still not observed very strictly, as far as I can find out, but I only know from the confessional and, therefore, cannot speak. I do not know what is to be done, but I think you cannot change her mind, for she said already she would act this way just because you do not like it. I guess a visitation would not do any harm. She is now, as it appears, trying to win over those who were opposed to her and, I am afraid, trying to spoil them only so as to keep the upper hand.[85]

Wimmer's decision to give aid and comfort to the disaffected sisters, together with Seidenbusch's unconcealed dislike for the mother superior, convinced Mother Benedicta and those nuns who supported her that as long as they remained in St. Marys there would be no chance for the female branch of the order to develop freely. The unrest in the convent seems to have centered on changes in the monastic regimen which some of the nuns regarded as a breakdown in discipline, as well as disagreement among the sisters about the propriety of Riepp's opposition to Wimmer. Trained to submit humbly to authority, particularly when it wore a miter, many of the nuns in St. Marys were scandalized by Mother Benedicta's refusal to accept submissively those decisions made by Wimmer that affected their lives. These nuns, finding allies in the authorities whom Riepp resisted, turned against the mother superior and in so doing received the approval and support of Wimmer and Seidenbusch.[86]

Recognizing the difficulty of her position with respect to her own community and finding her proximity to St. Vincent and its dependency in St. Marys intolerable since her every action was scrutinized and questioned by the abbot and prior, Mother Benedicta decided that she too should go to Minnesota if only to put greater distance between herself and the abbot of St. Vincent. In May she wrote Wimmer:

I cannot have peace of mind until I express my thoughts to you. I beg you to listen graciously to my earnest request and grant me your kind permission. It would be much easier here at St. Marys if there were fewer sisters. I ask you not to lose patience with me and kindly keep this matter confidential until I receive an answer from you. I have not spoken a word of it to anyone; perhaps now you can guess my thought. I myself would very much like to go to the West and that very soon, otherwise I feel my health will be considerably impaired. I feel very disturbed and under strain here, so much the more since I never was very happy at St. Marys and never had a desire to be here. You will be more pleased with me in the West than here; there, I shall do and work as they tell and advise me. It is not possible for me to remain here since contentment and inner peace are lacking, as well as happiness. I have tried to force myself in every respect, but I find that it is useless and impossible to do so; I can accomplish little good under these circumstances. You will perhaps smile when I say that I have become very shy and even do not wish to be among my own sisters. Here I feel inert and uninterested, I who in the past was so lively and full of zest. In the West I hope to regain this, be it from the right or from the left, on the land.[87]

Mother Benedicta's closest ally in her efforts to free the Benedictine sisters from Wimmer's control was Sister Willibalda Scherbauer, a twenty-nine-year-old Eichstätt nun who had come to St. Marys in 1855. Riepp and Scherbauer represented a group in the convent at St.

Marys who still hoped to liberate themselves from the authority of the abbot of St. Vincent. This group was determined to pursue its goal of independence and began at once to prepare for the move to Minnesota. On May 22 Prior Rupert wrote Abbot Boniface that

they are already packing up for Minnesota and I think are intending to send their boxes away; they are, I heard, packing up all the good clothes, linen, etc., even of those sisters who do not wish to go along and use, as it were, a moral thumbscrew to force the sisters to go along. You should, I think, stop this injustice by coming soon and deciding that all those who have professed in St. Marys should stay here. . . . Hoping to see you soon, and that you settle all the trouble at once, by telling her [Mother Benedicta] that she has nothing to say here anymore, I ask your paternal blessing.[88]

Despite Seidenbusch's recommendation, Wimmer's initial reaction was to acquiesce to Mother Benedicta's and her companions' plan to move to Minnesota, though later he would adamantly claim that he had specifically forbidden Sister Willibalda to accompany the group.[89] The sisters continued their preparations. Then, in June, Prior Demetrius informed him that on account of the grasshopper plague the monks in Minnesota were having difficulty finding food for themselves and would therefore be unable to provide for the sisters. Riepp had written di Marogna that she and the other sisters planned to arrive at the end of June or the beginning of July. "This is truly too hasty," the prior of Minnesota wrote Wimmer, and then he continued: "The things you have asked me to do are far from being completed and can not easily be carried out now since the people are so discouraged on account of the grasshoppers. I had not planned on doing them before next spring. Your letter gave me to understand that you, too, were not in a great hurry, as prudence demands." He counseled delay.[90] Father Demetrius's letter was followed a week later by one from Father Clement Staub, procurator at the St. Cloud Priory. Staub confirmed that financial matters were in such a poor state among the Minnesota monks that no arrangements for the reception of the sisters could be made.[91]

With this information in hand Wimmer informed Mother Benedicta that she would have to postpone her plans to leave St. Marys until conditions in Minnesota improved. He also announced that the four sisters whom he had sent to the Indiana Priory in order to prepare for the missions in Minnesota would not be going to St. Cloud after all. Their desire to go to Minnesota had been precipitated by their unwillingness to live under Mother Benedicta's rule, and he could hardly send them to St. Cloud if Riepp was eventually going to settle there as well. For that reason he directed the sisters in Indiana to go instead to Newark where nuns were needed to teach in the school attached to St. Mary's Parish. At the end of June Abbot Boniface went to the newly established priory in Newark to make arrangements for the arrival of the sisters from Indiana, and it was while in Newark that he received news that Mother Benedicta, together with ten sisters, two postulants, and a twelve-year-old girl, had arrived in Erie on the first leg of an unauthorized journey to Minnesota.

Mother Benedicta had obviously had enough of what she regarded as the abbot's oppressive rule. In a spirit of independence that reflected more her conviction of the limits of Wimmer's authority than willful disobedience, Riepp determined to go West where she might work and live a monastic life in an atmosphere of freedom which St. Marys' proximity to St. Vincent did not afford. Her action again infuriated Wimmer, who interpreted it as a clear case of disobedience and indiscipline. He immediately wrote Bishop Young asking that he detain the nuns in Erie. The bishop replied on July 4 that an advance party from the group had already departed the see city for the West. Of the fourteen, seven had gone to Minnesota: Sisters Willibalda Scherbauer, Gregoria Moser, Evangelista Kremeter, and Gertrude Kapsner: the postulants Marianna Wolters and Prisca Meier; and the twelve-year-old orphan, Josephine Lejal. The bishop agreed to keep the others in Erie but, most disconcerting of all, reported to Abbot Boniface that Mother Benedicta Riepp and Sister Augustina Short, with the bishop's permission, had already left Erie bound not for Minnesota but for Rome, "for the purpose of collecting funds and . . . to discover the mutual extent of her authority and of yours." Before Mother Benedicta arrived in Erie, the bishop continued,

I was unaware of the existence of any difficulty of the kind; and I should have been better *prepared to treat it scientifically* if you had availed yourself of an earlier opportunity to apprise me of it. If she is gone, however, you can dispose things to your liking in accordance with your powers as superior— without the embarrassment of her presence and opposition, and at the same time by letters to Europe put things in train so that this shall all turn out for the advantage of this particular community, and of religion in general.

It is fair to say, however, that while Sister Benedicta expressed a great deal of obstinate determination in the course she had resolved on, she was at the same time profuse in the expression of her devotion to you and in the acknowledgement of your kindness. She seemed willing to be deposed for the sake of peace and discipline; but I suppose you have ample opportunities to judge the worth of this.[92]

Meanwhile the seven sisters arrived in St. Cloud unannounced and unexpected. On June 28, while in St. Paul on business, Prior Demetrius was informed that the nuns were in town and staying with a community of Sisters of St. Joseph. Both surprised and annoyed that they had come, he wrote Abbot Boniface that their arrival had been "overhasty." He found them temporary shelter in St. Cloud and soon afterward rented a house for them. He reported that "all the sisters appeared pale, emaciated and ailing."[93]

Abbot Boniface took the four nuns from Indiana to Newark at the end of July. After settling them there, he considered what action he might take to apprise ecclesiastical authorities in Europe of his conflict with the Benedictine women in America. He was also worried about how to answer what he expected would be provocative questions Mother Benedicta would pose both in Munich and in Rome. Knowing that she intended to go first to Bavaria, he wrote a lengthy letter to his principal advisor at the Ludwig Missionsverein, Father Joseph Müller, detailing the events up to that time as he perceived them, explaining the authority he considered himself to have over the sisters, and justifying his actions with regard to them. He was, he said,

no longer pleased with the superior, because she is too self-willed, does not take advice, and still does not perform her duty satisfactorily. I never took it upon myself to rule the sisters.[94] I have neither the wish nor the time for that, but I thought myself *justified* and *obliged* to see to it that they obey the Holy Rule properly, and follow it according to our own Statutes as much as possible, so that they will be trained to become good nuns and teachers and that they also support themselves in the temporal sphere by a well-ordered domestic economy.

Wimmer said that his hope had always been that, following the example of the monks, the nuns in America would establish a strong motherhouse, a common novitiate, a common house of studies, and a close union among the individual convents "with at least one abbess under the leadership of the president and General Chapter" of the American Cassinese Congregation. He said that as founder of their convent, abbot of St. Vincent, and president of the American Cassinese Congregation, he considered himself their "highest superior." Neither the bishop of Erie nor the prioress of Eichstätt could effectively rule the American nuns because the former did not understand the problems of the order and the latter not only was too far away to exercise control but also did not understand American conditions. In 1855, he said, he had unsuccessfully petitioned Rome to establish such an organizational structure for the nuns, and now, under the present circumstances, discipline in the convent was on the verge of totally breaking down.

His first serious conflict with Mother Benedicta, Wimmer explained, was occasioned by her sending the sisters to Erie in 1856 with neither his permission nor the bishop's formal approval. He had opposed the move because the young sisters who had gone were inadequately formed both in education and in the monastic life. Moreover, they received no property in Erie from the bishop, and it was a cardinal principle of his never to accept a mission without also receiving title to the property on which it was located. Finally, he objected to the fact that Sister Scholastica Burkhardt, whom Mother Benedicta had named superior in Erie, could not be spared at St. Marys where she was needed as novice mistress.

Another serious falling out between the abbot and Mother Benedicta, according to Wimmer, occurred when he transferred Father Benedict Haindl from St. Marys to St. Vincent in 1856. As prior in St. Marys Haindl had been confessor for the sisters. "A very worthy and excellent man," he was loved by all. Wimmer characterized him as "a good gentleman without will power over against a willful woman." He could "never say 'No' when the Lady Superior said 'Yes.'" Haindl felt uncomfortable in this position and asked the abbot to transfer him. Wimmer replaced him with Father Rupert Seidenbusch, "a younger priest who was far superior to Fr. Benedict in ability and learning." Seidenbusch had been pastor in St. Marys for several years, and in fulfilling his duties he had come into conflict with Mother Benedicta on more than one occasion. The sisters, Wimmer said, reacted strongly against the appointment of Father Rupert as prior. "Good things and bad things were tried. Entreaties, letters, etc. came to keep Fr. Benedict, and not to have Fr. Rupert, all to no purpose!" The sisters ostracized Seidenbusch, calling him to the convent only for confessions. Whereas "Fr. Benedict had taught pedagogy and asceticism, and was asked for advice five or six times a day, poor Rupert had complete leisure." For several months the sisters "pursued" Father Benedict with letters. Some of these letters from Mother Benedicta and Sister Willibalda, the new novice mistress at St. Marys, contained "secrets of confession." Finally Wimmer put an end to the correspondence. He himself visited St. Marys every three months as extraordinary confessor for the nuns, and when Mother Benedicta and Sister Willibalda continued to complain about Father Rupert, he allowed them to confess to Fathers Aegidius Christoff and Roman Hell of the St. Marys Priory. But still "the Abbot and Fr. Rupert were in disgrace, and that's where it stayed! He and I were spoken of only with contempt. Sister Willibalda used only nicknames when speaking of him. Any of the nuns or sisters who allowed themselves to show confidence or attachment to the Abbot or Prior, fell out of favor, and soon it was strictly forbidden and even the use of our names was punished."

As novice mistress, Wimmer said, Sister Willibalda exercised inordinate power in the community. Upon her appointment after the departure to Erie of Sister Scholastica Burkhardt, she "was very soon the boss in the house; whatever she wanted came to pass; without her permission no one could speak to the Superior." But she allegedly did nothing for the novices and even discontinued their spiritual instruction: "Nothing was done for the novices any more; the instruction was omitted; even music was neglected though she [Willibalda] was well qualified to teach; the Superior and novice mistress bantered with each other like children, took their meals together, and neglected the spiritual exercises more and more until finally—from March to the end of May— prayers in choir, and all order of the day stopped."

Wimmer reported that many of the other sisters in the convent reacted strongly against the disrespect shown the abbot and the prior. "They deplored the fact that there was no order, especially when (without any necessity) the Superior took in a one-year-old girl who screamed day and night and disturbed the sleep, spiritual reading, and the choir." Wimmer said that he had received bitter complaints from many nuns in the community. He tried to make use of "the confessional and conferences to bring the Superior to a change of mind, all in vain." His efforts, he said, proved detrimental for those sisters suspected of complaining to him. The dissenting nuns "were hated so much more and persecuted." The abbot said that he attempted to solve the problem by forcing the mother superior to admit young members of the community to solemn profession in order to have a chapter that would "bring the Superior to insist on the better observance of order, the distribution of duties, etc." But this effort also failed because the only sisters Mother Benedicta would admit to solemn vows and the chapter were, with the exception of one, "all timid women. Two very sickly young women, who would not trust themselves to say a word, were accepted." Subsequently several sisters, including Sisters Walburga Dietrich and Emmerana Bader, two of the twelve nuns in the community who had come from Eichstätt, approached Wimmer, saying that they could no longer remain at St. Marys on account of the disorder. The abbot "deliberated with my priests and as a result of this I informed the Superior, after the profession of vows was over, that I was choosing Sister Emmerana and four or five other nuns and sisters, to send them, in time, to the West (Minnesota)." Until arrangements for the trip to Minnesota could be made, he decided to take the sisters to Indiana, Pennsylvania, "where Fr. Ulric Spöttl, a very good and wise man, would prepare them for the mission." When Mother Benedicta rejected this proposal "*flatly* and *firmly*," Abbot Boniface "demanded that the question be brought before the whole convent." He called a meeting of the community at which both he and Seidenbusch were present. There he "presented the case dispassionately, and left it to their judgment, with the statement that I wished to hear the result after dinner, and that if they absolutely did not want to take into consideration my advice and wish, then I would not bother myself with them any more. *Naturally*, I received a 'Yes,' a unanimous one, from the Chapter."

On March 26, 1857, Wimmer, Seidenbusch, and four sisters left St. Marys bound for Indiana. Wimmer said that he and Mother Benedicta had parted in peace ("on my part, at least"), but on the journey he learned from the sisters "that the Superior spoke hateful words about all of them." For three months these nuns worked and taught in Indiana, and in July the abbot "decided to send the sisters from Indiana to Newark and to send others to the West from St. Marys."

Not long afterward Mother Benedicta herself wrote that she too wanted to go to Minnesota where she would "begin anew and would take pains to give satisfaction in every way." Wimmer said he was "simple enough to believe her and gave the permission," but he warned against haste and told her to wait until Prior Demetrius could make preparations for the arrival of the sisters in St. Cloud. In June he was in Newark making preparations for the sisters from Indiana when he received news that Mother Benedicta, together with thirteen sisters, had arrived in Erie. From there Sister Willibalda led six sisters to Minnesota, and Mother Benedicta, together with Sister Augustina, had gone to Europe. Wimmer reported that he "had to return to St. Marys, restore order, and declare Mother Benedicta banished, once and for all, from St. Marys." He was outraged and said that he "would not tolerate Benedicta or Willibalda" any longer.

How much trouble, annoyance, travelling, writing, money and time these two women cost me, and then, they also want to go to Rome to complain about me—that I assume sovereign authority over them to which I have no right! I should be good enough to pay, but I should not say anything? We will see who is master! Just now, I still am. For well-behaved sisters I am prepared to do almost anything for the order, but for such tramps as Benedicta and Willibalda I will not do anything. . . . For her to question whether the Abbot-President of our Congregation is also the Superior of the sisters, before the forum of Bishops and of the Pope, is not only unwise and inopportune, it is also prejudicial to the peaceful development of the order. We are unanimously determined not to tolerate any sisters of our order near us who want to be independent of us, since we are their confessors and have troubles, vexations, and expenses enough with them, until they are able to help themselves. Bishop Young of Erie, to whom I had to report the recent events, also seems to question my rights. However, because I am his vicar general, he gave me full authority for this purpose. I wrote him, though, thanking him and informing him that I wanted to handle this affair as head of the order, not as vicar general; I will not endure disobedient, undisciplined sisters near my people. There is, moreover, no sister who would not be satisfied and grateful for this, except Mother Benedicta, Mother Willibalda and the "uncouth" Maura who was left behind so that we would have our cross![95]

Wimmer's long and detailed letter to Müller is remarkable for its candid, often intemperate, and extremely harsh assessment of the actions and motives of Mother Benedicta and Sister Willibalda. He was angry that these two sisters had rejected his authority and defied his will. Those who had gone to Minnesota with Sister Willibalda, he said, were merely pawns led astray by the mother superior and novice mistress. In July he wrote Prior Demetrius that the sisters newly arrived in Minnesota should neither be recognized as religious nor cared for by the monks at St. Cloud until they submitted unconditionally to the abbot's authority. Sister Willibalda, moreover, was to resign her position as superior and be expelled from the convent. Wimmer directed that Sister Evangelista Kremeter be made superior of the Minnesota nuns and that she have no further communication with either Mother Benedicta or Sister Willibalda.

In August Prior Demetrius wrote Abbot Boniface and informed him that the sisters in St. Cloud had agreed to submit to his jurisdiction. A mature, judicious, and fundamentally kind man, di Marogna assumed the role of peacemaker and asked Wimmer to allow Sister Willibalda to stay with the sisters. The sisters were distraught at the abbot's harsh treatment of Sister Willibalda, he said, and Sister Willibalda herself was ready to submit. He said that he had urged her to write the abbot for pardon. "I ask you, therefore, to prescribe a penance for her, to pardon her, and to permit her to remain."[96]

Sister Willibalda wrote Wimmer saying that she had never considered herself expressly forbidden to go west, but since the abbot insisted that such was the case, she asked his forgiveness and promised amendment and fidelity. "I will certainly be an obedient and sincere child from now on."[97] Sister Evangelista also wrote Abbot Boniface that she would comply with his directives. She protested, however, her appointment as superior and said that she could not follow his instructions to have nothing more to do with Mother Benedicta and Sister Willibalda without violating her own conscience: "[I]t is impossible for me not to associate with Rev. Mother Superior and Mother Willibalda without any reason on my part for such conduct; and . . . since I do not possess the required knowledge and experience necessary to maintain order and discipline in a cloister, I believe these will be sufficient reasons for you to spare me from such a responsibility. If [your commands] must be complied with, I feel constrained to leave and seek my salvation in a stricter order."[98]

Prior Demetrius, too, clearly considered the abbot's treatment of the sisters overly harsh. In his letter of August 27 he delicately suggested that though the sisters might have been wrong in coming to Minnesota, Wimmer may not have been entirely dispassionate in his treatment of them. "In the whole sad affair the sisters were very wrong," he wrote, "but there may have been fault and mistakes on the other side, too."

I did not say much about it to the sisters; many questions and much talking merely confuse. What hurts the sisters most, as they say, is the often repeated accusation on the part of the brothers that the sisters live at the expense of the monks, as if they were lazy women afraid of work. The more strictly they can keep the enclosure, the less they have to come in contact with the fathers and brothers, the more they like it, and the more peace and order is to be found in the convent.[99]

In October 1857, during the visit to Minnesota when he brought Father Benedict Haindl to St. Cloud and appointed Father Cornelius Wittmann to replace Father Demetrius as prior, Abbot Boniface visited the sisters and satisfied himself that their submission to his jurisdiction was sincere. He therefore gave his tentative blessing to their undertaking and confirmed Sister Willibalda as superior for three years. On his return to St. Vincent, he wrote Mother Scholastica Burkhardt of the Erie convent that Mother Willibalda

requested me earnestly to regard her and her fellow sisters as I do the other sisters. I did not want to consent to it; but after I had convinced myself that they could get along (the monks will give them wood), I gave in. I recognized her as prioress, gave the habit to Prisca and Marianna, and permitted the new prior, Father Cornelius, to read holy mass in the convent on Sundays and Communion days. I also had the brothers bring them firewood and help them to get their own home. I gave Sister Willibalda a piece of my mind and spoke the plain truth. If she will be truthful and prudent, things will go well. Josephina Lejal likes it there; I had left her there before. Peace reigns once more.[100]

Jurisdiction over the Benedictine sisters in America seemed securely in the hands of the abbot of St. Vincent when he left Minnesota in October. He had instructed the nuns not to receive novices without his authorization, and together with his delegate, Prior Cornelius Wittmann, he had taken over the financial affairs of the convent. He felt confident that he had resolved the conflict in his own favor and that he was, as he wrote Father Joseph Müller in July, still "master" of the nuns.

In the meantime, however, Mother Benedicta continued her efforts to gain a hearing for her cause in Europe. She had gone first to Bavaria, where she was received coldly both in Eichstätt and Munich. At the order of Bishop George von Öttl of Eichstätt she composed a list of six "points on which I cannot agree with the Right Reverend Lord Abbot Boniface Wimmer." These were (1) that Wimmer brought girls to the convent and invested them without consulting the mother superior and the chapter; (2) that he expected all the novices to whom he had given the habit to be allowed to make profession, even if the mother superior and the chapter did not agree; (3) that despite overcrowding in the sisters' convent he frequently brought postulants ("who had neither money nor clothes") to join them, and that when Mother Benedicta tried to relieve the crowding by sending nuns to Erie and Minnesota, he objected "because I, not he, had transferred them"; (4) that Wimmer had expropriated $4,000 that King Ludwig had sent to the sisters in St. Marys; (5) that he "expected the brothers to be with the sisters and work with them" and that he allowed dissatisfied and discontented sisters to send notes and letters to him through students and lay brothers; and (6) that he placed confessors at St. Marys who agreed with him and who gave the sisters "many false ideas of religious life."[101]

Baron Rudolph von Oberkamp, treasurer of the Ludwig Missionsverein, informed Wimmer of Mother Benedicta's complaints against him, and in November the abbot answered the charges, asking von Oberkamp to make his views known to both Bishop von Öttl and Archbishop von Reisach. Abbot Boniface said that he "did *not* bring a *single girl* [into the convent] without having obtained the permission for admittance from Sister Benedicta. But she, without my knowledge and a few times against my formally expressed wish, admitted eight or nine sisters." With regard to the complaint that he had decided which novices might make profession, Wimmer said, "It is an untruth and as much of a lie as the one above. . . . After a year novitiate, one makes profession in our order, and without a good reason, this may not be postponed. However, I have never insisted that it must be made right after one year, much less that all who had received the habit be allowed to make profession, and again much less, that this happen without the superior and community being allowed to say anything." Von Oberkamp had told Wimmer that another complaint against him was that he had not satisfactorily provided the sisters with material necessities. The abbot said that this was untrue and offered proof that he had supplied them sufficient food ever since they had come to St. Marys. He also called it "a wicked lie" that he had brought unwanted candidates to the convent in St. Marys each time he came from St. Vincent. "When I travel to St. Marys, I do so by horseback. My saddle cloth is not wide enough to stick a postulant into it!"

In his lengthy letter to Baron von Oberkamp, Abbot Boniface called Mother Benedicta's accusations blatant falsehoods and offered to contradict them with sworn testimony. With regard to his appropriation of funds intended for the sisters, he said that if he charged them for all the property, fuel, food, and necessities he had given them since their arrival in America, "there would be little left of the 8,000 florins" that King Ludwig had donated. "Have these sisters no feelings at all, that for all these sacrifices and benefits they can offer only false suspicions and calumnies?" Wimmer said that he had always "insisted strongly on enclosure" in the St. Marys convent, and he called Sister Benedicta's accusation that he allowed his monks to break the *clausura* "an infamous lie." Moreover, with regard to an accusation she had made that he had come into conflict with Prior Benedict Haindl over the nuns, Abbot Boniface said, "I have no priest who does not agree with me, that is who does not obey me. And if I had one, then I would be a real jackass if I made him prior."

Wimmer's letter to von Oberkamp was a virulent, bitter polemic against Mother Benedicta. In it he said that not only he, but "the entire clergy is against her. The sisters are against her. All the prioresses and nuns of the four convents are against her. Even her confederate Willibalda has fallen away from her and has most humbly asked for forgiveness. (I can produce her letter upon request.)" The abbot said that he would welcome back Sister Augustina Short, who had gone to Europe with Mother Benedicta, provided that she recognize and confess her guilt. But he hoped that Mother Edwarda Schnitzer and Bishop George von Öttl would not permit Mother Benedicta to return. "In America there is no longer any place for her."

His own efforts to direct the sisters, Abbot Boniface said, were made because he hoped to see the order in America grow.

This position is no benefice but a burden. Only love for the order and zeal for its expansion can determine me to hold it. I do not usurp anything for myself, but I hold fast whatever regard for the welfare of the order requires. The Bishop of Erie (and all bishops here) do not interest themselves in the sisters and cannot do so because of the great distance, ignorance of the language and of the Rule. Does not love demand it, if the law does not, that I interest myself in the sisters of the order, after I summoned them? Certainly. I acted and now act correctly when I do it out of love for the sisters. . . . Everything is in confusion; I must help put things in order; I established prioresses everywhere for three years; out of one monastery three are made; we have now four prioresses: in St. Marys, Erie, Newark, and St. Cloud. All posts are filled; for Benedicta there is none left, through her own fault. *Sic transit*, etc.[102]

In November 1857 Wimmer indeed seemed to have things under control. The four prioresses—Mother Theresa Vogel in St. Marys, Mother Scholastica Burkhardt in Erie, Mother Emmerana Bader in Newark, and Mother Willibalda Scherbauer in St. Cloud—had all accepted his authority and submitted to his jurisdiction. It appeared that the affair was finally settled and that in all matters his own will had prevailed.

Four months later, however, with the aid of Bishop Young of Erie, Bishop von Öttl of Eichstätt, and Archbishop von Reisach of the Roman Curia, Mother Benedicta succeeded in presenting her case to the Holy See, and in April 1858 Wimmer received a letter from Cardinal Alexander Barnabo, prefect of the Sacred Congregation for the Propagation of the Faith, informing him that

[t]he religious woman, Benedicta Riepp, who is in charge of the monastery of St. Marys in Pennsylvania, has written to His Holiness, Our Lord Pius IX, to obtain certain solutions about some articles expressed on the adjoining page, about which she cannot agree with your Reverence. Furthermore, the aforesaid nun makes a summary of the reasons on account of which she differs from you, which I do not think need to be related here because I think you have clearly understood them. But truly, since the matter concerns these differences between her and your Reverence, it is wholly fitting that, before any decision is made in regard to the matter, the pertinent information be sought from you. Wherefore, I shall expect that you will reply to me in regard to this matter, and in the meantime I am asking God that He may bestow on your Reverence all success and blessing.

The adjoining page listed the complaints Mother Benedicta had sent to the pope, essentially those detailed in the document she had earlier prepared by order of Bishop von Öttl. The cardinal's list also included a query from Propaganda about "accusations made by the sisters against the Superior of the Convent in St. Marys immediately before her departure from St. Marys as well as after her departure."[103]

Wimmer answered the charges as he had answered them for Baron von Oberkamp. In addition, he proposed four steps that Rome could take to bring order out of the chaos he claimed Mother Benedicta had caused. First, he asked that the convents in St. Marys, Erie, and

Newark be recognized as independent priories and incorporated into the American Cassinese Congregation under the jurisdiction of the congregation's president.[104] Second, he urged that the sisters be permitted to make solemn vows without being obliged to adhere to the customary monastic enclosure. Third, he requested that they be allowed to teach in public and private schools; and finally, he proposed that on account of their teaching burdens, they be permitted to substitute the Little Office of the Blessed Virgin for the Benedictine Office in their community prayer.[105] His petition to Rome was part of his overall strategy to establish a unified Benedictine response to the exigencies of the American missions and, at the same time, to create for the nuns an institutional structure that would assure them independence from episcopal control and organize them in a manner consistent with Benedictine tradition and conducive to their work and monastic observance in the United States.

At the end of July 1858 Wimmer wrote Abbot Utto Lang of Metten that his correspondence was "in arrears on account of the great work that my rebellious nun—or rather her case—has caused me." He said that he found much satisfaction and consolation

with my sisters. Generally speaking, their conduct is excellent. Their former prioress had for some time caused me much disappointment. . . but the greatest anguish is over. The tooth is pulled out. She set the snare for herself by deserting her position without being forced to. I was thus given the convenient opportunity to take action *propria auctoritate* and appoint prioresses as I saw fit for the four new priories. She returned after being absent for seven months in Europe in the beginning of May. I did not permit her to enter in St. Marys any more, nor in Erie. She didn't have the courage to go to Newark, so she was ordered to go immediately to St. Cloud and stay there under obedience to the prioress whom she is already starting to annoy. She is also causing trouble for the prior, Father Cornelius Wittmann. The only thing for her to do is to either submit herself or leave the order entirely.

She had made accusations against me in Rome from Erie and from Eichstätt. I was notified from Rome of this and told to explain my actions against her. I had already informed our procurator general [Abbot Angelo Pescetelli] who had approved all steps taken by me. I wrote Cardinal Barnabo, our procurator and at present the prefect of the Propaganda, and defended my claim of jurisdiction over the sisters of our order as *praeses congregationis.* I hope that it cannot be denied. (Naturally it is not a *beneficium* but an *onus gravissimum.*) I made the statement [to Cardinal Barnabo] that in the places where I have our fathers stationed I would not permit the nuns of our order without having jurisdiction over them. And I said that I would not consent to allow the obstinate mother superior to return to the convent. Having been given the opportunity to write Cardinal Barnabo, I made certain propositions regarding the matters of discipline for our sisters, concerning their exemption and incorporation into our congregation. It would not be good to shrink from difficulties if something for the better is to be done. The sisters are all on my side because they know too well that without my assistance they cannot achieve their purpose and that I am not mistaken. I do not mix in their affairs, but I had to take steps against Benedicta since she has acted wrongly for some time and would not listen to any well-considered counsel.[106]

Cardinal Barnabo responded to Wimmer's proposals in November that because the question both of jurisdiction and of solemn vows for the sisters had been raised, he had turned the matter over to the Congregation of Bishops and the Congregation of Religious. "I also asked the bishops of Pittsburgh and Erie," the cardinal said, "to take care to relate to me whatever they know that pertains to the controversy."[107]

In the meantime Wimmer precipitated another controversy with the sisters. In the fall of 1858 King Ludwig I donated 3,000 florins to the convent in Minnesota. As with his previous donations to the nuns in America, the king sent the money to Wimmer, but instead of giving it to the sisters, Abbot Boniface used the money to purchase land for the monks in St. Cloud. When Mother Willibalda learned of the misappropriation, she informed the king, and on March 15, 1859, King Ludwig's chaplain, Father Joseph Müller, wrote Wimmer asking if he really thought he had "the right to withhold the money from the sisters."

I consider it an injustice. This is the third time: 1) in St. Marys; 2) in Newark[108]. . . and now St. Cloud. You will lose the good will of His Majesty. I succeeded in excusing your action because of your great need and of the great advantage that accrued to you, but you must repay the sum of 3000 fl. by September 1, 1859. I have already had to inform Mother Willibalda about this. The Missionsverein was informed by the King to withhold 3000 fl. from the amount allotted to you in case you do not repay. This is how things stand now. I advise you not to do the same in the future. The women are too demanding. I do believe that you are in need of money and that you could take advantage of great opportunities. This does not, however, give you the right to take what was allotted to others, no matter how honestly you mean it.[109]

As soon as he received Müller's letter, Wimmer wrote immediately to King Ludwig acknowledging that he had made a mistake, but in an uninhibited gesture of ingratiation the abbot explained that he had acted "out of love for you. I wanted by all means to found a monastery (not a small priory, but a formal monastery that could become an abbey) which would carry the name St. Ludwig, and which should be a memorial of the everlasting gratitude of the American Benedictines towards the great donor, King Ludwig of Bavaria, for all times." Wimmer explained that 1,280 acres of land had been claimed by the Minnesota monks for the abbey, but unless they had paid for it immediately they would have lost their option on the property.

Then came the 3000 fl., just at the right time, when we must either pay and secure possession, or give up everything. Now the decision was easily reached: we must, for the honor of our good King, have a monastery. If we do not want to lose this land forever, we must pay for it now. The money for that is here; it is the King's own donation. It is really meant for the Benedictine Sisters, but surely only under the condition that it will be well spent, but this is certainly not the case. His Majesty would, therefore, not oppose it if it were used for St. Ludwig's, provided the proper explanation were made. . . . Love of Your Majesty inspired this reasoning. The temptation was strong. I submitted and committed the sin, in that with Your Majesty's own money I bought a capital tract of land for a Benedictine abbey in Your Majesty's honor! I am not sorry that I cannot repent; and moreover, it pleases me now still more because otherwise we would not have obtained a monastery in honor of St. Ludwig.

Wimmer went on to explain to the king the whole history of his relationship with the Benedictine sisters since their arrival in America. The future of the convent in St. Cloud, he said, was doubtful because its nuns continued to resist his authority.

I am certain Your Majesty does not have the intention of giving to a group of undisciplined and adventurous nuns the means to settle permanently near my good brothers, or to encourage them by your support and to strengthen them indirectly in their disorderly conduct. . . . It is really an injustice to me when in these circumstances my honesty is doubted; especially when this is done by the sisters themselves. They really do not deserve that I concern myself further about them. I believe I can best judge the needs of my brothers and sisters according to time and circumstances, and also the ways and means, how and when they should be helped. I am in debt myself. Everywhere are debts, but the heart of the order is in St. Vincent. Should the pulse stop here, it will stop everywhere. I must be concerned about that first. May these lines attain what they are meant to: Your Majesty's conviction that at all times I acted rightly, unselfishly and far-seeingly, and that I will always be concerned about the trust Your Majesty so kindly places in me.[110]

In June court chaplain Müller wrote Abbot Boniface that King Ludwig had accepted his explanation and had decided that there was no need for the abbot to repay the 3,000 florins to the sisters until Rome had decided the fate of the Benedictine nuns in America. Their case was at the moment before the cardinals in Rome, and the king did not want to give the money to the sisters if the future of their convent in St. Cloud was in doubt.[111]

It took Rome more than a year to review the case, but finally, on December 6, 1859, the Holy See handed down a decision. The decree reached America several weeks later, and from it Abbot Boniface learned that all of his most important petitions had been denied. Jurisdiction over the Benedictine nuns in America would henceforth rest not with the president of the American Cassinese Congregation but rather with the bishops of the three dioceses in which the sisters had settled. In addition, the sisters would no longer be bound to solemn vows but now only to simple vows, from which they could be dispensed by the local bishop. The decision settled the problem of *clausura* because as simply professed religious they were not bound to it.[112]

The Roman decision was a grave disappointment for Wimmer, not so much because he had personally been denied jurisdiction over the nuns but because he recognized that by refusing the Benedictine women in America the right to profess solemn vows and by placing them under the authority of the bishops, Rome had put them in the same category as contemporary diocesan sisterhoods and compromised their uniquely Benedictine identity. Still, he tried to cast a positive light on the Roman decree. "The decision from Rome is *not* unfavorable," he wrote Mother Scholastica Burkhardt, superior of the convent in Erie.

I won out in the dispute with Sister Benedicta and obtained everything I asked for the sisters except the *exemption*.[113] If that dispute had not come up, we surely would have obtained that too. I held to the papal confirmation of the three convents—St. Marys, Erie, and Newark—and to their recognition as priories, and then on that account, you remain under me and my successors in office, the parish priests.[114]

And now, the exemption. You have not yet, formally, been recognized by Rome, but it was given some thought (as it is expressly stated) and was earnestly recommended to the Rev. Bishops to acknowledge it. Naturally, because the sisters, under Sister Benedicta, did such mischief, one did not really trust them anymore and kept a little aloof. Furthermore, because Sister Benedicta had accused me of the greatest arbitrariness in the treatment of the sisters, and here was guilty of the rudest disobedience toward me, the Rev. Cardinals thought that most likely we might get angry again, and [the sisters] should, therefore, be under the jurisdiction of the bishops. But, because [the cardinals] knew that I, as the founder, according to canon law, should really have jurisdiction over you, they gave the bishops to understand that they should leave it to me so that I will receive you from them, but they could interfere in disputed matters.

However, I cannot do that, for, as an exempt abbot, I am under no bishop but, instead, directly under Rome. But if I do not want to have jurisdiction over you,[115] I would have to acknowledge the bishop as arbitrer over me in controversies, and in that way I myself would lose the exemption. I cannot do that even if the bishop would gladly give it. However, I am not afraid that you and I, or Sister Teresa and I, will quarrel with each other, but I cannot and will not give up my freedom. That does not say that I do not want to do anything for the sisters anymore. My priors, who are your confessors and spiritual guides and also your spiritual messengers, are subject to me, and can, and will, act for you according to my wish and your interest.

A beautiful idea—a community, a novitiate, a common cultural school for the whole order—will surely go to the grave with this. Yet, if you do what is right, and live and work in the spirit of our holy order, the Lord will make everything right. Indeed, I believe it is better this way because Rome has determined it to be so.[116]

Propaganda sent copies of the decree to Bishop Thomas Grace of St. Paul, Bishop James Bayley of Newark, and Bishop Josue Young of Erie. Bishop Young also received instructions to order Mother Benedicta Riepp to return to the Priory of St. Walburga in Eichstätt. In January Young wrote Abbot Boniface: "You can suggest to me, if you please, what ulterior steps I may have to take to carry out the wishes of the Sovereign Pontiff and the Congregation, if there are any. I think you can dispose of Sister Benedicta without further interference on my part, since she is not, as I am advised, in this diocese, but I know not where. I suppose, perhaps, I should have to communicate this matter to her, unless you think it best to take the whole care of it upon yourself."[117]

By this time Mother Benedicta was with her sisters in St. Cloud. She had returned to the United States from Europe in May 1858 and found the doors of all the other convents closed to her. With Wimmer's acquiescence she had gone to Minnesota, and when the Roman decree of December 6, 1859, was promulgated and the order issued that she return to Eichstätt, her health had deteriorated to such an extent that her ability to take the long journey back to Bavaria was out of the question. Learning that she was suffering from the final stages of tuberculosis, Bishop Thomas Grace of St. Paul urged Abbot Boniface to allow her to spend her last days in Minnesota, and both Wimmer and Bishop Young concurred. With her body racked by the ravages of consumption and her spirit broken by the long conflict with Abbot Boniface, Mother Benedicta lived quietly in Minnesota for two more years. In December 1861 she wrote her confessor:

With a weak hand I would like to write you a few lines to thank you for the information contained in your esteemed letter. I can only be amazed and grateful to God and the most blessed Virgin Mary that they show me so much mercy. I at once wrote to Rome and not only withdrew my opposition, but asked that the convents of Benedictine sisters be admitted into the Congregation. I consider myself fortunate, and the dear Lord may let me live or die. I am able to look into the future in peace. I have one great favor to ask of you, namely, that you be so kind and in my stead beg the Right Reverend Lord Abbot to forgive me for the displeasures I caused him. Now I must close; I feel too weak to write more. Do remember me in your good prayers.[118]

Three months later, on March 16, 1862, Mother Benedicta Riepp died in the convent of St. Cloud: she was thirty-six-years old.

The Roman decision of 1859 effectively separated the Benedictine sisters in the United States from the American Cassinese Congregation and its president, just as Benedicta Riepp had desired. But the consequences of that separation proved in some ways to be a heavier burden for the sisters than anything they had experienced or feared in the period when Wimmer claimed jurisdiction over them. As institutions falling under the authority of local American bishops, the convents lost the autonomy Riepp had wanted to ensure, and their struggles during the next century included even that essential one of maintaining their identity as Benedictines.

The sisters experienced enormous pressures from the bishops who

ruled them to abandon defining elements of the Benedictine vocation—elements such as the vow of stability that bound them to a particular community, the common recitation of the divine office, and
the right to freely choose their own prioresses. They were pressured to
conform to the pattern of modern institutes of teaching sisters whose
rules and customs were not compatible with a full expression of
the Benedictine charism.[119] Their identity as Benedictines was even
questioned by such European Benedictines as Bishop William B.
Ullathorne, O.S.B., of Birmingham, England, who wrote in 1880 to
Mother Scholastica Burkhardt of Erie:

From all that I have heard about the Benedictine women in the United
States, and I have had visits first from two of one house, then from one of
another, you do not appear to be true religious in the canonical sense of the
term, but rather a pious Institute bearing the Benedictine name, and an Institute which as yet has only Episcopal authority, so that your vows are not
only simple but technically or legally speaking they are only private vows:
that is to say, your bishop can deal with them and even dispense with them,
without the intervention of the Holy See, because you have not received the
formal approval of the Holy See.

Having no enclosure, either Pontifical or Episcopal, having but simple
vows, and doing the active works of Sisters of Charity, you bear the character of a third order, but the Church has never provided a third order of Benedictines, as it has of Dominicans and Franciscans. Third orders are not
bound to the great office as a rule, they usually have the little office of the
B.V.M.

You do not therefore belong to any form of the Benedictine Order which
the Church has formally approved. You are simply an Institute resting on
Episcopal authority and are bound to nothing but what you bind yourselves
to, and the obligation rests not on the authority of the Church but on the
authority of your bishop.[120]

No one really won in the controversy between Wimmer and Benedicta Riepp. In the aftermath of the 1859 Roman decree, Wimmer,
though he continued to work with the sisters, to assist them, and to
invite them to establish communities and teach schools in parishes
where his monks had the care of souls, was unable to forge a coherent, unified strategy with them for addressing the needs of the immigrants whom both the monks and the nuns had come to serve. For
her part Benedicta Riepp lost her bid to gain a greater measure of autonomy for Benedictine women when Rome placed the sisters under

American bishops who often proved less sympathetic and less understanding of their special needs as monastic women than Wimmer had. Both the abbot and the mother superior, of course, had worked for what each considered the best interests of the order and the Church. That they failed to agree on the means to do so is one of the greatest misfortunes of American Benedictine history.[121]

5 ✹ *Visions and Rebellions*

IN MAY 1860 Abbot Boniface wrote a long discursive letter to Abbot Utto Lang of Metten detailing recent events at St. Vincent and describing the conditions that prevailed in the American Benedictine communities. Two priests, Theodore von Gründer and Philip Vogg, had just been ordained, and Wimmer had assigned them to Texas and Kansas, respectively. Twenty-four clerics were currently preparing for orders, and these included seven he intended to send to Minnesota and four to Kansas. There were only three novices in the monastery in May, but the abbot said twenty scholastics would enter the novitiate in July. Michael O'Connor had just resigned as bishop of Pittsburgh, going east to join the Jesuits, and the Holy See had named Michael Domenec, C.M., a Spanish priest with twenty years' experience in the American missions, to replace him.

Wimmer wrote that in the near future he intended to build a small brewery at St. Vincent. Although the monastery had received permission from Rome in 1852 to brew beer, the abbot had refrained from using the privilege because of O'Connor's persistent opposition. But now that the Irish bishop, a leading proponent of the temperance movement in the American Church, was safely cloistered in a Jesuit novitiate in Maryland, no obstacle—certainly not the new Spanish bishop, who understood the desires of European immigrants to maintain their traditions—blocked the way of the Bavarian monks' fulfilling their old hope of providing the monastery table with inexpensive beer.

Abbot Boniface reported to Abbot Utto that frost had destroyed the wheat crop the previous year and that he had consequently been obliged to spend $3,000 for grain to feed the monks and students at St. Vincent. The crops planted by the monks in Carrolltown, St. Marys, and Indiana had also failed, and financial affairs at the abbey were consequently in a bad state.

This year, however, there is a wonderful outlook on nature. May God be pleased to keep it that way. Otherwise it will be bad for us because the pressure of money is felt everywhere. Commerce and business are at a standstill, and at the same time there is not enough food on the table for certain hypochondriacs. . . . All the trouble piles up on the poor abbot. Nevertheless our customary tendency to move forward must continue. Forward, always forward, everywhere forward. We cannot be held back by debts, by the difficulties of the times, by unfortunate years. Man's extremity is God's opportunity. . . . Everywhere there is need for priests, especially in the Far West. Very often I must turn down opportune offers because I do not have the people and do not like to divide the work of my priests too much. All over America churches are being built; many are very beautiful. The Kingdom of God is increasing at a remarkable rate despite the attacks from all sides (especially from German Freemasons; they are devilish people). . . . I never forget Metten at mass. In the Holy Sacrifice we find real consolation. Let us meet one another there under the cross where we will always discover new courage and gather fresh hope.[1]

The Benedictine movement forward was a movement westward, and as he indicated in his letter to Abbot Utto, Wimmer was enthusiastic about the mission potential of the new territories. "Today we stand with one foot on the west bank of the Mississippi in Minnesota," he wrote, "and with the other on the west bank of the Missouri in Kansas. In a few years you may find us near the Rocky Mountains and a little later in California on the Pacific Ocean. So it has to be. The stream of immigration moves ever westward and we must follow it."[2]

Wimmer missed no opportunity to instill his own enthusiasm for the West in the priests and brothers at St. Vincent, but he was often frustrated by the reluctance of many of them to go there. The priories in Minnesota, Kansas, and Texas were generally not well regarded by the monks in Pennsylvania. Texas had gained a reputation as a place where one was almost certain to contract tuberculosis; Kansas was renowned for its broiling summers, Minnesota for its fierce winters. A grim joke at the abbey during this period was that in the West a Benedictine's choices were Siberia (Minnesota), the Sahara (Kansas), or the grave (Texas).

Still, over the preceding four years the priories in those places had shown encouraging signs of growth and effectiveness. In Minnesota the monks served the pastoral needs of Catholics in an area encompassing six hundred square miles of central Minnesota and operated a small seminary (or "college") in St. Cloud. The five monks who had gone west in the spring of 1856 had established or assumed responsibility for parishes in St. Cloud (site of the priory), St. Augusta, Sauk Rapids, St. Joseph, St. James Prairie, Richmond, and St. Paul. Under Prior Demetrius di Marogna's able leadership, they had quickly completed and dedicated their monastery chapel, and in June 1856 they formally inaugurated monastic observance in Minnesota with the regular recitation of the divine office in the new chapel. A grasshopper plague struck the region two months later, bringing untold hardship to the settlers, and the community was forced to seek assistance from St. Vincent, which Wimmer gladly provided. But the St. Cloud monks quickly recovered from the setback and moved ahead with their pastoral and educational programs. They traveled to remote areas to seek out and bring the sacraments to Catholic settlers; they opened schools and provided catechetical instruction for children and adults; they educated young men for the priesthood in their small seminary in St. Cloud. In June 1857, at the invitation of Prior Demetrius, the Benedictine sisters from St. Marys arrived to teach in the parish school in St. Cloud and establish the Minnesota community that would eventually become one of the most active and important Benedictine convents in America.

From the beginning Abbot Boniface regarded St. Vincent's daughterhouse in Minnesota with particular affection and preferred it, after St. Vincent itself, above all of his other foundations. Indeed, at times he seemed to prefer it even above St. Vincent and on several occasions wrote that he wanted nothing better than to retire from his responsibilities in Pennsylvania and go to Minnesota to work as a missionary there.[3]

At the congregation's general chapter of 1858 the Minnesota priory, like the one in Kansas, had been declared independent of St. Vincent, though Wimmer, as president of the congregation, continued to exercise oversight of its administration and development. The chapter had also elected Father Benedict Haindl to replace Father Demetrius di Marogna as prior in Minnesota. Wimmer sent monks from St. Vincent to St. Cloud nearly every year between 1856 and 1860 so that by 1860 the St. Cloud priory numbered eight priests and ten brothers. Using the money diverted from King Ludwig's donation to the Benedictine sisters in Minnesota, Wimmer purchased 1,280 acres of prime land in the "Indianbush" northwest of St. Cloud, which the monks had claimed under the Land Act. A few years later the community would move the priory from St. Cloud to the Indianbush site, and within five years the priory would become the Abbey of St. Louis on the Lake and then St. John's.[4]

In Kansas, where Father Augustine Wirth and Casimir Seitz had gone in April 1857, the monks continued their mission work among the settlers and by 1860 had opened a college. Upon their arrival in Doniphan, Fathers Augustine and Casimir completed the church/ residence building Father Peter Henry Lemke had started and initiated their ministry to the Catholic families of the town. By June they were traveling to the river towns north and south of Doniphan to bring the sacraments to newly arrived Catholic settlers. Their mission journeys took them as far north as Omaha in the Nebraska Territory and as far south as Atchison and Leavenworth. The principal concentrations of Catholics were in Doniphan and Atchison Counties, which counted, respectively, one hundred and fifty and sixty Catholic families.

In September 1858, after the general chapter at St. Vincent in which the community was declared independent and Father Augustine was elected to a three-year term as prior, Wimmer sent Brother Paul Pfeifer from St. Marys, Pennsylvania, to assist as cook in the small Doniphan priory. When Wirth returned from the general chapter, one of the first things he began to plan was a move from Doniphan to Atchison. The reason for this was that he accurately foresaw that as Kansas grew in size and economic importance, Doniphan would be in a less favorable position to keep up with the development than Atchison. Wirth had seen that within a single year, because of more and more settlers moving in, the Catholic population of Atchison had increased by a factor of ten, so in August 1858 he had accepted from General Benjamin F. Stringfellow the donation of a tract of land on the northern edge of Atchison for the purpose of building a Catholic church and school. On this land he immediately put up a small frame church and soon began to make plans for establishing a small college.

The number of Catholics in Doniphan continued to decline as that of Atchison steadily increased. At the end of 1858, therefore, Wirth moved the priory to Atchison. King Ludwig I contributed the money that made the move possible. In October 1859 the monks opened St. Benedict's College in Atchison with four students. By the end of the year enrollment had increased to twelve, and by the following year the number had risen to twenty. Bishop Miége sent six seminarians to study philosophy and theology at St. Benedict's, and Bishop James M. O'Gorman, O.C.S.O., of the Nebraska Vicariate sent two. Wimmer assigned Fathers Edward Hipelius and Edmund Langenfelder from St. Vincent to assist Wirtz and Seitz in running the frontier school. Thus, by 1860 the Benedictines of St. Benedict's Priory were educating boys and young men for the priesthood in Atchison and providing pastoral care to Catholic settlers throughout eastern Kansas and Nebraska.[5]

As civil war loomed on the American horizon, the Benedictines of the United States were threatened with new hardship and adversity, but the developing material security and spiritual maturation of the communities, as well as Wimmer's own determination to move "forward, always forward," promised to carry the American monks through the difficult times to come. Steeled by the experience of disputes, deception, and outright revolt, they would emerge from the decade-long "era of troubles" stronger and better prepared to serve the American Church, to confront the challenges of postwar America, and to pursue their missionary and monastic goals into the 1870s and 1880s.

Not long after Rome had settled the question of jurisdiction over the Benedictine nuns in favor of the American bishops, and less than a year before the death of Mother Benedicta Riepp, another unexpected crisis arose which Abbot Boniface feared would destroy the peace and harmony that had been achieved at St. Vincent and the other American Benedictine communities. The episode that he called "the insurrection of the brothers" caught him completely by surprise.

Before coming to Pennsylvania in 1846 Wimmer had conceived a plan for organizing his monastery in the United States in a manner different from the organization of those he had known and helped revive in Bavaria. Unlike the Bavarian Benedictine communities, which had few lay brothers, the monastery of St. Vincent had from its earliest days a greater number of lay brothers than clerical monks. Wimmer had foreseen this development as early as 1845, when he wrote in his article for the *Augsburger Postzeitung* that in America the Benedictine Order would be required to adapt itself again to circumstances and begin anew. To acquire a considerable tract of land in the interior of the country, upon which to found a monastery, would not be very difficult; to bring under cultivation at least a portion of the land and to erect the most necessary buildings would give employment for a few years to the first Benedictine colony, which would consist of at least two or three priests and ten to fifteen brothers skilled in the most necessary trades. Once the colony is self-supporting, which could be expected in about two years, it should begin to expand so that the increased number of laboring hands might also increase the products and revenues to be derived from the estate. A printing and lithographing establishment would also be very desirable. Since the Holy Rule prescribes for all, not only manual labor and the chanting of the divine office, but also that the monks should devote several hours a day to study, this time could be used by the Fathers to instruct the Brothers thoroughly in arithmetic, German grammar, etc., thereby fitting them to teach school, to give catechetical instruction and in general to assist in teaching children as well as grown persons.[6]

Wimmer's original plan called for the integration of the brothers, clerical students, and priests into a single community in which they would all possess the same privileges, share the responsibilities of instructing the German students, and participate jointly in the communal prayer life, specifically in the recitation of the divine office. This plan emerged not from contemporary practice in Bavarian monasteries but from exigencies in America and Wimmer's own innovative thinking based on his reading and knowledge of the institution of the lay brotherhood in medieval Cistercian communities. Anticipating criticism of such integration, Wimmer wrote the *Ludwig Missionsverein* that the brothers would contribute not only to the material good of the monastery but also, by their simple piety, to its spiritual development as well.[7]

Not long after the monks' arrival in America, however, it became apparent that the plan was not practicable. Wimmer soon realized that a distinction between the lay and clerical members of the monastery, based upon social class, education, and function in the community, was unavoidable. The young clerical candidates who arrived at St. Vincent to study for the priesthood generally came from families who belonged to the small landowning, mercantile, and bourgeois classes of Bavarian society, families who could often provide secondary and sometimes even university education for their sons. Those, on the other hand, who came as candidates for the nonclerical brotherhood were skilled and unskilled laborers, generally from the poorer classes, who normally had only an elementary education. The differences between the two groups, as well as the economic and educational needs of the community itself, led to an inevitable division of labor and status at St. Vincent and in the priories founded from it.

The clerical members of the community devoted their energies before ordination to study, and then afterward to teaching, sacramental ministry, and the organization and administration of Catholic congregations, first in Pennsylvania and later in Minnesota, Kansas, New Jersey, Kentucky, and Texas. Upon the nonclerical members, or lay brothers, devolved the responsibility of filling the great demand for manual laborers necessary for building the monasteries, farming the lands, and feeding and clothing the American Benedictine communities. Thus while the priests taught and catechized, the brothers worked in the fields, kitchens, and craft shops.

Among the lay brothers, who made up nearly 70 percent of the American Cassinese Benedictine family through most of the nineteenth century, there were farmers, millers, brewers, herdsmen, saddlers, blacksmiths, machinists, locksmiths, carpenters, cooks, bakers, brewers, tailors, bootmakers, weavers, printers, and a host of other workers. There were also among them architects, artists, and teachers, but the vast majority were skilled and unskilled manual laborers, with limited formal education, whose work was essential to the success of the Benedictine communities Wimmer established.

The wide gap in status between the lay brothers and clerical members of the community developed gradually. Wimmer arrived in America with eighteen candidates for the monastic life: four students for the priesthood and fourteen postulants for the lay brotherhood. Even though European class consciousness was among the baggage the Bavarian Benedictines brought with them to the United States, and while canon law dictated a hierarchical structure that placed clerics above laymen in religious communities, the Benedictines at St. Vincent quickly absorbed the democratic ideals of their new home. Wimmer was a strong proponent of the principle that Benedictines should be prepared to adapt, as much as possible, to the conditions of the place in which they found themselves. His flexibility in this regard extended to a willingness to create a monastic organization in which the brothers, at least at the beginning, were permitted to make solemn vows and to share in the decision-making processes of the community. At the same time, he insisted that the clerical monks share with the brothers the labor of the fields, a policy that brought him into conflict with his first prior, Father Peter Lechner.

His efforts to "democratize" the monastery soon showed signs of fundamental weaknesses. Within days of establishing the monastic horarium at St. Vincent, Wimmer realized that the brothers, none of whom had studied Latin, were unable to follow the intricacies of the monastic breviary and thus were not benefiting fully from the prayer life of the community. He therefore instituted a dual system of communal prayer in which the clerical monks continued to recite the hours of the divine office in Latin but in which the lay brothers followed a separate prayer regimen consisting of the recitation of the rosary and the "Little Office" of the Blessed Virgin in German. Then, as more clerical monks were accepted into the community, he ended the practice of permitting the lay brothers to participate in deliberations of the monastic chapter, where decisions concerning the community's temporal policies, leadership, and spiritual regimen were made. In this he was following the requirements of canon law, which limited participation in the chapter to clerics in major orders, but he was also sympathetic with those clerical monks who argued that the brothers, a majority in the community, did not possess sufficient knowledge and education to make positive contributions to the deliberations of the monastic chapter.

Still, Wimmer attempted to grant as much equality as canon law allowed to the lay brothers. In 1852, when St. Vincent was elevated to the rank of canonical priory, he received the vows of all the members of the community. Each of them, including the brothers, pronounced solemn vows, although the decision to permit the brothers to make solemn vows, rather than the less binding simple profession, was not reached without opposition from some clerical members of the monastery.[8] In any event, though they were allowed to make solemn vows, the brothers no longer had the right to participate in the deliberations and decisions of the monastic chapter. By 1860 the social structure that divided clerical and lay members of the monastic communities in the American Cassinese Congregation was firmly institutionalized, and this caused dissatisfaction among some of the lay brothers at St. Vincent.

Serious problems did not arise for nearly ten years after Wimmer received the first solemn vows of the lay brothers. Then, in April 1861, Brother Joseph Sailer, one of the pioneers to come to St. Vincent with Father Boniface in 1846, addressed a lengthy letter of complaint to Pope Pius IX in which he alleged that the brothers at St. Vincent were being treated unfairly and even taken advantage of by the abbot and the other clerical monks. Sailer wrote that when they were leaving Europe in 1846 Wimmer had promised that in establishing the order in America there would be no distinction made between the brothers and the priests, that all would enjoy the same rights and privileges. He said, for example, that Wimmer had promised the brothers separate cells such as the priests would have and that they would be given the right to vote as full-fledged members of the monastic chapter. According to Sailer, none of these promises was kept. He complained that the brothers were looked down upon by the priests and clerics, who did not consider them part of the community; that they could be dismissed by Wimmer at the abbot's whim, solemn vows notwithstanding; that they were forced to work so hard "that no slave in America is treated with greater severity"; and that several brothers had been dismissed for no reason. "A thousand times" they had been promised the statutes that would instruct them in their rights and privileges, Brother Joseph said, but they had never received them and it was a hard thing "to have spent one's youth and lost one's health in working hard, and then to be sent away or to be treated in such a manner as to be obliged to go away and close one's life in a poor-house, in a country where one cannot even speak the language." Finally Brother Joseph protested that though great demands were made of the brothers, who were bound by the "gravest obligations," no corresponding rights and privileges were granted them.[9]

Wimmer did not learn of Brother Joseph's letter for three months. In July he was surprised to receive two communiqués from Rome, one from the Sacred Congregation for the Propagation of the Faith, the other from his friend Abbot Angelo Pescetelli. Pescetelli wrote:

To my letter of June 25 I add this one in order to render futile another attack of the Devil, who, to your glory, does not desist from lying in wait for your heel. . . . [Recently] Cardinal Barnabo handed me an appeal against you which was sent to the Propaganda by Brother Joseph Sailer, and which was dated April 30th. . . . I hasten to inform you that the Propaganda has asked the bishop of Pittsburgh for information in the matter. Speak to the bishop, therefore, and explain everything to him so that he may send a report in accordance with truth and justice.

Pescetelli detailed the charges Brother Joseph, who claimed to speak for a majority of the brothers, had made against Abbot Boniface, and said:

You see how well this upstart knows how to exploit democratic principles by misusing the words "fraternity" and "equality." I have already made a reply to Propaganda, but it would be good if you would explain to me your methods of governing the brothers, especially in securing them a subsistence in old age and sickness. The Bull of Innocent XI, in which he approves the Bavarian Congregation, does not speak of brothers at all. This appeal has caused me to withdraw my petition [that you be declared abbot of St. Vincent for life] because however much Cardinal Barnabo may be favorably disposed towards us, there are some, and among these perhaps is von Reisach, who consider you a severe man, arbitrary and obstinate in your opinions. You see, my dear Wimmer, that you will receive the reward of your many and fatiguing labors in Heaven. On earth you will find nothing but thistles and thorns. Console yourself, though, with the thought that this is the Way of the Cross, which all saints, especially founders, have followed.[10]

Cardinal Barnabo's letter outlined the complaints of Brother Joseph and informed Wimmer that the Propaganda Fide had directed Bishops Michael Domenec of Pittsburgh and Josue Mary Young of Erie to investigate conditions among the brothers at St. Vincent. On behalf of the other cardinals of the Sacred Congregation Barnabo asked Wimmer to respond to the charges made by Brother Joseph.[11]

Abbot Boniface composed his response at once. In his lengthy letter to Propaganda he claimed that Brother Joseph's charges against him were false and unjust. In every instance regarding the lay brothers at St. Vincent, he said, he had followed the customs and practices of the Bavarian Congregation. It was true that he had originally planned a greater integration of them in the community and had even hoped that some of the brothers might become teachers in the school. But he had been obliged to abandon this plan "in order to preserve harmony among them." He acknowledged that he had been forced to expel certain members of the community, including some lay brothers in solemn vows, after they themselves had abandoned the monastery and been declared *fugitivos,* but in every case he had used the Holy Rule as his guide.[12]

In September Bishop Domenec and his German-speaking secretary, Father John Stibiel, arrived at St. Vincent and instituted an investigation into the matter on behalf of the Sacred Congregation for the Propagation of the Faith. The bishop interviewed all the brothers in the community and having settled the affair in his own mind, wrote Propaganda that "some of the brothers state that promises of privileges for brothers have not been kept, and could not be kept. Several want a legal right to the property of the monastery, like the priests. The Right Reverend Abbot is too easy in receiving monks and brothers. This may give rise to troubles, but he has the very best of intentions. I propose that the brothers make only simple vows in the future."[13]

Bishop Young wrote Wimmer that he also had been instructed by Propaganda to visit St. Vincent and investigate the complaints of the brothers, but rather than do this, Young asked Wimmer to compose a letter that he could "conscientiously" send to Rome in answer to Propaganda's inquiries. In the meantime the bishop of Erie visited the priory at St. Marys, interviewed the brothers, and "found all pleasant and agreeable." Shortly afterward Bishop Young wrote Cardinal Barnabo that "after making investigations among the abbot, the fathers, and the brothers at St. Marys Priory, I heard no whisper of complaint. I have the honor of enclosing the abbot's report. It satisfied me, because I know the man, and should be more ready to accuse him of excess of indulgence towards the fractious and erring, than being severe with any one."[14]

In October the chapter at St. Vincent, composed of priests and clerics in major orders, met to debate the matter and after discussing the charges of the brothers determined that there was no substance to them. They drafted a letter to Rome indicating the results of their deliberations and exonerating Wimmer of any fault.[15] Wimmer himself wrote:

It is not on the part of any of the lay brothers that this thing set forth, but from Brother Joseph alone: none of the other brothers knows anything concerning it. This all the brothers and this Joseph Sailer himself positively and candidly declared, having been interrogated concerning it.

It is a pure lie (a) that I bore myself arbitrarily against the lay brothers, (b) that I am of the opinion that the lay brothers are able to be easily dismissed after pronouncing religious vows in the order. Since coming to America I have turned none of the lay brothers from the monastery, but have redeemed [several of them], even at great hazard, which can also be proven not only from the testimony of all the rest of the lay brothers, but also from the declarations of all the fathers of the chapter.

Wimmer went on to explain that in two cases he had been forced to formally expel two brothers in solemn vows who had abandoned the monastery and caused grave scandal, but that he had not initiated the action. He had rather instituted procedures called for in the Rule under such circumstances: "Whether this is a crime, let others judge. I, however, confess that I do not know how the discipline of the Rule is able to be sustained if anyone is freely permitted to travel here and there, to cause the greatest scandal, to disturb the whole peace and quiet of the congregation, etc."[16]

In December Pescetelli wrote from Rome that after receiving Wimmer's letter and that of the monastic chapter, he had drawn up a report for the cardinals of Propaganda

demanding the punishment of Sailer and the reparation of your honor. The cardinal, who is very well disposed towards you, told me that the bishops of Erie and Pittsburgh had sent in their reports and that he had ordered them to be given to me. . . . The bishop of Erie deplores in general the spirit of insubordination among the lay brothers, and praising your gentleness of mind, commends your conduct and sends to the Propaganda your own letter to him. The bishop of Pittsburgh reports that having heard the brothers, he has found: 1) that some promises of privileges had not been kept and that they could not be kept, 2) that the brothers want a legal right to the property of the monastery like the priests, 3) that the abbot is too easy in receiving monks and brothers, and that this will give rise to much trouble. But, as he adds, the abbot has the very best intentions. I have already made answer to those unreasonable pretensions of the brothers, and I have made the proposition that henceforth the brothers be allowed to make only simple vows and that they be subject to dismissal in the same manner that they are received, by decision of the monastic chapter as is the case in the Cassinese Congregation. Without this check there is no way of keeping the brothers under proper control. I will interview the cardinals composing the Sacred Congregation, and I hope they will do you justice.[17]

After that the matter seemed to die as quickly as it had begun. Satisfied with the reports of Bishops Domenec and Young, as well as with the information and defense of Wimmer supplied by Pescetelli, the cardinals of the Propaganda Fide issued no formal statement changing the structure of the lay brotherhood at St. Vincent. In 1866, however, while Wimmer was in Rome on other business, the Sacred Congregation handed down a decree at his request declaring that in the future *fratres conversi* of the American Cassinese Congregation would not be allowed to make solemn vows, though those who had already pronounced them would be bound to them. In one sense the decision of Propaganda was anticlimactic. After the problems generated by Brother Joseph Sailer, Abbot Boniface took matters into his own hands with regard to vows, and after 1861 no more brothers at St. Vincent were permitted to make solemn profession.[18]

Meanwhile, as Wimmer struggled with the problems caused by the "insurrection of the brothers," he was also dealing with the question of his lifetime abbacy, which he had tried unsuccessfully to resolve at the general chapter of 1858. At that time Wimmer had been elected abbot of St. Vincent for life, but the Propaganda Fide, on account of irregularities in the election process, had confirmed him only for another three years, at the end of which a second election was to be held. The term would expire in September 1861, and in August 1860 Wimmer wrote Abbot Pescetelli telling him that it would be extremely difficult to hold the chapter as scheduled. Recalling all the monks to the abbey would mean that the most distant missions would suffer greatly. Not only would they be left without priests for a long period of time, but also the money expended by each of the missions to send priests back to the motherhouse would cause severe hardship at a time when economic conditions all over the United States were bad. Moreover, the political situation in America had deteriorated to such an extent that it might be impossible for the priests in some of the distant priories, in Texas for instance, to return home at all should war break out.[19]

Apologizing for his failure to respond sooner, Abbot Angelo wrote the following January that Cardinal Barnabo had suggested that Pescetelli submit a letter to the Propaganda informing the cardinals of the difficulties calling a general chapter for the election of a lifetime abbot at St. Vincent would involve. Abbot Angelo said that Barnabo suggested further that

it might be good to have a letter from the bishop of Pittsburgh, and also from some other friendly bishop, directed to me or to the Sacred Congregation, and that I should then urge that you be confirmed for life or at least for

ten years if a confirmation for life cannot be secured. I hope you will approve
my plan, which has gone out from me alone, independently of you. I am
well acquainted with matters in Rome, and I assure you that there is no other
way of getting out of it. Moreover, if we obtain our object, *non curamus de
modo* so long as it is honest and does not compromise your honor.[20]

In February Wimmer wrote Pescetelli that serious internal problems had developed in the American Cassinese Congregation and for
that reason he wondered whether he should remain abbot at all. He
accused Prior Augustine Wirth of Kansas of trying to wreck the successes the American Benedictines had achieved. Wirth was attempting to organize his own novitiate in Kansas and thus break one of the
principal ties that bound the Kansas community with St. Vincent.
Wimmer said that Wirth, to a great extent, had been responsible for
the opposition and defections which the community had suffered in
1860, and that the motivating factor for his insubordinate behavior
was Wirth's own unprincipled ambition. Prior Augustine, Abbot
Boniface explained, had hoped to be elected abbot of St. Vincent in
1858. When his scheme failed, he asked to have his vows transferred
to the Kansas priory. Wimmer had not agreed. Even though the
Kansas community, like the one in Minnesota, was an independent
priory, the decision of the general chapter of 1858 remained in force
that all monks of the American Cassinese Congregation would continue to be bound by the vow of stability to the Abbey of St. Vincent.
Now Wirth was attempting to build up the priory in Atchison so that
it might be an abbey and he be elected abbot. In accordance with this
scheme, Prior Augustine had recently opened his own unauthorized
novitiate. Wimmer informed Pescetelli that the creation of another
American abbey would not displease him but that Wirth was not
suited for the job of abbot. He pointed out that the prior of Kansas
had come to St. Vincent in 1851 after being dismissed from the novitiate at Metten and that he had never demonstrated the humility that
a monk ought to have. His actions in Kansas clearly demonstrated
that he was unfit to be an abbot, and Wimmer said that because
of his impatience and ambition, Wirth was causing him no end of
trouble.[21]

Abbot Angelo answered in June that despite the difficulties caused
by Wirth's ambition-driven efforts to divide the American Benedictine community, Wimmer should not be discouraged. Especially he

Father Augustine Wirth (1828–1901), founder of the Benedictine community in Kansas that became Saint Benedict
Abbey, Atchison. (ASVA)

should not contemplate withdrawing as abbot of St. Vincent. Assuring him that Rome would never give the Kansas community permission to establish a novitiate or a house of studies separate from those
at St. Vincent, Pescetelli asked Abbot Boniface to explain a little more
clearly the relationship between the independent priories in Kansas
and Minnesota and the mother abbey at St. Vincent. "To settle all
questions," he continued,

I, for my part, will demand your confirmation, simple and absolute, the
more so since the war, which is now raging so furiously in America, renders

it impossible to hold a chapter. In case therefore that no directives shall have come from Rome by the 18th of September, do not become uneasy and send questions or doubts, for you know what consequences they had three years ago. But hold the chapter as best you can, following the general principle that all those are to be called who have a right to take part, and then let those come who can and desire to do so. I believe that in this way the monastic affairs in America will find a lasting adjustment and all intrigues and ambitions will be frustrated.[22]

Less than a month later Abbot Angelo wrote once again to inform Wimmer that Cardinal Barnabo was of the opinion that the general chapter slated for September 18, 1861, should be postponed for a year and that all the monks of the American Cassinese Congregation should remain where they were until the political situation in the United States had resolved itself. Pescetelli, on the other hand, recommended that "if you can assemble more than half the members of the chapter, you should hold a chapter meeting, for the longer you wait the more discord and trouble the adherents of Wirth will be able to make. . . . In case you send letters or petitions to the Propaganda, let them pass through my hands so that I may regulate myself according to circumstances."[23]

Abbot Boniface answered Pescetelli's queries concerning the organizational structure of the American Cassinese Congregation by pointing out that according to the decrees of the general chapter of 1858, which had been approved and confirmed by Rome, the independent priors of the American Cassinese Congregation were subject in all things to the authority of the president of the congregation, as was the custom and practice in the Bavarian Congregation. The monks of these independent priories, moreover, were to remain canonically attached to the Abbey of St. Vincent until such time as the future of the priories had been assured. The members of the Minnesota community had applied for a transfer of stability, but no decision had yet been made, nor had the transfer of stability from St. Vincent been approved for any of the monks in Kansas. Wimmer emphasized that Prior Augustine, by establishing his own novitiate and house of studies in Atchison and by continually petitioning St. Vincent for more priests, was destroying the order of the American Benedictines so that Kansas might gain a greater degree of independence and so that his own inordinate ambition to become abbot might be fulfilled.[24]

Before Wimmer's letter of August 3 had time to reach Rome, Abbot Angelo wrote again telling him that Cardinal Barnabo had come to a decision about the election of a lifetime abbot for St. Vincent. The election was to be definitively postponed for twelve months. "I thought it would be best if the chapter were held," Abbot Angelo wrote, "but Cardinal Barnabo said that those who would be legitimately absent might claim such an election invalid and that the Holy See would not confirm it. Do not be uneasy, therefore, about the legitimacy of your authority since you have had proper recourse to Propaganda." On September 15, 1861, the Sacred Congregation for the Propagation of the Faith officially ruled that the general chapter at St. Vincent be postponed for one year. In the meantime Wimmer would remain abbot "at the pleasure of the Holy See."[25]

In the spring of 1862 Abbot Boniface sent Father Wendelin Mayer, novice master at St. Vincent, and Father Louis Fink, prior of the recently established Chicago priory, on visitation to Kansas. The two visitators examined the books and interviewed the monks of the Atchison community, and at the end of their investigation issued a stinging denunciation of Prior Augustine's administration. They criticized Wirth for his financial administration and censured him for his efforts to reject the authority of the abbot of St. Vincent by opening a novitiate and admitting five novices to simple vows. The visitation was such a success, Wimmer reported, "that Father Prior Wirth surrendered completely, dissolved the novitiate and ordered everything in the priory according to the Rule and the sacred canons. . . . There was hardly the shadow of regular life in the house; three of the pseudo-professed promptly left the order; one came to St. Vincent to make his novitiate." Wimmer told Pescetelli that Wirth had repented his wrongdoing. "You can easily understand what a relief this is to me. It is a great triumph for our policies. I have freely forgiven all. . . . The opposition is now without head."[26]

But Wimmer's triumph was short-lived. In June Prior Augustine, anticipating a confrontation at the forthcoming general chapter, wrote Father Edward Hipelius, a St. Vincent monk studying in England who planned to visit Rome, and asked him to secure from the Holy See copies of any decrees that might be useful in his bid to challenge the power of Abbot Boniface. In September delegates from all the distant priories arrived at the abbey in Pennsylvania for the general chapter at which they would elect an abbot of St. Vincent who would rule for life.

The first order of business was the election. For this nearly all the priests of the congregation had gathered, and it seemed clear that they were prepared to elect Wimmer a second time. Before the balloting could begin, however, the rebels made their move. Prior Augustine Wirth rose and introduced a letter from Father Edward in which Hipelius maintained that according to a papal decree of May 7, 1859, not only monks in solemn vows, but also those in simple vows had the right to vote in abbatial elections. This was an obvious ploy to oust Wimmer, and the conspirators seemed for the moment to have gained the upper hand. Most of the opposition to the abbot's rule existed among the younger members of the community. With their ranks bolstered by the young clerics not yet in solemn vows and by the simply-professed brothers (many of whom had just recently joined Brother Joseph Sailer in the "insurrection"), Wirth and his supporters had reason to believe that they could accomplish their goal. A heated debate broke out about the validity of Father Edward's position. Wimmer realized that if he did not permit the simply-professed monks to participate, then the election might be challenged by his opponents as invalid and the matter would end up before the cardinals of Propaganda once again. On the other hand, he knew that if he permitted the simply-professed monks to vote, then there was a good chance he would not be chosen. He was convinced that the younger monks were trying to have Father Alphonse Heimler, a thirty-year-old native of Bavaria, elected. Heimler, Wimmer said, had joined the ranks of the rebels to spite the abbot when he (Wimmer) refused to appoint him director of St. Vincent College. He had aligned himself with Prior Augustine and had even requested that his vows be transferred to Kansas.[27] With this popular monk in their ranks (Heimler was one of the most respected professors in the college), Wimmer's opponents were even more powerful than before. Understanding all this, Abbot Boniface did the only thing he could in view of the circumstances. He postponed the election.

The postponement of the election was a heavy blow to both Wimmer and the community. For the fifth time they had been frustrated in their efforts to secure the future of the abbey by choosing a lifetime abbot of St. Vincent. On each of the four previous occasions Rome had stepped in and prevented them from doing so, either by failing to raise the community to abbatial status in 1852, by appointing Wimmer abbot for three years in 1855, by overturning an election because of irregularities in 1858, or in 1861 by ordering a twelve-month delay in the election to allow all eligible members of the congregation to be present. Now Wimmer himself had been forced to postpone the election because of a revolt among some of his most talented and influential monks. His frustration was palpable.

With his plan for the election in shambles and realizing the extent of the opposition to him among the younger monks of the community, a discouraged Wimmer moved on to the other business of the general chapter. He named an executive committee to represent the four principal houses of the congregation and released the other priests to return to their priories. The executive committee consisted of Prior Benedict Haindl and Father Cornelius Wittmann of Minnesota, Prior Augustine Wirth and Father Emmanuel Hartig of Kansas, Prior Alto Hörmann of San José in Texas, Prior Othmar Wirtz of St. Vincent, and Abbot Boniface himself. These seven monks then addressed themselves to the pressing affairs of the congregation.

They decided first of all to petition the Holy See for the elevation of the independent priory of St. Cloud in Minnesota to the rank of abbey. Then they voted to petition Rome for the elevation of the community in Texas to the status of independent canonical priory. Next they named Father Amandus Kramer, who had gone to Texas just before the outbreak of the war, to replace Father Alto Hörmann as prior. Hörmann had managed to return to St. Vincent for the general chapter, but because of the Union blockade of the South, he was unable to return to his post.

In order to avoid further problems like those arising when Father Augustine opened a novitiate in Kansas, the delegates confirmed the decrees of the general chapter of 1858 that established a common congregational novitiate and house of studies for clerics at St. Vincent. The delegates also formally designated Father Wendelin Mayer, novice master at St. Vincent, as novice master for the entire congregation. They next ruled that the abbot-president and elected visitators would periodically make visitation to each of the monasteries of the congregation to ensure that they were faithfully following the Rule of St. Benedict and the statutes of the Bavarian Congregation and properly observing the monastic discipline. Despite his opposition to Wimmer's rule and over his own protestations against reappointment, Wirth was reconfirmed as prior of St. Benedict's Priory, Atchison, for another three-year term. Father Benedict Haindl had asked that he be replaced as prior in Minnesota, so the general chapter directed that an election for a new superior be held in St. Cloud.

Next the delegates took up the matter of the "reformation of the congregation." From the earliest days of the Benedictine presence in America Wimmer and his monks had struggled with the problem of monastic observance. The abbot's own ideal of Benedictine monastic life was founded upon his belief that the most creative period in monastic history was that of the eighth and ninth centuries when Benedictine saints like Boniface, Willibald, and Ansgar sallied out from their monasteries, the Holy Rule in one hand, the Gospels in the other, to bring the Christian faith to the continental pagans north of the Rhine. These monks, coming principally from England, had founded the first German, Scandinavian, and Slavic abbeys and had created a northern European monastic culture that endured throughout the early Middle Ages. Their active missionary and educational apostolates had Christianized pagan peoples and stamped those peoples' faith with an indelible monastic character and an ongoing Benedictine religious and educational tradition that Wimmer saw as his own. His ambition was to replant that tradition in American soil.

He had articulated his ideals as early as 1845 when he wrote in the *Augsburger Postzeitung:* "Let us remember that here in Bavaria from the year 740 to the year 788 not less than 40 Benedictine monasteries were founded and the communities were composed almost entirely of natives from the free classes, who had enjoyed the advantages of freedom in the world and could have chosen the married state without any difficulty or hindrance. Why should we not reasonably expect the same results in the United States where the conditions are so similar?"[28]

Inspired by the achievements of the eighth-century Benedictines in Bavaria, Wimmer had worked for almost two decades attempting to create something similar in America. But there was another medieval monastic tradition that vied with the active missionary monasticism of the eighth and ninth centuries to inspire European monks during the nineteenth-century Benedictine revival. This was the tradition of the French abbey of Cluny. In the eleventh and twelfth centuries Cluny initiated a new phase in the history of European monastic spirituality. Altering the traditional Benedictine balance between work and prayer, Cluniac custom required that monks devote their lives almost entirely to liturgical ceremony, with the result that at Cluny liturgical ceremony became the raison d'etre of monastic observance and reached a degree of splendor unequaled in the annals of Christian monasticism. Traditional Benedictine emphasis on manual labor, educational work, and missionary activity had no place in its observance. During the high Middle Ages Cluny came to represent an influential monastic ideal, one partially revived by several outstanding Benedictine leaders during the European Romantic Age.

Three of these leaders were, like Wimmer, secular priests who founded monasteries where their monastic ideals could be put into practice: Prosper Guéranger founded the Abbey of Solesmes in France in 1833; the brothers Maurus and Placidus Wolter, who became monks in Italy in 1859, founded the Abbey of Beuron in Germany's Rhineland in 1863. Solesmes and Beuron modeled their monastic observance upon a contemporary understanding of the heritage of Cluny. Both emphasized liturgical ceremony and theological scholarship as the essential elements of Benedictine life, and both regarded the active apostolic work of such contemporary Benedictine missionaries as the Italian Pietro Casaretto, the Frenchman Jean-Baptiste Muard, the Englishman Bede Polding, the Spaniard Rosando Salvado, and the Bavarian Boniface Wimmer as inconsistent with the Benedictine monastic ideal.[29]

In the 1860s many of the younger American monks had assimilated the ideals that had inspired the founders of Solesmes and Beuron. These young monks now began to call for reform within the American Cassinese monasteries. As early as 1847 reformers led by Father Peter Lechner of Scheyern had questioned the active monastic life Wimmer was attempting to introduce to the United States and had urged that a more contemplative, scholarly, liturgically oriented life be adopted by the monks of St. Vincent. Reform-minded monks periodically called for a stricter monastic regimen at St. Vincent, and in 1862 another movement for reform had developed significant support at the abbey. Led principally by Prior Othmar Wirtz and novice master Wendelin Mayer, this movement gained momentum and adherents and was chiefly responsible for the call for reformation made by the general chapter of 1862.

It is clear that Wimmer did not necessarily regard such efforts to instill new devotional practices and a more contemplative spirit into the monastic life of the American Cassinese Benedictines as antagonistic to his own more active ideals. So long as they did not conflict with his plans to expand the order in America and to strengthen the various communities he had founded, he permitted and even encouraged them, frequently expressing a hope that such movements would bring a deeper spiritual life to the community. He opposed them only when they threatened the growth and internal harmony of the American monasteries.

Indeed, Wimmer consistently depended upon the reformers for leadership and often entrusted them with important temporal and spiritual responsibilities. Still, there continued to exist a tension between the reformers and those who were satisfied with the status quo. The struggle that Wimmer and his monks faced in the New World was essentially one of maintaining a spiritually sound monastic observance on the one hand and of serving the pastoral needs of the American Church on the other. There existed within the congregation strong disagreement as to how to strike a balance between these two purposes. The progress the Benedictines made in the missions during their first fifteen years in America had not been achieved without a degree of compromise in the area of monastic observance. Wimmer himself was not reluctant to adapt to the environment in which he found himself, and some of his compromises earned criticism from Benedictines both in America and Europe. Abbot Placidus Wolter of the Abbey of Maredsous in Belgium, for example, wrote

We have just received the new *Ceremoniale Monasticum* which has been issued by St. Vincent's Abbey. We are glad that they are doing something there, but the book of course has use only for the congregation over there. We do things quite differently here in many ways. For example, our method of accepting novices and our profession form are quite different. The melodies they suggest for the music are different. It has for us only an historical interest. I think that it is a shame that in these matters they take such a modern view and do not cling firmly to that which is ancient and monastic. For example, their willingness to give up certain privileges of the abbot! The Rt. Rev. Abbot Boniface has written to me that he has given up the practice of many of them as being unsuitable to our times. But is that good?[30]

Despite his willingness to adapt and even compromise, however, Wimmer by no means neglected his obligation to establish sound monastic observance in the monasteries he founded. In Kansas he had seen the debilitating effects on community life that resulted from a neglect of monastic discipline, and when zealous men proposed reform in the American Cassinese Congregation during the general chapter of 1862, he supported them.

One of the perennial problems the early communities faced was the tendency to disregard the importance of monastic enclosure. Because they were missionaries, the monks themselves were often unable to observe all the niceties that such enclosure demanded. Many of them were forced to travel great distances from the monastery and to remain away for long periods of time. Therefore they could not always live the regular life within the cloister that the Rule, tradition, and canon law required. In addition, in some cases laymen were allowed to visit monks within the enclosure because other meeting spaces were not available, and this irregularity occasioned concern and protest from many of the monks. The issue had come to such a head by 1862 that the general chapter found it necessary to legislate that the monastic *clausura* would be strictly observed in the monasteries of the American Cassinese Congregation. The chapter also passed legislation calling for a more careful observance of monastic poverty and for greater attention to religious and devotional practices in general. It handed down specific directives concerning the required reading of novices and professed monks alike. Included among the works the monks were to possess and read regularly were Holy Scripture, the Holy Rule, the *Imitation of Christ,* the *Tyrocinium Religiosum,* and several manuals of asceticism. The chapter ruled that the monks in America were to follow the customs of the Bavarian Congregation with regard to spiritual reading, devotional practices, and liturgical observances. Finally, the delegates to the general chapter censured several monks in the congregation for their failure to observe monastic discipline carefully enough. The three-day meeting ended on September 18, and the Minnesota and Kansas representatives returned to their communities.[31]

In October 1862 Abbot Boniface conducted a visitation of the priory in Minnesota. Father Benedict Haindl had resigned as prior, and the general chapter had directed that an election for his replacement be held as early as possible, so Wimmer called the election upon his arrival in St. Cloud and presided over the balloting. Father Othmar Wirtz, prior at St. Vincent, was chosen to succeed Father Benedict as the fourth prior of the Minnesota foundation and Wimmer immediately confirmed his election. As was customary in the American Cassinese Congregation at the time, the thirty-one-year-old Wirtz was given a three-year mandate to rule the community.[32]

Wimmer returned to St. Vincent toward the end of October, and in December he wrote King Ludwig of the results of the general chapter as well as of other affairs among the Benedictines in America. The abbot said that he was planning to send two clerics, Adalbert Müller and Innocent Wolf, to Italy to join Father Edward Hipelius, who had gone from England to Rome to continue his theological studies. The three monks would form the nucleus of a house of studies Abbot Boniface hoped to establish in the Eternal City. Unfortunately the war with the South had prevented him from taking any definitive steps toward achieving this goal, but he hoped to report more on the matter later. In the meantime, he said, monks from St. Vincent had taken over Assumption College in Sandwich, Ontario, at the request of the bishop of London, Ontario, Pierre Adolphe Pinsonnault. The people of the Canadian diocese were largely French and Irish, but despite the fact that it was not a German institution serving German needs, Wimmer was confident that his monks would meet with success in the college nonetheless. Bishop Pinsonnault had given one hundred acres to the Benedictines, and there were at present two priests, two clerics, and several lay brothers from St. Vincent there under the capable leadership of Father Oswald Moosmüller.[33]

The darkening clouds that hung like a pall over the nation in 1862 led Wimmer to turn his attention to Europe and Canada where he could establish monastic centers to carry on his work in the event that economic and political disaster struck and he was forced to abandon part or all of his enterprises in the United States. Things never looked bleaker for the Union than during the second year of the war. The effects of the conflict upon the monastery of St. Vincent, moreover, were immediate and grave. Economic conditions at the abbey, and indeed in all the American monasteries, grew precarious, and communications among Benedictine missionaries throughout the United States became increasingly difficult. Two months before southern guns opened fire on Fort Sumter in Charleston harbor, Wimmer wrote Abbot Angelo Pescetelli that the Benedictine missions in the South were almost entirely cut off from the motherhouse. "Our fathers in Texas, Nashville, Richmond, and Covington, and most probably in Kansas," he said, "have been separated from us so completely that we cannot communicate with them by letter."[34] Then when the war finally did break out, Wimmer's missionary activity ground to a halt. The success of the Benedictine ventures was threatened by the expanding conflict, and during the period between 1861 and 1865 he attempted only one foundation—at Assumption College in Canada—and accepted only three relatively "safe" parishes in Chicago (1861), Elizabeth, New Jersey (1863), and Newark, New Jersey (1864). By the end of 1863 he was forced to withdraw his monks from Canada because he had neither the money nor the manpower to carry on there.

After 1862 no communication at all was possible with the monks in Texas. Brother Michael Böhm died in San José on December 7, 1862, but the war was nearly over before word of his death reached Wimmer. Eventually communication between St. Vincent and the Kentucky priory was restored, and contact between the monks in Pennsylvania and those in Kansas was never effectively terminated. In Richmond, however, Father Leonard Mayer was completely isolated from St. Vincent until the city fell to Union forces in the spring of 1865.

In January 1861, when communication with the South was still possible, Wimmer answered a call for assistance from Bishop James Whalen, O.P., by sending Father Emmeran Bliemel from the priory in Covington to the Diocese of Nashville. Father Emmeran, who for a while had been professor of mathematics at St. Vincent College, took up residence at the German parish of the Assumption in Nashville, but soon after his arrival most of his male parishioners were drafted into the Confederate army. Bliemel asked Bishop Whalen's permission to follow them. Two years passed before he could get the bishop to agree, but in October 1863 he enlisted in the 10th Tennessee Regiment of the Confederate army. Bliemel went to Georgia to join the soldiers from his parish, and less than a year later, during the Battle of Atlanta, he was killed while administering the Church's last rites to wounded soldiers near Jonesboro, Georgia. He is remembered as the only Catholic chaplain of either army to be killed during the war.[35]

Besides the burdens it placed on the monks and missions in the South, the war caused considerable hardship at St. Vincent itself. Twenty of the one hundred and forty-two students in the college came from southern states and were unable to return to their homes when the fighting began. Wimmer wrote Archbishop Scherr of Munich in 1863 that these students "already owe us $6,000 for board and tuition, and most probably we will never receive payment." His patience and charity were tried, moreover, when the southern students seemed bent on aggravating trouble with their Yankee classmates. On one occasion the patriotic fervor of the "rebels" caused Abbot Boniface serious difficulties with local farmers. According to an account written forty years after the event, several of the southern boys prevailed upon a local seamstress to make a Confederate battle flag for them. In the dark of night they unfurled the banner atop one of the high buildings at St. Vincent, and at dawn it waved bravely over the monastery and college. When neighboring farmers, taking their produce to market in Latrobe, saw the rebel flag, they angrily marched up to St. Vincent and demanded an explanation from the abbot. Wimmer had not been aware that the flag was flying over his preserve. When it was brought to his attention, he summoned the southern students and directed them to furl their colors. They did, and a peace of sorts came to the Yankee campus once again.[36]

But more serious problems faced Wimmer and the American Benedictines in 1862 on account of the war. The Union's Conscription Act was passed that year, and as a result several of the monks at St. Vincent were drafted. Wimmer sent some of these priests and brothers to Assumption College in Canada to escape military service. Later he sent a number of clerics in similar circumstances to Europe, among them Boniface Krug, who eventually transferred his vows to the ancient Italian abbey of Montecassino where he was later elected archabbot.[37] In November 1862, with the help of Archbishop Francis Patrick Kenrick of Baltimore, Wimmer successfully petitioned the War Department in Washington to exempt from military service several of the monks who had been drafted.[38] But early in 1863 Congress passed a new, more stringent draft law, and more monks from St. Vincent were called up for military duty. In February 1863 Brother Bonaventure Gaul was drafted and assigned to the 61st Pennsylvania Regiment. A month later Brother Ulric Barth followed him. In all six priests and eight brothers were drafted: Brothers Ildephonse Hoffmann, George Held, Leo Christ, and Gallus Maier from St. Vincent; Father Valentine Lobmayer from St. Joseph's Parish, Johnstown, Pennsylvania; Fathers Bernard Manser, Casimir Seitz, and Erhard

Vanino from St. Mary's Parish, Erie; Father Benno Hegele from Newark Priory; and Father Isidor Walter and Brothers Martin Beck and Philip Bernard from St. Benedict's Priory, Carrolltown. Two priests and two brothers were released when the monastery paid the $300 exemption fee for each, and four others were declared unfit to bear arms by army doctors. But five brothers—Ildephonse, George, Leo, Ulric, and Bonaventure—remained in the army until the war ended, and one, Gallus Maier, was wounded at Antietam and after a brief hospitalization returned to St. Vincent in 1863.

In June 1863 Wimmer wrote President Lincoln asking that his monks be released from military service on account of their total unsuitability as warriors and thanking him for granting the release of several monks in 1862. Since the new conscription law made clerical exemptions void, he appealed again to the president's "well-known benevolence" for protection. There were four reasons, he said, why monks and clerics should be exempt:

First, I cannot believe that the law intends to press clergymen (of any denomination) into military service, because as a general matter these men are very warlike indeed if the fight has to be done with their tongues or pens, but otherwise they keep at a good distance from danger, and what should the Government gain if some hundred cowards were in the army?

Second. These learned men in Congress cannot well have been ignorant of the fact that nowhere and at no time among civilized nations ever a law existed by which clergymen or monks had been obliged to go to war. Indeed, in the middle ages we find sometimes bishops and abbots at war, but not in their clerical capacity, and only if they held lands from a sovereign. Congress, therefore, could not well have passed a law that is in contradiction with the feelings of the whole world. . . .

Third. If the law with regard to the clergy of all denominations does not intend to press them into the Army, and to take them away from the pulpit and the altar, and if it be satisfied if they ransom themselves for a certain sum, it would not make a very great difference whether the money had already been spent for the benefit of the country or shall be spent at the time of the draft. I mean to say if I had given last year all my fortune, say some thousand dollars, for charitable or religious purposes, not expecting or suspecting that I ever as a clergyman could be drafted, and if, nevertheless, I would now be drafted and had to go to war because I had not so much money any more to pay for my exemption, should the fact that I had given all my fortune for the best of the country not deserve any regard, and excuse me from paying of $300?

President, this is in fact the case with me. I am a good many years now living in this country. No necessity compelled me to emigrate; it was my own good and free will. I came to devote all I was and all I had to the moral and material aid of my countrymen. . . . All my confreres who came over from Germany have done the same; have deposited their fortunes into our common stock, little or much as it was. . . . Having spent all my own, all our common money, for the benefit of this country, I must blushingly confess I cannot pay. I have not money, and the law then answers: Shoulder arms. Is there such a law in this country?

Do we not deserve any regard on account of our money spent, though we have at present none to spare to pay the exemption? I do not like to boast or to glory, Sir; I am ashamed that I am compelled to say it. I cannot be drafted, I am too old for that, but I must speak for those of my confreres who may be drafted.

Fourth. The question of conscience I will not touch. Suffice it to say that we cannot go to war unless we act in a grievous manner against our conscience.[39]

Despite Wimmer's lengthy and colorful appeal to the president, the monks were not released from military service. Lincoln endorsed the letter and forwarded it to the War Department where Secretary of War Edwin Stanton issued an order transferring them to the hospital corps. They were released from the onus of bearing arms, but for two years they served the wounded on the battlefield amid the horrors of war.

Some of the war correspondence of the brothers has survived and interesting anecdotes of their military service abound. Thus Brother Bonaventure wrote Wimmer from Virginia during the final campaign of the war, "We dug trenches so close to the rebels that we could talk to them." Brother Leo Christ was severely wounded in the leg during the Petersburg Campaign of 1865 and suffered from the wound until his death in 1883. Brother Bonaventure was with Grant's army during the last days of the war, and three days after Lee's surrender he wrote his confrere, Brother Ildephonse Hoffmann, describing the last battle.

On April 1, at 9:30 in the evening, our Sixth Corps began the battle with a furious cannonade at Five Points, and the other batteries followed along the line. The next morning at four o'clock our Corps made a storm charge which broke the rebel line. The defeated forces fled to the right and to the left like sheep. Then we drove towards General Lee's headquarters. If we had reached them fifteen minutes earlier, we would have captured him. He had abandoned everything. From there our troops stormed towards Petersburg, and pursued General Lee in double-quick step through swamps and woods by day and by night, marching and fighting continually. We did not even allow the rebels enough time for cooking and eating. Mules fell by the roadside from sheer exhaustion, and we captured much war material. I must acknowledge that we also found out what it means to be almost continually on the march for 109 miles. Our boys, however, advanced like tigers to prevent the General from escaping. We marched over rocks and through water, in rain and sunshine getting scarcely any food.

On the last day, half our men dropped out of the ranks, chiefly because they had slept little for a whole week. On the eighth, at Appomattox Station, 25 miles from Lynchburg, the rebel army surrendered. On Palm Sunday, at 5 p.m., General Lee handed over his sword, and just as we were attacking again, his troops surrendered to the Sixth Corps. It was a glorious moment to witness, to hear the shouting and to listen to the Hurrahs. To me it was worth a thousand dollars. Then all the divisions of the Sixth Corps celebrated the event. Finally ration wagons were sent to save the troops that had surrendered. This assistance was very necessary. At that time we were only a short distance from the rebels. The Sixth Army Corps deserved all the honors which it received from the higher officers, and it is now relieved of field duties. I believe that we will soon come home. The President promised it at Petersburg. On Tuesday, after a long march through mud which was knee-deep we came back to our base. Many wagons got stuck in the mud. Our fare was only coffee and hard-tack. I hope the war will be over soon. Thanks to God a thousand times. These hardships will not easily be forgotten.

The Benedictines were discharged from the Army during the summer of 1865. Brother Gallus Maier, who after being wounded had returned to St. Vincent in 1863, later decided to leave the order, but the others remained. Brother Bonaventure Gaul earned a reputation in subsequent years as infirmarian of the college. Well trained in military hospitals during the war, he brought from the army a recipe for liniment that was popularly called "wizard oil" at the school and that helped heal a host of student sports injuries. Brothers Ulric, Leo, George, and Ildephonse all remained at St. Vincent until their deaths, quietly and unobtrusively fulfilling the duties they had been called from to go to war. Four weeks after the Confederate surrender at Appomattox the effects of the war were brought home even more dramatically to St. Vincent when the funeral train carrying the body of Abraham Lincoln passed through the monastery lands along the main line of the Pennsylvania Railroad less than a mile from the abbey and college. Monks and students lined the tracks to pay their final respects to the man who had saved the Union.[40]

Great as was the impact of the Civil War at St. Vincent, it was not the only cause of disruption in the life of the monastery in the 1860s. Further trouble plagued the burgeoning abbey in Pennsylvania when its abbot and community, for a time, fell victims to a hoax that almost succeeded in bringing about the collapse of the structure Wimmer had worked so long and hard to establish. The "insurrection of the brothers" had not yet gained momentum and the status of the Benedictine sisters was being decided in Rome when, in the summer of 1859, a twenty-three-year-old postulant from the district of Rheno-Prussia entered the novitiate at St. Vincent. George Keck was an intelligent, affable young man who before coming to America had studied acting and for a while had acted professionally in Germany. At St. Vincent he was to successfully play for nearly three years the most ambitious role of his career.

Soon after his arrival at the monastery Keck, who took the name Paul in religion, was received into the novitiate. Several weeks later he became sick and was sent to the monastery infirmary by novice master Wendelin Mayer. It was in the infirmary that on September 18, 1859, he claimed to have had a vision of "a Benedictine monk in choir garb with his head covered by a cowl and holding a cross in his right hand."[41] Keck informed Father Wendelin of the vision and the novice master immediately consulted Father Othmar Wirtz, at the time subprior at St. Vincent and a doctor of homeopathic medicine. The two men, fully believing the story, informed Wimmer, who instructed the novice to attempt to communicate with the spirit. On November 21, the last day in the octave of Benedictine All Soul's Day, Keck demanded in the name of Christ what the spirit desired. In the reply, recorded for posterity by Wimmer, the spirit allegedly said:

My name is Paul. I passed from this world seventy-seven years ago and am still suffering for sins I committed against monastic poverty. So far I have been allowed to appear every eleventh year, but until now all to whom I appealed refused help. I beg you to have seven masses offered, to make a novena of nine full days in great silence, and to recite the *miserere* for thirty days with bare feet and your head covered with the cowl.

Wimmer reported that while the vision was taking place, a priest was in the presence of Keck, but only the novice heard or saw anything. Considering all the circumstances, Abbot Boniface said that he could "hardly doubt the phenomenon."[42]

In February Wimmer wrote Abbot Angelo Pescetelli giving a detailed account of Keck's visions, which the novice claimed had frequently recurred. "When the sixth mass was offered by the sub-prior," Wimmer said, "the novice saw the spirit freed from Purgatory. Finally, on Christmas Day, after the seventh mass was offered, he beheld him radiant with joy."[43] News of the apparition quickly spread. In January court chaplain Müller wrote from Munich warning Wimmer to be very careful in the matter. "We had such a 'vision' in Munich which proved to be a fraud. I do not doubt that they may occur, but I also know that the imagination can play a prominent part in such cases."[44]

But at this stage of the deception Abbot Boniface accepted Keck's claims without reservation. On February 26, 1860, the *Pittsburgh Dispatch* published an article about the visions, saying that a spirit had appeared to the entire community at St. Vincent during conventual mass, had informed them that purgatory did not exist, and had revealed to them that in the long history of the Catholic Church only two priests had ever found their way to heaven. Abbot Boniface wrote the paper to clarify the article's misrepresentations. According to Wimmer, "The truth is that at St. Vincent's Abbey near Latrobe a Novice saw from the 18th of September until the 19th of November, every day from eleven to twelve o'clock a.m. or from twelve to two o'clock at night, the apparition of a Benedictine monk in full festive dress." The spirit, Wimmer said, had asked the novice to pray for him and for all the souls in purgatory and had revealed, sadly, "that of the five priests who had already died at the abbey, no one was yet in Heaven, but suffering in Purgatory."[45] The story of the apparition was greeted with skepticism. The *Pittsburgh Catholic* editorialized:

We have been urged by many to state what we think of the apparition said to have occurred at St. Vincent's, an account of which, as contained in the letter of Abbot Wimmer, we gave last week. We should have preferred confining ourselves, as did the Abbot, to giving a true account of the novice's version, leaving it to our readers to "give it the credit it deserves." We do not think it our duty to sit in judgment on every one who believes he sees a vision. Those who circulate such accounts must be satisfied with the uncertainties with which they are clothed. It would be too much to expect formal inquiries to be instituted on every statement of this kind which may be put forward.

As some insist, however, on knowing what we think this story to be worth, we have no hesitation in saying that our opinion is that it is worth nothing at all. The whole affair rests on the testimony of the novice who told the story. The ghost is said to have spoken to him, while another member of the community was present, but that other member neither saw nor heard anything. The question then turns on the truth of the novice's statement. Now, we know nothing of this gentleman's character to induce us to rely implicitly on his word or judgment in such an affair, and as a general very safe rule, we disbelieve all such statements until they are properly substantiated. The fact of his having been received a few months ago, and being yet kept on probation in the monastery, is proof that he is considered of good moral character, but we know nothing of his claims to that sound judgment that would entitle him to credit on a subject where fancy and other causes play pranks. We would add that the minutiae of the revelations of the spirit appear to us unworthy of their alleged authorship, and other circumstances, to which we need not refer more particularly, confirm us in the belief that no messenger from the Suffering Church had anything to do with the novice's vision.

We give this as our own opinion. We do not pretend to say that its truth is demonstrated or demonstrable. We think the fact that the opposite is neither the one nor the other, a sufficient reason for refusing to adhere to it. If any of our readers think otherwise, as it is possible some may, we can only say: let every one have his own opinion. When God will furnish any supernatural interposition for our benefit, He will surround it with evidence that will bring its truth home to us. In disbelieving these unproved private allegations we exercise a prudent caution which will save us, in most cases, from vain imaginings, and even if by this course we lose the benefit of some real manifestations, we have abundant truth for all useful purposes in the teachings of faith, and only forego some private communication not intended for us.[46]

Others, however, including Abbot Angelo Pescetelli in Rome, were convinced that the apparitions were genuine. In May Pescetelli wrote Wimmer: "I believe firmly in the apparitions of that monk Paul. . . . We have consulted our necrology and have found that seventy-seven years ago a monk with the name Paul, who was *cellararius*, died in the monastery at Brescia. The name and the occupation make it probable that he is the one who appeared. *Cellararii* are frequently guilty of sins against poverty."[47]

The initial success of the novice's fabrication emboldened him to elaborate his story. Claiming to have received further revelations, he advised the community that it was the divine will that a more strict monastic observance be followed in the monastery. He directed that certain pious practices be adopted by all the monks, that each, for example, attach a rosary to his belt and follow the Cistercian custom of affixing "Maria" to his name in religion. Perhaps the fame of the apparitions at Lourdes two years earlier had inspired Keck to concoct his own revelations, and it is likely that the perennial agitation on the part of some of the monks at St. Vincent, among whom were both the novice master and the subprior, for a more contemplative, devotional life in the monastery had suggested his proposed reforms. In any event Keck's visions at once became the center of an intense controversy not only at St. Vincent but in the priories of Minnesota and Kansas as well.

Led by Fathers Wendelin Mayer and Othmar Wirtz, who was made prior at St. Vincent several months after the novice's first "vision," a strong party of reformers gathered around the young novice. Following his directives, each of them adopted the name "Maria" and urged that a more contemplative and ascetic form of monastic life be inaugurated at St. Vincent. Division within the community was immediate. Those who believed in the supernatural origin of Keck's visions aligned themselves with Mayer and Wirtz and called for a thorough reform of the monastic regimen. Those who were skeptical opposed any efforts for reform. The controversy split the community into two strong camps. Wimmer, who at this stage seems to have been thoroughly deceived by the claims of Keck, was left in the middle of the ideological combatants.

On the one hand were those who demanded that the abbot abandon his long-held opinions about the active role of the order in America, suspend the missionary apostolates, and enforce a more rigorous ascetical and contemplative life at the abbey. To some extent Wimmer sympathized with these views, but at the same time he was reluctant to give up his ideal of missionary service to the Church, which he regarded as both proper and essential to the spread of religion and the growth of the order in America. Thus he sought ways to effect a compromise between the reformers and those members of the second ideological camp who shared his active spirit, pressed for more missionary enterprises, and urged the dismissal of Keck and an end to all the nonsense about heavenly visions. The acrimonious debate within the community built in a crescendo of angry exchanges and hard feelings until it reached a head at a chapter meeting in August 1860 at which the St. Vincent monks considered Keck's petition, upon completion of his novitiate, for admission to simple profession. Though strongly supported by the reformers, Keck was rejected for vows by a simple majority of the chapter members and was told to leave the monastery. The anti-reform party seemed to have secured the upper hand.[48]

In fact the victory was short-lived. As a tense peace returned to the abbey in Pennsylvania, internal divisions over the question of what role the Benedictines should play in America spread to the community in Minnesota. Just as at St. Vincent, there was disagreement in the West over the missionary work the monks were engaged in. Like their counterparts at St. Vincent, some members of the St. Cloud Priory believed that the monastic observance and spiritual development of their community had suffered on account of an overcommitment to the missions. They sympathized with the Keck party at St. Vincent and called for a spiritual reform of the community. On April 11, 1861, a quasi chapter of Minnesota monks met in St. Joseph, Minnesota, and voted to accept Paul Keck into their ranks.[49] The four Minnesota monks who made this decision—Demetrius di Marogna, Cornelius Wittmann, Bruno Riess, and Clement Staub—did so independently of the recently appointed prior of St. Cloud, Father Benedict Haindl, and without inviting the newer chapter members to participate. That Abbot Boniface did not repudiate the transactions of the quasi chapter indicates, in part at least, the extent of his sympathy for the visionary.

Meanwhile the winds had shifted at St. Vincent. In April 1861, less than nine months after Keck's dismissal, the monastic chapter in Pennsylvania voted to receive him back into the novitiate. Abbot Boniface explained to Abbot Angelo Pescetelli: "At first the members of the house opposed [Keck]. But gradually the majority became his friends and supporters. What I stated earlier about those apparitions and manifestations should be kept confidential until I am able to give you better arguments to confirm either their truth or falsehood."[50]

In the novitiate once again, Keck was having more visions, and before long a form of hysteria began to sweep the monastery. Two more monks at the abbey claimed to be visited by spirits and to have been given the gift of prophecy. The prophets, who quite clearly were under the influence of Keck, informed Abbot Boniface that suffering, hardship, and disloyalty would be his future lot if he did not follow the directives of Keck who, they claimed, was relaying authentic messages of the divine will delivered to him by an angel in the form of "a beautiful young boy."[51] In November 1861 Keck claimed that Martin Luther had appeared to him and revealed that he was not in hell but in purgatory, a revelation that was greeted by the staunchly Catholic Bavarians of St. Vincent with considerable consternation. Other apparitions to Keck revealed that unless reform were immediately imposed in the Pennsylvania monastery the entire community would be drafted into the army, a revelation that gained much credibility when the draft notices began to arrive soon afterward.

As if on cue, the troubles of Abbot Boniface started to multiply. Divisiveness and dissension once again gripped the community. It was during this period that Prior Augustine Wirth inaugurated his effort to weaken the bonds between the Kansas foundation and the motherhouse in Pennsylvania by opening his own novitiate, and it was after Keck informed Wimmer that Wirth was "up to no good" that the abbot, acting on the novice's instruction, decided to send Fathers Wendelin Mayer and Louis Fink (another of the visionary's supporters) on visitation to Kansas.[52] Inspired by his incredible success Keck shortly, as Wimmer later admitted, "seemed in fact to assume the government of the whole monastery."[53] He dictated parochial assignments, after "learning" from his revelations who should become the monastery's procurator, who should be student prefects, who should be prior in this or that parish, who should be transferred from one place to another, who was not properly observing the monastic life. Wimmer, to his credit, did not act precipitately and often refused to follow Keck's advice, claiming that he, Wimmer, was abbot of St. Vincent and not Keck or his guardian angel. Nevertheless, the abbot listened to the visionary and increasingly acted on his advice. More and more monks began to credit the novice's visions. Before long a majority of the chapter was voting under the influence of Keck's powerful lobby.

On April 12, 1862, Wimmer received the simple profession of the novice Paul George Keck, and on the same day ordained him to the minor orders in the abbey church.[54] In the meantime news of Keck's apparitions had reached Rome, and on July 9, 1862 the Sacred Congregation for the Propagation of the Faith addressed a series of questions to Wimmer regarding the alleged visions.[55]

If Abbot Boniface had residual doubts about Keck's probity and honesty during the summer of 1862, they must certainly have been strengthened shortly before the inquiry arrived from Rome when he received a short note from Francis Patrick Kenrick, archbishop of Baltimore, complaining of Keck's behavior in the archdiocese. Kenrick reported to Wimmer, who had acceded to the *Geisterseher's* unusual request to be allowed to visit friends in Maryland, that while in Baltimore, Keck had been observed "going about spreading the works of a certain woman, which are detrimental to peace and obedience."[56] Wimmer took no action at the time, but his suspicions were raised and he began to examine more carefully the actions and behavior of the newly professed monk. In September 1862 he presided over the second general chapter which undertook the reformation of the American Cassinese Congregation. There is no doubt that the reform legislation the delegates passed during that meeting was strongly influenced by Keck. Citing the authority of his alleged visions, the young monk had advanced principles of monastic observance that achieved formal expression in the decrees of the general chapter. There is equally no doubt that Keck's power in the monastery was now at its zenith. Those monks who believed his claims became a kind of spiritual elite in the community, and in the fall of 1862 they constituted a majority at St. Vincent. They followed Brother Paul's directives to the letter, embracing ascetical disciplines and devotional practices that had not previously been customary among American Benedictines, including the addition of the name "Maria" to their religious names. Under Keck's steadily growing influence they even passed legislation directing all monks in the congregation to do the same.[57]

In October 1862 Wimmer was still convinced of the authenticity of Keck's visions. In answer to the questions of the Propaganda Fide, the abbot wrote a spirited defense of the visions and remarked that the whole affair had brought a deeper spiritual life to the monastery.[58] Soon enough, however, he began to have reason to regret his uncritical acceptance of the visionary's directives. Keck made his first serious mistake when he informed Wimmer that he had been instructed by his visions to seek immediate ordination to the priesthood. Though there is no documentary evidence to support the theory, it seems plausible that Keck had higher ambitions than merely influencing the monastic observance of the community from behind the scenes. Wimmer's attempts to hold an election for a lifetime abbot of St. Vincent had just failed for the third time. The abbot's own popularity among many of the monks was in decline, and Keck must have suspected that he could control a majority of votes in the chapter when the time finally came for the decisive election. Only as an ordained priest, however, would he himself be eligible for the office. In any event and for whatever reasons, Keck insisted that he be ordained. Wimmer, noting that the young cleric had not completed even a minimum of the required studies, refused his request.

For the first time since the affair began, Keck turned on the abbot. With the full might of his supernatural patrons behind him, he accused Wimmer of playing into the Devil's hands, of being, in fact, an instrument of Satan. Without much difficulty he was able to convince a good many of his followers that this was the case. Setting out with two confreres from St. Vincent, he went to Pittsburgh where he told his story to Bishop Michael Domenec. But Domenec, together with a majority of the diocesan clergy, had considered him an imposter from the outset and refused to ordain him. Not to be discouraged, Keck next went to Erie with the blessings of Prior Othmar and Novice Master Wendelin where he hoped to be ordained by Bishop Young. In Erie the deception he had woven so expertly and for so long began to unravel.

At St. Mary's Priory in Erie he was received by the monks, most of whom stood in awe of him. Several of them, wanting to introduce their famous confrere to lay friends in the city, took him to a party in the home of one of the parishioners where until late in the evening Keck and his companions talked and drank and sang in what Wimmer described as a secular environment thoroughly inappropriate for monks. Returning to the priory with one of the priests, whom Keck later claimed to be intoxicated, the visionary attempted to seduce the man. The priest, however, angrily rejected the cleric's homosexual advances and denounced him before the community. The full story quickly became known not only to Wimmer but to Bishop Young as well. Keck defended himself vehemently. He insisted that he had done nothing wrong, arguing that he had taken off the priest's clothes because the priest, in a drunken state, was unable to do so himself. He claimed that he had merely given the priest the kiss of peace, a custom which Keck had encouraged many of his followers to perform as part of the spiritual renewal taking place in the congregation under the influence of the visionary's alleged revelations. Keck said, moreover, that it had been the priest and not himself who had attempted the seduction.

Wimmer was horrified by the events. He rushed back to Pennsylvania from Sandwich, Ontario, where he had been visiting the monks at Assumption College, and opened a full-scale investigation. He summoned the monks who had attended the party in Erie and questioned them extensively. He took testimony from the priest who accused Keck and interrogated the visionary himself. He met with both the supporters and the opponents of Keck at St. Vincent and carefully examined the devotional practices that had developed in the community under the visionary's influence. The evidence he accumulated pointed to the appalling conclusion that the spiritual reformation of the monastery concealed a homosexual subculture whose leading proponent was Keck himself. Formally he accused Keck of five offenses against obedience, chastity, and monastic discipline:

1) That without my knowledge and without my consent he tried underhandedly to receive holy orders, and by telling lies he tried to persuade Father Othmar to assist him in this endeavor and had gone with him to Erie; 2) that in Erie, hoping to be ordained a priest in two days, he remained until almost midnight with other priests in the home of a layman and scandalized the people by singing and playing; 3) that on returning home, he kissed one of the fathers, whom he thought to be drunk, and committed other acts which, according to this father, certainly should cast the gravest suspicion on him; 4) that he communicated the whole affair to the bishop, when he knew perfectly well that I was to come to Erie in a few days, and 5) that although not required to do so, he attached an oath to his statement.[59]

Wimmer was outraged to discover that Keck continued to have the support of many in the community. All but two of the priests whom he summoned to testify in the case defended him. A few of the defenders were Keck's intimate companions, but most, aware that he had given his testimony under oath, were simply convinced that the young cleric was telling the truth, that his visions were authentic, and that he was being maligned by those who opposed the reforms.

Wimmer was certain now that the young man was a fraud, and that rather than true spiritual renewal, he had brought deception,

corruption, and vice to the community. Because of its scandalous nature, he was reluctant to reveal to the community all the evidence he
had gathered. He suspected, moreover, that even with the evidence he
had, based as it was on the testimony of a few, many would accuse him
of being won over by the calumny of those who hated Paul Keck. For
a while he hesitated to take decisive action, but then he received a letter from Bishop Josue Mary Young who said that after conducting his
own investigation he was convinced that Keck's testimony was per-
jured. Without further ado, and refusing to consult with the monks
in a chapter meeting where he felt certain many of them would defend the "visionary," he expelled Keck from the monastery for "grave
sins against the sixth commandment."[60] On January 31, 1863, a mortified Wimmer wrote his friend Abbot Angelo Pescetelli that he was
"herewith retracting all I wrote to you and the Sacred Congregation
about the humility, obedience, and the chastity of Paul Keck. As I
have now the facts on hand, we know that he is a proud man, disobedient to the Holy Rule. I acknowledge that I was deceived and am
amazed that I did not discover the error for so long a time. As far as I
am able, I will now try to repair the losses and scandals. I hope that I
succeed in this in a short time."[61]

Pescetelli responded in February expressing his dismay and "sympathy on account of the sad things that have come to pass to Paul and
through Paul." The Roman abbot urged Wimmer "not to say anything in the future about visions and visionaries when you write the
Propaganda, because Rome, understanding the great impostures of
many, does not believe in such things except after a thorough examination of the life and heroic virtue of the persons who claim to have
such visions." Abbot Angelo said he suspected that Keck might have
been calumniated, but he told Wimmer that "I believe it is good that
he has been dismissed from the order on account of the suspicions regarding him, to which he gave occasion, and on account of the divisions which he caused among his confreres."[62]

Abbot Boniface spoke of his own shocked reaction to the sordid affair in a letter to Archbishop Gregory Scherr of Munich. With regard
to Keck's visions and revelations, Wimmer said,

I doubted many very strongly, but I considered several as authentic since
many prophecies were fulfilled exactly, and several real miracles have been
worked. For example, a noticeable cure, the conversion of a calloused sinner

on his deathbed, etc. Since the earliest days I did not want to believe what was said about the appearance of Luther, . . . his recantation and refutation and that he is only in Purgatory. But of one thing I was certain: this man Keck could not have made up this story by himself. So I gave the order that he was never to be left alone. I was certain that when he wrote, he could not have plagiarized it. Moreover, I remembered that at one time in Munich Fathers Fortunatus and Augustine presented the same thesis to me (that Luther is not in Hell). . . . On hasty reading of what was written by Keck, the idea seemed orthodox. Therefore I considered it at least possible that the case had some foundation, especially since Father Prior and Father Novice Master, who were closer to the seer than myself, vouched for the excellence of his character. The case reached sensational heights in the house, and almost all the fathers were divided either for or against the seer. The most zealous were all for him while the more lax ones repeatedly came forward with angry misrepresentations or obvious lies against him, and really the hand of God seemed to have touched several persons through this. So naturally it was impossible for a long time for me to decide what I should think of the matter, particularly since I myself could give evidence that I became more zealous in good deeds through it, as was also certain to a greater or lesser degree with all his friends. Your Excellency probably knows that I am not a man who is easily misled. But . . . while I was on a journey for five weeks, many things occurred which placed the morality of the seer in grave suspicion. When I investigated closer, I soon found out that my good novice master and prior were dominated by him, and that he was not watched over while writing, and that usually he had many breaches of the Holy Rule to confess. Soon afterwards my judgment was formed, and I expelled him from the order. His friends were very indignant over this, and it caused much irritation in the monastery. But now everything has been in order for a good while. The only thing is that the novice master ran away with this fellow and has not come back yet.[63]

Father Wendelin Mayer's flight from the monastery with the expelled cleric Paul Keck clearly suggested that the troubles had not ended, and Wimmer soon learned that order would not be restored to the abbey and congregation as quickly as he had expected. The ideological split in the community at St. Vincent was profound, and the division between the "Keckites" and those who adamantly opposed the *Geisterseher* continued to grow and spread into the wider reaches of the American Cassinese Congregation. Expelled from the abbey in Pennsylvania, Keck went with Father Wendelin to Minnesota, where the two of them sought refuge with Father Othmar Wirtz, former prior at St. Vincent who in October 1862 had replaced Father Benedict Haindl as superior of the St. Cloud monks. Keck and Mayer arrived at the priory of St. Cloud on January 19, 1863, and received a warm welcome from Prior Othmar and several of the Minnesota Benedictines.[64] A strong party of supporters, including Mayer, Wirtz, and Father Louis Fink, prior of St. Vincent's Priory in Chicago, gathered around the visionary and did everything they could to have the young man ordained. Among the bishops they petitioned were Francis Patrick Kenrick of Baltimore, Thomas Grace of St. Paul, and James Duggan of Chicago. In each case, the bishops contacted Wimmer, who prevented the ordination from taking place. Bishop Grace wrote Abbot Boniface in January, "I have the pleasure to acknowledge the receipt of your kind letter giving me warning in regard to a certain novice of St. Vincent. I am truly sorry that such a subject has been admitted into the community of St. Cloud. Of course, whatever depends on me to prevent that danger I shall do."[65] Thus as Keck and his admirers attempted to obtain his ordination and achieve a measure of ecclesiastical recognition for their movement, Abbot Boniface worked successfully to thwart their plans and prevent them from achieving their goals.

Meanwhile Wimmer continued to conduct an investigation into the nature of Keck's spiritual movement and the effects it had had on the community at St. Vincent. He was shocked by what he discovered. He was especially appalled by the intimacy that characterized the relationships among Keck's more ardent admirers, an intimacy that passed under the guise of fraternal charity and that he had not been fully aware of until now: "I soon learned that even in the monastery Paul was accustomed to embrace his friends most tenderly and to kiss them by putting his tongue in their mouths, as scarcely any chaste friends would do and which . . . I consider gravely impure. His manner of comportment manifested a certain womanly tenderness and effeminacy, even when he sang, for which he was looked upon askance by many laymen and clerics." Wimmer confessed that he could not understand how he had been deluded for so long, and how, moreover, the majority of monks in the community had been deceived by the *Geisterseher*. He concluded that only Keck's talent for acting and masterful ability to appear holy had blinded him and his confreres.

If someone were to ask me how I can now assail Paul, when only a few months ago I commended him so highly, I would simply reply that this is not a matter of my inconsistency, and still less is it to be attributed to any passion or malice. Quite simply I had a very great opinion of Paul's holiness which caused me to fail to act on doubts or suspicions that frequently occurred to me. [But then] all at once I learned that he was not obedient, nor chaste, nor a lover of poverty, nor humble, nor given to mortification, nor reverent, nor sincere, nor meek, neither truly loving God nor his neighbor, but arrogant, hypocritical, and a pious imposter—and in this judgment, with five or six exceptions, all the confreres now agree with me.[66]

But Keck was not to be easily thwarted. His deception had been complete for nearly three years, and he did not intend to give up without a fight the charade that had brought him to such prominence and power. Audacious as ever, he refused to be defeated by his expulsion from St. Vincent or by the refusal of the five American bishops to ordain him. Confident of his abilities and charm, and aware that his case was now under investigation by the cardinals of the Sacred Congregation for the Propagation of the Faith, Keck decided to meet the challenge head on. In March he left Minnesota for Rome to defend himself.

In April 1863 Father Wendelin Mayer, who had returned to St. Vincent after Keck's departure for the Holy See, addressed a long letter to Pope Pius IX in which he defended Keck, outlined the extent to which monastic discipline had declined at St. Vincent on account of Wimmer's leadership, and requested that he be permitted to come to Rome himself to explain the matter fully and to serve as an advocate for the visionary. Mayer resurrected many of the complaints against Wimmer that had cropped up before among those monks in the community who since 1847 had been calling for a stricter monastic observance among the Benedictines in America. The novices at St. Vincent, he said, were not given the opportunity to be trained properly in religious life because Wimmer was constantly calling on them to perform duties, such as teaching in the college, which were not consistent with a canonical novitiate. He objected to the abbot's practice of assigning priests to parishes and not granting them the right to lead a monastic life within the walls of the monastery to which they were bound by vows.

The walls of the monastery posed a special problem for the congregation's novice master. He complained that they were constantly being breached. Wimmer permitted laymen to enter the cloister almost at will, and the monks under his influence seldom observed any of the rules of monastic *clausura*. Mayer complained that because of the abbot's inattention to the details of monastic observance it was impossible for the monks "to pray the divine office together; even other holy exercises are often neglected, and the holy discipline has disappeared and has made room for secular customs. Frequently young monks have to rely upon themselves and live without supervision or example, or help and counsel, and often the greatest temptations and scandals occur." On the whole Mayer's letter to the pope contained well-worn but unsubstantiated charges against Abbot Boniface, whose rule he wanted to see ended. It was essentially an emotional outburst in which he called upon the Holy Father to investigate conditions at St. Vincent in order to see for himself to what a low ebb monastic life among the American Benedictines had fallen. Mayer labeled Keck's accusers slanderers and implied that it was the young visionary's efforts to reform a corrupt monastery that had caused enmity between him and the lax members of the community and had resulted in his expulsion. Father Wendelin called upon the pope to see that justice be done.[67]

Upon Keck's arrival in Rome, Pescetelli wrote Wimmer: "At first I feared that his coming might be prejudicial to you, for I supposed that he was incensed against you. I tried to see him and to assist him. . . . He has shown himself to be attracted to us and has promised never to say a word that could be injurious to yourself."

Abbot Angelo said that Keck had been called before the cardinals of the Holy Office of the Inquisition to retract anything he may have said contrary to the Catholic faith. Wimmer might expect the cardinals to order that all of Keck's writings be sent to Rome.

Since there are among these writings many things about the state of conscience and also the sins of certain persons, I beg you to make an assortment of those writings and to burn everything that might reflect on certain individuals of the order. You will be able to do this because the command of the Holy Office will reach you after my letter. The other doctrinal writings and such as treat of other matters you should send when you receive the order. It is two hours since I got knowledge of this. For mercy's sake do what I tell you, and burn also this my letter without saying anything to anyone, for the whole affair may become a matter of greatest importance for the good of the order.[68]

In September Wimmer received the order from Propaganda to send the writings of Paul Keck to Rome. He designated Father Alto Hörmann, sometime prior both in Texas and at St. Vincent and a consistent opponent of Keck and the reformers, as his emissary. On October 5, 1863, Father Alto arrived in Rome with the Keck papers and turned them over to the Propaganda Fide. In the meantime Father Wendelin Mayer had also arrived in Rome, where he had been summoned before the cardinals of Propaganda and there censured for his disobedience to Abbot Boniface and for his continued support of Paul Keck after the cleric had been expelled from the monastery. Cardinal Barnabo, prefect of the Sacred Congregation, sent Mayer to Abbot Angelo for absolution, and Pescetelli, in turn, sent him to Montecassino to make a retreat and to write a letter of apology and submission to Wimmer.[69]

Two other St. Vincent monks were in Rome at the time, and both were among the reformers whose party, since the expulsion of Keck, had begun to lose power and influence in the Pennsylvania monastery. Father Edward Hipelius, whose letter had prevented the abbatial election at the general chapter of 1862, had gone to Rome to study theology the previous year. He and Boniface Krug, one of the St. Vincent clerics who had left the United States when he received his conscription notice for the U.S. Army, were residing at the Benedictine house of studies, San Callisto, in Rome. Abbot Pescetelli had sent Paul Keck to San Callisto to await the pleasure of the cardinals who were examining the case. When Father Alto arrived, Pescetelli instructed him to take up residence at San Callisto as well, but Wimmer's emissary refused. Hörmann told the Roman abbot "that he would not come on account of Paul, that I should dismiss Paul and then he would come at once." Pescetelli answered that he could not send Keck away without offending the cardinals of the Propaganda Fide who had recommended the supposed visionary to his care until the case should be settled. Moreover, Pescetelli said that Keck had done nothing at San Callisto to warrant his expulsion. Pescetelli wrote Wimmer that "taking into considerations the interests of America, I decided it would be better to keep [Keck] in the monastery (in the dress of a secular clergyman) rather than allow him to roam about the City." Pescetelli felt that there was "no danger for Edward, Boniface, or anyone else since Keck himself has become convinced that all his visions came from the Devil by whom he believes himself to have been possessed."

But still Hörmann refused to take up residence at San Callisto. Instead, he went to Cardinal Barnabo, who was in charge of the investigation of Keck's case, and denounced Pescetelli as an enemy working against Wimmer and the interests of the American Cassinese Benedictines. Hörmann's excessive enthusiasm for the cause led him to act and speak injudiciously. He told Pescetelli that if he were to come to San Callisto, he would "make war on Paul because he is a charlatan, on Edward because he has been raised from a dung-hill. . . on Boniface because he came to Rome without permission of his abbot to follow Paul of whom he is an abettor, and on Wendelin who should go and do penance where he committed the fault."

Abbot Angelo attempted to mollify Hörmann by sending him to the Irish Benedictine, Dom Bernard Smith, who would "advise him to be a little more careful, not to injure [Wimmer's] cause and especially not to write everything that comes into his mind." In the meantime, however, Father Alto had begun to compose a defense of Abbot Boniface, and Pescetelli told Wimmer that

I myself have learned things from his writings of which I was ignorant before, and which would cause a painful sensation in Rome were they made public. . . . Dear Wimmer, be not offended at the severity of my judgments. I hope that I may be mistaken and that I may be a false prophet, but I believe that Father Alto will do you much harm, and considering only his first steps, he has already done so. If I have received your monks in San Callisto and Montecassino, it was done to give you new proof of the fraternal love which I feel towards you. But if you wish to dispose of them otherwise, do so freely. Do not, however, place your confidence in the counsels of Father Alto. They are counsels full of passion and imprudence. . . . We, who are advanced in years, understand each other better. The young ones are imprudent and presumptuous.[70]

Pescetelli's support of Wimmer had been constant since 1855 when he had successfully pressed the Propaganda Fide for the elevation of St. Vincent to the rank of abbey and the appointment of Wimmer as its first abbot. Abbot Boniface's awareness of this support and his deep appreciation for Abbot Angelo's invaluable services convinced him that Pescetelli, rather than Father Alto Hörmann, was the man most likely to settle the affair now before the cardinals of the Sacred Congregation. Hörmann's inexperience in Vatican protocol, as well as his imprudence and excessive zeal in defense of Wimmer's interests, clearly made him unsuitable to play the role of the American Benedictines' advocate before the Roman tribunal. Abbot Boniface therefore wrote his Italian agent confirming his confidence in him and repudiating the actions of Hörmann.[71]

In January 1864 Abbot Angelo answered Wimmer's letter thanking him for his friendship and confidence and renewing his commitment to defend the interests of the American Cassinese Benedictines before the Holy See. With regard to Father Alto, Pescetelli said that the overzealous monk, after writing "a most impertinent letter to Cardinal Barnabo," had left Rome for Bavaria. "Without a streak of insanity his conduct cannot be explained, and it has certainly done injury to the interests of the congregation. I told the cardinal that you had disavowed the actions of Alto and that you had sent an apology for him. The cardinal was satisfied. . . ."

Insofar as Keck was concerned, Pescetelli had become convinced that "this fellow is a solemn imposter. I tried to get rid of him at once; he had gotten it in his head to become a novice with us. I hope I shall soon succeed; it is a very delicate matter." Pescetelli also said that Father Edward Hipelius had at last turned his attention from the Keck affair to study because he was "very anxious to receive his doctorate. . . . If he has said some bitter words when he was irritated, he nevertheless sincerely loves St. Vincent and his confreres." Frater Boniface Krug's temporary vows had expired and he was eager to make solemn profession, but he had requested permission to transfer his stability from St. Vincent to Montecassino because he could not return to the United States without being subject to arrest by military authorities for his draft evasion. Pescetelli said that Krug desired "to have nothing more to do with Paul." Father Wendelin Mayer was "doing well at Montecassino and all are well satisfied with him. You see, therefore, that instead of being scandalized, we have rather been edified by your monks."[72]

In the meantime Prior Othmar Wirtz of the St. Cloud Priory, without the consent of Abbot Boniface, had written the Sacred Congregation for the Propagation of the Faith asking that the Minnesota foundation be immediately elevated to the rank of abbey. When Wirtz had been elected prior of St. Cloud by the Minnesota monks in 1862, it was with the understanding that should the Holy See raise the priory to the dignity of abbey before his three-year term of office expired, he would automatically become abbot. His petition was part of an effort undertaken by the Minnesota monks to promote Wirtz to the abbacy and with his help to establish a "reformed" monastery in America that would follow the statutes of the medieval abbey of Cluny and would not be under the control of the abbot of St. Vincent. Upon Pescetelli's advice Propaganda denied the petition, but Prior Othmar, who still supported Paul Keck, continued to hold out hopes for vindication. He wrote Father Wendelin at Montecassino that

he who has humbled [Keck] will also exalt him. . . . Let us trust in God and patiently wait for the time he has appointed for us all. Even though Minnesota will not be raised to the status of an abbey, and though we have no Cluniac statutes as yet, do not let this discourage you. Do not be afraid and deceived. Come to Minnesota gladly and quietly and help me in the difficult position which I am to maintain.

Only be patient. We are not at the end yet even if the Abbot may think so. Not I, however, oh no. We have not even started yet. For our further progress God will have to help us, and will do so despite all opposition.[73]

Father Othmar's hopes were never to be realized. In March 1864 Paul Keck, having been denied admission into several Roman monasteries and seminaries, enlisted in the Papal Zouaves. In April he was summoned before the cardinals of the Sacred Congregation for the Propagation of the Faith to answer questions, and in June his case was formally submitted to the Holy Office of the Inquisition.

In July Wimmer himself was summoned to Rome to answer questions about affairs at St. Vincent, but because of the difficulties of travel occasioned by the American Civil War, he could not leave St. Vincent immediately. In September he wrote Pescetelli that he would "start at the earliest time because the mandate says 'come as soon as possible.' At present all are at peace in our monastery. The spiritual and temporal affairs were never in better condition."[74]

Wimmer was unable to leave America for another four and a half months, but on February 11, 1865, he departed the port of New York bound for the Eternal City. It was his third trip to Europe since he had come to the United States, his second to Rome. He anticipated that it would be his most difficult. Not only were the Roman cardinals preparing to question him about reports of indiscipline, divisiveness, and disorder within the communities of the American Cassinese Congregation, but in addition his own judgment and integrity had been called into doubt.

The crossing lasted two weeks, and, as on previous visits, he went first to Munich to consult with friends and advisors there. Father Joseph Ferdinand Müller, the faithful supporter and generous benefactor of the American Benedictines for almost two decades, had died the previous year, and Wimmer felt the loss deeply. He would have welcomed Müller's counsel in this latest crisis which threatened both his own good name and the future of the Benedictine mission in the United States. But he took comfort in the advice and support he received from Müller's successor as secretary of the Ludwig Missionsverein, Baron Rudolph von Oberkamp, and from his former conovice and abbot, Gregory Scherr, now archbishop of Munich and president of the mission society. He also sought the counsel of several Benedictine abbots, including his old friends Utto Lang of Metten and Rupert Leiss of Scheyern.

He left Munich at the end of March and arrived in Rome during Holy Week, as he had done ten years earlier. There he was warmly welcomed by Abbot Angelo Pescetelli who informed him that Father Wendelin Mayer and Paul Keck had gained some advantage in their efforts to discredit him before the Roman authorities. Keck had obtained commendatory letters from "a certain prelate," and these, Pescetelli suggested, might influence some bishop to ordain him. In addition, the visionary had succeeded in ingratiating himself with some of the cardinals and had even managed to obtain an audience with the pope.[75] Several of the cardinals who would judge the case were showing evidence of reluctance to place much confidence in the American abbot since he had first given what seemed like unqualified support for Keck's claims concerning his visions and afterward had repudiated Keck in what appeared to be a precipitous manner, expelling the cleric from St. Vincent without the formal support of the monastic chapter. This sudden *voltafaccia* raised doubts in the minds of the cardinals about the abbot's wisdom and discretion.

Wimmer attended Holy Week services at St. Peter's and on Easter Tuesday celebrated pontifical mass at the Abbey of St. Paul's Outside the Walls where he was honored not only by the abbot and monks of that Italian community but also by Benedictine prelates from France, England, Spain, Germany, and Australia who were visiting the abbey.

"At St. Paul's," Wimmer wrote, "there were also four Italian abbots, and we all ate together at one table—a real Benedictine feast!" The welcome he received from his Benedictine confreres was warm and encouraging and helped steel him for the ordeal he now had to face.

The following week Pescetelli arranged for him to make calls on several of the more influential cardinals—including Leonardo Antonelli, Alexandro Barnabo, Karl von Reisach, and the French Benedictine Cardinal Jean Baptiste Pitra—to lay out his case and counter the doubts that had arisen about him because of his handling of the Keck controversy. He had heard that Cardinal Barnabo was opposing him in the case and was happy to discover that the prefect of the Propaganda Fide received him very cordially. The other cardinals, he learned, particularly Pitra and von Reisach, strongly supported him. Wimmer also visited King Ludwig, now living year-round in retirement in Rome, and received from the monarch both encouragement and a donation of $1,500 for the Benedictine missions in America.

The most gratifying meeting, however, was the one held on May 19 with the pope. Pescetelli had arranged the audience so that Wimmer could make an appeal directly to Pope Pius IX. Accompanying him to the audience was Father Edward Hipelius, who was serving as his secretary. Wimmer reported that the half-hour audience went extremely well. The pope "received me in a very fatherly manner. He is considerably weaker than ten years ago, but still looks good and works unbelievably hard." Abbot Boniface was delighted that the pope gave every indication that the case would be settled in his favor, and Father Edward wrote that the Holy Father, amused to discover that the clean-shaven monk whom he had named abbot ten years before had returned to Rome with whiskers, bid him farewell with the words, "Long live Abbot Wimmer and his magnificent beard."[76]

In June he was summoned before the cardinals of the Holy Office to answer questions concerning the Keck case. The trial lasted more than three months. In the course of it Wimmer became more deeply aware than ever before of the extent of conflict that existed within the community at St. Vincent and of the degree of animosity that many of the monks held toward him personally. Some of his monks had denounced him to the Holy See for permitting Keck to sow the seeds of discord and manipulate the community for almost three years. Others accused him of sacrificing monastic discipline and the full development of an authentic religious life at St. Vincent on the altar of his own ambitions. In July an embattled Wimmer wrote Prior Rupert Seidenbusch at St. Vincent that "the whole affair proceeds very slowly. Everything will turn out all right, but not before several months yet. Whether I'll stay here that long, I don't know, but in any event I shall put everything in order."

A great deal had to be put in order. In Rome Wimmer learned that Father Othmar Wirtz, who had assured him that he had repudiated his support for Keck, was as ardent in his defense of the *Geisterseher* as he had ever been. Abbot Boniface had intercepted three of Wirtz's letters to Mayer in which Wirtz had reaffirmed his faith in the revelations of Keck and from which Wimmer discovered that Fathers Louis Fink, Paulinus Wenkmann, and Agatho Stübinger were still working with the prior of St. Cloud to have the Minnesota monastery declared an abbey which could become a refuge for the congregation's most zealous reformers and supporters of Keck. With the evidence in hand Wimmer wrote to Wirtz:

The three letters you sent to P. Wendelin could not be delivered to him, since he was never at the place to which you addressed them. They therefore came into my hands, and I must say they made a very painful impression on me (1) because I know now that you are not sincere in dealing with me, (2) because I am now certain that you are still above your ears in superstition, (3) because I learned further that your soul is in great danger because you still foster the arrogant thought that you are destined to be the reformer of the order, and (4) because I also see that for three years you secretly tried to divide the order and break up the congregation rather than, as far as it is necessary and possible, to strengthen and improve it.

Concerning Wendelin, you have nothing to regret. He has not read your letters. But you are greatly mistaken if you think you can expect him to carry out your secession. He is as proud as you are. Like you, he too does not want to help with the reformation. That is too little for such selected tools, chosen by God. No, he himself wants to be the reformer of the order, as the founder of a monastery. He has already abandoned the idea of discipline. He has already discovered that wine is better than water and sleeping late more practical than rising early, etc. He is, however, already unmasked, and his plan for starting a new monastery has come to an end. However, he still believes firmly in Paul, so that what you wrote is true: "we are two incorrigibles." How far you will succeed in this, the future will tell.[77]

Under the pretext of going to Germany for his health, Father Wendelin had collected 300 francs from the archabbot of Montecassino and had promptly used the money to travel to Rome in order to help defend Paul Keck before the Inquisition. Wimmer called him "a thoroughly dishonest man" and wrote Rupert Seidenbusch at St. Vincent:

He wanted to go to Rome and find an opportunity to defend his Paul, to speak with the pope, and to promote the foundation of a monastery. He wants to found monasteries! Unfortunately for him, I stepped in. Although he was here for six weeks, prowling around town like a fox among the cardinals and monsignors with whom he had gained entrance, he obtained no audience with the pope. Cardinals von Reisach and Barnabo, to whom he brought accusations against me, ridiculed him and considered him crazy. Barnabo said to him: "You say such and such but Abbot Wimmer says the opposite. One of you is a liar. We have known Abbot Wimmer for ten years. And one cardinal here, von Reisach, has known him to be an honorable man for more than twenty years. We don't know you at all. Therefore . . ." So good Wendelin had to leave Rome before he was thrown out of town. Even so, his earlier calumnies found their way to the Holy Office of the Inquisition and it fell to me to disprove them. I was forced to tell the truth about him in order to frustrate his plans to found a monastery. . . . As you can see, my business here is a sad and unpleasant one. I must clean up a mess of ten years, and must contend with dishonesty among my own confreres almost constantly. I have chased the devil from St. Vincent, but from there he fled to Rome and now hides behind the authorities. Nevertheless, I find the authorities full of good will to rectify all this and am satisfied to hope that it will turn out all right.[78]

In the meantime Abbot Boniface was gaining credit and support among cardinals at both Propaganda and the Holy Office. It was becoming increasingly evident to everyone that even though the ideals of the reformers might have been commendable, their methods of pursuing their goals were divisive and destructive of peace and good order in the American Cassinese Congregation. The reformers wanted a stricter monastic observance at St. Vincent and had rallied around the questionable banner of Paul Keck. When it became clear that their goals could not be achieved in Pennsylvania, they had begun agitating for the establishment of a monastery in Minnesota free from Wimmer's control and subject to the monastic statutes of medieval Cluny. In order to reach this end they had inaugurated a campaign against Abbot Boniface in Rome. But their efforts were all doomed to failure.

Several weeks after his letter to Prior Rupert Seidenbusch, Wimmer wrote his nephew, Father Luke Wimmer, subprior and novice master at St. Vincent, that he expected a decision from the Inquisition soon. He said that the cardinals had decided not to call for an apostolic visitation at St. Vincent after all because he had given sufficient proof that only Wendelin Mayer and Othmar Wirtz still held tenaciously to the cult that had flourished around Paul Keck. Moreover, Wimmer reported that he himself had been exonerated of any suspicion of wrongdoing. On the other hand Father Wendelin had been severely censured by the Roman officials. His attempt to discredit the abbot had met with utter failure, and Wimmer told his nephew that on July 20, when he had gone to the offices of the Propaganda Fide on official business, the secretary of the Sacred Congregation had informed him that Cardinal Barnabo was at that very moment "exorcising" Father Wendelin.

When I said that I did not understand, the secretary opened the door of the cardinal's office. There stood poor Wendelin before the cardinal and his whole staff. The cardinal read a terrible condemnation: "Tu es apostatus, tu mentiris, tu non noscis ABC in vita religiosa. Disce obedire etc. etc." Father Wendelin was bold enough to contradict him and by so doing provoked the cardinal even more. With this I had to be satisfied to see this self-styled reformer of the order stigmatized in my presence as a liar and a traitor, who before had calumniated me without being reprimanded.[79]

The case, however, was not to be concluded for two more months. Finally, on September 16, 1865, the cardinals of the Holy Office handed down their decision. They declared "that the visions and revelations of George Keck deserve no credence. On the contrary, they contain grave errors, and the two monks who are their principal supporters must be placed under surveillance."[80] On October 11, 1865, the decree was formally promulgated, and six days later Wimmer wrote Prior Othmar Wirtz in St. Cloud informing him of the decision of the Holy Office and relieving him of his duties as superior in Minnesota.[81] Following instructions of the Holy See, Wimmer also directed that all the capitulars of the American Cassinese Congregation sign a document renouncing support for Paul George Keck and declaring their submission to the decision of the Holy Office.[82]

Father Othmar informed Wimmer that he would abide by the Roman decision, and he wrote Father Wendelin in December that he wished to comply entirely with the repudiation of Keck. With his hopes of founding a Cluniac monastery finally destroyed, he submitted in every way to his superiors and from St. Cloud went to St. Paul, Minnesota, where he worked as assistant to Father Clement Staub in Assumption Parish until his death in 1874.[83] Father Wendelin Mayer continued for a while to oppose the decision of the Inquisition. His faculties were suspended, and he was severely censured by the cardinals. Finally, convinced of his error, he requested absolution from the Congregation De Penitentiaria on May 16, 1866. After formally declaring his submission to the Roman decree concerning Paul Keck's visions and apologizing to Abbot Boniface for the calumnies he had spoken against him and the scandals he had brought to St. Vincent, Mayer was absolved of all censures by the Roman Congregation on December 26, 1866.[84] He had returned to the United States with Wimmer in September, and for the next fifteen years he worked quietly in parishes in Pennsylvania and New Jersey until his death in 1881. Of Paul Keck, the actor and archimposter who for nearly six years had occasioned unparalleled furor and contentiousness in the Benedictine communities of the American Cassinese Congregation, no more was ever heard.

But Wimmer's business in Rome was not ended. There was still the "mess of ten years" to be cleaned up, and with the Keck case out of the way he turned to other matters that would keep him occupied in Rome for the next nine months. The decisions of the general chapter of 1862 awaited the approval of the Propaganda Fide. Of particular concern to the cardinals was the question of tenure for American abbots, and though the American Benedictines had made clear their desire for permanent elected abbots in conformity with practice in the Bavarian Congregation, the cardinals favored the custom, observed by the Italian Congregation, of limited abbatial terms. The petition to elevate the priory in Minnesota to an abbey and the community in San José, Texas, to a canonical priory had also to be decided, and questions regarding vows for lay brothers in the American Cassinese Congregation and the vows and liturgical obligations of the Benedictine sisters in the United States remained to be resolved.

Wimmer began the tiresome task of convincing the Roman officials that his solutions to these questions were the most judicious. He favored lifetime tenure for abbots in the American Cassinese Congregation, supported the creation of an abbey in Minnesota on his terms and not those of Prior Othmar Wirtz and the reformers, now reluctantly opposed the elevation of San José to canonical status because it was clear that war and sickness had made the Benedictine presence in Texas untenable, and urged that the right of lay brothers in the American Cassinese Congregation to make solemn vows be rescinded.

In December 1865 he wrote Prior Rupert at St. Vincent that he was somewhat discouraged by the slow progress of the proceedings. "Rome cannot be taken by sudden attack," he lamented. "Apparently victory will come only after a long siege."[85] In fact the siege was much longer than Wimmer anticipated. In January 1866 he wrote that because his secretary, Father Edward Hipelius, had failed to make sufficient preparations for their presentation, the questions would not even reach the Propaganda until April. In April he wrote that no decision would be made until May, commenting that "so far I have worn out three pairs of shoes making calls to inquire about the progress of our cases, asking questions, answering objections, and correcting false opinions." In May he wrote, "Next Monday, June 4, our cases will be debated in the Sacred Congregation of the Propaganda. On the following Sunday the decisions will be submitted to the Holy Father, and on the next day I will be informed of the result. I hope to leave Rome about the middle of June."[86]

It was not until June 30 that Wimmer received the welcome news from Cardinal Barnabo that all his petitions had been decided in his favor, approved by the Propaganda, and confirmed by Pope Pius IX. According to the Propaganda decree which Cardinal Barnabo gave him, abbots in the American Cassinese Congregation who were canonically elected would be "nominated for life in accordance with the rules of the Bavarian Congregation." The petition to elevate the priory in Minnesota to the rank of abbey was also granted, although approval of the decision of the general chapter of 1862 to elevate the monastery in Texas to the rank of independent priory was, upon Wimmer's recommendation, deferred because the future of the Texas community was in doubt. Wimmer's petitions that his decision to exclude *fratres conversi* from solemn vows be upheld and that the Benedictine sisters in America be granted the right of reciting the Office of the Blessed Virgin instead of the regular divine office on weekdays were granted. Propaganda also reconfirmed its earlier decree that the sisters profess temporary simple vows after the novitiate and perpetual simple vows after three more years of religious life. Finally, the Sacred Congregation deferred the question of establishing a congregation of American Benedictine sisters, as well as the question of canonically recognizing the Benedictine convents that already existed in America, until the American bishops could be consulted when they convened at the plenary council scheduled to take place in Baltimore within four months.[87]

Thus the major problems facing Abbot Boniface during the years between 1856 and 1866—his "era of troubles"—received definitive solution. His plan for an active missionary role for the Benedictine Order in the American Church was confirmed by Rome with the censure of those monks who had called for a reform of the American Cassinese Congregation; abbots in the American Cassinese Congregation would henceforth be elected for life; the status of Benedictine lay brothers and sisters in the United States was clarified; and the direction of the missionary apostolate undertaken by the Benedictines in the United States was formally approved with the elevation of the Minnesota priory to the rank of abbey. Most gratifying to the abbot, however, was the vindication of his monastic ideals and administration. His achievements in the American missions had been gravely threatened by those who styled themselves reformers and whose storms of protest had carried all the way to Rome. But now his era of troubles had ended. On July 27, 1866, Boniface Wimmer, having "contributed to the faith in a wonderful way," was appointed abbot of St. Vincent *ad dies vitae* by the Holy Father.[88] Two days earlier he had marked the twentieth anniversary of his departure from Munich for the American missions.

6 ❧ Consolidation and Further Growth

ABBOT BONIFACE WIMMER left Rome on July 1, 1866. It had been his second trip to the Eternal City in a decade, and as on the previous occasion he had managed to wend his way skillfully and effectively through the labyrinth of the Vatican bureaucracy. He had overcome obstacles that might have defeated less capable churchmen, and he had emerged from the fray battered but successful in his efforts to achieve greater security for the twenty-year-old Benedictine mission in America. At the end of his fifteen-month struggle in Rome not only was his vision for the monastic institute in the United States ratified by the elevation of a second American abbey, but he also enjoyed the satisfaction of knowing that his often controversial policies had been vindicated by the Holy See. After an unhappy series of challenges and accusations, and despite strong opposition from certain of his own confreres, he was named permanent abbot of St. Vincent Abbey and president of the American Cassinese Congregation of Benedictines *ad dies vitae.* When Wimmer left Rome that July, the troubles of a decade were behind him.

Together with Father Edward Hipelius, the young St. Vincent priest who had just received his Roman doctorate, and Wendelin Mayer, the humbled rebel who carried with him the burden of a Roman censure, and in the company of Cardinal Karl August von Reisach, the former archbishop of Munich who had blessed the Benedictine mission to America twenty years earlier, Wimmer traveled by coach and rail to Munich, where he hoped to recruit candidates and raise money for the monasteries in the United States. From the Bavarian capital he wrote the perennial benefactor of the American Benedictines, King Ludwig I, expressing his deep gratitude for all the monarch had done in advancing his cause in Rome. The new abbey in Minnesota had not been named, Wimmer said, but he had "intentionally not given it a name except the indefinite descriptive one 'near St. Cloud.' For a very long time our intention was to name it after Your Majesty, but because I could not know if I would succeed in Rome to carry out my plan of erecting the new abbey, I could hardly come to you with such an untimely request."

Now that matters had been settled, however, and the abbey created, Abbot Boniface wanted to show his appreciation for all the monarch had done for the American Benedictines. Accordingly, he asked permission to name the new abbey in Minnesota for the king. "On the banks of the 'Father of Waters,' not very far from its fountainhead, we American Benedictines wish to erect a monument in honor of Your Majesty, a memorial of our gratitude and reverence."[1] The king granted Wimmer's request, and the community in Minnesota became known as the Abbey of St. Louis on the Lake. Three weeks later the abbot wrote the Bavarian monarch once again, remarking that the monks in America

feel greatly encouraged by the lively interest Your Majesty takes in the prosperity of our order, both in Europe and in America. . . . Through the very sad events in our present modern times and during the past several decades, our order has been practically exterminated in most countries of Europe. . . . But in Bavaria it flourishes once more under your protection, and I am sure it happened not without special dispensation of Divine Providence that from Bavaria it was transplanted to America.

Wimmer told the king that he had spent the previous weeks visiting monasteries in Bavaria "to share my experience with the superiors and also to learn theirs." He said that "with one single exception all the abbots in and outside Germany received me very cordially" and generally were quite willing to cooperate in providing the data he needed for the album he planned to publish with information and statistics from the world's Benedictine monasteries, "whereby we Benedictines will learn to know and get closer to one another for mutual support, be encouraged to intellectual and spiritual communication, compensated for local losses and comforted by the success in other localities, and become conscious of our numerical, scholarly, and pastoral strength, which is still considerable." He promised to send the king a copy of the *Album Benedictinum* as soon as it was published.[2]

The outbreak of the war between Prussia and Austria hampered his efforts to raise money for the American missions, one of the main reasons for his lengthy visit to Munich. Bavaria had allied herself with the Austrians, and taxes to finance the war overburdened would-be contributors. Many potential candidates for the monastery in America, moreover, were conscripted for military service, and as for those who did not enter the army, Bavarian conscription laws prohibited the emigration of men between the ages of sixteen and fifty. The same problem had occurred in 1855, during the Crimean War, when Wimmer had last visited Bavaria in hopes of recruiting candidates for the American missions. Thus, when he departed Munich at the end of August 1866, he was accompanied only by Fathers Edward and Wendelin.

The three priests traveled through Germany to France, and on September 10, 1866, embarked from Brest for the United States. It was more than a year and a half since the abbot had left St. Vincent, and he longed to return home. On September 23, after a particularly rough crossing, he and his companions reached New York where they disembarked and collected their baggage. They spent the next two days relaxing with the monks of St. Mary's Priory, in Newark, New Jersey, and on the morning of September 26 they left New York for Pennsylvania. Traveling by train along the main line of the Pennsylvania Railroad, they reached Johnstown in the early afternoon. Wimmer decided to stop for a visit of several hours with the Benedictine priests assigned there, so they did not reach the Latrobe station until midnight.

The monks and students at St. Vincent had made extensive preparations for the abbot's return. They had erected a triumphal arch at the monastery gate, decorating it with laurel branches from Chestnut Ridge, autumn flowers from the monastery garden, and small blue and white Bavarian flags. They had strung welcoming banners across the road, placed a large American flag on the "abbot's tower," and positioned the school band atop the tower to greet him with music when the carriage bringing him from the train station came into sight. Unfortunately, they had made all these preparations early in the day, for they expected him to arrive on the afternoon train. His stopover in Johnstown had delayed him, and when the afternoon train arrived without him, some said that he had deliberately missed his connection to avoid the pomp and ceremony that he knew the community was preparing.

The organizers were not to be disappointed in their attempt to prepare an appropriate welcome for the father they had not seen in nineteen months. Anticipating a nighttime arrival now, students gathered logs from the surrounding woods and built huge bonfires all around the campus. The brothers placed candles in the windows of the monastery and college. When the midnight train arrived, a delegation of priests met Wimmer at the station in Latrobe and escorted him in a triumphal procession back to St. Vincent. As the abbot's carriage, surrounded by blackclad horsemen, climbed the hill, the bonfires and candles were lit and the student band trumpeted a welcome. At the monastery gate Prior Rupert Seidenbusch greeted the abbot with a short speech, and the monks and students cheered his return. It was a dramatic and moving moment, but Wimmer was exhausted and after a few brief words of thanks he urged everyone to go to bed. The next day he celebrated pontifical high mass for the community and later was guest of honor at a reception and dinner the monks prepared for him.[3]

There was much for him to do at St. Vincent in the days that followed. His long absence meant that a great many matters had been postponed that now required his immediate attention. Although Prior Rupert Seidenbusch had done a commendable job managing the temporal and spiritual affairs of the community in the previous year and a half, there were some things that only the abbot could attend to. There were the preparations he had to make for the election of an abbot in Minnesota, for example, and unsettling reports from Kansas indicated that in the previous year Prior Augustine Wirth had so mismanaged affairs at St. Benedict's Priory that the Atchison community was now on the brink of spiritual and financial bankruptcy. Wimmer's desk was piled high with papers, but he was not able to remain long at the abbey to deal with the problems they contained. Within two weeks he had to travel to Baltimore to attend the Second Plenary Council of the Catholic Church in the United States.

Archbishop Martin John Spalding had called the council to consider the many problems confronting the American Church in the aftermath of the Civil War. It was the first time since 1852 that the archbishops and bishops had gathered in a body to discuss the critical issues facing the American Catholic community, and Wimmer was one of two mitered abbots—the other was the Trappist abbot of Gethsemani, Kentucky—who participated in the deliberations. The council focused on discipline and doctrine in the American Catholic Church. The bishops perceived the need for greater uniformity of church administration in the nation's dioceses and issued a series of decrees designed to harmonize ecclesiastical procedures throughout the country. They confirmed the recommendation of the Holy See that religious women in the United States pronounce simple rather than solemn vows, and they urged the creation of schools and orphanages for the children of the millions of Catholic immigrants streaming into the United States. One of the actions of the Plenary Council that would have an important impact on Wimmer and the Benedictines of St. Vincent was the bishops' call for religious communities to open schools and other institutions to serve the educational and spiritual needs of the freed black slaves. The Benedictines were among the few religious communities in the United States to heed this call when a decade later Wimmer opened a school for African Americans in Georgia.[4]

The Baltimore council also broke new ground in another way. For the first time in the history of the American Church the bishops jointly issued a series of statements on theological topics that were not clearly understood by Americans, Catholic and Protestant alike. The theological topics they discussed included revelation, the church as custodian of revelation, the doctrine of "outside the church there is no salvation," the nature and necessity of faith, Sacred Scripture, the mysteries of the Trinity, creation, redemption, sanctification, the future life, and veneration of the Blessed Virgin Mary.[5] Wimmer played an important role in the formulation of some of these statements by serving as vice-president of the theological committee chaired by Bishop James Frederic Wood of Philadelphia.[6]

On October 17 Abbot Boniface asked leave of the council in order to travel to New York to bid farewell to a contingent of young St. Vincent monks he had chosen to send to Rome to pursue advanced studies. During his extended stay in the Eternal City, he had made arrangements to establish a Roman house of studies for the American Benedictines, and upon returning to St. Vincent he had appointed Father Oswald Moosmüller, prior in Newark, to be rector of the Roman community. With Moosmüller went three recently ordained priests of St. Vincent: Fathers Adalbert Müller, Innocent Wolf, and Hilary Pfrängle. Writing to Father Bernard Smith, O.S.B., at the time a professor in the Urban College of the Propaganda Fide, the abbot said that he was sending his men to spend "three or perhaps four years in Rome, in order to qualify themselves as professors for our College." Wimmer told Smith that he wanted his men to study philosophy under the Dominicans and then to take courses in dogmatic theology. Father Adalbert was particularly talented in languages and should go on to study Hebrew after finishing philosophy. Likewise Father Innocent should turn to the study of mathematics and physics. Abbot Boniface said that within a year he hoped to send one or two more St. Vincent monks to Rome. "I have some very fine young men among my clerics and scholastics. Until we get professors here I cannot help sending the worthiest of them to Rome. It would cost me little or nothing to have a few at Munich, but I'd sooner pay a heavy outlay for them at Rome to make sure that they get fully reliable teachers." Because Smith knew the Roman colleges and the most prominent professors well, Wimmer asked his advice and help in placing the American students where they would be most benefited. "Besides, I am sure you take a lively interest in the first American Benedictine enterprise."[7]

Abbot Boniface had taken a two-day leave of absence from the Plenary Council to dispatch his Roman students from New York, and he returned to Baltimore in time to participate in the council's solemn closing session, which was attended by President Andrew Johnson. At the beginning of November he returned to St. Vincent, but again he could stay only briefly at the abbey. Soon he was on the road again, this time bound for St. Cloud, Minnesota. He arrived in St. Cloud during the second week of December, and on December 12 he presided over the election of the second abbot of the American Cassinese Congregation.

Twelve monks of the Minnesota foundation had transferred their vows to the new abbey, and nine of them now assembled with Wimmer in the Indianbush farmhouse that since the move from St. Cloud had served as the priory. Father Demetrius di Marogna, founding prior of the community, had gone to Florida to recover his health, but like Fathers Clement Staub, pastor in St. Paul, and Eberhard Gahr, pastor in Shakopee, he had appointed a proxy.

After the deposition of Prior Othmar Wirtz, Wimmer had named Father Benedict Haindl as administrator in Minnesota. Haindl, who earlier had served a three-year term as prior in St. Cloud, had not transferred his vows to the new abbey, but as interim prior he celebrated the solemn high mass *coram abbate* at nine o'clock in the morning of the election in the humble chapel that was now an abbey church. After mass Wimmer led the nine electors into the place that served as the community's chapter room. Accompanied by his secretary, Father Edward Hipelius, he addressed the capitulars, urging them to choose an abbot who was outstanding in wisdom and virtue. He said that if they could not arrive at a decision to elect one of their own number, they were free to choose any priest in the congregation. When Wimmer concluded his preliminary remarks, the voting began. The election proceeded smoothly and quickly. Father Edward Hipelius tabulated the results of the first ballot and announced that Father Rupert Seidenbusch, claustral prior at St. Vincent, had been elected first abbot of the Abbey of St. Louis on the Lake.[8] Seidenbusch, who had entered the monastery at St. Vincent in 1851, had been one of Wimmer's most dependable monks for many years. In addition to serving as prior at St. Vincent, he had been superior in the priories of St. Marys, Pennsylvania, and Newark, New Jersey, and his talents would be further recognized by the American Church when, within ten years of his election as the second Benedictine abbot in the United States he would be named bishop of the vicariate of Northern Minnesota.

Wimmer remained with the Minnesota monks "only until the result of the election was three times recorded and copied." He then visited St. Cloud, St. Paul, and Shakopee where some of the monks of the new abbey were stationed. He crossed the frozen Mississippi on foot "while carrying a heavy sack" and as a consequence sprained his arm. Undaunted, he went on to Milwaukee, where he held meetings with his old friend, Bishop John Martin Henni, and then to the Benedictine priory of St. Joseph in Chicago where four priests and two brothers from St. Vincent were stationed. In Chicago the abbot rested for several days and conducted a visitation. From there he traveled to Erie, where he visited the monks of St. Mary's Priory, and afterwards to St. Marys, Pennsylvania, where he spent Christmas with the monks and nuns. He returned to St. Vincent on January 5, 1867, after an absence of six weeks. "It was a difficult and expensive trip," he wrote Abbot Utto Lang, "but I was amply rewarded for my labor by the sincere love and delight with which I was hospitably received and feted by my confreres. A second abbey has been erected, a second abbot elected, and thus a guarantee given us for the propagation of our order and faith." Wimmer told Lang that the community in Minnesota was strong. The monastery owned about fourteen hundred acres of land, and during the previous summer the monks had erected a new large stone building about a mile and a half south of the farmhouse monastery in the Indianbush. The new structure was located near a beautiful lake, and though it was not ready for occupation at the time of the election, it would soon become the permanent home of the monks in Minnesota: "The surroundings are excellent. The lake is almost a square mile in area and has many fish. The forest is entirely deciduous. Bordering the creek that runs past the building are a few hundred acres of natural meadow land. Pheasants, rabbits, deer, and bear are plentiful."

Meanwhile at St. Vincent two more buildings were under construction, one to be ready for occupancy in the spring. Now that he was back home, Abbot Boniface was "again paying more attention to our seminary. I had left it pretty well to Father Edward." He said that he often had to "laugh at my Bavarian confreres. Because I am an American, I can do as I please without waiting for the permission of a royal minister, or the president. I am sure of success if I undertake something good and use common sense. But I do not laugh too loudly, for even here not everything is completed."[9]

Still Wimmer had every reason to be sanguine. When the Civil War ended, a major obstacle to the further expansion of the Benedictines in America disappeared. The abbot, who by this time had gained fame throughout the American Church as a dynamic missionary, received many new requests from bishops throughout the United States to send monks to establish monasteries in their dioceses. Among the prelates who asked for Benedictines were Bishop William Henry Elder of Natchez, Bishop Thaddeus Amat, C.M., of Monterey-Los Angeles, Bishop John B. Lamy of Santa Fé, Bishop Patrick Lynch of Charleston, and Archbishop John Mary Odin of New Orleans.[10] But despite the freedom of movement the new peace afforded, consolidation of existing foundations rather than the establishment of new ones was his first concern.

By 1867 the Abbey of St. Louis was firmly rooted in the soil of Minnesota. At St. Benedict's Priory in Kansas, however, it was a different story. The financial stability of the Kansas priory was in serious doubt, and there was growing disenchantment among the monks there with the superior, Father Augustine Wirth. Wirth still had ambitions of becoming abbot in Kansas, and to prepare for that great day he had begun an expansion project that would ultimately bring about his downfall. In the summer of 1867 the construction of a large and impressive abbey church, a church that was intended to be a memorial to the outstanding monastic leadership of Prior Augustine, was underway at St. Benedict's. Wirth, however, had not taken a realistic look at the prospects for raising money for the building, and its construction was forcing the community deeper and deeper into debt. As a consequence serious questions arose as to whether the Kansas priory could even survive.[11]

Prospects in the other communities of the American Cassinese Congregation were much brighter than in Kansas. St. Mary's Priory in Newark prospered under the leadership of Prior Roman Hell, who succeeded Father Oswald Moosmüller when Wimmer tapped Moosmüller to organize St. Elizabeth's House of Studies in Rome. With Father Roman in Newark were three priests and two lay brothers. At St. Joseph's Priory in Covington, Kentucky, Prior Celestine Englbrecht, with three priests and two lay brothers, made encouraging headway in the pastoral and educational work the Benedictines had begun there in 1857. Established from St. Vincent in 1860, St. Joseph Priory in Chicago had a community of four priests and two lay brothers in 1867 under the leadership of Prior Louis Fink. The monks in Chicago attended to the spiritual needs of one thousand Catholics and had recently completed a magnificent church "in the best basilica style."[12]

Other priories and parishes served by St. Vincent monks in 1867 included St. Mary's in Richmond, Virginia, where Father Leonard Mayer, brother of Father Wendelin, was pastor; St. Benedict's in Newark, served by monks from St. Mary's Priory since its establishment in 1864; and St. Walburga's in Elizabeth City, New Jersey, where seventy-one-year-old Father Peter Henry Lemke, Abbot Boniface's old friend and nemesis, was pastor.

In Pennsylvania three of the priories Wimmer established from St. Vincent in the 1840s and 1850s also fared well in 1867. St. Benedict's Priory in Carrolltown was the home of eight brothers and four priests under the direction of Prior Aegidius Christoph. The monks in Carrolltown continued to serve parishes and missions throughout northern Cambria County. In St. Marys, Pennsylvania, Prior Ferdinand Wolf, brother of Father Innocent, together with three priests and nine brothers, served the German population of Elk County. And at St.

Mary's Priory, in Erie, Prior Benno Hegele, together with two priests and one brother, ministered to a large German congregation.

At the Abbey of St. Vincent there were nearly one hundred and forty monks, half of whom were lay brothers. A hundred boys were enrolled in the gymnasium, and forty philosophers and theologians studied in the seminary. In the Diocese of Pittsburgh Benedictine priests from St. Vincent administered thirteen parishes, the most important of which were St. Mary's in Allegheny, St. Joseph's in Johnstown, Blessed Sacrament in Greensburg, St. Bernard's in Indiana, and St. Vincent itself. Wimmer had spent the months after his return from Rome visiting most of the foundations.

In the summer of 1867 he traveled to Kansas for a visitation, and in August, after returning to Pennsylvania from Kansas, he wrote King Ludwig I that "if up to this time St. Vincent alone and with very meager means has achieved so much that the order is already introduced in ten dioceses, it will now, with the support of a second abbey, be able to accomplish proportionately more." In his letter to the Bavarian monarch Wimmer spoke of the house of studies that the American monks had established in Rome. He had great hopes for this project, which he noted "is perhaps as important as the new abbey. Because our work is, in the first place, to educate and train good, efficient priests and to further Catholic learning, I had to keep in mind that I must provide teachers trained in Rome." Many of the priests and several of the bishops in America, Wimmer said, were trained at the Urban College of the Propaganda Fide. In order to be regarded as equal to them, his own priests, he felt, needed to be educated by Roman professors. "But even apart from that, genuine Catholicism is *Roman* Catholicism alone. The special German philosophies and theology taught in Germany at the present time are tainted more or less by rationalism." Such rationalism would not affect his students in Rome, however, because the Roman schools, above all else, were orthodox. "Besides this," he went on, "we need a permanent agent in the capital of Christendom." This was necessary in order to protect the American Benedictines against encroachment upon their prerogatives by episcopal authority. "To be sure, it takes a goodly sum of money to maintain four or six students in Rome, for there is no endowment in Rome itself. But we cannot avoid even greater sacrifices when it is a question of such a serious nature."[13]

On August 17, 1867, delegates from the two abbeys and eight priories gathered at St. Vincent for the third general chapter of the American Cassinese Congregation. The crucial question facing them was the plight of St. Benedict's Priory in Kansas. Prior Augustine Wirth and Father Timothy Luber represented the Kansas monks, and though Wirth said he had forgotten to bring the community's financial records to the meeting, he reported that the Benedictine debt in Kansas amounted to more than $10,000. Complaints against Wirth had come to Wimmer from a number of the monks in Atchison, including Father Timothy, and it was generally agreed that both the financial affairs and spiritual life of the community had deteriorated dangerously on account of Prior Augustine's weak leadership. The Kansas monks complained that the only sign of community life at the Atchison priory was the common table. Common recitation of the divine office, an essential in any Benedictine monastery, was almost entirely neglected. The prior, they said, held all the property in his own name and mismanaged the temporalities of the house. He refused to legally incorporate the priory and surrender the deeds to the community as required by canon law. He wrangled constantly with the other monks, whom he severely mistreated, and his chronic drunkenness promised to cause grave scandal should it become public knowledge.[14]

Still the delegates did not insist on appointing a new superior. The visitation Abbot Boniface had conducted earlier in the summer had convinced him that Wirth, who promised to amend his life, could solve the problems there, and so he left the prior in charge, much to the chagrin of the community. The delegates to the general chapter passed two statutes that attempted to solve immediate problems in Kansas. They voted that the clerics in Atchison should study their philosophy and theology at St. Vincent despite Prior Augustine's renewed claim that it would be cheaper to educate them in Kansas. Wimmer insisted that only by educating the young Kansas monks at St. Vincent would monastic life in Atchison achieve a par with other communities in the congregation. The chapter also directed that the priory be incorporated and that all property be registered in the name of the corporation.

The general chapter lasted three days. Among its other legislation was a decree formally erecting the Roman church of St. Elizabeth's and its adjacent property as the congregation's house of studies in Rome. Father Oswald Moosmüller was confirmed as rector of the community and named procurator general and general agent for the American Cassinese Congregation, though Wimmer made it clear that he wanted Abbot Angelo Pescetelli, who had been his agent in Rome for more than ten years, to continue functioning as before. The chapter handed down directives designed to ensure a uniform observance of the divine office and monastic discipline in all houses of the congregation, and in what was doubtless the least important but most oddly interesting decree passed by the delegates, the chapter favorably voted on the proposal of the abbot-president that "all monks, both priests and lay brothers, should, in the manner of our fathers who founded the Bavarian Congregation, wear beards. Novices before profession are formally obliged to do so."[15]

The general chapter closed on August 19, and the capitulars returned to their communities. A few days later Wimmer wrote Abbot Utto Lang that he never ceased to wonder at why he had been chosen "to be the instrument of such an undertaking as ours. But America is a poor country, and the average man is often looked upon as an outstanding person."[16]

Six months later Abbot Boniface was still downgrading the significance of his own contribution to the Benedictine achievement in America. Writing to the directors of the *Ludwig Missionsverein,* he said that there was nothing extraordinary or especially interesting to relate "because nothing of that sort readily appears in our work." Nevertheless, he reported that the blessing of Abbot Rupert Seidenbusch, which had taken place at St. Vincent the previous May, was "impressive," particularly since neither Wimmer nor any of his confreres had ever witnessed an abbatial blessing before. "In this regard," he said, "I came off badly." The Holy Father had appointed him to the abbatial office and had given him a private blessing. Abbot Rupert's was the first public and formal blessing of a Benedictine abbot in the United States.

When, upon my arrival at St. Vincent twenty-one years ago, I gave the Benedictine habit to my companions, future prospects were naturally quite gloomy. I do not know whether, apart from me, even one of them had the firm expectation that we would bring a monastery into being. Despite many difficulties and dangers from within and without, however, the work we began went forward, flourished, and became consolidated once it obtained papal authorization. [Since then] it has spread mightily into eleven dioceses and eight states! Is it not wonderful how here also God is glorified by bring-

ing into being a great work with insignificant means? I say a *great* work because if calamitous events don't disturb us, without any doubt our order will
spread all over America and through the care of souls and the teaching and
training of priests will exercise a great influence on the population.[17]

It was for the care of souls and the teaching and training of priests,
of course, that Wimmer had come to America, and as the order spread
to distant states and territories, Benedictine parishes and schools multiplied proportionately. By 1868 the American Cassinese Benedictines
were operating nineteen parishes in the United States and serving
nearly thirty other congregations with nonresident pastors. Benedictine sisters taught in elementary schools at most of the Benedictine
parishes in Pennsylvania, Minnesota, Kansas, New Jersey, Kentucky,
and Illinois, and the monks administered and taught in six secondary
schools ("colleges") they had established in Pennsylvania, Minnesota,
Kansas, New Jersey, Kentucky, and Virginia. The total enrollment in
the colleges was more than five hundred students, three hundred of
whom were candidates for the Benedictine Order. In addition, major
seminaries at the abbeys of St. Vincent and St. Louis on the Lake prepared nearly sixty young men from a dozen American dioceses for the
priesthood.[18]

The prototype of the Benedictine educational program in the
United States was the school at St. Vincent, so a brief review of the St.
Vincent model will be useful for a clearer understanding of the nature
of the schools operated by American Benedictines throughout the
nineteenth century.

There were four programs of study at the abbey in Pennsylvania.
In the first of these, the major seminary, ten Benedictine clerics and
forty diocesan seminarians were enrolled in 1868. The diocesan students came from New York, Charleston, Erie, Chicago, Richmond,
and Covington. (The diocese of Pittsburgh had opened its own seminary, and for that reason few Pittsburgh seminarians studied at St.
Vincent during this period.) A student normally began his studies in
the seminary at age eighteen or nineteen, although older men were
sometimes accepted if recommended by a bishop or accepted by the
monastic chapter. Benedictine students were required to undergo a
year's novitiate before entering the major seminary. The seminary offered a three-year program of philosophy and theology to young men
who had completed their classical secondary education either at St.

Vincent or in some other Catholic secondary institution. The curriculum included courses in Scholastic philosophy, moral theology, dogmatic theology, Sacred Scripture, biblical languages, liturgy, and ecclesiastical history. Seminarians who were native English speakers were expected to learn German, and native German speakers English. All were expected to know Latin and German thoroughly, for classes were taught in those languages.

The second program of study available at St. Vincent was the "classical course." This was one of two divisions in the secondary school, or college, which, following Bavarian tradition, was also known as the gymnasium or Latin school. The classical course consisted of a six-year program of study that encompassed the traditional liberal arts disciplines taught in Bavarian secondary schools. The principal disciplines were classical and modern languages (Latin, Greek, English, and German), history, mathematics, science, music, and religion. Students in the classical course ranged in age from twelve to eighteen. Most were candidates for the priesthood, though some planned after graduation to enter universities and professional schools to study medicine or law. Those among the classical students who desired to enter the Benedictine Order lived, worked, and prayed together in the "scholasticate," but their program of studies was the same as that of the other classical students.

The commercial course was the third division in the educational program at St. Vincent. It provided a three-year course of secondary-level training for students who desired practical preparation for careers in business, but there was also a strong liberal arts component in the curriculum. Boys in the commercial course were of the same age as those in the classical course and often attended the same classes. They studied modern languages (English, German, and French), mathematics, history, bookkeeping, penmanship, geography, natural philosophy, chemistry, and religion. In September 1868 there were more than two hundred secondary students enrolled at St. Vincent about evenly divided between the classical and commercial courses.

A fourth educational program operated by the monks in Pennsylvania was the elementary school. Wimmer had established this school shortly after his arrival at St. Vincent in order to afford children from poor families in the neighborhood, "especially those of German descent, an excellent opportunity of acquiring a thorough knowledge of elementary principles of the English and German languages." Its curriculum embraced the study of reading, spelling, writing, religion, penmanship, arithmetic, and geography. In 1868 there were thirty-three pupils enrolled in this school.[19]

The St. Vincent faculty and administration in the 1868–1869 academic year numbered twenty-two professors of whom all but one was a monk. (Lay professor Joseph Maurice Schwab, the Bavarian-born instructor of music, whom Wimmer had brought to St. Vincent in 1851, was the exception.[20]) Father Edward Hipelius was rector of the seminary and Father Alphonse Heimler president of the college. Heimler, a brilliant but tempestuous man, had received his degree in philosophy at the University of Munich before coming to St. Vincent in 1855. In 1859 Wimmer sent him to study physics and astronomy at Georgetown where he earned a master's degree in 1860. He was the first Benedictine to obtain a graduate degree from an American university. Upon his return to St. Vincent Heimler expected to be named president of the college, but when Wimmer failed to appoint him to the post immediately, he allied himself with those in the congregation who opposed the abbot and for a while promoted himself as successor to Wimmer. At the general chapter of 1862 he joined Father Augustine Wirth and some of the younger monks in a successful effort to thwart the election of Wimmer as lifetime abbot of St. Vincent. It is a measure of the abbot's tolerance and patience with the talented young monks who often challenged his leadership that shortly after the general chapter he appointed Heimler to the position he longed for, a position Father Alphonse held for the next ten years.[21]

Other Benedictine professors at St. Vincent in 1868 included Hipelius, the first St. Vincent monk to be sent for studies to Europe, where he studied hermeneutics in England and received his doctorate in canon law from the Sapienza in Rome, and Father Ulric Spöttl, who had studied philosophy and theology at the universities of Munich and Würzburg before entering the monastery in Pennsylvania. Besides Heimler, Hipelius, and Spöttl, the monks teaching at St. Vincent in 1868 had all received their postsecondary educations in the seminary in Pennsylvania. In many cases professors in the college were clerics working as part-time instructors as they completed their theological course in the major seminary. Wimmer complained that the Benedictine professors during this period were on the whole academically undistinguished. He recognized the monks' need for more thorough intellectual training and for that reason established St. Elizabeth's House of Studies in Rome and sent Fathers Oswald Moosmüller, Adalbert Müller, Innocent Wolf, and Hilary Pfrängle to study there in 1866. Other St. Vincent monks who under Wimmer's auspices received European educations during the 1860s and 1870s included Cyril Elder and William Walter, who studied theology and history at the University of Munich; Xavier Baltes and James Zilliox who studied theology and sacred scripture at Innsbruck and Rome; and Gerard Pilz, Bonaventure Ostendarp, and Cosmas Wolf (a lay brother) who studied art in Munich.[22]

The academic year at St. Vincent began during the first week of September and finished at the end of June. It consisted of two sessions of five months each, at the conclusion of which an examination of all the classes was made and reports sent home to the parents of the students "to inform them of the conduct, health, and improvement of their sons or wards." When a student presented himself for admission, which could be granted at any time during the year, he was examined and placed in a class "for which his previous attainments may have fitted him." Those coming to the college from other institutions were required to produce satisfactory recommendations from the presidents of those institutions, and the college catalogue stated that "no one will be admitted for a shorter period than one session."[23]

Students, both in the seminary and college, were recruited from all the dioceses in which the Benedictines had parishes. Wimmer placed special emphasis on providing the means for poor boys to study for the priesthood at St. Vincent. "It used to be said that American boys had no inclination for the priesthood," he wrote.

But this is not true. The sons of wealthy parents, of course, seldom dedicate themselves to the religious life, but this is general. The poor, however, especially in large cities, do so if they can find the opportunity. [The poor] frequently find it difficult to achieve independent positions in the populated areas. It is easier for them in the country districts. Thus we recruit mostly from our city parishes, where we select the best and most talented boys from the school for ourselves. All the orders do the same, as do the bishops. . . . We have more candidates for our order than for the secular clergy. This scarcely needs justification. But in the end the proportion adjusts itself, for some of our scholastics leave before entering the novitiate or making profession and become secular priests. Not rarely they make profession but leave the order before solemn profession or give such indications of a lack of a religious vocation that we do not admit them to solemn vows but turn them over to the secular clergy. In this way we have sent very many secular priests to the bishops.[24]

Two such candidates for the Benedictine Order, who both left the scholasticate in 1860 and entered the secular priesthood, were John A. Watterson of Blairsville, Pennsylvania, and Joseph A. Rademacher of Westphalia, Michigan. In 1880 Watterson was named bishop of Columbus, Ohio, and in 1883 Rademacher became bishop of Nashville, Tennessee, and ten years later was transferred to the diocese of Fort Wayne, Indiana.[25]

An interesting account of student life at St. Vincent during the late 1860s survives in the "fugitive recollections" of Father Henry Ganss, a student at the college in 1868. Ganss, who later became a priest in the diocese of Harrisburg and gained a notable reputation as a Reformation scholar and a composer of sacred music, wrote that

in 1868 the monastery and college, measured by the standard of the ancient Benedictine nurseries of civilization, who counted their histories by centuries and not years, was still in its swaddling clothes, though giving every evidence of being a healthy, lusty, vigorous youngster. Like Emerson's estimate of Amherst College in its infancy, it looked as if "the infant college would be an infant Hercules." Still it seemed so impressed with its own insignificance at this early period of its chrysalis state that it did not as yet even dare wing its flight for a state charter to confer academic degrees.[26]

Among the numerous stories told by Ganss about people and events at St. Vincent between 1868 and 1878 is one he called the "radical raid episode." The presidential election of 1868 had caused great excitement throughout the nation. Wimmer had declared himself a Democrat soon after coming to the United States because the Democratic party generally defended the immigrants while the Republican party was often identified with the anti-immigrant, anti-Catholic elements in American society. It was well known in the neighborhood of the abbey that the monks would cast their ballots against the Republican candidate, Ulysses S. Grant. Several weeks before the election Abbot Boniface and Father Alphonse Heimler had received anonymous letters to the effect that unless "the whole institution would cast its vote for the Republican ticket . . . the monastery and college would be raided." Not to be intimidated, Wimmer instructed his monks to vote for the Democratic slate. The day of the election arrived and the voting took place. That evening mysterious lights appeared at several points on the perimeter of the campus. An old shack several hundred yards from the main buildings caught fire and was quickly consumed by the flames. The tension and excitement among both monks and students reached fever pitch when

Father Alphonse with choked voice and excited gesture came into the senior study hall with the announcement that "the radicals are here and every student should come to the defense of his alma mater." The speech had little of the military ring about it, but there was not a student there whose heroic soul did not leap at the prospect of a scrap. On the ball field, midway between the college and the cherry path. . ., the army of defense, consisting of priests, clerics, brothers, workmen, and now students, was assembled. Armed with every imaginable weapon of defense and carnage, from antiquated army muskets to obsolete cavalry revolvers, from sledgehammers to candle-extinguishers, they awaited the word of command. Father Abbot of course assumed generalship. Some of the cooler heads and more safely armed were posted as sentinels; others, more brave and bellicose, were sent out in reconnoitering squads with proper countersigns.

But no Radical Republicans were discovered, and Ganss said he suspected the whole affair was a student prank. "The fact that the collegiate scouts were said to have centered all their vigilance on the brewery" seemed to support his argument. In any event the evening study period had been completely disrupted as brave men from academic halls and cloister met the challenge of the phantom foe. When morning came, peace reigned at the abbey and college of St. Vincent once again. The armaments of war were returned to their resting places, and Abbot Boniface put aside the mantle of warrior. He could not have been entirely happy with the outcome, however, since not only had one of the buildings on campus been destroyed but also by then news was clicking along the telegraph lines that the country had once again elected a Republican president.[27]

In the same month as the "Radical Raid" Wimmer wrote a revealing letter to Father Martin Marty, O.S.B., superior of the Benedictine community of St. Meinrad's in Indiana which had been founded fourteen years earlier by monks from the Swiss Abbey of Einsiedeln. Marty had been corresponding with Wimmer, asking advice and seeking assistance, since the arrival of the Swiss monks in America. By 1868 St. Meinrad's had achieved a level of stability that would permit it to successfully petition the Holy See for elevation to the rank of abbey two years later. Wimmer had encouraged Marty to pursue the elevation as early as 1866, when he met with him at the Second Plenary Council of Baltimore. He hoped that as the third abbey in the United States St. Meinrad's would join the American Cassinese Congregation. Marty, however, was reluctant to sever the ties that bound the community in Indiana to the motherhouse at Einsiedeln, and in this he was supported by the abbot of Einsiedeln, Henry Schmid, who warned Marty that Wimmer was trying to put "abbatial lice" on the prior of St. Meinrad.[28] During this period Marty had written several times to Wimmer describing conditions at St. Meinrad's and discussing his ideas about what form the monastic life should take in America. Marty and his Swiss confreres tended to disagree with Wimmer's vision of a wide-ranging, proactive missionary monasticism, prompting the abbot of St. Vincent to respond:

The things you said in your letter to me against the idea of a common novitiate and house of studies marks you as a real, true Switzer. It makes me wonder that as you were writing you did not get homesick and feel tempted to set out with bag and baggage and return to your father at Einsiedeln, so as to spend there all the days of your life at his side or at the side of his successor in a cozy, comfortable life together, just like many of your fellow countrymen who never left the valley where they were born or who if leaving it, died abroad out of sheer homesickness when they couldn't return home.

Wimmer objected to what he considered the provincial attitudes of the Swiss monks with regard to the Benedictine vow of stability. "That stability is a fundamental concept in the Rule, I will grant. I deny however that stability is to be understood only in regard to place or that it is to be restricted according to your interpretation of it. For you must note that the stability of which St. Benedict speaks is also a stability of state." If, as Marty suggested, the idea of St. Benedict was that monks were bound never to leave their monasteries under any circumstances,

how in the world could the order spread? How could the Benedictines have converted England, Germany, Hungary, Sweden and the rest? What about our St. Boniface, St. Willibrord, St. Otto, and the others? What would we be without them? What about you and me? It was against the gyrovagues and sarabites of his time that St. Benedict introduced stability, not only the stability of place but also the stability of state, so that those who made their profession might not take off their habit and return to the world. If you insist on such a one-sided view of the stability of place, what can America expect from St. Meinrad's?

Wimmer said that the logical consequence of Marty's interpretation of the Rule would be stagnation for his community.

God forbid such an interpretation. . . . We would stifle all future development and would disappoint the hopes that young America places in us. Such an interpretation would demolish once and for all every prospect of filling up the gap that exists here, namely the lack of an order that makes it its special objective to supply America with a sufficient number of good priests. It is certainly not contrary to stability of place to have a common novitiate and house of studies as long as they exist in accordance with the express will of the respective abbots, just as it is not contrary to the vow if a priest goes out to a parish . . . or is sent away as a professor.

Wimmer cited numerous examples from history to prove that the Benedictine Order had never taken a narrow view of St. Benedict's admonition to stability, and he charged that the Swiss superior of St. Meinrad's was doing harm to the order and preventing future development of his own community by insisting that missionary work was not compatible with the monastic life. Engaging in an active missionary apostolate and taking a broad view of the vow of stability, said Wimmer, assured the order "that there would be natural offshoots, ever fresh and strong, stemming from an ancient rootstock, just as the Church in the course of time, though preserving her fundamental, essential, and unalienable character, has nevertheless been formed and molded so as to correspond to the needs of any particular time."[29]

But even as he composed this spirited defense of his interpretation of the Rule of St. Benedict to Marty, Wimmer was still coming under attack from some, including members of his own house, over the emphasis he continued to place upon the active missionary life. His vision of the role the Benedictine Order should play in the life of the Church had remained unchanged for thirty years, and it was his task now to ensure that it be passed on intact to the next generation of American Benedictines. To this end, he wrote his Roman student, the young Father Innocent Wolf:

I can glory in nothing but this: throughout my entire life as a Benedictine, all my wishes, all my endeavors have been directed toward the furtherance of our order's prosperity. I have been and still am misunderstood by many both in the Old Country and in America. I have been considered a farmer, an adventurer, a reckless administrator. But whatever I did, and whatever I continue to do, is intended not just for the welfare of our abbey but of our entire order. I may have been mistaken at times, and surely I have often been wrong in the means I chose for attaining this end. . . . But this much is certain: the blessing of God was upon the work.[30]

Success, however, did not blunt the edge of criticism that some of Wimmer's own monks continued to level against his methods, nor did it ease the pain of discovery that many of those in whom he had placed his greatest hope for the future had rejected his vision of the Benedictine Order's role in the American Church. Father Edward Hipelius, the first of St. Vincent's Roman students, returned to America in 1866 with the experience of continental monasticism behind him. During his studies in England and Italy he had had the opportunity to witness firsthand the remarkable monastic revival taking place in Europe at the time. In France Abbot Prosper Guéranger's restoration of the medieval Abbey of Solesmes and Abbé Jean-Baptiste Muard's revival of Benedictine life at the Abbey of Pierre-qui-vire, in Italy the reforms of Abbot Pietro Casaretto at Subiaco, and in Germany the establishment of the Abbey of Beuron by the brothers Maurus and Placidus Wolter were all part of a spiritual and liturgical renewal in Benedictine life that excited and inspired young American Benedictines. Unlike the earlier revival of Benedictine monasticism in the Bavarian houses of Metten, Scheyern, and Munich, of which Wimmer was one of the leaders and which represented a nationalistic attempt to restore a conservative Bavarian Catholic tradition whose suppression had lasted no more than thirty years, the blossoming of monastic life at Solesmes, Subiaco, and Beuron was the result of a wave of romantic interest in the Middle Ages and a general belief among restoration leaders that an imitation of late medieval achievements and institutions was the best way to combat the threats to religion posed by the Enlightenment. As noted earlier, the result of this renewal was a new monasticism exemplified by asceticism, strict discipline, and an emphasis on liturgical devotion.[31]

Upon his return to St. Vincent, where he took charge of the seminary and served as Wimmer's secretary, Hipelius grew highly critical of monastic observance at the abbey. To him Benedictine life at St. Vincent did not compare favorably with that of the abbeys he had visited in Europe. He condemned both what he regarded as a lack of discipline among the American Cassinese communities and the extensive missionary activity undertaken by them. It was a constant refrain. Wimmer had faced the same kind of opposition in the 1840s from Fathers Peter Lechner, Thaddeus Brunner, and Andrew Zugtriegel, and again in the 1850s and early 1860s from Fathers Othmar Wirtz and Wendelin Mayer. Now, in 1868, with the voice of Father Edward, one of the most brilliant and talented monks of the congregation whom the abbot had identified as a key leader of the future, speaking out against Wimmer and "pronouncing precipitately a verdict against us all on account of certain defects in the house," Abbot Boniface was frustrated and distressed.

It was a painful discovery. He wrote that his "Roman Doctor" had betrayed him, that Father Edward had not given "great proof of modesty and humility. *Quia scientia inflat, nisi pietate et humilitate solidata* [For knowledge breeds arrogance unless strengthened by piety and humility]." He said that "no abbot would feel disposed to send his people to Rome if through indiscretion or for some other motive they afterwards denounced him and their community" as Hipelius had done. With a heart bearing as much disappointment as anger, Wimmer dismissed Father Edward from his position as rector of the seminary and banished him to St. Marys. He cautioned his other Roman students to remain "patriotic" to St. Vincent. If they "should turn out to be of the same stamp" as Father Edward, he wrote, "neither I nor any other abbot would feel disposed to send his folks to Rome. . . . I hope, though, that Father Edward will be the only instance of such ingratitude and that you and your future conduct will justify the propriety of my acquiring a house in Rome for the American Benedictines."[32]

Unlike earlier "reformers" Hipelius never managed to gather a following at St. Vincent. Perhaps it was his own arrogance (*"scientia inflat"*) that prevented this, or perhaps it was the fresh memory among his potential allies of the Keck affair and its adherents' abortive attempt to reform the congregation. In any event, Father Edward went off quietly to St. Marys where he served in the parish for a while before leaving the monastery and the order. His departure, however, did not end the dissatisfaction that hovered below the surface of life at St. Vincent among those idealistic young monks, always a force in the community, who believed that Wimmer's policies were misguided and that his views about the nature of Benedictine monasticism were outdated, unenlightened, and fundamentally wrong.

As Wimmer focused his energies on developing the monastic life and educational work of the community at St. Vincent, and on consolidating the nearly quarter century of missionary labors the Benedictines had undertaken in the United States, events were unfolding in the wider world that would have long-term impact on the Catholic Church and would bring important elements of the young and vibrant American Church into conflict with the conservative movements that were coming to dominate Roman Catholicism in the second half of the nineteenth century.

As a young institution in what Rome continued to regard as a mission country, the American Catholic Church was relatively isolated from if not indifferent to contemporary currents of European thought. These currents had stimulated debate and controversy in Catholic intellectual circles in mid-nineteenth-century Europe and resulted in the emergence of clearly defined and deeply divided parties that identified with either progressive liberalism or ultramontane conservativism. At the time, the American Church faced the challenge of caring for the millions of Catholic immigrants arriving in the eastern ports of the United States, and American church leaders had neither the leisure nor inclination to engage in doctrinal disputes whose outcome had no practical value in a mission country. Still, some issues were paramount and called for response from American bishops. The primacy of the bishop of Rome, papal infallibility, freedom of thought in the Church, and the relationship between church and state were important matters that had both practical and political implications for American Catholics.

American bishops tended to be relatively progressive on these issues. On the question of papal infallibility, for example, four-fifths of them either opposed the doctrine outright or believed that its official proclamation was politically provocative and therefore inopportune. With regard to the relationship between church and state, the overwhelming majority of American bishops defended the uniquely American practice of separation of church and state and staunchly defended freedom of religious thought in a manner that made conservative European churchmen uncomfortable.[33] Especially in the matter of papal infallibility, Wimmer tended to be considerably more conservative than the majority of the members of the American hierarchy.

In order to confront the intellectual and theological issues that European liberalism and science raised, as well as to centralize and reconfirm Roman control of the Church's authority and administration, Pope Pius IX summoned an Ecumenical Council of patriarchs, cardinals, bishops, and religious order leaders to Rome in 1869. As president of the American Cassinese Congregation, Wimmer was among the prelates called to attend the council, and on October 1, 1869, he and two clerics of St. Vincent, James Zilliox and Xavier Baltes, whom he had selected to pursue studies in Rome, left America for Europe. On board the *Ville de Paris* the abbot found himself in the company of twelve other priests and three American prelates going to the council, Bishop John B. Miége of the Kansas Vicariate, Bishop Ignatius Mrak of Marquette, and Bishop Augustin Verot of Savannah who would gain notoriety as the *"enfant terrible"* of the First Vatican Council. Also on board were one hundred and ten French Canadian volunteers for the papal army on their way to Rome to help defend papal independence against Italian revolutionaries. The young Canadians' "joyous frame of mind, their public devotions, and their excellent entertainments contributed much to the voyage."

The crossing took ten days. It was Wimmer's third trip to Rome, his fourth to Europe, in less than twenty years, and as usual he went first to Munich to meet and consult with his friends and advisors. He was pained that one of his greatest benefactors was no longer alive. King Ludwig I had died in 1868. Wimmer visited his former confrere Archbishop Gregory Scherr of Munich, the monks of St. Boniface where he had taught, and the directors of the Ludwig Missionsverein. After seeing Fraters James and Xavier off to join the other monks from St. Vincent at St. Elizabeth's House of Studies in Rome, Wimmer visited Metten where he made arrangements to travel to Italy with Abbot Utto Lang, president of the Bavarian Congregation. He also visited friends in Regensburg, Weltenburg, Hinheim, and Scheyern and distributed copies of the *Album Benedictinum* recently published at St. Vincent. "I am still determined to lead a wanderer's life," he wrote Abbot Rupert Leiss of Scheyern,

like our doves in North America. The nest remains at St. Vincent, and every year I make it wider and more spacious so that it is becoming a real dovecote from which the young brood fly away to establish new nests and cotes. But I also dislike travelling. I already feel a noticeable decline of physical strength and suspect that I don't have much more time, even though otherwise I am healthy. My sole desire is to see St. Vincent so well established that it will stand not only as mother but also as motherhouse for our order in America and especially as *alma mater* in scholarship. And so I send my best men to Rome for school in order to have a good school at St. Vincent. Of course this costs me much money, but as usual it comes in time, even if I am no longer around. I see the distress of our time, the spread of unbelief, the dearth of good priests, and would like, as far as possible, to stop the misery that must follow.

He told the abbot of Scheyern that there were twenty-one novices studying at St. Vincent, and fifty scholastics were preparing to enter the novitiate. These young men would help ensure the future of the order in America. He was constantly in debt, he said, because of the buildings he had to construct to house the many monks joining his ranks. "But God blesses all my undertakings. . . and our means and income grow from year to year."[34]

Wimmer left Munich with Abbot Utto on November 22 and arrived in Rome six days later. As the lowest ranking churchmen at the council, Wimmer and Lang led the fathers into St. Peter's Basilica for the solemn opening on the Feast of the Immaculate Conception, December 8, 1869. The prelates, vested in miter and cope, made obeisance to the pope, cardinals kissing his hand, the bishops his right knee, and the abbots his right foot. The first session lasted from 8:30 a.m. to 3:30 p.m., and afterward Abbot Boniface "had to wait for three-quarters of an hour for a carriage. It was in vain, however, until the abbot of Metten and I were taken along by the kindness of a Carthusian prior."[35]

The diary Wimmer kept throughout the council is a fine, often minute account of the proceedings. Together with twenty letters he sent to the *Wanderer*, a German Catholic weekly in St. Paul, Minnesota, founded by monks of the Abbey of St. Louis on the Lake, it provides an especially vivid portrait of his own reactions to the dramatic and historical event in which he was taking part.[36] On December 19 Bishop James Roosevelt Bayley of Newark informed Wimmer that the American bishops had unanimously voted to invite him to all their meetings, and he attended the first of them on December 22. He also met regularly with the Benedictine bishops, abbots-nullius, abbots, and theologians participating in the council. He widely distributed copies of the recently published *Album Benedictinum* and received gracious thanks and congratulations from Roman officials and Benedictine confreres alike for making this substantial contribution to fraternal cooperation and unity within the order.

On January 1, 1870, Wimmer received the solemn profession of James Zilliox at St. Elizabeth's. He had invited a number of people to the ceremony, including Abbot Leopoldo Zelli of St. Paul's-Outside-the-Walls, Benedictine Bishop Rosendo Salvado of Australia, his old friend Abbot Angelo Pescetelli, Abbots Benedict del Bufalo and Augustino Pucci of the Cassinese Congregation, Archabbot Carlo de Vera of Montecassino, and Abbot John Chrysostom Kreutz of St. Martin's Abbey, Pannonhalma, Hungary.[37]

On January 11 Wimmer signed a petition presented to him by the abbot of Metten urging the pope to define his infallibility *"in rebus Fidei et Morum."* It was a petition he could readily support since he had aligned himself early with the American pro-infallibility party and the Bavarian conservative party. Indeed he had spent part of his time in Munich during October and November discussing the issue and making his support of papal infallibility and his disenchantment with the "poison" being spread by Johann Ignatius Döllinger, his former professor at the University of Munich, known to Bavarian churchmen. In February he wrote his former confrere, Abbot Rupert Leiss of Scheyern, describing some of his impressions of the council.

The sessions are in St. Peter's, that is, on the right side of the north transept, which is divided off for this purpose from the rest of the church by a wooden partition beautifully painted on the exterior. The result was a hall, 175 feet long, 200 feet high, and eighty feet wide. In the center was an aisle, and to the right and left were seven rows of benches, with writing-desks and covered with green cloth, one higher than the other, and on these sat the primates, archbishops, bishops, and abbots. Almost one-third of the area, however, was occupied by a platform, to which one ascended from the aisle by several steps. On it was nothing except, in the middle, the tables for the apostolic protonotaries, for the secretary and subsecretary, for the five cardinal presidents, and, at the far end, an altar where, every day before the beginning of the session, an archbishop celebrated the mass of the Holy Spirit. In the semi-circle around it sat the cardinals and patriarchs.

But it was soon found out that the speakers could not be understood, and so a portion of the hall was cut off by a curtain, so that now it is only about

125 feet long. Then a cloth ceiling was stretched over the pulpit from one wall to the other, that is, eighty by about twenty feet, and four more benches were placed to the right and left of the aisle and also on the platform (where *we* now sit in front of the cardinals and beside the patriarchs), so that now every speaker can be understood everywhere, if he speaks clearly and slowly.

Thus far we have had twenty-six sessions, which always last from nine to one or one-thirty. Because secrecy has been imposed on us I cannot tell you anything about them. However I may say, since it is already known from the newspapers, that the poison spread by Döllinger seems to be operating significantly. There prevails among many bishops, in particular the Germans and the French, a spirit of distrust and suspicion of the Apostolic See which is distressing. Much prayer is needed if anything beneficial is to come about. The great majority of the bishops (and of course we abbots also) are on the pope's side. But, as the speeches indicate, there is still a strong opposition. Hence the matter is dragged out. There is too much freedom of speech and no profit is apparent in it. The pope is bitterly disappointed and out of temper and seems very tired. But perhaps this has to be, and God will direct all to the best. But if things don't change, we will still be sitting here a year from now. Some Fathers are for introducing a different order of business, and then things will probably move faster.

Just let us pray fervently for humility for the Council. The gentlemen are too clever. However, peace and decorum and good understanding prevail outwardly.[38]

As the sessions dragged on, Wimmer became increasingly impatient with the long-winded and tiresome speeches delivered by the bishops and theologians. Until the rearrangement of seating described to Abbot Rupert, he found it difficult to hear much of what was going on, and after the tenth secret session he remarked that during the speech of Archbishop Benevenuto Monzon y Martin of Grenada, Spain, he could not understand a thing "because two cardinals behind me were steadily chatting away."[39] In April he wrote a lengthy letter to Leiss providing an account of recent events at the council and of his own reactions to them.

Once again I must tell you a little about the Council. From March 18 we had four to five sessions every week, and since the new order of business had already been introduced, we moved forward a bit. The introduction *(proemium)* to all decrees and the first four chapters of *De Fide Catolica* were so far completed that they can be published next Sunday *(in Albis)* in the first public session. They treat only of the *preambula Fidei* and are directed against materialists, atheists, traditionalists, Hermesians, and rationalists (in the canons). Each section of these single parts was always explained by a bishop as *relator* of the *Disputatio pro Fide* in general session and was then put to a vote. Since the text was distributed to us some days previously, and each, if he so desired, could criticize it and submit his remarks in writing, which were then printed and again distributed to all the Fathers, the Council had the option of accepting the text of the *Disputatio pro Fide* (which consists of twenty-four prelates) or these criticisms *(emendationes).* The *emendatores* defended their views, then the *relator* defended the text, and the Council decided for one or the other by majority vote.

So it went. The subsecretary read aloud the numbered *emendatio*, of which there were sometimes more than 100, and then said: "Whoever is for this, stand up." The tellers then counted those standing unless almost all had risen. Then he said a second time: "Whoever is against it, stand up." The president then declared: "The *emendatio* is admitted (or excluded)." In this way we had to stand up fifty, sixty, or more times until a section was completed. If any amendments were accepted, the text had to be reprinted and again distributed to all the Fathers, and in this form be again put to a vote until the *proemium*, the four chapters, and the *conclusio* with all the pertinent canons had been taken care of. Only then was a vote taken on the *whole*, no longer by rising or remaining seated, but orally in the roll call. But again 148 amendments were introduced. Hence, once more the *relator* mounted the pulpit to defend the wording of the text.

In this balloting the one voting could say *"placet," "non placet,"* or *"placet juxta modum"* (with qualification). These last then had to place their qualifications in writing in a small basket held by a teller. The cardinals voted first, then the patriarchs, primates, archbishops and bishops, the abbots nullius, the abbots general of congregations, and finally the generals of orders. There were 598 voting because rather many were absent. No one voted *non placet*, but there were eighty-three *placet juxta modum* and 515 *placet*. (From the eighty-three *placet juxta modum* came the above-mentioned 148 new *emendationes*. And so there had to be a further vote on these 148 improvements, only two of which were accepted.) Now in the public session there will be a further public voting, but then each must say either *placet* or *non placet*. I do not doubt that not a few will vote *non placet*, because several were not pleased that the majority rejected their amendments. Then, so it is said, infallibility will come up for consideration.

On this there is significant lack of accord. Very recently Cardinals Schwarzenberg and Rauscher and Bishops Dupanloup and Hefele produced pamphlets against it, while Archbishops Manning, Deschamps, Spalding, and *[unintelligible]* are for it. These pamphlets were sent to us at our lodgings and with many they were not lacking in impact. Most American bishops are against it, also some Orientals, at least twenty-five to thirty French, and most of the German and Austrian bishops. From what I hear, even many Italian bishops, who had petitioned for the declaration of infallibility, changed their minds because of the pamphlets. And indeed a person must be on guard in order not to make a mistake. But I am for it, because the Church is built on the rock of Peter and hence I wish to stand on it. Among the *relatores* of the *Diputatio Fidei* were Bishops Gasser of Brixen, Martin of Paderborn, and *[unintelligible]*. Gasser is the right man for it; he has a clear enunciation, great learning, and an unassuming, attractive bearing, with great patience and consideration for opponents. If he becomes *relator* in this question, I hope, in spite of everything, that it will pass. Perhaps on this matter there is much misunderstanding that a lucid, disinterested mind can clarify, if he has in his favor a good *praejudicium*. But much prayer is necessary so that the Holy Spirit can work in all, in this question as well as in the other, on the primacy, which many bishops are not really willing to admit in the dogmatic constitution.[40]

Though he did not address the council himself, Wimmer confided in his diary the strong opinions he held with regard to the questions being debated and the interventions of those who spoke in the sessions. When on May 31 Archbishop Thomas Connolly, O.F.M. Cap., of Halifax addressed the sixtieth session of the council speaking against papal infallibility, Wimmer called the talk "annoying." And during another session, when Bishop William Clifford of Clifton, England, spoke in a similar vein, Wimmer said, "I didn't hear at all because I fell asleep." Bishop Michael Domenec of Pittsburgh, Wimmer's own ordinary, "ridiculed himself by speaking about the terrible consequences" of the definition of infallibility. Wimmer called the speech "good for nothing." And while being somewhat amused by the humorous and controversial remarks of Bishop Augustin Verot of Savannah, the abbot disparagingly called him "the most outspoken and violent Gallicanist" at the council.[41]

While he did not participate in the debates inside St. Peter's Basilica, Wimmer did find time between sessions to make his own intellectual contribution to the polemics by contributing the preface to a pro-infallibility book by the noted church historian, council *peritus* (expert), and Roman professor Giuseppe Pennachi. Pennachi had written a study of the condemnation of Pope Honorius I (625–638) by the Council of Constantinople, a condemnation that had been used by those who opposed the doctrine of papal infallibility to defend their position. In *De Honorii Romani Pontificis Causa in Concilio*

Sexto Pennachi argued that the conciliar condemnation of Pope Honorius in 681 did not provide valid historical proof against papal infallibility because Honorius's alleged heresy (a supposed defense of monothelitism, the heretical doctrine that while Christ had two natures, human and divine, he possessed only one will) was illusory. The writings of Honorius on the subject, Pennachi said, were hastily composed attempts to win over eastern heretics to true Catholic doctrine, and though perhaps imprudent, they were not in themselves heretical. After Honorius's death, Sergius I, patriarch of Constantinople, and the Emperor Heraclius developed his views into a full-blown heresy, and it was this heresy that the Council of Constantinople condemned, mistakenly attributing the heretical doctrine to the pope. Wimmer reviewed this complicated argument in his Latin preface to Pennachi's book and strongly asserted, with the Roman author, that the anti-infallibility party, like the Council of Constantinople, was wrong in attributing heresy to a pope.[42]

Wimmer's modest contribution to historical theology on this occasion was one of the few times he picked up his pen in the guise of a scholar. It was a role he had always longed to play, and indeed on several previous occasions he had written seriously on historical subjects. His very few publications included a brief history of the American Cassinese Congregation, published as a prologue to the *Album Benedictinum* in 1869; a German translation of Philipp Balzofiore's biography of the Italian holy woman Anna Maria Taigi, written during his long stay in Rome in 1865 and published in 1867, and a history of the medieval Benedictine monastery of Mallersdorf, which he had composed while attempting to restore Mallersdorf in 1841 and which he had published in 1842. As a student at the University of Munich he had also begun an ambitious history of the Benedictine Order in Bavaria, of which he completed fourteen chapters that carried the story up to the tenth century but which he never published. Wimmer's aspirations to be a serious historian were never realized not so much because he lacked the necessary intellectual ability and scholarly passion but because after 1845 and until the end of his life he devoted all his intellectual, emotional, and physical energies to the task of restoring the Benedictine Order to its former place in the spiritual economy of the Catholic Church. His vocation, as he understood and embraced it, was not to write history but to make it.[43]

Voting on the chapters of the constitution *De Romano Pontifice*, which contained the definition of infallibility and the statement on the Roman pontiff's primacy, took place on July 13. Among the 451 prelates to vote *placet* was Abbot Boniface Wimmer. Twenty-eight prelates from the United States cast their ballot, and of these, seventeen voted like Wimmer in unconditional favor of the constitution.[44] Five days later the decrees were confirmed by Pope Pius IX at a public session in St. Peter's. Wimmer wrote that

at that moment there was a thunderstorm and such darkness that [the Holy Father] could not read without a light. A great applause from the Fathers followed and was repeated by a thunderous exultation, over and over again, from the multitude in the hall. After the *Te Deum,* which was alternately sung by the choir and the Fathers and joined by the people, the Council came to a close. It was one o'clock when we passed the fortress. It rained on into the afternoon, then it cleared up. But later in the night the weather turned stormy again.[45]

The Franco-Prussian War had brought an early end to the council, and Wimmer, fearing for the safety of his six monks at St. Elizabeth's, entrusted the Roman house of studies to officials at the German College in Rome and left the city toward the end of July. Fathers Innocent Wolf, Hilary Pfrängle, and Adalbert Müller had completed their studies, and together with Father Oswald Moosmüller they returned to Munich with the abbot. Fraters James Zilliox and Xavier Baltes also left Rome with Wimmer, but instead of going on to Munich, they went to Innsbruck where they entered the Jesuit University to continue their studies.[46]

Perhaps fearing that this would be the last opportunity to visit his homeland, the sixty-year-old Wimmer lingered four months in Bavaria, calling on friends and supporters in Munich, Regensburg, Metten, and Scheyern and bidding them all farewell. At the end of November he and his confreres left Munich by train and traveled to England, and in the first week of December they departed Liverpool for New York. Writing to Abbot Utto Lang before they sailed, Wimmer said that their ship, the *Palmyra,* was "quite small. If we get rough weather we will suffer a great deal, and should the papers report that our boat is lost at sea, then you know that I'm in need of a *memento.*"[47] But there were no untoward incidents, and the abbot and his four companions arrived in New York two weeks later. After spending several days with the monks in Newark, they caught the train for Latrobe, arriving there two days before Christmas. Once again the monks and students at St. Vincent had prepared a grand celebration for his return, and Wimmer addressed the community with a speech in which he exalted the papacy and predicted that the Holy Father would one day overcome the persecutors who held him captive in the Vatican.[48]

In March 1871 Wimmer wrote Archbishop Gregory Scherr of Munich praising him for the work he had done in opposing those in Germany who led the attack against infallibility. The most prominent of the anti-infallibility leaders was Wimmer's old professor of history and canon law at the University of Munich, Johann Ignatius Döllinger, whom Scherr had recently excommunicated for his refusal to submit to the decrees of the Vatican Council. Wimmer told Scherr that the archbishop had done "very meritorious work" in confronting Döllinger and calling a meeting of the Bavarian bishops at Fulda to "secure victory of the Faith against reason, of the Church's authority against individual opinion, of the Church's very existence against its dissolution." Abbot Boniface predicted that on account of his decisive action the archbishop would "be the target of aggression. But that will make your name more well-known, your fame more eminent."[49]

The abbot complained that upon his return to America he had been immediately burdened by the financial plight of the Kansas priory. Under the misguided leadership of Prior Augustine Wirth the monks in Kansas had "run themselves down" by building a church for which they could not pay. In 1868 Wimmer had replaced Wirth with Father Louis Fink, formerly prior at St. Joseph's Priory, Chicago, and Fink reported to the abbot that the community in Atchison owed $50,000, most of it borrowed at an annual rate of 11 percent. The community's income from the parishes and college could not even pay the interest, and the monks in Kansas were desperate. In January Wimmer sent $3,000 to them from St. Vincent and looked for ways to pay off the remainder of the enormous debt.[50] "That is my Christmas gift this year, but I accept it willingly because 1) God's blessing has visibly rested upon St. Vincent and is still hovering over us, and 2) because by doing this my fathers and the various communities founded from St. Vincent will learn to consider themselves as one unit and thus learn to help each other when in need." On a happier note, Wimmer told Scherr that on September 30, 1870, the Holy See had erected a third Benedictine abbey in America. "It is the Priory of

St. Meinrad's in the diocese of Vincennes, Indiana. . . . Father Martin Marty is nominated as its first abbot and will receive the solemn blessing after Easter. I am invited to assist and have accepted the honor." Wimmer explained that St. Meinrad's was founded not from St. Vincent but from the Abbey of Einsiedeln in Switzerland. "But that makes no difference in our common work as Benedictines."[51]

In the meantime the success of Wimmer's American venture was becoming even more evident. In April 1870 the Pennsylvania state legislature issued a broad charter to St. Vincent College empowering it "to grant and confer degrees in the arts and sciences. . . as are granted in other colleges and universities in the United States."[52] And in December the Sacred Congregation of the Propaganda Fide informed the abbot that Prior Louis Fink of St. Benedict's, Atchison, had been chosen coadjutor to Bishop John B. Miége of the Kansas Vicariate.[53] The appointment of Father Louis, the first of Wimmer's spiritual sons to be elevated to episcopal rank, necessitated a major shift in personnel, and the abbot informed Rupert Seidenbusch that he had assigned Father Aegidius Christoph, claustral prior at St. Vincent, to succeed Father Louis as superior of the Kansas monastery. At first Christoph loudly and adamantly refused to accept the Kansas appointment. He said he would not go because of "financial, personal, historical, and hygienical" reasons. He fulminated against the assignment and then wept publicly before the chapter. But Wimmer ordered him under obedience to go, and on August 15, 1871, Christoph set out for the independent priory in Atchison. "I hope," the abbot remarked, "that Father Aegidius is smart enough to be independent in paying debts as well." Insolvency still handicapped the development of the Kansas Benedictines.[54]

Even as the business of consolidating the Benedictine work in America continued, plans for the celebration of the twenty-fifth anniversary of the arrival of the Benedictines in the United States were being made to coincide with the fourth general chapter of the American Cassinese Congregation. But before the delegates to the chapter arrived at St. Vincent, Wimmer received news that St. Joseph Priory in Chicago had been destroyed in the great fire of October 9, 1871. Father Leander Schnerr, O.S.B, prior in Chicago, telegraphed him that "the whole congregation lost everything. Our magnificent church, the altar which alone cost $8,000, the new priory, the sisters' convent all are in ruins." The anniversary year had begun, Wimmer said, with

Bishop Louis Fink (1834–1904), prior of St.
Benedict's Priory, Atchison, and later first
bishop of Leavenworth, Kansas. (ASVA)

"the misadventure in Kansas," and now it was ending "with the catastrophe in Chicago. St. Vincent—poor St. Vincent—is being bled
until its condition is nearly dropsical." But "God gives and God takes
away."[55]

Despite events in Chicago the general chapter and anniversary celebration went ahead as planned. Delegates from Minnesota, Kansas,
New Jersey, Kentucky, Illinois, and Pennsylvania gathered at the
motherhouse for the opening session of the chapter on October 20,
and after three days of deliberation, during which the calamitous financial condition of the Kansas priory and the recent disaster in
Chicago were the principal matters of business,[56] the anniversary celebration began.

Seven of the original band of monks who had been invested with the habit of St. Benedict on October 24, 1846, were still alive and present to take part in the celebration. In the twenty-five years since the founding of the community, membership had grown from nineteen to one hundred and eighty-seven monks at the abbey, dependent priories, and parishes. This did not include the monks at the two independent communities founded from St. Vincent, St. Louis on the Lake Abbey in Minnesota, where there were thirty monks, and St. Benedict's Priory in Kansas, whose community numbered sixteen.[57]

At the time of the celebration the American Cassinese Congregation was a well-organized union of monasteries with St. Vincent at its center. The monks at the motherhouse were engaged in teaching and parish work in the districts around the monastery. The ecclesiastical seminary had twelve Benedictine clerics and fifteen diocesan seminarians studying for the priesthood. The college boasted two hundred and fifty students, and priests from the abbey ministered to Catholics in six dioceses in five states with fifty parishes and mission stations.

In the Diocese of Pittsburgh, priests from St. Vincent were engaged in the pastoral care of ten thousand Catholics in Westmoreland, Indiana, Armstrong, Butler, and Allegheny Counties. From the parish church at St. Vincent they held regular services at St. Xavier's Convent, St. Boniface Chapel on Chestnut Ridge, Holy Trinity Church in Ligonier, St. Matthew's Mission in Saltsburg, Immaculate Conception Church in New Germany, Assumption Church in Penn, and the small Catholic chapel in Irwin. From time to time they assisted at other places, including Pittsburgh itself.

At St. Benedict's Priory in Carrolltown four priests and seven brothers served a large parish of two thousand souls, and Benedictine sisters taught one hundred pupils in the parish school. Priests from Carrolltown held regular services at St. Joseph's Mission at Hart's Sleeping Place, St. Lawrence Church in St. Lawrence (Glen Connell), St. Boniface Church in St. Boniface, and St. Nicholas Church in Nicktown.

Other Benedictine parishes with resident pastors in the Pittsburgh Diocese included St. Mary's Priory, Allegheny City, where four priests had charge of a large parish and several chaplaincies; Blessed Sacrament Church in Greensburg; St. Peter's Church in Butler; St. Bernard's Church in Indiana; St. Joseph's Church in Johnstown; and

St. Mary's Church in Cambria City. In the parochial schools attached to the Benedictine parishes in the diocese of Pittsburgh there were fourteen hundred pupils.

In the Diocese of Erie, St. Vincent monks staffed priories in St. Marys and the episcopal city. At the priory in St. Marys five priests and eleven brothers worked in a parish of four thousand souls and served a thousand more Catholics at nine mission stations in three counties. The Benedictine sisters taught one hundred and forty pupils in the parish school of St. Marys. St. Mary's Priory, Erie, had three priests who served a twenty-four-hundred-member congregation and a parish school with five hundred pupils directed by the Benedictine sisters. One priest from the Erie priory also served as pastor of St. John's Church in the see city.

In the Diocese of Newark five priests and two brothers were stationed at St. Mary's Priory in Newark and administered a parish with thirty-seven-hundred souls and a high school with fifty students. Monks from St. Mary's Priory also staffed St. Benedict's Church in Newark, St. Walburga's Church in Elizabeth City, and St. Mary's Church in Stony Hill. The Benedictine sisters in New Jersey taught eight hundred pupils in the two parishes at Newark and in St. Walburga's Parish, Elizabeth City.

In the Diocese of Covington, four priests were assigned to St. Joseph's Priory in the see city. They conducted services for a congregation of over two thousand members in Covington and attended six other parishes, with a total of twenty-two-hundred parishioners, in five Kentucky counties. The Benedictine sisters in Covington taught seven hundred children in four of the Kentucky parishes served by the Benedictine priests.

In the Diocese of Richmond, two priests were stationed at St. Mary's Church, Richmond. They had charge of eleven hundred German Catholics in the city, conducted a high school of fifty students, and operated a parish school with one hundred and sixty pupils taught by the Benedictine sisters. They also served a mission in Louisa County, Virginia.

In the Diocese of Chicago five priests were stationed at St. Joseph's Church, Chicago, and had the pastoral care of more than five thousand souls and eight mission stations in four Illinois counties. Five hundred pupils, taught by a community of Benedictine nuns, attended St. Joseph Parochial School. The Benedictine church and school in Chicago had recently been destroyed by the great fire of 1871, but at the time of the silver jubilee Prior Leander Schnerr, a future abbot of St. Vincent, was busily organizing the congregation's efforts to raise money for reconstruction.[58]

By 1871, principally under the direction of the community's two architects, Brothers Stephen Weber and Ewald Horn, a quadrangle of buildings at St. Vincent had been constructed on the south side of the abbey church. Lower down the hill on which stood the church, monastery, and the college were the barn, stables, brewery, gristmill, sawmill, printery, and workshops of the brothers. Each of these buildings, except the church, Sportsman's Hall, and the original parish house which the monks found when they arrived at St. Vincent, had been constructed by the lay brothers, who had charge of every aspect of construction from the cutting of timber and the making of bricks to the placement of crosses on the turrets. St. Vincent was a busy and vibrant center of work and prayer in 1871, and Wimmer and his monks had a great deal to celebrate on the twenty-fifth anniversary of their coming to America.

Present for the festivities on October 24 were Bishop Michael Domenec of Pittsburgh and two neighboring pastors, Fathers James Ambrose Stillinger of Blairsville and Jerome Kearney of Latrobe. That morning Abbot Boniface celebrated a solemn pontifical mass, and three of the four clerical students who, twenty-five years before, had been invested as novices at the same altar, assisted in the sanctuary. Father Benedict Haindl, claustral prior in Minnesota, served the abbot as arch-priest; Father Celestine Englbrecht, conventual prior of St. Mary's Priory, Allegheny City, was master of ceremonies, and Father Charles Geyerstanger served as chaplain to Abbot Rupert Seidenbusch who had come from Minnesota for the celebration. The pioneer brothers Andrew Binder, Jacob Raitmayer, Engelbert Nusser, and Conrad Reinbolt assisted in the sanctuary.

Bishop Michael Domenec delivered the anniversary sermon and praised the Benedictines for their contributions to the Diocese of Pittsburgh and the American Church. He said that "St. Vincent is already called the 'Montecassino of America'! May it become a similar light in the New World as the home of St. Benedict was in the Old World!"[59]

The mass was followed by a banquet in the monastery refectory attended by lay as well as clerical guests. A reporter from the *Pittsburgh*

Catholic, a student at the college in the 1850s, was present and wrote that

even in the years 1853–1856, when your correspondent had the honor—then thought a misfortune—of being one of St. Vincent's boys, such a change [as has come about at St. Vincent] was considered impossible. In those days of "Charley-come-back" and what we expected to be soup, the monks fared still worse. I don't think that Father Superior, now abbot, would have considered it a misfortune to the house if all the boys would have run away. The trials of the infant colony were terrific and required more than human courage and perseverance to overcome them. But by the blessing of God he has overcome them, and now finds himself at the head of a flourishing order of zealous, hard-working men, and of a College holding a foremost rank among such institutions in the United States.[60]

To memorialize the occasion the monks who formed the jubilee committee initiated plans for the construction of a bell tower in the monastic quadrangle, and Father Oswald Moosmüller was commissioned to write a history of the American Benedictines.[61] The fire in Chicago, however, had cast a pall over the festivities, and Abbot Boniface wrote that he had decided to permit only a "family feast" on account of it. He had ignored the promptings of the community and invited only a few special friends. Soon after the celebration ended, he left for Chicago to see what could be salvaged there. The work he had set out to do was still not completed, and there was really little time for the "frivolous" merrymaking that some of his well-wishers would foist upon him.[62]

In February 1872 Wimmer wrote Abbot Utto Lang of Metten that since Prior Aegidius Christoph had taken over in Kansas, things at St. Benedict's Priory had much improved. Attendance in the school established by the monks in Atchison was as good as it had ever been, and tuition brought in "much needed income." Under the circumstances it seemed that St. Benedict's Priory had become "a financially sound source," and there was "new hope that our people there can help themselves again." The abbot reported that the situation in Chicago also looked brighter. "My three beggar priests have thus far collected $11,000, and the temporary church is crowded on Sundays and feast days." The fire in Chicago, the abbot said, had "brought some good with it." The church had been located in a very undesirable spot and now the monks could rebuild so that it would be more convenient for them and the congregation. In the meantime the parish was operating out of a temporary structure "until the people have recuperated and are able to build a regular church."

In his letter to the abbot of Metten Wimmer also wrote of his former professor at the University of Munich, Johann Ignatius Döllinger. Several of the monks at St. Boniface's monastery in Munich had been attracted to Döllinger's teachings, and Wimmer said that

these blind ones must now see the truth about him. It is a pity that this poor man is going this way and only a faint hope is left of his return to the right faith. . . . Döllinger and his followers want to subject the Church to the state, but God is making use of their foolish tendencies to liberate His bride from the secular government. The Kingdom of God is passing through adversities as Bishop Wittmann predicted it would. . . . Döllinger, Lutz, and Bismarck shall live to see that all will be different from what they hoped it would be, despite their wishes and machinations. In the end they will be, however unwillingly, the very instrument of God's plan.[63]

In June Abbot Boniface was on visitation in Carrolltown where he presided over the installation of Father Amandus Kramer as prior of St. Benedict's Priory, and from there he wrote the abbot of Metten and asked him to receive the solemn vows of Xavier Baltes, one of the young St. Vincent monks studying at Innsbruck. "This favor will be one more bond which brings Metten and St. Vincent more closely together, for we are indeed the Bavarian Benedictine Congregation across the sea." Wimmer decried the current threats to the Church in Bavaria, saying that "it is necessary for the German bishops to stand firm and united. If they do not fail, the outcome will be immensely beneficial, but only after a terrible fight." By June 1872 the *Kulturkampf,* German chancellor Otto von Bismarck's effort to subject the Church to state control, had resulted not only in the subjection of all religious schools to state inspection but also in the suppression of the Jesuits in Germany. The German government's religious policy threatened the security and even the existence of other religious orders as well, and the abbot of St. Vincent was concerned about its effects on the Benedictines in Bavaria. If the persecution of the Church, he said, "is not just a military trick, then I am entirely confused about Bismarck. The man must have lost all his senses."[64] To Canon Michael Reger of Regensburg he wrote: "I had expected something

better of Bismarck. . . . I considered him more prudent and sensible."
On the other side of the ocean, in America, Wimmer reported that
"the whole country is excited about the coming election." The two
candidates, Grant and Greeley, were both Methodists, but "Greeley
had his daughters sent to a Catholic school to be educated. The Old
Democratic Party is the party of the people, but it seems to be losing
ground because of old age." Wimmer said that like Bismarck's Liberal
party in Germany, the Republican party in the United States welcomed those who opposed the Church and nurtured anti-Catholic
philosophies and attitudes. If Greeley were to align himself more
forcefully with the Democrats, Wimmer observed, then he would be
assured of the Catholic vote and would win the election.[65]

Political affairs in both Europe and America had begun to draw
Wimmer's attention more and more in the years following the Vatican Council, and the situation in Europe was particularly disturbing
to him. Though he had initially considered the unification of Germany desirable, the secular, anti-Catholic tendencies of the new government soon caused him to change his opinion, and he again wrote
Abbot Utto that "it seems Bismarck has lost his mind. With only a
grain of common sense he could foresee the ruin of Germany." The
abbot considered the expulsion of the Jesuits from the Fatherland an
evil omen for the Benedictines there, and he suggested that Abbot
Utto might have to oversee the abandonment of Metten. "If that is
the case, don't forget to bring the 50,000 florins along. Then we shall
establish a new Metten in America. . . . I did not dare give my foundation that name despite the fact that I was repeatedly asked to do so.
Perhaps that was providential" because now it looked as though the
abbot of Metten might himself be forced to move the abbey across the
sea. "God save our Fatherland; may the clergy persevere in faithful-
ness. Now there are Jansenists in Bavaria and the king is not unfriendly towards them. Archbishop Gregory had better show more resistance, and the bishop of Augsburg likewise."[66]

But Europe was a long way off, and despite Wimmer's concern for
the fate of the Benedictines in Bavaria, his greater concern was for the
order in America. As the end of his third decade in the United States
approached, he focused his attention more and more on parochial
and practical affairs at the abbey and priories in Pennsylvania. During the year 1872 he oversaw construction of a malthouse and a
slaughterhouse at St. Vincent as well as a new priory building in St.

Marys. The monks at St. Vincent, St. Marys, and Carrolltown, he reported, were blessed with an abundant harvest, but a bank failure had caused much hardship in the country, and Wimmer said that he was anticipating the inability of many of the students to pay for their tuition and living expenses: "All over workmen lost their jobs. Hundreds of them had nothing to eat and others had to work for half pay just to keep themselves alive. . . . We have to expect the worst. Even now we daily give food to thirty or forty strangers and shelter them in our exterior buildings."[67]

But despite difficult economic conditions in the country, 1873 was a very good year for the monks of St. Vincent. Wimmer managed to pay off some major debts of the abbey and was able to give the community in Kansas more financial help as well. That year St. Vincent assumed the administration of Sacred Heart Parish, in Wilmington, Delaware, where Wimmer assigned Father Wendelin Mayer, the monk censured by Rome in 1865 because of his part in the Keck affair, as pastor. Father Wendelin had emerged as one of Wimmer's most reliable pastors and was regarded by the faithful with whom he worked as a good and holy man. His capacity to win the confidence, esteem, and love of his parishioners was notable, and many thought him a saint. Mayer's move to Delaware marked the expansion of the American Benedictines to yet another state. Material and spiritual conditions in the Pennsylvania monastery were so positive in 1873, in fact, that Wimmer could tell Abbot Utto that if the monks of Metten were expelled from Germany, "they can expect from us the most kind welcome at St. Vincent. There is, for the moment, not much extra space, but in the different priories many can be housed. Also, we have made a hundred thousand bricks in preparation for a new building which we will begin during the coming spring."

At the end of the year there were sixty-two priests, twenty-three clerics, ninety-one lay brothers, and sixteen novices attached to St. Vincent Abbey.[68] In April Wimmer wrote one of them, Father Celestine Englbrecht, who had come with him to Pennsylvania in 1846, that because he must go to Chicago to make visitation and discuss with Bishop Louis Fink and Prior Leander Schnerr how to resolve the financial problems that had resulted from the destruction of St. Joseph's Church in the great fire of 1871, he would be unable to attend the silver anniversary celebration of Father Celestine's ordination. He apologized for his absence but sent Englbrecht his warmest congratulations. "Twenty-five years are by themselves a considerable length of time in human life," he wrote,

but still more so when they are as many years of service, as in the life of an officer or a soldier. What soldier would not be proud of having served his king for twenty-five years? But twenty-five years of service become still more important when they have been spent in the service of the Lord. And this you have done, Honored Jubilarian! How many holy masses have you said during this time! And with their merits you have given joy to heaven, consoled the poor souls, comforted the Church Militant, and averted innumerable punishments from her! To how many innocent children have you opened the gates of heaven through holy baptism in the course of this long period; how many suffering souls have you consoled and calmed on their beds of suffering; to how many dying have you granted the assistance they needed in the hour of their utter distress and desolation; how many sinners' eyes have you opened; how many hearts touched in the holy sacrament of penance so that they stopped walking in the way of perdition and reconciled themselves again with God; to how many have you given the bread of life so that they could persevere in the struggle with their evil inclinations, the pernicious examples and attacks of the enemy; how many children have you instructed and, through your prudent guidance, saved from the snares of temptation!

At the same time you have always fought the good fight and have brought high honor to your state as a priest and a monk. You preserved a spotless character everywhere, and you were selflessly, and with joyful devotion, concerned about the holy interests of the Church, of the order, and of the parish which has been entrusted to your care. All the churches to which you were appointed bear special witness that you loved the cleanliness, the beauty, and the adornment of the house of God. Besides, I personally testify and feel myself in debt for your faithful attachment to me as your superior. Thus you have scattered many seeds during this long time and have zealously put out at interest your God-given talents so that they will be returned to you some day doubled and multiplied by the Lord.[69]

Despite the success he had tasted, Wimmer still faced problems in 1874 which continued to challenge his own God-given talents as a religious superior and temporal administrator. Besides the financial difficulties plaguing him in Chicago and Kansas, the success of some of his Pennsylvania missions had begun to attract the covetous attention of the secular clergy. Some diocesan priests in Erie complained that the Benedictines were monopolizing the pastoral care of the most prosperous congregations, and as a result the bishop of Erie, Tobias

Mullen, had decided to limit the areas of his diocese in which he would permit the St. Vincent monks to labor to the town of St. Marys and the parish in the see city itself.[70] Perhaps the most unsettling problem, however, was that among the monks themselves a certain discontent had arisen once again.

This time the problem was not disagreement over monastic discipline but rather ethnic tensions within the congregation. In 1873 Father Augustine Burns, of St. John's Abbey in Minnesota,[71] petitioned Abbot Boniface for permission to establish a monastery for Irish monks. While the Benedictine mission to the United States had from the beginning served Irish immigrants whenever the monks encountered them among the German communities that were the focus of their labor, and while the Benedictine schools in Pennsylvania, Minnesota, and Kansas attracted Irish students, and the monasteries Irish candidates, the dominant culture of the Benedictine communities Wimmer founded continued to be German, and more specifically Bavarian. Indeed, as he stated on several occasions, he regarded the American Cassinese Congregation as the "Bavarian Congregation across the sea." Ethnic tensions between German and Irish immigrants which continued to play an important part in the nineteenth-century development of the American Catholic Church also arose at St. Vincent, and though they were not as severe and divisive as the much graver conflicts in the contemporary American Church as a whole, they were significant and certainly had an effect upon how Irish candidates adjusted to life at St. Vincent, St. John's, and St. Benedict's.

The Irish, of course, were always a minority in the schools and monasteries founded by Wimmer. In 1873, out of a total of 284 monks, only 8 were Irishmen, though 10 percent of the Benedictine scholastics at St. Vincent College were of Irish descent. Many of the Irish monks found life in the Benedictine communities of Pennsylvania, Minnesota, and Kansas difficult. The language of the houses was German, and the dominant religious tradition and culture Bavarian. The Irishmen often found the prevailing atmosphere in the American monasteries cold and always foreign. They noted that a significant number of young men of Irish heritage had come to study at St. Vincent with the intention of joining the monastery, but few of them persevered on account of the unfamiliar customs, religious devotions, and social structures they encountered. Some of the Irish priests believed that more Irish postulants would become Benedictines if they could find a more familiar religious and cultural ambience in at least one of the monastic communities of the congregation.

With this in mind, Father Augustine, a forty-four-year-old native of Tipperary who had been a monk of St. John's Abbey since 1866, approached Bishop John Hennessy of Dubuque about the possibility of establishing an "Irish" monastery in Iowa. The bishop welcomed the idea. Father Augustine then petitioned Wimmer and Seidenbusch for permission to found an English-speaking community within the American Cassinese Congregation. After consulting with Seidenbusch, Wimmer gave his approval. "They will aid in spreading the order in America, Canada, and Ireland," he wrote, "and after a few years will bring salvation to many Irish."[72]

Toward the end of the year Burns purchased four lots in Creston, Iowa, as well as 240 nearby acres of farmland for the Irish priory. He was soon joined by Father Placidus McKeever of St. Benedict's Priory, Atchison. The undertaking had the full support of Wimmer, who considered an Irish community in the congregation an ideal means of attracting a wider range of candidates for the order in America. Having established the priory in Creston, however, Burns and McKeever discovered to their chagrin that of the five Irish monks at St. Vincent, only Father Eugene Phelan expressed any interest in joining the new community.

Despite the lack of strong interest in the project among the other Irish members of the congregation, Father Augustine pressed ahead with his plan. "Our prospects in every way are good for the new monastery," he wrote. "Funds will not fail us as every Irish priest in the West is with us."[73] Father Eugene made plans to visit Ireland to recruit candidates for the monastery, but before he could travel, tragedy struck the incipient community. On August 12, 1874, Father Augustine, while on a visit to Burlington, Iowa, to collect money for the foundation, died suddenly of a stroke. It was an unexpected blow, but it did not deter Abbot Boniface from supporting the plan to establish an Irish monastery in the West. He immediately appointed Father Eugene Phelan prior and pastor of St. Malachy's Priory in Creston, with Father Placidus McKeever as his assistant, and made plans to introduce the question of the Creston priory's future to the delegates of the congregation's forthcoming general chapter. Meanwhile, he made his own views on the matter clear to everyone. "We have to give the Irish a chance," he said, "for the interest of the order."[74]

Wimmer's consolidation of the Benedictine missions in America continued to progress. He devoted increased attention to the temporal affairs of the monasteries, assigned priors and pastors, transferred monks from one community to another, reviewed the building plans of his architects, oversaw construction of new buildings, organized and developed the curricula of the schools, and quietly began planning the next phase of Benedictine expansion into new mission fields. But as his work continued and his thoughts turned to new mission fields and effective ways of incorporating other ethnic groups into the expanding Benedictine family, he received another shock. He learned from friends that criticism of his life's work had once again emerged among an important and influential element in the order. This time, however, the criticism came not from his own monks but from monastic leaders in Europe.

The monastic revival on the Continent had made considerable headway by the 1870s despite secular movements and liberal ideologies that since the 1840s had dominated political and social life in Germany, France, and Italy. The Benedictines of Solesmes and Beuron continued their successful efforts to create new and attractive forms of monastic life based on late medieval models, and monks from the abbeys of Einsiedeln and Engelberg in Switzerland, where a secularist government threatened to thwart the development of religious life, were seeking to gain a foothold for this tradition in the United States. As potential refuges from political turmoil in Europe two Swiss communities had been established in America. In 1854 monks from Einsiedeln had established the monastery of St. Meinrad's in Indiana, which in 1870 had been elevated to the rank of abbey, and in 1873 two monks from the abbey of Engelberg, Fathers Frowin Conrad and Adelhelm Odermatt, established the monastery of New Engelberg near Conception, Missouri.[75]

The correspondence between Father Frowin Conrad and Father Placidus Wolter of Beuron reveals some of the attitudes in European monastic circles about Wimmer's missionary and educational activities in the United States. Neither Wolter nor Conrad advocated the monastic vision and theory of the American abbot. Both believed that Wimmer was overly inclined to sacrifice traditional Benedictine liturgical and monastic observance to the exigencies of the missionary, pastoral, and educational apostolates he had accepted. They asserted that these apostolates, rather than purer monastic ideals, as formulated and interpreted by the European restorers, dictated how Benedictine life had and would develop in the American Cassinese Congregation, and they were not pleased with this development. Wolter wrote Conrad:

It is a shame that our Benedictine brethren in America display so much zeal and expend so much energy and yet are so little blessed and are by far neither so well accepted nor as well appreciated as the members of the modern congregations in that country. . . . For conducting schools and widespread missions, the Jesuits and the Redemptorists have far greater ability than we Benedictines, and in such work they are more blessed than we are. But in that which is of far greater importance, that is, the ascetical life, the life of prayer and the service of God in the liturgy, the Benedictines are far more gifted. If Benedictines base their life on the Holy Rule, then their missionary work and their work in schools will have far greater blessing.[76]

Though Wimmer smarted under such criticism, he held fast to his original designs. He could admire the contemplative zeal of the continental reformers and the splendor of the liturgy in their abbeys, but he continued to insist that conditions in America were different from those in Europe and therefore demanded different approaches. There was a great need for priests in the missions, and Benedictines, he repeatedly said, were entirely suited to fill that need. He likened himself to a general in the field who in the midst of battle had to act decisively and quickly, depending on his intuition and his immediate appraisal of situations rather than upon a manual or the ideas of theoreticians many miles away from the front. What the Wolter brothers were doing at Beuron was good. But that was Beuron, and this was America. For a precedent he could point to the missionary activity of early medieval Benedictines, if that were necessary—and it often was.

Despite criticism, however, Wimmer was in the long run reinforced in his ideas by his own success as well as by the support he received from such ecclesiastics as the cardinals of the Propaganda Fide in Rome, the abbots of his own Bavarian Congregation, and the American bishops. And during the early months of 1875 yet another proof of the success of his venture came when he was informed that a second monk of the American Cassinese Congregation had been chosen by the Holy See for the episcopal dignity. On February 12, 1875, Rome established a new vicariate in northern Minnesota and named as its first bishop Abbot Rupert Seidenbusch of St. John's Abbey.[77]

In March Abbot Boniface wrote Abbot Utto Lang of Metten that his efforts to "prepare the ground-work for a great monastery" seemed to be bearing fruit. It was a tiring task, however. "If my body were not so tough," he said, "I would have died long ago. I am only a poor scholar who can find neither rest nor peace. I do find consolation and hope in the belief that my successor will follow in my footsteps. But if he does not, I cannot help it." Kansas and Chicago were still "sorespots," and even though he was pleased that Abbot Rupert had been chosen for the episcopacy (he noted that he was the "right man for the job" and had brought honor to the order in America) Wimmer remarked that the two bishops, Fink and Seidenbusch, were "lost to the order."

With regard to his health, the abbot said that his eyes continued to bother him and that he often felt frail. "The old sore spot on my heart, or nearby, is also bothersome, and my stomach will not take anything cold. I have to be satisfied with tea as my steady drink. Last winter I did not go outside the house because of the terribly bad weather which continues up to the present day." He did take a trip to St. Marys, Pennsylvania, for two weeks, however, and during the summer he expected "to be on the road a great deal."

Wimmer reported that the political situation in America looked brighter. During the previous fall the Republican party had lost heavily in the general election. "They consist mainly of German liberals and radicals with a mixture of fanatics and are responsible for the sad conditions we are living in now." Since the election, however, "the Democrats have the upper hand in the lower house [of Congress] and in the legislative bodies of most states." At St. Vincent "our situation is not greatly changed." Because of the unhappy financial state of the country, tuition was coming in very irregularly; nevertheless, "things are going smoothly." The brewery was making a profit at last, buildings were continuing to be constructed, and Wimmer was making "every effort possible for the expansion of the order."[78]

Three months later Wimmer was in Minnesota for the consecration of Bishop Seidenbusch and the election of his successor as abbot of St. John's. The consecration took place in St. Mary's Church, St. Cloud, which Seidenbusch had chosen as his procathedral. Wimmer was pleased that the principal German bishops of the United States had agreed to participate in the ceremony. The consecrating bishop was Bishop Michael Heiss of La Crosse, and he was assisted by Bishops Joseph Dwenger of Fort Wayne and Louis Fink, O.S.B., of the Kansas Vicariate. Bishop John Hennessy of Dubuque delivered the sermon, and Bishop-elect Franz Xavier Krautbauer of Green Bay was present in the sanctuary. The event marked an important milestone for the Benedictine Order in the United States, and as Wimmer witnessed the ceremony taking place in the frontier church packed with clergy, monks, and laity, he realized that indeed the ancient order he had brought to Pennsylvania in 1846 had gradually over the years become an integral part of the American Church. Upon the recommendation of the American hierarchy, Rome had raised the second of his spiritual sons to the episcopate. After nearly thirty years of struggle and effort, of work and prayer, his vision of the active role the Benedictine Order should take in the American Church had been in great measure confirmed and vindicated with the consecration of Rupert Seidenbusch.

When the ceremony and celebrations ended, Abbot Boniface and the Benedictines returned to St. John's Abbey to choose Abbot Rupert's successor. The Minnesota monks were determined to elect Father Innocent Wolf, claustral prior at St. Vincent, but when Wolf received the majority vote on the first ballot, Abbot Boniface overturned the election. He said that he could not afford to lose his prior, for he planned to groom Wolf as his successor at St. Vincent. He therefore called for another vote, and when after two more ballots the twenty-four capitulars could not agree on a candidate, the abbot exercised his prerogative as president of the congregation and appointed Father Alexius Edelbrock as second abbot of the Minnesota foundation. Father Alexius objected to the appointment, and several of the monks in the community registered formal protests against Wimmer's action. Wimmer took due note of the objections and sent them to Rome along with the results of the election. On August 15, 1875, the Holy See confirmed the election, and two days later Abbot Angelo Pescetelli wrote Wimmer that despite misgivings among some of the cardinals Propaganda was pleased to approve the appointment of Edelbrock[79]

In his Christmas letter to Abbot Utto Wimmer described the election:

Now I must make the new abbot of St. Louis on the Lake in Minnesota *[sic]*, as you did in Scheyern; partially because he is young (33); partially because he is sharp; partially because he is the *factotum* in the college. Because his elevation to the abbacy would have infringed on his college activities a small minority did not elect him, but rather my Prior Innocent with 13 of 24 votes, and in spite of my having stated from the very beginning that I would not consent either to Fathers Oswald [Moosmüller] or Innocent [Wolf] as abbot if they would elect one of them. I cashiered the election and gave them Father Alexius Edelbrock who received eight votes on the first and eleven on the third ballot. Two young and one old Father protested. I forwarded their protest to the Holy Father, together with the acts of the election and my report. The Holy Father *approbavit et confirmavit* my procedure, and now everyone is satisfied. The new abbot is Westphalian. As a child he came to America, and as a boy to Minnesota. He was rather a wild boy until our Father Alexius Rötzer of happy memory, from whom he took the name Alexius, taught him manners. Then he ran away from his father who was a rugged man in order to study at St. Vincent. He has great talents which he developed with unceasing industry, and after finishing his studies he returned to Minnesota. Under Abbot Rupert he contributed most to the development of the foundation and college whose director he also was. He is healthy, strong, smart, and will accomplish much for the honor of God and our order, I hope in God. Abbot Rupert bequeathed to him a great deal of work. He [Seidenbusch] had brought along from Europe a plan for a church drawn up by Riedl which was supposed to be and was built in St. Paul. The plan was exactly executed despite my repeated warnings orally and in writing. The church is all of stone with two beautiful towers and a basement church for winter. It is a magnificent structure. But debts, debts! So you may immediately send another 50,000 florins. Well the *Projektenmacher* is still an unusual person![80]

With the appointment of a new abbot in the West, Wimmer returned to St. Vincent for the opening of the fifth general chapter of the American Cassinese Congregation. The meeting began on August 18, 1875, and together with the abbot-president eleven other delegates attended: Abbot Alexius Edelbrock of Minnesota, Prior Innocent Wolf of St. Vincent, Prior Oswald Moosmüller of Kansas (who had replaced Prior Aegidius Christoph), and the conventual priors of Carrolltown, St. Marys, Covington, Erie, Richmond, Chicago, and Creston. The priors of Newark and Pittsburgh had been excused.

It was by far the busiest chapter held to date by the American con-

Abbot Alexius Edelbrock (1843–1908), second
abbot of St. John's Abbey, Collegeville,
Minnesota. (ASVA)

gregation. The delegates passed thirty-one decrees, almost equaling
the number of those passed by the four previous general chapters
combined. After approving legislation on religious observance in the
abbeys and priories, the delegates voted to petition the Holy See for
the elevation of the priory in Kansas to the rank of abbey. This was a
milestone development. It not only vindicated the work and sacrifice
of those monks who had struggled in Kansas against seemingly insurmountable odds for almost two decades, but it also marked the
end of the postwar period of consolidation in the American Cassinese
Congregation. While Kansas had been a troublesome daughterhouse
for nearly twenty years, under Prior Oswald Moosmüller many of the
more debilitating problems, both financial and spiritual, were on the
way to being resolved. Moosmüller had introduced a strong and dis-
ciplined monastic observance in the community, had raised the academic quality of the school, and had husbanded the resources and

economy of St. Benedict's to such a degree that it now showed promise of achieving financial solvency in a reasonably short time. The new circumstances in Kansas convinced Wimmer and the chapter delegates that St. Benedict's was now ready to take its place as the third abbey in the congregation.

With regard to St. Malachy's Priory in Creston, Iowa, opinions were divided. Some thought the priory, which had only two monks in residence, should be downgraded to parish and that the idea of establishing a canonical priory for Irish members of the congregation should be abandoned. Others (and Wimmer was among them) believed that the experiment should be given a chance to succeed. Urged by the abbot of St. Vincent, and after an eloquent plea from Father Eugene Phelan, the delegates decided to permit the Irish community to continue, but they expressed their intention of reviewing their decision at the next general chapter three years hence.[81] Five days after the close of the chapter, Abbot Boniface wrote the abbot of Metten that, happily, the community in Kansas would soon be an abbey. Under Father Oswald the Atchison priory had made remarkable progress, and now the community was "better situated than ever before."[82]

In December Wimmer traveled to St. Marys to conduct a visitation. The monks of St. Mary's Priory had recently opened a second parish, Sacred Heart, in St. Marys, and this one served an Irish rather than an exclusively German congregation. By now, three decades after the Benedictines had come to America, Wimmer was becoming increasingly aware that his future apostolates could not be limited to the German-speaking peoples he had originally come to serve. In fact if the order were to remain a vital and relevant force in the American Catholic Church, he would have to move gradually away from his original intent, whose goals had in any case been largely achieved, and undertake missions to new ethnic minorities who spoke languages other than German. His monks in the West were already working among the Indians, and he himself had approved the establishment of an Irish priory in Iowa. As time went on he was less and less reluctant to take on parishes and missions that served exclusively non-German congregations.[83] The work of consolidation, which had occupied Wimmer for a decade after the Civil War, was, in his mind, brought to fulfillment with the decision to elevate St. Benedict's Priory in Kansas to the rank of abbey. Now he was ready to initiate a vigorous new program of missionary activity that would mark another dramatic phase of expansion for the Benedictine Order in the United States. Just as the first missionary thrust from St. Vincent had been to the West, so in 1876 the abbot's eyes turned south, to the broken states of the Confederacy, for the second.

Monks from St. Vincent had been working in the South since 1858, when Wimmer had accepted Bishop George A. Carrell's invitation to take charge of the German parish in Covington, Kentucky. In 1859 the abbot had sent monks to San José in Texas; in 1860 he assigned Father Leonard Mayer to Richmond, Virginia: and in 1861 he had sent Father Emmeran Bliemel to Nashville, Tennessee. In each of these cases the parishes Wimmer accepted consisted of German-speaking congregations. But now he began to consider requests to establish missions among exclusively English-speaking Catholic congregations in the South, including missions to the freed black slaves. The new phase of expansion would take the monks from St. Vincent to North Carolina, Alabama, and Georgia.

Several weeks before the general chapter of 1875, Abbot Boniface had received a request from James Gibbons, bishop of Richmond and vicar apostolic of North Carolina, for monks to work in the western part of the North Carolina vicariate. An estate of five hundred acres in Gaston County near Charlotte had recently been donated to Bishop Gibbons by Father Jeremiah J. O'Connell, a priest who had worked in the Carolina and Georgia missions for thirty years. Gibbons wrote Wimmer that he had immediately thought of turning to the Benedictines of St. Vincent, "whose brethren, I trust, are destined to cultivate souls and land in North Carolina, as they had done in Europe" during the Middle Ages. The bishop told Abbot Boniface that since the land was well situated on the Richmond and Atlanta Railroad, it would be an ideal spot to establish a college. He reminded the abbot that no Catholic school of this kind existed between Washington and Mobile "except in Georgia." The property in North Carolina Gibbons offered the Benedictines was valued at more than $10,000, and the only condition Father O'Connell had placed on the gift was that he be allowed to occupy a room on the premises during his lifetime, "which in the order of nature is not destined to be long, as he is old and feeble." Gibbons said that there were scarcely any Catholics in the immediate vicinity of the property, and that the mission would provide a great opportunity for the sons of St. Benedict to do serious proselytizing in a heavily Protestant region. "May God inspire you to accept this offer."[84]

Wimmer noted on the letter that he could not accept the property at once but would "like to see it first." But Bishop Gibbons was persistent. He called upon Father Benno Hegele, prior of St. Mary's Priory, Richmond, and asked him to persuade his superior in Pennsylvania to make a positive decision as soon as possible. In January Hegele informed Abbot Boniface of the bishop's visit, and on January 19, 1876, Wimmer summoned the chapter at St. Vincent and presented the question to his monks. There was considerable opposition among the capitulars to accepting Gibbons's offer. As the bishop himself said, there were scarcely any Catholics in the area being offered them, and what was probably worse for the St. Vincent monks, there were no Germans either, Catholic or otherwise. In the five months since receiving and shelving Bishop Gibbons's letter, however, Wimmer had had time to reconsider the possibilities of a new kind of missionary apostolate in North Carolina, and at the chapter meeting he urged the St. Vincent monks to accept the bishop's offer. The place was poverty-stricken, Protestant, and "godless" and had as yet not recovered from the ravages of a catastrophic civil war. The bleaker the prospects the more eagerly Abbot Boniface seemed to want to take them on. This was not the sort of challenge he had ever turned away from in the past, and the opportunity to create an oasis of monastic and academic life out of the Protestant and primitive land of western North Carolina stirred his spirit. Monks of old had turned deserts into fertile fields, swamps into rich pastures, wasteland into flourishing agricultural centers. Wimmer saw no reason why his men could not also turn North Carolina into something worthwhile.

Such rhetoric had its effect on the monks. After a lengthy discussion, the formerly reluctant capitulars "unanimously" advised Wimmer to accept Bishop Gibbons's offer, and the following day Wimmer wrote Father Benno instructing the Richmond prior to inform Gibbons of the chapter's decision.[85]

Wimmer detached Father Herman Wolfe, O.S.B., a sixty-year-old native of Holstein and a convert from Lutheranism, from Richmond, where he had been serving as assistant to Father Benno, and assigned him to lead the mission to North Carolina.[86] In March he wrote Abbot Utto that "I let myself be convinced to accept a farm in North Carolina worth $10,000, but only under the condition that we might gradually build a monastery on it which ought to become the center of Catholic life and action in the state. There aren't many Catholics there. . . . I shall make a beginning with one priest, a cleric, and two brothers."[87]

Father Herman Wolfe, who had served as a doctor in the Confederate army, was a judicious choice as first Benedictine superior in North Carolina. His service to the South during the war would offset whatever objections Protestant North Carolinians might raise to a Catholic presence in their state. With characteristic humility Wolfe wrote Wimmer that "had I been at St. Vincent I would have voted in favor of accepting the place but certainly would not have chosen the man who is to go there to start it." Wolfe said that "at first I hoped that the bishop would raise objections on account of my age, but this wish came to naught. The community must assist me with its prayers."[88]

Father Herman visited the North Carolina property in February and wrote that he hoped Wimmer would provide enough monks for the mission so that he could open a school at once.[89] After much planning and preparation, Wolfe finally settled on the O'Connell estate in April. Wimmer visited North Carolina in May, and when he returned to St. Vincent he sent Brothers Bartholomew Freundl, Ulric Barth, Placidus Draude, and Philip Cassidy to assist in establishing a monastery. In July Father Herman wrote that "we are all well. The first work which I did on the place was to fit up a room in the house for a chapel. I blessed it, and from the first morning holy mass was offered every day. May God assist us that this Sacrifice will never be interrupted here."[90]

Bishop Gibbons had entrusted the Benedictines with the care of souls in the western North Carolina counties of Gaston and Mecklenburg, and Father Herman spent the early weeks of his assignment traveling about and visiting the scattered Catholics. He wrote Wimmer that "the people are very earnest about their religion, and I have good hopes of being able to take care of them in spiritual matters. I intend to visit them once a month, going about by railroad. This means that I must start on Sunday mornings at 4:30 and come back at 10:30 in the evening." The monks were making plans to erect a building that would serve as a school, and the superior reported that nine students were expected for the first school year. "So far we have three resident students; two from Richmond who are scholastics and pay fifty dollars and another from the neighborhood who pays $150." There were also six day-students, and Wolfe said he was "expecting help from St. Vincent, a priest or at least a cleric."[91]

Wolfe had named the monastery "Mariastein," Mary's stone, on account of a large circular stone he found on the property. An oral tradition held that the stone served at one time as a sacrificial altar for Indians in the region and more recently as a block upon which black slaves were sold.[92] Father Joseph Keller soon came from St. Vincent to assist Father Herman, and together with Father O'Connell, who became an oblate in the community, the two priests and the several brothers busily set about laying the groundwork for a monastery and school. Brother Philip Cassidy, a former Irish School Brother who was sent to teach at the new foundation, wrote Abbot Boniface that "the plantation is well-timbered with oak and pine; the ground is level and seems easy to cultivate. The place in general looks well, and I think it is healthy as the country is a rolling land. . . . It seems primitive enough but it has signs of improvement."[93]

In the meantime the establishment of a second new southern mission was underway. About the same time that Bishop Gibbons offered the Benedictines the property in Gaston County, North Carolina, several requests for priests had come to St. Vincent from German settlers in Tennessee and northern Alabama. In August 1875 Abbot Boniface dutifully presented a proposal to the monastic chapter to send monks into Tennessee. The large German congregation at Lawrenceville in the Diocese of Nashville had been unable to find a priest to attend to its spiritual needs, and with the encouragement of Bishop Patrick A. Feehan of Nashville they had turned to St. Vincent. Although Wimmer favored establishing a mission in rural Tennessee, at the time internal opposition to his missionary activity was at one of its frequent highwater marks at St. Vincent. The capitulars thought it wiser to conserve manpower at the motherhouse than to spread thin the monastic ranks by sending more missionaries into the field. The major concern of most of the monks at St. Vincent was for the development of the college and the seminary. They feared that by opening more missions, no matter how beneficial to the Church, they would drain talented teachers and essential resources from the schools at St. Vincent. Their fears were not unwarranted. From the beginning of his work in America Wimmer had shown an inclination to send his best men to distant missions where for all practical purposes they were lost to the faculties of the college and seminary in Pennsylvania. The schools invariably suffered when missions were accepted, and so when the monastic chapter met on August 30, 1875, to discuss the Tennessee proposal, they decisively voted it down.[94]

Six months later, however, the mood of the chapter had changed. In March, after agreeing to accept the property in North Carolina, Wimmer received a request from Bishop John Quinlan of Mobile to establish a Benedictine mission among a German colony which had been founded in northern Alabama in conjunction with the one in Lawrenceville, Tennessee. This second colony, near Huntsville, was called St. Florian. Bishop Quinlan offered to give Wimmer and the community at St. Vincent "charge of Cullman Station, where there are 100 families, of St. Florian, with its 30 families, and all the property under my control. I will also give you charge of Huntsville." The bishop said that in Huntsville a church had already been constructed for which $19,000 had been expended. The debt on the church which the Benedictines would have to assume amounted to little more than $3,000. When the abbot brought the proposal before the chapter, he pointed out the advantages of accepting a mission where much of the groundwork—such as the building of a church and the gathering of a worshipping congregation—had already been laid. A lengthy debate ensued in which some objected to the commitment of financial and human resources the mission would entail, while others pointed out the advantages Alabama, with its German congregations and completed church, had over the mission in North Carolina. Wimmer urged the monks to accept the mission, and in an about-face that frequently characterized the decisions of the chapter, the community, with only two dissenting votes, agreed to send a band of monks to Alabama.[95]

Wimmer assigned Father Gabriel Guerster from the priory in St. Marys, Pennsylvania, as well as Brothers Majolus Mathey and Thaddeus Weber from St. Vincent, to St. Florian, and in April he accompanied the three monks to Alabama where, in addition to the land given him by the bishop, he purchased one thousand acres for $3,500. He spent two weeks in Alabama, meeting the bishop, familiarizing himself with the mission, and introducing himself and his monks to the people at Cullman Station, St. Florian, and Huntsville. From Alabama he went to the new priory in North Carolina. It was his first visit to the North Carolina mission, and he saw at once the implications of the difficulties the monks faced there. There was no Catholic congregation; Southern Catholic parents could be expected to resist sending their sons from the eastern cities to this outback place, and anti-Catholic Protestant neighbors were sometimes openly hostile. Nevertheless, Wimmer determined to forge ahead with the North Carolina foundation. He saw it eventually emerging as an important center of Catholicism in the rural South and entertained hopes that it would form the axis of a Benedictine mission to the freed black slaves. After only a few days in North Carolina, Wimmer then went to Richmond to meet Bishop Gibbons and visit his monks at St. Mary's Priory. When he finally returned to St. Vincent he was exhausted, but the news that came to him soon after his arrival revived him. In April the Holy See had approved his petition to elevate the priory in Kansas to the rank of abbey. Word of the approval reached St. Vincent at the end of May, and Wimmer was delighted. He told Abbot Alexius Edelbrock of Minnesota that the elevation of St. Benedict's meant that the American Cassinese Congregation was at last legally constituted. According to the Bavarian statutes that governed the American Congregation, three abbeys, one of whose abbots would serve as president and two as visitors, were necessary for the formal constitution of a congregation. With the creation of an abbey in Kansas and the forthcoming election of its abbot, the American Benedictines had finally fulfilled all the requirements for a fully functional Benedictine congregation in accord with Bavarian Benedictine precedents.

Wimmer also told Edelbrock that he hoped the monks of St. Benedict's would now begin planning for the foundation of daughterhouses in the West and Southwest. He himself, he said, was thinking of sending one of the priests of St. Vincent "to the western territories and California" in order to raise money for the missions. "Perhaps he can also become a missionary to the Germans and look for a place to build another monastery."[96]

In August Wimmer wrote Canon Michael Reger of the Ludwig Missionsverein informing him of the chapter's decision to accept the missions in North Carolina and Alabama. He said that in order to meet the challenges of these two missions successfully, the St. Vincent community would have to sacrifice both money and men, but he was determined to see the two new communities firmly planted in the fertile soil of the South. Now that the monastery in Kansas had been raised to abbatial dignity, it was time for the Benedictines to move forward into new fields of missionary endeavors: "It is a great comfort to me that we have a third abbey. . . . It took ten years for St. Vincent to become one, ten years likewise for St. Louis in Minnesota, and eighteen years for Atchison. Eternal thanks be to God for all this. All three abbeys have healthy and favorable locations for themselves, as well as for external work and wider dissemination of the order—providing God, on whom all depends, gives His blessing to it."[97]

In September Abbot Boniface left St. Vincent for Atchison where the election of the first abbot of St. Benedict's Abbey was to take place. Stopping first in Creston, Iowa, he conducted a visitation of St. Malachy's Priory and wrote Abbot Utto that the monks in Creston were doing pastoral work among families who lived in a forty- to fifty-mile radius of the priory. Mentioning that he had recently taken over the two missions in the South, he said that he had sent monks to North Carolina and Alabama in order "to make room for the growing number of young Benedictines as well as to help the poor bishops in that part of the country who have great concern for their neglected sheep, both white and black."

Wimmer said that he was well satisfied with the work God had allowed him to accomplish in America. "If I should be called from this world today or tomorrow, I will have left everything in order, at least externally. Internally, it's a different matter." He expressed concern that the quality of monastic observance in the American Cassinese houses was not of the high standard that he believed it would become. Still, he had great hopes for the American Benedictine capacity to perfect the monastic life through discipline, prayer, and study, though he himself doubted that he would live to assist his confreres in this task.

It seems very clear to me that I shall not last much longer. My end is very near, and now I have certain doubts. I am sure it was my duty to be a good Benedictine, but whether I was truly called to spread the order in this country, I am not so certain. I know only this: I honestly felt that it was my duty, my obligation, if not my destiny to do what I did. I think—rather, I know that it was my intention to do all for the honor of the order, for the glory of God, and for the salvation of souls. But *de facto* the Benedictine did not do so well, and the man who helped spread the order not much better. For all these failures my confreres in Metten are largely to blame. They should not have trusted such an important work to one who was so reckless. They

Abbot Innocent Wolf (1843–1922), first abbot of
St. Benedict's Abbey, Atchison, Kansas. (ASVA)

should have undertaken the work themselves. But what is past is past. I hope only that you keep me in your fervent prayers while I live, as well as after I am gone.[98]

The abbot was suffering more and more from ailments of the eye and stomach, but he had happily overcome the problems with angina he had experienced for quite some time. The "cure" had come when he boldly drank down a pitcher of lemonade "without a care for the consequences." Much to his surprise and delight this had effected a temporary respite from the complaint. He wrote that it was the first real relief he had gotten in years, and he recommended American lemonade to Abbot Utto as a sure cure for any similar ailments among the monks of Metten.[99]

On September 25, 1876, the sixty-seven-year-old Wimmer left Creston for Kansas. Four days later he conducted the abbatial election in Atchison. The monks of St. Benedict's Priory had undergone severe trials since the priory's founding in 1857. The Civil War and the postwar financial crisis had taken their toll at St. Benedict's. Under the administration of Prior Augustine Wirth the community had gone deeply into debt. Assistance had come not only from the Ludwig Missionsverein but also from St. Vincent and several European monasteries, notably Montecassino and Metten, and early in 1875 Abbot Boniface had sent one of his ablest monks, Father Oswald Moosmüller, to assume charge of the monastery and attempt to put it on sound financial footing. Soon after arriving in Atchison Prior Oswald had written Wimmer that "the condition of this monastery is so bad that I cannot see the least chance to be able to reduce the debts. . . . At present they amount to $50,000, the greater part of which is at 10 or 12 percent interest. Moreover, the College now has fewer students than several years ago. . . . Next to our prayers, the College is the only source of revenues, because the parishes and missions in Kansas are utterly unable to contribute anything for our support."[100] In less than two years, however, Moosmüller had accomplished the impossible and reduced the debt at St. Benedict's Priory to a manageable sum. By the time Wimmer arrived for the abbatial election in September 1876 a mood of optimism prevailed in the community that had not been known since its foundation.

Seven monks of St. Benedict's were present for the election of the first abbot and four others were voting by proxy. As he had done before at the two previous abbatial elections in Minnesota, Abbot Boniface instructed the capitulars that they were free to choose any monk in the congregation as their first abbot. He stipulated only that they not elect Father Innocent Wolf, claustral prior at St. Vincent. Abbot Boniface hoped that Father Innocent would succeed him as abbot of St. Vincent, and for that reason he ordered the Kansas monks to choose someone other than the prior of St. Vincent.

Wimmer's own choice for the first abbot of St. Benedict's was Father Oswald Moosmüller.[101] For more than a decade Moosmüller had been one of the abbot's most trusted and dependable men. He had

Father Oswald Moosmüller (1832–1901), Benedictine missionary and monastic reformer. Moosmüller helped found Benedictine communities in Kentucky, Ontario, Kansas, Georgia, Alabama, and Illinois. Elected abbot of Maryhelp Abbey, North Carolina, he declined the honor in order to work among African Americans in Georgia. (ASVA)

served as superior of St. Vincent's offshoots in Sandwich, Ontario; in Newark, New Jersey; in Covington, Kentucky; in Rome; and now in Kansas, and everyone agreed that he would make an excellent ab-bot.[102] But Prior Oswald would hear nothing of it. Despite Wimmer's objections he began a quiet campaign to have Father Innocent elected to the post Abbot Boniface had been preparing for Moosmüller him-self. Moosmüller's benign conspiracy was totally successful, and when the first ballot was tallied it was clear that Wimmer had lost the fight. Father Innocent Wolf received eight of the eleven votes. Reluctant as he was to acquiesce to the will of the majority, the abbot remembered how the objections raised by the Minnesota monks to his overturning of the election of Wolf in 1875 had led to annoying questions from Rome. How could he explain to the Holy See that for the second time in two years he had voided the election of Wolf? Not wanting to repeat the painful experience of appointing an abbot and then enduring the protests of those who would have to serve under him, the beleaguered Wimmer reluctantly agreed to approve the Kansas monks' choice of Father Innocent as their first abbot and to submit his name to Rome for confirmation. It seemed the easiest solution.[103]

With the election in Kansas accomplished, Wimmer began his return journey to St. Vincent. He stopped first in Chicago to inspect the buildings being constructed at St. Joseph's Priory to replace those destroyed in the disastrous fire of 1871 and to discuss the finances of the project with Prior Leander Schnerr. He made a month's progress toward the abbey, stopping first in Erie and then in St. Marys to visit the monks and nuns in each place. On the way he quietly celebrated the thirtieth anniversary of his arrival at St. Vincent. It had been thirty long years of work and prayer. He had grown old in America, but there was still much work to be done. He reached the abbey on November 1, and soon thereafter bid farewell to Father Innocent, who left for Kansas in tears.

When Wolf departed, Wimmer appointed Father Andrew Hintenach, a thirty-two-year-old native of Baden and a professor of theology, as the new prior of St. Vincent. Perhaps he had some inkling that it would be Hintenach who would succeed him as abbot, but if his thoughts turned in this direction, he did not allude to them in his correspondence. Losing Father Innocent had been a disappointment; it was now time to turn his attention to other matters. As the New Year dawned, he returned to his perennial preoccupation with the missions. The next decade would be his last, and he moved into it with the same vigor that characterized his earlier labors. And yet he had mellowed in the three decades since he had set out from Metten. More trials and challenges would come before he ended the journey, but this time he would handle them more expertly, more deftly, with the quiet wisdom that characterized his old age. "As autumn in the circle of years is the most beautiful season," he wrote, "so is old age in life! The young ones don't want to believe this, and yet it is true. In growing white one also grows wise—or at least wiser than one was. I am glad the hot season of my life has passed; I would not want to go through it again even if I could. A burnt child, you see, shuns the fire."[104]

7 ❧ *Laughter and Tears*

O N J A N U A R Y 14, 1877, Wimmer celebrated his sixty-eighth
birthday. Looking back over thirty years of work in the American missions, he said that he did not know "whether to laugh or to
weep. It must be that I had the vocation to bring the Order of St.
Benedict here, otherwise I would never have been able to do it. This
is a great grace—but! but! In this case laughing and weeping are very
close akin!" In some ways he felt that he had failed. There were times
when he did not "see the spirit of the order, nor genuine love for the
order, nor zeal for the honor of the order" among his confreres. "And
this moral deficit will be reckoned to my account!"[1]

But his successes seemed to far outweigh what failures he accused
himself of. By 1877 three abbeys, twelve priories, seventy-five parishes
and mission stations, six secondary schools, two major seminaries,
and nearly three hundred and seventy-five monks provided ample evidence that his efforts to transplant the ancient Order of St. Benedict
from Germany to the New World had borne abundant fruit. Three
decades after they had settled at St. Vincent, Wimmer's Benedictines
served more than forty thousand souls in seventeen states and nineteen dioceses and vicariates apostolic of the United States, and two of
his monks served as bishops—Louis Fink in Kansas and Rupert Seidenbusch in Minnesota. In the elementary schools attached to American Benedictine parishes there were more than four thousand pupils
taught principally by the Benedictine sisters whom Wimmer had first
introduced to the United States in 1852. More than four hundred students studied in secondary schools and major seminaries operated by
the monks, and approximately one hundred and seventy young men
who had studied at St. Vincent since 1847 had been ordained for the
diocesan priesthood.[2] "The past," Wimmer wrote to Bishop Rupert
Seidenbusch, "often appears to me like a dream. Sometimes I feel like

Adam before Eve was made. I see nobody like me. I am surrounded by young monks. I am like an old tree in the middle of young underwood. . . . In many ways I can consider myself happy—far more happy than I would ever have expected. There are disappointments, of course. But I have it so good that I often apprehend great troubles or calamities ahead."[3]

In February Wimmer wrote Abbot Utto Lang of Metten that despite his advanced age there was little rest: "Under the circumstances there is always more work. For us it is a time for growth, for development. I *must* make use of it. And even if I don't know where to put them I must take as many candidates as I have room for in order to be ready when necessity calls. . . . We feel the urge to expand, and that is the reason there is no rest. Something new is always turning up."[4]

To Munich's archbishop Gregory Scherr, his novitiate classmate and the superior who had tried to discourage him from going to America more than three decades earlier, Wimmer wrote that he was still looking for new places to send his monks: "Our order is in the process of growth. To hold it back means to kill it. I really don't know where to place all my people, but it makes no difference. I take in everyone who asks for reception and who seems to have a vocation, as many as I am able to house. I have them educated in the best possible way so that they can conduct schools or dedicate themselves to the missions." The abbot said that he foresaw many of his young monks themselves establishing monasteries in America, and that it was his "firm belief that Protestantism shall fall into ruin and its better part shall convert in great numbers by means of our order." For thirty years, he said, he had been building the order in America and educating priests for the German population. "I have done it, I am still doing it, and I shall continue to do it as long as I live. . . . It is absolutely necessary for the existence and propagation of our order." And now it was to the South that he was turning, for it seemed "predestined that our order go to this section of the country to convert the heretics and the pagan Negroes."[5]

Because of the devastation caused by the Civil War and Reconstruction, the South seemed ready to provide a new and fertile field for missionary activity from St. Vincent Abbey. By 1877 St. Vincent had men working in Kentucky, Virginia, North Carolina, and Alabama, and when Bishop William Gross, C.Ss.R., of Savannah requested priests from the Pennsylvania abbey to take over a small monastery in Georgia, Wimmer agreed to provide them.

In 1874 Gross had invited monks from the French province of the Benedictine Subiaco Congregation of the Primitive Observance to establish a community in Savannah and care for the emancipated black population. Two French monks from the Abbey of Pierre-qui-vire arrived in the spring of 1874, and settling on the Isle of Hope, some nine miles east of Savannah, they built a monastery and opened a novitiate. Two years later yellow fever struck the community and carried off the superior, Father Gabriel Bergier, as well as several novices and candidates. The remaining monks withdrew from Savannah and went to Oklahoma where they formed part of the nucleus that eventually became Sacred Heart Abbey.[6] Bishop Gross turned to Abbot Boniface for help in restoring the monastery on the Isle of Hope, and in February 1877, after the St. Vincent chapter voted to accept the mission, the abbot sent Fathers Oswald Moosmüller from Kansas and Maurice Kaeder from St. Vincent to Savannah.[7]

Wimmer explained to Abbot Utto that there were two reasons for his taking over the Georgia monastery. Not only did he have pity on "these entirely neglected Negroes," but also he wanted "another field for my young people to work in. . . . We must spread and expand ourselves, and the South, where there are very few Catholics, is the place we must do this. How wonderful! I am staggered with dizziness, and I am too glad to do it."[8]

Moosmüller and Kaeder arrived in Georgia on March 2, 1877, and immediately took possession of the small monastery on the Isle of Hope. Three black brothers, the only remaining members of the original community, joined the two priests in their efforts to reestablish monastic life in the Georgia mission, and on March 20 Prior Oswald wrote Abbot Boniface that plans were underway to establish a school near Savannah for African-American boys. Because the monastery on the Isle of Hope was still infected with the yellow fever, Moosmüller said that he was investigating the possibility of purchasing land on nearby Skidaway Island where he had found a more suitable place for a monastery and school. In the meantime the prior reported that Bishop Gross and the people of Savannah had warmly received the Benedictines from Pennsylvania and that prospects for the community in Georgia were bright: "Next week we will get our charter under the title 'The Benedictine Order in Georgia' with a capital of $10,000 invested in real estate for the 'Education of Youth, especially of the Colored Race.' The Bishop will transfer that property to our corporation for the purpose of 'conducting a manual labor school for colored boys.' So far we have three colored brothers. Two will be able to teach ordinary branches in school, the third to do housework. I hope that soon we get more."[9]

As Moosmüller began construction of a monastery and school on Skidaway Island, Kaeder set out on a missionary journey through central Georgia to bring the sacraments to Catholics scattered along the railroad that extended three hundred miles from the coast to the interior of the state. He also sought out Protestants to evangelize, and Wimmer reported to Archbishop Scherr of Munich that Father Maurice

goes everywhere, to any place that does not have a pastor (there are only a dozen priests in the entire diocese of one million people) to seek the scattered sheep, to support them, and to convert Protestants. He gives lectures on religious truths, which are attended by the most renowned people. He is a very talented man, a good theologian, and an out-of-the ordinary preacher, a Rheno-Prussian educated at St. Vincent. There are good prospects for him to make a number of conquests for the Church, especially in the small town of Thomasville where in the July heat of 105 degrees he delivered three lectures in the town hall. The entire class of better citizens of this town filled the auditorium, and there were many requests afterwards for catechisms. In this manner we plan to attack the devil in his own realm. In the southern states there is hardly one Catholic among 100 souls. I have made plenty of plans, but [until now] I could not realize a single one because I was called to help in the North too often. Naturally everything depends on the grace of God, who must provide the right people and right means, and also must point out the proper circumstances. Everything has arranged itself properly without my searching for it.[10]

In September Moosmüller opened a school for black students at the Isle of Hope, and eight months later the Benedictines moved their monastery and school across the Skidaway River to Skidaway Island. Twelve boys entered the school in September 1878, and Wimmer sent four monks from St. Vincent, including Brother Philip Cassidy, a former Irish School Brother, and Brother Rhabanus Cononge, a black monk from New Orleans who had recently entered the monastery at St. Vincent, to assist in the teaching of the students and in the agricultural work of the seven-hundred-acre farm Bishop Gross had given the Benedictines. Moosmüller's plan was to establish an agricultural school for the black population of coastal Georgia, but when he discovered that many of the families he hoped to serve preferred that their sons have the opportunity for professional studies, he modified the plan and created a school "designed to benefit two classes of students: . . those who wish to get a business education qualifying them for such positions" and those "whose circumstances or wishes incline them to seek a more limited and practical course of instruction in farming as a profession." Moosmüller intended that the institution would "elevate the vocation of farmer, and give him a scientific as well as a practical instruction for his pursuits." The school would do this by putting the student "in possession of knowledge of the most improved methods of cultivation which are now used." The Benedictines' purpose in establishing the school was "to counteract the increasing tendency against manual labor, especially vindicating its dignity by showing that it is compatible with intellectual culture and social refinement."[11]

In order to develop further opportunities for the conversion of the five hundred African Americans living on Skidaway Island, Moosmüller arranged for the appointment of the young black cleric, Siricius Palmer, O.S.B., as schoolmaster in the public school recently established on the island, and he wrote Wimmer that "if Siricius is a good teacher, he has the chance to convert these children and with them the whole population of the island to the Catholic Faith."[12]

Meanwhile, as the mission in Georgia developed, events were unfolding that would lead to the establishment of another mission in the West from St. Vincent. In March 1877 Abbot Boniface had gone to Atchison, Kansas, for the blessing of Abbot Innocent Wolf, and there he had met Bishop James O'Connor of the Nebraska Vicariate who had come to St. Benedict's to participate in the abbatial blessing. O'Connor, brother of the former bishop of Pittsburgh, Michael O'Connor, and successor to Bishop James O'Gorman, O.C.S.O., was an old acquaintance of Abbot Boniface since the early days of the Benedictine presence in Pennsylvania. For a while he had served as chaplain to the Sisters of Mercy at St. Xavier's Convent near St. Vincent and as pastor of the English-speaking congregation in Latrobe. Recalling their old friendship, Bishop O'Connor asked Wimmer to send monks to Omaha in order to establish a monastery for the Czech colonists there.[13] Nearly twenty years earlier, Abbot Boniface had answered a similar request of Bishop O'Gorman and had sent monks to Nebraska to work among German settlers, but disagreements with Bishop O'Gorman, as well as pressing needs for priests in other parts of the country, caused him to withdraw from the Nebraska mission shortly afterward. In Atchison Bishop O'Connor told Wimmer of the desperate need for priests among the Czech settlers in Nebraska and invited the abbot to visit Omaha and examine firsthand the opportunities for establishing a Benedictine community there.[14]

The chance to open a mission among a new ethnic group that promised to develop into a significant presence in the American Church appealed to Wimmer. In 1877 nearly six thousand Czech Catholics lived in the Nebraska Vicariate, part of a wave of immigration from Eastern Europe that would grow dramatically in the years leading up to the First World War. By the end of the first decade of the twentieth century almost three hundred fifty thousand Czechs would settle in the United States. Like the Germans who preceded them, the Czechs settled primarily in rural America, concentrating in Nebraska, Texas, Wisconsin, Iowa, and Minnesota, and Wimmer believed that their settlements, as well as those of other immigrants from Eastern Europe, would prove to be rich new fields of missionary labor for the American Benedictines. He was therefore eager to respond favorably to Bishop O'Connor's request.[15]

Already several Czech immigrants had entered the monastery at St. Vincent, and Benedictines from St. Vincent served the Czech parish of St. Wenceslaus in Allegheny City, Pennsylvania. Wimmer saw the Nebraska offer as an opportunity not only to serve the needs of a new Catholic immigrant group but also to attract Czech candidates to the Benedictine vocation. He therefore accepted Bishop O'Connor's invitation and after the blessing of Abbot Innocent went to Nebraska where O'Connor offered him a Czech church and congregation in Omaha. When he returned to St. Vincent, he presented the bishop's proposal to the monastic chapter, and the chapter, without significant opposition, agreed to accept the offer. Wimmer then wrote Bishop O'Connor and detailed the conditions the St. Vincent community would place on the agreement. Ever since his first dealings with O'Connor's brother in the 1840s, Wimmer had always required that bishops who offered the Benedictines missions in their dioceses deed over the property unconditionally to the monks and agree not to hinder the future development of an exempt independent monastery within their jurisdictions. On April 21, 1877, O'Connor replied, accepting the conditions. Perhaps remembering the bitter conflict that followed Michael O'Connor's attempt to put restrictions on the establishment of St. Vincent in 1846, and certainly aware of the impressive achievements of the American Benedictines in the three subsequent decades, Bishop James O'Connor wrote that Wimmer should "draw up whatever paper you wish me to sign in relation to the Bohemian church and congregation. I would not invite any religious community to the Vicariate before being prepared to give them all reasonable security against being disturbed by myself or successors. I shall, of course, deed the church to you."[16]

Five weeks later Wimmer ordered Father Wenceslaus Kocarnik, a thirty-two-year-old native of Bohemia who had entered the monastery at St. Vincent in 1866 and who since 1874 had served as pastor of St. Wenceslaus Parish in Allegheny City, to Nebraska.[17] Kocarnik arrived in Omaha in early July 1877 and immediately began organizing the Czech Catholics into a parish. Before Father Wenceslaus's arrival, Bishop O'Connor had bought a building in the Czech section of Omaha for the parish, but Kocarnik discovered that he would have to do a great deal of work before the building would be suitable for religious observances. It had earlier been a saloon and dancehall and still retained much of its former character. Kocarnik wrote that "several ladies came with soap and brooms to clean the dance hall as much as possible. We had to force the lock because nobody seemed to know where the keys were. And that was a sight to behold! The good Irish ladies did not even want to step inside until I provided them with the weapon of holy water and they properly blessed themselves several times." The women worked all day cleaning the saloon, and early the next morning, with his "heart beating fast," Father Wenceslaus

went to the church and waited for my first parishioners. About fifty persons came. As best as I could, I explained to them the reason why I came, what this place had been until now, and what it would be in the future. I blessed the room with the simple blessing of homes; I brought in the altar stone and explained its meaning and placed it under the altar cloths. Everything was now ready for the beginning of mass, in a place which formerly was used for sinful entertainment and for insults to God. The people who were present recognized the significance of this moment, for as soon as I came to the altar, they began weeping so much that I had difficulty in continuing holy mass. A person has to experience something like this; it is impossible to describe in writing. At ten o'clock, there was a second mass with a sermon; and in the afternoon, devotional services in honor of the Blessed Virgin Mary, because I did not have the things needed for Benediction with the Blessed Sacrament. These were the first Czech divine services in Omaha.[18]

After making the arrangements for the Nebraska mission, which he hoped would eventually become a "Bohemian" monastery, Wimmer left St. Vincent for a four-week tour of St. Vincent's southern missions, the first in a series of long and exhausting journeys he would make during the eighth and final decade of his life.

Going first to Covington where the monks of St. Joseph's had recently purchased eighty acres of land, Wimmer directed that the vineyard on the property be immediately put into operation to provide sacramental wine for the Benedictine communities of the American Cassinese Congregation. He planned to establish a Benedictine community on the property and name it after St. Benedict's own monastery south of Rome. He wrote that the eighty acres in Kentucky provided "an exquisite place for a monastery and college—an American Monte Cassino."

The site is wonderful and on an elevation that commands a view of Cincinnati, Covington, and Newport and opens up a magnificent vista. The land is very good; the vineyard has the best location. Eight hundred mature pear trees and some hundred apple trees are also there. Two frame houses are still standing as well as the farm buildings, but the residence was gutted by fire. . . . We did not take over the farm until mid-May, and we have already sold $500 worth of fruits and vegetables, got almost 700 gallons of mass wine and 700 gallons of table wine, feed for two horses and two cows and so on. If the vegetables and wine, or only one of them, boomed a bit, then in favorable circumstances we could realize two to three thousand dollars. We could easily produce ten to twelve thousand gallons of wine and in addition some hundreds of dollars worth of fruit. This computation is not exaggerated, for the former owners once produced 17,000 gallons of wine in a year. The trees only recently have commenced bearing fruit.[19]

From Covington Wimmer set out to visit his monks in Alabama, Georgia, and North Carolina. "All these stations in the South," he said, "promise to become great Benedictine settlements." Nevertheless the motherhouse was forced to "suffer hard and prolonged labor pains" in order to give them birth, and Wimmer discovered that his financial reserves were being rapidly depleted on their account. "One has to prepare himself for the eventuality that much hope and expectation might come to nothing. Not a few undertakings are frustrated despite the careful thought and best preparations that go into them." Still, there was much cause for optimism. At St. Vincent, he wrote, "we are again blessed with an abundant harvest. Also we are expecting many students this year."[20]

The visit to the southern missions had a sobering effect on Wimmer. While all the communities showed signs of future material success, and prospects for the one in Georgia were especially bright for the evangelization of the freed slaves, the abbot was disappointed in the quality of the spiritual life he had found in the new monastic communities, particularly at Maryhelp Priory in North Carolina. The North Carolina monks were demoralized, and their monastic observance had begun to falter. Surrounded by Protestants, with no German congregation to sustain them, living in uncomfortable quarters, and experiencing great difficulty in making the farm productive, they felt isolated and homesick for Pennsylvania. Almost to a man they had sought to be transferred back to St. Vincent. Wimmer did what he could to encourage them, finally ordering them "to cease murmuring and start working."[21] But he blamed himself for the apparent lack of religious zeal he had encountered in the southern priories, and upon his return to St. Vincent he wrote Abbot Alexius Edelbrock that "people may think I have done great things, but God may judge I have greatly failed in doing what I chiefly ought to have done! Not to speak of all my private life as a priest and a religious and an abbot! I often think I should not have undertaken such a work at all. To do it right would require not only an energetic, assiduous, and a wise man, but a holy man. I am none of that. For this reason I am afraid of death, but likewise of a long life, since it is very doubtful if I can or will do much better."[22]

Despite these misgivings he forged ahead with the work of spreading the order to new and distant places. When a request came from Archbishop Napoleon J. Perché of New Orleans for a priest to take over a German parish in Covington, Louisiana, Abbot Boniface assigned Father Bernardine Dolweck of St. Mary's Priory, Richmond, to assume charge of the mission. Wimmer said that he had taken over the parish because the German people in the archdiocese of New Orleans were being neglected by the archbishop "to such an extent that two congregations had installed Methodist preachers as their pastors because their call for a priest was in vain."[23] An even more pressing reason in the abbot's mind for accepting the Louisiana mission was that a community of Benedictine nuns had recently settled in the parish, and like other German Catholics in the area, they lacked the spiritual ministrations of a priest. These nuns, who had gone from Covington, Kentucky, to New Orleans in 1869, had moved their convent to Covington, Louisiana, in 1873 in order to establish an academy there. Wimmer wrote Abbot Utto Lang of Metten that when he learned of the sisters' plight and their urgent need for a priest, he had immediately sent Father Bernardine to assist them.[24] Requests from Archbishop Francis Norbert Blanchet of Oregon City as well as from bishops of certain "Yankee states" had to go unfilled, however, because by now available missionary-priests at St. Vincent were scarce.

At the end of April 1878 Abbot Boniface assigned the recently ordained Father Willibald Baumgartner to the Richmond priory. Accompanying the young priest to his new assignment, Wimmer took the opportunity to visit his southern missions yet again. From the priory in Richmond he traveled to the community of Maryhelp in North Carolina where he found conditions slightly improved, though enrollment in the college was less than he had hoped. From there he went to Georgia with Father Melchior Reichert, a twenty-six-year-old Bavarian from St. Vincent whom he assigned to the Skidaway community. In Savannah Wimmer and Father Oswald Moosmüller met with Bishop Gross and accepted the bishop's offer to establish a parish for African-American Catholics in the see city. The abbot named Reichert superior of the monastery and school on Skidaway Island and assigned Father Oswald the task of organizing Sacred Heart Parish in Savannah. Then the abbot journeyed by boat to New Orleans to inspect the missions in St. Tammany Parish that the monastery of St. Vincent had recently acquired. Spending ten days in Louisiana, he next traveled to Alabama and the small colony of St. Florian. While in Alabama, he accepted the offer of Bishop John Quinlan of Mobile to take over mission stations in eight northern Alabama counties. From St. Florian the abbot went to Covington, Kentucky, to inspect the vineyard and priory of Monte Cassino, and four weeks after setting out on the journey he arrived back at St. Vincent. Despite slow progress in some cases, he said, growth in the newest foundations of St. Vincent was steady. Maryhelp in North Carolina was having the most difficulty, but in spite of the problems he encountered the abbot was convinced that "the South is becoming a very productive field for us."[25]

Soon after his return to the abbey from his extended trip to the southern missions, Abbot Boniface began preparations for the sixth general chapter of the American Cassinese Congregation. The meeting began on the morning of August 20, 1878, with a pontifical mass celebrated by the abbot-president. Fifteen monks were in attendance: the three American Cassinese abbots, their communities' delegates, and the nine priors of the congregation's dependent priories. The first order of business was to study the acts and decrees of previous general chapters. Additions and modifications were made to the body of existing legislation that dealt primarily with discipline and observance in the various monasteries of the congregation. Next the capitulars discussed current problems. They decreed that secular priests who entered the congregational novitiate at St. Vincent were not to be assigned to the missions during their novitiate except under rare and urgent circumstances. The capitulars also approved the practice of receiving penitent diocesan priests sent to the monasteries of the congregation by their bishops.

The most important matter of business at the sixth general chapter, however, was the question of canonical recognition for the Irish priory of St. Malachy in Creston, Iowa. The community, established in 1874, had been incorporated by an act of the Iowa legislature in 1876 and continued to serve the pastoral needs of Irish Catholics in and around Creston. Though St. Malachy's had not experienced the rapid growth many expected of it, Prior Eugene Phelan asked the general chapter to sanction the canonical erection of the community as an independent priory because he and his confreres believed that this "would materially assist the advancement of our Community and give permanency to our undertaking."[26]

The monks at St. Malachy's were making a bid to achieve the greatest possible measure of independence for their English-speaking community. They hoped that freedom from the control of Wimmer and other Bavarian officials of the American Cassinese Congregation would attract non-German candidates who could not identify with and assimilate the German traditions of the American branch of the order. Abbot Boniface had expressed his willingness to support the Irish undertaking, but when the question of canonical status arose, his response was to offer only a degree of independence to the community. As with the earlier foundations in Minnesota and Kansas, Wimmer wanted to grant the Creston priory merely semi-independent status until the future of the community was assured. Such status would mean that the monks assigned there would continue to be bound by the vow of stability to their original communities and that the abbot-president would exercise ultimate authority over the priory's temporal and spiritual affairs, retaining even the right to appoint and replace its superior. His reluctance to grant full independence to the community was the result of his doubts about its ability to develop and prosper in the same degree and as quickly as others believed it would.[27] At the general chapter Prior Eugene and a number of the delegates, including the chapter's secretary, Father James Zilliox, opposed Wimmer's plan. They called instead for the full independence of the Irish priory. While he argued against their proposal, Wimmer agreed to submit the question to Rome and allow the Holy See to decide. So with the matter of the status of St. Malachy's Priory left in abeyance, the sixth general chapter closed on August 23, 1878.[28] When the delegates dispersed, Wimmer sent the chapter's recommendations to the Sacred Congregation for the Propagation of the Faith, but he also wrote a strong defense of his own position and asked that his recommendations, and not those of the general chapter, be implemented.

Not long afterward Father James Zilliox drafted a letter to Abbot Angelo Pescetelli, still the American Cassinese Benedictines' procurator in Rome, and urged that the Irish priory in Iowa be given full canonical independence. Zilliox said that it was the opinion of most delegates to the general chapter that Wimmer's proposal to grant only semi-independent status to St. Malachy's Priory should be overruled, that indeed Bishop John Hennessey of Dubuque wanted the priory to be granted full independence, and that the monks of St. Malachy's themselves desired it. He asked Pescetelli, therefore, to support the opinion of the majority rather than that of Wimmer. To the abbot's dismay, the Sacred Congregation for the Propagation of the Faith, after reviewing the case, decided in favor of the dissidents and granted St. Malachy's full canonical status. Wimmer was surprised and disappointed by this decision, though he said he would implement it as instructed. He let it be known, however, that he considered the decision of Propaganda a serious mistake and predicted that the Creston house

Abbot James Zilliox (1849–1890). A native of Newark, New Jersey,
Zilliox was the first American-born Benedictine abbot in the
United States. He served as abbot of St. Mary's Abbey,
Newark, from 1885 to 1886. (ASVA)

would not prosper without strong control from St. Vincent. With the
suppression of the house after his death the abbot's prediction proved
in the end unhappily accurate.[29]

Shortly after the general chapter Abbot Boniface left St. Vincent
for Chicago to visit the monks of St. Joseph's Priory. Prior Giles
(Aegidius) Christoph administered the large German parish there
with the assistance of three priests and two lay brothers from St. Vincent. Christoph, formerly prior both at St. Vincent and at St. Benedict's, Kansas, had overseen the final phases of construction of the impressive neogothic church that replaced the church destroyed by the

fire of 1871. The parish in Chicago had a congregation of four thousand and operated a parochial school of five hundred pupils taught by the Benedictine sisters. Wimmer was on hand for the solemn dedication of the new church, and after a three-week visit with the monks of St. Joseph's Priory, he traveled south to Kentucky where he visited the monks of Monte Cassino Priory in Covington and attempted to resolve the financial problems that had arisen on account of the purchase of the vineyard there. His nephew, Father Luke Wimmer, was prior in Covington and oversaw the operation of the farm with eleven lay brothers. In the city of Covington Father Suitbert Demarteau, a forty-three-year-old native of Prussia, served as pastor of St. Joseph Parish, with two thousand parishioners, and was assisted by two priests and a community of Benedictine sisters who taught four hundred pupils in the parochial school. Returning to St. Vincent in the middle of November, the abbot initiated construction of a barn near the monastery. He was quite proud of this newest addition to the abbey. It would be, he said, "the largest barn in the country." But its cost, and that of several other newly constructed buildings at the Pennsylvania monastery had "emptied my treasury," and Wimmer wondered if the abbot of Metten could possibly spare some mass stipends.[30]

Even as growth and expansion presaged a bright future for the enterprise of the American Benedictines, discontent among certain members of the community at St. Vincent started to plague Abbot Boniface yet again. The monastic reforms in Europe, particularly those at Beuron, had once more begun to exert a strong influence on some of the monks at St. Vincent. Like many of the St. Vincent "reformers" who preceded them, these monks were young, pious, idealistic, and generally well educated. Like those who came before them, they felt deep dissatisfaction with Wimmer's vision of Benedictine life and its active missionary role in the American Church. They regarded the abbey's external apostolates as distractions from rather than essential elements of the Benedictine vocation, and they called for significant changes in the monastic regimen of the community. They opposed what they regarded as the abbot's obsession with the order's growth and expansion, his eagerness to take on virtually every mission offered him by the American bishops, his willingness to accept as members of the community almost anyone who expressed an interest to join, and especially his policy of assigning young monks, hardly

Scholastics at Saint Vincent in 1880 with their direcctor, Father William Mayer
(1856–1904). (ASVA)

weaned from the novitiate, to new and distant missions where they
had, in the reformers' opinion, little opportunity to mature and grow
in the monastic life. These young monks wanted a more contemplative life at St. Vincent, with greater emphasis on liturgical ceremony,
spiritual development, and theological study.

The first signs of this latest reform movement at St. Vincent occurred in 1878 when the director of music at the abbey, Father Ignatius Treug, whom Wimmer had sent to Beuron and other European abbeys to study the new methods of Gregorian chant being developed there, urged the abbot to replace the traditional Bavarian
liturgical forms at St. Vincent with the ancient plain chant being revived in many European monasteries. Wimmer, always disposed to
listen to new ideas that might contribute to the spiritual and monastic development of the community, agreed and gave Father Ignatius
leave to introduce at St. Vincent the Beuronese methods of celebrat-

ing the liturgy. Opposition from other members of the community, however, quickly developed. Many of the older monks at the abbey were entirely satisfied with the traditional Bavarian music and liturgical practices they had known since entering the monastery, and they succeeded in frustrating Treug's efforts to introduce the Beuronese liturgy at St. Vincent. Deeply disappointed by his failure, Treug petitioned the Holy See through Wimmer to have his vows transferred to the Beuronese Congregation and soon afterward left St. Vincent.[31] Several months later Wimmer wrote Abbot Placidus Wolter of the Beuronese Abbey of Maredsous:

Ignatius did not want anything but hymns, mostly polyphonic ones. Perhaps you remember what I wrote you about Gregorian chant. In my opinion Gregorian chant belongs in the choir and in the conventual mass, but not in parish masses or in pontifical masses, except when there is no music. However, nothing helped. We no longer have patterned mass. I let him have his way, but this exclusiveness created much opposition by other modern music teachers, whom we can not banish on account of the college. There always was some friction until Fr. Ignatius left. I was happy to give him travel money and wished him the best. Now we have as much singing as before, but also have other music as before.[32]

Despite the departure of Father Ignatius, the reform movement gained momentum at St. Vincent. In June 1879, just before the annual monastic retreat, Abbot Boniface uncovered what he described as a plot by two of his most trusted monks who had encouraged a group of young clerics to seek a more contemplative life in stricter monastic communities. He wrote Abbot Innocent Wolf in Kansas that "a number of clerics were ready to leave the monastery on account of the low state of religious discipline and go to the Trappists or Beuron. And now it develops that the prior and master of novices are part of the plan, the latter also ready to go along with them. I found this out through the Abbot of Gethsemani." Wimmer said that the whole affair seemed to have been perpetrated by Father James Zilliox, the thirty-year-old novice master whom Wimmer had earlier sent to Rome, Austria, and Bavaria for theological and monastic studies. But Prior Andrew Hintenach, who had given his blessing to the clerics' plans, was also a central figure in the plot. For that reason, Wimmer said, both men would have to be replaced: "In the face of all these things I am not making any outcries, still less am I harboring any hostility. But in spite of an easy-going temperament, it is not a small penance. This is now the third instance of treachery at the hands of friends . . . treachery to me and to the monastery of St. Vincent under the pretext of piety and zeal."[33]

Several days later, without mentioning that he had become aware of what was happening, Abbot Boniface sent Father James to St. Mary's Priory, Newark, and a week after his departure wrote him a paternal letter wishing him well in his new assignment. Wimmer began his letter by informing Zilliox that he had recently become aware that opposition among several monks of Maryhelp Priory in North Carolina had arisen against Prior Herman Wolfe, and that the opposition looked very much like a conspiracy "with reasons that are no reasons and accusations containing no quick at all." Wimmer said that he "gave therefore to the young fellow, in whose mouth such a petition sounded particularly wrong, a good scolding, and to Father Stephen, who timidly had seconded it in a letter of his own, a warning, and since that time I have heard nothing more of it. Of course I told nothing of it to Father Herman, in order to save him the cruel disappointment of finding two enemies and supplanters in the very confrères he supposed to be his sincere friends." The parallel between the situation in North Carolina and the one in Pennsylvania was hard to miss. Zilliox had written Wimmer to inquire about the trouble in North Carolina, and the abbot's reply was a masterful double entendre. Everything he said about the disloyalty of the monks in North Carolina applied to Zilliox's own disloyalty to Wimmer. But in case Father James missed the point, Wimmer informed him that before the retreat recently conducted at St. Vincent began "I got a letter from Gethsemani, notifying me that a cleric had made application there, with the remark that others would go to Europe. On inquiry I found out, that my good P. Magister [novice master] himself wanted to be of the party." Abbot Boniface said that he had "cooled off" in the meantime, but, continuing to refer to Zilliox in the third person, he said "I thought it best for him and for me to remove the *occasio proxima,* considering at the same time that he had really too much to do. . . . Therefore I accept your resignation as Master of Novices, so that you can breathe easier."[34]

The fortuitous discovery of the plot effectively ended active opposition to Wimmer's regime for the time being. The abbot replaced Zilliox as novice master with Father Sebastian Arnold but decided to permit Father Andrew Hintenach to remain as prior. The principal reason for Wimmer's decision to retain Hintenach was that Father Andrew had had experience in the job for nearly four years, and such experience would be valuable, if not essential, during Wimmer's forthcoming trip to Europe. A practical and experienced hand would be needed to direct the community at St. Vincent during the abbot's absence.

Abbot Boniface's trip to Europe was planned to coincide with the celebration of the fourteen-hundredth anniversary of the birth of St. Benedict. As early as 1876 Wimmer had sent a circular letter to all the Benedictine abbots of the world inviting them to participate in a solemn celebration of the anniversary at the Abbey of Monte-cassino.[35] Ever since 1869, when he attended the First Vatican Council and met many of the Benedictine leaders of Europe, Wimmer had entertained the hope of bringing together the world's Benedictine monasteries into a federated union in which they could share experiences and support each other's monastic observance and apostolic work through regular dialogue and the exchange of ideas. The publication of the *Album Benedictinum* at St. Vincent in 1869, a work that gathered into one place detailed information about Benedictine monasteries throughout the world, was the first step Wimmer had taken toward achieving this goal, and though he met with indifference and even resistance on the part of some European abbots, who jealously guarded their traditional independence, his suggestion that an international meeting and celebration take place at Montecassino in 1880, and that to honor St. Benedict the abbots of Europe and America make a substantial donation to the restoration of the Abbey of Montecassino, which had suffered extensive losses during the Italian wars, earned an enthusiastic response from many monastic leaders. In October 1876 twenty-four Bavarian and Austrian abbots meeting in Salzburg endorsed his proposal, and when he learned of the Salzburg meeting Wimmer again wrote to all the abbots urging their universal cooperation.[36] Upon receiving Wimmer's second letter, Archabbot Nicolas D'Orgemont of Montecassino sent his own circular letter to the abbots of the order in which he said:

The letter which we received from the Right Reverend Boniface Wimmer of St. Vincent Abbey, Pennsylvania, filled us with wonderful joy. His unexpected zeal immediately aroused in us an enthusiasm, as if these proposals had arisen from one mind and were animated by one spirit. Afterwards he informed us of the approval of this plan by the illustrious abbots who attended the consecration of the Most Reverend Albert Eder of Salzburg. We must not wonder that these confreres who are separated from us by a wide ocean bear testimony of such a perfect harmony with us. When the question arises how God is to be honored in his saints, it is well to note that we are not separated from one another by space nor age nor class.

In a formal letter of thanks to the monks of St. Vincent, D'Orgemont wrote: "The generous plan of Abbot Wimmer became for us not an occasion to satisfy our vanity, but rather seemed to us to be a voice from God. It was as if it were a marvelous echo of that Divine call that raised one who was already dead four days to life. Now we want to answer this summons that it may be for us a means of resurrection, and if our confreres help to carry on this work which we have begun, we shall live forever."[37]

Wimmer's idea for an international meeting of Benedictine abbots and a worldwide Benedictine effort to assist Montecassino soon gained the support of other European abbots, including Maurus Wolter of Beuron and John Chrysostom Kreutz of Pannonhalma, Hungary, and in July 1877 Pope Pius IX endorsed it. "Montecassino has always contributed men and means for the upbuilding of the kingdom of God in many lands," the pope said. "It is therefore appropriate that this humble and impoverished monastery should be assisted by them."[38]

In the meantime, as plans for the international celebration and the first-ever gathering of the world's Benedictine abbots proceeded, the monks of St. Vincent began making preparations for a specifically American commemoration of the Benedictine jubilee. That commemoration took place at St. Vincent on April 4–6, 1880, and included the celebration of three masses by Abbot Boniface, Prior Andrew Hintenach, and Bishop John Tuigg of Pittsburgh; the delivery of three anniversary sermons honoring St. Benedict and the American Benedictines by the renowned Redemptorist preacher Father Wilhelm Watrich of Baltimore, by Monsignor Richard Phelan, vicar general of the Diocese of Pittsburgh, and by church historian Father Arnold A. Lambing of Pittsburgh; and dramatic and musical presentations by the students of St. Vincent on each of the three evenings of the *triduum*. In addition, several scholarly publications and artistic works by St. Vincent monks were presented to the guests during the celebration to mark the jubilee: Father Oswald Moosmüller's *Europäer in Amerika vor Columbus,* Father Augustine Schneider's commentary on the Rule of St. Benedict, Father Aurelius McMahon's English translations of the Benedictine Rule and St. Gregory the Great's *Life and Miracles of St. Benedict,* two dramas by Father Agatho Stübinger, Father Bonaventure Ostendarp's 20 x 8 foot oil painting entitled *Benedictines in Heaven and on Earth,* and Brother Cosmas Wolf's votive altar in honor of St. Benedict.[39]

Abbot Boniface departed for Italy ten days after the celebration at St. Vincent. It was his fifth trip to Europe since 1846, and he knew that it was likely to be his last. Together with Abbot Alexius Edelbrock and Subprior Peter Engel of St. John's and Abbot Innocent Wolf of St. Benedict's, he embarked from New York on April 20, 1880, aboard the steamer *Arizona.* Nine days later the *Arizona* docked in Liverpool. From England the American Benedictine leaders went to France, and after a brief stop at the Marian shrine at Lourdes, they left for Italy, arriving at Montecassino on May 12.[40]

The fourteenth centenary celebration at the monastery of St. Benedict began on May 14, and more than fifty Benedictine abbots, bishops, and archbishops from all over the world participated. After three days of liturgical and extraliturgical festivities the abbots gathered for a meeting to discuss business affecting the entire order. Abbot Maurus Wolter of Beuron proposed that Wimmer, as the senior abbot present and the person who had in effect summoned the abbots, chair the meeting. Accepting the honor, Abbot Boniface appointed Abbot Placidus Wolter of Maredsous as secretary. After formally presenting a donation of money to Archabbot Nicolas D'Orgemont of Montecassino, the assembled abbots discussed organizing the institution of oblates, but no practical resolutions were passed because the abbots disagreed on the nature of the institution of oblates. Then the matter of greater unity for the order was proposed. Abbot Maurus Wolter urged that a single unified organization be created for the order and that an abbot-general be given authority over it. The Beuronese and Italian abbots heartily supported the proposal, but most of the other German abbots, the English abbots, and the American Cassinese abbots, with Wimmer as their principal spokesman, opposed such centralization. For them the strength of the order was directly proportionate to the richness and diversity of the various abbeys and congregations, and Wimmer was among the first of those to stand against centralization of the order under a single abbot-general. "Unity," he said, "but not centralization." When a compromise was proposed by the prior of Metten that at least the ceremonials of the various monasteries be brought into harmony, even that was voted down by the majority. But the abbots did agree to pursue a federative unity along the lines of the contemporary congregational organization. To this Wimmer agreed, urging further that the order establish a central house of studies in Rome to which all monasteries could send monks.[41]

The meeting ended on May 21, 1880, and though it succeeded in achieving neither the formation of a federation of Benedictine monasteries nor the establishment of an international Benedictine house of studies in Rome, it did lay the groundwork for the eventual realization of both these objectives before the end of the century. Wimmer's part in the work of bringing the world's Benedictine abbots together for the first time in order to focus on issues of concern to all of them was universally acknowledged. He was recognized not only as the driving force behind the meeting but also as preeminent among the abbots by virtue of his age, his unquestioned achievements in America, and his exceptional contributions to the restoration of Benedictine monasticism in the Church.

From Montecassino Wimmer, accompanied by Abbot Innocent Wolf, went to Rome. In the Eternal City he was unable to gain a private audience with Pope Leo XIII. He "had to be satisfied with a public one because the Holy Father is granting very few private audiences these days." After negotiating for the purchase of the St. Elizabeth's property, which from 1866 to 1870 he had leased and used as the house of studies for the American Cassinese Benedictines in Rome and which he now hoped to revive, Wimmer left Italy for Germany.[42]

Throughout June Wimmer visited monasteries and friends in Austria and Bavaria. He traveled to Salzburg, Regensburg, Metten, and Munich, but most of the old friends he had known before going to America were dead. It was a melancholy homecoming, and a cold he had caught in Montecassino had developed serious complications. On July 1, 1880, the seventy-one-year-old patriarch was admitted to Munich City Hospital with a chest infection that he predicted would be the end of him.[43] Confined to the hospital indefinitely, Wimmer had to postpone his return to America, but two months later, having rallied his strength and renewed his spirit, he departed his Bavarian homeland for the last time. Boarding a ship in Le Havre, France, on August 28, 1880, he arrived in New York eleven days later. He had become quite ill again during the voyage and so he stopped for a short while with the monks of St. Mary's Priory, Newark, to recover. If he were going to die, however, he wanted to die in only one place, and thus he "went on to St. Vincent, and there the misery of illness finally wore out. Since then I am as well as I was before the journey, thank God."[44]

Back at St. Vincent Abbot Boniface turned his attention once again to the missions. The Benedictine work in the South was going well, and in January 1881 he responded to a call for assistance from Bishop Peter Joseph Baltes of Alton, Illinois, by sending Fathers Engelbert Leist and Augustine Schneider, together with two lay brothers, to establish a Benedictine community in southern Illinois. The monks built a church in Wetaug, Illinois, and undertook the pastoral care of Catholics in the Illinois towns of Anna and Cobden, as well as in Doniphan and Poplar Bluff, Missouri.[45]

In January Wimmer also oversaw publication of the second edition of the *Album Benedictinum* which, because he had been able to make personal contact with most of the world's Benedictine abbots at the celebration in Montecassino, was much more complete than the first edition of 1869.[46] Meanwhile, despite the apparent tranquility that existed on account of his successes in the missions, Wimmer discovered that new opposition to his leadership had arisen among his confreres. "My illness last year," he wrote, "and the rumor of its fatal issue has laid bare the hearts of men and allowed me to perceive that most of my confrere priests would have been happy had I failed to return. They were dissatisfied with my regime (and probably are still)." Abbot Boniface said that the opposition existed among young and old, *"boni et mali"*. "Not a few injurious denunciations have been made that were difficult to bear. But I managed to overcome my own hard feelings."[47]

In May the abbot set out on one of those lengthy journeys that had marked his career and that now belied his advanced age. He traveled to the Benedictine missions in Alabama, Kentucky, and Illinois. When he returned to St. Vincent early in June, he wrote Bishop Quinlan of Mobile that he hoped to continue his efforts to strengthen the Alabama missions despite the fact that "I meet with some opposition in my own house if I seem *too much* for the South."[48] The opposition he spoke of continued to weigh heavily on him, and he wrote Abbot Innocent Wolf that the "general dissatisfaction about my regime" was caused by a feeling at St. Vincent "that I do not go [to the community] for advice and that I am not led by the Holy Spirit because I do not pray enough." He admitted that some of these charges may have been true, but he said that he called upon the Holy Spirit "more often than some gentlemen believe. I cheerfully agree that there is much that should be done. . . . But things are not as bad as they are made out to be. The outcries come from naturally-gifted scolds. . . . My undertakings in the South will speak for and justify themselves."[49]

Two months later the seventh general chapter of the American Cassinese Congregation was held at St. Vincent. The superiors and delegates arrived at the end of July, but in lieu of a lengthy meeting, they surprised Wimmer with a celebration in honor of the fiftieth anniversary of his ordination. Abbots Innocent Wolf and Alexius Edelbrock were there, as were most of the priors of the American Cassinese monasteries. The Benedictine bishops of Minnesota and Kansas, Rupert Seidenbusch and Louis Fink, came, as well as the Swiss Benedictine bishop of the Dakotas, Martin Marty. Bishop John Tuigg of Pittsburgh and Abbot Frowin Conrad of Conception Abbey were also present. Abbot Boniface said that he received "so much praise that I have to suffer great humiliations in order to make amends."[50] And he wrote to Archabbot John Chrysostom Kreutz of Pannonhalma, Hungary, that during the celebration "I sat there as if on needles, not knowing whether to laugh or weep. It was too much of a good thing. I was all of a sudden marked as a patriarch, and I had to be told of exploits carried out in the line of duty of which I knew nothing."[51]

But if the celebration lifted his spirits, there remained the gnawing concern that there were monks in his own community whose opposition to him was growing daily. He wrote Abbot Utto Lang of Metten that "some of my professors are not very faithful in attending choir. This is especially the case with the professor of moral theology. He insists that as a professor of theology he has the *privilege of being absent from choir!*" And when confronted with arguments to the contrary, "this moralist quotes canon law at me!"[52]

The professor was Father Maurice Kaeder, the monk whom Wimmer had sent with Father Oswald Moosmüller to the Georgia missions in 1877. Disenchanted with the difficult life of a missionary,

Kaeder had returned to the more comfortable life at St. Vincent. Together with a number of unlikely confederates, including the pious James Zilliox, whom Wimmer had long since forgiven for his part in the plot to lead some of the younger members of the community to Gethsemani and Beuron and who had since been appointed claustral prior at St. Vincent, Kaeder was fomenting rebellion within the monastic ranks. But Abbot Boniface was oblivious to the extent of the opposition sparked by Kaeder. Not realizing that it would soon erupt into full-scale revolt, he censured those monks who were consistently absent from choir, ordered all privileges (including the daily mug of beer) taken from them, and turned his attention to the southern missions once again, satisfied that the "evil spirit" had been driven from the abbey. In January 1882 he wrote his nephew, Father Luke Wimmer, O.S.B., prior of the monastery of Monte Cassino in Kentucky, that "during the last two years, especially since my return from Europe, I have suffered very much. Perhaps it was a trial, perhaps even a castigation. Anyhow, I was victorious."[53]

But the abbot had spoken too soon.

In March Wimmer wrote Abbot Utto that the squabble about choir attendance had been squelched. "Even the professor surrendered and since then is going to choir in the early morning and all the time unless detained by duties. . . . The others will follow him and will also find time to say holy mass."[54] But Kaeder was merely biding his time. Shortly after the general chapter in August he had convinced Prior James Zilliox that Wimmer's administration was corrupting the souls of the most dedicated monks in the community. Zilliox was an intelligent and pious man who commanded much respect among the members of the community, but he was exceedingly scrupulous. By playing on this scrupulosity—whether out of malice, bitterness, or a sincere desire to improve the quality of spiritual life at St. Vincent—Kaeder managed to enlist him in a plot to overthrow Abbot Boniface. The plan clearly was to force Wimmer's resignation and elect a superior in his place—possibly Zilliox himself—who could be more easily manipulated by Kaeder and his allies.

There were no more unlikely companions in rebellion than Father Maurice and Father James. Kaeder, the portly, pompous, self-willed cleric who had quoted canon law to support his own negligence in monastic duties, and Zilliox, the gaunt, ascetical, humble monk who sought a more contemplative life than the one offered at St. Vincent, were men cut from two different patterns. Father James was well loved among all manner of men in the community and commanded the respect and admiration of Wimmer himself. Father Maurice was a bone of contention, an arrogant man who did not make friends easily. But when Kaeder designed the plot to overthrow the abbot, it was to Zilliox he turned for support. He used the prior's office as well as Father James's naive idealism to his own advantage. He played upon Zilliox's frustration with the active life of the American Cassinese monks, when he himself thought the monastic regimen at St. Vincent was too strict, and he convinced the gullible prior to join him in his insurrection against Abbot Boniface. In August 1881 the two men composed a letter of protest to Rome.

In March of the following year Wimmer received a startling communiqué from Cardinal Giovanni Simeoni, prefect of the Sacred Congregation for the Propagation of the Faith. Simeoni informed him that the Propaganda had received a document from two monks of St. Vincent that raised serious questions about monastic observance in the abbey and even the moral behavior of the members of the community.

It is reported that your monks do not observe any law of enclosure, that they go out and wander here and there, that they talk and feast with women outside the cloister, that sometimes they go to the city to visit the theater, that they receive women within the enclosure as well as in the dormitories of the abbey. And so it happens that monks are considered most scandalous, ensnared in shameful habits, pursuing earthly, not heavenly things.[55]

The letter struck Wimmer like a lightning bolt. The seventy-three-year-old abbot reeled back from the blow in shock and dismay and wrote Abbot Innocent Wolf of Kansas: "Father Maurice and Father Prior have brought accusations against me at the Vatican to the pope. They have made charges for a hearing. The affair will probably end with my resignation. They are hounding me to death. Of course I will give account of my actions. But it will be a sorry story for St. Vincent and for the entire congregation on account of the way in which we have been portrayed."[56] Wimmer also wrote to Abbot Alexius Edelbrock telling him of the affair and saying that he and Abbot Innocent might have to come as visitators to St. Vincent in order to make an official report to the Holy See.[57]

Edelbrock replied that "certainly Father James Zilliox as well as Father Maurice Kaeder will be considered very scandalous because of their lie against their monastery and their abbot, burdened with years and merits as he is."[58] But Wimmer answered that "Father James is an innocent sheep! Father Maurice, however, is a haughty ruffian. He is a bitter enemy of mine" on account of assignments the abbot had given him, such as the appointment to the Georgia mission, that did not suit his pleasure.[59] Abbot Boniface's initial reaction to the news of the protest registered in Rome had been a weary resignation to the state of affairs. He said that he was an old man and not well suited for the fight he had now to face. As a younger man he had brooked opposition of this type, sometimes malicious attacks on him and his life's work, and he had entered the frays with confidence and energy. Now, however, he was old and tired of battling his enemies. He thought that perhaps he should resign and let someone else carry on his work.[60]

On the other hand, his resignation under these circumstances would certainly seem like an admission of defeat, proof that what Kaeder and Zilliox had said about the abbey was true. Besides, a bright spot had risen on the horizon. When the letter of protest arrived in Rome, Bishop John Tuigg of Pittsburgh had been at the Holy See on his *ad limina* visit consulting with officials of the Propaganda Fide. Cardinal Simeoni questioned him about the accusations against Wimmer and the abbey, and he responded by denouncing the charges of Kaeder and Zilliox as vicious lies and by giving a glowing report on conditions at St. Vincent and on the probity and judiciousness of Wimmer as abbot. In a spirited defense of Abbot Boniface, Tuigg wrote:

Alone he planted and watered in the United States the Benedictine tree, which now has spread over the whole land. He created St. Vincent Abbey out of nothing. He can be judged by the fruits, and these fruits show a most kind-hearted man of unbounded charity, indefatigable in work, eminent in learning and prudence, wise in temporal as well as in spiritual matters. As I know him well, I cannot be convinced that he should have done or omitted anything through his fault and that he will do or omit anything from which Religion or his subjects should suffer harm. I visit the abbey several times a year for ordinations or other purposes, and I must confess that I never saw anything which would be considered a grave violation of the Rule of religious perfection. On the contrary I was always highly edified by the monastic silence which the monks observe.[61]

In addition to this unexpected support from the bishop of Pittsburgh, Wimmer was gratified to discover that he commanded greater respect and support among the monks of St. Vincent than he had at first realized. Most of the monks did not like Father Maurice at all, and despite the fact that Kaeder had enlisted the well-loved prior in order to sidestep the personality conflicts he had with his confreres, the monks of St. Vincent rallied around the abbot. Father Leo Haid, rector of the major seminary at St. Vincent, expressed the sentiments of many of his fellow monks when he wrote:

Our discipline is not only very lax, but in a word we have no monastic discipline. We go to theaters, loaf around the country *ad libitum,* eat and drink whatever and whenever we please, take women into our cells, etc. Hang it! The recital alone is enough to make St. Hermenegild lose his patience. . . . We are not all saints, but after all we try to be Benedictines. I have been here for nearly 21 years and only once did I see a woman in the monastery— accidentally having lost her way. And good Father Charley of happy memory nearly threw the poor thing down the stairs.

Father Leo said that only malice "and a good dose of crankiness" could have caused Kaeder to pen such accusations. He was sorry that Abbot Boniface's "declining years should be embittered by such ingratitude. He need not fear. His fathers love him and will gladly defend him against every attack. Had he given us our way, we would have smoked the coon out and given him a chance to face all his slandered brethren in the Chapter."[62]

So Abbot Boniface prepared to engage the foe. "The coarsest allegations," he wrote, "were characteristically presented by Father Maurice." He forgave both men, however, though he reluctantly admitted that he would have to remove Father James from the office of prior. With less reluctance he dismissed Father Maurice from the seminary faculty and transferred him to a parish assignment away from St. Vincent. In the meantime, after he had "cooled off," he drafted a reply to Rome. "I did not make any recriminations but reported that choir is being faithfully attended—even by Father Maurice."[63]

At the end of April he left St. Vincent for a month's tour of the newest priories and missions. He visited the parishes in Baltimore and Richmond and the missions in North Carolina, Georgia, Alabama, Kentucky, and southern Illinois. When he returned to St. Vincent, he was able to report that the Benedictine work in the South was progressing despite the usual setbacks and frustrations. In the most troublesome place, Maryhelp in North Carolina, where fourteen monks under the new prior, Father Placidus Pilz, worked in the missions and operated a small college of fewer than forty students, the community continued to experience serious problems that included low enrollment in the school, little income from the missions, poor productivity on the farm, and living conditions that disheartened most of the monks assigned there. Some of the monks in Georgia, too, were demoralized. They complained of the terrible heat of the Georgia summers, the unhealthful conditions on Skidaway Island, and their inability to understand and relate to the culture of the blacks they worked with. When Brother Fridolin Stehle wrote a letter to several of the lay brothers at St. Vincent painting a bleak picture of life in the Georgia priory, speaking contemptuously of the blacks, and predicting that the Benedictine mission in Georgia would end in failure, Wimmer intercepted the letter and wrote a searing rebuttal that revealed his attitudes about both monastic obedience and the importance of the Benedictine mission to the freed black slaves in the South.

You did not go to Skidaway to do *your will* (otherwise you would not be a religious with the sacred vow of obedience), but to do *my* will or that of your immediate superior who rules in my name; whereas *I* also may not follow *my own will,* but do command that which I recognize as the will of God, namely, to found an institution for Negroes whereby many Negroes will retain their Catholic faith or be converted, and their immortal souls, bought with the Blood of Christ, will be snatched away from the devil and be won for God.

Perhaps you may think that Skidaway is not the right place for this, or that I do not correctly understand the affair: "many men, many minds." That, however, is not your business because I am the superior, not you. It also should not be Fr. Oswald's or Fr. Melchior's concern, because I, not they, am the superior. The subject may *think* this or that way and may also politely *express* his opinion *to him* if he is asked. But he may not *murmur,* and may not *find fault* in the presence of others, or *grumble* or *incite* them. That deserves punishment because it is strictly forbidden and must be forbidden since it is *revolutionary* and *rebellious,* and in a religious community extremely detrimental, because it is for the other brothers a temptation that leads to disobedience and contempt for their superiors. Some time ago you wrote a letter to the Brothers here which I only recently got to see. This letter was overflowing with arrogance and in it you treated and ran me down as though I were a little boy; as if it were nonsense to convert the Negroes, who are not worth anything, who are full of arrogance, brutish, etc.

That is not language for a Brother to use when speaking of his superior, and besides it is too stupid for me to refute. Even if all were true what you have written, we should make even greater efforts to help these unfortunate Negroes. They are also people and God's children, and Christ has also died for them. Therefore under pain of mortal sin you must love them as you love yourself. That means to pray for them and work for their conversion as much as you can; otherwise you yourself have a black heart, although your face is white, and you are no child of God.

Whether I am attacking the matter in the right way or not, that is not your concern, because I am the boss; you just do what you are told and then it will be all right. And if it does not succeed, our efforts will not have been in vain because God values more the good intention than the result. . . .

But if you brand the place and instead of gathering you destroy, then you will only do harm and hinder the success, instead of supporting it. If you preach contempt and hatred of the Negroes, you are indeed hardly disposed to do any good for them. But you will be severely punished by God for that, both here and in the next world. Therefore, I have asked Rev. Fr. Prior P. Melchior to order you to make at least a five-day retreat, so that you have the time to read the Holy Rule and to think about it, and especially to meditate on Christ's Passion and his love for *all* mankind. In this we must follow Him if we want to be some day in heaven with Him. For this we have a good opportunity especially through our efforts concerning the Negroes. In Dakota we work among the *Indians*. Fr. Paul and five Brothers from St. Meinrad and several sisters from Atchison and Ferdinand are there. We work among the *Negroes* in Skidaway and Savannah and also soon in other places. That is a privilege, a joy and it brings great merit for us. Let us thank God for it![64]

In June the abbot received word from the prefect of the Propaganda Fide that Rome was satisfied with the reports it had received from the bishop of Pittsburgh and the American Cassinese abbots, and that having found no substance to them the Holy See would take no further action as a result of the denunciations of Fathers James and Maurice.[65] The affair had ended less with a bang than with a whimper. The abbot immediately transferred Father Maurice Kaeder to a parish in Crown Point, Indiana, and assigned Father James Zilliox as professor of moral theology to the seminary at St. Vincent. He wrote of his former prior: "It is he who brought all this trouble into our house with his show and praising of Beuron and his deprecation of St. Vincent. . . . There is no doubt that he and Maurice wanted to effect my deposition. . . . The only difference between the two is that Maurice was guided by hate and revenge because I transferred him (unjustly, he thought) from Covington. James, however, was guided by a sincere conviction that I am not the man for this place." Wimmer went on to say that the experiences of the past year had profoundly shaken him.

> I have been living under the delusion that I was, even if not loved, at least tolerated by my people and that in general they were satisfied by my government. Therefore I was surprised when Father James revealed to me with praiseworthy sincerity and honesty that the very opposite is the case, and when the attack was made openly, though I was prepared, the dosage was still very strong. . . . But I remain abbot for the time being—until I am deposed or resign.[66]

Abbot Boniface named Father Michael Hofmayer as prior to replace Zilliox. In October he traveled to St. John's Abbey, Minnesota, where he helped dedicate the new abbey church. He visited the priories in Chicago; in Creston, Iowa; in Wetaug, Illinois; and in Covington, Kentucky, before returning home. At St. Vincent once again he received a request from Bishop Winand Michael Wigger of Newark to take over Seton Hall College in South Orange, New Jersey, but he declined the offer, writing that he could not spare any men. The missions in the South were draining St. Vincent of its professors.[67]

On November 29, 1882, Abbot Boniface received word that Father Peter Henry Lemke, the missionary who had persuaded him to come to the diocese of Pittsburgh thirty-seven years earlier, had died at the priory in Carrolltown. The aging abbot attended the funeral and several days later wrote Abbot Utto Lang of Metten that "the year 1882 was in many ways most fruitful for me in trials. . . . For seven years a very bad feeling was predominant in our community on account of a certain courtship with the customs of Beuron. I tolerated it too long and tried to settle it peacefully. But it was in vain. Eventually the situation demanded that I act decisively, which I did. And now everything is peaceful once again."[68]

With the Kaeder-Zilliox affair safely behind him, Abbot Boniface turned once again to the work that would occupy his final years. The southern missions were gradually growing in strength, and the community in Newark, established in 1857, had recently built a new priory and after twenty-five years of development was long overdue for independence. In addition, the priory in Chicago was waxing strong and more monks had been sent to Wetaug in southern Illinois. Writing to Abbot Alexius Edelbrock, Abbot Boniface said that he would like to establish four more abbeys before he died: "One in the East: Newark, Elizabeth, Wilmington; one in the West: Chicago, Wetaug; one in the Southeast: Baltimore, Richmond, North Carolina; one in the South: Alabama; keeping for St. Vincent Carrolltown, St. Marys, Erie, Allegheny (Pittsburgh), Covington, and the Negro Mission [in Georgia]. Perhaps St. Marys and Erie might afterwards constitute an abbey too."[69]

In April 1883 Wimmer went to Newark to visit the monks of St. Mary's Priory and to speak with Bishop Wigger about his plan to make the priory an abbey. From Newark he went on to Wilmington, Delaware, Baltimore, Richmond, Maryhelp Priory in North Carolina, and then to Savannah. The purpose of this latest trip to the South was to review conditions in the Benedictine foundations there and to determine which dependencies of St. Vincent he would transfer to the new abbey he hoped to establish in North Carolina. When he returned to St. Vincent he wrote Abbot Innocent Wolf that he had firmly decided to make the Newark priory an abbey with dependencies in Elizabeth, New Jersey, and Wilmington, Delaware. He said he also planned to do the same for Maryhelp Priory in North Carolina with the missions in Richmond, Savannah, and Skidaway Island, Georgia, as dependencies. "In furtherance of this project St. Vincent, of course, will suffer some losses. . . . But the order will reap a great harvest."[70]

In the months that followed his inspection tour, Abbot Boniface wrote that "my chief occupation of thought and concern is for the new establishments in the South," but he continued to complain of the "antipathy" many of the monks at St. Vincent had for the missions in the southern states. "This makes it dreary work and difficult to make progress in North Carolina." With regard to his health, Wimmer said that things were "going downhill." "Soon there will be no place further to go. But then, I am cheerful in the Lord, and on the whole am still quite well for my age."[71]

In December Abbot Boniface celebrated yet another anniversary. Fifty years had passed since he had made his profession as a Benedictine monk in the Priory of St. Michael's, Metten, and his confreres in

America conspired once more to celebrate his jubilee. Before he got wind of the plans, invitations had gone out all over the United States. He tried to have the celebration cancelled, but Abbot Innocent Wolf wrote him from Kansas:

We must celebrate this jubilee, and you must not be a kill-joy. In this way it is proper that we punish those few critics. We owe you and your work such an honor. You suffered so much since your jubilee two years ago that God is giving you as a reward the joy of celebrating also the golden jubilee of your profession. I cannot bring you any presents, but offer you the unanimous joy of all members of our community that you will be honored, to undo the calumnies which were spread against you and your community.[72]

In the end, the abbot acquiesced to the celebration, and on December 29 several hundred guests descended on the abbey. Bishops Joseph Rademacher of Nashville, John Ambrose Watterson of Columbus, James O'Connor of Omaha, and Rupert Seidenbusch of Northern Minnesota, together with Abbots Alexius Edelbrock of St. John's, Innocent Wolf of St. Benedict's, and the two Swiss American abbots, Fintan Mundwiler of St. Meinrad's, and Frowin Conrad of Conception, were there. Because he was ill, Bishop John Tuigg of Pittsburgh was unable to attend, but his vicar general, Monsignor Richard Phelan, represented him. Wimmer wrote that representatives from the Franciscans, Capuchins, Carmelites, and Redemptorists were also present, as well as fifty-six pastors from the secular clergy who had received their education at St. Vincent.[73] And sisters from the Benedictine convents in Erie and St. Marys also came. The celebration proved to be a great boost to Abbot Boniface's spirits, and he felt especially uplifted by the opportunity to renew his monastic vows, using the same formula he had used fifty years earlier at Metten, before the hundreds of friends and confreres who had gathered in the abbey church. Not long afterward he received a telegram of congratulations from the Holy See informing him that he had been given the title "archabbot" and granted the privilege of wearing the *cappa magna*. In reply to the Benedictine sisters in Erie, who had sent him greetings and congratulations upon his jubilee, he wrote that "all this is very nice and well-meant. But it does not help me get to heaven, and I could easily get a few years in purgatory for it. I did not know whether to laugh or to weep, so I did neither. I just let them do with me what they wanted to do. Now I want to start all over again trying to be a good monk."[74]

Archabbot Boniface had delayed petitioning Rome for the elevation of the priories in New Jersey and North Carolina to abbatial rank until he had resolved the financial problems associated with the separation of the two communities from the motherhouse. He also encountered the problem that many of the monks at St. Vincent did not relish the idea of establishing two more abbeys at one blow because they would drain the motherhouse in Pennsylvania of much-needed monk-professors. He spent the first six months of 1884 lobbying the community for support of his plan, and in July, after obtaining the consent of the monastic chapter, he finally sent the petition to Rome. In an accompanying letter to Cardinal Simeoni of the Propaganda Fide Wimmer's tone was apologetic.

At first sight it may appear that I am asking for too much—petitioning for two abbeys at once. And there may be some doubt concerning the question whether or not it is premature, especially with regard to the second abbey proposed for North Carolina. However, I do not think I am wrong in my belief that there is danger in delay rather than in haste. Overmuch caution is usually harmful in undertakings for the glory of God and the progress of religion. At the time when St. Vincent itself was being founded, the excessive timidity of some people turned out to be very detrimental and sometimes almost nullified all our earnest efforts. Now however there is no denying that it is close to being the largest monastery in the whole order. The college it operates is like a small Propaganda in which native Americans, Irish, Germans, Bohemians, and Poles are educated for the clerical state and without charge. This was not due to any merit, skill, or prudence on my part, but was the result rather of making good use of the opportunities which America more than any other land had to offer. To have neglected them would have been sheer stupidity, indolence of the worst kind, or utter indifference. It will be the same also with the new abbeys. . . .

Not long hence it will be necessary to erect two more abbeys: one in the province of Alabama in the diocese of Mobile, the other in Chicago, Illinois. After these things have been taken care of, a more normal state of affairs than is now possible should find its way into the monastery of St. Vincent.[75]

In October Archabbot Boniface wrote Abbot Benedict Braunmüller of Metten, who had recently succeeded Abbot Utto Lang, that he had traveled to St. Meinrad's Abbey, Indiana, in September to help celebrate the silver jubilee of Abbot Fintan Mundwiler's ordination.

Accompanied by his secretary, Father Sebastian Arnold, subprior at St. Vincent, Wimmer had taken the opportunity to visit his monks at the priory of Monte Cassino in Kentucky, the mission at Wetaug in southern Illinois, and the priory of St. Joseph in Chicago. He reported that he arrived back at St. Vincent "fresh and in good health."[76] In November he was on the road again, this time to Baltimore where he took up residence with his monks at Fourteen Holy Martyrs' Parish and attended the Third Plenary Council of Baltimore. The archabbot was warmly received by the American bishops at the council, who gave him special recognition and commendation for his work in the missions and with penitent priests who were periodically sent to St. Vincent and the other monasteries of the American Cassinese Congregation.[77] The council lasted four weeks and was "very tiresome, especially for participants of advanced age." Afterward Wimmer returned to St. Vincent where Abbots Alexius Edelbrock and Innocent Wolf conducted the triennial visitation prescribed by the congregation's constitution. The visitation was followed by the eighth general chapter of the American Cassinese Congregation, held at St. Vincent in November.[78]

Even for a young man Wimmer's schedule and activities in 1884 would have been exhausting, but the seventy-six-year-old archabbot almost forgot his bodily weariness and infirmities when on his birthday, January 14, 1885, he received the apostolic briefs from Rome, dated December 1884, raising the communities in New Jersey and North Carolina to abbatial rank.[79] Four days later he joyfully wrote to Abbot Alexius in Minnesota:

The creation of two new abbeys in our congregation falls yet in 1884. St. John's Abbey was erected in 1866, Atchison in 1876, St. Vincent in 1855—so that always about 10-year intervals lie between. I hope it will not take ten years until in Illinois and Alabama two others can be erected. . . . Meanwhile St. John's will grow strong enough to commence bringing forth daughters in the Northwest too, and Atchison in the Southwest.[80]

The briefs authorized the monks of St. Vincent to elect abbots for New Jersey and North Carolina from among their own ranks, and on February 11, 1885, Wimmer assembled the community in the abbey church for the elections. One hundred and fifteen priests and subdeacons were entitled to vote, but not all were able to attend. Nine of the absent monks who named proxies did not follow the prescribed procedures and their votes were therefore excluded. Consequently one hundred and six votes were to be cast, of which fifty-four were required to constitute the absolute majority necessary to elect an abbot. Prior Michael Hofmayer celebrated a solemn high mass *coram abbate* at eight o'clock in the morning, and afterward the voting began. Before the first ballot was cast, however, Father Alphonse Heimler, former president of St. Vincent College who for many years had ambitions of his own, "arose and declared the whole proceedings nonsense and unreasonable." Why should the whole clerical community of St. Vincent be allowed to vote for two abbots under whom only a few monks would serve, he asked. It would make far greater sense to select permanent communities for New Jersey and North Carolina and then have these communities elect their own abbots. Wimmer answered that the procedure had been established not by himself but by the Holy See. "With that, Father Alphonse put his protest in writing, placed it on the table, and left in a fury. No one followed him."

As soon as this disturbance had ended, the monks elected three tellers to manage the proceedings. Since it was the oldest of the two communities, St. Mary's Abbey, Newark, was the first to be considered. The election took two ballots, and on the second turn Father James Zilliox, former prior of St. Vincent and sometime opponent of Wimmer, received sixty-two votes, six more than were needed to constitute a majority. The well-loved Zilliox "was applauded with much hand-clapping," and the election of an abbot for St. Mary's Abbey, Newark, was declared at an end. The monks adjourned for divine office and lunch, and at two o'clock in the afternoon they returned to the abbey church to elect an abbot for North Carolina.

On the first ballot of the election for North Carolina Father Oswald Moosmüller, pastor of Sacred Heart Church, Savannah, Georgia, received one more than the required fifty-four votes, and Archabbot Boniface declared him the first abbot of Maryhelp Abbey. There was tumultuous applause. "Everything went in the best of order," Wimmer wrote; "everyone was happy." Since Moosmüller was not present for the voting, news of the election was telegraphed to him via Bishop William Gross of Savannah. Wimmer then dismissed the monks, many of whom departed that afternoon for their various priories. Years later Abbot Leo Haid told a story that revealed something of the high spirits and optimistic outlook for the future of the order in America that many of the monks felt after the election of Zilliox and Moosmüller. As some of the fathers were walking to Latrobe after the election to take the evening train, Haid said, "they met two neighbors, who never were very friendly to St. Vincent and its activities. As they passed them, one of them remarked rather loudly to the other: 'God be praised, the priest factory is breaking up.' However one of the Fathers in a happy frame of mind quickly retorted: 'By no means. We are only swarming.'"[81]

Like all his monks, the archabbot was pleased. Two of his most talented and dedicated men had been chosen for the abbatial dignity. Zilliox, who had been dissatisfied with the way things were run at St. Vincent, now had an opportunity to order a community in his own fashion and according to his own vision. Perhaps he would even discover that being abbot over a monastery was more difficult than he had imagined. And Moosmüller, who had confounded his superior's plans by pushing for the election of Innocent Wolf as first abbot of Kansas, now had the honor and dignity of the abbatial office that Wimmer had always believed he deserved. The abbot had reason to be pleased.

Things weren't what they appeared to be, however. Later on in the evening of the elections, after many of the monks had left the abbey and begun their journeys home, Archabbot Boniface was handed a telegram on his way to compline. He read the message, "became very angry," grew sick with "terrible catarrh and with a sore neck and coughing," and was unable to continue on to the choir. The telegram was from Father Oswald in Savannah and stated briefly and simply: "Thank you for the honor, but I cannot accept." Wimmer was furious. It was as if his chosen disciple, the one in whom he had put so much trust and hope, had defied him. He immediately wrote Moosmüller a "well-deserved letter bitterly complaining that he should have known better. If he was so positively unwilling to accept the election, he should have let us know beforehand. The election was a great expense for many who had to travel some distance, and it was trouble upon trouble for me."[82]

But despite the archabbot's pleas that he reconsider, Moosmüller continued to refuse the abbacy. So on March 14, 1885, Wimmer petitioned the Holy See to confirm the election of James Zilliox and to permit the monks of St. Vincent to hold another election for an abbot in North Carolina. Writing to Abbot Bernard Smith, O.S.B., in Rome, he asked for support in his petition to permit a small group of ten monks, who would transfer their vows to the abbey in North Carolina, to elect the abbot, since another election of the same size as the previous one would cause burdens and incur expenses that both the archabbot and the monks of St. Vincent preferred to avoid.[83]

On June 10 confirmation of the election of Zilliox and permission for another election of a North Carolina abbot in the manner that Wimmer had suggested arrived from the Propaganda Fide. A month later the archabbot assembled those monks who would form the nucleus of Maryhelp Abbey, and on July 14, 1885, the abbatial election was held. On the first ballot Father Leo Haid, rector of the seminary at St. Vincent, was unanimously elected abbot of the community in North Carolina.[84] The election of the abbots of New Jersey and North Carolina marked a new phase in the history of the Benedictine Order in the United States. Haid, a native of Westmoreland County, Pennsylvania, and Zilliox, a native of Newark, were both American-born, and their election signified that Wimmer's hopes of creating an American branch of the order had reached fulfillment. Archabbot Boniface wrote that the elections had given him "quite enough work this year, and I'm very glad to see the end of them."[85]

Two new abbeys had been erected, and thus in a single stroke the number of abbeys in the American Cassinese Congregation was brought to five. But Archabbot Boniface still did not consider his life's work finished. He wanted to see at least two more abbeys spring from the fertile soil of America before he died, and the communities in Chicago and Alabama were his choices for the honor. By now, however, his health was failing, and that, together with the growing antimission sentiment at St. Vincent, militated against his ever achieving that goal. He wrote that he had little energy any more, and concern for his foundations was often the only thing that kept him going. "It would do no harm," he said

if I live a few more years yet. [Our foundations] still need assistance, and it is doubtful whether my successor will care much for them. There are some who think it would be more proper to pay our debts at St. Vincent before laying out so much for the other places. *De gustibus etc.* . . . Indeed someone told me that people are still dissatisfied with my government. That may be, but I don't care. I saw enough of that selfish spirit among the abbots across the ocean. I refuse to imitate it. I consider St. Vincent to be the motherhouse for other, indeed for many abbeys. And I mean to continue laying the foundations for new abbeys as long as I live.[86]

As for the two newest abbeys in the American Cassinese Congregation, Wimmer said that "Newark has the advantage of money (there is plenty of it in the East), and Maryhelp has the advantage of time (there is no competition there so far as other religious orders are concerned)." Moreover, Maryhelp would in time become, Wimmer predicted, "the Catholic educational center of the Atlantic states and the starting point for the conversion of the colored race."[87]

With the abbeys in New Jersey and North Carolina securely established, the archabbot turned his attention to affairs at St. Vincent. He directed the construction of several new buildings and attended to the needs of the college and seminary. The college, he wrote, was filled to capacity, and there were over a hundred scholastics preparing to enter the order.[88]

Wimmer's concern for the development of the college and seminary at St. Vincent had always kept pace with his concern for the missions, and he continued to make sure that his future professors received the best possible education. In October 1880, after a hiatus of ten years, he reestablished the American Benedictine house of studies in Rome in order to be able to send students from St. Vincent to the Eternal City for advanced academic work. In the 1870s the property of St. Elizabeth's had been sold to a community of Italian nuns, but in 1880 Wimmer was able to secure a lease on it once again. He immediately assigned Father Adalbert Müller as rector and sent four students to Italy: Fathers Vincent Huber, Philip Kretz, and Clement Stratman, and the cleric Robert Monroe. Upon their arrival in Rome these students took up residence at St. Elizabeth's and began courses of study in philosophy and theology under the Jesuits of the German College.[89] A year later they were joined by two more clerics from St. Vincent, Hugo Paff and John Kops. But the new venture at St. Elizabeth's lasted only three years. The property was condemned by the Roman city council to make room for a road, and in August 1883, after failing in their attempt to rent another facility, the St. Vincent monks returned home. Three of them had received their doctorates in philosophy, however, and two others their licentiates in theology.[90]

Though Wimmer's two attempts to establish an American Benedictine house of studies in Rome ended in failure, his efforts, in part

Bishop Leo Haid (1849–1924), born in Westmoreland County, Pennsylvania,
became the first abbot of Maryhelp Abbey (later Belmont Abbey),
North Carolina, and after 1888 also bishop of North Carolina. (ASVA)

at least, helped motivate Vatican officials to reconstitute the Benedictine Collegio di Sant' Anselmo in February 1887. Sant' Anselmo
was originally established in the eighteenth century as a Benedictine
house of studies by Pope Innocent XI but had been suppressed during the Napoleonic upheavals. Wimmer had proposed its reestablish-
ment during the meeting of Benedictine abbots at Montecassino in
the spring of 1880, and in October 1886 the Italian Cassinese abbots,

meeting at the Abbey of Melk, Austria, passed a resolution urging Pope Leo XIII to restore the old college as an international house of studies for the Benedictine Order.[91] Wimmer strongly supported the Italian plan, and when the college opened in September 1887, he assigned two St. Vincent monks, Fathers Adalbert Müller and Robert Monroe, to serve on the faculty. In addition he sent three clerics to study theology in the first class organized at Sant' Anselmo after the restoration—Candidus Eichenlaub, Raphael Wieland, and Lawrence Haas—and Wimmer expressed his pleasure that the young American branch of the ancient Order of St. Benedict could make this substantial contribution to the first joint enterprise of the international Benedictine family.[92]

In the meantime the college and seminary at St. Vincent were undergoing significant development. Father Hilary Pfrängle, one of St. Vincent's former Roman students who had received his doctorate at the Gregorian University in Rome, was directing the academic institutions in Pennsylvania. Pfrängle had succeeded Father Alphonse Heimler as president of St. Vincent College and Seminary in 1876, and he continued in that capacity until a year before Wimmer's death, when he was elected second abbot of St. Mary's Abbey, Newark. In 1885 there were nearly four hundred students in the various academic branches at St. Vincent, and more than one hundred of these were studying for the Benedictine priesthood.[93] Because the diocese of Pittsburgh had established a seminary of its own in Bishop Michael O'Connor's time, few students from Pittsburgh attended the schools of St. Vincent in the 1860s and 1870s. In 1876, however, the Pittsburgh diocese was briefly divided, and the short-lived Diocese of Allegheny, under the direction of Bishop Michael Domenec, sent its clerical candidates to St. Vincent. Three years later, when the new diocese was reunited with the Diocese of Pittsburgh, Bishop John Tuigg closed the diocesan seminary of St. Michael's and permitted his seminarians to choose their own place of study.[94] Many went to St. Vincent, which until then had been serving students from almost every American diocese *except* Pittsburgh.[95]

But despite his efforts to develop the schools at St. Vincent, the archabbot's principal preoccupation during his final years was, as it had been previously, with the missions. In November 1885 he journeyed with Abbots Alexius Edelbrock, Innocent Wolf, and James Zilliox to Charleston, South Carolina, where on November

Wimmer and the priests of Saint Vincent, June 8, 1885. (ASVA)

25th, Thanksgiving Day, Father Leo Haid received the abbatial blessing from Bishop Henry Northrop of Charleston in St. John's Cathedral Chapel. From Charleston the five American abbots went the next day by train to Maryhelp, and there Haid introduced his guests to the monks and students of the American Cassinese Congregation's newest abbey. Wimmer savored the two days he spent with his confreres at Maryhelp. He was proud of the Benedictine achievement in North Carolina, and he wrote that the small monastery offered "all that would be required for a speedy and prosperous development."[96] On November 30 the abbots parted company. Edelbrock, Wolf, and Zilliox returned to their respective abbeys, and Wimmer and Haid traveled to Georgia where they visited the Negro school on Skidaway Island and the parish of Sacred Heart in Savannah which Father Oswald Moosmüller had established to serve the black Catholic population of the city. Wimmer turned over the Georgia mission to Haid, and leaving his confreres in Savannah set out alone for St. Vincent's mission in Alabama.

By November 1885 the Benedictine efforts in northern Alabama had not developed as rapidly as the seventy-six-year-old archabbot might have hoped. Still, he had plans of raising the Alabama foundation to abbatial dignity and was pleased to find that some progress had been made there. Monks from St. Vincent served three Alabama parishes in 1885: St. Mary's in Huntsville, St. Florian's in Lauderdale County, and St. Mary's in Tuscumbia. It was Wimmer's opinion that Tuscumbia would be the best place for the new abbey. He had sent Father Athanasius Hintenach (Father Andrew's brother) to Tuscumbia in 1883, but Hintenach was among the party of monks in the congregation who thought Wimmer was spreading the order in America too far and too thin. Father Athanasius wrote that he admired the archabbot's "wonderful way of praising the Alabama missions," but he could not agree that another abbey should be established there. The school that the Benedictines had founded in Tuscumbia was not prospering, and even if more students enrolled after the cotton-picking season as expected, Hintenach said their tuition would hardly provide enough money to support an independent monastery in Alabama.[97]

So Wimmer left Alabama not sure of what to expect of the enterprise there. From Tuscumbia he traveled to the Benedictine priory in Covington, Kentucky, and from Covington he returned to St. Vincent in time to celebrate Christmas with the monks at the abbey.[98] In the meantime events were unfolding that would lead to the establishment of another foundation from St. Vincent.

Since the Civil War Wimmer had concentrated almost exclusively on the mission fields in the South. Except for sending monks to the Czech parish in Omaha at the request of Bishop James O'Connor and to southern Illinois at the request of Bishop Peter Joseph Baltes, he had established new missions only in the southern states ravaged by the conflict of the 1860s. With his southern missions developing in a manner that gratified him, however, the archabbot could now turn his attention to St. Joseph's Priory in Chicago, which he hoped shortly to raise to abbatial rank. But the new patterns of European immigration to the United States caused him to alter his plans for raising the Chicago priory to an abbey.

"I have to think about supplying the Bohemians, Poles, and Hungarians with priests," he wrote Prior Placidus Lacense of St. Boniface Abbey, Munich, because nobody else is doing it. We now have charge of one Polish and two Bohemian congregations. Twenty Bohemian students are in our scholasticate, but only two of Polish nationality because more did not apply. The Slovenes, as far as we are able to reach them, can be taken care of by Polish and Bohemian priests. The Jesuits and Redemptorists are doing all they can, but so far no national institute exists for these immigrants. The Swedes and Norwegians ought also to have missionaries. . . . I believe that the Benedictines should undertake this work and arouse the American monks to assist in these labors, as in the olden days they urged the Western Europeans to Christianize their eastern neighbors.[99]

The congregations Wimmer referred to in his letter to Lacense were the Czech parishes of St. Wenceslaus in Allegheny City, Pennsylvania (which St. Vincent monks assumed charge of in 1876) and St. Wenceslaus in Omaha, and the Polish parish of Mary Immaculate in Rockville, Illinois, established in 1879. In March 1884 Father Wenceslaus Kocarnik, pastor in Omaha, and Father Nepomucene Jaeger, pastor in Allegheny City, went to Chicago to conduct a mission at the Czech parish of St. Procopius. At St. Procopius the two Benedictines discussed with the pastor, Father William Choka, Wimmer's hope to establish a Czech monastery in America. Czech monks from St. Vincent had been working in Omaha for six years, but because the Omaha project was not developing as they had hoped Fathers Wenceslaus and Nepomucene believed that they would have to find a different site for the proposed monastery, preferably one near a large, concentrated Czech population. Father Choka proposed that the Benedictines of St. Vincent take over St. Procopius Parish in Chicago and promised to speak with Archbishop Patrick A. Feehan about the possibility of doing so. When Choka proposed the idea to Feehan, the Chicago archbishop expressed interest and wrote Wimmer inviting him to send monks to St. Procopius. In January 1885 Archabbot Boniface agreed. He assigned Father Nepomucene Jaeger as first Benedictine pastor of the parish and sent Fathers Wenceslaus Kocarnik and Sigismund Singer to assist him. Father William Choka left the parish and went to Omaha where he assumed the duties of pastor at the Czech parish of St. Wenceslaus, which the Benedictines now relinquished in favor of Chicago. "I dropped the plan of founding a Bohemian abbey in Nebraska," Wimmer wrote, "because such an undertaking became impossible. The aims of the order and the interests of the diocese could not be satisfactorily reconciled."[100] Later he wrote Father Nepomucene that "we incurred the displeasure of Bishop O'Connor to the full extent because we left Omaha for the benefit of the people of St. Procopius."[101]

With the establishment of the Benedictines at St. Procopius, Wimmer determined to devote his efforts toward raising an abbey in Chicago on the basis of the Czech parish rather than the German one at St. Joseph's. Father Nepomucene went immediately to work to achieve this end. The reason for Wimmer's change of plan was pragmatically based on demographics and the dynamics of contemporary immigration to America. A new wave of Eastern European immigrants was now arriving on the shores of the United States, and many of the newcomers were settling in the Midwest, particularly in Chicago and its environs. A large portion of these immigrants in Chicago were Czech Catholics whose need for priests who spoke their language and who could provide for their pastoral care was, because of their greater number, even more pressing than that of their compatriots in Nebraska. Wimmer correctly believed, moreover, that the Benedictines would receive greater financial support for a potential abbey and attract more Czech vocations to the monastic life from the large and concentrated Czech population of Chicago than from the rural and dispersed population of Nebraska. He therefore gave Father Nepomucene and the other Bohemian monks at St. Vincent a free rein to work among their countrymen in Chicago. On its own scale their effort proved to be as fully successful among Czech immigrants as Wimmer's had been among Bavarian immigrants forty years earlier.

In November 1885 Jaeger wrote the archabbot that "every month we have 100 baptisms, a dozen marriages, and 25 funerals. The school has 930 children in ten classes." Father Wenceslaus had traveled to Prague for the purpose of raising money for the future abbey and had returned with $2,500 and promises of equal contributions the following year. Although he found no young men willing to come to America to join the Benedictines, Jaeger felt confident that numerous Czech candidates for the order could be found among the people of Chicago.[102] The monks in Chicago were making good progress. They purchased more property and opened St. Procopius College in the fall of 1886, and Wimmer was quite pleased that the venture among the Bohemian immigrants in Chicago was bearing fruit so rapidly.

Forty years had passed since Wimmer and eighteen young candidates had arrived in Pennsylvania to establish the Benedictine Order in the United States. The order had grown and developed remarkably during that time, and Wimmer himself, even in his old age, continued to press forward with the work that had become the sole purpose of his life. But more and more he was having to leave the active labor of preaching and teaching to his younger confreres. "What else do you want to know?" he wrote to a friend on the board of directors of the Ludwig Missionsverein.

Certainly you want to know that we are active and are accomplishing something. When all the orders are advancing and prospering—the women no less than the men—it would be a shame if we Benedictines were not doing the same. There is in the whole Catholic Church a striving for and a promoting of religion, as well as a love of fellow-man, as never before. The whole hierarchy, all the secular clergy, all the religious orders and also the laity are performing miracles of zeal for the honor of God, for the salvation of souls, as well as for the temporal welfare. I regret sincerely that I am not able to do and accomplish more, and that the little I do is so imperfect! . . . I preach perhaps once a year. All I do is go to choir regularly and write letters at my desk, back and forth, listen to complaints, give answers to questions, make suggestions concerning the building, etc., send the young priests into "the fire" or bring them back and change them, see to it that not more money goes out than I bring in, etc. Now and then I make a long trip by train, where I can even sleep in a bed at night.

Despite the effects of illness and age, and his own commitments to the schools, parishes, and missions that his monks served, Wimmer still provided support for the Benedictine sisters in the United States. The sisters had established new communities and were now working as widely and successfully in the American missions as the monks, and he continued to seek aid for them from his benefactors in Europe. "It is not a small cross for me that I am becoming very forgetful," he wrote his friend, Father Rath, in Munich, "and my memory is not reliable."

I have, for instance, kept in my desk for a long time and forgot to send two receipts for money from the Missionsverein for the prioresses of Atchison and Elizabeth. (I enclose them here.) In like manner, I promised and again forgot to intercede for money for the prioress of Nauvoo, Illinois, from the Missionsverein. If I am not mistaken she has already, once or twice, received some money at the same time as the Benedictine sisters of Carrolltown and Elizabeth. But this was not much because the others were then in greater need. I had therefore given the larger amount to them.

May I suggest that at the distribution of money by the Missionsverein, the venerable central committee consider giving some money to the prioress of Nauvoo? Her name is Ottilia Hoevler. She writes English well, but her German is poor since only her father was German, but her mother was English. Nauvoo is the place of the old Mormon settlement in the West. It is a small place in the diocese of Peoria on the Mississippi.

For now this is enough. I am quite well, but I have very few teeth left. I may not drink beer or wine and suffer from ailments of old age, which make travelling very difficult for me. I hope you keep well and reach old age. That is a great blessing. One is fortunate in reaching old age if one is feeling fairly well.[103]

In February 1886 the archabbot received news from Newark that Abbot James Zilliox had been hospitalized on account of a serious lung ailment. Never a physically strong person, Zilliox had developed tuberculosis, and Wimmer wrote Abbot Innocent Wolf that "the doctors say there is no hope because the condition is so far advanced. He may live only until the fall." Having found the duties and responsibilities of the abbacy beyond his emotional and physical strength, and because of his ill health, Zilliox had petitioned the Holy See to relieve him of the office, but Rome had denied his request. Now Wimmer suspected that his young confrere would be "relieved of his troubles by God."[104] As it turned out, the archabbot would be relieved of his first.

He had been suffering from the usual eye and stomach problems, and now was experiencing difficulties with his kidneys and bladder. Nevertheless, he forged ahead. His days were numbered, but there was still much for him to do. In April 1886, responding to a petition of Bishop John Moore of St. Augustine, Florida, Archabbot Boniface sent Father Gerard Pilz to the large German colony of San Antonio in Hernando County, Florida. From Florida Father Gerard wrote that the place "is most beautiful in every respect. San Antonio is a splendid district for people to settle in and to make a good living." Pilz said, however, that he would suspend further judgment about the possibilities for a Benedictine foundation there until he had "some time to investigate matters."[105] In May, when it had become clear that his first impressions had been accurate, Father Gerard sent his recommendations to St. Vincent, and the monastic chapter voted to formally accept the Benedictine mission in Florida. Wimmer assigned Father Cyprian Creagh from Georgia and Brother Francis de Sales Zwiesler from St. Vincent to San Antonio. Pilz had already started a high school in Florida, and he reported that the monks from St. Vincent had won the full confidence and support of the colonists.[106]

Not long afterward Archabbot Boniface wrote Abbot Alexius Edelbrock in Minnesota giving a uniquely vivid picture of summer life at the abbey of St. Vincent. He himself was feeling "feeble and sick," he said, but there was no rest for him.

My prior is giving retreats for the sisters; my procurator is sick in bed, scarcely able to stand before his desk to make the necessary entries; the fathers are on vacation; the brothers are humming and buzzing like bees to get to the ridge; the workers are knocking and hammering to install pipes for the steam heating; the plasterers are not yet finished with the new kitchen building; the farm hands are driven out of the fields during the harvesting by rain showers; strangers make visits and nobody is here to show them around. The mail brings letters upon letters to be answered—and I am sitting here alone, hardly knowing where my head is. Today I was the only father at Prime, with 20 novices whom I clothed on July 10, five of whom, however, belong to Kansas. It's at times like this that I often become weary of life, because I feel I cannot cope any longer with my position.

Wimmer—who had carried his work from German-speaking to English-speaking Americans and who was now sending his monks to evangelize the Protestant people of North Carolina and Alabama, to educate and convert the Negroes of Georgia, and to serve the Czechs in the Midwest—commended Edelbrock for his efforts among the Indians in Minnesota. It had always been the dream of the archabbot to carry the Benedictine mission to Native Americans, and now that the monks of St. John's had undertaken the task, his ambition was fulfilled. Abbot Alexius's work "for the gradual conversion of the heretics and heathens," he said, would "braid new laurels into the wreath of your merits."[107]

To Father Celestine Englbrecht, one of the original band of monks to come with him to America, Wimmer wrote on the anniversary of their departure from Munich that "when one thinks back forty years, one must marvel at how much has been done or initiated in that time. We may thank God very heartily that He has chosen and used us as instruments for this work. For my part, it fills me with fear and trembling because I am not able to oversee and direct everything any more. But as long as I am still able to work I cannot afford to retire." He said that there were a good many monks at St. Vincent, but in assigning them to various duties, he had to be careful. "Unfortunately those whom one can really rely on are not too numerous." But he hoped this would improve in time.[108]

Among the monks upon whom he had often relied was James Zilliox. More than a year had passed since Father James had assumed the duties of abbot in Newark, and his reign had not been a happy one. He had carried the same zeal for contemplative monastic life to Newark that he had tried to instill among the monks of St. Vincent, but the monks there, like those in Pennsylvania, had resisted his efforts to alter their traditional observance, with its emphasis on parochial and educational work, to one that stressed withdrawal from educational work and pastoral care, a more complex spiritual regimen, intense theological study, and Beuronese liturgical practices. Both the Newark monks' adamant resistance to change and his own difficult struggle with the effects of the tuberculosis he had contracted at St. Vincent multiplied his frustrations and caused Zilliox to sink into depression. Because of this depression he had attempted to resign the abbacy early in 1886, but Rome had denied his petition to step down. Later in the year, however, he petitioned again, citing his poor health as a grave obstacle to his continuing spiritual leadership of the community, and this time, with support from Archabbot Boniface, he was successful. In November the archabbot informed the three other abbots of the congregation that Rome had accepted Abbot James's resignation. By then Zilliox was in Richmond, Virginia, critically ill, with poor prospects for recovery. Wimmer announced to the abbots his plans to travel to Newark for the election of Zilliox's successor.[109]

He went to St. Mary's Abbey in the second week of November, where on November 16 the monks of St. Mary's chose Father Hilary Pfrängle, director of the college and seminary at St. Vincent, as the second abbot of the Newark abbey. Wimmer telegraphed Pfrängle with news of the election, and Pfrängle replied at once that he could not accept the honor. Father Ambrose Hübner, prior in Newark, then wired St. Vincent urging Father Hilary to reconsider. A series of telegrams continued to flow between New Jersey and Pennsylvania

Father Celestine Englbrecht (1824–1904), member of the
pioneer band of Benedictines who came to the
United States in 1846. (ASVA)

throughout the day, but Father Hilary would not be moved. Finally
the archabbot, determined not to allow another of his monks to escape the responsibility of leadership as Oswald Moosmüller had done
the previous year, responded with a forceful letter that made clear his
intention to see Father Hilary elevated to the abbacy of Newark.

You were yesterday elected abbot with 9 votes out of 14, at the third ballot.
Your refusal caused great consternation and still more your second telegraph
to Father Prior. . . . He, as well as the other electors, feared that if another
election should become necessary, no one would receive a majority, so that

I, the Abbot [President] would have to select an abbot. This they dislike and so do I—even more than they. I think you should spare them and me the trouble and accept the election. You will quite certainly be a candidate for abbot of St. Vincent's when I die. However, it is possible that I may still have a few years to live. In your position, you are also a candidate for bishop, but in our diocese there is no prospect in the near future.

A brilliant future cannot be expected for Newark, but in a small diocese an abbot is an important man. Under a good abbot, the small abbey has a promising future. Since there are so many *Romani Doctores* in the East, the abbot should be a man who can lend dignity to his office. If I should be compelled to appoint an abbot, I cannot appoint one of the resident Fathers. That much I have learnt from the people here. They want no Newarker, though this does not reflect on anyone. Even Abbot James was not popular for this reason. The monastery too will suffer if the abbacy is refused. It will be a reflection either on the local Fathers, because it is rumored that Abbot James did not get along well with some of them, or on the abbey itself.

However, an abbot must not be so sensitive, and the Fathers in Newark are not so bad. In fact, there is a beautiful order in the monastery, much better than at St. Vincent. They attend choir regularly, there is no idea of neglecting mass, they do not miss chapter, waste time, or talk after recreation. As far as I can see, there is good understanding among them and they work diligently. In fact, it is a nice little monastery and the food is good and sufficient.

I cannot see why a good monk should shrink from assuming the government of such a community. I expect, therefore, that you will not allow previously conceived prejudices to prevent you from accepting the proffered dignity. It is my wish that you notify me of your consent by telegram so that I may not be detained here unnecessarily but return to St. Vincent by Saturday or Sunday morning.[110]

Recognizing the futility of resisting the archabbot's will, Pfrängle, upon receiving this letter, telegraphed his acceptance.

Wimmer had made arrangements for Zilliox to live in retirement at St. Vincent, and before returning home he ordered the resigned abbot's personal effects packed and shipped to Pennsylvania. A month later he wrote Abbot Alexius Edelbrock that as soon as confirmation of Abbot Hilary's election arrived from Rome, the abbatial blessing would take place at the monastery in Pennsylvania. He reported that because of some sour red wine he had drunk in Newark he was suffering from serious problems in the urinary tract. He had to be

Scholastics and Novices at Saint Vincent in 1886. (ASVA)

catheterized, and though he was assured by the doctors that there was no direct danger to his life as a result of the condition, he predicted that this was "the beginning of the end." Another monk in the community, Father Kilian Bernetzeder, had quite a different problem: "I have had an extra little stall built for Father Kilian in choir beside mine; nobody wanted to be next to him because he cannot control his water. So there I now stand in counterpoint beside him, watching in envy every time it runs with him because it remains so obstructed with me."[111]

In the meantime, and despite his difficulties, Wimmer was keeping up his frenetic pace in the mission fields. In September 1886 Bishop Joseph P. Machebeuf, vicar apostolic of Colorado and Utah, visited St. Vincent and asked for priests to work in his vicariate. Several months earlier a group of Benedictine sisters from the Priory of St. Scholastica in Chicago had, against the advice of the archabbot, been persuaded by a diocesan priest from Colorado to establish a convent and school in Breckenridge. The priest, a Father Chapuis who had served as their chaplain, soon departed the vicariate, and the sisters were left on their own. Bishop Machebeuf offered Wimmer a substantial mission field in Colorado, and when the archabbot learned of the sisters' plight in Breckenridge he agreed to send help.[112] In December he assigned Fathers Rhabanus Gutmann and Eusebius Geiger to Colorado and wrote Abbot Benedict Braunmüller of Metten that he "could not leave the people, the sisters, and the bishop without assistance. Father Rhabanus, a man of the best years [he was forty-one], a good horseman, strong and healthy, also somewhat adventurous, volunteered for the mission, and Father Eusebius, socius of novices, pious and healthy, is anxious to take part in the expedition."[113]

Fathers Rhabanus and Eusebius arrived in Denver on December 17, 1886. As Father Rhabanus later recorded it, the monks

found the bishop at home and were cordially received, but says the bishop you must leave this evening for Breckenridge at 8 o'cl. So we did and arrived at Breckenridge at 4 A.M., pitch dark, station closed, zero and below, 4 feet of snow, & no path to be seen. We will freeze to death I said to P. Eusebius, but behold at once we saw a light. The bishop had informed Mr. McNamara to meet us at the station, came a little late yet in time.[114]

In Breckenridge the two monks took up their duties, which included serving the Catholic missions in eight nearby small towns. On December 18 Father Rhabanus wrote Archabbot Boniface that he did "not know whether we are going to freeze this winter or not." The following month he wrote that "as far as our parish is concerned, which embraces two counties, we do not think that we shall suffer any great want. The people are willing and very generous, also devoted to the priest."[115]

Both Gutmann and Geiger suffered debilitating illnesses during the early months of their mission in Colorado, and for a while Geiger had to be hospitalized in the Union Pacific Railroad hospital in Denver. Nevertheless, the two monks continued their work among the Catholics of Breckenridge and its vicinity while they explored the possibilities for a more permanent Benedictine settlement in Colorado. Living conditions for both the priests and the sisters were primitive, and Gutmann wrote Archabbot Boniface asking that he send Brother Gregory from the abbey in Pennsylvania to help them build better quarters.

We *have* a house, yes, a dwarf's house—*domusculus*—inhospitable and cold as a dog kennel, and on an altogether poor site. The church is located at one corner of the town, the Chapuis house at another corner, and the Sisters' convent on a third. But, Your Grace, that would all be nothing. For, should you be able to form any conception of the force of the wind here, the depth of the snow, and the merciless character of the weather, then I'd surely know that your otherwise soft heart would grow softer still, and the order would not fail to be issued: *Gregori, vade ad fratres in frigore et inopia degentes* [Gregory, go to your brethren living in cold and in need]. If we are to do anything at all here, a beginning must be made and right away. The bishop wishes us to move the church next to the sisters' convent in the spring; all well and good, but that is why I need a man to manage things for me, and such men are precious as gold here. Where shall I dish up the gold? . . . Rt. Rev. Abbot and dearest Father, please do not let this letter get by you without some attention and without leaving a little favorable impression, for to whom should I go, *Abba Pater,* if not to you?[116]

In the meantime Wimmer was receiving encouraging reports about the progress of some of his other missionary ventures. "They laughed at me and I had to listen to a good many obstinate critics with regard to Maryhelp in North Carolina," he said. But the strong and decisive leadership of Abbot Leo Haid had brought the community in North Carolina through the earlier demoralizing crises of financial insecurity and low enrollment in the college. The monastery's financial condition had vastly improved, monastic observance under Abbot Leo was developing satisfactorily, and the school was operating at nearly full capacity. Many had thought a monastery in Protestant North Carolina would have no chance of success, he said, and that "it was money thrown down the drain." But Archabbot Boniface, who had just turned seventy-eight two weeks earlier, wrote Prior Nepomucene Jaeger of St. Procopius Priory, Chicago, that "Abbot Leo has given proof that the monastery and college are in the right place. The monks of North Carolina will be able to support themselves now."[117]

In February the archabbot learned that the Holy See had confirmed Abbot Hilary Pfrängle's election as second abbot of St. Mary's Abbey, Newark. He also learned that Rome was considering Abbot Leo Haid for the episcopal dignity. Haid would become vicar apostolic of North Carolina and was the third of Wimmer's spiritual sons to be made a bishop. Wimmer told Abbot Alexius Edelbrock that he expected Abbot Leo would remain superior at Maryhelp, however, despite the forthcoming appointment, so there would be no need for a new abbatial election.[118]

Abbot Hilary was blessed at St. Vincent on February 17, 1887, and all the abbots of the American Cassinese Congregation came for the ceremony. It was a joyful day for the archabbot. He knew that his days were drawing to a close and that this would doubtless be the last opportunity for him to see his brother abbots, all of whom had been his novices at St. Vincent. Alexius, Innocent, and Hilary all were infants when Boniface had arrived in Pennsylvania forty-one years earlier with his vision of transplanting the ancient Order of St. Benedict to the fertile soil of America, and James and Leo had not even been born. All five of these monastic leaders had come to St. Vincent as boys to be educated in the Benedictine tradition that under Wimmer's guidance and with their help had now become an American tradition as well. They represented an affirmation of his life's work and the hope of its continuation after he was gone.

In March Wimmer wrote the abbot of Metten that he was in the fourth month of his illness and was certain that his days were numbered. "I am saturated with suffering," he said. "I am an old and sick and half- dead man."[119]

On April 11, 1887, Father Benedict Haindl died in Minnesota. He had come with Boniface Wimmer to the American missions forty-one years earlier, and his death marked the end of an era at St. John's where he was the last of the pioneer monks. It also marked a transition for the Benedictines in America. The torch had been passed to a new generation. Only five of the pioneers who had come to Pennsylvania in 1846 were still alive: Archabbot Boniface, Father Celestine Englbrecht, Brother Joseph Sailer, Brother Conrad Reinbolt, and Brother Andrew Binder. When he learned of Father Benedict's death, Wimmer understood that the new generation had taken over from the old, a new generation made up of the young boys whom Metten's *Projektenmacher* had come to educate so many years before. They were the children of the immigrants whose cries he had heard in Munich an age ago. Now these boys, the four hundred and more monks who followed the Rule of St. Benedict in the monasteries he had founded during the preceding four decades, were the heirs of his grand design, the promise of his prophetic vision.

The archabbot rejoiced even as he complained of "the chronic in-

Saint Vincent in 1887. (ASVA)

flammation of the bladder" that would kill him. And there was still
much work to be done. He was a man racing, as all men ultimately
race, against time. In the same month that he learned of Father Benedict's death, Archabbot Boniface received a letter from Bishop Jeremiah O'Sullivan of Mobile offering to turn over the parish in Cullman, Alabama, to the Benedictines. This parish was in the center of
a strong German settlement and had a Catholic population larger
than that of all the other Benedictine parishes in Alabama combined.
Bishop O'Sullivan commended Wimmer for the work he and his
monks had done in the diocese of Mobile and offered continued support of their efforts in the future.[120]

Urged by Father Benedict Menges, O.S.B., pastor in Huntsville,
the archabbot accepted the bishop's offer and in May sent Father Andrew Hintenach, the former prior at St. Vincent, to take charge of all
Benedictine missions in Alabama. Though the parish in Tuscumbia
would continue for a while to be the center of Benedictine activity in
the Diocese of Mobile, it was Sacred Heart Parish in Cullman that
formed the nucleus of what later became, after Wimmer's death,

St. Bernard's Abbey. The archabbot sent his protege, Father Oswald Moosmüller, from Savannah to the Cullman parish. Fathers Andrew and Oswald were soon joined in the Alabama missions by Fathers Cyprian Creagh and Gammelbert Brunner, and by Brother Rupert Noll. Together with Fathers Urban Tracy and Joseph Keller, these monks continued the work in Alabama which had begun ten years before. Following the pattern of missionary development well established by Wimmer during the previous forty years, the Alabama monks served four parishes in a wide geographical area and established a central base at Tuscumbia where, in September 1887, they opened a college.[121]

Besides busying himself with the missions in Alabama during the spring of 1887, the archabbot was also collecting funds for the Collegio di Sant' Anselmo. By the end of April he had forwarded $8,000 from the American Benedictines and said that only a little more was required before the Americans would "catch up to" the Italian contributions toward the college.[122] In March Bishop Joseph P. Machebeuf of Colorado wrote Wimmer, offering the Benedictines of St. Vincent a 160-acre farm six miles from Boulder for the founding of a Benedictine monastery "which would be the head-quarters of your Fathers in Colorado." In May Wimmer, who was too ill to do so himself, instructed Prior Michael Hofmayer to call a meeting of the St. Vincent chapter to discuss the formal acceptance of the bishop's offer. The chapter meeting took place on May 5, and four days later the archabbot wrote Bishop Machebeuf:

Your favor of Breckenridge, March 22nd, came to hand in due time, but found me in great sufferings because of my afflictions of over five months standing. Consequently I was very little disposed to attend to business of importance or even to think on it earnestly. After Easter I was a little better, but not strong enough to convoke a chapter and preside over it. To avoid further delay I charged P. Prior to hold the chapter, to lay Your Lordship's letter and to take the votes of the P.P. capitulars and report them to me.

This was done on the fifth of May with fifteen affirmative votes among the twenty-six, only six were decidedly negative, the others being indifferent. As I am personally in favor of acceptance, I herewith send Your Lordship the official declaration *that I as abbot of St. Vincent Abbey*, with the consent of the majority of the chapter accept your offer . . . .

I understand perfectly the difficulties at such a distance of 1,800 or more miles to found a religious institution that necessarily must become a large

Archabbot Andrew Hintenach (1844–1927), Boniface Wimmer's
successor as head of the Benedictine monastery
of Saint Vincent. (ASVA)

house of missionaries, if it should answer its purpose, and a mother-house
of other similar institutions in the state of Colorado. But as the spiritual necessities of it manifestly require, that the bishop or vicar apostolic has the aid
and assistance of religious in attending to these spiritual necessities of the
faithful inhabitants of Colorado, I nevertheless thought it to be my duty not
to slight Your Lordship's urgent invitation, to give you so much help as circumstances allow us to give, trusting in divine providence that our good will
with God's blessing will be crowned with success.[123]

By now the seventy-eight-year-old archabbot was too weak to conduct the affairs of the monastery himself and was delegating more and
more authority to the prior. "I can scarcely sleep two hours at night,"
he wrote, "and twice a day I have to resort to the catheter. When that

stops working, I am finished. I say holy mass in my private chapel every morning, recite the divine office, and attend to the necessary correspondence. I go neither to choir nor to the refectory nor do I leave the house except for an occasional half-hour stroll in the garden. Father Prior, Father Procurator, and Brother Andrew have to do most of my work. Their main business is to keep me informed of whatever I need to know."[124]

Despite his physical suffering, Archabbot Boniface kept pace with the work and activities of his monks. In the last eight months of his life he wrote more than one hundred letters. He corresponded regularly with the abbots of the congregation, reporting on activities at St. Vincent and offering advice and encouragement. He informed Abbot Alexius Edelbrock, who, after himself, was senior abbot in the congregation, that he saw no reason why the ninth general chapter should not take place at St. Vincent during the summer as scheduled. He had noticed a change for the better in his health, he said, and was anxious to hold the chapter. "I need the instrument only twice a day now, whereas before I needed it three times daily."[125] He knew, however, that he was dying, and it was a slow and painful death. He wrote Father Celestine Englbrecht that "God is good to me. I regard it as a consoling sign of His mercy, that he has sent me this illness. I am therefore not sad, nor do I feel discontented or unhappy. Human beings are human beings, and suffering is suffering. . . . Perfect resignation to God's will is a great grace for which one cannot ask often enough."[126]

In June he wrote the abbots of the American Cassinese Congregation that because of his ill health he had decided to postpone the ninth general chapter after all.[127] In July he petitioned the Holy See to elevate the Bohemian monastery of St. Procopius in Chicago to the rank of independent canonical priory.[128] Later in the month, on the forty-first anniversary of his departure from Munich for America, he wrote his confrere, Father Celestine Englbrecht:

Today you and I are the only surviving clerics [of the original band]. And, if I am not mistaken, of the brothers only three are still alive. Near to death and slowly dying, I naturally think quite often about the days gone by and wonder how things turned out the way they did. No one imagined us capable of accomplishing anything significant, and yet we *did* accomplish something. God's grace was obviously with us. Our chief object—the establishment of the order in America—has been achieved, and our second major purpose—training and providing a sufficient clergy for our German Catholics—is well underway. May unbounded thanks be given to God a thousand times, for He chose and made use of us as instruments for the execution of His designs. For many, our foundations have had serious defects, but it could not have been otherwise without a miracle, and I firmly believe that it can be made better, once a well-regulated order is established in our abbeys and priories.

Hence we do not want to become faint-hearted or discouraged. Rather we want to work on confidently and courageously as well as we can. Inasmuch as things have come this far only with the evident protection and grace of God, so may we not expect from ourselves success in the future, but again only from the grace and protection of God, who cannot fail us so long as we work not for ourselves, but for Him, for His holy Church, for the order, and for souls.[129]

During the summer of 1887 Bishop Peter Schumacher of Portoviejo, Ecuador, came to St. Vincent looking for Benedictines to establish a colony in his diocese. At the time Wimmer was involved with a number of other ventures, including the Bohemian monastery in Chicago and the Collegio di Sant' Anselmo in Rome, and he wrote that he was unable to supply the South American diocese with monks.[130] He regretted that he had to turn down Bishop Schumacher, but he wrote in August to his nephew, Father Luke Wimmer, prior in Monte Cassino Priory, Kentucky, that perhaps his successor would be in a better position to help all those whom he had failed. He had great hopes for the future of the American Benedictines. He now no longer expected to see the communities in Alabama and Chicago elevated to abbatial rank in his lifetime. But it would come, he predicted, as would future abbeys from St. John's and St. Benedict's. In Colorado, moreover, there were good prospects for a monastery "from which all the territory in the neighborhood—like Nevada, New Mexico, and Mexico itself—could be evangelized and brought into our field of operations."[131]

The following month he received news that the Congregation for the Propagation of the Faith had elevated the community of St. Procopius to the rank of canonical priory.[132] "How happy I am, how filled with joy and consolation in my misery!" he wrote. "I cannot thank the good Lord enough for having ordained everything not less than miraculously."[133] And to Father Luke: "What more must I do before I am given my travelling papers for the journey home to my Father's house? It seems like a dream, these forty years at St. Vincent."[134]

In October he reported to the abbot of Metten that he was going to send several monks to the international Benedictine college in Rome. The missions in Alabama and Colorado were going well, but he admitted that he had "grown very indifferent to the outside world." Nevertheless, and despite the fact that he knew his last days were upon him, he was "still using the time given to me. . . . Great opportunities for the future of our order are open in the South."[135] Less than two weeks later he wrote once again to the abbot of the monastery where fifty-four years before he had made his profession as a Benedictine monk. A Bohemian monastery had been established in Chicago, he said, and the missions in Florida, Alabama, and Colorado flourished. "Our situation, generally speaking, is good. No need to say more. Why should I waste time? My health is neither better nor worse, but stable, near the point of crisis."[136]

His letter to the abbot of Metten was the last he ever completed. On the same day, October 15, 1887, he began a note to Father Maurus Kinter, O.S.B., editor of the Bavarian Benedictine journal *Studien und Mitteilungen zur Geschichte des Benediktiner-Ordens,* telling him about St. Procopius Priory. But he never finished it.[137] Overcome with weariness and the agonizing illness that had been slowly killing him for more than a year, he went to his cell for the last time. He asked the prior to anoint him, and then he waited.

Boniface Wimmer died less than two months later at ten o'clock in the morning on December 8, 1887, the Feast of the Immaculate Conception, and the bells in the abbey tower tolled over the countryside all day long. Hundreds came to pay their respects: the superiors of the Holy Ghost Fathers, of the Passionists, of the Capuchins, of the Carmelites; the abbots of St. John's, of St. Benedict's, of St. Mary's, of Maryhelp, of St. Meinrad's; the bishops of Pittsburgh, of Covington, of Nashville, of Scranton, of Erie. They were all there. And then there were the two funeral masses and the eulogies and the five absolutions chanted by the five bishops. When the time came to carry the casket to the hill behind the abbey church, to the spot which the abbot had chosen many years earlier, twelve lay brothers of St. Vincent were the pallbearers. They had been the basic fabric of his grand design. They had cleared the fields, harvested the crops, cut the timber, made the bricks, and built the buildings in all the communities that he had founded. And now they claimed the right to lay him in his final resting place. It was singularly appropriate that they should do so, for they had borne some of the greatest burdens of his abbacy, and he had always been grateful.

Epilogue

Two hours after the funeral, on December 13, 1887, the monks of St. Vincent gathered to choose an administrator for the abbey until an abbatial election could be held. The office fell to Prior Michael Hofmayer. Two months later, on February 8, 1888, the capitulars came together again to elect Wimmer's successor. Abbot Innocent Wolf was chosen, but he was unwilling to leave his post in Kansas, and when the capitulars voted again, they elected Father Andrew Hintenach, superior of the Alabama missions, as the second abbot of St. Vincent.

Hintenach reigned for only four years before he resigned. He built the basilica at St. Vincent which Abbot Boniface had planned, and he successfully petitioned Rome in 1891 to elevate the monastery in Alabama to the rank of abbey. His successor, Archabbot Leander Schnerr, petitioned for the elevation of the Bohemian Priory of St. Procopius to abbatial dignity in 1894, and Wimmer's missions in Florida and Colorado also became abbeys in 1902 and 1925, respectively. But after 1887 only one community founded from St. Vincent achieved abbatial status. St. Bede's monastery in Peru, Illinois, established as a college in 1891 under Archabbot Andrew, became an abbey in 1910.

Boniface Wimmer, the founder, was gone, and a new era had begun for the Benedictines in America.

Notes

Abbreviations Used in Notes

ABR	*American Benedictine Review*
ACA	Archives of Conception Abbey, Conception, Missouri
ACPF	Archives of the Congregation for the Propagation of the Faith, Rome
ADL	Archives of the Diocese of Linz, Austria
ALMV	Archives of the Ludwig Missionsverein, Munich
AMA	Archives of Metten Abbey, Metten, Germany
APH	Archives of St. Martin's Archabbey, Pannonhalma, Hungry
ASA	Archives of Scheyern Abbey, Scheyern, Germany
ASBA	Archives of St. Benedict's Abbey, Atchison, Kansas
ASJA	Archives of St. John's Abbey, Collegeville, Minnesota
ASMA	Archives of St. Meinrad's Archabbey, St. Meinrad, Indiana
ASPA	Archives of the Abbey of St. Paul's-Outside-the-Walls, Rome
ASPrA	Archives of St. Procopius Abbey, Lisle, Illinois
ASVA	Archives of St. Vincent Archabbey, Latrobe, Pennsylvania
RAB	Royal Archives of Bavaria, Munich

Notes to Chapter 1

1. Published sources on the life of Boniface Wimmer include Oswald Moos-müller, O.S.B., *Bonifaz Wimmer, Erzabt von St. Vincent in Pennsylvanien* (New York: Benziger, 1891); Sebastian Wimmer, "Biographical Sketch of Rt. Rev. Arch-Abbot Wimmer, O.S.B., D.D., Patriarch of the American Cassinese Benedictines," *Records of the American Catholic Historical Society of Philadelphia* 3 (1891): 174–93; Bernhard Lester, "Erzabt Bonifaz Wimmer, Das Bild eines deutschen Mannes in Amerika," *Frankfurter Zeitgemässe Broschüren* 12 (1891): 397–414; J. S., "Rt. Rev. Boniface Wimmer, O.S.B., Founder of St. Vincent's," *St. Vincent Journal* 18 (1909): 151–66; Felix Fellner, O.S.B., *Abbot Boniface and His Monks,* 5 vols. (Latrobe, Pa.: Privately published at Saint Vincent Archabbey, 1956); and Colman J. Barry, O.S.B., "Boniface Wimmer, Pioneer of the American Benedictines," *Catholic Historical Review* 41 (1955): 272–96. Substantial portions of the present biography appeared in the *American Benedictine Review* 22 (1971): 147–76; 23 (1972): 282–313; 24 (1973): 1–28; and 25 (1974): 1–32; and in the *Saint Vincent Alumni Magazine* 6 (1972): 4–5.

2. Moosmüller, *Bonifaz Wimmer,* 13.

3. Fellner, *Abbot Boniface and His Monks,* 1:6.

4. Henry Lachouque, *Napoleon's Battles: A History of His Campaigns* (London: Allen & Unwin, 1966), 233–49.

5. Karl Bihlmeyer, *Church History: Modern and Recent Times,* rev. Herman Tüchle, trans. V. E. Mills and F. J. Müller (Westminster, Md.: Newman Press, 1968), 306.

6. Bihlmeyer, *Church History: Modern and Recent Times,* 301–2.

7. Moosmüller, *Bonifaz Wimmer,* 14.

8. ASVA: Wimmer Scholastic Records (VAB I).

9. ASVA: Wimmer Scholastic Records (VAB I).

10. Fellner, *Abbot Boniface and His Monks,* 1: 9; Barry, "Boniface Wimmer," 280.

11. ASVA: Wimmer Scholastic Records (VAB I).

12. Moosmüller, *Bonifaz Wimmer,* 47; J. S., "Rt. Rev. Boniface Wimmer, O.S.B.," 151.

13. J. S., "Rt. Rev. Boniface Wimmer, O.S.B.," 155.

14. Fellner, *Abbot Boniface and His Monks,* 1: 11; Moosmüller, *Bonifaz Wimmer,* 24.

15. Fellner, *Abbot Boniface and His Monks,* 1: 11; J.S., "Rt. Rev. Boniface Wimmer, O.S.B.," 156.

16. ASVA: Wimmer Scholastic Records (VAB I).

17. Wimmer celebrated his first mass on Sunday, August 7, 1831, in Thalmassing; see Fellner, *Abbot Boniface and His Monks,* 1: 12. "At the time it was customary in many places to have a celebration featuring a banquet, dancing, and a pseudo-marriage; but before he returned home, Father Wimmer had to sign a paper in which he promised to refrain from such worldly amusements."

18. ASVA: Wimmer to Schneider, St. Vincent, no date (File TS 6).

19. Bihlmeyer, *Church History: Modern and Recent Times,* 313.

20. Bihlmeyer, *Church History: Modern and Recent Times,* 325; Barry, "Boniface Wimmer," 275; and Wilhelm Fink, O.S.B., *Beiträge zur Geschichte der Bayerischen Benediktinerkongregation: Eine Jubiläumsschrift 1684–1934* (Munich: Kommissionsverlag R. Oldenbourg, 1934).

21. Fink, *Geschichte der Bayerischen Benediktinerkongregation,* 327.

22. Fink, *Geschichte der Bayerischen Benediktinerkongregation,* 327. Determining the equivalency of early currency in modern terms is notoriously difficult to do, but one modern historian has estimated that a Bavarian florin, equivalent to about half a contemporary U.S. dollar in the 1830s and 1840s, would be roughly equal to $20.00 in 1996 currency. Thus 50,000 florins would be worth about $1 million today. See Bruce Seymour, *Lola Montez: A Life* (New Haven, Conn.: Yale University Press, 1996), 238.

23. Fellner, *Abbot Boniface and His Monks,* 1: 15; Moosmüller, *Bonifaz Wimmer,* 28.

24. Moosmüller, *Bonifaz Wimmer,* 28.

25. AMA: Wimmer to Nebauer, Altötting, May 22, 1832. This letter is translated in "Wimmer Letters," *Scriptorium* (St. John's Abbey) 17 (1958): 55–56.

26. ASVA: Wimmer Personal Documents (VAB I).

27. AMA: Wimmer to Nebauer, Altötting, July 16, 1832. See *Scriptorium* 17 (1958): 56–58.

28. AMA: Wimmer to Nebauer, Altötting, August 6, 1832. See *Scriptorium* 17 (1958): 58.

29. AMA: Wimmer to Lang, St. Vincent, May 14, 1882.

30. ASVA: Wimmer Personal Documents (VAB I); see *Scriptorium* 17 (1958): 58–59.

31. Fink, *Geschichte der Bayerischen Benediktinerkongregation*, 329–30.

32. Fellner, *Abbot Boniface and His Monks*, 1: 17.

33. AMA: Wimmer to Nebauer, Augsburg, November 5, 1835; see *Scriptorium* 17 (1958): 59–64.

34. ASVA: Wimmer to Höcker, Augsburg, May 22, 1836 (copy).

35. ASVA: Wimmer to Schwäbl, Augsburg, June 12, 1836 (copy).

36. ASVA: Ludwig I to Wimmer, Bath Brinkemau, August 3, 1836.

37. ASVA: Wimmer to Schwäbl, Augsburg, August 9, 1836 (copy).

38. ASVA: Wimmer to Utz, Edenstätten, April 8, 1837 (copy).

39. Fellner, *Abbot Boniface and His Monks*, 1: 18; Barry, "Boniface Wimmer," 276; Moosmüller, *Bonifaz Wimmer*, 23; ASVA: Wimmer to Schneider, St. Vincent, no date (File TS 6).

40. RAB: Wimmer to Ludwig I, Munich, November 29, 1841.

41. AMA: Wimmer et al. to Scherr, Munich, December 8, 1841.

42. AMA: Wimmer to Scherr, Munich, n.d., n.m., 1842.

43. Philip Taylor, *The Distant Magnet: European Emigration to the United States of America* (New York: Harper & Row, 1971).

44. Colman J. Barry, O.S.B., *The Catholic Church and German Americans* (Milwaukee: Bruce Publishing, 1953), 6.

45. Theodore Roemer, O.F.M.Cap., *The Leopoldine Foundation and the Church in the United States, 1820–1839* (New York: United States Catholic Historical Society, 1933).

46. Theodore Roemer, O.F.M.Cap., *The Ludwig Missionsverein and the Church in the United States* (Washington, D.C.: The Catholic University of America Press, 1933), 10–11.

47. Severus Brandus, *Die Katholisch-irisch-bischöfliche Administration in Nordamerika* (Philadelphia, 1840).

48. Roemer, *Ludwig Missionsverein*, 18, n14.

49. Roemer, *Ludwig Missionsverein*, 22–23.

50. Although this letter does not survive, Wimmer wrote in May 1845, "For three years in succession I have asked your permission to become a missionary"; see AMA: Wimmer to Scherr, Munich, May 28, 1845.

51. AMA: Wimmer to Scherr, Munich, July 22, 1843.

52. Roemer, *Ludwig Missionsverein*, 48–49.

53. Josef Salzbacher, *Meine Reise nach Nord-Amerika in Jahre 1842* (Vienna: Wimmer, Schmidt, & Leo, 1845).

54. See Lemke's autobiography, *Haudegen Gottes: Das Leben des Peter H. Lemke,*

ed. Willibald Mathäser, O.S.B. (Würzburg: Kommissionsverlag Echter Gesamtherstellung, 1971); Modestus Wirtner, *The Benedictine Fathers in Cambria County* (Carrolltown, Pa: Privately published, 1926), 27–65; Peter Beckman, *Kansas Monks*
(Atchison: Abbey Student Press, 1957), 29–43; and Terrence Kardong, "Peter Henry
Lemke: 'Brave Soldier of the Lord' or Gyrovague?," *Tjurunga: An Australian Benedictine Review* 24 (1983): 44–65.

55. Peter H. Lemke, O.S.B., "Autobiography," *Northern Cambria News* (Carrolltown, Pennsylvania), November 8, 1879. The letter to the Mainz *Katholic* is quoted
in Wirtner, *Benedictine Fathers in Cambria County,* 52.

56. AMA: Wimmer to Scherr, Munich, May 28, 1845.

57. AMA: Wimmer to Scherr, Munich, June 5, 1845.

58. ASVA: Lemke to Wimmer, Munich, June 15, 1845.

59. AMA: Wimmer to Scherr, Munich, June 30, 1845.

60. ASVA: Fransoni to Wimmer, Rome, July 3, 1845.

61. AMA: Wimmer to Scherr, Munich, August 5, 1845.

62. AMA: Wimmer to Scherr, Munich, October 29, 1845; see *Scriptorium* 18
(1959): 69–70.

Notes to Chapter 2

1. [Boniface Wimmer], "Über die Missionen," *Augsburger Postzeitung,* November
8, 1845, translated in "Boniface Wimmer Outlines the Future of the Benedictine Order in the United States, November 8, 1845," in *Documents of American Catholic History,* 3 vols., ed. John Tracy Ellis (Wilmington, Del.: Michael Glazier, 1987), 1:
280–88, and in Colman J. Barry, *Worship and Work: St. John's Abbey and University
1856–1992* (Collegeville, Minn.: Liturgical Press, 1993), 479$85.

2. AMA: Wimmer to Scherr, Munich, November 11, 1845.

3. Felix Fellner, O.S.B., *Abbot Boniface and His Monks* (Latrobe, Pa.: Privately
published at St. Vincent Archabbey, 1956), 1: 37; Colman J. Barry, O.S.B., "Boniface
Wimmer, Pioneer of the American Benedictines," *Catholic Historical Review* 41
(1955): 278.

4. Peter Henry Lemke, O.S.B., "Autobiography," *Northern Cambria News* (Carrolltown, Pa.), November 9, 1879.

5. AMA: Wimmer to Lang, Munich, December 18, 1845; Wimmer to Scherr, Munich, December 28, 1845, and January 26, 1846.

6. Abbot Gregory Scherr gave Wimmer formal written permission to undertake
the American mission on February 14, 1846. Wimmer attached a copy of the document to a letter he sent to the Ludwig Missionsverein requesting financial assistance
for the mission. See ALMV: Wimmer to Ludwig Missionsverein, Munich, February 26, 1846. Scherr wrote: "With this document I freely dismiss Boniface Wimmer,
a professed monk of this house in good standing, to this end: that he may labor in
the American missions for the honor of God and the salvation of souls and that with
legitimate authority he may establish one or more monasteries of the Order of St.

Benedict. Nor do I intend to revoke this permission except for grave cause or unless the project fails. Metten, February 14, 1846. Gregory, Abbot."

7. AMA: Wimmer to Scherr, Munich, March 16, 1846; see *Scriptorium* 18 (1959): 71–72.

8. ASVA: Students to Wimmer, Munich, February 16, 1846; Wimmer to Students, Munich, February 19, 1846.

9. AMA: Wimmer to Scherr, Munich, May 6, 1846; see *Scriptorium* 18 (1959): 72–73; Fellner, *Abbot Boniface and His Monks,* 1: 46–50.

10. ASVA: Ziegler to Wimmer, Linz, May 30, 1846.

11. AMA: Wimmer to Scherr, Munich, June 5, 1846; ADL: Wimmer to Ziegler, Munich, June 9, 1846.

12. AMA: Wimmer to Scherr, Munich, June 5, 1846.

13. AMA: Wimmer to Scherr, Munich, June 23, 1846.

14. ASVA: Lemke to Wimmer, St. Joseph's, May 28, 1846.

15. ADL: Wimmer to Ziegler, Munich, June 30, 1846; see also AMA: Wimmer to Scherr, Munich, June 30, 1846.

16. AMA: Wimmer to Scherr, Munich, July 16, 1846; see *Scriptorium* 18 (1959): 74–75.

17. ACPF: Morichini to Propaganda, Munich, July 26, 1846.

18. ADL: Wimmer to Ziegler, Mainz, July 30, 1846.

19. Fellner, *Abbot Boniface and His Monks,* 1: 52–53.

20. National Archives of the United States: Passenger list of the *Iowa,* September 16, 1846 (microfilm M–237, roll 64). Of the eighteen Benedictine candidates all but three were to persevere throughout their lives as Benedictine monks. George Wimmer and Leonard Hiller left the community of Saint Vincent before pronouncing final vows. Peter Seemüller, who took vows, left the monastery, attempted marriage, but was reconciled with both the order and the Church before his death in 1885. (ASVA: *Album Fratrum Conversorum.*)

21. Felix Fellner, O.S.B., "Archabbot Boniface Wimmer as an Educator," *National Benedictine Educational Association Bulletin* 25(1942): 9.

22. AMA: Wimmer to Scherr, Aboard the *Iowa,* September 1–11, 1846; see *Scriptorium* 18(1959): 76–82. Father Maximilian Gärtner, the Premonstratensian superior, kept a diary of the voyage which was published in *Annalen der Verbreitung des Glaubens* (Munich, 1847), 76–82 and 404–9.

23. See Colman J. Barry, *Worship and Work: Saint John's Abbey and University 1856–1992* (Collegeville, Minn.: Liturgical Press, 1993), 9.

24. Lemke, "Autobiography," *Northern Cambria News,* November 8, 1879.

25. See Peter H. Lemke, *Life and Work of Prince Demetrius Augustine Gallitzin,* trans. Joseph C. Plumpe (New York: Longmans, Green & Co.), 1940; Grace Murphy, *Gallitzin's Letters: A Collection of Polemical Works of the Very Reverend Prince Demetrius Augustine Gallitzin, 1770–1840* (Loretto, Pa.: Angelmodde Press, 1940); and Daniel Sargent, *Mitri; or, the Story of Prince Demetrius Augustine Gallitzin, 1770–1840* (New York: Longmans, Green & Co., 1945).

26. Modestus Wirtner, O.S.B., *The Benedictine Fathers in Cambria Country* (Carrolltown, Pa.: Privately published, 1926), 51.

27. ASVA: Wimmer to Meyringer, St. Vincent, December 30, 1846.

28. For a detailed account, see Henry Szarnicki, *Michael O'Connor, First Catholic Bishop of Pittsburgh, 1843–1860* (Pittsburgh: Wolfson Publishing, 1975), 55–56, 82–83.

29. ASVA: Theodore Brouwers papers and parish records.

30. See Omer U. Kline, O.S.B., *The Sportsman's Hall Parish, Later Named St. Vincent, 1790–1846* (Latrobe, Pa.: Archabbey Press, 1990); Vincent Huber, O.S.B., "Sportsman's Hall and St. Vincent Abbey," *St. Vincent Journal* 1 (1892); and Fellner, *Abbot Boniface and His Monks,* 1: 68–75.

31. ADL: Wimmer to Ziegler, St. Vincent, November 5, 1846. See Kline, *The Sportsman's Hall Parish,* 7, 63–66, 81–82, and 85–86.

32. ASVA: Parishioners to Wimmer, Youngstown, October 11, 1846; O'Connor to Wimmer, Youngstown, October 11, 1846.

33. Huber, "Sportsman's Hall," 301; Wirtner, *Benedictine Fathers in Cambria County,* 53–57; and Fellner, *Abbot Boniface and His Monks,* 1: 60–65.

34. ASVA: O'Connor to Wimmer, Youngstown, November 5, 1846.

35. ALMV: Wimmer to Müller, St. Vincent, October 26, 1846; quoted in Oswald Moosmüller, O.S.B., *Bonifaz Wimmer, Erzabt von St. Vincent in Pennsylvanien* (New York: Benziger Bros., 1891), 63–67; translated in Fellner, *Abbot Boniface and His Monks,* 1: 77–79.

36. Oswald Moosmüller, O.S.B., *Europäer in Amerika vor Columbus* (Regensburg: G. J. Manz, 1879), 169–70.

37. Fellner, *Abbot Boniface and His Monks,* 1: 55; Aloysius Plaisance, O.S.B., "Dom Pierre Joseph Didier, Pioneer Benedictine in the United States," *ABR* 3 (1952), 23–26; Peter Guilday, *The Life and Times of John Carroll* (New York: Encyclopedia Press, 1922), 1: 392–407.

38. Archives of Downside Abbey: Carroll to Pembridge, Baltimore, September 19, 1794. Carroll's letter is published in *ABR* 22 (1971): 175–76, and in *The John Carroll Papers,* 3 vols., ed. Thomas O'Brien Hanley (Notre Dame, Ind.: Notre Dame University Press, 1976), 2:128–29. See Rene Kollar, "Plans for an 18th-Century Benedictine Settlement in Western Pennsylvania: Bishop John Carroll and the English Benedictine Congregation" *Word and Spirit: A Monastic Review* 14 (1992): 3–11.

39. ASVA: Balleis Records; Fellner, *Abbot Boniface and His Monks,* 1: 55.

40. Fellner, *Abbot Boniface and His Monks,* 1: 55.

41. RAB: Wimmer to Ludwig I, St. Vincent, January 25, 1851.

42. ALMV: Wimmer to Müller, St. Vincent, October 26, 1846. See also ADL: Wimmer to Ziegler, St. Vincent, November 5, 1846. For a similar account of the horarium during the early days, see Oswald Moosmüller, O.S.B., *St. Vincenz in Pennsylvanien* (New York and Cincinnati: F. Pustet, 1873), 39–40; and Barry, "Boniface Wimmer," 281–82.

43. ASVA: Wimmer to Meyringer, St. Vincent, December 30, 1846.

44. ALMV: Wimmer to von Reisach, St. Vincent, December 17, 1846.

45. ASVA: *Album Capitularium.*

46. ALMV: Wimmer to Müller, St. Vincent, October 20, 1846; quoted in Moosmüller, *St. Vincenz in Pennsylvanien,* 39.

47. Archives of the Archdiocese of Milwaukee: Müller to Henni, Munich, March 1, 1847. See Theodore Roemer, *The Ludwig Missionsverein and the Catholic Church in the United States, 1838–1918* (Washington, D.C.: The Catholic University of America Press), 34–35.

48. ASVA: Müller to Wimmer, Munich, October 5, 1846.

49. ASVA: Müller to Wimmer, Munich, December 23, 1846.

50. ALMV: Wimmer to von Reisach, St. Vincent, March 1, 1847.

51. RAB: Wimmer to Ludwig I, Munich, January 25, 1851.

52. ASVA: O'Connor to Wimmer, Pittsburgh, April 14, 1847; translated in Fellner, *Abbot Boniface and His Monks,* 1: 93–94. Bishop O'Connor, like other American bishops of his day, believed that the canonical concept of "exemption" should not have been allowed to gain a foothold in the American Church. Hence, his opposition to many of Wimmer's plans can be understood in terms of his desire to keep the Benedictines firmly under episcopal control. For this reason O'Connor wanted Wimmer to "establish a seminary separate from the abbey, of which he, O'Connor, would act as rector." See Edward E. Malone, trans., "A Long Lost Letter of Boniface Wimmer," *ABR* 20 (1969): 311, n 6. O'Connor's concerns about exemption seem also to explain more fully his reluctance to support Wimmer's petition to establish St. Vincent as a canonical priory in 1848. When the monastery was finally elevated to the rank of priory in 1852, it remained nonexempt, and did not achieve the status of exemption until 1855 when it became an abbey.

53. See Fellner, *Abbot Boniface and His Monks,* 1: 89–90; and Willibald Mathäser, *Der Ludwig-Missionsverein in der Zeit König Ludwigs I von Bayern* (Munich: Druck der Salesianischen Offizin, 1939), 248–50.

54. ASVA: O'Connor to Wimmer, Pittsburgh, May 8, 1847. See Fellner, *Abbot Boniface and His Monks,* 1: 95–105; and Szarnicki, *Michael O'Connor,* 82–87.

55. ASVA: Wimmer to O'Connor, St. Vincent, May 10, 1847.

56. ASVA: O'Connor to Wimmer, Pittsburgh, May 13, 1847; translated in Fellner, *Abbot Boniface and His Monks,* 1: 94–96.

57. ALMV: Wimmer to Ludwig Missionsverein, St. Vincent, 1855; printed in *Annalen der Verbreitung des Glaubens* (Munich, 1856), 85.

58. ASA: Wimmer to Leiss, St. Vincent, October 12–31, 1847.

59. ASVA: O'Connor to Wimmer, Pittsburgh, November 2, 1847.

60. ASVA: O'Connor to Wimmer, Pittsburgh, February 15, 1848.

61. Father Gallagher left the community in June 1847 and went to Brownsville, Pennsylvania. Later he moved to Boston where he became an Augustinian. He served as pastor in Philadelphia and founded St. Nicholas Church, Atlantic City, New Jersey. See Fellner, *Abbot Boniface and His Monks,* 1: 114.

62. ASVA: O'Connor to Wimmer, Pittsburgh, February 15, 1848; translated in Fellner, *Abbot Boniface and His Monks,* 1: 104.

63. ASA: Wimmer to Leiss, St. Vincent, March 1, 1848.

64. ALMV: Wimmer to von Reisach, St. Vincent, March 3, 1848.

65. ASA: Wimmer to Leiss, St. Vincent, October 12, 1847.

66. ADL: Wimmer to Ziegler, St. Vincent, June 11, 1848.

67. ALMV: Wimmer to von Reisach, St. Vincent, July 2, 1847.

68. AMA: Wimmer to Scherr, St. Vincent, December 22, 1848.

69. ASA: Wimmer to Leiss, St. Vincent, March 12, 1849.

70. AMA: Brunner to Scherr, St. Vincent, June 18, 1849.

71. AMA: Lechner to Scherr, St. Vincent, April 21, 1849.

72. AMA: Brunner to Scherr, Carrolltown, July 2, 1849.

73. ASA: Wimmer to Leiss, St. Vincent, June 27, 1849. Bishop Maurice St. Palais of Vincennes, Indiana, unsuccessfully sought assistance from Wimmer to establish a Benedictine community in his diocese. Three years later St. Palais visited Switzerland and invited monks from the Abbey of Einsiedeln to establish a community in his diocese. This community became St. Meinrad Archabbey, the motherhouse of the Swiss American Congregation.

The "four priests of [his] own" to whom Wimmer refers in this letter were Charles Geyerstanger, Benedict Haindl, Placidus Döttl, and Celestine Englbrecht who had accompanied him to Pennsylvania in 1846. Bishop O'Connor ordained Haindl, Döttl, and Englbrecht on April 20, 1849. Geyerstanger had been ordained earlier, on March 18, 1847.

74. AMA: Wimmer to Leiss, St. Vincent, July 4–8, 1849; Wimmer to Leiss, St. Vincent, October 9, 1849.

75. AMA: Müller to Scherr, Munich, August 19, 1849.

76. ASVA: Müller to Wimmer, Munich, August 8, 1849.

77. ASA: Wimmer to Leiss, St. Vincent, March 27, 1850.

78. ASA: Wimmer to Leiss, Munich, December 28, 1850.

79. Lechner's commentary on Sacred Scripture was published at St. Vincent between 1881 and 1884. See Peter Lechner, O.S.B., *Die Heilige Schrift des Alten Testamentes nach der Vulgata und dem Grundtext erklärt* (Beatty, Pa.: St. Vincent Press, 1882, 1884); *Die Heilige Schrift des Neuen Testamentes nach der Vulgata und dem Grundtext erklärt* (Beatty, Pa.: St. Vincent Press, 1881). His other works included *Ausführliches Martyrologium des Benediktinerordens und seiner Verzweigungen* (Augsburg: B. Schmid, 1855) and *Leben der heiligen Benedikt, Ordenstifters und Abtes auf Monte Cassino* (Regensburg: G. J. Manz, 1857). For a complete list of Lechner's publications, see Oliver Kapsner, *A Benedictine Bibliography: An Author-Subject Union List*, Vol. 1, Author Part (Collegeville, Minn.: St. John's Abbey Press, 1962), 326–28, which includes twenty-nine items.

80. Peter Lechner, O.S.B., "Missionsbericht des P. Petrus Lechner," *Berichten der Leopoldinen Stiftung* (Vienna) 25 (1853): 79–94.

Notes to Chapter 3

1. [Boniface Wimmer, O.S.B.], "Über die Missionen," *Augsburger Postzeitung*, November 8, 1845; translated in *Documents of American Catholic History*, 3 vols., ed. John Tracy Ellis (Wilmington, Del.: Michael Glazier, 1991), 1: 287.

2. ALMV: Wimmer to Müller, St. Vincent, December 1848. See Felix Fellner, O.S.B., "Archabbot Boniface Wimmer as an Educator," *National Benedictine Educational Association Bulletin* 25 (1942): 95.

3. Fellner, "Archabbot Boniface Wimmer as an Educator," 95.

4. ALMV: Wimmer to *Missionsverein,* St. Vincent, November 7, 1851.

5. ALMV: Wimmer to von Reisach, St. Vincent, August 9, 1852.

6. AMA: Wimmer to Scherr, St. Vincent, August 14, 1850.

7. *Annalen der Verbreitung des Glaubens* (Munich, 1853), 396.

8. Joseph Maurice Schwab came to St. Vincent in 1851, and except for a brief period in 1856–1857 when he was director of music at St. Philomena Church, Pittsburgh, he served as professor of music and *kappelmeister* at St. Vincent until his death in 1875. For a full account of Schwab and his work at St. Vincent, see Fred J. Moleck, *Nineteenth-Century Musical Activity at St. Vincent Archabbey* (Ph.D. diss., University of Pittsburgh, 1971).

9. *Annalen der Verbreitung des Glaubens* (Munich, 1853), 16–18.

10. Moleck, *Nineteenth-Century Musical Activity at St. Vincent Archabbey,* 1–35. See also Fred J. Moleck, "Music at St. Vincent under Abbot Boniface Wimmer," *ABR* 14 (1963): 248–62.

11. ALMV: Wimmer to von Reisach, St. Vincent, July 3, 1851.

12. Quoted in Felix Fellner, *Abbot Boniface and His Monks,* 5 vols. (Latrobe, Pa.: Privately published, 1956), 2: 165.

13. *Annalen der Verbreitung des Glaubens* (Munich, 1853); quoted in Fellner, "Archabbot Boniface Wimmer as an Educator," 19.

14. Archives of the Abbey of Sancta Maria, Vienna: Wimmer to Schulte, St. Vincent [1853]; quoted in Fellner, *Abbot Boniface and His Monks,* 1: 114.

15. ASA: Wimmer to Leiss, St. Vincent, March 27, 1850.

16. ALVM: Wimmer to von Reisach, St. Vincent, March 1, 1847.

17. AMA: Wimmer to Scherr, St. Vincent, July 6, 1853.

18. ALMV: Wimmer to von Reisach, St. Vincent, March 27, 1850.

19. AMA: Wimmer to Scherr, St. Vincent, August 14, 1850.

20. ASA: Wimmer to Leiss, Munich, December 28, 1850.

21. ASVA: Wimmer to Propaganda, Munich, January 20, 1851; Wimmer to Friend (S.J.), Munich, January 20, 1851. See Fellner, *Abbot Boniface and His Monks,* 1: 136.

22. ASVA: Barnabo to Wimmer, Rome, February 1851.

23. RAB: Wimmer to Ludwig I, Munich, January 25, 1851.

24. ACPF: Von Spaur to Propaganda, Rome, May 22, 1851.

25. ASVA: Ludwig I to Wimmer, Rome, June 24, 1851.

26. ASVA: O'Connor to Kirby, Pittsburgh, August 13, 1851 (copy).

27. ACPF: O'Connor to Propaganda, On Visitation, August 18, 1851. See Henry Szarnicki, *Michael O'Connor: First Catholic Bishop of Pittsburgh: 1843–1860* (Pittsburgh: Wolfson Publishing, 1975), 91.

28. ACPF: Wimmer to Propaganda, St. Vincent, September 4, 1851.

29. ACPF: O'Connor to Propaganda, Milwaukee, October 22, 1851.

30. Archives of the Catholic University of America: O'Connor to Smith, Pitts-

burgh, November 20, 1851 (Bernard Smith Letters on microfilm). See Szarnicki, *Michael O'Connor,* 199.

31. ALMV: Wimmer to von Reisach, St. Vincent, January 1, 1852.

32. RAB: Fransoni to von Spaur, Rome, February 17, 1852.

33. ASVA: Fransoni to Wimmer, Rome, February 14, 1852.

34. RAB: Wimmer to Ludwig I, St. Vincent, February 13, 1852.

35. Beer brewing at St. Vincent caused some scandal during the nineteenth century and gave grist to the mill of anti-Catholic propaganda. The *New York Voice* published an "exposé" on April 21, 1898, under the headline "Students of St. Vincent's Monastic College Trained for Roman Catholic Priesthood Amid Fumes of a Brew-Pot Steaming Under Direct Authority of Pope Pius IX. Monks, Said to Be Trained to Absolute Self-Denial, Fight like Tigers Whenever Their Beer Is Assailed." And Philadelphia's *Griffin's Journal* of April 1, 1894, interpreted the initials "O.S.B." as "Order of Sacred Brewers."

Wimmer himself, even in retrospect, continued to regard the beer controversy as a serious matter. Writing to Bishop Mathias Loras of Dubuque in 1856, he said, "It may seem a laughable affair to bring such a question before the Apostolic See; but for us it was truly important. We are now ten years in this country; all of us have been used to drinking beer; here we have it not; it is too high in price to buy it for so many (we were at the time 100 men; now we are 150, not accounted 100 scholars); but it is cheap, if we would distill it ourselves; however, if we dare not sell any, we cannot afford either to brew it for our own use, it being yet too costly; and always being obliged to drink fresh water and nothing else, it is a thing which no religious orders, even the Trappists, Carthusians and Paulans are obliged to do. Therefore all religious orders, except Capuchins and Franciscans, were allowed everywhere to sell the wine of their own vineyards, or the beer of their own distilleries, in order to have from profit on the sale their own drinks gratis, and not only in barrels, but (of course not in the monasteries and by their own friars) even in retail in taverns kept for that purpose. . . .

"While I was in Rome last summer, even the Holy Father plagued me a little in an audience I had with him, about the beer-affair. I replied: 'Holy Father, you have a good saying about your Benedictines brewing and selling beer; but you forget that we don't drink any these nine years, and that we have no brewery.' 'Germans and not drinking beer,' he replied, 'that is much.' 'Yes, indeed,' I said, 'until now we could do so, being young; but when we grow older, we will probably be in necessity to make beer.' 'Of course,' he said, 'S. Paul also wrote to S. Timothy he should take a little wine for his weak stomach, and so you must have something'—and he laughed heartily.

"This is the fact Right Rev. Bishop, of which six years ago many a joke was made by Temperance-men, who indeed brew no beer, but drink strong ales, spirits and wines, and preach temperance to the hard working classes.

"I may have been imprudent in getting my hands into that business, but I could hardly help it, and from the notions I have of that business I could positively not foresee any difficulty or scandal, except from the temperance men; and with regard to these men, I only say, I divide them into two classes—in fools and hypocrites; and I could easily defend this thesis. The Apostolic See has at different times and repeatedly declared against this temperance system, which is of no Catholic character." Archives of the Archdiocese of Dubuque: Wimmer to Loras, St. Vincent, February 8, 1856. Quoted in Szarnicki, *Michael O'Connor,* 93–94, and in Colman J. Barry, "Boniface Wimmer: Pioneer of the American Benedictines," *Catholic Historical Review* 41 (1955): 287–88.

36. Archives of Holy Cross Priory: Bauer to von Riede, Regensburg, 1853. *Holy Cross Chronicle,* 3: 8. See Sister M. Hortense Kohler, O.P., *The Life and Work of Mother Benedicta Bauer, O.P.* (Milwaukee: Bruce Publishing, 1937), 94.

37. Kohler, *Mother Benedicta Bauer,* 96–97.

38. Kohler, *Mother Benedicta Bauer,* 97–100.

39. This is the view expressed by Kohler (footnote 36) and Crawford (footnote 40).

40. AMA: Wimmer to Scherr, St. Vincent, July 29, 1853. See Eugene Joseph Crawford, *Daughters of Dominic on Long Island* (New York: Benziger Brothers, 1938), 42.

41. Crawford, *Daughters of Dominic,* 39–62.

42. Crawford, *Daughters of Dominic,* 48.

43. Crawford, *Daughters of Dominic,* 50–53.

44. ASVA: Wimmer to Bauer, St. Vincent, September 18, 1853 (copy). This letter is quoted by Crawford with an important commentary, 53–62.

45. AMA: Wimmer to Scherr, St. Vincent, December 24, 1853.

46. AMA: Wimmer to Scherr, St. Vincent, February 28, 1854.

47. ALMV: Wimmer to von Reisach, St. Vincent, January 1, 1852; quoted in Joel Rippinger, *The Benedictine Order in the United States: An Interpretive History* (Collegeville, Minn.: Liturgical Press, 1990), 73.

48. For an account of the Benedictine sisters' arrival in America, see the MS memoirs of Sister Nepomucene Ludwig, O.S.B., in the archives of St. Joseph's Convent, St. Marys, Pennsylvania. These memoirs were written in 1913, but Sister Nepomucene entered the convent at St. Marys in 1855 and would have known the earliest traditions of the community. For other accounts of the arrival, see Sister Regina Baska, O.S.B., *The Benedictine Congregation of St. Scholastica: Its Foundation and Development, 1852–1930* (Washington, D.C.: The Catholic University of America Press, 1935), 8–12; Sister Grace McDonald, O.S.B., *With Lamps Burning* (St. Paul, Minn.: St. Benedict's Convent, 1957); Sisters Louis Morkin, O.S.B., and Theophane Seigel, O.S.B., *Wind in the Wheat* (Erie, Pa.: McCarty Publishing, 1956), 55–56; Sister Faith Schuster, O.S.B., *The Meaning of the Mountain* (Baltimore: Helican Press, 1953), 13–19; Fellner, *Abbot Boniface and His Monks,* 2: 156–59; Sister Incarnata Girgen, O.S.B., *Behind the Beginnings: Benedictine Women in America* (St. Joseph, Minn.: St. Benedict's Convent, 1981), 13–18; Jerome Oetgen, "Benedictine Women in Nineteenth-Century America," *ABR* 34 (1983): 296–98; and Ephrem Hollermann, O.S.B., *The Reshaping of a Tradition: American Benedictine Women 1852–1881* (St. Joseph, Minn.: Sisters of the Order of St. Benedict, 1994), 57–66.

49. ASVA: Church Book of St. Vincent Parish, July 15, 1852 (pp. 39–40).

50. ASA: Wimmer to Leiss, St. Vincent, October 8, 1852.

51. RAB: Wimmer to Ludwig I, St. Vincent, July 4, 1853; translated in Girgen, *Behind the Beginnings,* 28.

52. Hollermann, *The Reshaping of a Tradition,* 64–80. See also Baska, *The Benedictine Congregation of St. Scholastica,* 34–35.

53. ASA: Wimmer to Leiss, St. Vincent, October 8, 1852.

54. ASA: Wimmer to Missionsverein, St. Vincent, April 5, 1852; Fellner, "Archabbot Boniface Wimmer as an Educator," 20–21.

55. In several letters Wimmer mentions that fifteen lay brother candidates accompanied him from Munich. Evidence from other written records indicates that only fourteen brother novices were invested with the habit in October 1846. It is probable that a fifteenth candidate accompanied the missionary band to the United States but abandoned the mission before the community settled at St. Vincent.

56. Archives of the Abbey of Schottenstift (Vienna): Wimmer to Kremsmünster, St. Vincent, October 19, 1852. See Edward J. Malone, trans., "A Long Lost Letter of Boniface Wimmer (October 19, 1852)," *ABR* 20 (1969): 316–17.

57. RAB: Wimmer to Ludwig I, St. Vincent, July 4, 1853; quoted in Rippinger, *The Benedictine Order in the United States,* 37–38.

58. Modestus Wirtner, *The Benedictine Fathers in Cambria County* (Carrolltown, Pa.: Privately published, 1926), 23–24.

59. Wirtner, *Benedictine Fathers in Cambria County,* 106–8.

60. ASA: Wimmer to Leiss, St. Vincent, October 8, 1852.

61. *Annalen der Verbreitung des Glaubens* (Munich, 1848), 174–97.

62. John F. Byrne, *The Redemptorist Centenaries* (Philadelphia: Dolphin Press, 1932), 197.

63. AMA: Wimmer to Scherr, St. Vincent, August 14, 1850.

64. ASVA: Benzinger-Eschbach to Garner, Baltimore, July 21, 1850; quoted in Fellner, *Abbot Boniface and His Monks,* 2: 152.

65. ALMV: Wimmer to von Reisach, St. Vincent, January 1, 1852. See Remegius Burgemeister, *History of the Development of Catholicity in St. Marys* (St. Marys: Privately published, 1919).

66. Fellner, *Abbot Boniface and His Monks,* 2: 154.

67. Archives of the Abbey of Schottenstift (Vienna): Wimmer to Kremsmünster, October 19, 1852. Malone, "A Long Lost Letter of Boniface Wimmer," 312–13.

68. Fellner, *Abbot Boniface and His Monks,* 2: 175–76.

69. ADL: Wimmer to Ziegler, St. Vincent, November 7, 1851.

70. ASVA: O'Connor to Wimmer, St. Vincent, July 15, 1852. See Fellner, *Abbot Boniface and His Monks,* 2: 149–62.

71. Fellner, *Abbot Boniface and His Monks,* 1: 113–14 and 2: 153–54.

72. AMA: Wimmer to Scherr, St. Vincent, July 6, 1853.

73. Fellner, *Abbot Boniface and His Monks,* 2: 186.

74. ACPF: Wimmer to Pius IX, St. Vincent, November 10, 1853; Wimmer to Morichini, St. Vincent, November 11, 1853.

75. ACPF: Wimmer to Fransoni, St. Vincent, December 11, 1853.

76. ASVA: Morichini to Wimmer, Rome, January 15, 1854.

77. ASVA: Fransoni to Wimmer, Rome, February 7, 1854.

78. ACPF: O'Connor to Fransoni, Pittsburgh, April 12, 1854; see Szarnicki, *Michael O'Connor*, 99–100.

79. ACPF: Bedini to Propaganda, Rome, July 12, 1854.

80. ACPF: St. Vincent Monks to Pius IX, St. Vincent, December 8, 1854; this letter is quoted in Fellner, *Abbot Boniface and His Monks,* 1: 192–94.

81. ACPF: Wimmer to Fransoni, St. Vincent, December 18, 1854.

82. ASJA: Wimmer to di Marogna, Rome, April 9, 1855; AMA: Wimmer to Scherr, May 1, 1855. See Fellner, *Abbot Boniface and His Monks,* 2: 200.

83. ACPF: O'Connor to Fransoni, Pittsburgh, December 1854; quoted in Fellner, *Abbot Boniface and His Monks,* II: 200–02.

84. ACPF: O'Connor to Fransoni, Pittsburgh, February 13, 1855; see Szarnicki, *Michael O'Connor*, 101–3.

85. ACPF: Pescetelli to Fransoni, Rome, March 12, 1855.

86. ASJA: Wimmer to di Marogna, Rome, April 18, 1855.

87. ASJA: Wimmer to di Marogna, Rome, May 13, 1855.

88. ASVA: Roman Document, April 21, 1855.

89. ALMV: Wimmer to von Reisach, Rome, May 30, 1855.

90. ASJA: Wimmer to di Marogna, Rome, May 13, 1855.

91. RAB: Wimmer to Ludwig I, Rome, June 4, 1855.

92. ASJA: Wimmer to di Marogna, Rome, June 27, 1855; quoted in Fellner, *Abbot Boniface and His Monks,* 2: 216–17.

93. ASJA: Wimmer to di Marogna, Rome, July 29, 1855.

94. ASVA: Roman Document, July 30, 1855.

95. ASVA: Apostolic Brief, September 17, 1855.

96. RAB: Wimmer to Ludwig I, Munich, August 19, 1855.

97. Archives of Kremsmünster Abbey: Wimmer to Kremsmünster, Munich, August 17, 1855.

98. ASJA: Wimmer to di Marogna, Munich, August 22, 1855.

99. Fellner, *Abbot Boniface and His Monks,* 2: 230.

100. AMA: Wimmer to Scherr, On the Ocean, November 21, 1855.

101. ALMV: Wimmer to von Reisach, St. Vincent, December 14, 1855.

102. Fellner, *Abbot Boniface and His Monks,* 2: 233.

103. ASVA: O'Connor to Wimmer, Pittsburgh, December 14, 1855.

Notes to Chapter 4

1. [Boniface Wimmer, O.S.B.], "Über die Missionen," *Augsburger Postzeitung,* November 8, 1845; translated in *Documents of American Catholic History,* 3 vols., ed. John Tracy Ellis (Wilmington, Del.: Michael Glazier, 1991), 1: 287.

2. *Annalen der Verbreitung des Glaubens* (Munich, 1856), 374.

3. ALMV: Wimmer to Missionsverein, St. Vincent, February 26, 1857.

4. ASA: Wimmer to Leiss, St. Vincent, April 26, 1856. See also ALMV: Wimmer to Missionsverein, St. Vincent, March 7, 1856.

The chapter of 1856 was called the *Erstes Generalcapitel* and the acts of the chapter of 1858 the *Acta Secundi Capituli*. The chapter of 1862, however, was also called the "Second General Chapter" (its records are entitled *Acta Capituli Generalis Secundi*). The chapter of 1858, and not that of 1856, was officially counted as the first general chapter by the chapter of 1862 and all subsequent chapters.

The reason for this is that in 1856 there was only one independent monastery in the American Cassinese Congregation, St. Vincent. In order for a Benedictine congregation to be properly designated as such, it had to consist of at least three independent houses. This was not the case in America until the General Chapter of 1858, when the Minnesota and Kansas foundations were given independent status. Wimmer explained in a letter of November 1858 that the American Cassinese Congregation had been established in 1855 because at the time it seemed likely that the priories in St. Marys and Carrolltown were ready to become independent. (See ALMV: Wimmer to *Missionsverein*, St. Vincent, November 7, 1858.) This never occurred, and because there was only one independent monastery in the American Cassinese Congregation in 1856, later chapters considered that of 1856 a local rather than a general chapter. See ASVA: Chapter Records, 1856, 1858, 1862.

The records of the chapter of 1856 show that there were nineteen priests attached to St. Vincent in January of that year: Boniface Wimmer, first abbot and president of the congregation; Demetrius di Marogna, claustral prior at St. Vincent; Benedict Haindl, prior in St. Marys, Pennsylvania; Celestine Englbrecht, pastor at St. Vincent; Charles Geyerstanger, assistant pastor at St. Vincent ; Luke Wimmer, novice master at St. Vincent; Odilo Vandergrün, pastor in Saltsburg; Utto Huber, pastor in Butler; Rupert Seidenbusch, pastor in St. Marys; Amandus Krammer, pastor in Cooper Settlement; Augustine Wirth, pastor in Greensburg; Ulric Spöttl, director of the college at St. Vincent; Valentine Felder, pastor in Carrolltown; Clement Staub, procurator at St. Vincent; Kilian Bernetzeder, assistant in Carrolltown; Alto Hörmann, pastor in Indiana; Joseph Billon, pastor in Frenchville; Roman Hell, procurator in St. Marys; and Peter Henry Lemke, assistant in Carrolltown. Father Ildephonse Böld, prior in Carrolltown, had recently been killed in a fall from his horse while visiting parishioners in Cambria County. At the same time there were approximately one hundred and twenty lay brothers, clerics, and novices attached to the abbey. (See ASVA: Chapter Records, 1856; also see *Album Capitularium* and *Album Fratrum Conversorum*.)

5. AMA: Wimmer to Scherr, St. Vincent, March 10, 1856. A translation of this letter is published in the *Scriptorium* (St. John's Abbey), 19 (1960): 65–68. See also ALMV: Wimmer to Missionsverein, St. Vincent, February 1856, in which Wimmer writes: "The question whether we should think now or later about the foundation of new monasteries in the West occupies us intensely. There are reasons for it and against it. I would not be in America if I had not believed resolutely that now is the time and need for the Benedictine Order to spread out. I am of this opinion even yet because I believe it is easier to lock the gates of the fortress to an enemy when you

occupy it before him than to throw him out of the fortress if he gets there first. Also, if the general is not too neglectful, discipline is more strictly observed in the field than in the barracks. Therefore, I will miss no opportunity to establish a new colony of our order in the West where the stream of immigration now presses."

6. Modestus Wirtner, *The Benedictine Fathers in Cambria County* (Carrolltown, Pa.: Privately published, 1926), 27–66; Peter Beckman, *Kansas Monks: A History of St. Benedict's Abbey* (Atchison, Kans.: Abbey Student Press, 1957), 5–43; Willibald Mathäser, ed., *Haudegen Gottes: Das Leben des Peter H. Lemke* (Würzburg: Kommissionsverlag Echter Gesamtherstellung, 1971). See also Lemke's autobiography (the English version) published in the *Northern Cambria News* (Carrolltown, Pa.), vol. 1, 1879; Lawrence Flick, "Biographical Sketch of Reverend Peter H. Lemke, O.S.B.," *Records of the American Catholic Historical Society of Philadelphia* 9 (1898): 184ff; the introduction to Joseph C. Plumpe's translation of Lemke's *Life and Work of Prince Demetrius Augustine Gallitzin* (New York: Longmans, Green & Co., 1940); and Terrence Kardong, "Peter Henry Lemke: 'Brave Soldier of the Lord' or Gyrovague?," *Tjurunga: An Australian Benedictine Review* 24 (1983): 44–65.

7. ASBA: Lemke to Johnson, Westport, December 27, 1855.

8. Felix Fellner, *Abbot Boniface and His Monks,* 5 vols. (Privately published at St. Vincent Archabbey, 1956), 2: 262.

9. AMA: Wimmer to Scherr, St. Vincent, March 10, 1856. See also Fellner, *Abbot Boniface and His Monks,* 2: 261–73.

10. ASJA: *The Record,* February 1889. See Colman J. Barry, *Worship and Work,* 3rd ed. (Collegeville, Minn: Liturgi cal Press, 1993), 19 and 382. Barry's is the authoritative study of the history of the Minnesota foundation.

11. ASVA: di Marogna to Wimmer, St. Paul, May 7, 1856.

12. ASJA: "Memoirs of Alexius Hoffman, O.S.B." See Barry, *Worship and Work,* 61–62.

13. AMA: Wimmer to Lang, St. Vincent, November 28, 1856. A translation of this letter was published in the *Scriptorium* (St. John's Abbey), 19 (1960): 68–72.

14. Barry, *Worship and Work,* 43–45.

15. Beckman, *Kansas Monks,* 26.

16. ALMV: Wimmer to *Missionsverein,* St. Cloud, November 6, 1856.

17. ASVA: Miége to Wimmer, Leavenworth, March 14, 1857.

18. Beckman, *Kansas Monks,* 29–43.

19. ASJA: Wimmer to Edelbrock, St. Vincent, September 9, 1882.

20. ASA: Wimmer to Leiss, St. Vincent, October 12, 1847.

21. ALMV: Wimmer to von Reisach, St. Vincent, March 1, 1847, and ASVA: Balleis to Wimmer, Newark, November 19, 1847. See Fellner, *Abbot Boniface and His Monks,* 2: 274–76.

22. Archives of the Diocese of Newark: Wimmer to Bayley, Newark, October 3, 1854. This letter is edited and published in Giles P. Hayes, "Early Bayley-Wimmer Correspondence (1854–1857)," *ABR* 14 (1963): 480–81.

23. Archives of the Diocese of Newark: Wimmer to Bayley, Newark, September 12, 1854. Hayes, "Early Bayley- Wimmer Correspondence," 474–77.

24. ASVA: Bayley to Wimmer, Newark, September 25, 1854. See Hayes, "Early Bayley-Wimmer Correspondence," 478.

25. Bayley wrote Wimmer on March 30, 1857, asking him to reconsider the Newark offer. Wimmer's reply on April 9, 1857, indicated that he was concerned more about his foundations in the West than with any plans for a new one in the East, but Wimmer's letter crossed in the mail another sent by Bayley, dated April 11, 1857, which announced Hasslinger's sudden departure and asked for "a priest or two to take charge of the mission." On April 13, 1857, Bayley sent still another letter to Wimmer expressing regret that the abbot had apparently turned down his request, but by then Wimmer had received the bishop's letter of April 11 and appointed Father Valentine Felder to Newark. See Hayes, "Early Bayley-Wimmer Correspondence," 484–88.

26. ASVA: Felder to Wimmer, Newark, May 19, 1857.

27. Archives of the Diocese of Newark: Bishop's register, May 28, 1857. See Hayes, "Early Bayley-Wimmer Correspondence," 491, n53; Fellner, *Abbot Boniface and His Monks,* 2: 282–83; Oswald Moosmüller, *St. Vincenz in Pennsylvanien* (New York: Pustet, 1873), 241.

28. Archives of the Diocese of Newark: Wimmer to Bayley, St. Vincent, June 1, 1857. See Hayes, "Early Bayley- Wimmer Correspondence," 491–92.

29. Barry, *Worship and Work,* 95–99, 125–27.

30. RAB: Wimmer to Ludwig I, Carrolltown, August 10, 1857.

31. ASVA: Seitz to Wimmer, Doniphan, June 4, 1857; Wirth to Wimmer, Doniphan, May 10, 1857—quoted in Beckman, *Kansas Monks,* 40–41.

32. RAB: Wimmer to Ludwig I, Carrolltown, December 7, 1857.

33. ALMV: Wimmer to Missionsverein, St. Vincent, July 14, 1858.

34. The land problem that the Minnesota monks faced at this time is discussed in Barry, *Worship and Work,* 51–52.

35. AMA: Wimmer to Lang, St. Vincent, July 27, 1858.

36. AMA: Wimmer to Lang, St. Vincent, July 27, 1858.

37. ASVA: Müller to Wimmer, Munich, February 28, 1858.

38. ALMV: Wimmer to Missionsverein, St. Vincent, July 14, 1858.

39. ACPF: Wimmer to Barnabo, St. Vincent, April 28, 1858.

40. RAB: Wimmer to Ludwig I, St. Vincent, July 13, 1858. See also ALMV: Wimmer to Müller, St. Vincent, June 13, 1858.

41. ASPA: Wimmer to Pescetelli, St. Vincent, August 16, 1858.

42. ASVA: Pescetelli to Wimmer, Rome, August 30, 1858.

43. ASVA: Chapter Records, September 18, 1858; ASPA: Wimmer to Pescetelli, St. Vincent, September 18, 1858; ALMV: Wimmer to Missionsverein, St. Vincent, November 7, 1858. See also Fellner, *Abbot Boniface and His Monks,* 3: 318–19.

44. ASVA: Chapter Records, September 20–21, 1858.

45. ACPF: Wimmer to Barnabo, St. Vincent, September 18, 1858.

46. AMA: Wimmer to Lang, St. Vincent, November 8, 1858.

47. ALMV: Wimmer to Missionsverein, St. Vincent, December 10, 1858.

48. RAB: Wimmer to Ludwig I, St. Vincent, December 12, 1858.

49. ASVA: Barnabo to Wimmer, Rome, November 11, 1858.

50. ASVA: Pescetelli to Wimmer, Rome, December 10, 1858.

51. ASVA: Roman Document, December 20, 1858; Barnabo to Wimmer, Rome, December 29, 1858.

52. ASPA: Wimmer to Pescetelli, St. Vincent, February 16, 1859.

53. ASVA: Pescetelli to Wimmer, Rome, April 12, 1859. See Fellner, *Abbot Boniface and His Monks,* 3: 325–26.

54. ASPA: Wimmer to Pescetelli, St. Vincent, June 15, 1859.

55. A brief survey of the history of this community, which eventually became St. Mary's Abbey, is found in Malachy McPadden, *The Benedictines in Newark 1842–1992* (Newark, N.J.: Privately published, 1992).

56. ASA: Wimmer to Leiss, St. Vincent, January 16, 1859; Wimmer to Leiss, Carrolltown, February 25, 1859.

57. ASA: Wimmer to Leiss, St. Vincent, January 16, 1859.

58. Robert J. Brennan, "Benedictines in Virginia," *ABR* 13 (1962): 26.

59. ASVA: Letters from Prelates, 1856–1861. See also Oswald Moosmüller, O.S.B., *Chronicon Monasterii St. Vincent in Pennsylvania,* a handwritten chronicle in two volumes containing copies of letters from American bishops requesting priests from St. Vincent.

60. ASVA: Odin to Wimmer, Galveston, March 12, 1859.

61. RAB: Wimmer to Ludwig I, St. Vincent, July 25 1859. For accounts of the Texas foundation see Fellner, *Abbot Boniface and His Monks,* 3: 356–68; Willibald Mathäser, "San José in Texas," *Studien und Mitteilungen* 60 (1946): 309–30; and Moosmüller, *St. Vincenz,* 264–74.

62. ASPA: Wimmer to Pescetelli, St. Vincent, December 18, 1859.

63. *Cincinnati Wahrheitsfreund,* October 8, 1862.

64. Recent studies of the early history of the Benedictine nuns in America have shed much light on the conflict between Boniface Wimmer and Benedicta Riepp and resulted in a better understanding of the causes and consequences of their disagreements. Sister Incarnata Girgen's *Behind the Beginnings: Benedictine Women in America* (St. Paul, Minn.: St. Benedict's Convent, 1981) is an invaluable source for translations of all contemporary correspondence and documents relating to the controversy. Sister Judith Sutera's *True Daughters: Monastic Identity and American Benedictine Women's History* (Atchison, Kans.: Mount St. Scholastica, 1987) is a careful and competent examination of the canonical and ecclesiastical context within which the conflict played out. Sister Ephrem Hollermann's *The Reshaping of a Tradition: American Benedictine Women 1852–1881* (St. Joseph, Minn.: Sisters of the Order of St. Benedict, 1994) includes a superb scholarly examination of the Wimmer-Riepp controversy and provides considerable insight into the experiences of the earliest Benedictine communities of women in the United States. See also Judith Sutera, "Pioneers in Search of an Identity," *Benedictines* 35 (1980): 25–36. For the discussion that follows I am indebted to the work of each of these scholars, though some of the conclusions I draw are different from theirs.

65. ALMV: Wimmer to Müller, Pittsburgh, July 24, 1857; see Girgen, *Behind the Beginnings,* 87.

66. "No official collection of church law was made from 1317 until 1917. In the six centuries which intervened, the laws of 1317 were added to through the decrees of ecumenical and national councils, decisions of Roman congregations, and various kinds of papal documents. To clarify a point of law, one had to consult an immense number of works and to deal with ordinances that were contradictory, some of which had been repealed, and others which had become obsolete through long disuse. Longstanding custom also had the force of law. The situation was further complicated by the fact that the United States was considered until 1908 to be mission territory and hence under the jurisdiction of the Roman congregation of the Propaganda rather than general church law." Mary Ewens, *The Role of the Nun in Nineteenth Century America* (New York: Arno Press, 1978), 14. Quoted in Sutera, *True Daughters,* 5.

67. Sutera, *True Daughters,* 5–18, and Hollermann, *The Reshaping of a Tradition,* 1–53.

68. Garrett Francis Barry, *Violation of the Cloister* (Washington, D.C.: The Catholic University of America Press, 1942), 85.

69. [Emmanuel Drey et al.], *Die Abtei St. Walburg (1035–1935): 900 Jahre in Wort und Bild* (Eichstätt: St. Walburga Abbey, 1934); translated by Gonzaga Engelhart as *Spring and Harvest* (St. Meinrad, Ind.: Grail Press, 1952), 36. See Hollermann, *The Reshaping of a Tradition,* 58.

70. *The New Catholic Encyclopedia,* s.v."exemption"; A. Scheuermann, *Die Exemtion nach geltendem kirchlichen Recht mit einem Überblick über die geschichtliche Entwicklung* (Paderborn, 1938); and J. D. O'Brien, *The Exemption of Religious in Church Law* (Milwaukee: Bruce Publishing, 1943).

71. See above, ALVM: Wimmer to Müller, Pittsburgh, July 24, 1857; translated in Girgen, *Behind the Beginnings,* 87. "According to the *jus canonicum,* the sisters always enjoy the same rights and privileges as the monks do; they would, therefore, be exempt here and the President of the Congregation at the time would be their highest superior, as I have considered myself to be."

72. Stephanus Hilpisch, *Geschichte der Benediktinerinnen* (St. Ottilien: Eos Verlag der Erzabtei, 1951), translated by Joanne Muggli as *A History of Benedictine Nuns* (Collegeville, Minn.: St. John's Abbey Press, 1958); Mary David Olheiser, *From Autonomy to Federations* (Ph.D. diss., The Catholic University of America, 1977).

73. AMA: Wimmer to Scherr, St. Vincent, October 17, 1852; translated in Girgen, *Behind the Beginnings,* 18–19. In this letter Wimmer says that eleven of the "novices" were American-born and one Bavarian-born. As a result of her research Hollermann concludes that six were American-born and four Bavarian-born. The place of birth of two of them cannot be determined from the extant records at St. Joseph's Convent. Another inconsistency is that these twelve young women were not formally invested as novices until October 16, 1853, though in his letter to Scherr of October 17, 1852, and again in his letter to King Ludwig I of July 4, 1853, Wimmer says that the novitiate had already been opened. It is likely that between October 1852 and Octo-

ber 1853 the twelve candidates followed the monastic regimen as postulants and were not formally recognized by the three Eichstätt nuns as novices until the investiture of 1853, though Wimmer called them "novices" from the time of their entry into the convent. See Hollermann, *The Reshaping of a Tradition,* 66–68.

74. RAB: Wimmer to Ludwig I, St. Vincent, July 4, 1853; printed in Willibald Mathäser, *Bonifaz Wimmer und König Ludwig I von Bayern* (Munich: A. G. Manz, 1937), 49; translated in Girgen, *Behind the Beginnings,* 29.

75. AMA: Wimmer to Scherr, St. Vincent, July 6, 1853; Girgen, *Behind the Beginnings,* 30.

76. RAB: Wimmer to Ludwig I, St. Vincent, July 4, 1853; Mathäser, *Bonifaz Wimmer und König Ludwig I,* 48–49; Girgen, *Behind the Beginnings,* 28.

77. On August 1, 1855, Wimmer petitioned the Sacred Congregation for the Propagation of the Faith for the independence of St. Joseph's Convent, St. Marys, Pennsylvania, from the Priory of St. Walburga, Eichstätt. The petition at this time was denied. See ACPF: Wimmer to Barnabo, Rome, August 1, 1855; Girgen, *Behind the Beginnings,* 50–51.

78. Girgen, *Behind the Beginnings,* 48–49; see Grace McDonald, *With Lamps Burning* (St. Paul, Minn.: St. Benedict's Priory, 1957), 14.

79. Mathäser, *Bonifaz Wimmer und König Ludwig I,* 119, n12; translated in Girgen, *Behind the Beginnings,* 49.

80. Louis Morkin and Theophane Seigel, *Wind in the Wheat* (Erie, Pa.: McCarty Printing, 1956), 81–83, and Hollermann, *The Reshaping of a Tradition,* 99–103.

81. ALMV: Riepp to the Ludwig Missionsverein, St. Marytown, April 13, 1857; Girgen, *Behind the Beginnings,* 61–62.

82. ALMV: Wimmer to Müller, Pittsburgh, July 24, 1857; Girgen, *Behind the Beginnings,* 88.

83. ASVA: di Marogna to Wimmer, St. Cloud, March 10, 1857; Girgen, *Behind the Beginnings,* 60–61.

84. See Hollermann, *The Reshaping of a Tradition,* 122–24.

85. ASVA: Seidenbusch to Wimmer, St. Marys, April 24, 1857; Girgen, *Behind the Beginnings,* 63–64.

86. Wimmer's view was that the unrest in the community was the result of a breakdown in discipline, which included neglect of the divine office and the spiritual exercises. A nun at St. Marys who witnessed the problems and wrote a memoir sixty years after the events she describes seems to confirm Wimmer's assessment. Sr. Nepomucene Ludwig wrote: "How many tears were shed when we had to remain in bed even during the time of the holy sacrifice of the Mass. We would then rise, dress and go to breakfast. And how about the saying of the divine office? How was this function performed? In the refectory after breakfast, we knelt, four or five in groups around one of the sisters who knew some Latin, to recite the divine office in low murmurs. Who would ever imagine that one woman [Sr. Willibalda Scherbauer] would dare to bring about such changes, but these are facts. Those were days of trial and deep anguish for us all. . . . " Archives of St. Joseph's Monastery, St. Marys, Pa.: Nepomucene Ludwig, "Convent Foundations of the Benedictine Order in North

America" (Manuscript, c. 1913), translated by Timothy Seus, p.7; quoted in Hollermann, *The Reshaping of a Tradition,* 118.

87. ASVA: Riepp to Wimmer, St. Marys, May 3, 1857; Girgen, *Behind the Beginnings,* 65–66.

88. ASVA: Seidenbusch to Wimmer, Benziger P.O., Elk Co., May 22, 1857; Girgen, *Behind the Beginnings,* 67.

89. ALMV: Wimmer to Müller, Pittsburgh, July 24, 1857; Girgen, *Behind the Beginnings,* 92.

90. ASVA: di Marogna to Wimmer, St. Cloud, June 15, 1857; Girgen, *Behind the Beginnings,* 68.

91. ASVA: Staub to Wimmer, St. Cloud, June 22, 1857.

92. ASVA: Young to Wimmer, Erie, July 4, 1857; Girgen, *Behind the Beginnings,* 69–70.

93. ASVA: di Marogna to Wimmer, St. Cloud, July 14, 1857; Girgen, *Behind the Beginnings,* 71–73.

94. Exactly what Wimmer meant by this statement is difficult to understand in the light of his earlier actions and his comments later on in this letter.

95. ALMV: Wimmer to Müller, Pittsburgh, July 24, 1857; Girgen, *Behind the Beginnings,* 86–99.

96. ASVA: di Marogna to Wimmer, St. Cloud, August 20/27, 1857; Girgen, *Behind the Beginnings,* 81–82.

97. ASVA: Scherbauer to Wimmer, St. Cloud, August 27, 1857; Girgen, *Behind the Beginnings,* 83.

98. ASVA: Kremeter to Wimmer, St. Cloud, August 22, 1857; Girgen, *Behind the Beginnings,* 84.

99. ASVA: di Marogna to Wimmer, St. Cloud, August 20/27, 1857.

100. ASVA: Wimmer to Burkhardt, St. Louis, November 15, 1857; Girgen, *Behind the Beginnings,* 100.

101. Archives of St. Benedict Convent: Baraga Collection, undated letter of Riepp; Girgen, *Behind the Beginnings,* 110–13.

102. ALMV: Wimmer to von Oberkamp, St. Vincent, November 23, 1857; Girgen, *Behind the Beginnings,* 113–21.

103. ASVA: Barnabo to Wimmer, Rome, March 17, 1858; Girgen, *Behind the Beginnings,* 109–10.

104. It is noteworthy that Wimmer did not also ask for recognition of the St. Cloud Priory as an independent monastery. Hollerman suggests that Benedicta Riepp's presence in Minnesota (she had returned to the United States and gone to live with the St. Cloud nuns in May 1858) may have made Wimmer reluctant to seek independent status for the community there. "Perhaps he also believed that the community had little chance of survival, due to the famine caused by the grasshopper plague and the hostile attitude of the townspeople toward parochial education" (*The Reshaping of a Tradition,* 168). As late as April 1859 Wimmer, in justifying his appropriation of funds destined for the convent in Minnesota, described the com-

munity in St. Cloud as "a group of undisciplined and adventurous nuns." See RAB: Wimmer to Ludwig I, St. Vincent, April 9, 1859; Girgen, *Behind the Beginnings,* 148.

105. ACPF: Wimmer to Barnabo, St. Vincent, July 11, 1858; Girgen, *Behind the Beginnings,* 122.

106. AMA: Wimmer to Lang, St. Vincent, July 27, 1858; Girgen, *Behind the Beginnings,* 129–30.

107. ASVA: Barnabo to Wimmer, Rome, November 11, 1858; Girgen, *Behind the Beginnings,* 123–24.

108. In November 1857 King Ludwig I had sent 1,500 florins to Wimmer for the Benedictine sisters in Newark, but Wimmer did not turn the money over to the sisters, justifying his action by saying that he had recently given a house to the sisters worth more than 6,000 florins and had taken the 1,500 florins donated by the king as partial repayment for the house. See RAB: Wimmer to Ludwig I, St. Vincent, April 9, 1859; translated in Girgen, *Behind the Beginnings,* 149. See Hollermann, *The Reshaping of a Tradition,* 126–27.

109. ASVA: Müller to Wimmer, Munich, March 15, 1859; Girgen, *Behind the Beginnings,* 140–41.

110. RAB: Wimmer to Ludwig I, St. Vincent, April 9, 1859; Girgen, *Behind the Beginnings,* 142–50. Mathäser, *Bonifaz Wimmer und König Ludwig I,* 115–24.

111. ASVA: Müller to Wimmer, Munich, June 1, 1859; Girgen, *Behind the Beginnings,* 151.

112. ASVA: Roman Document, December 6, 1859; Girgen, *Behind the Beginnings,* 156.

113. Wimmer was wrong here. He had also failed to obtain the right for the sisters to make solemn vows. Because they would now be bound by only simple vows, they would not be obliged to maintain enclosure or recite the full monastic office. On the other hand, as simply professed religious they would be able to teach in parochial and public schools without a special dispensation.

114. Again Wimmer was wrong in his interpretation of the Roman decree. Rome clearly placed the sisters "under the jurisdiction of the bishops of the same places" where their convents were located. The decree, however, did permit the bishops "to use the abbot spokesman as a founder to choose their rule [way of life] and even to depute as confessors monks of the aforesaid congregation, provided there are no opposing obstacles." ASVA: Roman Document, December 6, 1859; translated in Girgen, *Behind the Beginnings,* 156.

115. Surely Wimmer means here "if I want to have jurisdiction over you."

116. ASVA: Wimmer to Burkhardt, Carrolltown, April 26, 1860; translated in Girgen, *Behind the Beginnings,* 160–61.

117. ASVA: Young to Wimmer, Erie, January 25, 1860; Girgen, *Behind the Beginnings,* 155–56.

118. Archives of St. Benedict Convent: Riepp to Reverend Father, St. Cloud, December 30, 1861; Girgen, *Behind the Beginnings,* 166. See McDonald, *With Lamps Burning,* 19; Fellner, *Abbot Boniface and His Monks,* 3: 310; and ASPA: Wimmer to Pescetelli, St. Vincent, May 30, 1862.

119. "Besides intervening in prayer life, ministry, and other areas . . . , the bishop was basically free to guide and control in any area where he felt there was need. Some saw no problem with changing the process and length of initial formation, the habit, or even the superior of the community. The suppression of a community in order to benefit another or the importing of a prioress from another monastery were within the bishop's power even if they were hardly in keeping with the tradition of ceno-bitic authority and were seldom conducive to internal peace and harmony." See Sutera, *True Daughters*, 59.

120. Archives of Mount St. Benedict, Erie: Ullathorne to Burkhardt, Birming-ham, January 4, 1880; printed in Sutera, *True Daughters*, 152. A twentieth-century Benedictine historian wrote, "The Benedictine Sisters of North America, insofar as time and circumstances demanded, took on a form of development which differed from the Benedictines of the old world, the more the longer they have been sepa-rated. They have received a structure built upon the principle of a congregation or a province, not upon the old monastic principle of stability of place. With this they came to resemble the third orders which do not profess solemn, but only simple vows" (Mathäser, *Bonifaz Wimmer und König Ludwig I,* 135; quoted in Girgen, *Be-hind the Beginnings,* 168). See also Hollermann, *The Reshaping of a Tradition,* xx: "The Roman Decree of 1859 set the adaptation of Benedictine women to the cul-tural and religious circumstances of America on a course which eventually led to their redefinition within the law of the church. When the canons governing religious institutes were definitively codified in 1917, groups of American Benedictine women came to be redefined as communities dedicated to the works of the apostolate, over against the definition for monastic institutes of men and women—a redefinition that has prevailed and shaped American Benedictine women until recent times."

121. Despite the conflict between Abbot Boniface and Mother Benedicta, and even after the Roman decision of 1859, Benedictine monks and nuns continued to work closely together in the American missions. Virtually every nineteenth-century foundation from St. Vincent was soon joined by a foundation of Benedictine sisters. For details of these foundations, see Regina Baska, *The Benedictine Congregation of St. Scholastica: Its Foundation and Development 1852–1930* (Washington, D.C.: The Catholic University of America Press, 1935) and Hollermann, *The Reshaping of a Tra-dition.*

Notes to Chapter 5

1. AMA: Wimmer to Lang, St. Vincent, May 17, 1860.

2. ALMV: Wimmer to Missionsverein, St. Vincent, February 26, 1857; quoted in Joel Rippinger, *The Benedictine Order in the United States: An Interpretive History* (Collegeville, Minn.: Liturgical Press, 1990), 33–34.

3. Wimmer's comment to Abbot Angelo Pescetelli in 1858 was typical. "Our elec-tion will be held soon. We are forty-nine capitulars, of whom fifteen will vote by proxy. I would prefer that Father Demetrius di Marogna or Benedict Haindl be cho-sen for the abbatial dignity. Such a change would allow me to go to Minnesota where

I have good friends, and we will be able to build another monastery. We have a large farm there, and I would like to live as a missionary among the Indians." ASPA: Wimmer to Pescetelli, St. Vincent, August 16, 1858.

4. Colman Barry, *Worship and Work: Saint John's Abbey and University 1856–1992* (Collegeville, Minn.: Liturgical Press, 1993), 26–66.

5. See Peter Beckman, *Kansas Monks: A History of St. Benedict's Abbey* (Atchison, Kans.: Abbey Student Press, 1957), 29–50.

6. [Boniface Wimmer, O.S.B.], "Über die Missionen," *Augsburger Postzeitung,* November 8, 1845; translation in *Documents of American Catholic History,* 3 vols. , ed. John Tracy Ellis (Wilmington, Del.: Michael Glazier, 1987), 1: 284–85.

7. *Annalen der Verbreitung des Glaubens* (Munich, 1848), 384. See also Archives of the Diocese of Linz: Wimmer to Ziegler, Munich, June 9, 1846. "The motherhouse [Metten] has a large choir of priests and clerics. We will have only five. The absence of priests will be keenly felt. Therefore we might try to recite the same office, and after considering this question for a time, I came to the conclusion that it would be best to instruct the Brothers sufficiently to recite the office with the clerical members." Quoted in Felix Fellner, O.S.B., *Abbot Boniface and His Monks,* 5 vols. (Latrobe, Pa.: Private Published, 1956), 3: 340.

8. AMA: Brunner to Scherr, St. Vincent, July 2, 1849.

9. ACPF: Sailer to Pius IX, St. Vincent, April 30, 1861. See Fellner, *Abbot Boniface and His Monks,* 3: 330–31.

10. ASVA: Pescetelli to Wimmer, Rome, July 16, 1861.

11. ASVA: Roman Document, July 13, 1861.

12. ACPF: Wimmer to Barnabo, St. Vincent, August 5, 1861. See also ASPA: Wimmer to Pescetelli, St. Vincent, August 3, 1861, and August 5, 1861.

13. ACPF: Domenec to Propaganda, Pittsburgh, September 1861. See Fellner, *Abbot Boniface and His Monks,* 3: 332.

14. ACPF: Young to Propaganda, Erie, September 1861; ASVA: Young to Wimmer, Erie, September 12, 1861. See Fellner, *Abbot Boniface and His Monks,* 3: 332.

15. ASVA: Chapter Records, October 2, 1861. ACPF: St. Vincent Monks to Propaganda, St. Vincent, October 3, 1861. Fellner, *Abbot Boniface and His Monks,* 3: 332.

16. ASVA: Wimmer to Young, St. Vincent, September 25, 1861.

17. ASVA: Pescetelli to Wimmer, Rome, December 13, 1861.

18. ASVA: Roman Document, June 23, 1866. See also *Album Fratrum Conversorum* in ASVA. The practice of granting only simple vows to lay brothers was continued in the American Cassinese Congregation for more than one hundred years and was abandoned only in 1967.

19. ASPA: Wimmer to Pescetelli, St. Vincent, August 24, 1860.

20. ASVA: Pescetelli to Wimmer, Rome, January 21, 1861.

21. ASPA: Wimmer to Pescetelli, St. Vincent, February 12, 1861, and May 12, 1861. See also Beckman, *Kansas Monks,* 72–73.

22. ASVA: Pescetelli to Wimmer, Rome, June 25, 1861.

23. ASVA: Pescetelli to Wimmer, Rome, July 16, 1861.

24. ASPA: Wimmer to Pescetelli, St. Vincent, August 3, 1861.

25. ASVA: Pescetelli to Wimmer, Rome, August 8, 1861, and December 13, 1861.

26. ASPA: Wimmer to Pescetelli, St. Vincent, May 30, 1862. See Beckman, *Kansas Monks*, 73–74.

27. ASPA: Wimmer to Pescetelli, St. Vincent, October 1, 1862. See Beckman, *Kansas Monks*, 74–75.

28. "Boniface Wimmer Outlines the Future of the Benedictine Order in the United States, November 8, 1845," in *Documents of American Catholic History*, ed. John Tracy Ellis (Wilmington, Del.: Michael Glazier, 1987), 1: 287.

29. For useful discussions of the origins and development of the various movements within the nineteenth- century Benedictine revival, see David Knowles, *Christian Monasticism* (New York: McGraw Hill, 1969), 170–76; Daniel Misonne, "La restauration monastique du XIX siècle," *Revue Bénédictine* 83 (1973): 26–40; and Rippinger, *The Benedictine Order in the United States*, 11–18.

30. Archives of Conception Abbey (Mo.): Placidus Wolter to Frowin Conrad, Maredsous, August 9, 1875; quoted in Edward E. Malone, O.S.B., *A History of Conception Colony, Abbey, and Schools* (Elkhorn, Nebr.: Michaeleen Press, 1971), 101.

31. ASVA: Chapter Records, September 15–18, 1862.

32. Barry, *Worship and Work*, 68.

33. RAB: Wimmer to Ludwig I, Newark, December 2, 1862.

34. ASPA: Wimmer to Pescetelli, St. Vincent, February 12, 1861.

35. Aloysius Plaisance, "Emmeran Bliemel, O.S.B., Heroic Confederate Chaplain," *ABR* 17 (1966): 106–16; Fellner, *Abbot Boniface and His Monks*, 3: 351–53; and Peter Meaney, "Valiant Chaplain of the Bloody Tenth," *Tennessee Historical Quarterly* 41 (1983): 37–47.

36. AMA: Wimmer to Scherr, St. Vincent, February 26, 1863. Louis Haas, O.S.B., *St. Vincent's* (Latrobe: Abbey Press, 1905), 27. For statistics on students at St. Vincent during this period, see *The Saint Vincent College Catalogue, 1863–1864* (St. Vincent, 1864).

37. Alfonso Capecelatro, *Commemorazione di Don Bonifacio Maria Krug, abate di Montecassino* (Rome: Desclée & cie: 1910).

38. ASVA: Civil War Papers (VH–41). The document of release, signed by Brigadier General C. P. Buckingham of the War Department and dated November 28, 1862, reads: "Francis Patrick Kenrick, Archbishop of Baltimore, and Right Reverend B. Wimmer, Abbot of the Benedictine Monastery, Latrobe, Pennsylvania, having represented to this Department that four monks of the Order of St. Benedict have been drafted into military services of the United States, that by their religious belief and doctrine it is unlawful for them to bear arms and that the monks are bound irrevocably to the order by solemn vows, their mission being a mission of peace, it is hereby ordered that the members of the Benedictine Order are relieved from military duty."

39. ASVA: Wimmer to Lincoln, St. Vincent, June 10, 1863 (copy). This letter, as well as one of June 11, 1863, that Wimmer sent Secretary of War Edwin M. Stanton, is published in *Official Records of the War of Rebellion* (Washington, D.C.: Government Printing Office, 1880), Series 101, 3: 33–36 and 341–45.

40. ASVA: Gaul to Wimmer, Virginia, March 12, 1865; Gaul to Hoffmann, Virginia, April 12, 1865. "Obituary: Brother Bonaventure Gaul, O.S.B.," *St. Vincent Journal* 6 (1896): 38–39. See Fellner, *Abbot Boniface and His Monks,* 3: 249–50.

41. ASPA: Wimmer to Pescetelli, St. Vincent, December 15, 1859. See Oswald Moosmüller, *St. Vincenz in Pennsylvanien* (New York: Pustet, 1873), 178; and Fellner, *Abbot Boniface and His Monks,* 3: 333–34.

42. ASPA: Wimmer to Pescetelli, St. Vincent, December 15, 1859.

43. ASPA: Wimmer to Pescetelli, St. Vincent, February 12, 1860.

44. ASVA: Müller to Wimmer, Munich, January 26, 1860.

45. Wimmer's letter to the *Pittsburgh Dispatch,* written on February 26, 1860, appeared in the *Pittsburgh Catholic* on March 17, 1860, in the *Cincinnati Wahrheitsfreund* on March 15, 1860, and in several other German and English newspapers.

46. "The Ghost Story," *Pittsburgh Catholic,* March 24, 1860.

47. ASVA: Pescetelli to Wimmer, Rome, May 28, 1860.

48. ASJA: Wimmer to di Marogna, St. Vincent, August 10, 1860.

49. Barry, *Worship and Work,* 66.

50. ASPA: Wimmer to Pescetelli, St. Vincent, May 12, 1861.

51. ASVA: Pescetelli to Wimmer, Rome, June 25, 1861.

52. ASPA: Wimmer to Pescetelli, St. Vincent, May 30, 1862. See Beckman, *Kansas Monks,* 73–74.

53. ACPF: Wimmer to Barnabo, St. Vincent, June 20, 1863.

54. ASVA: *Album Capitularium.* The entry for Keck states, "Vulgo: Geisterseher!—Dismissus—15 November 1862."

55. ASVA: Roman Document, July 9, 1862.

56. ASVA: Kenrick to Wimmer, Baltimore, July 23, 1862. Archbishop Kenrick did not reveal the nature of the works Keck was spreading or the identity of the woman.

57. ASVA: Chapter Records, September 15–17, 1862. Wimmer signed the minutes of this chapter "Bonifacius M[aria] Wimmer." The extent of his acceptance of the reform inspired by Keck might be gauged in part by his readiness to assume the pious practices commanded by the *Geisterseher.* Between 1861 and 1863 much of his correspondence is signed "Bonifacius Maria Wimmer." See, for example, his letters to King Ludwig I (December 6, 1861), to Father Luke Wimmer (December 20, 1861), to Bishop Henni of Milwaukee (February 26 1863), and to Father Eberhard Gahr, O.S.B. (July 27, 1863).

58. ASVA: Wimmer to Barnabo, St. Vincent, October 1, 1862.

59. ACPF: Wimmer to Barnabo, St. Vincent, June 20, 1863.

60. ASVA: Paul Keck Papers (VH–34). The expulsion is dated November 15, 1862, and is signed by Wimmer.

61. ASPA: Wimmer to Pescetelli, St. Vincent, January 21, 1863.

62. ASVA: Pescetelli to Wimmer, Rome, February 5, 1863.

63. AMA: Wimmer to Scherr, St. Vincent, February 26, 1863.

64. Barry, *Worship and Work,* 68, 79–81.

65. ASVA: Grace to Wimmer, St. Paul, January 14, 1863.

66. ACPF: Wimmer to Barnabo, St. Vincent, June 20, 1863.

67. ACPF: Mayer to Pius IX, St. Vincent, April 29, 1863.

68. ASVA: Pescetelli to Wimmer, Rome, June 24, 1863; ACPF: Wimmer to Propaganda, St. Vincent, June 20, 1863.

69. ASVA: Roman Document, September 16, 1863.

70. ASVA: Pescetelli to Wimmer, Rome, October 19, 1863.

71. ASVA: Wimmer to Pescetelli, St. Vincent, November 22, 1863.

72. ASVA: Pescetelli to Wimmer, Rome, January 4, 1864.

73. ASVA: Wirtz to Mayer, The Indianbush, May 22, 1865. See Barry, *Worship and Work,* 80.

74. ASPA: Wimmer to Pescetelli, St. Vincent, September 28, 1864. See Fellner, *Abbot Boniface and His Monks,* 3: 372.

75. ASJA: Wimmer to Seidenbusch, Rome, June 9, 1865.

76. AMA: Wimmer to Lang, Rome, May 29, 1865; ASA: Wimmer to Leiss, Rome, June 15, 1865; Oswald Moosmüller, *Bonifaz Wimmer, Erzabt von St. Vincent in Pennsylvanien* (New York: Benziger, 1891), 210; Fellner, *Abbot Boniface and His Monks,* 3: 375–385.

77. ASJA: Wimmer to Wirtz, San Callisto, August 27, 1865.

78. ASJA: Wimmer to Seidenbusch, Rome, July 3, 1865.

79. ASVA: Wimmer to Luke Wimmer, Rome, July 21, 1865.

80. ASVA: Roman Document, October 11, 1865. See Fellner, *Abbot Boniface and His Monks,* 3: 340.

81. ASVA: Wimmer to Wirtz, Rome, October 17, 1865.

82. ASVA: Paul Keck Papers (MV–92), November 13, 1865.

83. ASVA: Wirtz to Mayer, St. Joseph, Minnesota, December 26, 1865. See Barry, *Worship and Work,* 81.

84. ASVA: Roman Document, December 26, 1866.

85. ASJA: Wimmer to Seidenbusch, Rome, December 18, 1865.

86. ASJA: Wimmer to Seidenbusch, Rome, January 29, 1866; February 20, 1866; April 22, 1866; May 31, 1866.

87. ASVA: Roman Document, June 23, 1866; Barnabo to Wimmer, Rome, June 30, 1866. Wimmer had petitioned that on weekdays the Benedictine sisters in the United States be permitted to recite the Little Office of the Blessed Virgin instead of the full divine office. See ASVA: Wimmer to Burkhardt, San Callisto, June 28, 1866; translated in Incarnata Girgen, *Behind the Beginnings: Benedictine Women in America* (St. Joseph, Minn.: St. Benedict's Convent, 1981), 187–88. He had also sought to unify the ten American communities of Benedictine women in a single congregation, with a mother general and a common novitiate. The cardinals granted the first petition and indicated their support of the second. Before permitting a congregation, however, they told Wimmer to seek the approval of the American bishops who were to meet in Baltimore in October. Wimmer returned to the United States too late to have the item put on the bishops' agenda, and though he strove over the next two decades to help create a union of communities of American Benedictine women, the first congregation did not come into being until 1927. See Girgen, *Behind the Beginnings,* 185–86; Judith Sutera, *True Daughters: Monastic Identity and*

American Benedictine Women's History (Atchison, Kans.: Mount St. Scholastica, 1987), 39–40; and Regina Baska, *The Benedictine Congregation of St. Scholastica: Its Foundation and Development, 1852–1930* (Washington, D.C.: The Catholic University of America Press, 1935).

88. ASVA: Apostolic Brief, July 27, 1866.

Notes to Chapter 6

1. RAB: Wimmer to Ludwig I, Munich, July 22, 1866.

2. RAB: Wimmer to Ludwig I, Munich, August 16, 1866. King Ludwig died in 1868, a year before the *Album Benedictinum* (Beatty, Pa.: St. Vincent Press, 1869) was published.

3. *Cincinnati Wahrheitsfreund,* October 24, 1866. See Fellner, *Abbot Boniface and His Monks,* 3: 386–87.

4. James Hennesey, *American Catholics: A History of the Roman Catholic Community in the United States* (New York: Oxford University Press, 1981), 161; Jerome Oetgen, "The Origins of the Benedictine Order in Georgia," *Georgia Historical Quarterly* 53 (1969): 165–83.

5. Hennesey, *American Catholics,* 160. See also James Hennesey, "The Baltimore Council of 1866: An American Syllabus," *Records of the American Catholic Historical Society of Philadelphia* 76: 165–72.

6. AMA: Wimmer to Lang, St. Vincent, January 28, 1867; published in the *Scriptorium* 19 (1960): 73.

7. ACPF: Wimmer to Smith, Newark, October 18, 1866.

8. Colman Barry, *Worship and Work: St. John's Abbey and University 1856–1992* (Collegeville, Minn.: Liturgical Press, 1994), 93–95.

9. AMA: Wimmer to Lang, St. Vincent, January 28, 1867.

10. ASVA: *Chronicon;* Archives of the Diocese of Charleston: Wimmer to Lynch, Rome, April 23, 1866.

11. Peter Beckman, *Kansas Monks: The History of St. Benedict's Abbey* (Atchison, Kans.: Abbey Student Press, 1957), 75–86.

12. ALMV: Wimmer to Missionsverein, St. Vincent, February 25, 1868.

13. RAB: Wimmer to Ludwig I, Erie, August 10, 1867.

14. Beckman, *Kansas Monks,* 80–81.

15. ASVA: Chapter Records, August 17–19, 1867.

16. AMA: Wimmer to Lang, St. Vincent, August 28, 1867.

17. ALMV: Wimmer to Missionsverein, St. Vincent, February 25, 1868.

18. *Catalogus Monachorum Ord. S. P. Benedicti Congregationis Americano-Bavaricae Cassinensi Affiliatae* (St. Vincent: Abbey Press, 1873).

19. *St. Vincent College Catalogue, 1868–1869* (Beatty, Pa.: St. Vincent Press, 1869).

20. Fred Moleck, "Nineteenth-Century Musical Activity at St. Vincent Archabbey" (Ph.D. diss., University of Pittsburgh, 1971).

21. Heimler owed more to Wimmer than his position as president of St. Vincent College. In 1855, when he was refused ordination in Bavaria because of a deformed

right hand, he came to St. Vincent where Abbot Boniface first arranged for a surgeon to make an incision in the deformed hand so that he could hold the host and then obtained a dispensation from Rome so that Heimler could be ordained. He completed his novitiate at St. Vincent in 1856 and was ordained in 1857. See Felix Fellner, *Abbot Boniface and His Monks,* 5 vols. (Latrobe, Pa.: Privately published by St. Vincent Archabbey, 1956), 3: 401 and 409.

22. Felix Fellner, "Archabbot Boniface Wimmer as an Educator," *National Benedictine Educational Association Bulletin* 25 (1942): 84–114; Fellner, *Abbot Boniface and His Monks,* 3: 391–401.

23. *St. Vincent College Catalogue, 1868–1869* (Beatty, Pa.: St. Vincent Press, 1869).

24. ALMV: Wimmer to Missionsverein, St. Vincent, February 25, 1868.

25. See Fellner, *Abbot Boniface and His Monks,* 5: 620.

26. The charter was not obtained until 1870.

27. ASVA: Henry Ganss, "Fugitive Recollections, Musical and Unmusical: 1868–1878," typescript, n.d. A native of Darmstadt, Germany, Ganss studied for the priesthood at St. Vincent and was ordained by Bishop John Tuigg in 1878. He served as pastor in several central Pennsylvania towns, including Carlisle and Lancaster. Because of his work at the U.S. government's Indian school at Carlisle, Cardinal James Gibbons appointed him financial agent of the Catholic Indian Missions. He was an authority on Martin Luther and wrote articles for such Catholic journals as the *Catholic World,* the *American Catholic Quarterly,* the *American Ecclesiastical Review,* and *Ave Maria.* He was also a composer of note whose compositions included piano pieces, sacred and secular songs, hymns, and five masses. One of the masses was a requiem for Boniface Wimmer. See Moleck, "Nineteenth Century Musical Activity at St. Vincent Archabbey," and the articles on Ganss in *The New Catholic Encyclopedia* (Washington, D.C.: The Catholic University of America Press, 1967), 6: 280–81, and Georgina Pell Curtis, *The American Catholic Who's Who* (St. Louis: B Herder, 1911), 230.

28. ASMA: Schmid to Marty, Einsiedeln, April 1, 1868. Joel Rippinger, "Martin Marty: Monk, Abbot, Missionary, and Bishop," *ABR* 33 (1982): 231–32.

29. ASMA: Wimmer to Marty, St. Vincent, November 22, 1868. In view of Martin Marty's opinions about Benedictine stability, it is ironic that after being elected abbot of St. Meinrad in 1870, he spent much of the remainder of his life away from his abbey as a solitary missionary among the Sioux in the Dakota Territory. See Rippinger, "Martin Marty: Monk, Abbot, Missionary, and Bishop," 223–40, 376–93.

30. ASBA: Wimmer to Wolf, St. Vincent, July 30, 1868.

31. David Knowles, *Christian Monasticism* (New York: McGraw-Hill, 1969), 170–76.

32. ASBA: Wimmer to Wolf, St. Vincent, July 30, 1868, and November 17, 1868.

33. Hennesey, *American Catholics,* 168–69.

34. ASA: Wimmer to Leiss, Munich, October 21, 1869. See Fellner, *Abbot Boniface and His Monks,* 4: 481–82.

35. ASVA: Wimmer Diary of the Vatican Council, December 8, 1869, 3.

36. See the *Wanderer* (St. Paul), June 1, 1870, to July 18, 1871.

37. ASVA: Wimmer Diary , December 19, 1869, and January 1, 1870, 8, 15; Wimmer to Leiss, Rome, February 20, 1870.

38. ASA: Wimmer to Leiss, Rome, February 20, 1870.

39. ASVA: Wimmer Diary, January 14, 1870, 24.

40. ASA: Wimmer to Leiss, Rome, April 22, 1870.

41. ASVA: Wimmer Diary, May 31, 1870, 92; May 25, 1870, 87; June 3, 1870, 93; June 10, 1870, 99.

42. Giuseppe Pennachi, *De Honorii I Romani Pontificis causa in Concilio VI. Dissertatio Josephi Pennachii in Romana Studiorum Universitate Historiae Ecclesiasticae Professoris Substituti ad Patres Concilii Vaticani. Praefatus est P. Bonifacius Wimmer, O.S.B., Abbas S. Vincentii et Praeses Congregationis Americo-Bavaricae Benedictinae* (Regensburg: Pustet, 1870).

43. See *Prolegomena Historica Congregationis Americano-Cassinensis* in *Album Benedictinum* (Beatty, Pa.: St. Vincent, 1869); Philipp Balzofiore, *Lebensgeschichte der ehrwürdigen Dienerin Gottes Anna Maria Taigi (1769–1827). Aus der approbirten italienischen Ausgabe übertragen von P. Bonifaz Wimmer, O.S.B.* (Regensburg and New York: Pustet, 1867); *Einige Notizen über Kloster Mallersdorf* (Landshut: J. A. Attendorfer, 1842). ASVA: Wimmer Writings, and Fellner, *Abbot Boniface and His Monk,* 2: 163, 171; 3: 390; and 4: 486, 494.

44. James Hennesey, S.J., *The First Council of the Vatican: The American Experience* (New York, 1963), 273–74. ASVA: Wimmer Diary, July 13, 1870, 116.

45. ASVA: Wimmer Diary, July 16, 1870, 118.

46. Fellner, *Abbot Boniface and His Monks,* 4: 489.

47. AMA: Wimmer to Lang, Liverpool, December 5, 1870.

48. *Wanderer* (St. Paul, Minnesota), January 7, 1871; also, Fellner, *Abbot Boniface and His Monks,* 4: 491.

49. 49. AMA: Wimmer to Scherr, St. Vincent, March 16, 1871.

50. Beckman, *Kansas Monks,* 87–91.

51. AMA: Wimmer to Scherr, St. Vincent, March 16, 1871.

52. ASVA: State Charter, April 18, 1870.

53. ASVA: Propaganda to Wimmer, Rome, December 18, 1870; Fellner, *Abbot Boniface and His Monks,* 4: 458.

54. ASJA: Wimmer to Seidenbusch, St. Vincent, July 30, 1871. On Christoph's initial refusal, see Beckman, *Kansas Monks,* 92.

55. AMA: Wimmer to Lang, St. Vincent, November 2, 1871.

56. ASVA: Chapter Records, October 20–23, 1871.

57. See Oswald Moosmüller, *St. Vincenz in Pennsylvanien* (New York: Pustet, 1873), 326–53, which provides a list of all Benedictines in the United States in October 1871.

58. Fellner, *Abbot Boniface and His Monks,* 4: 497–99; Moosmüller, *St. Vincenz in Pennsylvanien,* 321–23.

59. Fellner, *Abbot Boniface and His Monks,* 4: 499; *Pittsburgh Catholic,* November 4, 1871; *Cincinnati Wahrheitsfreund,* November 8, 1871.

60. *Pittsburgh Catholic,* November 4, 1871.

61. The bell tower, constructed in 1871, was a landmark at St. Vincent until its destruction in the fire of 1963. Moosmüller's history, *St. Vincenz in Pennsylvanien,* survived the ravages of time and remains one of the most important sources of early American Benedictine history.

62. AMA: Wimmer to Lang, St. Vincent, November 2, 1871.

63. AMA: Wimmer to Lang, St. Marys, February 7, 1872.

64. AMA: Wimmer to Lang, Carrolltown, June 21, 1872.

65. ALMV: Wimmer to Reger, St. Vincent, August 4, 1872.

66. AMA: Wimmer to Lang, St. Vincent, August 24, 1872.

67. ALMV: Wimmer to Reger, St. Vincent, November 14, 1872; AMA: Wimmer to Lang, St. Vincent, November 12, 1872.

68. *Catalogus Monachorum O.S.B. Congregationis Americano-Bavaricae Cassinensi Affiliatae* (Beatty, Pa.: St. Vincent Press, 1874).

69. ASVA: Wimmer to Englbrecht, St. Vincent, April 19, 1874.

70. ASPA: Wimmer to Pescetelli, St. Vincent, March 23, 1874.

71. The chapter in Minnesota changed the name of the abbey from St. Louis to St. John's not long after the death of King Ludwig I in 1868.

72. ASJA: Wimmer to Edelbrock, St. Vincent, February 13, 1875.

73. ASBA: Burns to Phelan, Mendata, June 8, 1874.

74. ASJA: Wimmer to Edelbrock, St. Vincent, December 29, 1875. Fellner, *Abbot Boniface and His Monks,* 4: 507–13; Beckman, *Kansas Monks,* 192–94; and Marion Kotinek, "Arrival of Benedictines in Southwest Iowa," *Messenger* (Des Moines), October 29, 1948.

75. Albert Kleber, *A History of St. Meinrad's Archabbey, 1854–1954* (St. Meinrad, Ind.: Abbey Press, 1954); Edward E. Malone, *A History of Conception Colony, Abbey, and Schools* (Michaeleen Press, Elkhorn Nebr., 1971); and Rippinger, "Martin Marty: Monk, Abbot, Missionary and Bishop," 223–40, 376–93.

76. Archives of Conception Abbey: P. Wolter to F. Conrad, Beuron, April 17, 1874; this letter is translated in Edward E. Malone, "Placidus Wolter and the American Benedictines," *ABR* 16 (1965): 310–25.

77. Barry, *Worship and Work,* 125–27.

78. AMA: Wimmer to Lang, St. Vincent, March 28, 1875. *Scriptorium* 19 (1960): 75–81.

79. ASVA: Pescetelli to Wimmer, Rome, August 17, 1875; Barry, *Worship and Work,* 128–30, 403–4.

80. AMA: Wimmer to Lang, St. Vincent, December 16, 1875.

81. ASVA: Chapter Records, August 18–20, 1875; ASJA: Wimmer to Edelbrock, St. Vincent, December 29, 1879.

82. AMA: Wimmer to Lang, St. Vincent, August 25, 1875.

83. ALMV: Wimmer to Reger, St. Marys, December 13, 1875; and AMA: Wimmer to Lang, St. Marys, December 16, 1875.

84. ASVA: Gibbons to Wimmer, Richmond, August 1, 1875. For a discussion of Gibbons's invitation, and some of the misleading statements he made to Wimmer

in his letter, see Paschal Baumstein, *My Lord of Belmont: A Biography of Leo Haid* (Kings Mountain, N.C.: Herald House, 1985), 31–32.

85. ASVA: Wimmer to Hegele, St. Vincent, January 20, 1876.

86. ASVA: Chapter Records, January 19, 1876; and ASJA: Wimmer to Edelbrock, St. Vincent, February 13, 1876.

87. AMA: Wimmer to Lang, St. Vincent, March 9, 1876.

88. ASVA: Wolfe to Wimmer, Richmond, January 26, 1876.

89. ASVA: Wolfe to Wimmer, Richmond, April 5, 1876.

90. ASVA: Wolfe to Wimmer, Mariastein, July 5, 1876.

91. Wolfe to Wimmer, Mariastein, July 5, 1876. The grade ledgers in the archives of Belmont Abbey show only four students in the autumn of 1876, apparently all residents. (Information supplied by Father Paschal Baumstein.)

92. Fellner, *Abbot Boniface and His Monks,* 4: 517. The name of the mission soon changed to "Maryhelp" in honor of Mary, Help of Christians. Still later the monastery became known as Belmont Abbey. In 1965 the stone after which it had first been named was moved to the baptistry of the Belmont Abbey Cathedral and today serves as a baptismal font. A plaque on the font reads: "UPON THIS ROCK, MEN WERE ONCE SOLD INTO SLAVERY. NOW UPON THIS ROCK, THROUGH THE WATERS OF BAPTISM, MEN BECOME FREE CHILDREN OF GOD."

93. ASVA: Cassidy to Wimmer, Mariastein, October 27, 1876. See Fellner, *Abbot Boniface and His Monks,* 4: 514–18.

94. ASVA: Chapter Records, August 30, 1875.

95. ASVA: Quinlan to Wimmer, Mobile, March 20, 1876; Chapter Records, March 26, 1876. For the early history of the Alabama mission, see Ambrose Reger, *Die Benediktiner in Alabama* (Baltimore: Benziger, 1898), translated by Gregory Roettger in *An Historical Overview of St. Bernard Abbey* (Cullman, Ala.: St. Bernard Abbey, 1991).

96. ASVA: Apostolic Brief, April 7, 1876; ASJA: Wimmer to Edelbrock, St. Vincent, June 2, 1876. Wimmer's hope to establish a monastery in California was never fulfilled. In 1886, however, he sent monks to Colorado, where they established a community that became Holy Cross Abbey in 1925, and in 1896, nine years after Wimmer's death, monks from St. John's went to the state of Washington and established the community that in 1914 became St. Martin's Abbey. With the founding of St. Martin's, the American Cassinese Benedictines finally spanned the continent.

97. ALMV: Wimmer to Reger, St. Vincent, August 7, 1876.

98. AMA: Wimmer to Lang, Creston, September 24, 1876.

99. ALMV: Wimmer to Reger, St. Vincent, August 7, 1876; and AMA: Wimmer to Lang, Creston, September 24, 1876.

100. ASVA: Moosmüller to Wimmer, Atchison, January 10, 1875.

101. ASPA: Wimmer to Pescetelli, St. Vincent, September 14, 1876; ALMV: Wimmer to Reger, St. Vincent, November 12, 1876.

102. Jerome Oetgen, "Oswald Moosmüller: Monk and Missionary," *ABR* 27 (1976): 1–35.

103. ASPA: Wimmer to Pescetelli, Atchison, October 3, 1876. See Beckman, *Kansas Monks,* 112–14.

104. ASJA: Wimmer to Edelbrock, St. Vincent, January 4, 1877.

Notes for Chapter 7

1. ASJA: Wimmer to Edelbrock, St. Vincent, January 4, 1877. See the Rule of St. Benedict 2:7, 37–38.

2. *Catalogus Exhibens Nomina Monachorum Ord. S.P. Benedicti Congreg. Americano-Casinensis Omniumque Locorum, Quibus Curam Gerunt Animarum 1879* (Latrobe, Pa.: St. Vincent Press, 1879), 52–59.

3. ASJA: Wimmer to Seidenbusch, St. Vincent, January 14, 1877.

4. AMA: Wimmer to Lang, St. Vincent, February 1877.

5. AMA: Wimmer to Scherr, Newark, February 25, 1877.

6. Joseph Murphy, O.S.B., *Tenacious Monks: The Oklahoma Benedictines (1875–1975)* (Shawnee, Okla.: Benedictine Color Press, 1974). In 1924 Sacred Heart Abbey became part of the American Cassinese Congregation and in 1929 changed its name to St. Gregory's Abbey.

7. Jerome Oetgen, "The Origins of the Benedictine Order in Georgia," *Georgia Historical Quarterly* 53 (1969): 165–83, and Felix Fellner, *Abbot Boniface and His Monks,* 5 vols. (Latrobe, Pa.: Privately published at St. Vincent Archabbey, 1956), 4: 556–71.

8. AMA: Wimmer to Lang, St. Vincent, April 4, 1877.

9. ASVA: Moosmüller to Wimmer, Isle of Hope, March 20, 1877.

10. AMA: Wimmer to Scherr, St. Vincent, August 27, 1877.

11. ASVA: Prospectus of the Manual Labor School for Colored Boys on Skidaway Island.

12. ASVA: Moosmüller to Wimmer, Skidaway, December 9, 1878.

13. ASVA: J. O'Connor to Wimmer, Omaha, October 3, 1876.

14. Fellner, *Abbot Boniface and His Monks,* 4: 574.

15. Jay Dolan, *The American Catholic Experience: A History from Colonial Times to the Present* (New York: Doubleday, 1985), 135, 138; Vitus Buresh, *The Procopian Chronicle: St. Procopius Abbey 1885–1985* (Lisle, Ill.: St. Procopius Abbey, 1985), 3–5.

16. ASVA: J. O'Connor to Wimmer, St. Vincent, April 21, 1877.

17. See Fellner, *Abbot Boniface and His Monks,* 4: 573–80.

18. Reconstruction from the Czech translation of a letter from Kocarnik to Wimmer, Omaha, July 17, 1877; quoted in Buresh, *The Procopian Chronicle,* 6.

19. ASJA: Wimmer to Seidenbusch, St. Vincent, December 29, 1877.

20. AMA: Wimmer to Lang, St. Vincent, September 4, 1877.

21. Paschal Baumstein, *My Lord of Belmont: A Biography of Leo Haid* (Kings Mountain, N.C.: Herald House, 1985), 38.

22. ASJA: Wimmer to Edelbrock, St. Vincent, December 29, 1877.

23. AMA: Wimmer to Lang, St. Vincent, April 2, 1878.

24. Fellner, *Abbot Boniface and His Monks,* 4: 583–86. Father Bernardine Dolweck

was joined by Father Severin Laufenberg in April 1879, but in the fall of that year, when Dolweck was stricken with yellow fever, Wimmer withdrew his monks from Louisiana and turned the parish over to the archbishop of New Orleans. In 1890 monks from St. Meinrad's Abbey, Indiana, went to Louisiana and established a monastery in Covington which eventually became St. Joseph's Abbey, a community of the Swiss American Congregation. See Joel Rippinger, *The Benedictine Order in the United States: An Interpretive History* (Collegeville, Minn.: Liturgical Press, 1990), 71, and Jonathan De Frange, *Century of Grace: A Pictorial History of St. Joseph Abbey and Seminary* (St. Benedict, La.: Privately published, 1989), 2.

25. ASJA: Wimmer to Seidenbusch, St. Vincent, June 7, 1878; Wimmer to Edelbrock, St. Florian, May 20, 1878.

26. ASVA: Chapter Records, August 20–23, 1878.

27. ASPA: Wimmer to Pescetelli, St. Vincent, August 3, 1878.

28. ASVA: Chapter Records, August 20–23, 1878.

29. ASPA: Zilliox to Pescetelli, St. Vincent, August 29, 1878. See also Zilliox to Pescetelli, September 18, 1878. On June 26, 1879, the Sacred Congregation for the Propagation of the Faith issued a decree elevating St. Malachy's Priory to full independent status according to the desire of the majority of the delegates at the General Chapter of 1878 (ASVA: Roman Document, June 26, 1879). Despite this action, however, Prior Eugene Phelan's hopes for the growth of the community did not materialize. The priory never received the anticipated vocations, and in 1893 it was suppressed. See Peter Beckman, *Kansas Monks* (Atchison, Kans.: Abbey Student Press, 1957), 192–96; and AMA: Wimmer to Lang, St. Vincent, December 22, 1878.

30. AMA: Wimmer to Lang, St. Vincent, December 16, 1878; ALMV: Wimmer to Reger, St. Vincent, December 22, 1878.

31. ASVA: *Album Capitularium,* 40. Treug became a monk of Erdington Abbey, England, a monastery of the Beuronese Congregation. He suffered from mental illness in the final years of his life and died at Erdington in 1910. See Fellner, *Abbot Boniface and His Monks,* 5: 619.

32. Archives of the Abbey of Maredsous: Wimmer to Placidus Wolter, St. Vincent, January 31, 1879.

33. ASBA: Wimmer to Wolf, St. Vincent, July 14, 1879.

34. ASVA: Wimmer to Zilliox, St. Vincent, July 29, 1879.

35. ASVA: Wimmer to Benedictine Abbots, St. Vincent, May 1, 1876.

36. ASVA: Wimmer to Benedictine Abbots, February 8, 1877.

37. ASVA: D'Orgemont to Benedictine Abbots, Montecassino, April 1877; D'Orgemont to Wimmer, Montecassino, June 9, 1877.

38. ASVA: Kreutz to Wimmer, Pannonhalma, July 30, 1877.

39. Oswald Moosmüller, *Europäer in Amerika vor Columbus* (Regensburg: G. J. Manz, 1879); Augustine Schneider, *Erklärung der Regel des heiligen Benedikt, Patriarch der Mönche des Abendlandes* (Regensburg, New York, and Cincinnati: F. Pustet, 1879); Aurelius McMahon, *Rule of St. Benedict, Patriarch of Western Monks* (Baltimore: J. Murphy, 1879); Aurelius McMahon, *The Life of St. Benedict, Patriarch of Western Monks, Translated from the Second Book of the Dialogues of St. Gregory the*

Great (Baltimore: J. Murphy, 1880). The dramas of Father Agatho Stübinger, which have not been located, were entitled *Die Weihnachtsbaum* and *Der Weinachtstraum.* See Fellner, *Abbot Boniface and His Monks,* 5: 595–96.

40. ASVA: Wimmer to Hintenach, on board the *Arizona,* April 26–28, 1880; Wimmer to Hintenach, Montecassino, May 12, 1880.

41. ASVA: Wimmer to Hintenach, Montecassino, May 20, 1880. See also *Studien und Mitteilungen* 3 (1881): 120.

42. ASVA: Wimmer to Hintenach, Rome, May 26, 1880.

43. ASJA: Wimmer to Seidenbusch, Munich, July 3, 1880; ASBA: Wimmer to Wolfe, Munich, July 8, 1880.

44. APH: Wimmer to Kreutz, St. Vincent, November 4, 1880.

45. Archives of the Diocese of Springfield: Wimmer to Baltes, St. Vincent, January 10, 1881. See Fellner, *Abbot Boniface and His Monks,* 5: 684–92.

46. *Album Benedictinum* (St. Vincent, 1881).

47. ASBA: Wimmer to Wolf, St. Vincent, May 2, 1881.

48. Archives of the Diocese of Mobile: Wimmer to Quinlan, St. Vincent, June 12, 1881.

49. ASBA: Wimmer to Wolf, St. Vincent, June 16, 1881.

50. ASVA: Wimmer to Meyringer, St. Vincent, August 28, 1881; Chapter Records, August 3–5, 1881.

51. APH: Wimmer to Kreutz, St. Vincent, August 30, 1881.

52. AMA: Wimmer to Lang, St. Vincent, December 27, 1881.

53. ASVA: Wimmer to L. Wimmer, St. Vincent, January 17, 1882.

54. AMA: Wimmer to Lang, St. Vincent, March 18, 1882.

55. ASVA: Simeoni to Wimmer, Rome, February 25, 1882.

56. ASBA: Wimmer to Wolf, St. Vincent, March 18, 1882.

57. ASJA: Wimmer to Edelbrock, St. Vincent, March 23, 1882; Wimmer to Seidenbusch, St. Vincent, March 23, 1882; ASBA: Wimmer to Wolf, St. Vincent, March 23, 1882.

58. ASVA: Edelbrock to Wimmer, St. John's, April 3, 1882.

59. ASJA: Wimmer to Edelbrock, St. Vincent, April 7, 1882.

60. ASBA: Wimmer to Wolf, St. Vincent, March 18, 1882.

61. ACPF: Tuigg to Propaganda, Rome, February 6, 1882.

62. ASBA: Haid to Wolf, St. Vincent, April 5, 1882.

63. ASBA: Wimmer to Wolf, St. Vincent, April 7, 1882; ASJA: Wimmer to Edelbrock, St. Vincent, June 21, 1882.

64. ASVA: Wimmer to Brother Fridolin, St. Vincent, December 11, 1880; ASA: Wimmer to the Abbot of Scheyern, St. Vincent, May 29, 1882; ASJA: Wimmer to Edelbrock, St. Vincent, June 21, 1882.

65. ASBA: Wimmer to Wolf, St. Vincent, June 22, 1882.

66. ASJA: Wimmer to Edelbrock, St. Vincent, September 9, 1882.

67. ASJA: Wimmer to Edelbrock, St. Vincent, November 27, 1882.

68. AMA: Wimmer to Lang, St. Vincent, December 5, 1882.

69. ASJA: Wimmer to Edelbrock, St. Vincent, March 9, 1883.

70. ASBA: Wimmer to Wolf, St. Vincent, May 23, 1883.

71. APH: Wimmer to Kreutz, St. Vincent, November 13, 1883.

72. ASVA: Wolf to Wimmer, Atchison, December 20, 1883.

73. ACPF: Wimmer to Pucci, St. Vincent, April 19, 1884.

74. ASVA: Wimmer to Erie Sisters, St. Vincent, January 8, 1884 (copy).

75. ACPF: Wimmer to Simeoni, St. Vincent, July 7, 1884.

76. AMA: Wimmer to Braunmüller, St. Vincent, October 9, 1884.

77. ASVA: Wimmer to Hofmayer, Baltimore, November 22, 1884.

78. AMA: Wimmer to Braunmüller, St. Vincent, December 20, 1884.

79. ASVA: Apostolic Briefs, December 19, 1884.

80. ASJA: Wimmer to Edelbrock, St. Vincent, January 18, 1885.

81. Quoted by Fellner in *Abbot Boniface and His Monks,* 5: 632.

82. ASBA: Wimmer to Wolf, St. Vincent, February 17, 1885; ASJA: Wimmer to Edelbrock, St. Vincent, February 15, 1885; ASVA: Chapter Records, February 11, 1885; AMA: Wimmer to Lang, St. Vincent, March 22, 1885. See Baumstein, *My Lord of Belmont,* 19.

83. ACPF: Wimmer to Smith, St. Vincent, March 1885.

84. ACPF: Wimmer to Propaganda, St. Vincent, July 17, 1885. See Baumstein, *My Lord of Belmont,* 22–24.

85. ASJA: Wimmer to Edelbrock, St. Vincent, July 15, 1885; ASBA: Wimmer to Wolf, St. Vincent, July 14, 1885; ACPF: Wimmer to Simeoni, St. Vincent, July 17, 1885; ASPA: Wimmer to Pucci, St. Vincent, July 20, 1885.

86. ASJA: Wimmer to Seidenbusch, St. Vincent, December 27, 1880.

87. ASJA: Wimmer to Edelbrock, St. Vincent, St. Vincent, June 15, 1885.

88. ASVA: Wimmer to Amberger, St. Vincent, October 25, 1885.

89. ASJA: Wimmer to Seidenbusch, St. Vincent, December 27, 1880.

90. Fellner, *Abbot Boniface and His Monks,* 5: 646.

91. Fellner, *Abbot Boniface and His Monks,* 5: 651.

92. Felix Fellner, O.S.B., "Archabbot Boniface Wimmer as an Educator," *National Benedictine Educational Association Bulletin* 25 (1942): 9.

93. *St. Vincent College Catalogue, 1885–1886* (St. Vincent, 1886).

94. *Pittsburgh Catholic,* August 31, 1878.

95. It was not until 1914, nearly seventy years after Boniface Wimmer arrived in America, that St. Vincent became, by order of Bishop Regis Canevin, the official school of theology for the diocese of Pittsburgh.

96. ASVA: Wimmer to Amberger, St. Vincent, January 15, 1886; quoted in Baumstein, *My Lord of Belmont,* 57.

97. ASVA: Athanasius Hintenach to Wimmer, Tuscumbia, October 31, 1883, and November 19, 1883.

98. AMA: Wimmer to Braunmüller, St. Vincent, December 21, 1885.

99. Archives of St. Boniface Abbey, Munich: Wimmer to Lacense, St. Vincent, August 21, 1884.

100. *Studien und Mitteilungen* 7 (1895): 423.

101. ASVA: Wimmer to Jaeger, St. Vincent, November 15, 1886. The history of St.

Procopius, which became an abbey in 1894 and moved to Lisle, Illinois, in 1914 is told by Vitus Buresh, in *The Procopian Chronicle: St. Procopius Abbey 1885–1985* (Lisle, Ill.: St. Procopius Abbey, 1985).

102. ASVA: Jaeger to Wimmer, Chicago, November 3, 1885.

103. ALVM: Wimmer to Rath, St. Vincent, November 20, 1885.

104. ASBA: Wimmer to Wolf, St. Vincent, February 16, 1886.

105. ASVA: G. Pilz to Wimmer, San Antonio, May 14, 1886.

106. Fellner, *Abbot Boniface and His Monks,* 5: 693–700.

107. ASJA: Wimmer to Edelbrock, St. Vincent, July 16, 1886.

108. ASVA: Wimmer to Englbrecht, St. Vincent, July 25, 1886.

109. ASBA: Wimmer to Wolf, St. Vincent, November 2, 1886.

110. ASVA: Wimmer to Pfrängle, Newark, November 17, 1886.

111. ASJA: Wimmer to Edelbrock, St. Vincent, December 22, 1886.

112. ASBA: Wimmer to Wolf, St. Vincent, November 26, 1886; Fellner, *Abbot Boniface and His Monks,* 5: 702.

113. AMA: Wimmer to Braunmüller, St. Vincent, December 12, 1886.

114. Quoted in Urban J. Schnitzhofer, "First Monks in the Colorado Rockies," *ABR* 12 (1961): 234.

115. ASVA: Gutmann to Wimmer, Breckenridge, December 19, 1886, and January 3, 1887; Schnitzhofer, "First Monks in the Colorado Rockies," 242, 244. See also Fellner, *Abbot Boniface and His Monks,* 5: 702–3. For a brief history of the Colorado community that became Holy Cross Abbey, see Martin J. Burne, "Holy Cross Abbey—One Hundred Years," *ABR* 37 (1986): 423–32.

116. ASVA: Gutmann to Wimmer, Breckenridge, January 15, 1885; translated in Schnitzhofer, "First Monks in the Colorado Rockies," 247–48.

117. ASPrA: Wimmer to Jaeger, St. Vincent, January 28, 1887.

118. ASJA: Wimmer to Edelbrock, St. Vincent, February 2, 1887.

119. AMA: Wimmer to Braunmüller, St. Vincent, March 12, 1887.

120. ASVA: O'Sullivan to Wimmer, Mobile, April 26, 1887.

121. Fellner, *Abbot Boniface and His Monks,* 5: 675–83; Ambrose Reger, *Die Benediktiner in Alabama und Geschichte der Gründung von St. Bernard* (Baltimore: Kreuzer Bros., 1898).

122. ASJA: Wimmer to Edelbrock, St. Vincent, May 1887.

123. ASVA: Wimmer to Machebeuf, St. Vincent, May 9, 1887 (copy); printed in [Urban J. Schnitzhofer], "First Monks in the Colorado Rockies, II," *ABR* 12 (1961): 371–72.

124. AMA: Wimmer to Braunmüller, St. Vincent, May 19, 1887.

125. ASJA: Wimmer to Edelbrock, St. Vincent, May 24, 1887.

126. ASVA: Wimmer To Englbrecht, St. Vincent, June 2, 1887.

127. ASJA: Wimmer to Edelbrock, St. Vincent, June 16, 1887; ASBA: Wimmer to Wolf, St. Vincent, June 16, 1887.

128. ACPF: Wimmer to Simeoni, St. Vincent, July 12, 1887.

129. ASVA: Wimmer to Englbrecht, St. Vincent, July 24, 1887.

130. ASBA: Wimmer to Wolf, St. Vincent, June 27, 1887.

131. ASVA: Wimmer to L. Wimmer, St. Vincent, August 20, 1887.

132. ASVA: Simeoni to Wimmer, St. Vincent, August 22, 1887.

133. AMA: Wimmer to Braunmüller, St. Vincent, September 19, 1887.

134. ASVA: Wimmer to L. Wimmer, St. Vincent, September 28, 1887.

135. AMA: Wimmer to Braunmüller, St. Vincent, October 2, 1887.

136. AMA: Wimmer to Braunmüller, St. Vincent, October 15, 1887.

137. ASVA: Wimmer to Kinter, St. Vincent, October 15, 1887.

Bibliography

1. Archives

Abbey of St. Paul's-Outside-the-Walls, Rome
Conception Abbey, Conception, Missouri
Congregation for the Propagation of the Faith, Rome
Diocese of Erie, Pennsylvania
Diocese of Linz, Austria
Diocese of Pittsburgh, Pennsylvania
Diocese of Milwaukee, Wisconsin
Holy Cross Priory, Regensburg, Germany
Ludwig Missionsverein, Munich, Germany
National Archives, Washington, D.C.
St. Benedict's Abbey, Atchison, Kansas
St. John's Abbey, Collegeville, Minnesota
St. Joseph's Monastery, St. Marys, Pennsylvania
St. Martin's Archabbey, Pannonhalma, Hungary
St. Meinrad's Archabbey, St. Meinrad's, Indiana
St. Michael's Abbey, Metten, Germany
St. Procopius Abbey, Lisle, Illinois
St. Vincent Archabbey, Latrobe, Pennsylvania
Scheyern Abbey, Scheyern, Germany
Royal Archives of Bavaria, Munich, Germany

2. Newspapers and Journals

American Benedictine Review
Annalen der Verbreitung des Glaubens (Munich, Germany)
Augsburger Postzeitung (Augsburg, Germany)
Berichte der Leopoldinen-Stiftung im Kaiserthume Österreich (Vienna, Austria)
Cincinnati Wahrheitsfreund
Pittsburgh Catholic
Records of the American Catholic Historical Society of Philadelphia
St. Vincent's Journal (St. Vincent College, Latrobe, Pennsylvania) *Scriptorium* (Saint
   John's Abbey, Collegeville, Minnesota)

Studien und Mitteilungen zur Geschichte des Benediktiner-Ordens und seiner Zweige (Munich, Germany)

Der Wanderer (St. Paul, Minnesota)

3. Primary Sources

Album Benedictinum. Beatty, Pa.: St. Vincent Abbey Press, 1869.

Album Benedictinum. Beatty, Pa.: St. Vincent Abbey Press, 1880.

Balzofiore, Philipp. *Lebensgeschichte der ehrwürdigen Dienerin Gottes Anna Maria Taigi (1769–1827). Aus der approbirten italienischen Ausgabe übertragen von P. Bonifaz Wimmer, O.S.B.* Regensburg, N.Y.: Pustet, 1867.

Bartscherer, Giles, translator. *Tyrocinium Religiosum: School of Religious Perfection Based Upon the Holy Rule of S. Benedict.* Latrobe, Pa.: Archabbey Press, 1896.

Brandus, Severus. *Die Katholisch-irisch-bischöfliche Administration in Nordamerika.* Philadelphia, 1840.

Catalogue of St. Vincent College and Seminary. Published at St. Vincent College annually, 1860–1887.

Catalogus exhibens nomina Monachorum Ord. S.P. Benedicti Congregationis Americano- Cassinensis Omniumque Locorum, quibus curam gerunt animarum. Latrobe, Pa.: St. Vincent Abbey Press, 1879.

Catalogus Monachorum Congregationis Americano-Cassinensis sub Titulo Sanctorum Angelorum Custodum. Collegeville, Minn.: St. John's Abbey Press, 1893.

Catalogus Monachorum Ord. S.P. Benedicti Congregationis Americano-Bavaricae Cassinensi Affiliatae. Latrobe, Pa.: St. Vincent Abbey Press, 1873.

Catalogus Monachorum Ord. S. P. Benedicti Congregationis Americano-Cassinensis. Latrobe, Pa.: St. Vincent Abbey Press, 1878.

Ganss, Henry. "Fugitive Recollections, Musical and Unmusical: 1868–1878." Typescript, n.d., located in the Archives of St. Vincent Archabbey.

Lechner, Peter. *Ausführliches Martyrologium des Benediktinerordens und seiner Verzweigungen.* Augsburg: B. Schmid, 1855.

———. *Die Heilige Schrift des Alten Testamentes nach der Vulgata und dem Grundtext erklärt.* Beatty, Pa.: St. Vincent Press, 1882, 1884.

———. *Die Heilige Schrift des Neuen Testamentes nach der Vulgata und dem Grundtext erklärt.* Beatty, Pa.: St. Vincent Press, 1881.

———. *Leben der heiligen Benedikt, Ordenstifters und Abtes auf Monte Cassino.* Regensburg: G. J. Manz, 1857.

———. "Missionsbericht des P. Petrus Lechner." *Berichte der Leopoldinen-Stiftung im Kaiserthume Österreich* 25 (1853): 79–94.

Lemke, Peter H. "Autobiography." *Northern Cambria News* (Carrolltown, Pennsylvania), June 7–November 22, 1879. Passim.

———. "Brief eines deutschen Missionaers in Amerika an den Redakteur des Katholiken." *Der Katholik* (Speyer) 15 (1835): 259–79.

Ludwig, Nepomucene. "Memoirs of Sister Nepomucene Ludwig." Manuscript c.

1913, located in the archives of St. Joseph's Monastery, St. Marys, Pennsylvania. Translated by Timothy Seus.

Pennachi, Giuseppe. *De Honorii I Romani Pontificis causa in Concilio VI. Dissertatio Josephi Pennachii in Romana Studiorum Universitate Historiae Ecclesiasticae Professoris Substituti ad Patres Concilii Vaticani. Praefatus est P. Bonifacius Wimmer, O.S.B., Abbas S. Vincentii et Praeses Congregationis Americo-Bavaricae Benedictinae.* Regensburg: Pustet, 1870.

Sadlier's Catholic Directory. New York: Sadlier's, 1888.

Salzbacher, Josef. *Meine Reise nach Nord-Amerika in Jahre 1842.* Vienna: Wimmer, Schmidt, & Leo, 1845.

Wimmer, Bonifaz. *Einige Notizen über Kloster Mallersdorf.* Landshut: J. A. Attendorfer, 1842.

Wimmer, Boniface. The Letters of Boniface Wimmer. Unpublished correspondence to and from Wimmer, located in the archives cited above. Copies (and some originals) in the Archives of St. Vincent Archabbey.

[Wimmer, Boniface]. "Über die Missionen." *Augsburger Postzeitung,* November 8, 1845. Translated in "Boniface Wimmer Outlines the Future of the Benedictine Order in the United States, November 8, 1845." In *Documents of American Catholic History,* 3 vols, ed. John Tracy Ellis, 1:280–88. Wilmington, Del.: Michael Glazier, 1987.

4. Secondary Sources

"Archabbot Boniface Wimmer, Founder of the First Czech Benedictine Abbey in the United States." *Central Blatt and Social Justice Review* 28 (1935): 215ff.

Aubert, Roger. "XIX Century Monastic Restoration in Western Europe." *Tjurunga: An Australian Benedictine Review* 8 (1974): 5–24.

Barry, Colman J. "Boniface Wimmer, Pioneer of the American Benedictines." *Catholic Historical Review* 41 (1955): 272–96.

———. *The Catholic Church and German Americans.* Milwaukee: Bruce Publishing, 1953.

———. "The First Hurrah: Boniface Wimmer, O.S.B." *American Benedictine Review* 28 (1977): 30–40.

———. *Worship and Work: St. John's Abbey and University 1856–1992.* Collegeville, Minn.: Liturgical Press, 1993.

Barry, Garrett Francis. *Violation of the Cloister.* Washington, D.C.: The Catholic University of America Press, 1942.

Baska, Regina. *The Benedictine Congregation of St. Scholastica: Its Foundation and Development, 1852–1930.* Washington, D.C.: The Catholic University of America Press, 1935.

Baumstein, Paschal. *My Lord of Belmont: A Biography of Leo Haid.* Kings Mountain, N.C.: Herald House, 1985.

Beckman, Peter. *Kansas Monks: A History of St. Benedict's Abbey.* Atchison, Kans.: Abbey Student Press, 1957.

———. "Oswald Moosmuller in Kansas." *American Benedictine Review* 7 (1957): 263–81.

"Die Benediktiner als Jugenderzieher in Amerika." *Studien und Mitteilungen* 1 (1880): 155–64.

Betschart, Ildephonse. *Der Apostel der Siouxindianer, Bischof Martinus Marty, O.S.B.* Einsiedeln, Switzerland: Benziger, 1934.

Betschart, Ildephonse. "Bishop Martin Marty, O.S.B., 1834–1896." *Records of the American Catholic Historical Society of Philadelphia* 49 (1938): 97–134, 214–248, and 50 (1939): 33–64.

Bihlmeyer, Karl. *Church History: Modern and Recent Times.* Revised by Herman Tüchle. Translated by V. E. Mills and F. J. Müller. Westminster, Md.: Newman Press, 1968.

Blied, Benjamin. *Austrian Aid to American Catholics, 1830–1860.* Milwaukee: Bruce Publishing, 1944.

"Bonifaz Wimmer und Gregor Scherr." *Alt und Jung Metten* 4 (1926): 3–64.

Brennan, Robert J. "Benedictines in Virginia." *American Benedictine Review* 13 (1962): 25–40.

Bridge, Gerard. *An Illustrated History of St. Vincent Archabbey.* Beatty, Pa.: St. Vincent Abbey Press, 1922.

———. "St. Vincent College and Ecclesiastical Seminary." In *Catholic Builders of the Nation,* 5 vols., ed. C. E. McGuire, 5:313–22. Boston: Continental Press, 1923.

Buresh, Vitus. *The Procopian Chronicle: St. Procopius Abbey, 1885–1985.* Lisle, Ill.: St. Procopius Abbey, 1985.

Burgemeister, Remegius. *History of the Development of Catholicity in St. Marys.* St. Marys, Pa.: Privately published, 1919.

Burne, Martin J. "Holy Cross Abbey–One Hundred Years." *American Benedictine Review* 37 (1986): 423–32.

Byrne, John F. *The Redemptorist Centenaries.* Philadelphia: Dolphin Press, 1932.

Campbell, Stephanie. *A Love that Impels: A History of the Benedictine Sisters of Ridgely, Maryland.* Erie, Pa.: Benet Press, 1986.

Capecelatro, Alfonso, Cardinal. *Commemorazione di Don Bonifacio Maria Krug, abate di Montecassino.* Rome: Desclée & Cie: 1910.

"Congregations of Benedictine Sisters in North America." *Benedictines* 26 (1971): 91–92.

Connelly, James F. *The Visit of Archbishop Gaetano Bedini to the United States of America: June 1853–February 1854.* Rome: Gregorian University, 1960.

Corti, Eugon C. *Ludwig I of Bavaria.* London: T. Butterworth, 1938.

Crawford, Eugene Joseph. *Daughters of Dominic on Long Island.* New York: Benziger Brothers, 1938.

Danzer, Beda. *Die Benediktinerregel in der Übersee.* St. Ottilien: Eos Verlag der Erzabtei, 1929.

DeFrange, Jonathan. *Century of Grace: A Pictorial History of St. Joseph Abbey and Seminary.* St. Benedict, La.: St. Joseph's Abbey, 1989.

Dirrigl, Michael. *Ludwig I: König von Bayern, 1825–1848.* Munich: Hugendubel, 1980.

Dolan, Jay. *The American Catholic Experience: A History from Colonial Times to the Present.* New York: Doubleday, 1985.

Doppelfeld, Basilius. *Mönchtum und Kirchlicher Heilsdienst: Entstehung und Entwicklung des nordamerikanischen Benediktinerums im 19 Jahrhundert.* Münsterschwarzach: Vier-Turme-Verlag, 1974.

[Drey, Emmanuel, et al.]. *Die Abtei St. Walburg (1035–1935): 900 Jahre in Wort und Bild.* Eichstätt: St. Walburga Abbey, 1934. Translated by Gonzaga Engelhart as *Spring and Harvest.* St. Meinrad, Ind.: Grail Press, 1952.

Ellis, John Tracy, ed. *Documents of American Catholic History.* 3 vols. Wilmington, Del.: Michael Glazier, 1991.

Engelhart, Gonzaga. "The Daughters of St. Walburg Cross the Ocean." *Benedictine Review* 7 (Winter 1952): 29–32.

———. *Spring and Harvest.* St. Meinrad, Ind.: Grail Press, 1952.

Ewens, Mary. *The Role of the Nun in Nineteenth-Century America.* New York: Arno Press, 1978.

Fallon, Clarisse. *Waters of Promise, 1874–1974.* Nauvoo, Ill.: St. Mary Priory, 1974.

Fellner, Felix. *Abbot Boniface and His Monks.* 5 vols. Latrobe, Pa.: Privately published at Saint Vincent Archabbey, 1956.

———. "Archabbot Boniface Wimmer and Historical Sources." *Records of the American Catholic Historical Society of Philadelphia* 37(1926): 299–304.

———. "Archabbot Boniface Wimmer as an Educator." *National Benedictine Educational Association Bulletin* 25 (1942): 90–106.

———. "Oswald Moosmüller." *Records of the American Catholic Historical Society of Philadelphia* 34 (1923): 1–16.

———. "The Reverend Theodore Brouwers, O.F.M." *Records of the American Catholic Historical Society of Philadelphia* 24 (1914): 356–63.

———. *Die St. Vincenz Gemeinde und Erzabtei.* Latrobe, Pa.: St. Vincent Abbey Press, 1905.

Fendl, Josef, ed. *Thalmassing: Eine Gemeinde des alten Landgerichts Haidau.* Regensburg: Studio Druck, 1981.

Fink, Wilhelm. *Beiträge zur Geschichte der Bayerischen Benediktiner-kongregation: Eine Jubiläumsschrift, 1684–1934.* Munich: Kom- missionsverlag R. Oldenbourg, 1934.

———. *Entwicklungsgeschichte der Benediktinerabtei Metten.* 3 vols. Munich: Kommissionsverlag R.Oldenbourg, 1926–1930.

Flick, Lawrence. "Biographical Sketch of Reverend Peter H. Lemke, O.S.B." *Records of the American Catholic Historical Society of Philadelphia* 9 (1898): 184ff.

Fogarty, Gerald P. *The Vatican and the American Hierarchy from 1870 to 1965.* Collegeville, Minn.: Liturgical Press, 1985.

Gallivan, Ricarda. *Shades in the Fabric: Excerpts from the Nauvoo Benedictine Story.* Nauvoo, Ill.: St. Mary Priory, 1970.

"Gaul, Brother Bonaventure, O.S.B.: Obituary." *St. Vincent's Journal* 6 (1896): 38–39.

Girgen, Incarnata. *Behind the Beginnings: Benedictine Women in America.* St. Joseph, Minn.: St. Benedict's Convent, 1981.

————. "The Schools of the American Cassinese Benedictines in the United States: Their Foundation, Development, and Character." Ph.D. diss., Saint Louis University, 1944.

Gleason, Philip. *Keeping the Faith: American Catholicism Past and Present.* Notre Dame, Ind.: University of Notre Dame Press, 1987.

Gollwitzer, Heinz. *Ludwig I von Bayern, Königtum in Vormärz: Eine Politische Biographie.* Munich: Süddeutscher Verlag, 1986.

Guilday, Peter. *A History of the Councils of Baltimore (1791–1884).* 1932; reprint, New York: Arno Press, 1969.

————. *The Life and Times of John Carroll.* New York: Encyclopedia Press, 1922.

Haas, Louis. *St. Vincent's: Souvenir of the Consecration of the New Abbey Church, August 24, 1905, on the Fiftieth Anniversary of the Elevation of St. Vincent's to an Abbey.* Latrobe, Pa: St. Vincent Press, 1905.

Hammill, Martina, R.S.M. *The Expansion of the Church in Pennsylvania.* Pittsburgh: Privately published, 1960.

Hanley, Thomas O'Brien, ed. *The John Carroll Papers.* 3 vols. Notre Dame, Ind.: Notre Dame University Press, 1976.

Hansen, Marcus Lee. *The Atlantic Migration, 1607–1860.* Cambridge, Mass.: Harvard University Press, 1940.

Hayes, Giles P. "Early Bayley-Wimmer Correspondence (1854–1857)." *American Benedictine Review* 14 (1963): 470–94.

Hennesey, James. *American Catholics: A History of the Roman Catholic Community in the United States.* New York: Oxford University Press, 1981.

————. "The Baltimore Council of 1866: An American Syllabus." *Records of the American Catholic Historical Society of Philadelphia* 76 (1965): 165–72.

————. *The First Council of the Vatican: The American Experience.* New York: Herder and Herder, 1963.

Higby, Charles Penn. *The Religious Policy of the Bavarian Government during the Napoleonic Period.* 1919; reprint, New York: AMS Press, 1967.

Hilpisch, Stephanus. *Das Benediktinertum im Wandel der Zeiten.* St. Ottilien: Eos Verlag der Erzabtei, 1950. Translated by Leonard J. Doyle as *Benedictinism through Changing Centuries.* Collegeville, Minn.: St. John's Abbey Press, 1958.

————. *Geschichte der Benediktinerinnen.* St. Ottilien: Eos Verlag der Erzabtei, 1951. Translated by Joanne Muggli as *A History of Benedictine Nuns.* Collegeville, Minn.: St. John's Abbey Press, 1958.

Hollermann, Ephrem. *The Reshaping of a Tradition: American Benedictine Women, 1852–1881.* St. Joseph, Minn.: Sisters of the Order of St. Benedict, 1994.

Huber, Vincent. "Sportsman's Hall." *Records of the American Catholic Historical Society of Philadelphia* 3 (1888–1891): 142–73.

————. "Sportsman's Hall and St. Vincent Abbey." *St. Vincent Journal* 1 (1892): passim.

J.S. "Rt. Rev. Boniface Wimmer, O.S.B., Founder of St. Vincent's." *St. Vincent Journal* 18 (1909): 151–66.

Johnston, Helen. *The Fruit of His Works: A History of the Benedictine Sisters of St. Benedict's Convent.* Bristow, Va.: Linton Hall Press, 1954.

Kapsner, Oliver. *A Benedictine Bibliography: An Author-Subject Union List.* 2 vols. Collegeville, Minn.: St. John's Abbey Press, 1962.

Kardong, Terence. "Peter Henry Lemke: 'Brave Soldier of the Lord' or Gyrovague?" *Tjurunga: An Australian Benedictine Review* 24 (1983): 44–65.

Karolevitz, Robert. *Bishop Martin Marty.* Freeman, S. Dak.: Pine Hill Press, 1980.

Kenneally, Finbar, O.F.M. *United States Documents in the Propaganda Fide Archives: A Calendar.* 9 vols. to date. Washington, D.C.: The Catholic University of America Press, 1966- .

Kleber, Albert. *A History of St. Meinrad Archabbey, 1854–1954.* St. Meinrad, Ind.: Abbey Press, 1954.

Kline, Omer U. *The Sportsman's Hall Parish, Later Named St. Vincent, 1790–1846.* Latrobe, Pa.: Archabbey Press, 1990.

Knowles, David. *Christian Monasticism.* New York: McGraw-Hill, 1969.

Kohler, M. Hortense. *The Life and Work of Mother Benedicta Bauer, O.P.* Milwaukee: Bruce Publishing, 1937.

Kotinek, Marion. "Arrival of Benedictines in Southwest Iowa." *Messenger* (Des Moines), October 29, 1948, 2–3, 5.

Lachouque, Henry. *Napoleon's Battles: A History of His Campaigns.* London: Allen & Unwin, 1966.

Lambing, A. A. *A History of the Catholic Church in the Dioceses of Pittsburg and Allegheny.* New York: Benziger Bros., 1880.

Lemke, Peter H. *Life and Work of Prince Demetrius Augustine Gallitzin.* Translated by Joseph C. Plumpe. New York: Longmans, Green & Co., 1940.

Lester, Bernhard. "Erzabt Bonifaz Wimmer, Das Bild eines deutschen Mannes in Amerika." *Frankfurter Zeitgemaesse Broschueren,* 12 (1891): 397–424.

Lynch, Claire. *The Leaven.* St. Paul, Minn.: North Central Publishing, 1980.

————. "The Shakopee Story: Episodes in Oppression." *Benedictines* 31 (1976): 6–15, 35–37, and 58–63.

Malone, Edward E. *A History of Conception Colony, Abbey, and Schools.* Elkhorn, Nebr.: Michaeleen Press, 1971.

————, trans. "A Long Lost Letter of Boniface Wimmer." *American Benedictine Review* 20 (1969): 309–320.

————. "Placidus Wolter and the American Benedictines." *American Benedictine Review* 16 (1965): 310–25.

Martin, Aquinata. *The Catholic Church on the Nebraska Frontier, 1885–1954.* Washington, D.C.: The Catholic University of America Press, 1957.

Marty, Martin. *Dr. Johann Martin Henni.* New York: Benziger Bros., 1888.

Mathäser, Willibald. *Bonifaz Wimmer O.S.B. und König Ludwig I von Bayern.* Munich: J. Pfeiffer, 1938.

———. "Erzabt Bonifaz Wimmer in Spiegel seiner Briefe." *Studien und Mitteilungen* 60 (1946): 234–302.

———, ed. *Haudegen Gottes: Das Leben des Peter H. Lemke.* Würzburg: Kommissionsverlag Echter Gesamtherstellung, 1971.

———. "König Ludwig I von Bayern als Forderer des Deutschtums und des Katholizismus in Nord-Amerika." *Gelbe Hefte* (Munich) 1 (1924–1925): 616–19.

———. "König Ludwig I von Bayern und die deutschen Katholiken in Nordamerika." *Der Auslandsdeutsche* (Stuttgart) 9 (1926): 317–20.

———. "König Ludwig I von Bayern und die Gründung der ersten bayer-ischen Benediktinerabtei in Nordamerika." *Studien und Mitteilungen* 43(1926): 123–82.

———. *Der Ludwig-Missionsverein in der Zeit König Ludwigs I von Bayern.* Munich: Druck der Salesianischen Offizin, 1939.

———. "San José in Texas." *Studien und Mitteilungen* 6 (1946): 309–30.

McAvoy, Thomas T. *A History of the Catholic Church in the United States.* Notre Dame, Ind.: University of Notre Dame Press, 1969.

McDonald, Grace. *With Lamps Burning.* St. Paul, Minn.: St. Benedict's Convent, 1957.

McMahon, Aurelius. *The Life of St. Benedict, Patriarch of Western Monks, Translated from the Second Book of the Dialogues of St. Gregory the Great.* Baltimore: J. Murphy, 1880.

———. *Rule of St. Benedict, Patriarch of Western Monks.* Baltimore: J. Murphy, 1879.

McPadden, Malachy. *The Benedictines in Newark, 1842–1992.* Newark, N.J.: Privately published, 1992.

Meaney, Peter J. "Valiant Chaplain of the Bloody Tenth [Emmeran Bliemel, O.S.B.]." *Tennessee Historical Quarterly* 41 (1983): 37–47.

Meyer, Consilia. "Communities of Benedictine Women: Foundations in North America, 1852–1970." *Benedictines* 28 (1973): 79–83.

Misonne, Daniel. "La restauration monastique du XIX siècle." *Revue Bénédictine* 83(1973): 205–43.

Mizera, Peter F. *Czech Benedictines in America: 1877–1961.* Lisle, Ill.: Center for Slav Culture, St. Procopius College, 1969.

Moleck, Fred J. "Music at St. Vincent under Abbot Boniface Wimmer." *American Benedictine Review* 14 (1963): 248–62.

———. "Nineteenth-Century Musical Activity at St. Vincent Archabbey." Ph.D. diss., University of Pittsburgh, 1971.

———. "The Wimmer Music Collection." *Benedictine Confluence* 6 (1972): 25–30.

Moosmüller, Oswald. *Bonifaz Wimmer, Erzabt von St. Vincent in Pennsylvanien.* New York: Benziger, 1891.

———. "Die Negermissionen der Benediktiner in Georgia." *Studien und Mitteilungen* 2 (1881): 351–55 and 3 (1882): 146–49.

———. *Europäer in Amerika vor Columbus.* Regensburg: G. J. Manz, 1879.

———. *St. Vincenz in Pennsylvanien.* New York: F. Pustet, 1873.

Morkin, M. Louis, and Theophane Seigel. *Wind in the Wheat.* Erie, Pa.: McCarty Publishing, 1956.

Morris, William S. *The Seminary Movement in the United States: Projects, Foundations, and Early Development, 1833–1866.* Washington, D.C.: The Catholic University of America Press, 1932.

Murphy, Joseph. *Tenacious Monks: The Oklahoma Benedictines (1875–1975).* Shawnee, Okla.: Benedictine Color Press, 1974.

Murrman, Warren, trans. "Boniface Wimmer to Archbishop von Reisach [Wimmer Letter of March 1, 1847]." *Benedictine Confluence* 6 (1972): 19–23.

———. "The Wimmer Correspondence: A Collection and a Project." *Benedictine Confluence* 6 (1972): 16–18.

Necrologium Congregationis Americano-Cassinensis, O.S.B., 1846–1946. Collegeville, Minn.: St. John's Abbey Press, 1948.

O'Brien, J. D. *The Exemption of Religious in Church Law.* Milwaukee: Bruce Publishing, 1943.

O'Connell, Jeremiah. *Catholicity in the Carolinas and Georgia.* New York: D. & J. Sadlier, 1879.

Oetgen, Jerome. *An American Abbot: Boniface Wimmer, O.S.B., 1809–1887.* Latrobe, Pa.: Archabbey Press, 1976.

———. "Benedictine Women in Nineteenth-Century America." *American Benedictine Review* 34 (1983): 396–423.

———. "A Bibliography of American Benedictine History." *Benedictine Confluence* (Latrobe, Pa.) 6 (1972): 6–15.

———. "Boniface Wimmer." *Saint Vincent* 6 (1972): 4–5.

———. "Boniface Wimmer and the American Benedictines: 1856–1866." *American Benedictine Review* 23 (1972): 283–313.

———. "Boniface Wimmer and the American Benedictines: 1866–1876." *American Benedictine Review* 24 (1973): 1–28.

———. "Boniface Wimmer and the American Benedictines: 1877–1887." *American Benedictine Review* 25 (1974): 1–32.

———. "Boniface Wimmer and the Founding of St. Vincent Archbbey." *American Benedictine Review* 22 (1971): 147–76.

———. "The Origins of the Benedictine Order in Georgia." *Georgia Historical Quarterly* 53 (1969): 165–83.

———."Oswald Moosmüller: Monk and Missionary." *American Benedictine Review* 27 (1976): 1–35.

Official Records of the War of Rebellion. Washington, D.C.: Government Printing Office, 1880.

Olheiser, Mary David. "From Autonomy to Federations." Ph.D. diss., The Catholic University of America, 1977.

Plaisance, Aloysius. "Dom Pierre Joseph Didier, Pioneer Benedictine in the United States." *American Benedictine Review* 3 (1952): 23–26.

———. "Emmeran Bliemel, O.S.B., Heroic Confederate Chaplain." *American Benedictine Review* 17 (1966): 206–16.

Rees, Daniel. "The Benedictine Revival in the Nineteenth Century." In *Benedict's Disciples,* ed. D. H. Farmer, pp. 294–317. Leominster, England: F. Wright Books, 1980.

Reger, Ambrose. *Die Benediktiner in Alabama und Geschichte der Gründung von St. Bernard.* Baltimore: Kreuzer Bros., 1898.

Renner, Emmanuel. "Riepp, Mother Benedicta." In *Notable American Women: A Biographical Dictionary,* ed. Edward T. James, 160–61. Cambridge, Mass.: Belknop Press of Harvard University Press, 1971.

Reuss, Francis X. "Memoir of the Rt. Rev. James Zilliox, O.S.B., D.D.: First Abbot of St. Mary's Benedictine Abbey, of Newark, N.J." *Records of the American Catholic Historical Society of Philadelphia* 11 (1900): 129–55, 257–80.

Rippinger, Joel. "Adapting Benedictine Monasticism to Nineteenth-Century America." *U.S. Catholic Historian* 3 (1984): 294–302.

———. "The Benedictine Missionary Impulse of the Ninteenth Century." *Tjurunga: An Australian Benedictine Review* 27 (1984): 46–57.

———. *The Benedictine Order in the United States: An Interpretive History.* Collegeville, Minn.: Liturgical Press, 1990.

———. "Martin Marty: Monk, Abbot, Missionary, and Bishop." *American Benedictine Review* 33 (1982): 223–40 and 376–93.

———. "Monastic Formation in the Nineteenth-Century American Benedictinism." *American Benedictine Review* 28 (1977): 244–47.

———. "The Origins and Development of Benedictine Monasticism in the United States." In *The Continuing Quest for God,* ed. William Skudlarek, O.S.B., 160–69. Collegeville, Minn.: Liturgical Press, 1982.

———. "Some Historical Determinants of American Benedictine Monasticism: 1846–1900." *American Benedictine Review* 27 (1976) 63–84.

———. "Some Models of *Conversatio:* The American Benedictines." *American Benedictine Review* 36 (1985): 100–103.

———. "The Swiss-American Congregation: A Centennial Survey." *American Benedictine Review* 32 (1981): 87–99.

Roemer, Theodore. *The Leopoldine Foundation and the Church in the United States, 1820–1839.* New York: United States Catholic Historical Society, 1933.

———. *The Ludwig Missionsverein and the Church in the United States.* Washington, D.C.: The Catholic University of America Press, 1933.

[Roettger, Gregory]. *An Historical Overview of St. Bernard's Abbey 1891–1991.* Cullman, Ala.: St. Bernard's Abbey, 1991.

St. Joseph's Convent. *The Hundredth Anniversary of the Benedictine Sisters, 1852–1952, Cradle of the Order in the United States, St. Joseph's Convent.* St. Marys, Pa.: Sisters of St. Benedict, 1952.

St. Walburg Convent. *The Challenge: Saint Walburg Convent Centennial, 1859–1959.* Covington, Ky.: St. Walburg Convent, 1959.

Sargent, Daniel. *Mitri; or the Story of Prince Demetrius Augustine Gallitzin, 1770–1840.* New York: Longmans, Green & Co., 1945.

Sauer, Walter. "Unpublished Viennese Letters of Benedictine Mission-aries: Boniface Wimmer and John Bede Polding." *American Benedictine Review* 26 (1975): 369–80.

Scheuermann, Audomar. *Die Exemtion nach geltendem kirchlichen rech mit einem Überblick über die geschichtliche Entwicklung.* Paderborn: F. Schoningh, 1938.

Schmid, Placidus. *Die Benediktiner in Conception, Missouri.* St. Louis: Herder, 1885.

Schneider, Augustine. *Erklärung der Regel des heiligen Benedikt, Patriarch der Mönche des Abendlandes.* Regensburg, N.Y.: F. Pustet, 1879.

Schnitzhofer, Urban J. "First Monks in the Colorado Rockies." *American Benedictine Review* 12 (1961): 232–56 and 369–89.

Schuster, Faith. *The Meaning of the Mountain.* Baltimore: Helican Press, 1953.

Schwaiger, Georg, and Paul Mai. *Johann Michael Sailer und seine Zeit.* Regensburg: Verlag des Vereins für Regensburger Bistumgeschichte, 1982.

Skudlarek, William, ed. *The Continuing Quest for God: Monastic Spirituality in Tradition and Transition.* Collegeville, Minn.: Liturgical Press, 1982.

Sutera, Judith. "Pioneers in Search of an Identity." *Benedictines* 35 (1980): 25–36.

———. *True Daughters: Monastic Identity and American Benedictine Women's History.* Atchison, Kans.: Mount St. Scholastica, 1987.

Szarnicki, Henry. *Michael O'Connor, First Catholic Bishop of Pittsburgh, 1843–1860.* Pittsburgh: Wolfson Publishing, 1975.

Taylor, Philip. *The Distant Magnet: European Emigration to the United States of America.* New York: Harper & Row, 1971.

Tegeder, Vincent. "The Abbot Smith Letters and the American Benedictines." *American Benedictine Review* 6 (1955): 24–38.

Weber, Willibald. "Erzabt Bonifaz Wimmer." *Alt und Jung Metten* 44 (1977–1978): 4–37.

Wilson, Debora. "Benedictine Higher Education and the Development of American Higher Education." Ph.D. diss., University of Michigan, 1969.

Wimmer, Sebastian. "Biographical Sketch of Rt. Rev. Arch-Abbot Wimmer, O.S.B., D.D., Patriarch of the American Cassinese Benedictines." *Records of the American Catholic Historical Society of Philadelphia* 3 (1891): 174–93.

Windschiegl, Peter. *Fifty Golden Years, 1903–1953: A Brief History of the Order of Saint Benedict in the Abbacy Nullius of St. Peter.* Muenster, Saskatchewan: St. Peter's Abbey, 1952.

Wirtner, Modestus. *The Benedictine Fathers in Cambria County.* Carrolltown, Pa.: Privately published, 1926.

Wolfsbruger, Coelestin. "Bonifaz Wimmer an Sigismund Schultes." *Studien und Mitteilungen* 15 (1894): 478–86.

Zimmerman, Conrad., et al. "Wimmer Letters." *Scriptorium* (Saint John's Abbey, Minnesota) 17 (1958): 53–64; 18 (1959): 67–82; and 19 (1960): 61–83.

Züricher, Franz. *Die Benediktiner in Amerika.* Würzburg: Leo Woerl, 1877.

Index

An American Abbot: Boniface Wimmer, O.S.B., 1809–1887 was composed in Adobe Garamond by Graphic Composition, Inc., Athens, Georgia; printed on 60-pound Glatfelter Supple Opaque and bound by Thomson-Shore, Inc., Dexter, Michigan; and designed and produced by Kachergis Book Design, Pittsboro, North Carolina.